THE GREAT GATES

THE GREAT GATES

The Story of the Rocky Mountain Passes

978
S_0739
1981

By

MARSHALL SPRAGUE

with illustrations and maps

University of Nebraska Press

Lincoln and London

First Bison Book printing: 1981
Most recent printing indicated by the first digit below:
1   2   3   4   5   6   7   8   9   10

Library of Congress Cataloging in Publication Data

Sprague, Marshall.
  The great gates.

    Reprint of the ed. published by Little, Brown, Boston.
    Bibliography: p.
    Includes index.
    1. Rocky Mountains—Passes. 2. Rocky Mountains, Can.—Passes. I.
Title.
[F721.S76 1981]   978   80–21994
ISBN 0–8032–4122–4
ISBN 0–8032–9119–1 (pbk.)

Published by arrangement with Marshall Sprague
Manufactured in the United States of America

IN MEMORY OF
JOHN LEONARD McDONALD

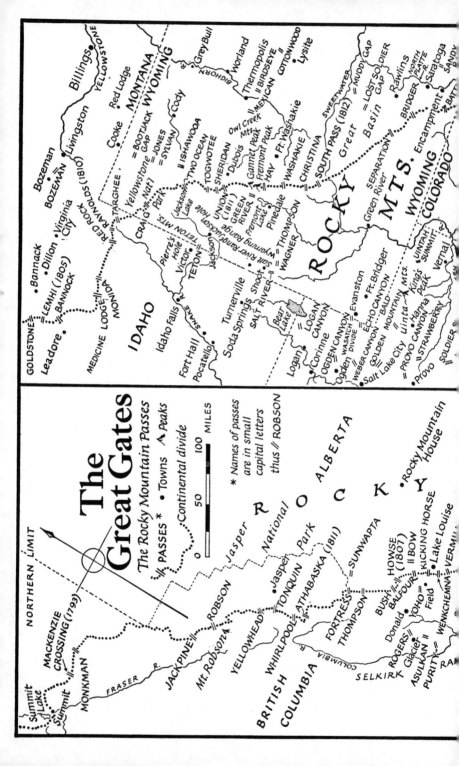

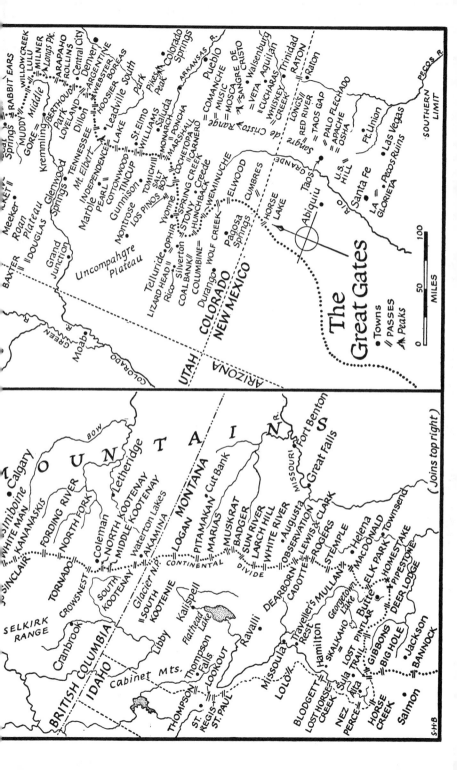

The Great Gates

• Towns
‖ Passes
⋀ Peaks

0 50 100
MILES

(Joins top right)

Foreword

In threading together this story of the Rocky Mountains in terms of passes I have used a common definition of the chain. It starts at Horse Lake Pass in the San Juans of northern New Mexico and extends northward for two thousand miles along the Continental Divide deep into Canada. There, beyond Jasper National Park, I cease to be concerned because the Rockies dwindle away and part company with the Divide.

The Divide is the backbone, and I include the passes of ranges which spur off from it — the Sangre de Cristos of northern New Mexico, the Elks of Colorado, the Wasatch and Uinta Mountains of Utah, the Big Horns and Tetons of Wyoming, and, also, the Selkirks of British Columbia — which are not defined as Rockies at all. The story opens with the sixteenth-century Spaniards, and runs through the pass adventures of British and American explorers and trappers until the whole chain stood revealed around 1830. The narrative continues with the development of passes by army engineers, empire-building politicians, gold-seekers, scientists, railroaders, and, at last, motorists.

I would say a word about the sketches of some eight hundred Rocky Mountain passes in the back of the book, listed by state or country — Canada, Colorado, Montana-Idaho, northern New Mexico, Utah, and Wyoming. I prepared the list originally to help me memorize the ranges and drainage systems and different kinds of terrain. I needed it also to give me a standard of altitude figures and of name spellings, since these vary from source to source. Later on, I saw that the list had become a catch-all for material which I could not work into the story. I present it, therefore, hoping that it has a little something for a variety of readers. Students of the history of the West, for instance, can learn what David Thompson meant when he wrote of "Saskatchewan Pass," what John Mullan meant by "Father's Defile," what heroine is honored by "Pitamakan Pass." The list gives pass locations exact enough so that those who like to trace old paths or visit out-of-the-way spots can reach them without too much difficulty. If a pass can be crossed by standard car, the list makes note of it. If a four-wheel-drive vehicle (4WD) is needed, the list records the fact. Passes in the roster lacking these designations have to be crossed on foot or horseback. Of course today's trail — 1963 — is tomorrow's 4WD road, or even highway. Travelers on uncommon pass roads and trails should inquire locally about what they can expect.

M. S.

Contents

(Illustrations appear between pages 244 and 245.)

CONTENTS

THE GREAT GATES

1

The Earliest Gates

THE FIRST EUROPEANS to use a Rocky Mountain pass were twenty-two members of a Spanish scouting party, and the time of their crossing was a crisp autumn day in 1540. The party belonged to the army of a Spanish grandee, General Don Francisco Vásquez de Coronado, governor of New Galicia Province in Mexico. The pass is called La Glorieta today, which is a good name for it because it is, and was in 1540, a hub of routes like a "glorieta," or square of a Spanish town. A four-lane highway, U.S. Route 84–85, from Santa Fe, New Mexico, goes over it in a twenty-mile arc through sandy hills, fragrant with piñon and juniper, at the southern tip of the Sangre de Cristo Mountains.

Like Hernando Cortes, who had conquered Mexico twenty years earlier, Coronado had dreams of conquest, and also of loot in the form of gold and silver, for king, church, country and his own prestige. Through the spring and summer of 1540 he had led his army north from New Galicia Province for two thousand miles —"250 horsemen, 70 Spanish footmen and several hundred friendly Indians," plus pack animals and herds of cattle for food. His trail paralleled the present Guadalajara-Nogales highway in Mexico, and then his army worked through the uplands along the Arizona–New Mexico border to a pueblo of the Zuni Indians. This Zuni Pueblo was rumored to be one of the wealthy Seven Cities of Cibola. But Coronado found only a poor mud village.

As he prepared for the long trek back home, Indians arrived at Zuni from Pecos Pueblo to the east and told the General about the "humpbacked oxen" in the Great Plains east of La Glorieta Pass. They implied that Coronado would find in the east the real Seven Cities of Cibola ("cibola" means "bison" — a hump-backed ox — in Spanish) and so the General continued east over the Continental Divide and wintered on the Rio Grande some forty-five miles south of the present Santa Fe. From this point on the shallow river, he could look northward up the valley and see on the right the southern end of the Sangre de Cristo Mountains and, on the left, the foothills of the San Juan Mountains — twin beginnings of the Rockies.

There was still time to reconnoiter before winter closed in. For this task, Coronado assigned his captain of artillery, Hernando de Alvarado, and a chaplain, sixteen cavalrymen and four crossbowmen — twenty-two in all. The Alvarado party rode along trails up the Rio Grande and veered northeast to reach the oasis of golden cottonwoods and cornfields and garrulous magpies around Taos Pueblo. Alvarado took notes on Taos and so its lazy charm became a matter of record in 1540, at least twenty-five years before the founding of another American antique — St. Augustine, Florida. The mountains above Taos would later be named the Sangre de Cristos by Spanish priests reminded of Christ's blood by the hues of the rising and setting sun on those 13,000-foot peaks.

Coronado's scouts saw nothing of value in Taos Pueblo. Since it was the last of a line of farming villages up the Rio Grande Valley, they penetrated no further northward into the unknown Rocky Mountains. However, they learned about Indian trails which ran over the Sangre de Cristos to the plains of northern New Mexico. The main trail went up today's Fernando de Taos Creek to the top of present Palo Flechado Pass (9107). At least two trails branched off from the upper part of this

Fernando de Taos Creek trail to reach the top a few miles south of Palo Flechado Pass at the passes known now as Apache and Osha. A third trail went due east from Taos Pueblo up Taos Creek and, near the top, crossed over to Fernando de Taos Creek and on over Palo Flechado. The Taos Indians in 1540 needed these different pass trails to avoid ambush by the nomadic Apaches, who came over the Sangre de Cristos to trade or to raid.

Having finished their investigation of Taos, the Spanish scouts retraced their steps, passing through Picurís Pueblo in the foothills thirty miles to the south. From near Picurís, a trail ran over the Sangre de Cristos southeasterly to the plains and Pecos Pueblo, as State Route 3 runs over U.S. Hill and Holman Hill to Mora and Las Vegas, New Mexico. However, the explorers kept on south and southwest to the Rio Grande and down it again.

And so, from the hill-pocked environs of present Santa Fe, their Pecos Indian guides led them east over La Glorieta Pass. That was four centuries ago, but four centuries is hardly a comma in time's endless punctuation. La Glorieta in the autumn of 1540 looked much as it does now, with flocks of piñon jays flashing blue among the scrub oak and with the yellow rabbit bush fading along the trail. And the Spanish were much the same in mind and body as men today, for all their harquebuses, flintlock pistols, metal hats and high leather boots rolled down at the thigh.

LA GLORIETA does not seem like much of a pass, as Rocky Mountain passes go. It is only four miles up Galisteo Creek out of the wooded hills and six miles down to the detour which leads to the ruins of Pecos Pueblo. La Glorieta does nothing psychologically stirring like crossing the Continental Divide. It merely crosses the mesas between the drainage of the Rio Grande and the drainage of its main tributary, the Pecos. It is narrow at both ends and a quarter-mile wide in the middle.

Deep arroyos like Apache Canyon fall into it here and there. The climb over is nothing for cars on U.S. Route 84–85, or for sleek passenger trains of the Santa Fe Railroad — a mere 500 feet, from 7000 to 7500 feet above sea level. But the grade of 158 feet per mile — steepest, except for the Raton Pass grade northeast of it, on the entire Santa Fe line to California — is too much for freights, which are routed through lower terrain to the south.

For all its modesty, La Glorieta, and Pecos Pueblo particularly, must have made an impression on the Spaniards. Of Pecos, Coronado's chronicler wrote: "A very strong village four stories high, a village of nearly 500 warriors . . . One can go over the top of the whole village without there being a street to hinder . . . The houses do not have doors below, but they use ladders, which can be lifted up like a drawbridge . . . The people of this village boast that no one has been able to conquer them . . ."

At Pecos, Captain de Alvarado heard about the kingdom of Quivira far to the east. His informant was the "legendary Turk" — a Plains Indian held captive by the villagers. This Turk seems to have been a professional creator of illusions for the exploitation of suckers. Quivira, he told Alvarado in confidence, was a land of a lot more than Seven rich Cities of Cibola. The Turk, of course, worked for the Pecos Indians, who had the correct idea that the Spanish had come up from Mexico to rob them. The myth of gold in Quivira would lure them out on the Great Plains, where they might get lost.

Alvarado took the Turk's lure, rejoined Coronado on the Rio Grande, and told him about the wealth of Quivira. In April, 1541, Coronado and a large part of his army followed the Turk beyond La Glorieta Pass and into the wide flat eastern yonder. Somehow they reached Quivira in the middle of Kansas, but it was just windy space and Caddoa Indians in straw villages. The Conquistadores garroted the lying Turk and were back on the Rio Grande by way of La Glorieta by September,

1541. They returned to Mexico in the spring of 1542, bringing to a frustrated end the first episode in the story of Rocky Mountain passes.

AND STILL TALL TALES persisted about gold in Quivira and also about pearls in the Western Sea which Spaniards might reach overland through New Mexico, if they could find a way. Spanish authorities in New Spain began to understand that the Upper Rio Grande had promise as a farming colony. Soldiers and priests wandered east and west of La Glorieta Pass, but nobody, not even Governor Juan de Oñate, who led the first Spanish colonists to New Mexico in 1598, reported any penetration of the country north of Taos on the west side of the Sangre de Cristos or north of La Glorieta Pass along the east side.

We do have a legend. In those days, the Indian trail from the Rio Grande villages to Kansas and Quivira went east from La Glorieta Pass and down the Canadian River four hundred miles before turning north toward the Arkansas River. The legend relates that in 1593–1594 Captain Francisco Leyda de Bonilla and Captain Antonio Gutierrez de Humana and their friends trailed out this Great Plains road seeking gold in Quivira. Gutierrez quarreled with Leyda and murdered him. On the return trip from Quivira-Kansas, the Spaniards approached the Rockies in sight of Pikes Peak by riding west up the Arkansas and up a southward branch past the Spanish Peaks on the Indian trail toward Raton Pass.

Just short of Raton, all of them were attacked and killed by Apaches on the banks of a rushing stream shaded by cottonwoods — the future site of Trinidad, Colorado. No priest was in the party to absolve Captain Gutierrez of the murder of his friend Leyda and that is why the stream came to be called El Rio de las Animas Perdidas en Purgatorio (The River of Lost Souls in Purgatory) — the Purgatoire, or "Picketwire," as the cowboys made it.

Santa Fe was founded in 1610 as the capital of New Spain's Province of New Mexico. However, the Rio Grande colonists were too busy controlling their Pueblo Indian serfs and fending off wild mountain Indians to do much exploration of passes during the rest of the seventeenth century. We are told that, just before the Pueblo Indian Revolt of 1680 against the colonists, some Taos Indians ran off to the Arkansas River rather than build a church free for a priest. Don Juan Archuleta and twenty soldiers went after them over Palo Flechado Pass and possibly over Raton Pass to the Purgatoire and down that — or the Huerfano River — to capture the runaways out on the plains of Colorado.

After putting down the revolt, Governor Don Diego de Vargas led an expedition in 1694 from Santa Fe upriver along the course of today's U.S. Route 285. His explorers passed the mouth of Chama River, marking the south end of San Juan Range, as the river forked northwest from the Rio Grande. From the Chama mouth, they rode on up the Rio Grande into the spacious San Luis Valley. But De Vargas went into the Rockies north of Taos only to the Conejos River on the San Juan side of San Luis Valley, and to Culebra Creek on the Sangre de Cristo side — a mere seventy miles beyond the point which Coronado's scouts had reached in the autumn of 1540.

It was during De Vargas's regime that the Rio Grande Spaniards began to worry about invasion from the northeast by the French, following La Salle's descent of the Mississippi to its mouth in 1682. Concurrently, the Apache Indians, pedestrians from time immemorial, started to acquire Spanish horses from the colonists, at first to eat them, then to ride them, and finally to use them in attacking the Rio Grande settlements. For years, the colonists sought help from Mexico City — especially those founding families of the Spanish town of Don Fernando de Taos (or simply Taos, as distinguished from the ancient Taos Pueblo three miles north of it). At last, in the summer of 1706, Captain Juan de Ulibarri set out with one hundred and forty soldiers, settlers and Pueblo Indians from Santa Fe to awe the Apaches, to look for signs of invading Frenchmen, and to bring back runaway Picurís Indians from the Arkansas.

The Captain took his men from Taos over Palo Flechado Pass (the Spanish phrase "palo flechado" means "arrow-shaped tree" — the shape of the Engelmann spruce and blue spruce up there).[1] Perhaps he enjoyed the sixty-mile traverse, in spite of difficulties with underbrush and boulders. His route today forms one of the nicest highways in New Mexico, moving sixteen miles up Fernando de Taos Creek through widening meadows to the top of the Sangre de Cristos. Then it runs down Cieneguilla (Little Marsh) Creek through a treeless park to Eagle Nest Lake and descends Taos Gap, a ravine of colored cliffs, to the sage flats and hills extending northeasterly to the foot of Raton Pass (7888).

The Ulibarri troop headed for Raton, shortest and easiest crossing of the Raton Mountains, but turned north short of the pass when scouts reported hostile Comanche Indians ahead. This roundabout trail took them up the Canadian River some miles toward its source and over the Raton Mountains by way of what we call Long's Pass, which lies fifteen miles west of, and a little higher than, Raton Pass.

THE RATON MOUNTAINS are a series of blocky piñon-and-juniper mesas which extend east from the Sangre de Cristos along the New Mexico–Colorado border. "Raton" means "mouse" in Spanish and signifies nothing because the Rockies are all full of mice. The Indians called the spur "Chuquirique" in honor of the pack rats, but the tableland has no monopoly on them either (its distinctive beast is the domestic goat). Fishers Peak, a bald flattop 9586 feet high, rises like a fort above Raton Pass and above the towns of Trinidad, Colorado, and Raton, New Mexico, which are twenty-five miles apart at either end of the pass. The Raton Mountains run due east for a hundred miles or so in descending steps until they sink into the arid plain. They spur off from the Sangre de Cristos below Culebra (Snake) Peak, a shapeless pile which is the most southerly of the fifty-four peaks rising above 14,000 feet in the Rockies — all of them in Colorado, as it happens.

The east-west Raton Mountains do not divide watersheds as you might expect. The Arkansas River does its eastward flowing a hundred miles *north* of the Ratons, and so all Arkansas tributaries would seem to start on the north side of the Raton Mountain barrier. They do not. Some Arkansas tributaries rise on the *south* side, notably the Cimarron and Canadian rivers, which flow southeast as though to join the Rio Grande and then change direction to wind up at the Arkansas in Oklahoma. Technically and paradoxically, the Raton Mountains lie in the Arkansas River drainage system.

The wide, busy U.S. Route 85–87 runs from Trinidad up Raton Creek, a branch of the Purgatoire, and leaves it to sweep along the ridge and over Raton Pass in great curves around which the diesel trucks roar like mighty doom. The double tracks and tunnels of the Santa Fe Railroad and all the earlier Raton Pass roads and trails lie a few hundred yards west of and a bit below the highway. The variety of routes over the same pass demonstrates Raton's adaptability to the needs of any age. On the highway, the vertical climb to the top of the pass is 1834 feet in eleven miles. The descent to Raton town is less steep — 1434 feet in fourteen miles.

The view from the top on a clear day shows how different two states can be even though divided by an abstraction — the thirty-seventh parallel of latitude. Southward, New Mexico spreads away like a Dali landscape, a vast carpet of ordered space with tawny mesas and buttes rising like islands in a tropical bay. Northward is Colorado, rugged and weather-beaten as an old cowhand's face — volcanic and coal hills in the foreground, the Spanish Peaks in the middle distance and, far, far north, a blue implacable dominance, Pikes Peak (14,-110). It is one hundred and fifty miles away.

Raton Pass and Long's Pass, which Ulibarri used in 1706, are not the only gaps through the Ratons. Nine miles east of Raton Pass, beyond Bartlett Mesa, is San Francisco Pass (8200), one of three passes of the same name in this area where so much naming of things was done by Spanish admirers of St. Francis of Assisi. This San Francisco Pass trail connects Barela, Colorado, and Sugarite, New Mexico. Further east is Trinchera Pass (6000) on the road from Trinchera, Colorado, to Johnson Mesa and the Cimarron River ranches. West of Long's Pass is a minor Red River Pass (9200), not to be confused with the well-known Red River Pass in the New Mexican mining region between Eagle Nest and San Luis Valley. The minor Red River Pass is on the private road from Tercio, Colorado, to Vermejo Park Ranch of New Mexico, a five-hundred-thousand-acre principality of fences and padlocked gates in a vastness of Sangre de Cristo grassland and forest.

The Raton Mountain country up the Purgatoire River west of Raton Pass is a sheltered upland of adobe homes in cottonwood groves swarming with goats, chickens, pigs, sheep, dogs and brown children. The population is composed partly of "Anglos" (white Americans), and partly of Spanish Americans, including descendants of Rio Grande colonists and of Apache Indians who stayed put during the eighteenth century when Comanche Indians came from Wyoming to occupy northeastern New Mexico.

The area is full of roads, but they are on the old private Sangre de Cristo and Maxwell grants. Even if you get past the padlocked gates, very few natives can explain where the roads go. One of them leads from Vermejo Park over the Sangre de Cristos by way of Costilla Pass (10,100) and through the rugged wilderness of Costilla Canyon to San Luis Valley at Costilla, New Mexico — a forty-mile trek. A faint jeep trail runs west from Tercio through another San Francisco Pass (8560), winding up eventually in San Luis Valley near San Luis, Colorado's oldest town. San Francisco Pass number three (9500) is crossed by a private road up Badito Canyon (Purgatoire drainage) south of Stonewall, Colorado, to the headwaters of the Vermejo River (a Canadian River branch).

All these passes are for 4WD cars only and the roads over them can be slippery when wet. For ordinary travelers, there is the charming State Route 12 from Trinidad up the Purgatoire past the big dike at Stonewall, through Cucharas Pass (9994) and down the north side west of the Spanish Peaks through the rich valley of Cucharas River.

WE LEFT CAPTAIN JUAN DE ULIBARRI and his army some pages back on Long's Pass in the Ratons during that summer of 1706. After coming down Long's Canyon to the Purgatoire, the men clambered over the coal hills to Apishapa River, passed the Spanish Peaks and crossed the Huerfano.[2] Then they moved along the Wet Mountains to the Arkansas at Fountain Creek, with Pikes Peak looming forty miles ahead.

Soon after, they caught up with their Picurís runaways in the curious Jicarilla Apache farming community on the Arkansas out in the plains near present Las Animas, Colorado, which the Spanish called El Cuartelejo, "The Far Quarter." In addition, Ulibarri came upon disturbing proof that Missouri Frenchmen were indeed pushing west into Quivira and other lands which the Spaniards considered to be theirs by right of Coronado's travels. The proof consisted of a new French rifle which one of the Apache chiefs had bought from the Pawnee Indians on the Platte not more than three hundred miles away.

2

Horse Lake and Sangre de Cristo

For many years after Ulibarri, the Rio Grande Spanish rode plainsward, always plainsward, avoiding the Rockies as assiduously as had Coronado and Governor Oñate. In 1719 it was Governor Valverde, heading northeast for the Arkansas again in search of French invaders. He led a mélange of soldiers, settlers, Pueblo Indians and a thousand horses from Santa Fe and Taos on the old trail over Palo Flechado Pass and Raton Pass. The assorted warriors battled snow, bears and poison ivy all the way to The Far Quarter, where evidence of Gallic penetration seemed more ominous even than in 1706.

And during the next summer, Valverde received intelligence from the Spanish viceroy in Mexico City that six thousand French soldiers were poised at The Far Quarter on the Arkansas for the descent on the Rio Grande.[1] Valverde sent his assistant, Pedro de Villasur, and a scouting party of forty-two soldiers, three settlers and sixty Pueblo Indians to check the report. The soldiers let down their long hair and painted their faces with almagra to look like Comanche Indians. Finding only resident Apaches at The Far Quarter, Villasur plunged on north and east, perhaps to the South Platte–North Platte junction, and beyond. Near present North Platte, Nebraska, the scouts were attacked by Pawnee Indians who were not deterred by the Comanche disguise. Villasur and thirty-three soldiers were killed and scalped. When the survivors arrived back in Santa Fe via Raton, they had to admit that not a sign of any of the six thousand Frenchmen had been found.

Thereafter, the Rio Grande settlers gradually lost their French psychosis, though it revived slightly when the dreaded enemy did show at last, arriving from the Arkansas over Raton and Palo Flechado and on down to Santa Fe from Taos. The date was July 22, 1739. The invaders — all eight of them — were almost barefoot, almost naked, utterly defenseless and very tired of traveling. Only one was a real Frenchman. The others were French-Canadian peddlers from the Illinois country led by two brothers, Pierre and Paul Mallet.

They had come, they explained, for personal reasons, to try to do a little business with the merchants of Santa Fe. For a time, Spanish officials thought of hanging them as spies, but could not bring themselves to it. After nine months, the viceroy sent an order to release the prisoners. On May 2, 1740, the Mallet brothers left New Mexico through La Glorieta Pass, and floated on a raft down the Canadian, the Arkansas and the Mississippi to complete their ramble at New Orleans in March, 1741.

SPANISH AFFAIRS at the extreme south end of the unknown Rockies drifted along until the end of the French and Indian War in 1763, when France handed over all of French Canada to England and all of Louisiana west of the Mississippi — the river's total west-side drainage, wherever that was — to Charles III, King of Spain. Charles knew no more about what lay north of Taos then had Governor de Vargas after his brief look at the San Juan Mountains from San Luis Valley in 1694.

But the King felt that the time had come to strengthen Spain's colonial defenses in the immense area north of Mexico which the Spanish claimed by right of exploration. When Russian hunters from Alaska began to appear along the Pacific coast in search of sea otter, Charles shipped soldiers in 1769 to block their way, and to build forts and missions in California from San Diego to Monterey. Between 1772 and 1775, Spanish seamen sailed northward up the West coast past present Oregon and Washington as far as Nootka Sound off Vancouver Island.

The King's leadership inspired support and produced a remarkable aide — Juan Bautista de Anza, perhaps the greatest frontiersman in the 278 years of Spanish colonialism in New Mexico. De Anza's first act was to find a way in 1774 from central Mexico north through Arizona and over San Carlos Pass into California — fruition of the old dream of a route overland to the pearls of the Western Sea. Two years later, De Anza founded San Francisco after leading 240 settlers there through the snows of the Sierras from Culiacan, Mexico, two thousand miles away.

In 1777, Charles III appointed De Anza governor of New Mexico, with the particular task of subduing the Comanche Indians, who had been growing troublesome in their new career as raiding horse Indians. But before De Anza went after the Comanches, the New Mexican scene was brightened by the explorations of two young, muscular, rash and energetic Franciscan priests. Their names were Silvestre Vélez de Escalante and Francisco Atanasio Dominguez. They set out from Santa Fe in July, 1776, with an unarmed party which consisted of an astrologist, a Ute Indian interpreter, the mayor of Zuni, four Spanish traders and (later) two runaway serfs from the Chama River frontier village of Abiquiu. Their aim was to blaze a looping trail to connect Spanish New Mexico and Spanish California. It would pass through the wilds of southwestern Colorado and central Utah, which were presumed to be high and cool. If so, the new route would preserve them from the arid discomfort and Indian perils of De Anza's route to California through Arizona.

The fathers smoked cigars, carried no arms to speak of, ate porcupine when necessary, and traveled most of the way on foot wearing long robes, wide-brimmed hats and sandals. They did not try to explore the main chain of what would turn out to be the Rockies, due north. Instead they followed trails which Spanish traders had been developing for decades along the south and west sides of what they called the "Sierra de las Grullas" (cranes) — the San Juan Mountains. Then they pushed far beyond these.

They saw bits of today's Mesa Verde National Park and a hundred other sights. But they never reached California, mostly because the friendly Ute Indians of Colorado, charmed by their gaiety, lectures on monogamy, gospel singing, and naive disregard of their own danger in the wilderness, kept leading them in the wrong direction to show them the Uncompahgre and Roan plateaus, the jewel lakes of Grand Mesa, deep canyons of the Upper Colorado River, the swift-running White River, the future Dinosaur National Monument and other Colorado tourist attractions.

Part of the route of the fathers would be known later as the Spanish Trail from Santa Fe to Los Angeles. Dozens of the Spanish names which they gave to landmarks survive. And they were the first to report in detail on the existence of La Plata Mountains above Durango, Colorado, the needle-spired San Miguels, the magnificent orange and green Elk Mountains as seen from Gunnison River, the Cathedral Bluffs up White River, and those fringe Rockies of Utah — the Uinta and Wasatch ranges. The approach of winter stopped their westward progress at Utah Lake near Salt Lake. To escape the snow, they came home through northern Arizona, arriving back in Santa Fe on January 2, 1777.

The eleven Spanish tourists went through several passes. On August 4, 1776, they crossed the Continental Divide at Horse Lake Pass (7675) by way of the Rio Grande and its rambling Chama River branch one hundred miles northwest of Santa Fe. Since ancient times Indians had used this trail winding among the sage mesas and arroyos to reach the fertile valleys of San Juan River. Horse Lake Pass cuts the southern tip of the San Juan Mountains in the same way that La Glorieta Pass cuts the south end of the Sangre de Cristos. But Horse Lake Pass is on no major route today and is hard to find among the back roads of the Apache Indian Reservation. The pass lies some twenty miles northwest from U.S. Route 84 at Park View (near Tierra Amarilla), New Mexico, by way of Rutheron and Horse Lake Creek. From the top it is about fifteen miles down the west side to civilization again at Dulce. When the air is right in that lonely Horse Lake country, visitors have heard the toot of a locomotive whistle on the Denver and Rio Grande narrow-gauge railroad tracks seven miles due north of the pass.

On August 22, 1776, the young fathers followed a Ute Indian guide from San Miguel River near present Naturita, Colorado, *eastward* over the crest of the windswept and treeless Uncompahgre Plateau. They could have used Columbine Pass (8500), a wind-swept desolation which is crossed now by State Route 97. Some writers believe that the priests moved further up San Miguel River as far as present Placerville, Colorado, and then crossed the plateau to Uncompahgre River over Dallas Divide (8735). Today's tourists use Dallas Divide when they drive from Ridgway up State Route 62 to the great San Juan peaks around the fascinating mining town of Telluride.

From Uncompahgre and Gunnison rivers, the fathers worked still farther eastward and then around the vast, forested Grand Mesa. They forded Colorado River on September 6, 1776, in the lovely valley short of De Beque Canyon and toiled up Roan Creek under the Book Cliffs among the ridges and bushy ravines of Roan Plateau. One stony ride was so steep that two pack animals slipped and rolled twenty yards. Father Escalante named the ridge "La Cuesta del Susto" — "Hill of the Scare."

After forty miles of climbing and nine miles along the crest of what was even then — as today — superb deer and elk country, they reached Douglas Pass (8268). They descended to White River through Douglas Canyon, which they called

Painted Canyon because of Ute war pictures scratched on the canyon walls. Altogether, it took them four days (September 6 to 10) to cross that divide between the Colorado and White rivers. Today motorists make it from Loma to Rangely through Douglas Pass in two hours. From White River, the priests pushed west into Utah to and across Green River and then up Duchesne River, Strawberry River and Diamond Creek (U.S. Route 40, more or less). Their Indian trail brought them through the Wasatch Range by way of Spanish Fork Canyon (U.S. Route 50), and so on down to the shore of Utah Lake, where the Rocky Mountain portion of their great trek ended.

GOVERNOR JUAN BAUTISTA DE ANZA arrived at Sante Fe from California late in 1778 to tackle the problem of the terrorist Comanches who now ruled all the old Apache country, except pockets of Jicarilla Apaches in the Raton Pass area, from Taos northeast to The Far Quarter on the Arkansas. The Comanches were whimsical terrorists, stealing horses and Pueblo, Navajo or Ute Indian slaves from one Spanish hacienda and selling them to another. A few of them owned guns which they had bought from French traders who worked out of the small new town below the junction of the Missouri and Mississippi rivers, St. Louis.

The Comanches had an able and picturesque chief, Cuerno Verde ("Greenhorn"), who could frighten his enemies by wearing a leather cap to which he attached buffalo horns painted green. De Anza described Cuerno Verde as "a scourge of the Spanish kingdom who had exterminated many pueblos." He decided to demolish the chief and to transform his tribe into buffer allies of the Spanish colonists on the order of the remnant Jicarilla Apaches on Cimarron Creek at the East end of Palo Flechado Pass, and the Utes beyond Horse Lake Pass on San Juan River. But De Anza declined to emulate earlier governors by useless chases to the Arkansas through Raton Pass. Instead he planned to come to grips with the Comanches "through regions different from those which have been followed."

And that is how it finally happened — the first penetration of the Rocky Mountains by Europeans, and the official discovery of four of the chain's most useful southern gates.

The time was during August of 1779, 238 years after Coronado's brief appearances at La Glorieta Pass. Some Comanches were reported to be assembling in San Luis Valley for raids on the Rio Grande settlements. On August 15, De Anza put together a force of 103 soldiers, and 470 colonists and Pueblo Indians and rode after them. He led his army along the same route which Governor de Vargas had used in 1694 — north from Santa Fe up the Rio Grande to the end of the Camino Real at the Spanish outpost of Ojo Caliente, and on from there by Indian trail to Conejos River, which flowed down out of the San Juan Mountains to the valley at a point 115 miles from the capital.

De Anza didn't stop going north as De Vargas had stopped. He pushed on through the sage swells of San Luis Valley with the Rockies rising higher and higher on his left — the San Juans — and on his right — the Sangre de Cristos. Also on his right, a few miles off, he could see the green line of cottonwoods marking the course of the Rio Grande. De Anza's notion of this Spanish river was the official notion. It originated thousands of miles to the north, perhaps near the North Pole.

He was baffled, therefore, when the Rio Grande's bed trended westward across his northward path. And it was then that he learned from his Ute guides the truth. Contrary to the opinion of all reputable cartographers, the Rio Grande went no further north than this. Its source was not near the North Pole, but right here in the San Juans a mere 120 miles west, where there was a high pass to the wilds beyond (it was Stony Pass, 12,594). De Anza could see for himself the region of the pass, at the west end of a great bend in the Continental Divide which the river had scooped out.

And west of the pass? The Utes conveyed to the Governor something of the beauty of the soaring multicolored ridges in today's Silverton-Ouray mining area. De Anza knew, from Father Escalante's report, that that was where many Rocky Mountain streams began — the Animas, the Dolores, the Uncompahgre, the Gunnison, all of which the priest had seen in 1776 from the other side of the San Juans. But the Governor, busy chasing Comanches, could hardly have comprehended so much complex terrain.

And much more confusing geography was still ahead of him. His army forded the Rio Grande and rode north next day across La Garita Creek to Saguache Creek. These streams, he found, were not Rio Grande tributaries. They ran from the mountains out into San Luis Valley and disappeared. Saguache Creek, he observed, flowed from an immense sag in the Continental Divide to the west — a sag so low as to give the illusion that the San Juan Mountains had vanished altogether. The sag, the Utes explained to De Anza, was their Cochetopa Pass (10,032). It had always been — for Utes and animals both — the easy, all-weather gate to the glowing Gunnison River Valley between the Elk Mountains on the north and the San Juans on the south. Beyond were many well-worn trails to Utah.

The trail of De Anza's elusive Comanches seemed to grow warmer as the army pressed on north of Saguache Creek. On August 27, it led the men out of San Luis Valley and over Poncha Pass (9011), a twenty-mile saddle which separated the drainage of the Rio Grande from that of Upper Arkansas River. In the canyons of this gentle pass ("poncha" means "mild" in Spanish), the northern terminals of the San Juan and Sangre de Cristo Mountains met. On the other side of Poncha, the descending army came upon one of the most stirring of Colorado views. Below the soldiers was the verdant valley of the South Fork of the Arkansas, coming down from today's Monarch Pass (11,312). Northward was the blue thread of the main Arkansas, far different in its clean, bright appearance from the same thin, sluggish stream out on the plains of The Far Quarter.

Lining the Arkansas on the west was the massive contin-
uance of the San Juans, the Sawatch Range. Later surveys would
prove that every one of these twelve stately Sawatch peaks was
above 14,000 feet. Among them were the four highest summits
in the Rockies — today's Mount Elbert (14,431), Mount
Harvard (14,420), Mount Massive (14,418) and La Plata Peak
(14,340). Above the Arkansas on the east rose the piñon-and-
juniper ridges of the Mosquito Range, and it was across the
river and into the Mosquitoes that De Anza took his men —
up and over the crest near Cameron Mountain, where Pikes
Peak could be seen presiding over the land fifty miles to the
northeast.

The Spaniards crossed the parklike valleys and piney hills of
the west Pikes Peak country, feasted on buffalo near the
present village of Guffey and diverged from the Indian trail
which ran around the north side of Pikes Peak. This trail
reached the plains down a variant of today's Ute Pass (9183).
Instead of following it, the army rode south of the peak across
the future gold hills of Cripple Creek, past St. Peter's Dome
and down the Little Fountain Creek trail. At the edge of the
plain, they trapped the Comanches at last — a thousand of
them enjoying family life in their lodges among the cottonwoods of Fountain Creek, twenty-five miles below present Ute
Pass at Colorado Springs.

The engagement of August 31, 1779, was brief. The Comanches lost to De Anza their big horse herd, baggage, eighteen warriors, and thirty-four women and children. Unfortunately, Chief Cuerno Verde and two hundred of his warriors
were absent, being on their way to raid Taos. The Governor
went galloping after them with most of his cavalry. He caught
up with them thirty miles south of the Arkansas below Greenhorn Mountain, which marks the southern end of the Wet
Mountains near the Spanish Peaks.

The second battle was brief, too, because Cuerno Verde had
on his leather hat, which made him feel invincible and im-

mortal. He rode proudly out in the open and was killed at the start. His son, four captains, a medicine man and ten warriors died also. The rest fled, which was all right with De Anza, who knew that he had achieved his aim. He had greatly reduced the Comanche power around the settlements for all future Spanish time.

ON THIS COMANCHE CHASE, De Anza had ridden completely around the west and north sides of the Sangre de Cristo Mountains. After his victory of September 3, 1779, he was halfway down along the east side toward Raton Pass, familiar terrain since at least 1700. The Governor camped his army in the willows of Huerfano River near the brown stub of Huerfano Butte ("huerfano" is Spanish for "orphan"). The setting sun painted the Sangre de Cristos blood red, and in the twilight De Anza could see how a Huerfano branch came down from a graceful dip in the range to the southwest.

Early next morning, De Anza followed his Ute guides up the Huerfano toward that graceful dip. South of him, thrusting out into the plain away from the range, were the poetic landmarks, the Spanish Peaks. Close on his left was a great gray dike. The brown block of Sheep Mountain was a little to the right ahead, and then, ridge on ridge behind, were the white caps of the 14,000-footers, Blanca and Mount Lindsey. De Anza noted how Wet Mountain Valley, pressed between the Sangre de Cristos on the west and the lower Wet Mountains on the east, could be entered up a short northering branch of the Huerfano as well as from Arkansas River forty miles northwest.

By midafternoon, the Governor and his men had climbed three thousand feet vertically in twenty miles, on a trail which veered left up South Oak Creek from the Huerfano and the red-patched stack of Badito Cone. The grade brought them to the spruce-covered top of the dip. Beyond was a big grassland hemmed in by a glory of aspen turning gold. De Anza named the place Sangre de Cristo Pass (9459). The descent from the top down Sangre de Cristo Creek to San Luis Valley was no longer than the ascent, and the grade was easier. At times De Anza had an unobstructed view across that gray-green valley for ninety miles to the edge of the San Juans along which he had ridden a fortnight earlier. He could not see the faraway dips of Cochetopa Pass and Poncha Pass. They were hidden by the shoulder of Blanca Peak.

It was plain to the Governor that Sangre de Cristo Pass would be an immediate boon to the Rio Grande settlements. With the Comanches subdued, all the Sangre de Cristo region could be colonized. Now Spanish traders from Taos could reach the Great Plains far east on the Arkansas by crossing only one pass, instead of being obliged to struggle over Palo Flechado and Raton. De Anza had noticed a trail (today's La Veta Pass highway, U.S. Route 160) which forked east at the top of Sangre de Cristo Pass. This trail joined the Cucharas Pass trail leading south to the Raton Pass area. A second trail from the top (today's Pass Creek Pass road) ran due north to enter Wet Mountain Valley.

Very good. But De Anza, the visionary pioneer, looked beyond the Rio Grande. He perceived the relation between Sangre de Cristo Pass, easy gate to the plains, and Cochetopa Pass and Poncha Pass, easy gates through the Rockies to the west and north. Father Escalante's rambling route over Horse Lake Pass was a good start toward California. But Sangre de Cristo Pass and Cochetopa promised much greater things toward achieving a cohesive Spanish empire stretching from the Great Plains to the Pacific.

DE ANZA'S DREAM did not materialize, of course. Even as the Governor crossed Sangre de Cristo Pass, King Charles III of Spain lost interest in New Mexico, and turned his attention and his resources to Spanish affairs nearer home. Without his strong support, the Rio Grande colonists could not extend their wild frontier. When Charles died in 1788, De Anza's dream of empire died with him.

So ended the pass history of Spain in the Rockies. From Coronado's time to that of De Anza, the horse-loving colonists had managed to push from La Glorieta Pass only as far north as Poncha Pass on the Upper Arkansas and Ute Pass at Pikes Peak, a meager three hundred miles.

But all the while an entirely different sort of men were setting the stage to find Rocky Mountain passes from an entirely different direction.

3

Victory at Lemhi

And for entirely different reasons. The "different sort of men" had none of the Spanish love for king, for church, for horses, for the dreamy ranch life which the colonists enjoyed with their Indian serfs along the Rio Grande. The "different sort" were rugged, restless Frenchmen and Englishmen — two centuries and more of them — paddling their fragile birchbark canoes wherever water ran west from the North Atlantic. Their incentive was commercial — the search for beaver to meet the demand for fur in fashionable dress, which had been growing since the days of Geoffrey Chaucer.

Jacques Cartier began the beaver push toward the Pacific by discovering for France the St. Lawrence River in 1536, while Coronado was in Mexico City hearing about the Seven Cities of Cibola. In 1610, Santa Fe's first year as capital of New Mexico, Henry Hudson discovered Hudson Bay for England. In 1673, Père Marquette and Louis Joliet mapped the mouths of the Missouri and Arkansas rivers. In 1742–1743, the gallant Vérendrye brothers may have proved the existence of the Wyoming-Montana Rockies by following the Tongue River into the massive Big Horns at the foot of Granite Pass.[1]

And Canada? In 1754–1755, Anthony Hendry of Hudson's Bay Company, which held the Canadian trade monopoly for the Hudson Bay drainage, explored Lake Winnipeg and saw how Saskatchewan River flowed down from passes of high mountains — the Canadian Rockies — which blocked the way to the Pacific Ocean. Finally, as we have seen, France lost the French and Indian War in 1763. She withdrew from North America, leaving to Spain and to England all this beaver country — the entire St. Lawrence and Mississippi drainage areas.

At that precise time, the world's demand for fur began to exceed the capacity of known beaver grounds to supply it. The result was the speeding up of the tempo of exploration, particularly British exploration in western Canada with its myriad chains of blue lakes and streams and short portages for canoe travel. The horsey Spanish, who had no enthusiasm for beaver or canoes, talked of finding passes west at the headwaters of their new "Louisiana" possessions, the Missouri, the Arkansas, the Platte rivers. Talk was about as far as they got.

By 1790, when ex-Governor de Anza knew for sure that Spain's advance north from Santa Fe was stalled forever at Ute Pass on Pikes Peak, British traders had mapped their vast forests and plains right up to the Canadian Rockies — and along them north and south for five hundred miles. Beaver became plentiful again in fur markets because of these new Canadian areas east of the barrier. There was no urgent need to breach the Rockies on that account. And still some traders were aware of another imperative to get along to the Pacific. One of these traders was a quiet young Scot from the Hebrides named Alexander Mackenzie, aged twenty-six.

The young Scot came to Canada in 1779 while George Washington was trying to hold the Hudson River against the British for the new United States. He had learned the fur trade at Montreal and, in 1785, journeyed by canoe far west and north to take charge of Fort Chipewyan, a bleak spot on Lake Athabaska in the northeast corner of present Alberta. This post was the Peace River headquarters for the North West Company, the upstart Canadian rival of the English Hudson's Bay Company.

Mackenzie kept up on world affairs and he heard even at

remote Peace River about the booming trade in sea otters which British, and Boston-American sailors, as well as the earlier Russians, were buying in the 1780's from Pacific Northwest coast Indians and selling at huge profits to wealthy Chinese at Canton. England, the Scot decided, ought to own that Northwest coast. The way to win it was to find an overland route to the Pacific through the Rockies.

He thought of going southwestward up the Peace from its mouth near Lake Athabaska, but decided to go northerly down the adjacent Slave River instead, expecting to be carried right to the Pacific sea otters. On June 3, 1789, he left Fort Chipewyan with a canoe party of four French Canadians, two of their wives, a German, two Indian guides and an Indian chief with two more wives. After forty-one days and fifteen hundred miles of hardship in that wasteland, the canoes reached the ocean. Unfortunately, it was the wrong ocean — the ice-packed Arctic, not the Pacific. Mackenzie named his Slave River extension the Disappointment — today's interminable Mackenzie — and got back to Fort Chipewyan on September 12, 1789. The only effect of his failure was to make him determined to do better next time. He should have gone up the Peace after all.[2]

He took a year off for preparation. During 1791–1792, he went to England and crammed on mathematics and astronomy, navigation and geography. While cramming, he learned that Spain had been persuaded by England in effect to give up exclusive claims to coast lands north of Spanish California.[3] But he could not have heard so soon about a far more prodigious portent for the future of North America — the discovery in mid-May, 1792, of the mouth of a great new river, the Columbia, on the Pacific coast. The discoverer was Robert Gray, captain of the Boston sailing ship *Columbia* and a citizen of General Washington's United States, which had somehow won its war with England.

In the fall of 1792, Mackenzie returned to Fort Chipewyan,

moved south up Peace River four hundred and fifty miles, and made winter camp near present Peace River town. He spent his hibernation sifting Indian gossip about passes through the Rockies and, on May 9, 1793, he left camp on his brave trek with six French Canadians, two Indian guides, and a Scots clerk. The conveyance for the ten men and their three thousand pounds of food and supplies was a twenty-five-foot canoe.

The country southwestward became heavily and handsomely wooded as they neared the low Rockies, which rose only 6000 feet above sea level. Timberline was at 5000 feet, in contrast to the 11,500-foot timberline of the Sangre de Cristos and San Juans in Governor de Anza's part of the Rockies far southward. Then, on May 17, the explorers had an unpleasant surprise. They came to an unnavigable canyon — today's Peace River Pass. For a painful week, the men exhausted themselves dragging the big canoe over the mountain trail which humped up through the forest for ten miles around the canyon to the river again.

And that was only part of their troubles. Peace River Pass cut completely through this thin belt of Rockies, which meant that the Rockies Western Slope here was not on Pacific drainage. Where was the Continental Divide? Three weeks later, Mackenzie found it in forest uplands by paddling south up the Parsnip, a fast-water fork of the Peace. The Continental Divide itself was barely perceptible, a mere 3000 feet above sea level. It involved a brief portage of eight hundred yards between two lakes from the Parsnip to a small turbulent Pacific stream, Bad River, which became McGregor River and, finally, the Fraser. Bad River was Mackenzie's name for today's James Creek. The Divide crossing was eighteen miles west, and a little south, of present Monkman Pass (3550).

The great date of this crossing was June 12, 1793. Continuing, the Mackenzie party reached, on July 20, 1793, the salt Pacific at Bella Coola Bay, three hundred miles north up the coast from the present United States border. The ten heroes

could tell themselves that they were the first whites to make it
overland to the ocean through the Rocky Mountains.[4] But
that historic portage at the source of the Parsnip can hardly be
found today. It does not deserve to be called a pass, and it has
no other identification. The Rockies part of the Mackenzie
trail is approximated roughly by Hart Highway, running 471
miles from Peace River (town), Alberta, to Prince George,
British Columbia, by way of Pine River Pass (2850) and
Summit Lake (3060). The latter high point — source of the
Parsnip's Crooked River branch — marks the Continental Divide forty miles west of Mackenzie's crossing of it from the
Peace-Parsnip rivers of the Arctic drainage to the Pacific-bound
Bad-McGregor-Fraser rivers.

Mackenzie's men had some perilous hours, particularly in
their affectionate efforts to keep the big canoe afloat.[5] But, on
the whole, their excursion was a relatively easy matter. The
weather was good. Nobody got hurt. Food was plentiful. They
wasted only two weeks on wrong trails — a total of one hundred and forty miles. The journey west — a thousand miles excluding the wrong trails — took only seventy-two days, May 9
to July 20. They covered the thousand miles back to their base
camp on Peace River in an astonishing thirty-two days, July 23
to August 24, 1793.

Nevertheless, the trip was sufficiently painful to cure Alexander Mackenzie of his urge to explore. Thereafter, he stuck to
the beaver business, returned to England in 1799, wrote a book
of his transcontinental adventure, was knighted, and became a
country squire in Scotland, where he died in 1820. His pioneer
crossing to the Pacific was a principal basis for England's claim
to sovereignty in the Northwest. But the Mackenzie route itself to Bella Coola Bay was not practical and was seldom used
again.

DURING THE middle 1780's, when Mackenzie was dreaming of
canoeing to the Pacific, a much greater explorer, even though

by armchair, was dreaming of it too — Thomas Jefferson, United States Minister in Paris. And, while Mackenzie was at Bella Coola Bay in 1793, Captain Robert Gray of Boston was informing Secretary of State Thomas Jefferson about his year-old discovery of the mouth of the Columbia. Jefferson assumed that a close relation existed between this river and the Missouri, and he developed a need to know for sure. The need became an obsession with President Thomas Jefferson when he learned that Napoleon was repossessing for France all of Spanish Louisiana, including the unlocated headwaters of the Arkansas and Missouri rivers in the still mostly unknown Rockies.

And then, in December, 1801, Jefferson read Mackenzie's just-published book of his trip overland eight years before from Fort Chipewyan to the shores of the Pacific Northwest. Reports were reaching him too of Canadians moving down from the north to trade with the Mandan Indians on the Upper Missouri. England and France threatened to gobble up everything! As far as the President was concerned, the United States could not survive if France owned Louisiana and England seized all the Pacific Northwest. Jefferson discussed Mackenzie's book, and also his own acute sense of crisis, with his private secretary, Captain Meriwether Lewis.

This Lewis, a veteran of frontier army duty, had been longing for a decade to have a chance to solve the Missouri-Columbia-Rockies mystery. When Jefferson mentioned a scheme to explore westward, Lewis lit up like a lamp and the Lewis and Clark expedition was born. And so in January, 1803, Congress secretly approved sending an American party up the French-owned Missouri and on to the British-coveted Northwest, led by Lewis and his old army friend, Captain William Clark. The expenses would be met by a magnificent appropriation of twenty-five hundred dollars. Napoleon's attitude toward this American traverse of French soil was not an issue, for he sold all of Louisiana to Jefferson three months later in a deal so stunningly unexpected as to be beyond belief to this day. Jefferson paid Napoleon fifteen million dollars for the Louisiana Purchase of 909,130 square miles, which more than doubled the existing 869,735 square miles of the United States.[6]

Captain Lewis had grown up under Jefferson's wing in the Virginia piedmont around Charlottesville. His great hero was the plumed Governor Spottswood, who had discovered a new world in 1716 by crossing the Virginia Blue Ridge through Swift Run Gap (3585). Lewis combined data in Mackenzie's Pacific journal with Spanish-French guesswork and Indian gossip to conclude that the Missouri River began at a modest pass in low Rocky Mountains. The range at that point would be thin, as at Mackenzie's Peace River Pass, and would run simply and regularly south to north like the Blue Ridge. After portaging half a mile over the Swift-Run-Gap-like pass, the explorers would reach the source of the mighty Columbia, which would carry the canoes swiftly through the one hundred and fifty miles or so of piedmont between the Rockies and the Pacific — terrain and distance being similar to that between Swift Run Gap and Chesapeake Bay.

The trek, clearly, would not be difficult, but Lewis prepared himself as carefully as had Mackenzie. He, too, studied the natural sciences, and he designed a portable boat for negotiating rapids like those in Mackenzie's Peace River Pass. He took his time, wintering some of his party near St. Louis from December, 1803, to May, 1804. On May 14, he and his men headed up the Missouri. By October 26 they had keelboated sixteen hundred miles to the nine villages of the Mandan Indians (near today's Bismarck, North Dakota), which was the end of the known portion of the Louisiana Purchase.

This second winter (1804–1805) passed pleasantly enough. Captain Lewis was thirty years old by then. Captain William Clark, also a native of the Blue Ridge country, was thirty-four. Besides the two leaders, the party consisted of thirty assorted people. Most of them had been recruited along the Ohio River by Captain Clark, who followed Lewis's order that they be "good hunters, stout, healthy, unmarried men, accustomed to the woods and capable of bearing bodily fatigue in a pretty considerable degree."

There was Clark's cheerful Negro slave, York, whose black skin always excited the Indian squaws. There were three army sergeants. The twenty-two privates — mainly Kentuckians plus two French voyageurs — included a taciturn thirty-year-old hunter from Virginia named John Colter. One interpreter was an aging French Canadian, Toussaint Charbonneau, who had secured for Lewis from Minnetaree Indians much data on Missouri headwaters and their Rocky Mountain passes.

Charbonneau was no great shakes professionally, but he had a special value. Among his casual wives was a quick-minded Snake Indian girl of sixteen whom a delighted posterity would know as Sacajawea ("boat woman" or "bird woman"). Charbonneau had bought Sacajawea from the Minnetarees, who had captured her from the Snakes in 1799 far up the Missouri where the river split into three forks. During that Mandan winter of 1804–1805, Sacajawea had told Charbonneau that she wanted to visit her people, who were horse Indians on the Pacific slope just across the Rockies. She felt that she could find the pass to their village over the Divide if Lewis got her to the forks.

Lewis may have been intrigued by the notion of a girl guide-interpreter. But Sacajawea was pregnant and not precisely married. He solved matters by supplying rattlesnake rattles in February to ease her labor and by presiding at her sort-of-wedding to Charbonneau. That made all three of them — Sacajawea, Charbonneau and their baby, Baptiste — United States government explorers in good standing. Soon after, Captain Clark became involved in Sacajawea's affairs by taking a fancy to Baptiste, whom he nicknamed Pompey, or "my boy Pomp."

Meanwhile, rumors reached Lewis during the spring of 1805 that Alexander Mackenzie's old colleagues might be heading west (actually, Simon Fraser of the North West Company planned a trek to the Pacific that summer by way of Peace River

Pass). And so it was that, on April 7, 1805, two pirogues, red and white, and six canoes carrying thirty-two members of the Lewis and Clark expedition, plus Lewis's Newfoundland dog and an iron boat frame, set forth into the unknown under two compulsions. One was an Anglo-American race to the Pacific, with the richest continent on earth as a prize. The other was the domestic problems of a sixteen-year-old Snake girl and her baby.

ONE HUNDRED SPRING DAYS flew by as the young men towed and rowed and sailed their eight boats a thousand miles up the temperamental, tawny, turbid Missouri from the Mandan villages to present Great Falls, Montana. The leaders packed their journals with the color and drama of the wilderness — the vast flowering prairie teeming with buffalo and elk, mule deer and scudding antelope, whirring mallards and teal, hungry mosquitoes. Sacajawea nursed "my boy Pomp" while gathering artichokes, and saved the pirogues from Charbonneau's inept boatmanship. Lewis saw a big black woodpecker (our Lewis woodpecker) and wrote: "It is as black as a crow with a long tail and flies like a jay-bird." [7] But the portable boat was a failure.

On April 25, the explorers entered the plains of Montana at the mouth of the Yellowstone which, Charbonneau said, might have branches leading to Missouri headwaters (Billman Creek does at Bozeman Pass), and even to headwaters of "Spanish" (Green) River (as Wind River, a Yellowstone tributary, does at Union Pass). Green River flows to the Gulf of California after joining the Colorado. Two weeks later, they saw Milk River and the Larb Hills on the right, and then, on the left, the burbling blue Musselshell, where Lewis found freshwater mollusks. As their altitude above sea level rose to 2500 feet, higher forested uplands appeared — the 6000-foot Little Rockies and the Judith Mountains above Judith River, both of which Clark named for his Virginia girl and future wife, Judy Hancock.

But it was early June before they reached the mouth of Marias River (Lewis had a girl, too — Miss Maria Wood), and found themselves staring at the real Montana Rockies, the first white men to record doing so. The mountains rose in blue majesty one hundred ten miles away — the 8000-foot barrier of the Lewis Range straight west and the Big Belts tumbling south toward the soaring Absarokas and Yellowstone Park. All of them were snowcapped and receding in depth; not remotely like the thin Blue Ridge around Charlottesville, Virginia. With dismay Lewis revised his estimate of what lay between his expedition and the Pacific Ocean. He scouted thirty miles up the northbound Marias toward Marias Pass (5215 feet), which the Great Northern Railway would cross a century later to Columbia drainage by way of Flathead and Clark Fork rivers. But he agreed with Captain Clark that they should continue up the south-trending Missouri, having abandoned hope of a short portage from the navigable Missouri to the navigable Columbia beyond the Continental Divide. The immense mass ahead was too high and too thick for that.

And so a great deal of Lewis's preparation had come to nothing. Success depended now on Stone Age intelligence instead of modern science. The Lewis and Clark expedition had to have many horses to carry their eight boatloads of gear up and over the Montana Rockies. Getting horses depended on the ability of Sacajawea, the child bride, to find the pass which led to the camp of her horse Indian people.

The red pirogue was stored on a small island at the mouth of the Marias and, from June 21 to July 15, the men hauled their supplies and boats eighteen miles around Great Falls, cached the white pirogue, and made shirts and breeches of elkskin to replace their tattered army-issue clothes. The namers of Judith River and Marias River named Smith's River, which came down to the Missouri from the Big Belts, after their Secretary of the Navy, Robert Smith. Lewis nursed Sacajawea tenderly through various female complaints, and he longed for horses. With them he could have hunted for passes which might exist directly west up the Sun or Dearborn rivers (today's Cadotte, and Lewis and Clark). Lewis named the fast-running Dearborn for Secretary of War Henry Dearborn.

The thirty-two travelers continued south up the narrowing valley of the Missouri, pressed between the Montana Rockies proper, which rose to 10,500 feet now on the west, and the Big Belt and Crazy Mountains on the east. On July 18, they toiled through the spectacular five-mile canyon, Gate of the Mountains, and avoided streams around present Helena which would have brought them in a day's march to Little Blackfoot River drainage of the Columbia by way of MacDonald, Priest or Mullan Pass. The heat of summer magnified their fear of getting lost but, on July 22, Sacajawea bucked them up by announcing that she knew exactly where they were.

Three days later, sure enough, they camped among the willows in the meadowlands surrounding Three Forks, where their Indian girl had been captured in 1799, some one hundred and sixty miles south of Great Falls. Lewis and Clark named the first fork, to the east, the Gallatin (for Secretary of the Treasury Albert Gallatin). A mile or so up stream, the river forked again. They named the east fork the Madison (Secretary of State James Madison), and the largest west fork the Jefferson. Thus 2465 miles from St. Louis on the 437th day of their trek, they marked the official end of the Missouri River.

The next week brought more cheer and excitement as they began to approach Sacajawea's crossing of the Continental Divide. On August 3, they went by Pipestone Creek, up which a great road would run in time over Pipestone Pass (6418) to the copper kingdom of Butte. Beyond Pipestone Creek, they entered the vast grasslands of the Big Hole country, Montana's supreme cattle region, enclosed by the Bitterroot and Pioneer Mountains on the west, and the Ruby and Madison ranges on the east. They passed the mouths of the Big Hole River and Ruby River and named them the Wisdom and the Philanthropy, honoring Jefferson's personality.

On August 8, Sacajawea recognized the Snake Indian landmark, Beaverhead Rock, near the river (the Jefferson is called the Beaverhead above the Big Hole), and Captain Lewis saw indications of a pass (Lemhi) over the Bitterroots sixty miles to the northwest. That was too much for him. At daybreak next morning, he hurried ahead on foot with three of his men. They passed the site of present Dillon and the Rattlesnake Cliffs at Rattlesnake Creek, and turned west up the trickle of Horse Prairie Creek (near Armstead), instead of following the main stream to Monida Pass (6823) and Red Rock Pass (7056). The latter is a popular gate today from the Big Hole to U.S. Route 20 and Yellowstone Park.

The quartet had, on August 11, the eerie thrill of spotting a man fleeing from them on a horse toward Sacajawea's Lemhi Pass, the first human they had seen in four months.[8] They lost him on his trail east, which climbed out of the bleak grassland and into cooler sage and sparse pine uplands of the Bitterroots.[9] And next day, August 12, 1805, they reached the grassy top of Lemhi Pass (7373) after drinking at a final rivulet, the extreme source of the waterway which had been Lewis's objective through much of his adult life.[10] The pass was not high or otherwise distinctive for these Rockies. But, to Easterners used to the 4000-foot crests of the Alleghenies, it was stupendous.

They stared for awhile westward across Lemhi Valley at the stark, treeless hills of Idaho and descended three-quarters of a mile down the steeper west slope of Lemhi, where Lewis drank at another rivulet which he called the Columbia. Actually, it was Agency Creek — which became Lemhi River at the foot of Lemhi Pass, and then Salmon River twenty miles to the northwest along the Bitterroots, and then Snake River one hundred and forty miles west of *that*, and *then* the Columbia, three hundred miles down the Snake. Beyond the mouth of the Snake, the Columbia had to flow nearly three hundred and fifty miles west before it came to its Pacific mouth, which Captain Gray had discovered in 1792.

Lewis found and made friends with Sacajawea's timid Snake people next day in their sand-and-sage summer camp a few miles north down Lemhi River from the west foot of Lemhi Pass. There were four hundred of them, and they had many horses and mules with Spanish brands and saddles and bridles. Sacajawea's brother, the Snake chief Cameahwait, told Lewis by sign language how the horses had filtered north by trade from De Anza's Santa Fe and Taos over Cochetopa Pass, or by way of Father Escalante's Horse Lake Pass and Douglas Pass to "Spanish" (Green) River, and on north. Or to Utah Lake, Great Salt Lake and north.

The Captain had no clear idea where Santa Fe and Taos were, though he placed them south of the unexplored Red River, the southernmost Mississippi drainage of Jefferson's Louisiana Purchase, provided that the Red rose where it was supposed to rise — at the Continental Divide in the Rockies. On the whole, Lewis was hard put to visualize from Chief Cameahwait's descriptive fingers these confusing threads of Spanish-Indian commerce. It is not surprising that he saw the vast terrain incompletely and incorrectly.

The fortnight which followed was full of business. Lewis bought horses and mules, and recrossed Lemhi Pass with them and with Cameahwait's warriors on August 16 to meet the Clark Party. Captain Clark, "my boy Pomp" and Sacajawea went over Lemhi on August 19. Sacajawea sucked her fingers on the way, meaning "these are my people" in sign language. Lewis rejoined them at the Snake camp a week later, after sinking the canoes for storage in a pond near the mouth of Horse Prairie Creek and loading the baggage on thirteen horses. On that third crossing, one of his lady Indian helpers lagged, but caught up with him on the down slope an hour later and proudly displayed the baby to which she had given birth beside the brook near the top. It was the first of many babies reported to have been born from time to time on Rocky Mountain passes.

VICTORY AT LEMHI was a thrilling event for the explorers, who knew that all outdoors west of the pass could become American by their claiming. And still there were worries. The navigable Columbia seemed a long way off on August 24 when Captain Clark reconnoitered north down the Lemhi, and then down the Salmon to its west turning. A brief examination of this Salmon with its canyons and rapids convinced him that travel to the Snake and Columbia was impossible that way.[11] The only solution was to push over the Bitterroots again to the valley beyond in order to pick up the Columbia-bound Indian trail which their need for horses had forced them to bypass in mid-July at the Gate of the Mountains.

Over the Bitterroots again, but *not* back east over the Continental Divide — as Clark learned from his new Snake Indian guide, an old man named Toby. One of the Divide's innumerable quirks is its abrupt eastering departure from the Bitterroots at Gibbons Pass, sixty miles north of Lemhi Pass, after being a part of the Bitterroots all the way north from Red Rock Pass and Yellowstone Park.[12] And so, on September 1, the expedition left the Lemhi River Snake camp — the exact same thirty-two people who had left the Mandan villages on April 7, 1805, for Sacajawea came along, and Pompey too, a bouncing seven-month-old tourist now. Charbonneau's young wife, it seemed, was to keep on seeing the world instead of settling down near Lemhi Pass with the home folks.

The chill air reminded them that winter was coming as they tramped up the North Fork of the Salmon. This small stream remained winsome and cheerful even on September 3, when the trail became very steep and rough in the forest uplands, and snowy, too. They noted Dahlongo Creek on their right

(Gibbonsville), but in the slippery gloom old Toby missed the trail, which ran up a right branch of that North Fork of the Salmon to the Divide at the future Gibbons Pass. Instead, having lost the trail, he took his employers ten miles farther along the North Fork, and they camped that night — the most miserable of the whole trip so far — with little to eat, near the crest of the Bitterroots, two miles or so south and west of Gibbons Pass.

Next day, September 4, they toiled along the snowy ridge of the crossing which we now call Lost Trail Pass (6951) until they found the trail again at Gibbons Pass (6982). But they stayed on the Western Slope, descending 2000 vertical feet on Camp Creek through the just-turning aspens. Soon Toby brought them to the junctions of Camp and Cameron creeks and the East Fork of Bitterroot River — known later as Ross's Hole. Here they found a village (near Sula) of four hundred friendly and intensely curious Flathead Indians, who had never seen such weird people before. The Flatheads posted Lewis and Clark on Western Slope geography and sold them eleven horses, bringing their string up to forty.

The beautiful Bitterroot Valley is thirty miles wide between the 8000-foot forested crest of the Sapphire Mountains on the east and the 8000-foot Bitterroot crest on the west. It is the garden spot of the entire Rockies today, but it was far from fruitful in the fall of 1805. Game was hardly to be found as the hungry explorers moved eight-five miles from Lost Trail Pass down Bitterroot River to make camp at the mouth of Lolo Creek. They named the camp Traveller's Rest. From camp, they scouted eleven miles farther north to the junction (today's Missoula) of the Bitterroot with what they called Clark Fork of the Columbia. The friendly Flatheads had told them how several good trails led directly east up branches of this lovely Clark Fork and over the Continental Divide to the Missouri buffalo country by the very passes which they had missed in their horse-hunting detour to Lemhi. If they had had horses on

July 18 at Gate of the Mountains they would have reached Traveller's Rest on July 28, instead of September 9 — 145 easy miles instead of 415 difficult miles.

The Flatheads stressed, however, that Clark Fork was of no use to them downstream to reach the Columbia. It looped north even more interminably than the Missouri looped south to Lemhi. But one of the Flatheads offered to guide them to the Columbia by an ancient Indian shortcut — Lolo Trail up Lolo Creek from Traveller's Rest, and over the Bitterroots by Lolo Pass (5187).

Captain Lewis decided to take a chance. He hired the Flathead guide and, on September 11, the enduring thirty-two rode south and west up brightly-bubbling Lolo Creek. On the thirteenth, they climbed into the pungent lodgepole pines and came to Lolo Hot Springs — which Lewis judged to be hotter than Hot Springs, Virginia — beyond Swift Run Gap. They passed Needle Rock, crossed Lolo Pass two miles from the Springs, and pitched briefly down toward Lochsa River through blazing fall foliage.[13]

But then Lolo Trail moved to the high, brushy ridges of the Clearwater Mountains. For a week they stumbled over a hundred miles of hill and dale through snow and mud to reach at last a Nez Perce village at the forks of North and South Clearwater rivers (Ahsahka, Idaho). Here the Rockies ended for good, and the altitude was a mere thousand feet above sea level. From the village, it would be sixty miles by canoe down the widening Clearwater Valley to Snake River, and then an easy float of one hundred and fifty miles to the Columbia.

They were exhausted — except "my boy Pomp," who never seemed to get tired. And yet they were pleased, even though their "portage" of the Rockies was not quite what Captain Lewis had expected. Instead of a half-mile carry over one low pass from Missouri to Columbia headwaters, they had journeyed five hundred miles over three passes higher than they dreamed could exist. Instead of lasting one day, the "portage" lasted from July 18 to September 20, 1805.

THEY SPENT THE WINTER in reasonable comfort on the Pacific at the mouth of the Columbia (Fort Clatsop, November 14, 1805–March 23, 1806), and arrived back in Bitterroot Valley at Traveller's Rest by way of Lolo Pass soon after sunset, June 30, 1806. They were homesick now, but had two more exploring jobs to do. On July 3, Captain Lewis and nine soldiers rode east on the direct buffalo trail to the Missouri River. Simultaneously, Captain Clark headed south again up the Bitterroot River toward Lost Trail Pass with eighteen soldiers, his Negro slave York, Pompey and seventeen-year-old Sacajawea, who had been promoted to official guide for this side trip.

With efficiency and speed, the Indian girl led them and forty-nine horses over Gibbons Pass, down Trail Creek in the peak-girdled spaces of Big Hole River Valley near present Wisdom, south up the Big Hole, and over to Beaverhead drainage and Horse Prairie Creek. The divide here is called Big Hole Pass (7357) — not the Continental Divide pass of the same name which exists south of Lost Trail.[14]

The hustling Clark party covered two hundred miles in four days and raised the canoes from the pond at the mouth of Horse Prairie Creek. Then they practically flew (most of them) by canoe down the Beaverhead and Jefferson to Three Forks — one hundred miles on that single day, July 11. The horses and wranglers trailed after. At Three Forks, Clark sent eleven boatmen on north down the Missouri to meet Captain Lewis's eastering buffalo trail explorers at Great Falls.

Clark himself, with Sacajawea, Pompey, Charbonneau and seven others, spent some happy days escorting the forty-nine horses up the delicious Gallatin River to near present Bozeman, and east over the lodgepole intervales of the Bridger Mountains to Yellowstone River, which poured down from the

Absaroka Range and Yellowstone Park. Perhaps they crossed from Gallatin to Yellowstone drainage by the lowest and straightest pass trail — over Bozeman Pass (6002), just south of Sacajawea Peak (9665). But they could have used other nearby crossings such as Bridger (6139) or Flathead (6770). In any event, they reached the Yellowstone on July 15 near its junction with a smaller river which they named after Private John Shields. Three weeks later (August 3), their new-made dugout canoes brought them to the Yellowstone-Missouri junction near the Montana–North Dakota border, and they began watching for Captain Lewis. Their forty-nine horses did not do so well. On the way east, Crow Indians stole them all from Clark's wranglers, thus starting the proud record of the Crows' as the best horse thieves of the Plains.

THE LEWIS DETACHMENT of ten made good progress on the shortcut trail east, starting July 3. From present Missoula the trail led through Hell Gate and up Blackfoot River branch of Clark Fork to a spot in thick pine forest eleven miles east of today's Lincoln summer resort. Here, the boiling Blackfoot forked — Alice Creek to the left, Cadotte to the right. The trail forked too, and Lewis chose the Alice Creek trail, which brought his men in fourteen miles to the woody top of the Continental Divide — today's Lewis and Clark Pass (6323).[15]

The day was Monday, July 7, 1806. If Lewis had picked the righthand trail up Cadotte Creek, they would have crossed by Cadotte Pass (6044), three miles southwest from Lewis and Clark Pass. The next pass just south of Cadotte was lower still (Rogers Pass, 5609). Rogers is used now by State Route 20 from Missoula to Great Falls, one hundred and sixty miles. Beyond Lewis and Clark Pass, the buffalo trail brought the men to Dearborn River branches, but then moved northward to Sun River, by which they reached Great Falls of the Missouri on July 11. A week later, they were joined there by Captain Clark's eleven canoemen from Three Forks.

As chance would have it, the unhappiest and most dangerous moment of the whole Lewis and Clark expedition occurred
near the end. On July 6, Captain Lewis, with George Drewyer
and the Fields brothers, rode from Great Falls to see if Marias
River trended north far enough to tap the Saskatchewan River
beaver lands, which were enriching the fur merchants of England and Montreal. They pushed over the hot Montana plain
to the desolate spot where Marias River becomes Cut Bank
Creek and Two Medicine Creek, twenty airline miles west of
present Shelby, Montana. Then they followed the white clay
gash of Cut Bank Creek north until they found it veering
southwest near today's oil town of Cut Bank, Montana, instead of continuing north into Canada. They pursued the
creek anyhow to within ten miles of the Rocky Mountains'
Lewis Range and future Glacier National Park, where the
stream rises at Cut Bank Pass (7800).

It was all Blackfoot Indian country in 1806, and it remains
the Blackfoot Indian Reservation today. Lewis saw campsites
often as they crossed the dozen miles of Carlow Flat to Two
Medicine Creek — the same Carlow Flat through which the
Great Northern Railway runs along the line of Two Medicine
Creek and its Summit Creek branch to Marias Pass fifty-five
miles east. On July 26, the party met eight Blackfoot men
near Two Medicine Creek. Greetings followed, and Lewis gave
out three gifts, since three of the eight claimed to be chiefs.
The twelve red men and white men camped together that
night in the wide, grassy Two Medicine Creek bottom below
high bluffs.

At dawn next morning, July 27, Captain Lewis woke to find
that the Indians had stolen all of their four guns. In the
scuffle to recover them, Reuben Fields stabbed one Blackfoot
dead. Soon after, Lewis shot and killed another who was trying
to steal his horse. The exact spot of these killings can be
reached today by driving thirteen miles south from Cut Bank
on the Valier road and walking a mile farther south over the

flat prairie to the high banks of Two Medicine Creek. There are ranches in this Alkali Lake area but it is still a very wild place.

Lewis feared that the main Blackfoot camp was in the vicinity, and it was imperative to clear out. The day was cooled by occasional light rains, the plain was level, and Lewis found that the Blackfoot horse which he had caught was better than the one which had been stolen from him. By 3 P.M., July 27, the fleeing white men had made sixty-three miles. They rested an hour and a half and covered seventeen miles more by dark. After two more hours rest, they pushed on toward the mouth of the Marias by moonlight through shadowy herds of buffalo — a grand total of one hundred miles from Two Medicine Creek by 2 A.M. They rested again until daybreak, rode twenty miles more, though Lewis was "so soar from my ride yesterday that I could scarcely stand," and then joyfully joined the seventeen other soldiers, who had canoed down from Great Falls, at the Missouri-Marias junction. A week later, they passed the Yellowstone's mouth and on August 12, 1806, caught up with Clark's party. All thirty-two explorers ended their epic trek in fine health except Captain Lewis. Peter Cruzatte had shot him in the rear, harmlessly but painfully, the day before, thinking that he was an elk.[16]

THE LEWIS AND CLARK EXPEDITION endures as one of history's most entrancing adventure stories. Besides, it established solid American claims to Washington and Oregon, inasmuch as its Canadian rival, Simon Fraser of the North West Fur Company, was stalled that year far up Stuart River of the Fraser. He had crossed the Continental Divide in the spring of 1806 at Summit Lake where, as we have seen, Hart Highway crosses it now.

On the debit side, the achievement was of limited value in spreading knowledge of the Rocky Mountains as mountains. The Nicholas Biddle account of the Lewis and Clark journals was not published until 1814, when Americans were distracted by their war with England. Furthermore, the Blackfoot killings of July 27 was a factor in provoking that powerful tribe to keep trappers out of the Montana and Canadian Rockies until its fatal weakening by smallpox in the late 1830's. Nearly a half-century passed before the United States government (Northern Pacific Railroad Survey of 1853) ventured again into those Montana Rockies.

But, from this book's special viewpoint, the expedition could not have been more successful. It gave to Americans their first Rocky Mountain passes, none of them as dramatic or as important as some we will meet later, but all charming and accessible — Lemhi and Lost Trail, Gibbons and Lolo, Lewis and Clark, Big Hole and Bozeman.

These were our very first, but others were about to be discovered by another American soldier who was not looking for passes at all. On August 12, 1806, while Clark's group and Lewis's group rejoined near the North Dakota–Montana border, this soldier was a thousand miles south, leading a small army party from the Osage Indian country of present Missouri west toward the Arkansas. His name was Zebulon Montgomery Pike. On that very day he had been promoted from lieutenant to captain.

4

Pike's Gap—and a Shot in Time

As LEWIS AND CLARK headed home, Captain Pike's explorers rode west from the Missouri Osage country under quite different auspices. President Jefferson and Congress did not authorize the Pike expedition. The President's knowledge of it was casual. Though approved by Secretary of War Dearborn, it was conceived by one of America's ranking scamps, General James Wilkinson, governor of Upper Louisiana and also commander in chief of the United States Army.[1]

Wilkinson — handsome, plausible, charming — was a Maryland-born citizen of Kentucky who held the two highest offices in western America as the price of his loyalty to the government in Washington. To keep his price high, he carried on intrigues with Spain, and with Jefferson's vice president, Aaron Burr, whom he soon double-crossed. Wilkinson talked of setting up his own nation west of the Alleghenies. Technically, this was treason. Actually, in those days of states' rights, when thousands of Kentuckians had separatist leanings, it was more like ruthless politics played by a ruthless man. In 1806, President Jefferson was involved in a dispute with Spain over the southern boundary of his Louisiana Purchase. He could not fire the commander in chief of the only force he had in the Louisiana area. He had to play along with him, and hope for the best.

When Zebulon Pike headed west under Wilkinson's orders,

he was twenty-seven years old — a small, compact, tactful, red-cheeked, blue-eyed young officer with wide swinging shoulders and a nose as straight as any Greek god's. He was army through and through, born in New Jersey of army parents. He became almost a protégé of General Wilkinson's at Fort Washington (Cincinnati) in 1793, and he fought at the Battle of Fallen Timbers with Meriwether Lewis, whom he knew later also at the army's frontier post, Kaskaskia, Illinois. In 1801, he showed his romantic temperament by eloping to Cincinnati with, and marrying, a Kentucky belle, Clarissa Brown.

All the while, he worked hard to please General Wilkinson, and to be a better soldier. He learned to speak French at Kaskaskia, and how to use a telescope, compass, watch and quadrant for rough mapping. He was forthright rather than perceptive, more stubborn than judicial. He handled his men kindly (providing grog) but with discipline (wenching was out). They admired him because he led them well and yet remained one of them, enduring what they endured. And they admired him for his stamina, which he demonstrated during the bitter winter of 1805–1806 in the frozen wastes of Minnesota while hunting the source of the Mississippi for Wilkinson.[2]

What Lieutenant Pike knew, or thought, of his friend's treasonable plotting he confided to nobody. The General's orders to him, issued June 24, 1806, after he returned to St. Louis, were clear and legitimate. They were also simple — an easy summer's outing quite unlike the grandiose Lewis and Clark expedition to find passes by which to journey all the way to the Pacific. Pike was to explore the Arkansas River to its unknown source — presumably in the Rockies. No passes to find. Then he would move south along the range below the Continental Divide until he intercepted the Red River which began, theoretically, in the Rockies too. He would canoe down the Red a thousand miles or so to join Wilkinson's boundary-watching army camped near Natchitoches in southern Louisiana. Along the way, he would gather all information about the Spaniards of New Mexico which might be useful to Jefferson in settling the boundary dispute.

These were the orders. Pike was trained to obey them, whether or not the spy data obtained might be useful to the schemer Wilkinson, bent on out-maneuvering both the President of the United States and Spain to win a western empire of his own. The young Captain understood the technicalities. The Upper Arkansas River marked the Spain–United States boundary by usage, if not by treaty, west of the 100th meridian (today's Dodge City, Kansas). The illusive Red River was that region's real boundary, as the French had defined Louisiana from the seventeenth century on. Pike had a right, therefore, to explore south of the Upper Arkansas as far as the Red, but Wilkinson advised him not to be caught doing it. The Spanish of New Mexico might not accept the French definition.[3]

The just-promoted officer and his party left their river boats with the Missouri Osages and pushed by pack train across Kansas to visit the Republican River Pawnee village in Nebraska (near Red Cloud) — the same Pawnee band that had killed Villasur and thirty-three of his men in 1720. There they heard of the safe return to St. Louis of Lewis and Clark.[4] They heard also that a Spanish troop under Lieutenant Don Facundo Melgares had ridden from Santa Fe to stop them — six hundred dragoons on white horses using the old river trail east from La Glorieta Pass (Red River, Pike guessed; but it was the Canadian) and then north to the Arkansas. The dragoons had come a month too early and had gone back by Sangre de Cristo Pass to Santa Fe.

The Pike party reached the Great Bend of the Arkansas on October 28, 1806, and entered Colorado two weeks later. The flat prairie had changed to a rolling terrain. The brisk air, the clear sunlight, gave the explorers that exhilaration of mind and body that comes in arid lands more than four thousand feet high. Colorado blazed still with autumnal gold — golden grasslands back from the bluffs of the winding Arkansas, great golden leaves falling from the river's ribbon of cottonwoods. There was the clatter of parent magpies and their trailing young. Twice they saw wild horses grazing with buffalo — beautiful Arabian horses of every color with speed greater than that of their own horses. The eerie sight of these horses was a startling reminder that this was not unclaimed wilderness. It was Spanish country, and had been for two and a half centuries.

No Rockies in sight, and November already! Pike knew now that the trip would run well into winter. They had summer clothes only but that was not too great a problem. Of these sixteen travelers, twelve had been with Pike on the Minnesota expedition, also in summer overalls, and they had made out somehow with blankets and skins. Pike's present roster included Sergeant William E. Meek, Corporal Jeremiah Jackson, Spanish Interpreter Vasquez and eleven privates. They were resourceful soldiers, good horsemen and hunters, congenial, and too fond of adventure to mind hardship.

Besides, a young surgeon, Dr. John Hamilton Robinson, had volunteered to come along. Robinson, a twenty-four-year-old Virginian, was a civilian friend of General Wilkinson's. His apparent reason for taking the trip, trumped up by Pike, was to collect a bill in Santa Fe owed by Baptiste La Lande, a Creole trader, to one of Pike's friends back in Kaskaskia, Illinois.[5] The real reason must have been to gather information for Wilkinson. Captain Pike, of course, should not visit the Spanish capital of New Mexico at this time of tension and suspicion over the United States–Spanish boundary. Pike felt, however, that Robinson could do Wilkinson's spy work if he went in alone with a bill to collect.[6]

AND SUDDENLY the Rockies appeared. The explorers topped a ridge and there they were — Pikes Peak, sprawling snowcapped to the northwest beneath the bluest of skies; the Spanish Peaks, slate-gray pyramids to the southwest. The time was 2 P.M. on

Saturday, November 15, 1806. The men cheered, as people do when the curtain rises on a good stage set. They were not overwhelmed, but glad to see their objective. Pikes Peak is one of the world's most deceptive landmarks. It can seem small and low at a distance, but it covers four hundred and fifty square miles and rises 14,110 feet above sea level. It was nearly two miles above the altitude of Pike's men, and one hundred and twenty miles away from them.[7]

But the Captain, like Lewis and Clark at Marias River in 1805, had eyes trained for nothing higher than the 4000-foot Alleghenies. The Rockies, he guessed, might be as much as fifteen miles off. But he adjusted toward the truth during the next week as his men advanced up the sandy Arkansas, treading "desert" which would be a garden in time for raising Rocky Ford melons, vegetables and Thanksgiving turkeys, nourished by snow water gathered at the Continental Divide.

The men noted Indian signs often; perhaps unseen Utes watching them for Lieutenant Melgares. They met some Pawnees. They observed the low place straight ahead where the Arkansas emerged from the blue range. At left were the Wet Mountains and Spanish Peaks from which Arkansas tributaries flowed down to them at intervals — the Purgatoire (Raton Pass), Apishapa (Apishapa and Cucharas passes), Huerfano (Sangre de Cristo Pass), St. Charles (De Anza killed Cuerno Verde on its Greenhorn branch). The mysterious Red River, they knew, had to lie beyond these Arkansas tributaries.

At the site of the present steel city of Pueblo, some of the soldiers built a breastworks for protection against Utes or Spanish dragoons. Captain Pike, Dr. Robinson, and Privates John Brown and Theodore Miller took the afternoon off (November 24) to hike up Pikes Peak. The quartet began by way of Fountain Creek, which came down to their breastworks from Ute Pass. They hiked twelve miles on the twenty-fourth, crossed the bleak mesa west to Turkey Creek on the twenty-fifth (twenty-two miles), getting more and more uncomfortable in their thin overalls and worn moccasins. They set up a base camp that night beneath the mountain, and headed for the top next day, scrambling up the rocks of Little Turkey Creek through piñon and pine.

They saw a buffalo, a strange partridge (dusky grouse) and a new kind of deer (mule). But night fell with the top out of sight somewhere above. They rested miserably in a cave, and, on Thursday, the twenty-seventh (Thanksgiving Day in a later era) struggled upward for an hour in a dazzle of sunshine; temperature, ten above zero (Fahrenheit).[8] The snow deepened to their waists as they hit the top of something — a minor ridge at 10,000 feet. From there, the round summit beckoned. It was "15 or 16 miles away" — over an obstacle course of immense woody ravines and satellite peaks. And almost a mile higher.[9]

That was the last straw. As Pike said, "no human being could have ascended to its pinical" from that ridge at that time. They retreated to warmer weather at their Little Turkey Creek base camp to find that magpies had made off with all their food except some deer ribs and a thin grouse. Next day, the four trudged on south down Turkey Creek through old Comanche camps like the big one which De Anza had attacked in 1779 (the Fort Carson Reservation today). They reached their Pueblo breastworks on November 29.

Their afternoon's hike had lasted six days. It was a failure, and it made Pike forever famous as the first American who didn't climb Pikes Peak.

THE EXPEDITION continued on up the Arkansas toward the tabletop mesas in front of present Canon City. The temperature sank almost to zero. It snowed and hungry magpies pecked at the sores on the backs of the pack horses. Pike, convinced by now that his peak was the highest ever seen by Americans on American soil, placed its height by triangulation at 18,581 feet above sea level. The figure was 4471 feet too high, but not bad at that. Much of his error came from estimating his posi-

tion near the Arkansas at 8000 feet above the sea instead of
5187. Excluding this, he made the top only 1658 feet higher
than it really was above the river.

Trails went off to the left, one of them the present Hardscrabble Pass road from Florence south to Wet Mountain Valley.
But the men persisted west, and found themselves on December
5 in the grassy glade above today's Canon City where Sand
Creek arrives from the north and the river tumbles from the
high walls of the Royal Gorge. It was a cul-de-sac in 1806,
hemmed in by multicolored crags, full of echoes by day and
wildcat screams by night — in sharp contrast to the plains world
they had lived in since July. They camped under Noonans Peak
with buffalo and deer and fat turkeys in sight, and they scouted
for four days to decide which of several streams falling in from
the rugged hinterlands was the Arkansas. Two soldiers clambered into the Royal Gorge for two of its eight miles and told
Pike that the stream had its sources a short way up.

Grape Creek to the south was no more promising. So they
headed their pack train northwest on December 10 — up Currant Creek for forty miles through the frozen pastures west of
Pikes Peak to Currant Creek Pass (9300).[10] The pass was the end
of the Arkansas, as far as Pike could judge. A few miles beyond
and below it he found a new river — the South Platte. Pike
knew that it had to be the Platte. He had crossed Platte drainage on the plains in October after visiting the Pawnee village.
And he had learned from the Pawnee party on the Arkansas
how the South Platte left the Rockies not far north of Pikes
Peak.

It was clear too that the South Platte's origins were in this
treeless, high basin of brown grass sprinkled with buttes which
spread away from him to peak-marked horizons — South Park.
The basin was rimmed on the west by a tapestried ridge — today's Mosquito Range.[11] Beyond it, Pike gazed at a much
higher barrier of granite and blue snow. It was, he surmised
correctly, the Continental Divide. It was also, though he

couldn't have known it, that supreme Sawatch Range portion of all the Rockies which we saw with De Anza in 1779 after crossing Poncha Pass from San Luis Valley.

Swinging his telescope northward, the Captain examined the high rampart there, and the dips in it which he thought could be South Platte passes. And were — Boreas Pass (11,482), Hoosier Pass (11,541) and others. And beyond them? The headwaters of Yellowstone River, to be sure! The Continental Divide was due west, wasn't it? The Platte was here in South Park. The next drainage system north of the Platte had to be the Yellowstone.

Having reached this conclusion, Pike concluded wrongly a second time. A large river flowed between the Mosquito Range and the Sawatch Range west of it. The river had to be the Red, since his men had determined that the Arkansas stopped at least eighty miles behind them. So the explorers trudged on west toward the "Red." Their trail took them through a very large Indian summer camp littered with corncobs, broken combs and other reminders of the Spanish culture south of them.[12] Near present Hartsel, they veered southwest from the main South Platte and climbed four easy miles out of South Park to the top of Trout Creek Pass (9346), and on down the gentle, sparsely-wooded west slope of the Mosquitoes to the river.

It snowed hard on December 19, obscuring the buttressed architecture of Mount Princeton (14,197) above them and making the stream a black foam-flecked turbulence. Next day, Dr. Robinson led thirteen men and the pack train downstream past the white cliffs of Chalk Creek and south toward Brown's Canyon and present Salida. Pike, with John Mountjoy and Theodore Miller, scouted upstream, up the piñon-and-cedar valley. They camped between Mount Harvard and Buffalo peaks and advanced on the twenty-second to the foot of Mount Elbert (14,431), the highest Rocky Mountain of all. The presumed Red, a small blue burble now, came from the Divide twenty-five miles north. Pike's telescope brought its sources close — Tennessee Pass and Fremont Pass. Westward, between Elbert and La Plata Peak, was the sag of Independence Pass (12,095), over whose crest today's summer music lovers gingerly wend toward the concerts at Aspen.

But Pike and his privates had seen enough. They hurried downstream and found the rest in a merry mood on a cloudy Christmas Eve. Just when they had seemed about to starve for lack of game, eight fat buffalo had waddled by. So Christmas Day, 1806, was for feasting around a log fire big enough to warm much of their campsite intervale four miles above present Salida and under Cameron Mountain. The Captain donned his dress uniform — faded blue trousers, scarlet cap and red coat lined with fox skins, but the elegant effect was reduced by his bare toes sticking out from what was left of his moccasins. The sixteen celebrants gorged on rich meat and sent Christmas carols ringing all over this wild place.

Some dreamed of home to be reached by floating in dugout canoes all the way down the Red to Natchitoches. Dr. Robinson caught and caged a peculiar greenish bird, and then a second bird, which pounced on and killed the first. Pike called them Carolina parakeets, but they were western evening grosbeaks, common winter residents in the high Colorado Rockies. If the Captain noticed De Anza's trail coming down to the river from Poncha Pass and San Luis Valley he did not report it in his journal.

The sad truth about the Red dawned slowly. They left Salida on the twenty-sixth, descending southwestward along the Grand Canyon of the Arkansas, where daredevil boatmen race each June these days. U.S. Route 50 has been blasted along the sixty-mile narrows, but there was no trail in 1806, and would not be for almost a century. For three days the Sangre de Cristo Range stayed close on their right as it trended south toward Taos and Santa Fe. But then the river channel turned at right angles to the northeast, just below present Coaldale and the

Hayden Pass 4WD road. The explorers slipped and slithered on the frozen edges of the river and tore their feet on the quartz-strewn shore. They threw dirt on the ice and still the pack horses fell, broke legs, and had to be killed. Food ran short again. Sleds had to be built to carry supplies which the battered, starving horses could no longer carry.

The Captain split his party into groups, some to hunt,[13] some to bypass this murderous passage right and left, as the earliest roads would do, and as U.S. Route 50 does now at the lower end. At Parkdale, where the Grand Canyon reaches its climax in the Royal Gorge, Pike admitted to himself at last that this was not Red River. On January 4, he plunged alone into that dark slot of wet vertical walls and ribboned sky, descending to the middle where the Denver and Rio Grande train stops to show tourists how its roadbed hangs over the torrent on girders.

There was no going on for him. Next day, his twenty-eighth birthday, he steeplejacked out of the gorge on the north side, climbed Noonans Peak and looked down, knowing exactly what his birthday present would be. Below him was the Canon City campsite.

HE SHOULD HAVE retreated down the Arkansas right then. His persistence, his recklessness with his own life and that of his men during the next fortnight, seem the product of plain obstinacy. He had promised Wilkinson to find Red River and to put Dr. Robinson in Santa Fe. These things he must do. Red River surely was just beyond the Sangre de Cristos. He had seen southbound Indian trails which surely led to passes over. As soon as his men reported in, he began to prepare. He sent them to gather venison and to build a small blockhouse from which to operate. And, between January 5 and 13, 1807, he built up their energy by daily feasts — an easy process since the explorers brought down a total of thirty-six deer. On the fourteenth, Captain Pike, Dr. Robinson and twelve others said goodby to Interpreter Vasquez and Private Patrick Smith, who would stay at the Canon City blockhouse and take care of the horses.

The fourteen Red River hunters headed south up Grape Creek on foot, each carrying arms, food and supplies weighing seventy pounds. They were fat from Pike's feeding, and full of cheer, but they looked like so many tramps in the last stages of disintegration. Pike owned the only hat among them. Their shoes were slabs of buffalo hide. They were stockingless. Their pants were breechclouts. The rest of them was covered by bits of blanket, legging canvas and deerskin.

Three days of tramping brought them forty miles to near present Westcliffe in Wet Mountain Valley, now a place of prosperous farms somewhat like Bitterroot Valley as Lewis and Clark knew it at Traveller's Rest. Wet Mountain Valley, however, is much narrower than Bitterroot, and nearly a mile higher. Its snow-covered peaks on the west — Crestone (14,-291), Crestone Needle (14,191), Kit Carson (14,100) — go up sheer like Swiss Alps, 7000 feet above the plain. Hemming the valley on the east are the Wet Mountains, rising to 12,000 feet.[14]

The next week was unrelieved nightmare. Snow kept falling. The temperature dropped drastically (and characteristically; in February, 1953, it dropped in a few hours from thirty above to fifty-three below at Westcliffe). Pike watched for ways to escape from the icebox. Such dips as he saw in the Crestones were too high and snowbound for use. The dips — Venable Pass (12,000), Comanche Pass (12,000), Music Pass (11,800) — are favorites with mountain climbers today. Privates Sparks and Dougherty came down with frozen feet and had to be left behind on the prairie with a supply of firewood and most of the venison. The remaining twelve pushed on south, fighting off starvation and freezing. Private John Brown, one of Pike's companions on the attempt to climb Pikes Peak, made mutinous remarks. Pike told him to shut up or be shot.

And then the food gave out completely, with the temperature at twenty below zero and two feet of snow on the ground. Seven more men collapsed with frosted feet, including the three official hunters. That night, the five who still walked could hardly keep the fires going. If the fires went out all would be lost. At dawn, Pike and Dr. Robinson slipped off, came upon an old buffalo and trailed him all day until dark without getting close enough to bring him down. They spent a sleepless night on the prairie fighting the cold, too exhausted and too ashamed of their failure to return to the camp of dying invalids. And suddenly in the early light they heard sounds of more buffalo. They crawled on their knees for a mile in the snow, and then they saw them — a dozen animals far out of range, but coming toward them.

It was now or never for the fourteen starving, freezing, separated and almost hopeless men. Both Pike and Dr. Robinson were too weak to hunt any more, almost too weak to hold their guns. It was Pike's responsibility to shoot first. He checked his powder and waited as long as he dared for the buffalo to come in range and still not get wind of him. He waited, and at last he acted. As he wrote later: "With great exertion I made out to run and place myself behind some cedars and by the greatest good luck the first shot stopped one, which we killed in three more shots, and by dusk had cut each of us a heavy load, with which we determined immediately to proceed to the camp in order to relieve the anxiety of our men. We arrived there about noon and when I threw my load down it was with difficulty I prevented myself from falling. I was attacked with a giddiness which lasted for some minutes."

Soon thereafter the weather moderated. The snow thinned out. On January 24, the twelve hobbled over Promontory Divide (9275), that bleak bit of Wet Mountain Valley marking the drainage division — Grape Creek flowing north to the Arkansas, Muddy Creek running south to the Huerfano. They had reached a sort of civilization — De Anza's Sangre de Cristo Pass area. They saw the familiar Spanish Peaks to the southeast.

Close to the southwest was a pass hardly much higher than they were. One more soldier, Private Hugh Menaugh, collapsed with frozen feet, but they had plenty of buffalo meat now. They parked him with firewood and food near today's spot on State Route 69 called Bradford. Then, on January 27, they walked over the pass to a creek which Pike drank of and declared to be Red River, as Meriwether Lewis had drunk of Agency Creek and called it the Columbia at Lemhi Pass in 1805.

PIKE NAMED this pass Pike's Gap, eastern fashion in the style of Kentucky's Cumberland Gap (1315). But the Spanish had named it already and that name survives, Medano Pass (9900). Today, from Private Menaugh's invalid bivouac at Bradford, a ranch lane winds west and southwest through the rolling vales of Muddy Creek for seven miles. Then a 4WD road climbs through the evergreens to the top — four very steep rough miles with gates to open, white-faced cattle to dodge and dusky grouse to stare at. Few people except cowboys come this way. The beauty of the west descent — tawny cliffs lining the slender valley — is increased by its isolation and made more appealing to some by the small trout in Medano Creek. Now and again, a vista opens, and San Luis Valley spreads off to the Continental Divide — exactly the gray-green valley which De Anza saw, and Captain Pike.

But Pike's Gap, or Medano ("sand dune" in Spanish), involves one of the phenomena of the Rockies. The pass, like the higher Music Pass eight miles north and the slightly lower Mosca Pass (9713) eight miles south, is a wind tunnel. For eons, sand-laden wind has buffeted through these three passes, dropping sand for ten miles along the base to form dozens of strange Sahara-like piles as much as six hundred feet high — today's Great Sand Dunes National Monument. This sand begins to show two miles below the top of Medano Pass, and soon the aspen groves and rabbit bush are deep in it. Near the bottom, Medano Creek loses its banks to sand and, turning south, simply flows in a thin sheet on the flat sand between the range proper and the dunes. The 4WD road takes to the sand-stream, which becomes mere damp sand in a mile. And then Medano Creek disappears altogether before the sand track reaches the checking station two miles farther south.

The billowing, insubstantial, iridescent dunes in the montane setting make a strange and implausible sight. Many legends have been built around them — of disappearances, of ghosts wandering by moonlight, of horses loping about on webbed feet, of weird music heard with special clarity at Music Pass. But Pike treated the dunes briefly in his journal and did not mention their vast monument on the south, Blanca Peak (14,317). He had problems, what with two men a hundred miles in the rear at Canon City, two dying of frozen feet at Westcliffe, and the lonely Private Menaugh at Bradford.

Besides, his Red River had vanished inconsiderately in the sand. But he was cheered on January 28, 1807. From the top of a dune, he saw a large river thirty miles southwest at present Alamosa. Three days later, his depleted expedition of eleven camped in a cottonwood grove five miles up a branch of this river. The branch was the Conejos, where Governor de Vargas had stopped his pioneer exploration of San Luis Valley in 1694.

The Captain realized soon that the large river was not the American Red but the Spanish Rio Grande, which solved the question of how Dr. Robinson would find Santa Fe to do his spying and bill collecting. On February 7, the doctor began his 125-mile hike downstream to the Spanish capital, while Pike's soldiers built a thirty-six-foot square log stockade which might deter Spanish officials from throwing him off Spanish soil until Robinson got back. During the next fortnight, two relief parties returned to Wet Mountain Valley and brought in the five men left behind, though Privates Sparks and Dougherty would be cripples for life as a result of having frozen their feet. The first of these rescue parties tried to avoid the tedious Medano Pass trail through heavy sand by using Mosca Pass, at the south edge of the dunes, but found too much snow near the top. The second group may have crossed Mosca.

Pike's later adventures, beyond the scope of our story, began on February 26, 1807, when a hundred Spanish soldiers turned up at his Conejos stockade and hauled everybody off to Santa Fe, and then to Chihuahua in Mexico for examination by Spanish officials there. A confused period followed — many days of questioning and nights of feting — which lasted more than a year for some of the American soldiers. Pike, Dr. Robinson and six others were released in late April and arrived — finally — at Red River and Natchitoches on July 1, 1807.

Posterity would not rank the sixteen-man Pike expedition in a place of glory equal to that of the longer Lewis and Clark trek. Red River had defeated Pike utterly. The Spanish had confiscated his maps, notes and secret papers. The Kaskaskia bill was not collected. Back home, Pike found that many Americans believed him to have been involved in General Wilkinson's harebrained conspiracy against the United States. It might not have pleased him could he have known that his fame would derive from the fame of Pikes Peak, which he neither discovered nor climbed nor named.

And still, he accomplished something, even if it were largely ignored. By heroism, leadership and endurance during the nightmare month of January, 1807, Pike met tests far more difficult than any of those met by Lewis and Clark in 1805–1806. During the ghastly fortnight's trip of a hundred miles from Canon City to Pike's Gap, he made a shot in time. The men he saved were the first of thousands of Americans to experience the paradox of the high Rockies — their marvelous capacity to let people live in circumstances, seemingly, too awful to be endured.

Furthermore, Captain Pike brought into the horizon of his new country the very highest of its mountains, the magnificent basins of South Park and San Luis Valley, and the whereabouts of two dozen passes, most of which are important crossings to-day.[15]

5

Teton Tourists

AND SO BEGAN the golden age of Rocky Mountain pass discovery. The preliminaries were over — a few southern Rockies passes first with Alvarado at La Glorieta in 1540, Escalante at Horse Lake and Douglas Pass in 1776, De Anza at Poncha and Sangre de Cristo in 1779. In the extreme north, Mackenzie made it up the Parsnip and over Canada's Continental Divide in 1793. Lewis and Clark crossed Lemhi Pass in 1805, which was the year of Simon Fraser's Summit Lake crossing near Mackenzie's pass. It took two centuries and more for white men to collect this handful, scattered along two thousand miles of Rockies.

But the slow pace ended with Pike's crossing of Trout Creek and Medano in 1806–1807. During the next twenty-five years, every Rockies gate to 10,500 feet would be found.[1] Compulsions pushing men west popped up everywhere. A business depression was on. Some took to travel because they had nothing better to do. Meriwether Lewis wrote President Jefferson in that year of 1807 about the potential for Rockies fur trade, and about the need for a trading post at the mouth of the Columbia to reinforce American claims to the Oregon region.

As a result, Jefferson encouraged plans for a Columbia post being made by John Jacob Astor, the German-born New York fur king. Astor was plotting with agents from Moscow and Paris and Canton not only to open the Rockies but to control much of the world's fur trade and to expand it by making beaver more in demand. Meanwhile, the young North West Fur Company of Montreal had built three far-north trading posts west of Summit Lake. And, in April 1807, the Spaniard, Manuel Lisa, left St. Louis up the Missouri to establish an American post for his Missouri Fur Company among the Crow Indians of the Yellowstone area.

The Rockies were still largely unknown — all the Canadian range south of Summit Lake, all of northern Montana, all of Wyoming's bizarre uplands, all of Colorado's great summits north of Pikes Peak. Pike, we saw, assumed that the Yellowstone began at what would be called Hoosier Pass in the center of Colorado. He mapped the South Platte correctly but could not visualize the larger North Platte, draining Colorado's high lonely North Park and much of Wyoming's ranchlands. Lewis and Clark thought that the Rio Grande carried north from Santa Fe and Taos almost to Yellowstone Park. They confused it with Escalante's Green ("Spanish") River which flowed from the west side of Wyoming's Wind River Range to join the Colorado in Utah, and on to the Gulf of California. Clark guessed right about Snake River's source, and wrong about the Bighorn which, he thought, started at Jackson Lake in Jackson Hole.

The Canadian mountain men of the North West Fur Company had the Fraser's source at Summit Lake mixed up with the Columbia. However, within a year, Simon Fraser discovered that the Fraser was not the Columbia by descending through its perilous canyons to near its mouth at present Vancouver, British Columbia.[2] The mouth was too far north up the Pacific coast to be the Columbia.

Everybody was traveling that spring of 1807. While Fraser canoed down his river, his colleague, David Thompson, started west on horseback from the company post, Rocky Mountain House. Thompson, a tall, sandy-haired, quiet Englishman of thirty years, had surveyed most of the Canadian plains and had found time on the side to marry a fourteen-year-old half-breed girl named Charlotte Small. Unlike Mackenzie, he explored for business purely, for beaver trade, not to enlarge the British Empire. The Summit Lake crossing was too far north for Indian business. Thompson sought a Rockies pass up the North Saskatchewan, which was only two hundred and fifty miles north of the 49th parallel, the United States–Canadian border east of the Continental Divide since 1792.

By June 6, Thompson, Charlotte and their three children were in the Rockies at the forks of the North Saskatchewan and Howse River, ninety-five miles north of today's resort of Banff, and ninety miles south of Jasper. What they were seeing was one of the world's great montane regions — the chaotic and perpetually whitecapped Canadian Rockies running north from Mount Assiniboine (11,780), west of Calgary at the south end of Banff National Park, and ending in Jasper National Park.

These famous mountains, a wilderness still, have more of the precipitous loveliness and élan of the Swiss Alps than any other Rockies excepting those in Glacier National Park, and the regal Wyoming Tetons mirrored in Jackson Lake. Several things give the Canadian Alps their breathtaking beauty. Though they are small and narrow as high Rockies go, the valley floor is low — four thousand feet or so, and timberline is less than seven thousand feet, so that almost a mile of streaked pinnacles and precipices tower above the trees to the snow. They are close to the viewer, and the rainfall is heavy west of the Continental Divide, making dense forests of big spruce and fir and cedar and larch and hemlock. Around the 52nd parallel is the one hundred miles square Columbia field of solid ice. There are deep lakes of poignant blue and crashing waterfalls and heavy clouds and mists producing a melodramatic effect unknown in the higher radiances south of Montana.

By June 22, 1807, David Thompson had made the easy climb up Howse River trail to Howse Pass (5000), where the Mount

Freshfield Ice Field almost seemed to fall in his lap. He called the crossing Mountain Portage, and it is reached still only by trail. For a week the family of explorers rode down the steep and difficult west-side trail along Blaeberry River to Columbia River near today's Donald Station.

Thompson was the first white man to report this greatest waterway of the Northwest in its Canadian phase.[3] He did not know that it was the Columbia, since it flowed northwest instead of south — completely the wrong direction. But it seemed promising for trade. Thompson made canoes, paddled eighty miles south upstream to Lake Windermere near the Columbia's source and built a small post, Fort Kootenay, where the family wintered. Twenty miles west of them were the rock crests of the 10,000-foot Selkirk Range and its big-tree forests below timberline. Just beyond the Selkirks, as Thompson would discover later, was the same Columbia (flowing south toward Oregon by then) which he had ascended south to Lake Windermere.

In April of the following spring, 1808, Thompson portaged less than two miles from the Upper Columbia Lake source of the Columbia to the Kootenay River, which he descended south almost to northern Montana in the Flathead country west of present Glacier National Park — a week's march north of Traveller's Rest and Lolo Pass. That was enough trading territory to find for the North West Fur Company in one year. Thompson returned north to Howse Pass and was back at Rocky Mountain House on the plain by June 24, 1808.

In October of that same year of 1807, the St. Louis trader, Manuel Lisa, and forty trapping employees reached by keelboat the Yellowstone-Bighorn junction, a bleak spot on the Montana plain which the Captain Clark party had passed in late July, 1806. Here, the trappers built Fort Lisa, a pile of logs as impermanent as a magpie's nest. The spot was within the Crow Indian nation, which adjoined the out-of-bounds Blackfoot na-

tion on the south. To the west, the Yellowstone led to Bozeman Pass (6002), to the great Absaroka Range bordering Yellowstone Park, and the further Big Hole region short of Lemhi
Pass. The Bighorn River came up to Fort Lisa from the unknown south, bounded on the east by the isolated Big Horns
and on the west by the Continental Divide.

One of Lisa's trappers, a somber Virginian of thirty years,
John Colter, should have become a national myth like the Minnesota lumber hero, Paul Bunyan. Colter's trouble was that he
really did some of the feats credited to him, which reduced his
mythical standing. He had served Lewis and Clark as one of
their best hunters. Only little Pomp had approached him in
stamina. While most of the explorers had come down with
everything from high-altitude bowels to venereal disease, Colter
never had a day's sickness.

By November, 1807, when Fort Lisa was finished, the Crows
had settled for the winter in their upland camps. Manuel Lisa
wanted them to know about the wares which he would trade
for beaver. Colter, who liked being alone, was willing to tramp
around the Crow country, and did tramp all winter. Hot debate
has raged ever since as to where he did the tramping. Students
agree that he walked mostly, and that he carried thirty pounds
of supplies including awls, vermilion and beads for presents. He
ascended the Yellowstone first for forty-five miles above Fort
Lisa and veered south up Pryor's Creek and on to Pryor's Gap
(4640) in the sandstone hills which Will James described so
well in his horse books. These Pryor Mountains divide the Bighorn from Clarks Fork of the Yellowstone. Next, Colter
reached Clarks Fork and plodded south by way of Pat O'Hara
Creek to present Cody and Shoshone River, the Bighorn tributary.[4]

From then on, the students part company. Colter's biographer, Burton Harris, sends his man briefly up South Fork of the
Shoshone, southeast by badlands to Greybull River, and over
the low east part of Owl Creek Range to the lovely Wind River

Valley. From near today's Crowheart, he is described moving northwest upstream along the route of U.S. Route 26-287 past Ramshorn Peak and over Togwotee Pass (9658), where he gazed on the splendor of the Teton Range and Snake River sweeping south through Jackson Hole.

After a trip west over Teton Pass (8429) to see the Tetons from the Pierre's Hole side, Harris's Colter returned east over Teton Pass and hiked north past Jackson Lake to West Thumb of Yellowstone Lake and Tower Falls. Harris believes that he observed many of the spouting geysers, bubbling paint pots, rainbow hot springs and thundering falls which make up Yellowstone Park's prime collection of cosmic freaks. Colter left the Park (Harris wrote) by Cooke Pass, walked down Clarks Fork to Sunlight Basin (Cooke-Cody road) and over Pryor's Gap to Fort Lisa. By then it was late spring, 1808.

This version of Colter's route is opposed by those who declare that the lone pedestrian stayed with South Fork of the Shoshone as far as Ishawooa Creek, crossed Ishawooa Pass (9870) over the Absaroka Range, and moved through the lodgepoles down Pass Creek–Thorofare Creek to Yellowstone River. He turned south then up the slight grade of the Yellowstone and Atlantic Creek to the barely perceptible Continental Divide at Two Ocean Pass (8200). Below the pass on the west side, he proceeded from Pacific Creek due north into Yellowstone Park, without detours to Jackson Hole.[5]

A third set of Colter students give him a real jaunt from the Bighorn River, sending him by Wind River branches straight over Wyoming's highest ice-packed Rockies, the Wind River Range.[6] The suggested crossing is Washakie Pass (11,160), on the old Snake Indian trail from present Fort Washakie up North Popo Agie River, and down Green River to near Pinedale. From there, Colter could have crossed the low Wyoming Range north of Lander Peak, over McDougal Gap (8500), and across Salt River Range by McDougal's Pass (9236) to Star Valley and on to Pierre's Hole. He would have returned to Fort

Lisa northward around the Tetons, through Yellowstone Park and over Cooke Pass.

Quite a winter's hike — 1050 miles — even for a legendary mountain man!

IT MAKES no great difference how Colter went, or whether, later in 1808, he crossed Bozeman Pass to be caught and stripped naked near Three Forks by some Blackfoot Indians. After surviving a gallop through their torture gauntlet, the story goes, he eluded them by diving into Madison River and coming up inside a beaver house. At dawn next morning our nude superman left his beavers and loped up the Gallatin, over Bozeman Pass and down the Yellowstone three hundred miles to Fort Lisa, where he arrived weary and still stark naked, but imperturbable and laconic.

The main thing was that John Colter learned enough from the Crow Indians to start solving the riddle of a wonderful part of the world, northern Wyoming — the massive Big Horns blocking the way from the east to the main Rockies; Green River, its source and westering flow; the one hundred-mile south-north barrier of the Wind River Range ending at Togwotee Pass, the Absaroka barrier north of Togwotee for one hundred and fifty miles to Bozeman Pass; Jackson Hole, enshrined by the Tetons; the lodgepole plateau of Yellowstone Park, with the Continental Divide winding through the geysers on its way to the Bitterroots and Gibbons Pass in Montana.

The findings of Colter and other Lisa trappers filtered east to St. Louis, encouraging men all along the Missouri to seek fur fortunes and adventure in this bright new land just south of Blackfoot territory. Manuel Lisa's Missouri Fur Company became a large corporation. John Jacob Astor chartered his American Fur Company in 1809 to oppose the Britishers of the North West Company and Hudson's Bay Company, and he began selecting personnel to find an overland route to his proposed Astoria post at the mouth of the Columbia.

In the spring of 1810, Colter and thirty other French and American trappers crossed Bozeman Pass and built a makeshift post near Three Forks. The Blackfeet objected, and killed several of them by piecemeal means startling enough to cure Colter of pioneering and to send him back to Missouri, where he spent his last years growing beans. Meanwhile Manuel Lisa had acquired a new partner, Andrew Henry, who decided to see about the Three Forks situation for himself during that same year of 1810.

He arrived there with a dozen friends, found swarms of Blackfeet with scalping knives and muskets ready, and escaped from them — not over Bozeman Pass but in a new direction, south up the tranquil Madison, roughly today's State Route 1 from Three Forks most of the way to the town of West Yellowstone. The hills right and left — Jefferson Range, Madison Range — rose into timbered mountains as high as Koch Peak (11,293). The terraced grassy valley widened into the present Missouri Flats of cow camps and ranches and small lakes, and ghost towns hidden in Gravelly Range to the west. After traveling a hundred miles, the trappers reached a Madison headwater, Mile Creek, and crossed the Continental Divide from Montana into Idaho, emulating Lewis and Clark at Lemhi, and John Colter at wherever he crossed — Togwotee, Two Ocean, Washakie.

The Henry crossing — a modest gap — would be named Raynolds Pass much later on. The party descended Timber Creek on the Idaho side to Henrys Lake, a pretty blue pond five miles square, full of floating islets. These islets had a way of sinking and surfacing like submarines and were revered by Bannock Indians, who buried relatives on them so that they could travel a bit after death. The Henrys Lake region in the summer of 1810 was a patchwork of beflowered clearings and evergreens, girdled by peaks. The main stream was Henrys Fork of Snake River. At the south edge of Henrys Lake was Sawtelle Peak (9930 feet) from the top of which the visitors could inspect the rolling terrain in all directions — the forest-and-grass Continental Divide of the Bitterroots and Big Hole Valley westward, Yellowstone Park eastward, and the potato bottomlands of Idaho to the south, adjoining Pierre's Hole.[7]

The trappers descended Henrys Fork sixty-five miles south to near present St. Anthony, Idaho, where they built some cabins and a dugout — Fort Henry, the first American trading post west of the Continental Divide. They wintered there, and the party's hunters, superb mountaineers named John Hoback, Edward Robinson and Jacob Reznor, explored the region thoroughly. They ascended Teton River past the great cottonwoods and thick willows of Pierre's Hole, climbed the steep brief pitch of Teton Pass, and, at the top, saw the Gros Ventre Mountains tumbling east beyond Jackson Hole to join Wind River Range at what would be known as Sheridan Pass (9100).

The three hunters were practical men looking for food on the hoof. They probably did not pay much attention to the magnificent Grand Teton scenery. They probed Snake River Canyon south of Jackson Hole and found Greys River, which divided the low Wyoming and Salt River ranges. They ascended the canyon of Hoback River to its source, and crossed The Rim (7921) to Green River, just as motorists do now on U.S. Route 187-189 from Jackson Hole to Pinedale, with Wind River Range rising just east.

But Fort Henry on Henrys Fork had a brief career. The trappers abandoned it the following summer. Most of them recrossed Raynolds (or maybe Targhee) Pass and then Bozeman Pass, and returned to civilization down the familiar Yellowstone and Missouri. However, Hoback, Robinson and Reznor chose to return a different way. They crossed Teton and Togwotee Passes to Wind River, the Bighorn, and then the Yellowstone to the Missouri.

MANY OTHER adventurers roamed the Rockies in those years. St. Louis traders led by Robert McKnight traveled (1811 or

1812) the Arkansas-Raton Pass trail to try to open commerce with Santa Fe, and wound up spending nine years in a Chihuahua jail. One of Manuel Lisa's trappers, Ezekiel Williams, and twenty friends went south up the Bighorn from Fort Lisa and arrived months later on the Arkansas below Zebulon Pike's Pueblo breastworks.

In letters to the *Missouri Gazette,* Williams wrote of this 1811–1812 trek with tantalizing lack of detail.[8] His men were the first of record to close the seven-hundred-mile Rockies gap between the Montana Yellowstone and the Colorado Arkansas, but how they closed it is a mystery. They had to cross the North Platte River, and they may have followed it into Colorado's North Park, and over the low Medicine Bows and Front Range to Cache la Poudre River and on south past Pikes Peak. Williams's letter did imply what time would confirm. The Colorado Rockies were much less fruitful from a fur-business standpoint than Wyoming's. The mountains were too high, the rivers too few and game too scarce for comfortable trapping and traveling. The Ute Indian population of Colorado was too small for much trade.

The Williams party may have seen the Sweetwater branch of the North Platte on their way south, though the men did not ascend it to discover South Pass. That was a critical matter. If some of those touring Americans did not find this greatest of Rocky Mountain gates soon, who would keep the British from seizing Oregon? [9]

6

South Pass: Fruit of Failure

David Thompson, at least, seemed in no hurry to claim the Columbia River for England. He delayed the task of floating down it to the sea from his Fort Kootenay, near Columbia headwaters north of the Montana border. This tall, studious Scot, hardly a prototype of the wild mountain men who would make the Rockies their own in the 1820's, kept finding beaver grounds south of Fort Kootenay after crossing the Continental Divide at Howse Pass in 1807. He enjoyed exploration. He responded to the charms of that exquisite land. But he liked most to trade, to build a monopoly for his North West Company, to outwit the Hudson's Bay crowd, to exchange trinkets for fur with the Kootenays, Pend d'Oreilles, Flatheads and other well-behaved red men on the Western Slope, mostly south of the 49th parallel.

Building a monopoly took time. For years his pack trains shuttled from his eastern base at Rocky Mountain House on the Alberta plains, up the North Saskatchewan and over Howse Pass to Fort Kootenay. From there he worked south, and then west on the Kootenai[1] to near present Bonners Ferry in northern Idaho. From the Montana stretch of the Kootenai he followed an Indian trail south across the Cabinet Mountains — perhaps today's Bull Lake road. That put him on Clark Fork of the Columbia, which led him west to Lake Pend Oreille. It led him also to the Coeur d'Alêne region and to the eastern edge of Washington, though short of that still unexplored lower part of the looping Columbia.

His French-Canadian employees may have been the traders who supplied the French word "cabinet" or "water closet" to the rock-walled Cabinet Gorge of Clark Fork, and "cabinet" was applied to the range. The lovely French phrase "coeur d'alêne" means "heart of an awl," which was what Thompson's sharp traders called their sharp Salish Indian clients — and vice versa. "Pend d'oreille" means "earbob," which seemed to fit the Pend d'Oreille (Kalispel) Indians. Thompson built Kully-spell House on Lake Pend Oreille and then Saleesh House on Clark Fork a mile from present Thompson Falls, Montana. In 1810, he ascended Clark Fork from Saleesh House past the mouth of Flathead River as far as present Missoula, where Meri-wether Lewis and nine companions had faced homeward in 1806 toward Lewis and Clark Pass and their unhappy date with the Blackfeet on Two Medicine Creek east of Marias Pass.[2]

Howse Pass suited Thompson fine for crossing the Rockies on his 425-mile shuttle between Saleesh House in Montana and Rocky Mountain House in Alberta. It also suited his Hudson's Bay Company rival, Joseph Howse, who began using it in 1809. But a crisis occurred during the spring of 1810, which warned Thompson that the Howse Pass days were numbered. Three of his men, Finan McDonald, Michael Bordeaux (Michel Bour-don?) and Baptiste Buche, left Saleesh House to go buffalo hunting with Flathead Indians, some of whom carried guns sup-plied to them by Thompson. The party's objective was the same Marias River–Cutbank Creek area where Lewis and Reuben Fields had killed the two Blackfeet.

From Flathead Lake, the hunters took a good horse trail up the Middle Fork of Flathead River, which becomes Bear Creek twelve miles short of the top of Marias Pass (5215). Just north of them rose the peaks of Glacier National Park. At the mouth of Skyland Creek, three miles short of today's limestone shaft at the top of the pass honoring Theodore Roosevelt, the party was ambushed by a crowd of partly-armed Blackfeet, who planned to wipe out these bow-and-arrow intruders quickly. Thompson's guns were a brutal surprise. The Flatheads and their white friends won the battle, and chased the Blackfeet on over Marias Pass, and then down Summit Creek and Two Medicine Creek toward Marias River.

So the Blackfeet, who had already blacklisted Lewis, Andrew Henry and John Colter, blacklisted David Thompson too, for arming their enemies. They would not allow any white men at all in their domain east of the Continental Divide, from Bozeman Pass and Yellowstone Park north for six hundred miles, which was as far as the plains went in Canada. Thompson did manage to slip east over Howse Pass in July, 1810. On his September return trip west, the Blackfeet turned back the four canoes which his voyageurs were paddling up the North Saskatchewan while he followed on horseback. Thompson had just heard of a pass on the watershed of the Athabaska River one hundred and fifty miles north in the muskeg and forest beyond the Blackfoot range. He decided to dump the canoes and go searching for it.

By late November, 1810, his pack train and men had reached and ascended the cold Athabaska as far as Jasper Lake just within present Jasper National Park. The lake is a turquoise prelude to the park's montane summer scene. But Thompson found no aesthetic joy when he saw it with the temperature at thirty below and six inches of snow on the meadows. Wild game is much less plentiful in the Canadian Rockies than it is in gentler climes south of the border. While building sleds and snowshoes for crossing the snowy rampart, Thompson's men could find no cinnamon bear, no mountain goats, not even a whistling marmot. They had to live on horse and dog meat. They talked mutiny and a few deserted. At last, a four-horse load of pemmican and other supplies arrived from Rocky Mountain House. By New Year's Day, 1811, the grumbling voyageurs trailed after Thompson in deepening snow past Maligne River mouth and today's Jasper town site, past the low Victoria peaks north, and the glacial summit of Mount Edith Cavell (11,033) fifteen miles south.

The Miette River flows into the many-channeled Athabaska here, and Thompson almost pointed his snowshoes up it. That would have made him the discoverer of Yellowhead Pass (3717), fifteen miles west of Jasper — the very low Rockies gate (to Fraser River and Vancouver) which would determine the path of the Canadian National Railway a century later. However, he avoided the Miette, pushed south up the Athabaska, and veered southwest on the icy Whirlpool River. The cold continued. For four days the Thompson group worked the dog sleds up the steep grade of the Whirlpool to timberline. The snow deepened to more than the length of a twenty-foot pole. Ahead was the north edge of the Columbia Ice Field — the 10,000-foot Continental Divide curling for two hundred frozen miles between Banff and Jasper.

Thompson scouted ahead and found Athabaska Pass (5724), squeezed between two ice fields. The top was a tiny tarn which would be called the Committee's Punch Bowl, presenting the same oddity as at Colter's Two Ocean Pass in Wyoming. One tarn outlet flowed to the Pacific by the Columbia. The other reached the Arctic by Athabaska, Peace and Mackenzie rivers. On January 10, 1811, the shivering group crossed Athabaska Pass between pendulous glaciers, and slithered down along a violent stream and out of the ice fields west of Fortress Lake to the thick alders of Wood River and the big trees of the Columbia-Canoe-Wood River junction.[3]

During that painful week, Thompson could gaze southeast on the blinding ice summit of Mount Columbia (12,294), second highest peak in the Canadian Rockies. The white towers which he saw were the upland climax of western Canada, the source of its main rivers — North Saskatchewan, Athabaska, Columbia, Fraser.[4] But, after crossing, poor Thompson endured many more weeks of trouble — snow blindness, hunger, spring freshets, desertions — before reaching Fort Kootenay with a few worn-out men and one lean dog. He continued to the Kootenay, to Saleesh House in Montana, to Kullyspell House in Idaho, to his new Spokane trading post in Washington.

Finally, he could forget his Kootenai beaver business and look to England's larger concerns on the Pacific slope. He began paddling down the Columbia from northeast Washington with a crew of eight. On July 9, 1811, at Snake River junction (Pasco, Washington), he set up a pine stake bearing a paper which assigned all the Columbia and its 259,000-square-mile drainage to King George III and the British Empire. The paper was an answer of sorts to Lewis and Clark, who had passed there already. Thompson thought that it might be of interest also to an American party from St. Louis which, he knew, was being sent overland by John Jacob Astor to the mouth of the Columbia on behalf of Astor's Pacific Fur Company.[5]

Though Athabaska Pass had been almost the death of him, Thompson promoted it as a summer trade route to get around the Blackfeet. And, for forty years, this crossing three hundred miles north of the border served as Canada's main Rockies fur trade gate, for all its circuitousness, stunning thunder, obstructive timber, and black flies conferring at the Committee's Punch Bowl.

WHILE THOMPSON was claiming the Columbia, Astor's pack train — largest in the Rockies since Governor de Anza's time — was about to head west from an Arikara village on the Missouri in north-central South Dakota. It was a party of sixty-five people — six Astor partners, forty-five French Canadians, eleven hunters, interpreters and guides, and Marie l'Aguivoise, Pierre Dorion's pregnant squaw, with two small children. It was led by Wilson Price Hunt, a twenty-eight-year-old native of Trenton, New Jersey, which was not exactly a training center for mountaineers. Hunt's further qualifications for conquering the Rockies included five years of tending store in the village of St. Louis, Missouri.

One Astor partner was the difficult Robert McClellan, of Hagerstown, Maryland; another was Ramsay Crooks of Scotland, aged twenty-four, who was sick at the start and acquired new ailments with great regularity. Both had joined Astor's over-landers after five years of trying to be Missouri fur traders on their own. Other partners were the fat Scotsman, Donald Mc-Kenzie; "a rough, warm-hearted, brave old Irishman," John Reed; and an ex-army officer from Pennsylvania, Joseph Miller, who hated all of the party's eighty-two horses and refused to ride one under any circumstance.

Fate protects the inexperienced. Wilson Price Hunt had meant to follow the Lewis and Clark trail up the Missouri to Three Forks and Lemhi Pass. But, on May 26, 1811, he had met those rugged individualists, John Hoback, Edward Robin-son and Jacob Reznor, as they canoed down the Missouri from Fort Henry past the mouth of the Niobrara in present Nebraska. The three explorers told Hunt stories about the vi-cious Blackfeet (Robinson untied and removed the kerchief from his head to show what a scalped skull looked like). Hunt persuaded them to turn about and guide the Astorians as far as Fort Henry and Pierre's Hole by a safe route.

And so it happened that the experts, Hoback, Robinson and Reznor, conducted the Astor mob due west on July 18, 1811, from near the mouth of South Dakota's Grand River. They abandoned the wide Missouri. That meant abandoning also the idea of reaching the Pacific on water, the idea which had spoiled the transcontinental plans of white men from the six-teenth century on. The Astorians — except Joseph Miller — put their trust in eighty-two horses, plus thirty-six more bought later from Crow Indians. This complete use of horses was enough by itself to make their trek a turning point in the transportation aspect of the passes story. Their trip would show once and for all what the Indians had learned from the Rio

Grande Spanish as early as 1660: the Rocky Mountains were for horses, not boats.[6]

The Astorians touched in southeast Montana across the Little Missouri and rode southwest for a month into northeast Wyoming's red hills and shallow dales, through the knee-deep grass, the sand, the pines, where the world was mostly a blue and optimistic sky. On August 17, they glimpsed the soft mass of the Big Horns against the western horizon — the first whites to see them from the east since the Vérendrye brothers approached them in 1742–1743 — up Tongue River, perhaps. They crossed the Little Powder along a Mandan-Crow trail, and then the Powder flowing between naked ridges — "a mile wide, an inch deep, and runs uphill" — and Crazy Woman Creek. They ate tender bighorn sheep and a tough wolf with equal gusto. They chewed gooseberries. They saw black-tailed deer (mule) with huge ears and looks of poignant inquiry. In late August they ascended Clear Creek to the sage oasis of present Buffalo, where they horse-traded with a band of Crows and watched a tiny two-year-old Indian boy handling a horse like a man.

Fall was coming as they moved up Clear Creek into the meadows and spruce or lodgepole groves of the wide Big Horns. In the west rose Cloud Peak (13,165), highest in the range — an indistinct swelling among other swellings. Some aspens had turned to old gold. Their Indian trail, aflame with red fireweed and purple asters, approximated the south and west course of U.S. Route 16 — a motoring delight today past the detour to Sheep Mountain Lookout and its closer view of the Cloud Peak company. After thirty miles of upgoing, they reached, on September 5, Powder River Pass (9666), at a forest grouping of headwaters which included the North Fork of the Powder and Crazy Woman Creek. And they helped the horses down the steep west slope by Tensleep Creek — ten sleeps, the Crows had explained, from their Absaroka villages which John Colter had found in his circuit of Yellowstone Park.[7]

Tensleep Creek dumped them into the dizzy pitches of Tensleep Canyon. Beyond they found a strange disturbance at the foot of the pass — rainbow badlands scarring the land for thirty miles west to Bighorn River and present Worland, hump after hump of cream and red and green and gruesome purple sand. At the junction of Tensleep and No Wood creeks, they rested in a green break in the gaudy desert — a garden of strawberries and thick grass and "a continuous barnyard" of tame elk, deer and buffalo. Next day they avoided the badlands and kept to the Indian trail south up No Wood Creek, over Cottonwood Pass (6727) and Sioux Pass (5400) to present Lysite. From there they followed Badwater Creek west to Wind River just upstream from Wind River Canyon and today's haven for rheumatics, Thermopolis.

The water is still bad along the Badwater of sage flats and draws. No road exists, but the old Indian route hums with other commerce — oil pipelines, telephone lines, tracks of the Burlington and of the Chicago and North Western. The Wind River which the sixty-five Astorians reached was three hundred feet wide. The locale is Boysen Reservoir now. West beyond it, Wind River Range rises in slow grandeur to culminate in the ice fields of Gannett Peak (13,785), almost the only American Rockies remotely like Canada's ice fields around Mount Columbia which Thompson saw. But neither Gannett nor any other glacial 13,000-footer of this Continental Divide can be seen from the east valleys because of the gradual elevation of the foothills.

Wilson Price Hunt could make out the course of Togwotee Pass one hundred and ten miles westerly as it divided Wind River and Absaroka ranges, and he noted migrating robins hurrying south toward warmer weather in New Spain. The old hands, Hoback, Robinson and Reznor, seemed unconcerned about the robins and winter and explained where the party was. They knew, because they had passed here months ago on their return from Fort Henry, Teton Pass and Jackson Hole down the

Wind-Bighorn to what was left of Fort Lisa, and on to the Missouri by the Yellowstone.

For a week, the three white hunters and two late-appearing Snake Indian guides led the Astorians up Wind River. They crossed the Popo Agie at present Riverton, and on up the Wind along Owl Creek Range to a spot beyond today's Dubois twenty miles short of Togwotee Pass. Here the Indians showed Hunt a pass trail which ran toward a dip in the southwest (the dip would be named Union Pass by a Civil War Union officer, W. F. Raynolds, for whom Raynolds Pass would be named). They told Hunt how the trail ascended the drainage of Warm Spring Creek off Wind River, and over this easy Union Pass (9210) to headwaters of Green River which flowed down from thence to — the Gulf of California, perhaps.

They confessed that the short way to Pierre's Hole and Fort Henry was over Togwotee Pass to Jackson Hole, Snake River and Teton Pass. Crossing Union Pass would involve getting over still another divide — the steep climb out of Green River Valley over The Rim and then down Hoback River to the Snake. But the food of the Astorians was running short. Game, the Indians said, might be scarce in Jackson Hole. There were enormous numbers of buffalo along the Green.

And so Hunt and his people followed the guides over Union Pass on September 16, 1811. The road is there today, rough in spots for cars, but no trouble for 4WD cars as far as the top (the west descent to Kendall is difficult). There is a pond — Lake of the Woods — just over the top which consists of a big cow pasture and a bit of forest like anybody's ranch — not the right setting somehow for the dramatic departure of water down Green River seventeen hundred miles to the Pacific, and other water bound down Wind River forty-two hundred miles to the Gulf of Mexico. This Wind River water makes one of the longest river trips in the world.

The Astorians observed the pond after winding up the Union Pass trail for fifteen miles through little parks of spruce and sage and crossing Warm Spring Creek branches time and again. The views were fine. Northward were the many-hued, rim-rocked Absarokas centered on Ramshorn Peak; west, the Gros Ventre Range; south and east, the brown blocks of lower Wind River Mountains, hiding Gannett Peak. But the sight of sights was the snow-covered spires of the Tetons, seen through the slot made by Gros Ventre River. Hunt called Grand Teton (13,766) Pilot Knob.

Next day they went down Wagon Creek to meet the Green at its bend below Green River Pass, and there were some who said that it was not the Pacific-bound Green at all but the Gulf-of-Mexico-bound Rio Grande.[8] They crossed The Rim up Beaver Creek from the Green with Wyoming Range in view twenty miles west across Green River Valley — Lander Peak (11,134), for instance, and Wyoming Peak (11,363). The trail over The Rim and down Fish Creek–Hoback River to Snake River was good, smoothed by the passing of countless travois, horses, dogs and red people since 1700. Hunt was thrilled by the scenery, and awed by the turbulence of the Snake at the mouth of the Hoback as it began its twenty-mile race through Snake River Canyon to Star Valley. He called it Mad River, explored the gorge for four days, and moved upstream fifteen miles north to Jackson Hole and the foot of Teton Pass. Here he was aston-ished to find a large herd of fat elk — animals which his guides had said would be rare in their argument for crossing Union Pass instead of Togwotee.[9]

The Astorians, Hunt wrote, went over Teton Pass on Octo-ber 5, 1811, "by an easy and well-beaten trail; snow whitened the summit and the northerly slope of the heights. The Snakes served us as guides, although last year our hunters [Hoback, etc.] had come into this region." Three days later, they com-pleted the Rockies part of the trip by reaching Fort Henry where "our hunters" left them. Then their real troubles began — troubles which would harass travelers in this region through the trapper and Oregon Trail periods.

Reviving the old water psychology, Hunt built canoes to descend the Snake. Soon one man drowned in an upset, and then another. They lost time waiting for Ramsay Crooks to recover from his newest illness, and more time trying to get the canoes around Twin Falls, trying to get their horses back from Fort Henry, trying to pass down the Snake in its narrows (still impassable) below Weiser, Idaho, trying to stay on the trail over Oregon's Blue Mountains (Huntington-Baker-Pendleton-Umatilla).[10] Food ran so low that they ate their horses and dogs (the dogs tasted much the best). Water also ran low (the French Canadians drank their own urine). Marie l'Aguivoise had her baby (the child, not as tough as Little Pomp, died at Umatilla).

The original group of sixty-five was split up by all these crises. Hunt took thirty-four over the low Blue Mountains — five to seven thousand feet — in late December and reached the Columbia on January 31, 1812. The junction was forty miles below the Snake-Columbia junction, so Hunt did not see David Thompson's posted claim to an Oregon empire which he had staked on July 9, 1811. The Hunt group reached the Pacific by canoe on February 16, 1812, where the Astor partners McClellan, McKenzie and Reed, plus eight hunters, had arrived a month before. The invalid Ramsay Crooks and John Day turned up in May. Besides the loss of the two drowned voyageurs, the party's number was reduced further by drop-outs. Some of these were thought to be lost or killed, though actually they were just wandering around the Snake River region with the Indians. Hoback, Reznor, Robinson, the horse-hater, Joseph Miller and a Martin Cass were trapping south of Fort Henry.[11]

Poor Hunt! At his long journey's end, he thought that his two-thousand-mile reconnaissance for Astor had come to very little. His Powder River Pass–Union Pass–Teton Pass route was as useless for transport as the looping Lewis and Clark route by Lemhi, Lost Trail and Lolo passes. And, at the end of it, he found only more misery — a discouraged Fort Astoria. It had been built by four other Pacific Fur Company partners who had arrived by sea in mid-March, 1811, on the ship *Tonquin*. These sea-going partners, Alexander McKay, Duncan McDougal, David Stuart and his nephew, Robert Stuart, Scotsmen all, had been lured by Astor away from the North West Company. When David Thompson had finally got down the Columbia for England on July 15, 1811, it was his old colleagues and countrymen the Stuarts whom he had found building Fort Astoria beneath a large American flag.

David and Robert Stuart poured out their woes to Hunt, who had more than enough woes of his own. Astor's good ship *Tonquin* was no more. It had sailed north from Astoria to trade the previous summer, and had been seized by a hundred Indians, who murdered Alexander McKay.[12] Then the ship had been blown up by four of its crew with the Indians still aboard. Trade with the Indians up the Columbia was poor. The Stuarts had nagging fears of possible North West Company competition, in view of what David Thompson seemed to have accomplished up the Kootenai. And how were affairs going between the United States and England these days? Suppose war should come over the old issue of freedom of the seas? In that case, how could Astor send supplies and trade goods from New York to Astoria? Not over Union Pass, certainly.

Meanwhile, Astor must be told the bad news about the *Tonquin*.

THE FOUR BEARERS OF THE BAD NEWS left Astoria for St. Louis and New York on June 29, 1812, led by young Robert Stuart, aged twenty-seven. He had migrated from Scotland to Montreal in 1807 and had been working for the North West Company when Astor made him a Pacific Fur Company partner. He had no more business heading the eastbound Astorians than had Wilson Price Hunt the westbound. Stuart counted on the experience of his companions, all of whom had made it west with Hunt and who, presumably, could show him the way back.[13]

One of the three was a real frontiersman, Benjamin Jones, from the Virginia and Kentucky mountains. The others were François Leclerc, a Canadian half-breed, and André Vallé, also a Canadian. At the last minute, Stuart was glad to have his undermanned group strengthened by Ramsay Crooks and that small bundle of nerves, Robert McClellan. The two had resigned in disgust as Astor partners, but they did not scruple to dump themselves on Stuart as the first transcontinental deadheads in American history.

It was not entirely certain that the Hunt men could retrace Hunt's route east from the Blue Mountains over Teton, Union, Cottonwood and Powder River passes. As a result, Stuart was intrigued on August 16, 1812, when he met, just beyond the Blues, one of Hunt's Teton Pass guides, a Snake Indian. The guide declared that "there is a shorter trace to the South than that by which Mr. Hunt had traversed the Rocky Mountains." It was, the Indian said, not only shorter but devoid of mountains. This last remark was hard for Stuart to believe.

He forgot about it until four days later when his party came across the indestructibles, John Hoback, Edward Robinson and Jacob Reznor, and also Joseph Miller as they fished for salmon on the banks of the Snake near present Bruneau (Brown Water), Idaho. They were naked, half-famished and they had been robbed of all they owned by various Indians — Snakes, Utes, Arapahoes — during a winter of touring where white men had never toured before.

They had gone, it seemed, south to Bear River and down toward Great Salt Lake. From that Utah border area, they had trailed east along the Uinta Mountains into southern Wyoming. They had crossed Green River and had kept on as far as Ute country southwest of present Rawlins — the dreary Sulphur Spring–Muddy Creek drainage of Little Snake River, a

Yampa River tributary. They did not go farther east over the low Sierra Madre Range of the Continental Divide.

Wherever they had gone, Indians had talked to them of the "shorter trace" over the Divide unimpeded by mountains. The trappers did not find it, but now they told Stuart where they thought it was from Snake River. They were not ready to leave their traps just yet to guide Stuart. However, Joseph Miller was homesick for Pennsylvania's hills. The ex-army officer would lead Stuart's party to the "shorter trace." And so began six weeks of futility, mixed with the sad comedy and ludicrous tragedy which panicky men can produce. In 1805 Lewis and Clark had wasted weeks of time and had gone two hundred and seventy miles out of their way in their Lemhi Pass ramble, but for good reasons — the lack of horses. There were no *reasons* for the Stuart ramble, which was motivated by fear of Indians, fear of hunger, fear of the unknown. On September 6, the party of seven left the Snake and moved up Portneuf River near today's Pocatello, Idaho.

They crossed to the broad valley of the Bear in its north-flowing upper reaches and followed up it south to near present Dingle, Utah. From here, they scrambled east over sage hills hoping to meet the Green because Miller guessed that they were far enough south to flank the mountains south of Teton Pass. They came to a small stream (Thomas Fork of the Bear) and, since Crow Indians were tailing them, they pushed up it north into a montane maze which baffles topographers still — Preuss Range, Sublette Range, Gannett Hills, and the confusion of Salt River and Wyoming ranges. They bypassed Thomas Fork Canyon by a long detour to its source at Salt River Pass (7616) in the Gannett Hills and descended Salt River into today's happy cheese factory, Star Valley.

It was September 16. In a last effort to find the south-flowing Green they struggled east up Cottonwood Creek and over the highest crest of Salt River Range at Sheep Pass (*ca.* 10,000) and down Sheep Creek to discover — a river. The Green? Impossible. This one flowed north "with great rapidity over a stony and gravely Bed." It was Greys River.

Robert Stuart wrote further: "On striking this watercourse we easily discovered how far we had failed in attaining the object in view; for, from all we had learned concerning Millers River [the Green] we ought to have struck it hereabouts, whereas the one we are on runs quite a contrary course and must be a branch of the Snake. Having thus lost the intended track by which we proposed crossing the Rocky Mountains knowing it must be to the South, and the great probability of falling in again with the Crows, the large Band of whom we did meet, our Horses would undoubtedly be sacrificed, other property forcibly taken from us, and our lives perhaps endangered, we at once concluded that our best, safest and most certain way would be to follow this River down and pass the first spur of mountains by the route of the Party who came across the Continent last year."

So, impelled by fear to take the wrong direction, they pushed north and west up Greys River to Snake River and present Palisade Reservoir, northwest down the Snake to the site of Heise, Idaho, north along the future line of the Union Pacific Railroad and east past Pitcock Hot Springs to Pierre's Hole. From thence they followed the broad trail over Teton Pass and The Rim. They arrived on Green River at last on October 12 below Union Pass near Kendall. The distance of the detour was two hundred and fifty miles; the time, twenty-six days. By ironic contrast, an Indian trail ran east over the Wyoming Range in five miles (from their point of departure on Greys River) to North Piney Creek, which reached Green River forty miles farther east at present Big Piney, Wyoming. A two-sleep trip!

Still, they wasted their time in interesting ways. The Crows caught up with them on the Snake and stole all their horses. At Pitcock Hot Springs, Ramsay Crooks had another sick spell which required the rest of the party to bathe him in the hot water, to give him castor oil, and to wait five days for him to get well. In Pierre's Hole, Robert McClellan refused to take his turn carrying beaver traps on the grounds that his feet hurt because of Stuart's bad management in making them wander through all this crazy country. On October 1, he went skulking off on his sore feet by himself, but not very far off. He didn't rejoin the other six until he ran out of food on Green River. By then, the rest were starving too. André Vallé's solution was to draw lots and odd man got eaten. Robert Stuart took Vallé's rifle from him, and rejected the plan. Next day a buffalo bull showed up as providentially as Pike's buffalo in Wet Mountain Valley. The bull was old and tough, but the voracious Astorians, who ate a good deal of him raw, proclaimed him to be delicious, and the cannibal crisis ended.

Young Stuart was a true Scot — stubborn, brave, patient. Wilson Price Hunt's Union Pass was in sight to the northeast, but he would have the "shorter trace" or nothing. "We intend," he wrote, "going down this [Green] River so long as it lies in our course or at least to the point of a mountain we see in the East near which we expect finding Missouri waters." The tired men trudged south and east, parallel to the massive Wind River Range, past the line of great peaks — Gannett (13,785), Fremont (13,730), Wind River (13,200), and a dozen more.

Much of their trail was down New Fork River, an east branch of the Green. It brought them to present Pinedale (many pines even then), and to three Indian mummies laid out tastefully with their feet pointed east at the entrance of a huge lodge. Two days later they met Snake Indians on Pocket Creek who pointed to the "shorter trace" forty miles farther on, and sold them a horse to carry their meat. The rest was a tedious trudge through sand and sage along the sinking range. They crossed Big and Little Sandy creeks to present Elkhorn, passed the source of Pacific Creek on October 21, 1812, and camped in a clump of aspens perhaps three miles short of (and southeast of) South Pass (7550). It was snowing a little.

And what did they see? What was South Pass precisely?

The seven Astorians and their overloaded horse saw an almost treeless table of gray-green sage where two streams approached within a mile or so of each other. The sage suggested the sea as it moved north to break against the tawny terminal cliffs of Wind River Range, toothed unevenly like a broken saw. There were no mountains in sight southward — only two buttes a dozen miles away, Continental Peak and Oregon Butte, and little black hillocks here and there. They believed that Pacific Creek which they had passed was a Green River branch bound for the Western Sea. It was just a trickle, having just started. The Atlantic-bound stream, which they could see ahead, was quite wide already. Its source was visible many miles to the northwest at a dip in Wind River Range. It would be named the Sweetwater River later on, starting below Sweetwater Gap under Atlantic Peak.

Though Stuart's men were sure that they had found South Pass, they could hardly see the grade, which was only seventeen feet per mile to the east, thirty-seven feet per mile to the west. And they could not even begin to imagine then the significance of their discovery. All the other gates in our story are slots permitting passage through rock barriers. South Pass is a slot in a subtler and more magnificent sense. It is the one watered place in the entire two thousand miles of Rocky Mountains where wagons and animals and people can cross the chain without climbing anything and without having to prepare any path at all. Furthermore, this watered South Pass band eighteen miles wide is not only of itself mountainless. From its southern edge at Continental Peak, the flatness continues without water for eighty miles southeast to a point below present Rawlins. Here the Rockies resume in the foothills of the Sierra Madre Range which extends to Rabbit Ears Pass in north-central Colorado.

The larger flatness at an average elevation of 7500 feet is a vast saucer of desolation measuring one hundred miles from east to west. It is known as the Great Basin, of which the Red Desert is a part. The rain which falls into the saucer never gets out of it. It simply dries up like the cat's dish of milk if the cat isn't hungry. When the single line of the Continental Divide hits the saucer it has to become two lines running around its edge until normal east-west drainage takes up again on the other side.

But the Astorians were in no mood to visualize saucers. They said goodby to Pacific Creek and crossed South Pass before breakfast on October 22, 1812, four miles south of the present highway and two miles south of the future Oregon Trail. Stuart was being cautious. The "shorter trace" down the Sweetwater, he had noted, was scarred with recent polings of many travois. He wanted no more meetings with thieving Crow Indians.

Unfortunately, he angled farther south while the Sweetwater angled north. Soon his party had lost contact with it, caught behind the Antelope Hills and the Great Basin's desolation below the Green Mountains and Crooks Gap (ca. 7500). On October 26, they stumbled through Lost Soldier Gap (ca. 7000) at today's Bairol, and on to Lost Soldier Creek which became, following Great Basin custom, a ghost stream floating off in thin air.[14]

Where, oh where was the Sweetwater? They made for a line of willows to the north, went along Muddy Creek through Muddy Gap (6350) between Green and Ferris Mountains and finally rediscovered the river at a spot one hundred miles east of South Pass. Another week along the Sweetwater led them to the North Platte beyond Devil's Gate and Independence Rock and beyond the range of our story. They wintered in the beautiful North Platte country around Torrington, Wyoming, and reached St. Louis by way of the Platte and the Missouri on April 30, 1813. Stuart learned then that the War of 1812 with England had been on for months, with prospects of the very kind of severe sea blockade that had worried him at Fort Astoria. Soon after, he delivered his bad news about the blowing up of the *Tonquin* to John Jacob Astor in New York.

Astor came to see the hopelessness of his position and resigned himself in the end to the inevitable. He allowed Astoria to be sold to the British North West Company. But of course this whole sad American failure in Oregon was inconsequential and temporary. Time would show that Hunt's westbound trek had proved something after all. And, when Robert Stuart found South Pass eastbound, he found a tool of destiny which made a transcontinental United States inevitable.[15]

7

Hell-bent for Taos

And still, for a dozen years after 1812, Robert Stuart's discovery of South Pass and the arid, eerie suspension of mountains between Wind River Range and the Sierra Madre had no effect on Rockies affairs. The Upper Missouri crowd of beaver hunters were persuaded by Indian restiveness to trap far east of the high country for the present. Their spirits were dampened by Astoria's fate and by the state of the fur market, which was depressed by the War of 1812 and by the business slump of 1819.

The sage prairie of South Pass, long Union Pass, steep Teton, spacious Togwotee, low Raynolds and Targhee and Bozeman passes had been found in five years. They were abandoned and half forgotten just as quickly. And, while these Missouri River Americans quit the mountains, the Canadians and English let things slide a bit too. Nobody seemed to be able to make Fort Astoria pay. Some ninety employees and hangers-on pulled out and went home by way of the Columbia to David Thompson's Boat Encampment and across Athabaska Pass, overhung with green ice as usual. In 1818, ownership of Fort Astoria was returned to the United States, which didn't seem to want it either. Officials of the North West and Hudson's Bay companies wore themselves out in disputes about territory east of the Canadian Rockies. The disputes continued until 1821, when the firms merged into one Hudson's Bay Company with a new dynamic young director, George Simpson.

The ex-Astorian, Donald McKenzie, tried to expand North West Company trade among the Indians of Thompson's Kootenai and Columbia rivers. In 1818, he built Fort Nez Perce at the Columbia–Walla Walla junction of eastern Washington. Then he sent a trapper brigade under Alexander Ross over the low Blue Mountains to the Snake-Bear-Jackson Hole region which had been so beloved by John Hoback and his pioneer hoboes. The results were mediocre. McKenzie retired then from such strenuous living and rode east one last time (1821) through the Columbia's forests of red cedar and white pine and over Athabaska Pass, a broad trace now up Wood River and down the Whirlpool, cleared of timber and fit for horses. Alexander Ross stayed on to open a new post, Flathead, for Hudson's Bay Company, near Thompson's Saleesh House on Clark Fork of the Columbia in Montana. For three seasons, Ross's men roamed the streams of the Bitterroot Range — some five hundred miles of it in all its convolutions and contours, from the Clark Fork breakthrough near Pend Oreille Lake southward to Ross's Hole near Gibbons Pass and then east to Targhee Pass and Yellowstone Park.

In 1823, a party of Hudson's Bay Company trappers under Finan McDonald, the old-timer who crossed Marias Pass in 1810, made an unusual trip from Flathead Post. As described by Dale Morgan in *Jedediah Smith*, they took the shortcut route east up Flathead and Jocko rivers and over Evaro Pass to present Missoula, then on east up Clark Fork through Hell Gate to its source near present Butte. The brigade crossed the low Continental Divide by Deer Lodge Pass (5902) — used today by U.S. Route 91 and the Union Pacific Railroad. They circled Pioneer Range, battled seventy-five Blackfeet below Lemhi Pass at a cost of seven men killed, trapped the Snake River as far south as Bear River, and then trapped the Missouri by way of the Beaverhead and Jefferson rivers as far north as present Great Falls, Montana.

Perhaps they returned west to Flathead Post over Lewis and Clark Pass. If so, they were the first party to risk crossing it since Meriwether Lewis in 1806. But the truculent Blackfeet still guarded Howse Pass under Freshfield Ice Field four hundred miles to the north of Lewis and Clark. That left Athabaska Pass — another hundred and fifty miles farther north — as Canada's sole Continental Divide gate to the Montana-Oregon trade area. As things developed, no white man would find any other crossing over the Canadian Rockies until the 1840's.

FAR TO THE SOUTH, meanwhile, the ghost of Governor de Anza was sad as Spanish power at the La Glorieta Pass end of his Rocky Mountain empire became a shadow without substance. In their weakness, Spanish officials guarded La Glorieta and Palo Flechado (Taos) passes against foreign invasion — and trade — even more closely than the Blackfeet guarded Howse Pass at the head of the Blaeberry in Canada. De Anza's dream of commerce between New Mexico and Spanish California with the help of Sangre de Cristo and Cochetopa passes was deader than Zebulon Pike had found it to be in 1807.

The St. Louis promoter Robert McKnight was still serving time in a Chihuahua *calabozo* for trying to do business on the Rio Grande. When young Auguste Pierre Chouteau, of the St. Louis fur dynasty, and Julius De Mun ascended the Arkansas to open trade (1815–1817) in a large way beyond Huerfano River and Sangre de Cristo Pass, the Spanish arrested them and confiscated their goods and supplies. These officials feared that such trade would strengthen the Mexican movement to become free of weary old Spain and her expensive Twin Majesties. As we saw in the days of Pedro de Villasur and the touring Mallet brothers, the Spanish could imagine themselves besieged with marvelous clarity. In 1818–1819, the old psychosis flared anew while talks were proceeding in Washington to set the United States–New Mexico boundary where it had been in practice anyhow since the Louisiana Purchase of 1803: along the Arkansas River west of the 100th meridian to its source at what came to be called Tennessee Pass, due north then to the 42nd parallel, and on to Canada with the Continental Divide.

It happened that the Spanish minister, Luis de Onis, came upon a mysterious report in French which seemed to have been prepared by spies working for the United States Army. It was a survey of New Mexico's frontier with descriptions of all passes fit for passage of wheeled artillery, and with comment on the province's military might, including intelligence that the entire New Mexican Army numbered 124 "badly armed militia" led by "ignorant under-officers." It discussed the excellence of the Great Plains terrain for wagons from St. Louis to the Spanish Peaks. It described the "easy footpath" thence up South Oak Creek between Sheep and Dike Mountains, over Sangre de Cristo Pass to San Luis Valley and south to Taos and Santa Fe.

It outlined the "very bad crossing" north of Sangre de Cristo, the appraisal of which applied to both of Pike's passes to the sand dunes, Mosca and Medano. It had something to say about the "difficult footpath" down "El Cañon de San Fernando" (Palo Flechado Pass) with its steep right fork leading from the top to Taos Indian Pueblo, even as a trail does now, instead of to the Spanish fandango center, Don Fernando de Taos. It mentioned the Pecos River crossing "El Vado" below La Glorieta Pass, and the road north from there along the east flank of the Sangre de Cristos through Mora and Black Lake to the east foot of Palo Flechado — which could hardly have been rougher than today's State Route 38.

In Mexico City, the Spanish viceroy who read the report was as ignorant of Rocky Mountain geography as viceroys had been two centuries earlier. He had been advised by Minister de Onis that General Henry W. Atkinson would head a force of a thousand United States soldiers up the Missouri to the mouth of the Yellowstone near the present Montana line in North Dakota. This was true, and it was all the viceroy needed to conjure a vision of a great American army flying up the Yellowstone to Two Ocean Pass above Jackson Hole where, he thought, the Rio Grande rose. The army would march down from there through San Luis Valley to decimate New Mexico's 124 warriors while seizing Taos and Santa Fe.

The viceroy could not have foreseen that General Atkinson's "Yellowstone Expedition" would become a wry joke through mismanagement and army numbness to elementary facts about the West. Its purpose was to awe Missouri River Indians and Hudson's Bay Company poachers with a show of American power and ingenuity. It had quite the opposite effect. It could get no farther than Council Bluffs in Iowa, hundreds of miles short of the Yellowstone, because the five steamboats used for transport wouldn't cooperate with the shallow Missouri. They broke down, and most of the soldiers got scurvy.

In a flurry of fear, the Spanish viceroy ordered Acting Governor Facundo Melgares in Santa Fe to prepare for the worst. Melgares had been a loyal supporter of King Ferdinand VII in 1807 when he had escorted Captain Pike to Chihuahua, but he was languidly on the fence by 1819. He knew that inside plotters, not outside imperialists, threatened Spanish New Mexico. He checked the frontier anyhow, hauled two rusty cannon to Palo Flechado Pass, and built a small mud fort on the east side of Sangre de Cristo Pass halfway down South Oak Creek, between the top and the Huerfano. He assigned six of his "badly armed militia" to the fort, where the poor fellows were attacked by "one hundred white men dressed as Indians," and five of them were killed. The attackers were probably Comanches.

In his own frontier survey, Governor Melgares implied that Raton Pass had been displaced as the popular trail to the Arkansas from the Rio Grande since De Anza's discovery of Sangre de Cristo Pass in 1779. The Muache Utes had taken to bothering horsemen among the yellow cliffs of Cimarron Canyon and Ute Park on the Palo Flechado–Raton Pass trail (today's U.S. Route 64 from Eagle Nest Lake to Cimarron town). Along Raton Pass itself, the Comanches had become troublesome. To avoid both, some Spanish traders and buffalo hunters trailed due east from Palo Flechado up Agua Fria Creek through piñon foothills of the Cimarron Mountains toward present Rayado and Springer, New Mexico. They veered north up the green valley of the Canadian to the foot of Raton Pass, and northeast into the Johnson Mesa region of sunshine and scenery. They crossed Manco Burro Pass (7762) from Chicorica Creek to Rathbun Creek, and Trinchera Pass (6000) over the dwindling Ratons into present Colorado, then down Trinchera Creek to the ragged gash of the Purgatoire and to the Arkansas. They could see Huajatolla, "Breasts of the World" (Spanish Peaks), and Pikes Peak rising in the northwest.

Governor Melgares's survey covered the terrain along Sangre de Cristo Range north of Palo Flechado to Sangre de Cristo Pass. In that sweep of snowy peaks and gray saddles, there were only "two or three unhandy footpaths" over; by which he meant Costilla Pass (10,100) leading to Purgatoire headwaters and the stern dike which we call Stonewall; San Francisco Pass (8560) above present San Luis, Colorado's oldest town; and Indian Creek Pass (9775), an old game trail crossing which linked San Luis Valley and Cucharas River below the Spanish Peaks. Finally, Melgares wrote of the "Road of the Narrow Gap" forking north from the main road near the top of Sangre de Cristo Pass by Pass Creek Pass (9400) to the Upper Huerfano River "where all roads unite for this province. They converge here from the Valley of the Huerfano, Valleys of the Soldiers [Spanish Peaks], and Valleys of the Sierra Mojada [Wet Mountains]."

They did converge, and do today in the sleepy adobe village of Gardner, Colorado. Gardner naps in the sun near Badito Cone which Taos-bound Spaniards knew as the place where they forked left from the Huerfano–Mosca Pass trail to proceed up South Oak Creek to Sangre de Cristo Pass.[1]

CAME THE REVOLUTION — August 24, 1821 — and a self-crowned Mexican emperor, Iturbide Augustin I. Melgares shifted smoothly from one king to another and continued as New Mexico's governor. He hauled the cannon off Palo Flechado Pass, let his mud fort dissolve in rain below Sangre de Cristo Pass, and staged an independence fiesta in Santa Fe on January 6, 1822, during which he proclaimed that Americans were very welcome now on the Rio Grande.[2]

Three groups of Missourians were already in Mexican territory, moved by rumor and intuition. One of them was a do-it-now kind of Kentuckian, Captain William Becknell, aged thirty-one. He hailed from the frontier town of Franklin, Missouri, where one of his teen-aged admirers was a sandy-haired boy named Kit Carson. The captain, a peddler of firewood, had been hearing tales of the Rockies from tale-spinners like James Purcell, who had visited South Park in Colorado a year or so before Zebulon Pike, and Ezekiel Williams, whom we watched in 1810 closing the Rockies gap between Yellowstone River of Montana and the Arkansas in Colorado.

Becknell was burdened with debt and longed to strike it rich to get his creditors off his neck. At last, on June 10, 1821, he advertised in the *Missouri Intelligencer* (Franklin) for "seventy men to go westward" to find fortunes among the Comanche Indians by trading cheap beads and awls for fine Rio Grande horses and mules which the Comanches stole from the Mexicans. On the side, they would capture "Wild Animals" to display in St. Louis for cash. Seventeen men answered the ad but only three were along on September 1, 1821, when Becknell's small pack train headed for the Arkansas by way of the Osage and Neosho rivers. The quartet traded briefly with the Comanches, who let them ascend the Purgatoire and toil over the gulches of Raton Pass between yellow cliffs. They moved south then in early November, spurning both Palo Flechado–Taos trails described by Melgares. At "El Vado" crossing of the Pecos near La Glorieta Pass, friendly Spanish soldiers showed them the old Santa Fe road which Coronado's scout, Alvarado, had used in 1540. The four were greeted warmly in the capital by Melgares on November 15, 1821.

Though Santa Feans were desperately poor, Becknell sold his wares for seven times their cost at St. Louis. By mid-December, he and his friends were bound homeward over Raton Pass, full of plans to return with a real load carried in wagons which could be bought for one hundred and fifty dollars each and sold in Santa Fe for seven hundred dollars. Raton Pass was impassable for wagons, but Becknell thought that he knew how to avoid it westbound by veering southwest from the Arkansas into the desert some two hundred miles short of the Purgatoire–Raton Pass trail and joining Cimarron River after sixty arid miles. This was not the Cimarron Creek which the Palo Flechado trail followed on its way to Raton Pass. This second Cimarron rose on the south slope of the Raton Mountains and from it easy roads led over the low divide to Canadian River waters and the New Mexican plains flowing south to the La Glorieta Pass end of the Rockies.

The Becknell quartet was back in Franklin, Missouri, on January 29, 1822, having made the La Glorieta–Raton trek from Santa Fe in the fast time of forty-eight days. On May 22, 1822, the Captain rode west once more, with twenty-one helpers and three wagonloads of wares. Near present Cimarron, Kansas, west of Dodge City, they waded the half-dozen sandy trickles of the Arkansas and started southwest over a dust bowl of thistles and yucca and tumbleweed in search of the Cimarron bypass around the Ratons. They ran out of water long before they could cover the sixty dry miles to the Cimarron, and survived by drinking blood from the ears of their mules. They killed a buffalo also, and drew water from its stomach. Then they retreated to the familiar Arkansas and the salubrious Raton trail, which involved taking apart the three wagons and carrying them in pieces over Raton Pass.

In Santa Fe, the Captain underplayed his Cimarron failure and overplayed the excellence of his profits, which encouraged some fifty Missourians to haul $12,000 worth of goods to Santa Fe during 1823 by both wet Raton Pass and dry Cimarron routes. Becknell himself was not pleased with the freighting total. He spent most of the next two years planning a grandiose Cimarron highway from St. Louis to Santa Fe on the scale of Marco Polo's thirteenth-century trade route from Venice to the Orient.

On May 16, 1824, he left home a third time as the leader of a caravan far more impressive than Wilson Price Hunt's pack train of sixty-five people in 1811. Before swarms of cheering Missourians, eighty-one Becknell adventurers paraded through Franklin with twenty four-wheeled dearborn carriages, two wagons, two carts, a small cannon, one hundred and fifty horses and mules, and $30,000 worth of trade goods. They endured twenty-four hours without water on the Cimarron Cut-Off, but nobody died of thirst except one dog. Then they descended from La Glorieta Pass into Santa Fe with much noise for the benefit of the Mexican girls. The date was July 28, 1824 — completing a journey of eight hundred and seventy miles in seventy-three days for an average of twelve miles a day. They arrived with most of their wares in fair enough shape to bring them $180,000 in coin and $10,000 in furs.

And so William Becknell won his place as the creator of the Santa Fe Trail which, along with the Oregon Trail, would bring the United States to its continental destiny during the next twenty-two years. In that period, a thousand merchants would haul at least $3,000,000 worth of goods from St. Louis to Santa Fe along the Trail, either by the short, dreary, dangerous Cimarron Cut-Off for well-equipped caravans, or the rugged healthful Raton Pass route for conservative travelers and pack trains.

Of course Raton Pass won out in the end, being crossed to-day by a scenic highway and the double tracks of the Santa Fe Railroad. The dread Cimarron Cut-Off has been abandoned to the thistles, the sand and the restless tumbleweed.

BUT WE ARE GETTING ahead of our pass chronology. In retro-spect, the year 1821 stands as a time when many independent forces coalesced for the development of the Rockies as a whole. Politically, the year brought Mexican independence, the presentation of one of many bills before Congress by John Floyd of Virginia for a "territory of Oregon," and demands by Senator Benton for a string of army posts from St. Louis to the Columbia's mouth. By 1821, everybody who was anybody had to own a beaver hat. Fur prices soared, which explained the Hudson's Bay Company absorption of the North West Company under George Simpson, and a lot of discussion, about starting new fur firms based in St. Louis, carried on by men like William Ashley, Ramsay Crooks and John Jacob Astor.

As we have seen, Iturbide's revolution south of the Arkansas put Becknell and other frontier Missourians to scurrying for the Spanish Peaks even before they knew that Mexico was free. These pioneers discovered the charms of Taos — sheltering cottonwoods, lenient ladies, homemade whiskey, benign win-ters, and gambling and fandangos around the clock. Among the discoverers were nine tourists from the big Osage post of Fort Smith on the Arkansas, led by Major Jacob Fowler, a fifty-seven-year-old Kentucky landowner. Fowler was distinguished by his advanced age, being twice as old as the average mountain man, and by his spelling, which was as noteworthy as William Clark's.

The Major, tenderly cared for by his Negro slave Paul, had left Fort Smith on September 6, 1821, had seen Pikes Peak from where Pike had first seen it, and had helped bury Lewis Dawson, who had got his head stuck in a grizzly bear's mouth so that "on examining a Hole in the upper part of his Wright temple We found the Brains Workeing out." In January 1822, Fowler built the first house in Colorado at present Pueblo and left at the end of the month with Paul and the rest on the Taos Trail, which ran south from Pueblo along Wet Mountains to Huerfano Butte, and up the Huerfano toward Badito Cone. Fowler wrote: "We now under Stand that the mackeson Provence Has de Clared Independance of the mother Cuntry and is desirous of a traid." His account of Sangre de Cristo Pass, the first of American record, read: "Set out Early about South . . . for about ten miles to a Crick [South Oak] and about five miles to Whar there the Remains of a Spanish fort [Melgares's] to apperence ocepied about one year back — Hear We Camped for the night Which Was Cold and Windey . . . Was like to frees."

And next day, February 4, 1822: "The Wind High and Very Cold We set out Early up the valley a little West of South for about two miles thence up the Point of a mountain and along a Ridge leave High Peeks on both Sides till We took up a High Hill and threw a Pine groave Whar the Snow is three feet deep — and at about five miles from Camp We Came to the top or Backbon of the mountain Which devides the Watters of the arkensaw from the Delnort Heare the Wind Was So Cold We Scarce dare look Round — South 5 miles to the top of the mountain We then Steered more West down the mountain to a branch of the delnort [Sangre de Cristo Creek] — and down that about South for nearly ten miles to Wheare the mountains are much lower Whear Capted for the (night) We Hear find no timber but Piny and Roal Some old logs off the mountain for fier Wood."

Reaching Taos "Satterday 9th Feby 1822," Fowler attended a fandango that evening with some social success, but nothing comparable to that achieved next night by his slave Paul, who was invited with two trappers to the home of "a Wife and two daughters both young Woman . . . but With Some Reluctance aledgeing that He Was not Settesfyed to go With out His master aledgeing . . . that there might be Some mis-cheef Intended and uder those doupts He Went as I before Stated and from the Statement of those two gentlemen I Will Indevour to State What followed."

Fowler continued: "It Is a Custom With the Spanierds When Interdused to Imbrace With a Close Huge — this Cere-money So Imbareshed Pall and maid Him So Shaimed that if a Small Hole Cold Have been found He Wold Sartainly Crept Into it. but unfortnetly there Was no Such place to be found. and the trap door threw Which the desended Into the Room being Shut down (for the Went In at the top of the House) there Was no Poseble Way for Him to make His Escape — now the Haveing but one Beed in the House and that So large as to be Cappeble of Holding the three Copple of poson — there Ware all to lodge to geather and the mother of the daughters being oldest Had of Corse the ferst Chois of Bows. and took pall for Hir Chap takeing Hold of Him and drawing Him to the beed Side Sot Him down with Hir arms Round His Shol-ders. and gave Him a Kis from Sliped Hir Hand down Into His Britches — but it Wold take amuch abeler Hand than mine to discribe palls feelings at this time being naturly a little Re-legous modest and Bashfull He Sot as near the wall as Was Poseble and it may be Soposed He Indevoured to Creep Into it for Such Was His atachment to the old lady that he kept His (eyes) turned Constently up to the trap door — and to His great Joy Some person oppened it to Come In to the Same Room — But Pall no Sooner Saw the light (for their Rooms are dark) than He Sprang from the old lady and Was out In an Instent — and maid to our lodgeing as fast as Poseble Wheare the other two Soon followed and told What Head Happened to Pall."

The venerable Major and bashful Paul piled up first after first during those winter months of 1822. On February 12, they set out to trap toward San Luis Valley with three others and eight horses, riding north to camp in cottonwoods of Conejos River two miles below Pike's stockade. Then they invaded a delightful region where no Americans had been before — the present South Fork of the sparkling Rio Grande below Wolf Creek Pass (10,850). Here the trapper Taylor "Came into Camp on futt Haveing lost the Hors With Sadle Bridle Blankets nek Roap and all." Next day "Taylor and Pall Began to Complain of Hunger of Which Taylor began gro black In the face and Pall Was gitting White With the Same Complaint" — foreshadowing the trials of Frémont's expedition of 1848–1849 near South Fork. The softhearted Major took himself from earshot when a horse was killed for food. During its death, somebody brought down two deer and "We Soon Head Suntious feest and much Plesentness . . . tho We lamented the fate of the Poor Hors — as now (we) Head no use for His flesh."

By March 11, Fowler and company had reached Wagon Wheel Gap in the great loop of the forested Continental Divide. The loop was formed by the Upper Rio Grande flowing down from Stony Pass (12,594) seventy miles west of Wagon Wheel. To south, west and north, the snowpacked San Juans glistened four to six thousand feet above the men. But there was none of the oppressive loneliness which David Thompson had found in the Canadian Rockies.[3] Fowler met people daily — Spanish peddlers in huge conical hats; other American trappers coming up behind him; short, fat, smiling Ute Indians. The Spaniards said that the Utes owned and roamed these stupendous Colorado Rockies all the way west to and beyond Green River, north to Wyoming's Great Basin, south to the Navajo grazing country above San Juan River.

The Utes, Fowler learned, numbered perhaps thirty-five hundred in six bands. They moved between the valleys of their uplands on ancient pass trials engineered by themselves and buffalo. Escalante had used Ute trails in 1776 over Horse Lake Pass from Santa Fe to the San Juan and Dolores rivers while pioneering part of the Spanish Trail to Utah Lake. From San Juan River, a deep-worn trace brought the Utes and their dogs and huge horse-herds northeast to San Luis Valley. This busy trail ran up Los Pinos River drainage from near the site of the present Ute capital of Ignacio, Colorado, and Vallecito Reservoir to cross the Continental Divide at Weminuche Pass (10,629), named for one of the Ute bands. From there, in the shadow of Rio Grande Pyramid (13,838), it descended Weminuche Creek to the Rio Grande forty miles upstream from Major Fowler's Wagon Wheel Gap camp. The trail's junction today is at the east end of Rio Grande Reservoir.

North from Wagon Wheel, as we have seen, was Cochetopa Pass (10,032), the main Ute gate from Eastern to Western Slope, from San Luis Valley and South Park to the Gunnison, Colorado, White and Green rivers, and northeast Utah. Fowler's Spaniards knew of no practical Continental Divide pass north of Cochetopa, and they predicted that Cochetopa traffic would increase. It was shorter that way west from Taos than by the old Horse Lake Pass route.

Back at Taos in May, the Major reported these matters to a flock of American newcomers who did not seem to share Paul's aversion to the village ladies. On June 1, 1822, the small Fowler party headed for home by Palo Flechado Pass, Agua Fria Creek and Fowler Pass (9189) over Fowler Mesa and the Cimarron Mountains — the area of today's famous Philmont Scout Ranch. They reached the Canadian, but missed the Manco Burro Pass fork of Chicorica Creek to avoid Comanches in Raton Pass. Instead they ascended Una de Gato Creek, and went over the piñon-juniper Ratons ten miles east of Trinchera Pass near the present Branson crossing of the Denver, Texas and Fort Worth Railroad. From there they rode down Chacuaco Creek past Mesa de Maya and another Fowler mesa. However, they departed from Chacuaco Creek before it reached the Purgatoire, moving twenty miles farther east where U.S. Route 160 runs today between Tobe and Kim to Two Butte Creek.[4]

It was a peculiar route over peculiar, dispirited moonlike terrain, where only pocket gophers and jackrabbits seemed able to savor life.[5] Still, Two Butte Creek brought them to the Arkansas at present Holly, Colorado — practically Kansas. And, on July 26, 1822, the Major reached home at Covington, Kentucky, looking no more the worse for wear than an antique of fifty-eight years should.

8

The Roaring Twenties

D URING THE NEXT THREE CROWDED YEARS after Major Fowler's pioneering at Wagon Wheel Gap, the American Rockies filled with people — well, several hundred, say — who used new and old gates from Bozeman Pass in Montana south to Horse Lake above Santa Fe. The Hudson's Bay Company crowd began a systematic cleanup of Snake River beaver. Missourians from Kentucky and Virginia moved up the Missouri toward many northwest headwaters, and southwest up the Arkansas toward Sangre de Cristo and Raton passes to see if it were true what Becknell said about Taos.

The conviction spread that Rocky Mountain trapping was the only way for a real man to live. It was entrancing, thrilling, the ultimate expression of liberty and the pursuit of happiness. The average trapper might smell a bit strong. He might not be able to read and write. But in the Rockies he stood supreme unto himself like a king. All twenty-four hours of any day belonged to him alone, and he owned a million square miles of a high, beautiful paradise where he might lose his scalp but never his self-respect.

From Taos, this new kind of human being rode off every which way with his dangling traps and unpredictable mules, never dreaming that his careless steps carried him to immortality. Ewing Young, Oregon's future First Citizen, and William

Wolfskill, both of whom had reached Taos with Becknell's train, crossed Horse Lake Pass in 1824 and trapped the San Juan River Ute country on the south side of Weminuche Pass. Later Wolfskill would help to advance the Spanish Trail beyond Utah over Mojave Desert and Cajon Pass to southern California.

The father-and-son team of Sylvester and James Ohio Pattie, Kentuckians, appeared in Taos in October, 1825, after rambling from the Missouri near present Omaha across the Smoky Hill divide of eastern Colorado to Becknell's Cimarron Cut-Off and Palo Flechado Pass. Young James Ohio described the Pattie treks of the next two years in an imaginative book so far beyond belief that many people believe it still. However, James Ohio really did trap the Arizona Gila River area in 1826 with various men, including Ewing Young, and he did explore the Colorado River north past Grand Canyon and Escalante's Crossing of the Fathers to the mouth of the San Juan River, which he and his men ascended.

Of the date April 23, 1827, young Pattie wrote in his book, *Personal Narrative*, that Navajo Indians showed them where to find the Los Pinos River branch of the San Juan, in the country of the Pewee tribes (Utes). Pattie continued: "Their chief village is situated within two days' of the low gap at which we arrived on the first of May. The crossing was a work, the difficulty of which may be imagined from the nature of the case and the character of the Mountains. The passage occupied six days, during which we had to pass along compact drifts of snow, higher than a man on horseback. Nothing is to be seen among these mountains but bare peaks and perpetual snow. Every one knows that these mountains divide between the Atlantic and Pacific Oceans. At the point where we crossed them, they run in a direction a little north of west and south of east, further than the eye can reach."

In matters of timing, topography and weather, this description seems to fit the Weminuche Pass trail better than any other Continental Divide traverse in the San Juan Range. If they did

cross Weminuche, the Pattie men would have found themselves
on the Upper Rio Grande above Wagon Wheel Gap. From
that point on to their arrival at Santa Fe three months later,
James Ohio's tale is chaotically confused — a colorful rag rug of
myth which he could have pieced together out of trapper tales.
He wrote of visiting the Bighorn, the Yellowstone, "the country
of the Flat Heads" and Clark Fork of the Columbia — a three-
thousand-mile safari which hardly could have been made in six
months, let alone three. But perhaps Pattie did cross Poncha
Pass from San Luis Valley, and Trout Creek Pass to South Park,
and so on to the plains by Ute Pass at Pikes Peak. He wrote of
"Long's Peak" — a common name for Pikes Peak then because
of Major Long's expedition past it in 1820. Today's Longs Peak
is the other great and beautiful Front Range eminence one hundred and twenty miles north of Pikes Peak.

Like the Patties, William Becknell got himself fired up about
the beaver boom, forgetting his Santa Fe Trail almost as soon as
he founded it and setting out over Horse Lake in the fall of
1824 along the Spanish Trail. He and his party of nine foun-
dered in the usual heavy snows of the San Juans above present
Durango, Colorado. They almost starved rather than eat their
horses because, Becknell explained, "they were our principal
reliance for effecting a retreat, so that to have eaten them would
have been like dining upon our own feet."

Becknell was one of many of the new Taos trapping society
who longed for an easy short route to Green River. Though the
Green below Wind River Range had never been systematically
trapped, pioneers of the 1810–1812 period — Lisa, Henry, Hoback, Reznor and such — had hinted at its beaver potential.
Ten years were enough to build their hints into a legend of the
stream's wealth — beaver so thick and tame you knocked them
down with sticks. But to get there from Taos was difficult, with
a mountain mass intervening of unimaginable height. Slipping
around it south by the Spanish Trail over Horse Lake Pass was
too roundabout. That left only one other rumored route — the

ancient Ute and buffalo traverse over the Cochetopa Hills, which Governor de Anza had observed in 1779.

Nobody knows who was the first American to cross Cochetopa Pass. In their book *Old Spanish Trail*, LeRoy and Ann Hafen present the claim of a William Huddart that he left Taos on August 24, 1824, with fourteen others and made it in a month by Cochetopa to some lower part of Green River. With him was the hard-boiled St. Louis Canadian, Etienne Provost, aged forty-two, and Antoine Robidoux, another St. Louis Frenchman of Quebec ancestry, who had served in the army's foolish Yellowstone expedition of 1819.

The black-haired, brown-eyed swarthy Antoine, born near St. Louis in 1794, was a brother of the St. Louis trader and future founder of St. Joseph, Missouri, Joseph Robidoux. Antoine may not have crossed Cochetopa Pass first, but he was the first American after Zebulon Pike to thoroughly penetrate the high Colorado Rockies. He was also the first pioneer of the vast, beguiling Gunnison River region of Colorado's Western Slope. As early as 1825, he began regular trade trips by pack train from Santa Fe and Taos over Cochetopa to Lower Green River. His choice of Cochetopa put American approval on what the LeRoy Hafens call "the north branch of the Spanish Trail," which joined the original Chama–Horse Lake Pass–San Juan River–Dolores River trace at a point near present Green River, Utah.

Soon Robidoux made up pack trains at his brother's establishment in St. Louis or at Fort Osage or Fort Smith part of the way west, and moved them directly to Cochetopa Pass, bypassing the Spanish settlements. To do this involved following the Sante Fe Trail up the Arkansas and then the Huerfano as far as the Spanish Peaks and Badito Cone, and continuing up the Huerfano to Mosca Pass instead of to Sangre de Cristo Pass. Though Mosca was much harder to climb than Sangre de Cristo, it had a rich grass valley for forage just below the top on the east side. Furthermore, it came down into San Luis Valley at the edge of the sand dunes north of the bulging hump of

Blanca Peak, which Antoine would have had to ride around otherwise. The saving in travel time was three days. From then on, Mosca Pass was usually called Roubideau's Pass by Americans, and was favored by Cochetopa-bound travelers from the Spanish Peaks.

From the sand dunes side of Mosca Pass, Robidoux trailed some seventy miles northwest up San Luis Valley, picking up Saguache Creek, which made its appearance in the sand along the way. Then he began the easy grade to the Continental Divide through a series of gray, barren hillocks, as you see them at the little red brick and white clapboard county seat of Saguache. Due west of him, the gray and green Cochetopa Hills stretched low across his horizon for sixty miles between the last great peak of the San Juans on the south, San Luis (14,149), and the stately first peak of the Sawatch Range, Mount Ouray (13,955), on the north.

The Cochetopa Hills terrain is not at all flat as South Pass is flat. But it is rounded gently enough so that the whole sixty-mile span is one wide Cochetopa Pass in effect rather than a particular narrow gap. Antoine's pack trains could have crossed the Divide at a dozen places among the aspen and spruce and grassy parks at the 10,000-foot level of Cochetopa Hills. Perhaps he chose the East Pass Creek route which the so-called North Cochetopa Pass (10,200) road follows today — the new 1962 short road from Saguache town to Gunnison River and U.S. Route 50 instead of the older gravel road which runs just south of it in more leisurely fashion over the original Cochetopa Pass (10,032).[1]

But crossing Cochetopa was the simplest part of the five-hundred-mile trek from Taos to Lower Green River south of the Uinta Range. From Cochetopa, Robidoux and his Taos colleagues had a choice of ancient paths made by animals and Indians. As we have said, these paths were formed by necessities — altitudes below timberline, running water, game for food, river crossings, year-around forage and climate which, if not always mild, could be endured. The paths rambled for good reasons — to avoid canyons, bogs, mosquitoes, rock slides. Problems of undergrowth and fallen trees, which drove David Thompson to despair in the Canadian Rockies, were less of a factor in the higher drier uplands south of Lewis and Clark Pass.

Beyond Cochetopa Pass, one westering Ute Indian route left the blue Gunnison River near the present town of Gunnison, ran north up Ohio Creek and over Ohio Pass and Kebler Pass. From these sagey West Elk Mountains it cut through aspens up Muddy Creek and down Divide Creek (or Mam Creek) just east of Grand Mesa to the boulder-strewn Colorado at today's Silt.[2] This Ute trail ascended Roan Creek from the Colorado, then to Douglas Pass — adorned with pictographs on granite, delicate as needlework — and on to White River. From thence it was placid going through sage and sand hills to Green River in today's Dinosaur National Monument.

Again from Cochetopa Pass, another Ute trail went down Gunnison River as far as its impassable Black Canyon near today's Curecanti Reservoir. Then it angled southwesterly and upward over Son-of-a-Bitch Hill (*ca.* 9000 — known now by the more polite name of Blue Mesa Summit) — and Cerro Summit (7909), which was the divide between Gunnison and Uncompahgre rivers. The country bypassing Black Canyon was not serene, being squeezed between Uncompahgre Peak (14,-301) on the south and the old Ute hunting ground of Thigunawat — Grand Mesa — on the north. The result was a mean trail of forty miles, the painful character of which can be felt still by any driver on the relocated U.S. Route 50 from Gunnison to Montrose. At the Uncompahgre, the Ute trail followed down that stream, and then the Gunnison, to the Colorado River crossing at present Grand Junction, and over Roan Plateau by Douglas Pass, or Baxter Pass a few miles west, to White and Green rivers.

WHILE MAJOR FOWLER and William Becknell were making Taos fashionable with trappers in 1822, a handsome man-about-St. Louis, William H. Ashley, was advertising for "one hundred enterprising young men" to make fur fortunes with him in the Rockies, as Becknell had advertised for adventurers the previous year. The energetic Ashley, a Virginian of forty-four years, was lieutenant governor of Missouri, a general in Missouri's new state militia, a manufacturer of gunpowder, a promoter of lead mines, a real-estate salesman, and a perennial suitor who acquired a new wife every so often. His knowledge of beaver was confined to the hat on his head, but his Missouri mining associate was our Raynolds Pass hero of 1810, Major Andrew Henry, and the Major knew all about the Rockies fur business.

The first two years of Ashley's Rocky Mountain Fur Company (that name came later) ended in disaster. The tow-mast of his first keelboat hit a tree branch on the lower Missouri, causing the boat to upset and sink with a cargo of trinkets and supplies. Some of Andrew Henry's advance party wintered on the Upper Missouri at the mouth of the Musselshell, where Meriwether Lewis had found mollusks in 1805 and Clark had named the nearby Judith River after his girl back home. In the spring of 1823, Blackfeet attacked the Henry party and killed four of them a bit farther up the Missouri, but still short of Gate of the Mountains and the actual Montana Rockies. Soon after, near the Missouri River departure point of Hunt's Astorians in South Dakota, Arikara Indians killed thirteen of Ashley's seventy men. A thousand soldiers, trappers and Sioux Indians made motions to punish them, but merely got in each other's way and accomplished nothing at all.

Meantime, what remained of Manuel Lisa's old Missouri Fur Company under Robert Jones and Michael Immell had bad luck too. They should have known better than to trap where they did. Crossing Bozeman Pass, thirty of them ascended Jefferson River past Three Forks and Pipestone Creek as far as the point where the Jefferson is formed by the inflowing Big Hole, Beaverhead and Ruby rivers. Trapping was poor, a meager twenty packs. But the uplands were fine to look at, and soothingly contoured — Gallatin and Madison ranges, Tobacco Roots, Highland and Pioneer Mountains, the neat, standoffish Ruby Range. And the Blackfeet left them alone — until they crossed Bozeman Pass again eastbound down the Yellowstone toward the mouth of the Bighorn. Then the Indians pounced, killing seven of them, including Jones and Immell. The twenty-three survivors reached camp stripped almost as bare as had been the marathon man, John Colter.

From such behavior, General Ashley judged that the Upper Missouri was off limits. Green River was the place to trap these days, if he could find how Wilson Price Hunt got there in 1811, and how Stuart's party returned to St. Louis over South Pass in 1812. Ashley's position after the Arikara calamity was depressing. He had commanded one hundred and eighty men in 1822. Only twenty-four trappers were with him now at Fort Kiowa on the Missouri in southern Dakota.

Except for Andrew Henry, his young employees were just names. He could not have foreseen that some of these ragged tenderfeet would have a permanent impact on Western history. One was Jedediah Strong Smith, a tall, stern New Yorker of twenty-four who carried a Bible and talked religion. Another was a natural-born geographer, James Bridger, aged twenty, from Richmond, Virginia — recently a St. Louis wharf rat and barkeep. Bridger's lean shape and plain face did not show how perfectly his mind and body would fit the Rockies environment with its peculiar demands and unsuspected amenities. Ruddy-cheeked, judicial Thomas Fitzpatrick was there — Jed Smith's age; Kentucky-born William L. Sublette, as tall and thin and anxious as a cornstalk in autumn; and a moody mountaineer named Captain John G. Weber — the Weber which would apply later to a Utah river, canyon, college and mountain.

By August of 1823, Ashley had only twenty-five packs of fur to show for his year's work, which was the same thing as facing bankruptcy. He set off downstream from Fort Kiowa to raise funds in St. Louis and to campaign for governor of Missouri, leaving instructions with Andrew Henry and the faithful twenty-four to find Green River and rediscover South Pass.

Early in September, 1823, the elderly Henry picked twelve of his youngsters and slipped up the Missouri and up the Yellowstone into friendly Crow country. Luck was with them. Only two were killed on the way — by Arikaras or Mandans. The legendary Hugh Glass — John Colter's counterpart for the Roaring Twenties — was clawed open in fifty places by a female grizzly and left for dead, spouting blood north, east, west and south. But he lived to tell the tale, over and over and over, after crawling three hundred miles on hands and knees back to Fort Kiowa.

At the Powder River–Yellowstone junction, Henry subtracted several men from his nine survivors, including a kind of cub reporter named Daniel T. Potts, and sent them off toward South Pass. Meanwhile he and the rest continued to the Bighorn's mouth, where they wintered. The Potts handful rode southwest up the Powder and over the Big Horns by Wilson Price Hunt's route of 1811 (Buffalo, Wyoming, to Tensleep today). But at the west (Tensleep) foot of Powder River Pass, they departed from Hunt's southward route and crossed the delirious pinto badlands to Bighorn River (Worland), and upstream to present Thermopolis, where Potts wrote a nice essay on the hot springs at the bottom of Wind River Canyon — or Bighorn, if you like. Potts added, "From thence across the 2d range of mountains to Wind River Valley. In crossing this mountain I unfortunately froze my feet."

The "2d range" was the dry, sandy, east end of the Owl Creek Mountains and they could have used any of three passes — Mexican (6253), Sheep Creek (8400) or Mervit (ca. 8105). Then the party rode up the Wind River trail toward Union and Togwotee passes as the Hunt men had ridden before them. It was the winter of 1824 now, and they camped near present Dubois, Wyoming, to wait for the other Ashley party of eleven men under Jed Smith, as green a greenhorn as the Rockies had ever seen. Jed had a reporter too. He was Ashley's recruiting officer, Jim Clyman.

The Smith-Clyman party was distinct from Andrew Henry's Missouri-Yellowstone group of thirteen from which Potts and his companions were detached. Leaving Fort Kiowa some weeks after Henry's early-September departure, Smith led his ten men due west up White River from the Missouri, over the Black Hills and Powder River toward the inviting Big Horns. That dull part of the trip was enlivened by passage through Clyman's famous "peetrified forest where peetrified birds on peetrified trees sang peetrified songs;" and by Smith's unpleasantness with a "grissly" which (Clyman wrote) "sprang on the capt taking him by the head first pitcing sprawling on the earth he gave him a grab by the middle fortunately cathing by the ball pouch and Butcher kife which he broke but breaking several of his ribs and cutting his head badly."

After ten days of Rockies therapy, Jed was in good enough repair to lead on west and up the shady Tongue to the crest of the Big Horns at Granite Pass (8950). Cloud Peak and its companions rose south between them and Powder River Pass so recently used by the Daniel Potts group. The descent down Shell Creek and Shell Canyon was dreadful — worse than Pike's scramble in the Royal Gorge of the Arkansas and David Thompson's crawl down the Blaeberry below Howse Pass, as any motorist on U.S. Route 14 can understand now. It was climaxed at the bottom by the same sort of slumgullion nightmare that scares travelers at the foot of Powder River Pass. But the Smith-Clyman party had no trouble thereafter joining the Potts group on Wind River near Dubois by way of Bighorn River and the Owl Creek Range bypass around Wind River Canyon.

The great moment of rediscovering South Pass was at hand. First, in February, 1824, Jed Smith tried to cross Union Pass, perhaps reaching the frozen Lake of the Woods at the top and glimpsing the fairy-castle Tetons. The snow was deep ahead on the six-mile Snake-Green-Wind River triple divide, and aswirl in a gale. Smith retreated down the Wind all the way to its Popo Agie branch (Riverton) and began flanking Wind River Range on the east with Tom Fitzpatrick, William Sublette, Jim Clyman and seven others. They ascended the Popo Agie past present Lander into a region of tiny pastures and tortured red canyons, and crossed the divide to the wriggling Sweetwater near today's triangulation station at Devil's Gap (*ca.* 7000). The stream, they thought, belonged to the Platte, or maybe the Arkansas.

The usual gale almost blew them apart as they rested near the later Three Crossings canyon of the Oregon Trail. Then they undulated miserably up the Sweetwater plain toward South Pass seventy miles west of them, crossed it while gorging meat of a buffalo, which had the misfortune to be going their way, and struck Green River on March 19, 1824. They began trapping for beaver at once near the mouth of the Big Sandy.

THE RESULTS OF THEIR TRAPPING were sensational. In June, Tom Fitzpatrick recrossed South Pass and trailed fifteen hundred miles down the Sweetwater, the North Platte, the Platte and the Missouri to tell William Ashley in St. Louis that his fortune was piling up in beaver skins on Green River. The General needed good news just then. His campaign for governor of Missouri was a flop, and his finances had gone from rather bad to much worse.

Fitzpatrick's report kindled within Ashley a bright flame of hope. He came down also with a raging itch to travel. This suave urbanite had been talking like a mountain man for three years now and had never got within five hundred miles of the Rockies. The time had come, he decided, to go to Green River to collect his fur, to do some exploring himself. Perhaps he could organize eventually a system of summer carnivals or rendezvous right where the beaver were. These rendezvous would attract white and red trappers from everywhere to do business with his fur company.

On November 3, 1824, Ashley left Fort Atkinson (Omaha) and began ascending the Platte River with twenty-five employees, fifty pack horses, a wagon, and teams to haul it. In the meantime, the same kind of frenzy for commerce and adventure which impelled him was impelling the whole beaver world. Director George Simpson of Hudson's Bay Company crossed Athabaska Pass —"wild and majestic beyond description"— in mid-October of 1824 to increase profits at Flathead Post on Clarks Fork in western Montana by installing the efficient Peter Skene Ogden there. Jed Smith's little Green River crew were trapping far and wide while Jed himself rambled over The Rim, down Hoback River to Jackson Hole and west over the steeps of Teton Pass. He wound up far north at Flathead Post with some Hudson's Bay Company trappers and Iroquois Indians, following the Lemhi Pass–Gibbons Pass–Evaro Pass trail. One of the Iroquois was "Old Pierre" Tivanitagon, whose first name was being applied to Pierre's Hole around present Driggs, Idaho.

During the summer of 1824, trappers had materialized out of thin air along Green River to augment Ashley's Smith-Clyman group. They numbered twenty-five by fall, when William Sublette, Jim Bridger and Captain Weber took them west to Bear Lake of the north-flowing Bear River and on to the beautiful Cache Valley of the Bear's south-flowing sector. Their trail was over the rolling treeless hills south of those Wyoming Mountains which had enmeshed Stuart's Astorians in 1812. Roughly it approximated the Sublette Cut-Off of later Oregon Trail fame — Big Sandy Creek due west to Green River, up Fontenelle Creek and over the low Green River–Bear River divide (8600) beyond Hams Fork to Bear Lake past today's Cokeville, Wyoming.

While preparing to winter in Utah's Cache Valley, Jim

Bridger built a little bullboat out of green buffalo hides and floated alone twenty-five miles down Bear River Canyon to discover the north end of Great Salt Lake, and to remark as he drank of it, "Hell, it's the Pacific Ocean!" At precisely the same time (the fall of 1824), our Taos friends, Etienne Provost and Antoine Robidoux were discovering Salt Lake's south end. They had arrived to winter in the region from Cochetopa Pass, Gunnison River, Douglas Pass, White River and Lower Green River. From there they ascended Utah's Duchesne River, Strawberry River and Strawberry Pass (8000) across the Wasatch Range, and down Provo Canyon to Utah Lake and Salt Lake. High tide of tourism! To almost complete the circular subjection of the Rockies from Athabaska Pass in northern Canada to La Glorieta in New Mexico, Peter Skene Ogden's trappers from Flathead Post discovered Great Salt Lake during May, 1825 — the third time it had been discovered since October.[3]

And still, wherever these experts roamed, the tenderfoot Ashley, who had traveled mainly on paper in a St. Louis tavern, went them two or three better. No beaten paths for him. His first effort as a Rockies explorer began badly when his wagon fell apart near Fort Atkinson, but his pack train endured through the winter of 1825. By early February, Ashley had reached the eastern Colorado plains facing the Front Range and chose to go up South Platte River instead of the North Platte "as affording more wood." When the South Platte turned south near present Denver toward Pikes Peak, he took the northbound Cache la Poudre fork below Longs Peak and stayed with it to its north branch source in the Front Range at Dead Man Hill Divide (10,288).

The General found no sign that white men had ever before been in this aspen-lodgepole region north of Red Feather Lakes.[4] From Dead Man Hill, with its deep snow and startling views south of the white peaks of Mummy and Never Summer ranges, the pack train struggled down into spring weather — the wide grasslands of Laramie River. The men rode north past Snowy

Range and west across the vanishing Medicine Bow Mountains by Rattlesnake Pass (7518) just north of Elk Mountain (11,162) and today's Saratoga. And so the caravan reached the North Platte, which the General should have followed in the first place.

Crossing the cottonwood-banked stream, the twenty-five slogged on through alkali dust and across the Continental Divide in the Bridger Pass (7523) part of the Sierra Madre Range. They crossed the Divide again without knowing it as they rode into that no-mountain sink, the Great Basin of Wyoming, near present Rawlins, and turned up at Lost Soldier Gap, which Stuart's eastbound Astorians had used while hunting the Sweetwater. From Lost Soldier, it was no trick to push west past Antelope Hills and over the South Pass area to Big Sandy and Green River, arriving April 19, 1825.

Those one hundred sixty-seven winter days — some of them very hard to take — of jogging seventeen hundred miles from Fort Atkinson merely gave Ashley his second exploring wind. If the Upper Green was so full of beaver, how about the Lower Green, beyond those huge mountains (the Uintas) through which the stream cut its way to the south? Within a week, the General had divided most of his combined forces to trap — Zacharias Ham and six men west to Hams Fork of the Green, Clyman and six northward toward the Green River Pass (10,370) source of the Green, Tom Fitzpatrick and six southward to Henrys Fork, where Ashley would rendezvous everybody on July 1. Ashley himself floated downstream in a bullboat and some sort of canoe with six converted sailors.

Motorists today on the remote road from Green River, Wyoming, to Vernal, Utah, can imagine what pleasures and trials lay ahead of those wildly rash undergraduates in the exploring field.[5] The Green was low-banked and agreeable until it began cutting through the 12,000-foot Uinta Range at the Wyoming-Utah border. Thereafter, each mile was the torment of portaging or the worry of smashing boats in the turbulence of red and yellow trenches half a mile deep, the walls of which exposed ages of geologic history. The erosion of these twisting grooves changed the river's color to an angry mustard shade.

The seven sailors survived Red Canyon and Flaming Gorge, Upper and Lower Disaster Falls of Lodore Canyon, and also Hell's Half Mile. They had twenty miles of brief respite, low banks and good hunting as they floated through Brown's Hole (Park), the future home of trappers and outlaws. They could relax, too, in the tiny cottonwood-and-meadow oasis of Pat's Hole (Echo Park), a Rocky Mountain Shangri-la hidden below the sheer cliffs of Steamboat Rock where the mustard Green meets the clear blue Yampa from central Colorado.[6] But they lost nearly everything in Split Mountain Canyon near today's Dinosaur National Monument headquarters, and gave up boating in mid-May, 1825, soon after meeting some of Etienne Provost's men from Taos at the mouth of Ashley Creek (Jensen, Utah). A real St. Louis reunion! The southern limit of their Green River descent was reached on May 24, 1825, some seventy miles below Jensen at the mouth of Minnie Maud Creek.

They returned upstream and ascended Duchesne and Strawberry rivers as Escalante had done in 1776, but continued over Strawberry Pass (8000) to present Heber, Utah, and on north to Weber River, which flowed north there in its ramble to Salt Lake. Etienne Provost himself appeared on June 7, and told Ashley how to reach Henrys Fork of the Green for his July 1 rendezvous. The route from Weber River was by way of Chalk Creek and Big Muddy Creek. The Ashley party of seven finished the six-hundred-mile circuit of the Uinta Range on June 30, 1825 — it had taken sixty-six days. The first of many Green River area rendezvous began next day as planned on Henrys Fork, attended by one hundred and twenty trappers, including twenty-nine renegades from Peter Skene Ogden's brigade of Hudson's Bay Company men. There was also an assembly of Indians who had never seen such goings-on in their lives.[7]

WILLIAM ASHLEY retired to St. Louis with a fur fortune after selling out to Jed Smith, William Sublette and David Jackson in July, 1826. By that date, his "enterprising young men," abetted by Robidoux and other Taos pioneers, had uncovered most of the American Rockies where beaver lived, except high bits of Colorado, and the three-hundred-and-fifty-mile Blackfoot stretch of the Continental Divide north of Deer Lodge Pass in Montana.

While Jed Smith led a dramatic life exploring the West coast (1826–1829), his men and those from Taos were prosaically at work surviving Indian battles, starvation, venereal disease, freezing and the sort of multiple injury which comes from riding horses. They became familiar with the internal rumbles and external theatrics of Yellowstone Park. Jim Bridger could claim discovery of that common headwater of Yellowstone and Snake rivers, Two Oceans Pass, provided John Colter had not reached it first.

A consequence of all this activity was steady development of pass routes. Three-quarters of the future Oregon Trail over South Pass was standard now. Becknell's Santa Fe Trail — by Cimarron Cut-Off or Raton Pass — tied St. Louis to the Rio Grande. Ashley's ascent of the South Platte and on over the Front Range to Laramie River and the North Platte led people into Colorado's North Park where the North Platte rose below Rabbit Ears Pass. During 1827, Thomas L. "Pegleg" Smith, history's beloved horse thief, directed the amputation of his own injured leg in North Park while trapping with Bill Williams and Ceran St. Vrain of Taos. After his recovery, the group crossed the Continental Divide, probably by Battle Lake Pass (9916) on the Colorado-Wyoming border, to the charming Little Snake River, a branch of Yampa River. Ute trails from there could have taken them to Vermilion Creek and Green River at Brown's Hole, through which Ashley had boated in 1825, and north to the main Green River beaver grounds.

The large Bean-Sinclair party from Fort Smith rode up the

Arkansas in 1830 to Pueblo, moved north past Pikes Peak and over Black Forest Divide to the site of Denver, and entered South Park by an easy trail up the North Fork of the South Platte across Kenosha Pass (9950). When winter threatened, they made for Taos across Pike's Trout Creek Pass to the Upper Arkansas under Mount Princeton, and followed buffalo tracks over Poncha Pass to the Rio Grande.

Certainly the wild Rockies were getting tamer, and still there was excitement left for youngsters coming up. In 1829, for example, eighteen-year-old Joseph L. Meek of Virginia joined the Jed Smith firm. In November, he rode with William Sublette's brigade over Raynolds Pass to today's Missouri Flats, and crossed the low Gallatin Range northeast some thirty-five miles to Yellowstone River. The Blackfeet attacked the intruders at dusk, and cut young Joe and his mule off from the rest. His lady biographer reported: "Poor Joe succumbed to the influence of thought, and wept." Then he composed himself, made a quick trip to Mammoth Hot Springs in Yellowstone Park, and found his lonely way over the Absaroka Range up Soda Butte Creek to Cooke Pass and down Clarks Fork of the Yellowstone to find friends at the boiling springs of the Stinking River (Cody).

All things considered, perhaps the great event of Rockies pass history during the 1820's was the discovery of the two preeminent peaks of our continent. These tremendous spires were alleged to have been found at Athabaska Pass, where they had never been reported before by the hundreds of Canadian trappers who had trudged by the Committee's Punch Bowl since 1811. The discoverer was the Scottish botanist for the Royal Horticulture Society, David Douglas, for whom the Douglas fir is named.

On his return from a botany trip to Oregon, Douglas reached Athasbaska Pass at 10 A.M. on May 1, 1827, and described the day as follows: "Being well rested, by 1 o'clock I set out with the view of ascending what seemed to be the highest peak. Its height does not appear to be less than 16,000 or 17,000 feet above the level of the sea. After passing over the lower ridge, I came to about 1,200 feet of by far the most difficult and fatiguing walking I have ever experienced. . . . The view from the summit is too awful a cast to afford pleasure . . . The majestic but terrible avalanches hurling themselves from the more exposed southerly rocks produced a crash, and groaned through the distant valleys with a sound only equalled by that of an earthquake.

"This peak, the highest yet known in the northern continent of America I feel sincere pleasure in naming Mount Brown in honour of R. Brown, Esq., the illustrious botanist . . . A little to the southward is one nearly the same height rising to a sharper point; this I named Mount Hooker, in honour of my early patron, the Professor of Botany, in the University of Glasgow. 'The Committee's Punch Bowl' is a small circular lake 20 yards in diameter, with a small outlet on the west end, namely one of the branches of the Athabaska."

A great day for Canada, honored for the next seventy years by every Canadian child whose geographies described the glory of those twin 16,000-foot monarchs of the Rockies.[8] But, in 1893, a treasonable Toronto professor, A. P. Coleman, claimed to have visited Athabaska Pass and found nothing high up there at all. Such an insult to British prestige was too much for the English alpinists, Hugh E. M. Stutfield and J. Norman Collie. Their expedition reached the Committee's Punch Bowl on August 24, 1898, after three weeks of trailing from Banff.

They found Mount Hooker and Mount Brown right where David Douglas had said they were, and measured them carefully with modern instruments. The figures brought anguish not only to Canadian schoolchildren but to atlas publishers everywhere. Mount Hooker was only 10,782 feet above sea level. Mount Brown, 9156 feet.

9

Soldiers Take the High Road

Tₕₑ MAGNIFYING MISTS OF THE CANADIAN ROCKIES mesmer-
ized David Douglas into error about Mounts Brown and Hooker.
Still, he was not the only traveler guilty of spreading whoppers.
Though the trappers found most of the gates of the Rockies,
they took such delight in tall tales that their reports could not
be depended upon. Their crude maps were full of mistakes.
Often they refused to tell exactly where they had been. As the
fur trade boomed and busted during its thirty-year career, other
men with other motives had to explore the passes all over again
and decide how they should be used in the future.

These other men were mainly soldiers, and their investigations were begun by Major Stephen H. Long, an officer of the
Topographical Bureau of the United States Army Corps of
Engineers, during the summer of 1820. The Long party
consisted of twenty-two explorers, including the botanist, Dr.
Edwin James, and the painter, Titian Ramsay Peale, the twenty-
year-old son of Charles Willson Peale (who won fame and fortune by painting George Washington over and over).[1] They
arrived by the South Platte at the site of Denver on July 7,
having observed and named Longs Peak in honor of Major Long
without getting very close to it. They seemed to be timid about
penetrating the mountains, which was what they were supposed
to do. At the entrance to Platte River Canyon, Dr. James made
notes on a rock wren but judged the canyon too dangerous to

ascend, and so the party did not attempt to find the Kenosha Pass entrance to South Park.

Four days later, the south-moving explorers crossed Black Forest Divide near present Palmer Lake, visited the Garden of the Gods below Pikes Peak, and camped on the grassy mesa under Cheyenne Mountain. Dr. James spied redheaded house finches while admiring the dark beauty of North Cheyenne Canyon. On July 13, he was at the foot of Ute Pass drinking water at the tulip-shaped bubbling spring and watching the French guide, Joseph Bijeau, as he scooped strings of beads out of the spring. The beads had been thrown in by pious Indians honoring the Great Spirit. Bijeau explained that he had sold the beads to the Indians in the first place and made a practice of recovering them from the spring to sell them again.[2]

Dr. James peered up Ute Pass as warily as he had peered up Platte Canyon and took no further action. His notes, the first of record on the route to South Park which millions use now each year, read: "A large and much frequented road passes the springs and enters the mountains running to the north of the high peak. It is travelled principally by the bisons, sometimes also by the Indians: who penetrate here to the Columbia." Penetrating "to the Columbia" from Ute Pass would have been quite a trek. Dr. James's road did not follow the canyon of Fountain Creek as U.S. Route 24 does today. It humped over ridges half a mile south of and parallel to the present highway.[3]

At noon on that same July 13, James and two companions set out from the bubbling spring to be the first men of record to climb Pikes Peak. By sunset, they had scrambled all of two miles to the top of Engelmann Canyon (hikers reach the Summit House in an afternoon now). Since it was getting cold, they built a big fire, cached their food and camped for the night. At dawn on the fourteenth, they struggled upward along the nine-mile line, more or less, of today's Cog Train track from Manitou, and reached the rubble summit of "ten or fifteen acres" at 4 P.M.[4] After half an hour of rest, they started down, but darkness caught them just below timberline, forcing them to spend a night without supper or blankets. At daylight, stomachs grumbling, they hurried to their earlier camp for breakfast. Their food cache was almost destroyed. Their big campfire of the thirteenth had set most of Engelmann Canyon ablaze. Pikes Peak's first careless campers!

The Long men found no trace at Pueblo of Captain Pike's breastworks of 1806, and they could not explore the Upper Arkansas because "their progress was intercepted by proximity of the hills to the river" — meaning the Royal Gorge. Moving downstream, they struck an Arkansas fork which Joseph Bijeau seemed to call Wharf River (Huerfano). James guessed that the name Wharf resulted "from the circumstance of its washing the base of numerous perpendicular precipices of moderate height." From the Huerfano, half of the Long group moved homeward down the Arkansas. Major Long, Dr. James, painter Peale and seven others went south and east in yet another futile search for Red River.

They ascended Timpas Creek from near present La Junta, Colorado, and then the Purgatoire and Chacuaco Creek. On July 26, 1820, they reached the top of the Raton Mountains fifty miles east of Raton Pass amid the pocket gophers and red ridges of Mesa de Maya.[5] They slithered down the rimrock to Cimarron River by Longs Canyon and Longs Mesa, and continued south in New Mexico to another river — the North Fork of the Canadian. They were sure it was the Red, until it brought them to the Arkansas near Fort Smith, instead of to the Mississippi in Louisiana.

The Long party put the height of Pikes Peak at 11,507½ feet above sea level — an underestimate of the actual 14,110 feet which was almost as bad as the 18,581 overestimate of Captain Pike. Mayor Long named it James Peak in honor of the doctor's pioneering as climber and fire-starter. The name, like the expedition as a whole, was not successful.

FIVE YEARS LATER, Senator Thomas Hart Benton of Missouri and other expansionists pushed a bill through Congress appropriating ten thousand dollars to survey and mark the Santa Fe Trail from St. Louis and Fort Osage "to the Mexican settlements." The leader was the Fort Osage trader, Major George C. Sibley, a friend of Pike's friend, Dr. Robinson. There were twelve in the Sibley party, and two loaded wagons. In late September, 1825, they had an easy traverse of the dry Cimarron Cut-Off, reduced from sixty to forty miles by now. Sibley planned the route straight to Santa Fe, but he heard that mean Indians were posted in La Glorieta Pass and he decided to mark and survey the Santa Fe Trail to Taos instead.

From the Cimarron, Sibley's twelve struck the old Palo Flechado trail and moved west on it up the other Cimarron (Creek) to "Taos Gap," at the mouth of Cimarron Canyon near present Cimarron, New Mexico. The Taos Gap mule trail through the canyon proved to be unfit for the two wagons, so the surveyors detoured southward over the sort of rolling country which Major Fowler had crossed eastbound in 1822. They meant to cross the Sangre de Cristo Range by Palo Flechado Pass, but trailed some ten miles too far south to Black Lake near the east foot of Osha Pass. Here the wagons were dismantled and carried up Osha's four-mile east-side trail. On the west side, they rolled on their own from the head of Tienditas Creek, which joined the Palo Flechado Pass trail soon down Fernando de Taos Creek to Taos.

Nobody was impressed by Sibley's idea of reaching Santa Fe by way of Osha Pass and Taos, and his markers soon disappeared. But, in crossing Osha with two wagons, even dismantled wagons, the Major showed the world what wheels could do in the Rockies. Osha Pass was 9800 feet above sea level. If wagons could go that high, they could go over anything. Two years later, Jed Smith's trappers hauled a wheeled cannon over South Pass and on to Bear Lake. In July, 1830, Bill Sublette and crew reached Wind River near the Popo Agie mouth with ten wagons pulled by five mules each. As we have noted, Antoine Robidoux was freighting over Cochetopa Pass at 10,-000 feet in the mid-1830's. By then, a few wagons had made it over Raton Pass at 7834 feet between Bent's Fort, the new trading post of the Bent brothers on the Arkansas, and Taos.

The first wheels in quantity to roll over South Pass belonged to the twenty wagons of Captain Louis Eulalie de Bonneville, and the date of their passage was July 24, 1832. Bonneville had a romantic background, having been born in Paris in 1796 as a protégé of the Marquis de Lafayette, and he emigrated to the United States because his father was "a fugitive from Napoleon's wrath." He graduated from West Point in 1815, and served in frontier posts because — in the words of his biographer, Washington Irving — he was "not much calculated for the sordid struggle of a money-making world." He was a crony of John Jacob Astor, and he was also a sometimes ragged Bowery bum who fell asleep on park benches while reading Corneille. All in all, he fitted the role of hero in a sentimental era.

While stationed at Fort Smith, Arkansas, in the 1820's, Bonneville had listened to the yarns of Santa Fe Trail tourists like Jacob Fowler and William Becknell. From Nathaniel Pryor of the Lewis and Clark expedition, he heard of the promise of Oregon. At last, he had to see the Rockies for himself, partly out of curiosity about the fur trade and what Englishmen were doing on the Columbia watershed. Failing to get government support for a reconnaissance, he took a leave of absence, raised money from rich New York friends — including an ex-Astorian — and headed up the Platte in May, 1832, with the twenty wagons, one hundred and ten trappers, and herds of horses, oxen and cows.

Bonneville built a sloppy log Fort Bonneville that summer in a Horse Creek oasis of cottonwoods and wild roses near Green River.[6] Trappers like William Sublette and Jim Bridger called it Fort Nonsense, holding it to be poorly situated for wintering, though fine for summer trading. In late August, 1832, he led his men northward along the Green to the big triple divide of Union Pass, and down into the elk paradise of Jackson Hole by Fish Creek and Gros Ventre River.

As Irving wrote of this Union Pass trail: "Their march lay up the valley of the Seeds-ke-dee (Green), overlooked to the right by the lofty peaks of the Wind River Mountains. From bright little lakes and fountainheads of this remarkable bed of mountains poured forth the tributary streams. Some came rushing down gullies and ravines; others tumbled on crystal cascades from inaccessible clefts and rocks, and others winding their way in rapid and pellucid currents across the valley . . . So transparent were these waters that the trout with which they abounded could be seen gliding about as if in the air; and their pebbly beds were distinctly visible at a depth of many feet."

The party marveled at the blue splendor of the Tetons, mirrored in Jackson Lake, and crossed the piney steeps of Teton Pass on September 3 from Jackson Hole to Pierre's Hole. From thence the men pushed into the Salmon River country west of Lemhi Pass. They spent the winter trapping in the Sawtooth Mountains and Big Lost River region, pulling out in time to attend the trapper rendezvous of July, 1833, on Green River near Fort Nonsense. At the close of this festival, Bonneville took part of his men to the Bighorn Basin by South Pass, Little Popo Agie River and Wind River Canyon. Some of them trapped the Big Horns around Cloud Peak, getting in by "Bad Pass," which was Powder River Pass. They rejoined the Captain in late August among the crazy-colored hummocks at the foot of the pass near present Hyattville, Wyoming.

Since hostile Indians were in the area, Bonneville thought it best to withdraw his brigade toward the Green, trapping on the way. He himself hurried ahead with three companions to get more traps at Fort Nonsense, but not by way of Union Pass up Wind River, which was too far north, or by South Pass to the south. Instead, the four ascended North Popo Agie, or perhaps Little Wind River, to find a good shortcut pass right over the middle of the Wind River Mountains.

Such a good pass is still missing, of course.[7] What Bonneville found was a vast tumbled highland of turquoise tarns, spruce groves, waterfalls and ridge on ridge of rimrock, with the glaciers of a dozen peaks beckoning beyond — a wilderness almost as remote today as it was in 1833. According to Irving, Bonneville managed to reach the top of one of these peaks to observe "the whole Wind River chain . . . to the south the gentle river, called the Sweet Water . . . the head waters of Wind River . . . to the north the upper streams of the Yellowstone . . . some of the sources of the Oregon, or Columbia, flowing to the northwest past those towering landmarks the Three Tetons . . . while, almost at the captain's feet, the Green River, or Colorado of the West, set forth on its wandering pilgrimage to the Gulf of California."

The peak Bonneville climbed could have been Gannett, Wyoming's highest.[8] He was certainly high up somewhere, giving "it as his opinion that it is the loftiest point of the North American continent." But Washington Irving had heard Englishmen boast about Mount Brown at Athabaska Pass, which had grown steadily since David Douglas climbed it in 1827. So he tempered the Captain's claim with a note of caution: "We rather incline to the opinion that the highest peak is further northward . . . and is the same measured by Mr. Thompson, surveyor to the Northwest Company who . . . ascertained it to be twenty-five thousand feet above the level of the sea."

IRVING'S BIOGRAPHY OF BONNEVILLE, which described two more years of the Captain's adventures out West, was published in 1837. Its popularity caused a clamor for more information about the Rockies, leading to the creation of a quite epochal government agency. It was called the United States Army

Corps of Topographical Engineers — entirely independent of the Corps of Engineers and its Topographical Bureau of Major Long's time. The new Topographical Engineers consisted of thirty-six officers, each of whom was supposed to lead exploring parties in the Rockies under the authority of the Secretary of War. As things developed, they found themselves to be commanded not by the Secretary of War but by Senator Thomas Hart Benton, who used them to instrument his plans for the conquest of Oregon, California and New Mexico. They did not mind being used and came to think of themselves as the private eyes of manifest destiny.

Benton's private eye of eyes was Lieutenant John Charles Frémont, his son-in-law, a slight, wiry, unpredictable figure whose impact on American history is evident in countless things named for him — towns, counties, creeks, mountains, trails, passes. He was a professional hero, differing from Captain Bonneville, the amateur, who was pleased to be heroic briefly and then resume normal existence.[9] Frémont was twenty-nine years old in mid-June, 1842, when he led his first expedition for Benton and the Topographical Engineers out of St. Louis to map the Oregon Trail as far as South Pass. In his party of twenty-four were trappers like Lucien Maxwell, who would own the vast Maxwell Grant around Raton Pass one day, and Kit Carson, who had just placed his half-Cheyenne daughter in a St. Louis convent. The two were at liberty because the Rocky Mountain fur business was over for good.

A touch of nepotism was supplied by the presence of Benton's twelve-year-old son Randolph, and his grandnephew Henry Brant, aged eighteen. A tall blond German, Charles Preuss, was Frémont's topographer. Preuss likened everything he saw to some sight in Europe, thus starting the American habit of describing the Rockies according to whether they did, or did not look like the Alps. The main group followed the Oregon Trail up the North Platte, while Frémont and several others detoured up the South Platte short of Longs Peak in search of sites for forts, rejoining the expedition at Fort Laramie. In his daily journal, Frémont wrote of the sunny climate, the uplifting scenery, and the sweet taste of freedom in the wilderness.

His journal gave the first official portrait of South Pass, which the expedition crossed westbound on August 8, 1842: "The ascent had been so gradual that . . . we were obliged to watch very closely to find the place at which we had reached the culminating point . . . I should compare the elevation which we surmounted immediately at the Pass to the ascent of the Capitol hill from the avenue, at Washington. It is difficult for me to fix positively the breadth of this pass. From the broken ground where it commences, at the foot of the Wind River chain, the view to the southeast is over a champaign country, broken, at the distance of nineteen miles, by the Table rock which . . . seems to stand on a comparative plain . . . It will be seen that it in no manner resembles the places to which the term is commonly applied . . . nothing of the gorge-like character and winding ascents of the Allegheny passes in America: nothing of the Great St. Bernard and Simplon passes in Europe." Frémont, who had never been in Europe, got the St. Bernard–Simplon comparison from Charles Preuss.

Since Bonneville had claimed to have climbed "the loftiest point of the North American continent," Frémont decided to climb something higher, and to measure the altitude with one of his new English barometers. The barometers kept breaking until only one remained, and that one had to be repaired by scraping a powderhorn thin and sticking it on the instrument with buffalo glue. To find a mountain, Frémont took his party beyond South Pass and north up New Fork of Green River on the west, or Anglo-American, side of Wind River Range. They pushed eighty miles into the spectacular lake country northeast of present Pinedale, Wyoming, to Island Lake, above timberline just under the Continental Divide, and to "three small lakes of green color" clouded by glacial flour — Titcomb Lakes.

For three days they struggled to reach a crest in that Indian

Pass country of sheer walls; then they gave up. But, on August 15, 1842, as most of them returned to the Island Lake camp, Frémont, Preuss and four others spotted a route with a spyglass. In a few hours, they reached a tiny slab summit and "fixing a ramrod in a crevice, unfurled the national flag to wave in the breeze where never flag waved before . . . The barometer stood at 18.293 . . . giving for the elevation 13,570 feet."

His summit was just south of the really highest peak, Gannett. It, or one very near it, would be named Fremont Peak.[10]

FRÉMONT AND HIS MEN were back in St. Louis by mid-October, but that expedition of 1842 was merely a warm-up. In May, 1843, Benton packed his son-in-law and Charles Preuss off again in a party of thirty-nine, with a cannon supplied by Colonel Stephen Watts Kearny from the St. Louis arsenal. The cannon suggested that the peaceful Topographical Engineers were getting more warlike every day.

This second expedition went out the Republican Fork of the Kansas and up the South Platte to spend July 7 near Cherry Creek in present Denver. Then the men moved south by Castle Rock (Poundcake) and Black Forest Divide on a mule-buying mission to Pueblo. On their return, they drank at the Ute Pass boiling springs "which Mr. Preuss found very much to resemble that of the famous Seltzer springs in the grand duchy of Nassau."

Frémont was especially anxious to find passes for military and emigrant use in those highest Rockies between Cochetopa Pass of southern Colorado and Bridger Pass in southern Wyoming. But he had no luck, even with Kit Carson and Tom Fitzpatrick in his party. He wrote: "It is singular that, immediately at the foot of the mountains, I could find no one sufficiently acquainted with them to guide us to the plains at their western base." Accordingly, the explorers took familiar trails north from Cache la Poudre drainage to the Laramie River, over the Medicine Bows by Rattlesnake Pass below Elk Mountain, across

Bridger Pass, and north through Muddy Gap to the Sweetwater.

It was good to return to civilization on the Sweetwater. Frémont wrote on August 6, 1843: "Here passes the road to Oregon; and the broad smooth highway, where the numerous heavy wagons of the emigrants had entirely beaten and crushed the artemesia, was a happy exchange to our poor animals for the sharp rocks and tough shrubs along which they had been toiling so long." South Pass itself was positively urban. "We crossed at the southern extremity, which is nearly twenty miles in width, and already traversed by several different roads."

The expedition continued beyond our Rockies range along the Oregon Trail to the Columbia, explored Nevada's Great Basin, and discovered Carson Pass (8600) into California on February 20, 1844. In the spring, the men returned to the Rockies at Utah Lake by way of southern California and the Old Spanish Trail. From Utah Lake, they used Escalante's Spanish Fork–Diamond Creek route over the Wasatch Range to Fort Uintah, and east to reach Brown's Hole on June 7, 1844.

The place was just another well-known trapper hangout by then, instead of the lonely oasis Ashley had seen in 1825. Taking the main trail east, Frémont led the way up Vermilion Creek, crossed the sage divide to Little Snake River and pushed up that willowy waterway along the present Colorado-Wyoming border to the mouth of Battle Creek at the west foot of Battle Lake Pass (9916). A woodsy road goes over the Sierra Madre and Continental Divide today by Battle Lake Pass from Slater, Colorado, to Encampment, Wyoming, on the south side of Bridger Peak (11,007). Frémont, however, circled north around the peak, crossing the divide a bit south of Bridger Pass by one of many Ute trails through prime antelope country. The trail led to Jack Creek of the North Platte from which "we saw spread out before us the valley of the Platte, with the pass of the Medicine Butte beyond." He was referring to Rattlesnake Pass and Elk Mountain. Frémont went on to explain his next action, which had been forming in his mind ever since his failure of the summer before to find gates through the Colorado Rockies from the Pikes Peak region:

"We were now about two degrees south of the South Pass, and our course home would have been eastwardly; but that would have taken us over ground already examined, and therefore without the interest which would excite curiosity. Southwardly there were objects worthy to be explored, to wit: the approximation of the head waters of three different rivers — the Platte, the Arkansas, and the Grand River fork of the Rio Colorado [Green]:[11] the Passes at the heads of these rivers; and the three remarkable mountain coves, called Parks, in which they took their rise. One of these Parks was, of course, on the western side of the dividing ridge; and a visit to it would require us once more to cross the summit of the Rocky Mountains to the west, and then to re-cross to the east; making, in all, with the transit we had just accomplished, three crossings of that mountain in this section of its course. But, no matter. The coves, the heads of the rivers, the approximation of their waters, the practicability of the mountain passes, and the locality of the THREE PARKS, were all objects of interest, and, although well known to hunters and trappers, were unknown to science and to history. We therefore changed our course, and turned up the valley of the Platte instead of going down it."

THE MOTOR TRIP TODAY from Saratoga, Wyoming, south to the Colorado border and on through North, Middle and South Parks of Colorado is one of the finest of Rocky Mountain journeys. Frémont's journal suggests that it was just as felicitous in June of 1844. As the party entered North Park, buffalo, antelope and elk gamboled among the North Platte willows. One of the men amused himself trying to lasso a grizzly bear. Frémont called this treeless basin New Park and Cow Lodge as variants of the trappers' Bull Pen. The Sierra Madre and Continental Divide rose fifteen miles west. The Medicine Bows were a dark blue line in the light blue eastern sky. Trailing on south, Frémont saw a westering road to Summit Lake and Buffalo Pass (10,200) which would have brought him to the Yampa Valley and Brown's Hole on the Western Slope.[12] Then "we fell into a broad and excellent trail, made by buffalo, where a wagon would pass with ease; and in the course of the morning we crossed the summit of the Rocky Mountains, through a pass which was one of the most beautiful we had ever seen."

This last was Muddy Pass (8772), the lowest Colorado gate of the Continental Divide, which trended east across their southward trail to the Front Range in present Rocky Mountain National Park. The divide at Muddy Pass is called Rabbit Ears Range because of the comical and prominent stone ears which stick above Muddy Pass and the adjoining Rabbit Ears Pass (9680). U.S. Route 40 descends on the west to Steamboat Springs from both of these passes in its run from Denver. Muddy Pass brought the Frémont party into the rolling ranges and forests of Middle Park, which is a thousand feet lower than North Park and with a gentler atmosphere. Its Muddy Creek led them to the Colorado River (at present Kremmling), the stream which had remained a mystery "to science and to history" longer than any other in the Rockies.

Frémont would have liked to search for the unknown source of the Colorado somewhere in the Front Range. However, a mob of Arapahoes in war paint appeared from the east, forcing him to give up exploration in that direction. On June 19, his men swam their horses across the river and hurried south up its Blue River branch in the little valley between Gore Range on the west and Williams River Mountains. At the site of present Dillon Reservoir, they observed that a trail came in with Snake River to the Blue from the east (as Loveland Pass highway from Denver comes in now). But no trail arrived with Tenmile Creek from the west, where motorists today scud over Vail Pass toward Glenwood Springs or over Fremont Pass toward Leadville.

There were Arapahoes in the woods all around them now. It seemed that these Plains Indians were trying to arrange a fight with Mountain Utes in South Park. Frémont continued south up the Blue past the mouth of Swan River, the course of "which afforded a better pass than the branch we were on." This "better pass" to South Park was Georgia Pass (11,598), but most of the Arapahoe warriors were using it, so "we continued our road — occasionally through open pines, with a very gradual ascent. We surprised a herd of buffalo, enjoying the shade at a small lake among the pines; and they made the branches crack, as they broke through the woods." There are many beaver ponds still south of Breckenridge along the rippling Blue River beneath Quandary Peak (14,252). "In a ride of about three-quarters of an hour, and having ascended perhaps 800 feet, we reached the SUMMIT OF THE DIVIDING RIDGE, which would thus have an estimated height of 11,200 feet." The "Dividing Ridge," Hoosier Pass, was higher than that — 11,541 feet above sea level.

That midafternoon of June 22, 1844, must have been a fascinating time for Lieutenant Frémont of the Topographical Engineers. At the top of Hoosier, he was like a man placing the last easy pieces of a difficult picture puzzle. He saw just below him "a green valley, through which ran a stream," which he knew had to be the source of South Platte River. It was not far below him, since South Park is the highest of all three Colorado Parks — 10,000 feet above sea level in its northwest (Fairplay) corner. "A short distance opposite rose snow mountains, whose summits were formed into peaks of naked rock." These were the 14,000-footers — Mounts Lincoln, Cameron, Bross and Democrat. "We soon afterwards satisfied ourselves that immediately beyond these mountains was the main branch of the Arkansas River." That was right, too. The mountains were the Mosquito Range, running south to Pike's Trout Creek Pass to separate South Park from the Upper Arkansas.

Next day a buffalo road brought them on south to intersect the trail Pike had used in 1806 in his search for Red River. The Arapahoes had found their Utes and, for a time, the explorers watched from "a low piney ridge" (present Hartsel) a wild melee between the two tribes. Then they moved southeast away from the South Platte toward Currant Creek Pass, with Pikes Peak rising ahead of them. Missing the pass, they worked through the broken country east of it. "After several days' laborious travelling, we succeeded in extricating ourselves from the mountains, and on the morning of the 28th encamped at their foot on a handsome tributary [Oil Creek] of the Arkansas River."

The rest of the second Frémont trip was a lark. On August 6, 1844, the men were back in St. Louis.

WE WILL NOT DWELL long on Frémont's last important pass-finding expedition. In August of 1845, he hurried up the Arkansas once more with sixty well-armed men, ostensibly to map the southern Colorado region around Bent's Fort for the Corps of Topographical Engineers. His real objective was much farther west — in Mexico's California — on behalf of Senator Benton and the other expansionists. His route up the Arkansas deep into Colorado was the same that Pike had taken all the way to Mount Elbert. From there Frémont continued due north up the Arkansas over ground which contained the gold and silver treasures of future Leadville. Beyond Leadville's site he did not choose the East Fork of the Arkansas to Fremont Pass (11,318). Instead he kept straight ahead across the high meadows of Tennessee Creek to a dip in the Continental Divide under Homestake Peak.

And so he discovered what would be called Tennessee Pass (10,424), a versatile and beautiful Rocky Mountain gate which has as many uses today as Raton Pass, as Montana's Pipestone and Marias passes, as the Canadian Kicking Horse Pass. But our professional hero had more important things on his mind now than merely finding gates. He and his sixty men were not Topographical Engineers any more. They were about to be converted officially into Mounted Riflemen, going west to conquer California with the blessing of President Polk himself![13]

10

The New Mountain Men

WHILE LIEUTENANT FRÉMONT was conquering California, General Stephen Watts Kearny and his Army of the West crossed the Arkansas near Bent's Fort on August 2, 1846, to conquer New Mexico. The enormous force consisted of seventeen hundred dragoons, infantrymen, artillerists, volunteers, hangers-on and Topographical Engineers — the largest crowd of white people ever before seen in the Rockies.[1] There were one hundred supply wagons, twenty-two howitzers and a great many mules.

The General sent parties of diplomats and scouts on ahead to Santa Fe, and also a number of stray Mexicans, so that Governor Armijo would be informed about the irresistible power coming at him. These parties did their work so well that the hardest part of the conquest was to get the Army of the West over Raton Pass. Kearny's route, the Bent's Fort (or mountain) branch of the Santa Fe Trail, was sixty miles longer than the Cimarron Cut-Off. Nevertheless, Kearny's young Topographical Engineer, Lieutenant James W. Abert, chose it because "the beauty of the scenery, the delightful freshness of the snow-cooled water of the mountains, with good grass and timber in abundance, give it greatly the superiority."

In his reconnaissance of the previous year, Abert had let his admiration for Raton Pass run away with him: "Every moment our eyes were arrested by the imposing grandeur of the precipitous cliffs . . . whilst continually several small rivulets borne from the cool springs of the mountain side burst from the dark crystal waters . . . I thought that the pleasure afforded us . . . seemed not inferior to that experienced whilst looking on the falling waters of the Niagara." [2]

Of the eighteenth-century Spanish trails to Raton Pass from the Arkansas, Abert had picked the Timpas Creek route — precisely that followed by the Santa Fe Railroad today southwest from La Junta, Colorado. This route was becoming standard with the increased use of wagons. The sixty-mile-long Timpas arose in the rolling piñon-juniper terrain thirty miles southeastward from Raton Pass, at a spring of fine water called the Hole in the Rock. The trail along it was first rate for wheels because it avoided the deep river canyons and winding dry arroyos which created a very broken field for travel on lower sections of the Purgatoire, Apishapa and Huerfano River branches of the Arkansas.

Beyond the Hole in the Rock, General Kearny's hundred wagons and twenty-two cannon were trundled over an easy divide from the Timpas to the Upper Purgatoire on August 4, and they were hauled up the Raton Creek grade above present Trinidad during the next two days. Some wagons were wrecked in the gullies of the south Coal Creek side of Raton Pass, and a lot of the lowland soldiers from Missouri thought that they were dying in the thin air at the top of the pass some 7800 feet above sea level. But the grassy, treeless passage was not difficult on the whole.[3]

From Raton, Kearny led his men southward close along the east side of the Cimarron Mountains and on to Las Vegas. An uneventful march followed through the small defile called Las Vegas Pass just beyond the mud town. Though Governor Armijo's Mexican militia was expected to defend La Glorieta Pass, no troops appeared there — not even at the Apache Canyon bottleneck on the Santa Fe side. Some members of the Army of the West had time to examine the brown ruins of

Pecos, which Alvarado had visited in 1540 when it was "a very strong village four stories high."

On the rainy evening of August 16, 1846, a detachment of Kearny's Americans tramped into the capital without opposition and prepared to raise the Stars and Stripes over the old adobe Palace of Governors. Through the night and all next day the rest of the army filtered in from La Glorieta Pass.

AND SO ALL THE ROCKIES of present New Mexico and Colorado — east and west slopes — became United States property. The Rockies of Wyoming and Montana — east and west slopes — had been exclusively American since June 15, 1846, when Great Britain accepted the 49th parallel as the southern boundary of British North America. The Mexican War ended two years later and the expansionist program of Senator Benton and his group stood triumphant. The triumph was enhanced vastly by an incredible stroke of luck — the discovery in California of the richest gold field of all time during that same year of 1848.

This Sacramento find was placer gold, lying free in stream beds, and waiting for any man willing to hurry out there and pick up a fortune. What with California's gold, Oregon's agriculture and Mormon developments in Utah, millions of Americans suddenly discovered the West. These hordes besieged Congress with demands for wagon roads, railroads, forts, telegraph lines and everything else to ease their path to a variety of promised lands.

The United States Army Corps of Topographical Engineers was ready for action in the Rockies. The action was begun by Captain Howard Stansbury, a civil engineer from New York City who had been pottering around the Great Lakes on dull survey jobs for years. Though a gentle person, Stansbury held rude, heretical views. He believed, for example, that the American Indian was getting a raw deal, and that the much-married Mormons were more moral than people who married once and cheated often. Stansbury's orders were to locate a supply route for the Mormons from South Pass to Salt Lake City, to map the Salt Lake area, and to come home through Santa Fe on the old Spanish Trail over Horse Lake Pass. The Captain was forty-three years old, and he leaped to his adventure with the joy of one reprieved from senility. On May 31, 1849, he left Fort Leavenworth and the Missouri with eighteen mountain men, five wagons and forty-six horses and mules, as well as six California emigrants.[4]

By mid-August, Stansbury had crossed South Pass and had reached Fort Bridger, a jumble of log buildings bound by a picket fence. He sent most of his men northwest on the Oregon Trail by way of Bear River, Soda (Beer) Spring and Portneuf River to examine Fort Hall on Snake River for military use.[5] He himself, with Jim Bridger as guide and two others, pointed west toward the north end of Salt Lake. They crossed Bear River amid the sage of present Evanston, Wyoming, and Medicine Butte, found Ogden Creek headwaters, and struggled down "a wild almost impassable canyon" of sheer pink cliffs (Ogden Canyon), partly by way of an Indian trail high on the south wall. That brought them to the beautiful crescent-shaped valley of Ogden's Hole in view of Salt Lake. The date was August 28, 1849.

During the next year, Stansbury completed the first real survey of the lake region. Meanwhile he became convinced that the Oregon Trail was a poor way to go west to Salt Lake because it ran so far north to get around the Laramie and Medicine Bow ranges. The southern Spanish Trail was still more roundabout, and seldom used by pack trains any more. He decided, therefore, to ignore his orders to return on the Spanish Trail. Instead, he would explore a new short route from Salt Lake to the Missouri which Jim Bridger had suggested to him. It would run somewhere between the Oregon Trail and the Spanish Trail.

The Stansbury party left the Mormon capital on August 28,

1850, ascended Parley's Creek east of town and crossed Golden Pass — named, mean people said, because of the high fee charged by Parley P. Pratt, the Mormon leader, to use his new Parley's Creek toll road. For several days, Stansbury gathered data on passages through the Wasatch Range, including Duchesne (Strawberry) Pass. He recommended Timpanogos Canyon (Provo Canyon today) as the best supply route from Salt Lake and Utah Lake through the range. He continued north and east — just as the Union Pacific runs down the Weber, up Echo Creek Canyon and over Wasatch Divide into Wyoming. On September 7, his little expedition arrived at Fort Bridger, where he learned that President Taylor had died on July 9 from typhoid, too much rich food and the Washington heat.

Three days later, Jim Bridger led Stansbury's men toward South Pass on the Oregon Trail, and left it to move east across Green River and past the striking Pilot Butte near present Rock Springs. Here they began to ascend a ribbon of bad-tasting, six-inch-deep water called Bitter Creek. They noticed the southbearing track to Vermilion Creek and Brown's Hole, and they crossed a barren divide where the alkali water was worse still. The only scenery was a glum butte one hundred and fifty feet high which they named The Haystack.

On September 18, they struck Muddy Creek in the same coyote-jackrabbit terrain of low sage which Hoback, Robinson and Reznor had visited in 1812. For a week, Stansbury's men had suffered depression, missing the civilized bustle of the Oregon Trail. Bridger's trail was too dim for anybody but himself to see. Jim made no one happier by telling how a force of Sioux Indians had murdered Henry Fraeb and his trapping crew in this bleak area nine years before. He pointed out the stern rock summit of Hahn's Peak to the far southeast and promised that better days would come when they crossed the Continental Divide to the North Platte by a pet pass of his. The men tried to believe Bridger, but suspected that they were lost as they pushed up Muddy Creek on September 20 past a sulphur spring and found themselves climbing lower slopes of the Sierra Madre (Park) Range.

Stansbury's official report described this crossing of Bridger Pass:

> We turned to the left up a beautiful pass about a mile and a half in length with a uniform gentle ascent to its summit. From the top of the pass we continued for four miles over a gently undulating country, sloping to the right into the drainage of the Muddy. Here were reached *the Dividing height between the waters of the Pacific and those of the Atlantic.* Our universal shout arose at the announcement of this fact, and visions of home and all its joys floated before the imagination in vivid brightness. That to which we had so long been looking forward, as a thing that might one day be, now seemed almost within our grasp; for we knew that the water which we had at length reached, flowed, in one unbroken stream, almost to the very feet of those who were dearest to our hearts . . . None but those who have experienced it know how much companionship there is in the gentle murmur of a flowing stream. Such were now our sensations as with light hearts and buoyant spirits we galloped down the grassy slope . . . a perfectly feasible, a most excellent route for wagon or railroad — easy grades, few bridges, no high, narrow, snow-filled canyons.

The party made good progress in the next week, moving down the "flowing stream" (Little Sage Creek) and across the North Platte in a grove of cottonwoods turning bright yellow, and following the road over the Medicine Bows by Rattlesnake Pass into the lush Laramie Valley. They had sport running down buffalo, though Stansbury disapproved of killing them for killing's sake. He was almost pleased when his aide, Lieutenant John W. Gunnison, shot his own buffalo-chasing horse in the head instead of the buffalo at which he was trying to aim. The horse tumbled down dead, and Gunnison was shaken in the fall, but not badly hurt.

The problem now was how to keep going straight east over the Laramie Hills rather than to detour one hundred and fifty miles southeast to Cache la Poudre headwaters and Longs Peak, on the path which Frémont had taken westbound in 1843. Jim Bridger solved the matter when he met an old Sioux friend who had earned the proud title of Chief Buffalo Dung. Using Buffalo Dung's directions, Bridger led the way on September 27 into the Laramie Hills up present Telephone Canyon (U.S. Route 30), or near it, and crossed the grassy ridge to Crow Creek by an old Indian traverse which Buffalo Dung called Cheyenne Pass. From Crow Creek, it was only a step north to the south fork of Lodgepole Creek. This last convenient waterway ran due east to join the South Platte eventually in the northeast corner of present Colorado.

Captain Stansbury arrived back at Fort Leavenworth on November 6, 1850, to announce that his Bridger Pass–Cheyenne Pass–Lodgepole Creek route from Salt Lake was at least a hundred miles shorter than the Oregon Trail–South Pass route. The finding of it foreshadowed the creation of the Overland Trail and Union Pacific Railroad, and climaxed his pioneer mapping of Salt Lake.[6] He could congratulate himself besides that he had endured seventeen months of Rocky Mountain travel very well for an oldster, in spite of a small contretemps on Chugwater Creek east of Cheyenne Pass when in a careless moment, he fell from his horse to sustain a slightly creased testicle.

STANSBURY'S SUCCESS stimulated clamor for a transcontinental railroad, the best route of which was the subject of passionate, angry, endless debate, sectional and local, North and South, and all between. In March of 1853, Congress, baffled by the route issue, passed a bill for four Pacific railroad surveys by the Topographical Engineers, two of which called for expeditions through the Rockies. Stansbury's buffalo-hunting aide, Lieutenant (later Captain) John W. Gunnison, led one of these from the Missouri at Westport (Kansas City) on June 23, 1853, headed along the Santa Fe Trail. The aim was to find a route for rails to Salt Lake by Sangre de Cristo Pass and Cochetopa Pass, the empire-building promise of which had been noted seventy-five years before by Governor de Anza.

Gunnison was a handsome New Hampshire native turned forty, a West Pointer and veteran of the Florida Seminole wars. His expedition had an escort of thirty-two Mounted Riflemen, sixteen six-mule wagons, an instrument carriage hauled by four mules, and a four-mule ambulance. This last was a surrey without a fringe on top in which officers carried their liquor, castor oil and other medicinal necessities for survival. The wagons were under Captain Charles Taplin, a survivor of the 1848–1849 Frémont disaster (Note 13, Chapter 9). The soldiers were commanded by an upstate New Yorker, Lieutenant Edward G. Beckwith. The scientific staff included Frémont's artist, Richard Kern; the astronomer, Sheppard Homans; and a stuffy German tourist, Dr. James Schiel, who hired on as surgeon and geologist, and signed his name with "M.D." after it. Schiel's only degree was Doctor of Philosophy, but any one with a college education qualified as surgeon for government expeditions in 1853.

The men passed Bent's Fort on the Arkansas in early August. They pushed forty miles up Apishapa River, but realized that this was the wrong stream and crossed to the Cucharas and Huerfano below the Spanish Peaks. Lieutenant Beckwith took a side trip to Greenhorn Creek where De Anza had shot down Chief Cuerno Verde in 1779. The creek was lined with farms now, and a Mexican farmer invited him to spend the night. He accepted and was rather hurt when the farmer's Pawnee wife set up his cot out in the yard. He felt better that evening as the farmer, the wife, and flocks of children, goats and turkeys poured from the house and bedded down beside him.

The old Spanish path up South Oak Creek past the ruins of Governor Melgares's fort of 1819 was too rough for wagons, so Captain Gunnison moved west a bit and had a six-mile trail cut to the top of Sangre de Cristo Pass. It had such a sidle in places that the Mounted Riflemen roped the wagons and hung on for dear life on the upside to keep them from toppling. Beckwith amused himself meanwhile by trying, and failing, to shoot down those floppy Rockies aerialists, the magpies. Astronomer Homans put the pass summit at 9219 feet — 240 feet under today's figure. He noticed the faint Pass Creek Pass trail forking due north from the top of Sangre de Cristo Pass toward Wet Mountain Valley.

The Captain pronounced the scenery to be "very fine, the views extending far back over the plains, buttes, ridges and streams. The bold peaks tower loftily above us, whitened here and there by lines of snow." During the easy descent to the army's new Fort Massachusetts in San Luis Valley, Gunnison explored southeasterly up Wagon Creek from Sangre de Cristo Creek to the crest of the Sangre de Cristos at present Veta Pass. From a peak up there he saw below him how Cucharas River rose to Cucharas Pass and Purgatoire headwaters, and also how the Indian Creek Pass trail crossed the crest five miles south of him.

On August 15, Beckwith went to Taos to pick up the mountain man, Antoine Leroux, who guided the expedition then from Fort Massachusetts around Blanca Peak to examine the sand dunes and "Roubideau's or Musca" Pass (Mosca). The three-mile road to the top was found to be washed out, "the sides . . . about five hundred feet high, rocky and precipitous . . . entirely impracticable for a railroad, and but little better for a wagon road." Gunnison and Beckwith rode up Pike's Gap (Medano-Williams), too, "through a grove of pitch-pine, beyond most gigantic sand-hills rising above the plain to half the height (apparently at least 700 or 800 feet) of the adjacent mountain, and shaped by the winds into beautiful and fanciful forms . . . High up on the sides are seen . . . single bushes of artemesia — the only vegetation seen upon them, and the only change discoverable since they were visited by Captain Pike, fifty years ago." A broad Indian road crossed this Pike's Gap, but Gunnison judged it "not as good as Roubideau's Pass."

From the dunes, Antoine led the men, wagons and mules north and west across San Luis Valley's present Baca Grant Ranch beneath the beautiful 14,000-footers — Crestone, Crestone Needle and Kit Carson Peak. On August 29, 1853, they camped on Saguache Creek below Saguache Butte at today's Saguache town. Captain Gunnison, Sheppard Homans and six others went off north exploring and found "the prettiest, best watered and grassed valley, with wood convenient for fuel, that I have seen in this section." The Captain called the place Homans Park (around today's Villa Grove on U.S. Route 285). The men continued north over "Puncha" (Poncha) Pass and on down to the Arkansas, where Gunnison saw "heavy Indian trails to South Park, Hardscrabble, Wet Mountain Valley, etc." Returning up Poncha Pass, he observed the trend of Poncha Creek west from his trail to a dip which would be known later as Marshall Pass. In his report, Lieutenant Beckwith renamed Poncha Pass "Gunnison Pass," adding, "As a testimonial of respect to the memory of the officer who explored it, I have given his name to this pass."

After the Poncha detour, Gunnison put his wagons to rolling up Saguache Creek from Saguache Butte toward the wide Cochetopa Pass lowering of mountains. The trail was west, and he wrote of the dip ahead that evening in his journal: "No mountain pass ever opened more favorably for a railroad than this . . ." and, furthermore, "the grouse at camp are abundant and fine, as are also the trout in the creek, several having been caught . . . weighing each two pounds." After twenty-two miles, the main Indian trail turned south along Saguache Creek through stands of spruce and aspen blocking the wagons from going that way. A second road ran north (today's North Cochetopa Pass highway).

Antoine Leroux explained to Gunnison that "Carnero Pass" over the Continental Divide was a hard day's march south up

Saguache Creek, with a steep east ascent. The tree-blocked main trail went south only two miles to take advantage of gentle grades, and turned west again up a Saguache Creek branch (it was present Luders Creek) to Cochetopa Pass proper. The wagons, Antoine concluded, would roll on west up steeper but more open terrain to rejoin the main Cochetopa trail some miles short of the top of the pass.

The expedition went over Cochetopa smoothly at noon on September 2. Astronomer Homans figured the altitude at 10,-032 feet above sea level.[7] Beckwith commented: "The width of this pass at the summit does not exceed six hundred yards. The ascent from the valley of San Luis . . . was very gradual . . . for a wagon road this pass is already practicable." Four hours of rock clearing on the western slope was enough to make a way for the wagons to slide down to Cochetopa Creek and on to the lovely, spacious, high valley of the Gunnison River.

They began to learn the truth about Cochetopa soon. The promising pass was a siren's invitation to threats of disaster beyond it. There was no getting through Black Canyon of Gunnison River, though the Captain pushed down ten of its fifty miles of gorge where walls rose sheer for three thousand feet, to form a river bed so narrow as to cause a perpetual twilight. The bypass southward around it over Son-of-a-Bitch Hill and Cerro Summit to Uncompahgre River was as brutal as Antoine Robidoux had found it to be in the 1820's on trips to his Fort Robidoux near present Delta, Colorado. Gunnison did get the wagons and fringe-topped ambulance over the two mesas, but the soldiers had to carry them part of the way. They toiled a fortnight to cover those forty miles, with fall coming fast.

September had ended when they reached Green River in Utah by way of the Colorado from present Grand Junction, Colorado. And it was mid-October as they crossed the Wasatch Range by what Beckwith called Wasatch Pass, near today's

Summit (7980) on State Route 10 to Salina, Utah, and Sevier River. Gunnison chose this route west from the Green up San Rafael River and southward through Castle Valley because it needed exploration, being a hundred miles south of the Utah Lake–Salt Lake region which Captain Stansbury had mapped.

Gunnison was a fine soldier, an earnest, admirable man, and it is not pleasant to bring him prematurely to the end of his life. On October 26, he and some of his party were exploring up Sevier River near Sevier Desert. An emigrant caravan had passed there lately and had shot down in a gamey mood the father of a Paiute chief. The chief and his band saw no sport in this and resolved to do in the next white men they met — which happened to be Gunnison and his party encamped. The Paiutes attacked the camp at dawn, putting fifteen arrows into the Captain before he stayed down. They also killed his botanist F. Creutzfeldt, his artist Richard Kern, and five others.

Lieutenant Beckwith inherited command of the expedition, wintered it in Salt Lake City and took it to California after reexamining some of Stansbury's routes from Salt Lake to Fort Bridger. Through no fault of Gunnison's, his death climaxed a trip which accomplished little, except to lend a mellifluous name to Gunnison River, Mount Gunnison, Gunnison County, Gunnison town and Gunnison Tunnel — all parts of a delightful and characteristic section of the highest Rockies. The passes explored by him were well known by 1853.[8] Though Cochetopa Pass was, and still is, a natural gap for a railroad, none ever got over it and perhaps never will.

But, you recall, Congress called for a second Rockies expedition in 1853 — the Northern Pacific Railroad Survey. Because of the dynamism of its leader, this second one would turn out to be the most important Rockies trek since Lewis and Clark's in 1805–1806.

11

The Last Wilderness

Isaac Ingalls Stevens was born in 1818 on a flinty farm near Andover, Massachusetts, a child so puny and undersized that his mother kept him in his cradle until he was three. In protest against such coddling, his father dipped him daily in a pail of ice water. He attended Andover Academy, graduated from West Point, married a Newport belle, and worked for years as an army engineer fortifying the Penobscot River in Maine. He emerged a major from the Mexican War, a rank which seemed to him to underrate his talents. He was still undersized, but the ice water baths and army life had made him into a tough, driving, military person who knew what he wanted and how to get it.

Major Stevens wanted to be governor of the new Washington Territory, which stretched from the crest of the Montana Rockies to the Pacific, and he got the job because he was a Franklin Pierce Democrat.[1] President Pierce put his small supporter in charge also of the Northern Pacific Railroad Survey, since Stevens told him bluntly that he was "the fittest man for the place." In a crushing assault on Secretary of State Marcy, Secretary of the Interior McClelland and Secretary of War Jefferson Davis, Stevens blasted all opposition and won a free hand to run the new territory and the survey as he pleased. The Secretaries had in mind something about the size of Gunnison's expedition. They did not realize that the force which the Governor assembled in the spring of 1853 totaled two hundred and forty men.

Stevens needed this large force of soldiers, scientists and engineers to put over his large ideas. If Washington Territory was to grow big enough beyond its four thousand population to be worth his time, it would have to have a railroad to it. He would prove that the northern route through Chicago and St. Paul was better than Gunnison's Cochetopa Pass route, favored by Benton, and better than the New Mexican routes, favored by Jefferson Davis.

But Montana remained a wilderness, except the enclave around St. Mary's Mission which Father De Smet had built in 1841 near Traveller's Rest in Bitterroot Valley. To explore Montana passes involved making terms with seven thousand Blackfoot Indians of various kinds who still kept the mountains north of Bozeman Pass off limits for white men, and whose raids west of the Continental Divide made life miserable for the cooperative tribes — Flatheads, Nez Perces, Kootenais, and so on. The Governor put one unit of his force under his Mexican War friend, Captain George B. McClellan, and sent it by sea to Puget Sound to explore the Cascade Range. Stevens's main party from St. Paul and a keelboat group from St. Louis met on the Upper Missouri and reached Fort Benton on the high plain in sight of the Montana Rockies on September 1, 1853.[2]

Within a week, the Governor began peace talks with the Blackfeet and had his soldiers scattering in all directions, like happy chickens loosed from a crate. Because of his elaborate preparations, he had exhausted the entire ninety thousand dollars allotted to the expedition, but he didn't let that worry him. He began issuing personal drafts which Congress would just have to honor later. To the consternation of the civilians — by tradition the pampered pets of government expeditions — Stevens treated everybody like a buck private, including Frederick W. Lander, his chief engineer and fellow Andoverite. Lander was a big, vain, contentious man who wasn't used to being ordered around, even by people his own size. But now he had to break his own mules and stand guard like the rest, and strike his own tent and walk part of each day's march. He had to bathe daily and take his turn catching trout and eat breakfast promptly at 4 A.M. — or else, Stevens told him amiably, he "would shoot him down like a dog."

During those mid-September days at Fort Benton, the Governor ordered Lander off north with a few men to examine Marias Pass. Lander didn't examine it, but he did obey Stevens's further orders to return south and cross Lewis and Clark Pass. From there, he was to move west down Blackfoot River and on through Hell Gate to a new trading post, Fort Owen, near Father De Smet's mission. However, Lander disliked the Blackfoot River trail and concocted a shortcut by angling south over the Garnet Hills to Clark Fork of the Columbia. Thereafter he pushed south up Flint Creek and then up Rock Creek, thinking that one of them must be the Bitterroot. Failing to find Fort Owen on Rock Creek, or any other sign of civilization, he took a dim westering trail used by Blackfoot horse thieves which brought him over the Sapphire Range. He arrived "in a jaded condition" at Fort Owen on September 26, 1853. To this day, reaching Fort Owen (Stevensville) by Lander's shortcut presents a mountaineering problem.

Stevens's first task was to find routes for wagons or rails around the Great Falls of the Missouri and the sixty miles of rough country further upstream toward Three Forks and Bozeman Pass. By good luck, he had a top notch explorer along. Lieutenant John Mullan was twenty-three years old and pure Irish — brogue, wild enthusiasm and all. He had chased Seminoles after graduating from West Point, but otherwise knew little of life beyond the salty limits of his native Norfolk, Virginia.

On September 9, young Mullan and five white companions left Benton to look at approaches to the mountains from above the Missouri canyons. They pushed southeast between the Little Belt and Judith Mountains to Musselshell River and a bit farther. They found a camp of Flatheads who had got religion from Father De Smet and prayed in French, but when Mullan tried his West Point French on them "they understood me not." The men rode west then to Musselshell source streams between the Little Belts and Crazy Mountains, crossed Smith River near White Sulphur Springs, and descended to the Missouri east of present Helena. On September 24, Mullan led his party up Sevenmile Creek and across the Continental Divide to the head of Little Blackfoot River.

It was an easy crossing over a low piney hill and is known still as Mullan Pass (6000). Its merits were plain to its discoverer. He wrote: "Here therefore exists in the mountains a broad open pass, through which it is possible that . . . a broad emigrant trail will lead from the Atlantic to the Pacific. Can it be otherwise?" Moving west, Mullan noted how Little Blackfoot River joined Clark Fork which was joined in turn by the main Blackfoot just short of "a perfect gate in the mountains, forming a well known and noted landmark. Hell Gate was named by Flatheads and others because Blackfeet Indians have committed so many robberies and murders here."

Next day, September 30, the Mullan men rode thirty miles up the Bitterroot to Fort Owen, which was beginning to resemble headquarters for a field army. Supply parties, forwarded eastward to Lake Pend Oreille and up Clark Fork from Puget Sound, had come and gone. The Governor himself had arrived from Benton a day ahead of his main train. He had crossed the Continental Divide by Blackfoot Pass at the suggestion of his hunter, a French-Canadian half-breed named Pierre Cadotte who had used it while trapping in 1851. From then on Blackfoot Pass was called Cadotte Pass (6044). It was just south of Lewis and Clark Pass (6323) on the same Dearborn River and Blackfoot River drainages.[3]

By Stevens's account, he had left Benton on September 22

with his artist J. M. Stanley, his surgeon Dr. George Suckley, and two others, riding southwesterly up Teton River, and crossing Sun and Dearborn rivers past Crown Butte and Bird Tail Mountain. On the twenty-fourth, "we moved forward to the dividing ridge, which was reached at four o'clock. As we ascended the divide, a severe pelting hail and rain storm, accompanied with high wind, thunder, and lightning, came upon us and did not abate until we had reached the summit . . . It was with great gratification that we now left the plains of the Missouri to enter upon the country watered by the Columbia; and it was the more especially gratifying to me as, looking to my future duties . . . I felt that I could welcome to my future home and the scene of my labors the gentlemen of the party . . . I was a good deal surprised to find how small an obstacle this divide was to the movement of a wagon-train."

At the wooded top of Cadotte Pass, before going down the Blackfoot River trail to Hell Gate and Fort Owen, Stevens conducted a ceremony which pointed up the picturesque power of the western pioneer. To all interested cottontails and larger game within earshot, he issued a proclamation announcing the existence of Washington Territory and creating its civil government, which was himself. There was a week of whirlwind activity at Fort Owen. The Governor sent Mullan twenty miles up the Bitterroot to build winter quarters, Cantonment Stevens, for Mullan and his men. The Governor lambasted Frederick Lander for wandering in directions different from his instructions. He put his surgeon, Dr. Suckley, and a companion aboard a bullboat of amateur design and sent them bobbing down Clark Fork to see if the thing would float to The Dalles on the Columbia (for a wonder, it did). His main train headed west on October 3, with orders to use the Clark Fork route. The Governor, artist Stanley and six others followed next day. To build character with the many Indians along the trail, they ate a lot of their cooked camass root "of a dark color, small, between the pear and onion in shape, and of a sweet, agreeable flavor."

The small Stevens party left Clark Fork at its big bend near present St. Regis, Montana, and rode up St. Regis River, which Father De Smet had named in honor of the sixteenth-century Jesuit leader, St. Francis (Regis) Borgia.[4] Stevens's aim was to cross Bitterroot Range by what he called Coeur d'Alêne Pass or Stevens Pass, from St. Regis headwaters to Coeur d'A-lêne River and Coeur d'Alêne Mission, which had been built in 1848 by De Smet's colleague, Father Ravalli. Coeur d'Alêne Lake was farther down, its Spokane River outlet joining the Columbia below the Hudson's Bay Company post, Fort Col-ville. The Governor understood that this trail was one hundred and seventy-five miles shorter than the Clark Fork trail around the north end of the Bitterroots to Pend Oreille Lake and then to the Columbia along Spokane River drainage.

St. Regis Valley above Clark Fork was lushly wooded and, after a dozen miles of it, the travelers forked left, away from the stream, because, the guide said, the main trail was blocked by fallen larch and spruce trees. It was late afternoon of October 10, 1853. Stevens wrote: "We ascended the dividing ridge, and reached a camp with good grass upon a small lake within a mile of its top. The lake, to which we were obliged to descend for water, is twelve hundred feet below the camp." Rain drenched their tents in the night, but next morning "the sky was clear and the air as soft and balmy as a morn in summer. After striking camp we ascended to the highest point of the ridge. Here we made a long halt, enjoying the magnificent view spread open to us, which I venture to say, can scarcely be surpassed."

The view is still magnificent on Stevens Pass and the little lakes are lovely on both sides of the ridge under Stevens Peak (6826) — which is near Wonderful Peak on Kootenai National Forest maps. Stevens Pass is not even a name any more, but Lookout Pass (4738) and St. Regis Pass (5000) were so near the Governor's camp that he could claim to be their official dis-coverer. U.S. Route 10 (Interstate 90) and the Northern Pacific

Railroad go over Lookout today. St. Paul Pass (5163) lies some miles south of Stevens Peak. The Chicago, Milwaukee and St. Paul Railroad goes under it through an 8771-foot tunnel.

THE GOVERNOR'S ROLE as Rockies pass explorer began at Cadotte in September, 1853, and ended three weeks later when he crossed Stevens Pass and continued toward the Columbia. But the parties he left behind at Forts Benton and Owen, and Cantonment Stevens carried on his road-hunting plans with might and main. The fledgling mountaineers flung themselves about Montana — in blizzard, storm or sunny weather, sub-zero cold or torrid heat — throughout the next year in a rash of reconnaissance such as the Rockies had never known, and has not known since.

From Cantonment Stevens in October, Mullan took several men over the Continental Divide to Big Hole River, the Horse Prairie Creek of Lewis and Clark, and Red Rock River. At Ross's Hole short of Gibbons Pass, Mullan met an old Flathead who recalled seeing Lewis and Clark there in 1805. He pushed south across the Continental Divide aagin by Medicine Lodge Pass (7650) — Father De Smet's "Father's Defile" which he had used in 1841 on his trip to Bitterroot Valley.

The Mullan group rested at Cantonment Loring near Fort Hall on Snake River and returned north over low Monida Pass (6823), a featureless Rockies crossing. From Jefferson River drainage they trailed to Clark Fork near present Butte by Deer Lodge Pass (5902) — "no obstacle whatever" — and on to Cantonment Stevens through Hell Gate. Mullan hurried to Fort Benton during March, 1854, and brought back a wagon over Mullan Pass. It was his own discovery, of course, and he saw no point in being modest about it. "The mountain itself," he explained, "is nothing more than a low prairie ridge. The ascent and descent are so exceedingly gradual that not only was it not necessary to lock the wheels of the wagon on descending but it was drawn with the animals trotting. One could scarcely have believed that there existed such a beautiful and easy pass in the mountains."

Leaving the wagon at Fort Owen, Mullan took a long swing north past Flathead Lake and the American part of South Kootenay Pass to David Thompson's Kootenai River and the Tobacco Plains. Indians welcomed the travelers everywhere as though they were prodigal sons. Mullan wrote that after one hard day's trek in April, a covey of Clark Fork squaws "turned out 'en masse,' pitched our lodge, packed our wood, built our fire and would probably have extended the limit of their kindness much farther had we not requested them to desist." [5]

Governor Stevens's interest in travel conditions inspired one of his youngsters, Lieutenant Cuvier Grover, to cross Cadotte from Fort Benton in the deepest dead of winter with four dogsleds. Grover did reach Fort Owen in three weeks, but not without trouble. The eleven dogs, bought from Fort Benton Indians, were as green as their drivers. The sleds were homemade ten-foot ash boards ten inches wide — very unwieldy when overloaded with bedding and food for five men and one hundred and sixty pounds of pemmican for the dogs.

Nevertheless, the five men left Benton full of hope on January 2, 1854, but ran out of snow in a few miles and Grover had to call up mules to drag the sleds to where the snow resumed. The dogs had some wolf friends who trailed along companionably. At night, the wolves would eat the dogsled harness unless it was hung beyond reach. It was cold crossing Cadotte Pass on January 11, and colder next day — thirty-eight below. That evening, Grover complained, "sometimes I had my mouth frozen open, and sometimes shut, according to the position it happened to be kept in for half an hour. It takes a long time to pick solid ice off your face after camping. As it is, the dogs crowd around the fire with the most uncompromising pertinacity till we get to bed and asleep, when they pile in on us, and, if one is kicked off he makes war upon some smaller dog who, being displaced, turns out his next inferior, and so on, keeping the camp in a continual row till they all get settled again."

One major Montana effort, Stevens's hoped-for inspection of Marias Pass, turned out to be a fateful frustration. Everybody had known, from 1810 on, where Marias Pass was on the Continental Divide — some fifty miles south of the border of British North America. It connected headwaters of Two Medicine Creek of Marias River and Middle Fork headwaters of Flathead River. And yet, when Stevens tried to find guides at Fort Benton who had crossed it, he got nowhere. Though it was supposed to be low, easy and direct, the half-breed trappers didn't even want to talk about it. The Blackfeet, they said, had made it bad medicine ever since the smallpox plagues of the 1830's when so many Blackfeet had died.

As we have seen, Lander hiked north along the base of the range and failed to find it. Stevens himself went out in its direction, and was recalled to Benton by a minor emergency. Finally, after deciding to forget about Marias Pass for the 1853 season, the Governor asked his old friend, Abiel W. Tinkham, to examine it from west to east. Tinkham had worked with Stevens for years on the Penobscot River fortifications. He was a mild, unambitious and inconspicuous civil engineer, but he had a mind of his own and he was not afraid of bad medicine.

He accompanied Stevens's main train west in September over Cadotte Pass and left it to look for a trail up Clearwater River to Jocko River, which bypassed Hell Gate and the Clark Fork windings beyond.[6] He missed the trail but reached the Jocko and led his party on north around the west side of Flathead Lake. He noted the charming coves of what has since become Montana's big blue heaven for summer people and wrote prophetically, if prosaically, "Residences on the lake will be most agreeably situated."

But Marias Pass was his objective. Soon his party reached the Flathead River forks beneath the towers of present Glacier National Park and turned east up Middle Fork, rather than north up the main Flathead toward British North America. It was the right trail at last — easy and direct — for twenty miles. Then it trended northeast, became steep between walls and climbed four thousand feet in twenty-eight miles. Finally Tinkham arrived at where "a bare rocky circular ridge closed the valley, over which the trail crooks and winds, and is often just wide enough for the feet of the horse. It is wholly impracticable as a wagon pass."

He and his men scrambled over this Continental Divide on October 20, 1853, as snow fell on Tinkham Mountain and the other great peaks which loomed above them. Though south of the border, these peaks were the beginning of the Canadian Rockies — smaller and lower than the American, but as stirring as any mountains on earth. From the top, Tinkham pitched down to the prairie, and checked in at Fort Benton a week later with James Doty, a technician whom Stevens had left in charge. Tinkham reported that he had crossed Marias Pass and that it was 7600 feet above sea level — more than two thousand feet higher than it was thought to be and of no use for railroad, wagon or even a two-wheeled cart. Next day, Tinkham left Fort Benton and hurried west again, over Mullan Pass this time.[7] He reached Cantonment Stevens seventeen days later.

James Doty was a skeptic. Through the winter of 1853-1854, he mulled over Tinkham's account of crossing Marias Pass. Tinkham's "bare rocky circular ridge" closing the valley did not sound like the Marias he had heard about. The stream which Tinkham had descended to the prairie ran southeast. That didn't sound like Marias either. Its stream was supposed to run northeast. Doty was still puzzled in mid-May when he rode north with three men to have a look at British North America as far as Chief Mountain, Waterton Lake, and the east end of South Kootenay Pass.

While fording Two Medicine Creek of Marias River, he met an Indian who pointed out where Marias Pass was. The Indian showed him also the location of a pass twenty miles farther north along the divide, and claimed to know that Tinkham had crossed that one. Doty pushed on toward Chief Mountain but returned to Two Medicine Creek three weeks later, and moved up it to forks near present Glacier Park village. From a nearby hill, he could see the straight southwest course of Marias Pass, which rose in a dozen miles or so to a low part of the Continental Divide.

He had to conclude that Tinkham had made a mistake, as indeed he had. Instead of Marias Pass (5215), he had gone over the popular Blackfoot traverse, Cut Bank Pass (7861), which is now called Pitamakan Pass. He had left Middle Fork of Flathead River too soon, perhaps ascending to the ridge under Tinkham Mountain by Nyack Creek, instead of by Bear Creek. To this day, Pitamakan Pass is sometimes called False Marias Pass.

But Tinkham was Doty's superior in the Northern Pacific survey. Doty was a tactful as well as a skeptical man. He did not express his belief that Tinkham had not crossed Marias. He merely questioned Tinkham's view as to its usefulness. "This pass," he wrote, "is not vouched for as a good railroad or pack-train route; yet it is believed worthy of further examination."

That "further examination" would be a long time coming.

THE TRAGIC TENSIONS which were bringing on the Civil War prevented the laying of any rails at all in the west after the Pacific Surveys of 1853. Nevertheless, Governor Stevens's work began the transformation of Montana's wilderness into today's bewitching public park. All told, Stevens's young men explored nine Continental Divide passes, and five across the Bitterroots. Among the five were the previously unreported Nez Perce Pass, at the south end of Bitterroot Valley, and the ancient, tedious Lolo Pass of Lewis and Clark.[8]

That last wilderness, of course, did not stop at the boundary of British North America. It ran on north beyond Jasper National Park to where the Continental Divide curves west away from what remains of the Rockies. An important effect of Stevens's exploration was to prod England into doing something about her own five hundred miles of the two-thousand-mile Rockies. It was a bother. Many Englishmen had never heard of these remote uplands. Alexander Mackenzie, David Thompson, Simon Fraser, Howse Pass — the Rockies fur trade — all had faded into legend. Only a few pioneers like Sir George Simpson of Hudson's Bay Company remembered the hundreds of pack trains which had used Athabaska Pass. Simpson's proud old North Saskatchewan posts — Rocky Mountain House, Fort Edmonton — were mere collectors of buffalo meat now to feed employees in the north.

Knowledge of the Canadian Rockies was mostly hearsay. Simpson had circled the globe in 1841 and seemed to have crossed the Rockies at a Simpson Pass. An emigrant party had crossed from Bow River to the Kootenay in that year, and their gap was called White Man Pass. The party crossed a Sinclair Pass also — from the Kootenay to the Columbia. Four seasons later, the rambling Father De Smet proselytized up the Kootenay and east over Sinclair Pass and White Man Pass all the way to Rocky Mountain House, returning by Athabaska Pass. He had put a wood cross on White Man Pass, and the stream below became Cross River.

Or so people said. Just one thing was known for sure by most Britishers in the mid-1850's. The Canadian Rockies possessed the two highest peaks in North America — Mounts Hooker and Brown, rising 16,000 feet above the sea. But Sir George Simpson, the Highland Scot, knew something more. The diplomats of Downing Street had erred monstrously in 1846. They should have demanded the Columbia River as their boundary in the west, instead of accepting the 49th parallel. As things stood, it was impossible to reach the Canadian Pacific overland from eastern Canada without going part of the way on United States soil. If Canada was to develop as a unit, a transcontinental route would have to be found through those western mountains, and not only as far as the Columbia River.

Fired up by Stevens's work in Montana, Sir George discussed the route problem with his fellow Highlander, Sir Roderick Murchison, who was president of the Royal Geographical Society. Sir Roderick talked with Henry Labouchere, Her Majesty's Secretary of State for the Colonies. Labouchere was granted £5000 by Parliament and began interviewing explorers, including a forty-six-year-old travel writer, Captain John Palliser, whose book, *Adventures of a Hunter in the Prairies*, was the toast of England in 1856.

The Captain's military record was not impressive — service in the Artillery Militia of Waterford County, Ireland, and a year as sheriff of Waterford. But he had toured the American West. And he knew a half-breed trapper, James Sinclair, who had crossed the Canadian Rockies partly by a gap of his own discovery, Sinclair Pass. Labouchere hired also, as surgeon and naturalist, a big, brash, handsome young Scot sent to him by Sir Roderick Murchison. Dr. James Hector, aged twenty-two, was fresh out of Edinburgh University with an M.D. degree and a conviction that his last wish on earth was to practice medicine. He needn't have worried, for he never did.

Members of the Palliser expedition, England's first official attempt to see what she had in western Canada, spent the year 1857 on the plains, wintered at Fort Carlton and moved up the South Saskatchewan in June, 1858. The party was a bit smaller than Stevens's Montana army. It consisted of six Britishers, one American, and ten Scottish and French half-breeds with names like Louis Tekakowakii, and Jack Sakarontikitato. Each man had his own modus operandi by the time spring came. Captain Palliser and his aide, Lieutenant Blakiston, did what duty required them to do — faithfully and well. Young Dr.

Hector did as he pleased, and usually preempted the best of the Scottish half-breeds to help him do it.[9] While Palliser kept close watch against Blackfoot attack, Hector went gaily among them as a healer, working wonders with calomel and simple syrup. Hector was the dynamic core of the Palliser expedition.

The party split into groups as it neared the Rockies. Lieutenant Blakiston and a few companions ascended Oldman River and crossed North Kootenay Pass (6774) to the Flathead on the Kootenai Indian trail to the buffalo plains. They pushed on west over the MacDonald Range and North Kootenay's second summit (6850) by Wigwam and Elk rivers to Kootenay River. Then they moved downstream to the Kootenai–Tobacco River junction just in the United States, which Mullan had visited in 1854. From there they returned to Canada's eastern slope on the other main Kootenai Indian trail, first over the American summit of South Kootenay Pass (7100) and then the Canadian South Kootenay (6903), past Blakiston Mountain and down Blakiston Brook in Waterton Lakes National Park.[10]

Meanwhile, Palliser, his botanist Monsieur Bourgeau, and four others followed their idea of the British boundary to the Continental Divide near Chief Mountain, which James Doty had seen earlier. Then they rode north along the range to Bow River and Old Bow Fort, a relic of better Hudson's Bay Company times, at the mouth of the Kananaskis. For four days they toiled up the misty river which the half-breed James Sinclair had described to Palliser years before. There were roaring falls and whirlpools, white goats and "siffleurs" (whistling marmots), and two high lakes and a great glacier.

On August 22, 1858, they crossed the rocky pass itself (7200) with Mount Joffre (11,316) just south of them. Other snow-streaked towers of Kananaskis, Bourgeau and Goat ranges spread away in east-sloping, "writing desk" grandeur toward the glories of modern Banff. Palliser wrote: "This pass I have called Kananaskis, after the name of an Indian of whom there is a legend, giving an account of his most wonderful recovery from the blow of an axe." They reached the Kootenay by what would be called Palliser River. Though they were only twenty miles south of the White Man Pass — Sinclair Pass trail to the Upper Columbia, they could not find it. So they rode downstream, returned east over North Kootenay Pass and were back at Fort Edmonton in September, 1858. The Kananaskis trip concluded Captain Palliser's pass-finding career.

EVERY SEASONED TOURIST has been to Banff, has marveled at Three Sisters, at Bow Falls, at Canada's own Buckingham Palace — the Banff Springs Hotel, at Lake Louise with Victoria Glacier and Mount Lefroy's stern battlement above. James Hector, Banff's first tourist, must have marveled too in mid-August, even though at twenty-three, nothing seems as marvelous as one's own self. He and four companions rode under a cliff which he named Mount Rundle. They were free as the wind and hunting, in a casual way, for a low railroad pass to the Columbia. What interested them more were the romantic wilds, and finding panthers to shoot, and watching birds — curlews, terns, avocets. They had an old Stoney Indian guide with an unpronounceable name, so Hector called him Nimrod. This Nimrod led them west over the Continental Divide by Vermilion Pass (5416). The crags of Castle Mountain — Mount Eisenhower today — loomed behind them, and another pyramid rose in the south. Hector christened it Mount Ball, honoring the Under-Secretary of State for the Colonies.[11]

From the top, they rode south down the Vermilion River to the trail from Simpson Pass (6954) and on. When they reached the Kootenay, they reversed their direction and rode northward up it to avoid the Kananaskis Pass terrain which Palliser was exploring. The grade was slight and the trail good for the horses all the way to the Kootenay's source at Beaverfoot Pass (6000), and on down the wide valley of the Beaverfoot. However, Nimrod complained that the country was new to him, and to Indians generally, for that matter. Since nobody came this way, or had ever come this way, Hector was not likely to find a route to the Columbia here.

And then — August 29, 1858 — near catastrophe occurred. The Beaverfoot came to an end at an unknown river as large as the Bow. Hector wrote:

> This river descends the valley from the north-west, and, on entering the wide valley of Beaverfoot River, turns back on its course at a sharp angle, receives that river as a tributary, and flows off to the south-west. Just above the angle there is a fall about forty feet in height, where the channel is contracted by perpendicular rocks . . . A little way above this fall, one of our pack horses, to escape the fallen timber, plunged into the stream, luckily where it formed an eddy, but the banks were so steep that we had great difficulty in getting him out. In attempting to recatch my own horse, which had strayed off while we were engaged with the one in the water, he kicked me in the chest, but I had luckily got close to him before he struck out, so that I did not get the full force of the blow. However, it knocked me down and rendered me senseless for some time. This was unfortunate, as we had seen no tracks of game . . . and were now without food; but I was so hurt that we could not proceed further . . . My men covered me up under a tree and I sent them all off to try to raise something to eat . . . Because of the accident, the men named the stream Kicking Horse River.

Dr. Hector could ride again in a day or so, but the lower canyon of the Kicking Horse blocked the way to the Columbia twenty-five miles to the northwest. The food shortage became serious — nothing but blueberries to eat. Reluctantly, Hector gave up the Columbia search and ordered a retreat to the eastern plains. The Kicking Horse had an upper, as well as lower, canyon and there were stretches of heavy timber. It was a three-day race against starving as the men hacked their way upstream past Ottertail River and Otterhead Creek, Mount Stephen and the milky-green inflow of Yoho River.[12]

The date of crossing the Continental Divide at Kicking Horse

Pass (5339) to Bow River drainage was September 3, 1858. Nimrod shot a moose on the east side, at once solving the food crisis. The pain from being kicked left Hector's chest. Before feasting on the moose, the hungry whites rode a short way to a Stoney Indian camp where there was a comfortable mossy space for them. The Stoneys could be as hospitable as Mullan's Pend Oreilles far to the south. Hector wrote: "On our arrival . . . the squaws took the whole management of our affairs, unpacked the horses, put up the tent, lined it beautifully with pine foliage, lighted a fire, and cut wood into most conveniently sized billets, and piled them up ready to hand. They then set about cooking us all sorts of Indian delicacies — moose nose and entrails, boiled blood and roast kidneys, etc."

THE MOTOR TRIP over Kicking Horse today is a great pleasure — fifty miles of soaring crags, ambling wild life, lovely woods along the milky-green stream, and a glimpse of the Canadian Pacific Railway spiral tunnel. The discovery of Kicking Horse was Hector's gift to England, the equivalent of South Pass in a sense, the high achievement of the Palliser expedition. But no one realized it in September, 1858. After the moose feast, Nimrod guided Hector and his friends north past Lake Hector and the Wapta-Waputnik Ice Fields over Bow Pass and down Mistaya River between Mount Murchison and Mount Forbes. The Mistaya (Hector's Little Fork) put them on the North Saskatchewan, which brought them down to Rocky Mountain House and winter quarters at Fort Edmonton.

When the next June rolled around, Dr. Hector headed for Old Bow Fort again, planning to find more passes to the Upper Columbia. From there he would seek a passage to Fraser River to give Canada its own route to the Pacific without using the Lower Columbia in the United States at all. Fate was against him. Nimrod guided his party up the Bow and over Pipestone Pass to the Siffleur and North Saskatchewan, but got panicky over glacier thunder and resigned by just vanishing. Hector took on Nimrod's job. He pointed his group west and stumbled on Howse River, which led him to Howse Pass, Blaeberry River and the Columbia not far north of the Kicking Horse. However, it was mid-September by then, with the smell of snow in the air — too late to go Fraser-hunting. And the awesome Selkirk Range, seemingly impassable, rose directly ahead. Hector and his men had to hurry south toward Fort Colville in Washington by the Columbia-Kootenay trail which he had hoped to make obsolete. Canada would have to wait for its transcontinental route.[13]

THERE WAS CURIOUS TALK in the mountains all through the 1850's while the Gunnisons and Stansburys, the Stevenses and Mullans, the Pallisers and Hectors toiled to help their countrymen reach lands of their dreams beyond the Rockies. The talk had a key word with an exclamation point after it — Gold! Gunnison had heard of it — gold in the sands of the Huerfano, the Rio Grande, Saguache Creek, the Gunnison, the Provo. Some of Governor Stevens's soldiers had panned color in what they called the Gold Creek branch of Clark Fork west of Mullan Pass. Dr. Hector found a party of American argonauts on his Bow River trail in 1859. They were crossing Kananaskis Pass and planned to find diggings far up the Fraser in the Cariboo region of present British Columbia.

Gold! What would it do to the Rockies which had existed up to now merely to be crossed as quickly and as easily as possible!

12

Over the Wall

THE GOLD RUSH which began around Denver in 1859 was a time of revolution in Rocky Mountain affairs. Before it subsided three decades later, a million Americans learned the meaning of discovering, conquering and falling in love with a strange world. The national character still bears the marks of the same rash optimism, relish and trust which propelled people into the wild West a century ago.

The attitude of these pioneers toward their high environment was new. The Spaniards, the explorers, the trappers, the traders, the emigrants to Oregon and California were apathetic on the whole about mountains, regarding them as a nuisance at best. Their interest was in streams for beaver and for travel rather than in the land itself. And they were transient. For every settler like Jim Bridger and Kit Carson there were a hundred Lewises and Clarks, Colters, Mullanses and Pallisers who came briefly and returned home for good. While visiting, they submitted as meekly as the Indians to what the environment required of them in matters of food, dress, shelter. Mountain topography determined where they could — and could not — go, and at what season of the year. But, after 1859, people came to the high country to stay, and to live as they pleased, where they pleased and when they pleased. They ate pork and canned peaches instead of beaver tail and berries. They had white, rather than Indian, wives. They wore store clothes and store boots in place of buckskin and moccasins. They slept in houses instead of bedding down on spruce boughs under the stars.

And, by chance, they began this living as they pleased in the one part of the American Rockies where men were not supposed to be able to live at all. Gold was the lure, and most Rocky Mountain gold was to be found in those highest altitudes where the earth's granite core had been exposed by its own up-lift and the washing away of the soil on top. Those highest altitudes began north of Father Escalante's Horse Lake Pass at 12,000 feet and twisted in majesty along the Continental Divide through most of present Colorado for five hundred miles to lower country at Rabbit Ears Pass and the Sierra Madre Range of North Park.[1] As we have seen, Antoine Robidoux made good use of Cochetopa Pass in the 1820's for the transport of wares from San Luis Valley to his store on the Gunnison. Frémont trailed south in 1844 through North, Middle and South Parks over Muddy and Hoosier passes, and then crossed Tennessee Pass westward in 1845 from the Upper Arkansas to the Western Slope.

And so we had four gates of record only — Muddy, Hoosier, Tennessee, Cochetopa — in all that stretch of the Continental Divide, as of May 6, 1859. That was when John Gregory of Gordon County, Georgia, found his outcrop of gold just short of this highest wall at a point forty miles west of and far above Denver. Within days, the whole world was on the march — from Omaha up the Platte, from Fort Leavenworth up the Arkansas, from Salt Lake City and California — to crowd behind him in his Gregory Gulch and begin pushing up, up, up where men had had no reason or desire to push before. Up, anywhere and everywhere, was the road to wealth and happiness in the new way of Rocky Mountain life. And, at the top of every gulch, in the thin chill air above the grass, above the timber, above the bleak moraines and lonely tarns, was a mountain pass, and beyond the pass, was another gulch, more promising, of course, than those on the near side.

In the mass scramble, the total invasion of the rampart which blocked Denver from the west, it took a little time for the new passes to achieve the distinction of names. The Denver mob in 1859 swarmed on foot by the thousands up Clear Creek, and up all its branches — especially North Clear Creek (Central City) and plain Clear Creek, where Idaho Springs, Georgetown and Empire would stand, until no more claims remained. George Jackson found placer gold in Chicago Creek above the future Idaho Springs, and those who tramped after him too late for claims kept right on south beneath Mount Evans (14,260), up and over in the area of present Guanella Pass (11,500) just off the Divide. They prospected down the south side of Guanella Pass on Duck, Gomer and Geneva creeks, which put them on the North Fork of the South Platte, and so on over Kenosha Pass and into South Park. They found placer gold in the sands of what they called Tarryall Creek in July, 1859, and the South Park rush was added to the Clear Creek rush.

The camps of Tarryall and Hamilton bloomed close together along the willowed creek which burbled down from the Engelmann spruce zone of the Continental Divide — fifty miles of wall running roughly east-west to separate South Park and Middle Park. Above the spruce three miles from the camps were the beautiful rounded domes of Boreas Mountain (13,058) and Mount Silverheels (13,835). Silverheels blocked from view the spur wall of the Mosquito Range a dozen miles west, beyond which were the sources of the Arkansas River and Tennessee Pass.[2]

The old Indian trail which ran west from Denver across the foothills to Kenosha Pass and South Park was much too rough to handle the traffic of men who followed the discoverers to Tarryall. Their endless parade of wagons, carts, horses, oxen, mules and pack trains carrying food, liquor, hardware, stoves, furniture and lumber, and equipment for saloons, newspapers, dance halls, churches, stores and gambling places took the longer easier way — down the old Santa Fe road along the Front Range to the Garden of the Gods and Pikes Peak, and up the Ute Pass trail.[3] The trail was bad at first, but Colorado City merchants at the foot of the pass spent fourteen hundred dollars to bridge a few creeks and move rocks which made it half fit for wagons on the first four miles of pitches to the top of Fountain Creek canyon. From there, the throngs went west through the West Pikes Peak grasslands as U.S. Route 24 goes now, more or less, to Lake George and the South Platte River. Here they turned north to Tarryall Creek and on up that past the picturesque Tarryall Mountains to the diggings below Silverheels.[4]

Meanwhile, Gregory Gulch–bound thousands ascending the Arkansas from Fort Leavenworth heard about South Park and altered their plans. They were welcomed near Pike's old spot at the mouth of the Royal Gorge by Canon City merchants and sent on north into South Park by the Currant Creek Pass road. Most of them drove straight to Tarryall, but some chose to pan the Middle Fork of the South Platte toward Hoosier Pass, or the South Fork toward a pass soon to be called Weston after the pioneer prospector Algernon S. Weston, who took a ranch later at its west foot on Weston Creek and began raising beef to supply the camps. Weston and others crossed the lower southern part of the Mosquito Range by Trout Creek Pass to the Upper Arkansas — still a clean blue rushing torrent confined by monumental highlands. The Mosquitoes rose abruptly from its east bank, dominated by Mount Sherman (14,037) and Ptarmigan Peak above Weston Pass. On the west were the Sawatch (Collegiate) summits of Princeton and Yale, and then of Elbert, Harvard and Massive — second, third and fourth highest of American peaks not counting Alaska.

These early birds found color in Arkansas branches everywhere north of Trout Creek. New diggings included those on a second Clear Creek twenty miles north of Trout Creek; on Cache Creek (Kelley's Bar) three miles north of Clear Creek; and on Lake Creek (Georgia Bar) which flowed down from Twin Lakes. Prospecting sallies were made far up Lake Creek west of Twin Lakes toward present Independence Pass, and up the creek's south fork on a Ute trail toward Lake Pass and the Upper Gunnison. Eventually, men pushed north up the Arkansas nearly to Tennessee Pass and struck placers so dazzling that an old forty-niner exclaimed, "I've got the whole State of Californy right in my pan!" That tiny branch of the Arkansas is still called California Gulch.

As early as August, 1859, the Tarryall diggings were nicknamed "Graball" by late comers who found no space left for them. A few moved west by Red Hill Pass to the main (Middle Fork) South Platte, which they mistook for the Arkansas. They named their camp "the Arkansas Diggings" and then, after discovering their error, Fairplay, as a jibe at Graball. An attraction near Fairplay in this still woman-scarce society was Johnson's Ranch where, the *Rocky Mountain News* of Denver reported, "dwells Mrs. Johnson and her daughter, a buxom lass of seventeen or eighteen summers." Most of Graball's claimless persons went up the lovely Tarryall through the aspen and sparse evergreens and blazing plots of wildflowers to a gap of the Continental Divide above the gale-bent limber pines. From the gap, the sea of South Park stretched away south to the Sangre de Cristos. Pikes Peak stood northeast — vast, calm, benign. The gold-seekers descended from the gap to Blue River and Middle Park along gulches which they named for their home states — Indiana, Illinois, Pennsylvania.

They called their Blue River camp Breckinridge, after Buchanan's vice president, John C. Breckinridge of Kentucky. Later, the town's Union Republicans learned that Breckinridge had joined the Confederate Army, but they were afraid to abolish the town name since it might confuse new arrivals. They compromised by spelling the word Breckenridge. By then, the

Continental Divide crossing from Tarryall was called Breckenridge Pass, and its altitude was 11,482 feet above sea level —
not that any argonaut cared a tinker's dam how high he had to
go for gold.

The winter of 1859-1860 passed quietly. When residents of
Breckenridge were snowed in for days, some of the men cut
long skis out of boards and crossed Breckenridge Pass to Tarryall, returning with fifty-pound sacks of flour strapped to
their shoulders. Illinois Gulch had slalom runs beyond their
skiing skill and so they slid down them "on our tails." April of
1860 brought a bursting out of new camps like lavender pasque-
flowers. At the west foot of Kenosha Pass, a huddle of log
cabins named itself Jefferson, and its residents panned their
way up Michigan Creek as the snow melted, and over Georgia
Pass (11,598) by June. This one resembled Breckenridge Pass
four miles west of it, except that the top was narrower and
made more dramatic by the red escarpment of Mount Guyot
(13,370) rising sheer above.[5] Georgia Pass was at the head of
Swan River (South Fork) — a Blue River branch — and Swan
River sands were full of gold, especially Georgia Gulch and
American Gulch below Humbug Hill.

Georgia Gulch had the usual minority of dreamers who were
not satisfied. For them, the search was the thing, not the gold
itself. They wandered off to find other sands — up the North
Fork of Swan River, for instance, and over the barren shoulder of Glacier Mountain at 11,750 feet to Bear (St. John's)
Creek and Snake River. This wildly montane sector of Middle
Park — a rumpled quilt of errant gulches — was less than twenty
miles west of the booming Georgetown–Idaho Springs–Empire
district. It might as well have been on the moon. The thick
Continental Divide wall had not been conquered here yet,
though people probed up Clear Creek toward what would be
Loveland Pass, leading to Snake River headwaters. Any one
reaching Bear Creek and the Snake from Georgetown had to
get in by way of Ute or Kenosha Pass, South Park, Georgia Pass

and Glacier Mountain — a trek of two hundred miles. Those who did get there in 1860 found nothing worth reporting.

Some dreamers tried French Gulch, two miles from Georgia Gulch, and panned up it south to French Pass, which was just over 12,000 feet. On the South Park side of French, they found a difficult descent for a mile or so until they struck French Creek headwaters and its small tranquil valley falling gently to the Georgia Pass trail and Michigan Creek. One party of a hundred men went down Swan River to its junction with the Blue four miles north of Breckenridge, and down the Blue to Tenmile Creek (Dillon Reservoir now) which they worked up westward toward the Vail Pass of a later day.

A few panned south up the Blue above Breckenridge beneath the tremendous hump of Quandary Peak (14,252) where Frémont had "surprised a herd of buffalo" in 1844.[6] They climbed his same Indian trail which wriggled steeply in its last two miles to the top of the Continental Divide and another stupendous view. Being natives of Indiana, they named the crossing Hoosier Pass (11,541), even though they condemned it for any practical use. From the top, they observed prospectors not far below them in the high, small source valley of the South Platte about to set up the town of Montgomery eight miles north of Fairplay.

Downstream from this infant Montgomery, Joe Higginbottom and his friends were panning color and planning to start a short-lived but merry camp. Joe, a nonconformist, had no use for store clothes. He made his own out of deer hide. That is why his stream became Buckskin Creek and his town Buckskin Joe. The next creek fuming down to the South Platte from the great gray Mosquito Range ridges was being prospected too, and the cabins of Mosquito Camp were being built in the spring of 1860, some eight miles up the north fork of Mosquito Creek. A mosquito, found squashed in the minutes' book during a meeting of miners, inspired the name. We can suppose that somebody kept climbing west, and up three cruel rocky miles to a big alpine wasteland, and then a mile more to stand at last on top of the range.

The small saddle — lichened rubble, moaning wind, black ravens, and pipits flicking about with good cheer and no sense of their incongruity in such a cheerless part of outdoors — would be known as Mosquito Pass. At 13,180 feet above sea level it was the highest Rockies crossing in North America. Three thousand feet below, at the foot of its terrifying rubble slope, was the tiny Arkansas River, and specks of humanity sluicing wealth from the gravel of California Gulch. The gold would be exhausted by 1867 but the great silver camp of Leadville would rise there in another decade.

IN THAT SECOND YEAR OF THE GOLD RUSH, the Continental Divide in Colorado was crawling with gold-seekers, on the eastern slope mainly, for one hundred and fifty miles from Gregory Gulch south to Kelley's Bar and Cache Creek on the Arkansas.[7] Many of them had left home to escape the approaching Civil War, but there was no escape, not even in remote mountains. Hot debate, fights, murders, divided families were as common in the gulches as they were back East. Though Union sentiment prevailed, the thousands of Southerners stood their ground — pioneer Georgians, in particular, such as John Gregory, who did not mind claiming that the diggings belonged to the slave states by right of discovery.

One of these Southerners did more than claim diggings. His name was Charles Baker, and he picked up in California Gulch a grubstake generous enough to outfit a small party for the whole 1860 season. His aim was to follow the Divide southward until it qualified to be part of the South, to find diggings for Southerners, and to use Santa Fe as a Southern supply center rivaling Denver. The Baker group panned down the Arkansas, crossed Poncha Pass to San Luis Valley, and took the new wagon road west over Cochetopa Pass, which had been built in 1858 by the army's Loring expedition.[8] The road led them to Lake Fork of

Gunnison River, which they ascended into heightening glory — Wetterhorn, Matterhorn and Uncompahgre peaks looming west of their trail; Redcloud and Sunshine peaks dead ahead. Some of these fourteen-thousand-footers were splashed with that red-orange color which makes the San Juan Range such an overwhelming sight. The men reached Lake San Cristobal, with its islets, coves and beaches — one of the few in Colorado which looks like a lake instead of a temporary puddle after rain. They saw the huge fold of splotched-yellow earth which had come down in ancient times to block Lake Fork and form San Cristobal.[9]

Upstream south of the lake, the great San Juans closed in on the little valley as mountains do nowhere else in the Rockies except Glacier National Park and Canada. Soon Lake Fork became a torrent tumbling down an interminable ravine of multicolored cliffs. The men struggled for days up those dozen miles of spray and boulders, into the alpine intervale between Edith and Whitecross Mountains, and then hard up the last thirty per cent grade under Handies Peak (14,049). The top of the range was an astonishing bright warm glow of grasses which carpeted the terrain down to timberline. The glow was why the crossing came to be called Cinnamon Pass — 12,600 feet above sea level.[10]

What Baker and his men gazed on beyond Cinnamon was the secret heart of the San Juan Range, technically the San Juan Uplift, and they were the first whites to tell the world about it. Today, blessedly, much of it can be seen by car on the superb Million Dollar Highway (U.S. Route 550) running south for seventy-three miles from Ouray through Silverton (Baker's Park) to Durango on Animas River. It comprises four million acres of highland splendor, mostly west of the Continental Divide, at an average altitude of eleven thousand feet. The Animas flows down the middle, but the San Juan Uplift is not a lineal affair like the Sangre de Cristo, Sawatch, Wind River or Bitterroot ranges. The peak clusters which Baker saw in the summer of 1860 were scattered about in magnificent disorder.

The closest cluster to Cinnamon Pass was made up of the bald summits which hovered over Baker's Park like nosey chaperones — Sultan, Grand Turk, Kendall, Storm, Eureka. Northeast were the monstrous Uncompahgres; north the huge gloomy cirque of Mineral Point under Engineer and Yvonne passes which led to Lake Fork of the Gunnison. The Sneffels Massif (sneffels means snow field in Icelandic) of snow and ice couloirs towered in the northwest above the future site of Ouray town. The San Miguel steeples and red-banded La Platas were to the southwest. In the south were the Grenadiers and Needle Mountains, seen today only by adventurers packing in from the Upper Rio Grande over Hunchback Pass (12,487), or from Animas River over Columbine Pass (12,600).[11]

Charles Baker found his gold diggings in August, 1860, on Upper Animas River near present Silverton, and got his party out of that spectacular cul-de-sac just before Baker's Park was locked in by the heavy snowfall which characterizes the San Juans. His southward route was about the same as today's Million Dollar Highway, avoiding Animas Canyon by way of Molas Divide and Coalbank Pass. In late October, he crossed Horse Lake Pass in New Mexico to Abiquiu and began promoting his Southern kind of Gregory Gulch in Santa Fe. The news of fabulous San Juan riches flew to Denver, and several parties set out for the region over Sangre de Cristo Pass and through Fort Garland. Some planned to get in by Cochetopa and Cinnamon passes.

Such disloyalty to the Pikes Peak area was too much for William Newton Byers, the brilliant editor of Denver's *Rocky Mountain News*. He opened fire on the San Juan region in his paper, in vituperative defense of local business. He charged Baker with being fifty different kinds of humbug, and a traitor besides. He warned that those foolish enough to quit the home camps which Denver merchants toiled so nobly to supply were risking their lives to reach those fake diggings away down there in — his contemptuous designation — "Mexico."

The *Rocky Mountain News* threw a cloud on Baker's Park, but it did not prevent Baker from leading, in the spring of 1861, a hundred men, women and children from Santa Fe over Horse Lake Pass to Animas River and the San Juan diggings. On the way, Baker platted the town of Animas City below Engineer Mountain in the charming lower Animas Valley fifteen miles north of present Durango. But the diggings petered out and, in July, the discouraged miners heard that the war between the states had begun. All of them abandoned the Park and the half-built Animas City. Baker himself hurried to Missouri and signed up as a captain in the Confederate Army. The San Juan resumed its lonely life for a bit longer.[12]

13

Mr. Berthoud, and "Gilpin's Lambs"

Around Denver, the subject of roads across the passes was of a major interest during the pioneer period. Territorial charters for toll roads were as easy to get from members of the legislature as election calling cards. The charter gave the builder of a road the right to collect toll on it, if he were man enough. The usual rates were a dollar for a vehicle and a one-span team; twenty-five cents for horsemen; ten cents a head for horses and cattle; a nickel for hogs, goats and sheep. Travelers on their way to funerals could pass free, provided the corpse was produced as proof that a funeral was about to be held. Most of the paper roads described in the charters were never built. Promoters found it profitable to use their charters in selling stock to suckers for imaginary roads to reach imaginary gold camps by imaginary routes.

The genuine builders were aware, from the experience of army Topographical Engineers, that a road of sorts in this peculiar high country could come into being simply by driving a wagon along and lining the wheel tracks with stone markers. Quite good roads cost as little as ten dollars a mile — better ones cost not over five hundred dollars a mile at most. Timber was too sparse to be obstructive. The light rainfall and well-drained gravel soil eliminated the mud problem. If a mudhole appeared, the driver detoured around it. Streams could be forded anywhere after the spring runoff, even by loaded wagons weighing two tons and more, by cutting ramps down to them.

Though the Continental Divide passes were atrociously high, the grades along the gulches were gentler than in the Alleghenies most of the way up. In a few weeks' time, a good crew could blast out and gouge out with mule-drawn iron scoops the last two miles or so of narrow shelf road up the final alpine pitch. Crews operated from comfortable base camps in the aspen groves below timberline. The gates of toll roads could be erected at company fords or bridges or canyon mouths. Most people were too lazy or too fearful of the wilds to try to sneak around the toll gates. There was some profit in serving meals at the toll house, or letting customers spend the night on the toll house floor; still more in selling them cheap whiskey like Tilton's or Slavin's, or the fiery homemade stuff from Taos. There was a market also for strong black "Virginia" tobacco grown in Missouri.

The free Ute Pass road held its Denver to South Park monopoly briefly. By the spring of 1860, Denver toll road builders had found three routes to Kenosha Pass through the labyrinth of foothills and streams which surrounded the South Platte's impassable canyons.[1] Wagons were crossing the Continental Divide at Breckenridge Pass in August from Tarryall on a kind of road fashioned by miners determined to get their possessions over the wall. In January, 1861, William Byers reported in the *Rocky Mountain News* that a Mr. Buford took eight wagons over Georgia Pass with the help of twenty men shoveling away snow. The Hoosier Pass trail became a road in late May for nine wagons moving from Breckenridge to Buckskin Joe and Fairplay. Wheels were crossing French Pass by then, southbound at least. Big freighters from Santa Fe loaded with flour and Taos lightening were making it to California Gulch from Canon City over Currant Creek and Weston passes. Most of these embryo roads were improved soon by the toll road people and tied in with the Kenosha Pass toll roads.

And still no road crossed the Continental Divide from Denver anywhere north of Georgia Pass. There seemed to be no good reason to make one. The gold belt stopped east of the Divide on Clear Creek headwaters, and on those of Boulder Creek which was the next South Platte tributary to the north. A few mountaineers did push up the middle fork of Boulder Creek from the small Boulder Creek camps of Gold Hill, Sugarloaf, Caribou Hill and such, and along the Indian trail past Lake Dorothy and the remnant Arapaho Glacier to Arapaho Pass (11,905). Other alpinists told editor Byers in 1860 of reaching Devil's Thumb Pass (11,700) five miles south of Arapaho, mainly to examine the up-stuck pollex at the top. Byers called the crossing Boulder Pass and described the thumb as "an isolated chimney rock, two or three hundred feet high, standing like a beacon on the very summit."

The view from both passes was of Middle Park's shimmering open phase — the wide valley of Colorado River west to Gore Range and Gore Pass beyond present Hot Sulphur Springs. The Park was bounded on the north by the Rabbit Ears Range, and, on the south, by a confusion of forest uplands — Williams Fork and Vasquez Mountains.[2] The Divide itself was colossal, dominated south of Devil's Thumb by James Peak, named for our careless camper, Dr. Edwin James, who, you recall, saw it from afar. Colossal, but utterly different from the riotous, unpredictable San Juans which Baker saw from Cinnamon Pass. The Front Range athwart Denver was gray, rounded, ponderous, intransigently conservative — a long line of stone pachyderms.

And suddenly, late in 1860, there were urgent reasons to cross the part of the wall due west of Denver. Abraham Lincoln was elected President. South Carolina seceded. Troops guarding South Pass and the Oregon Trail from Indian attack began to be recalled East to fight the Civil War. The North was determined at last to build that Pacific railroad to hold California and Oregon to the Union. The Santa Fe Trail was Confederate property now. With no safe Oregon Trail, Denver might find itself isolated from the far West. It might lose the railroad also, not having a realistic route to offer. Booster William Byers was just whistling in the dark when he suggested that "a fine railroad could be run from Denver over Kenosha Pass and Breckenridge Pass easier than the Baltimore and Ohio had been run to Wheeling over the Alleghenies."

At this critical point, Byers and other Denver leaders called a mass meeting for March 2, 1861. Money was raised at the meeting and a slender young miner from Golden was hired to penetrate that wall. The young miner was Edward Louis Berthoud, and he was known for his exquisite goatee, his courtly manner, his knowledge of French wines and his friendship with William A. H. Loveland, the Golden tycoon. William Byers was about to publish a guide book of Berthoud's (written with S. W. Burt) called *The Rocky Mountain Gold Regions*. At thirty-three, Berthoud was an all-around engineer. Though Swiss by birth, he had grown up in Cooperstown, New York, and had graduated from Union College in 1849 with an engineering degree. His Cooperstown neighbor and friend, James Fenimore Cooper, got him a job building the railroad across the Isthmus of Panama, and then he did the same kind of work all over the Middle West.[3] He and his wife turned up in Golden in March, 1860, after crossing the plains in a four-mule wagon.

Berthoud had done some pass-hunting up the main Clear Creek west of Georgetown for Loveland, who dreamed of a crossing to which he could affix his name. However, the engineer wanted professional help for his new task and, by purest coincidence, he got it. As the historian, LeRoy R. Hafen, has explained, the important Central Overland California and Pikes Peak Express Company was about to schedule daily stages from Leavenworth, Kansas, over South Pass to Salt Lake City. The C.O.C. had its eye on a proposed government contract to carry mail from Denver to California, and sent the old topographical genius, Jim Bridger, to Denver to investigate the Cherokee Trail as a possible route. Bridger, now fifty-seven, and partly crippled with arthritis, had retired to his Missouri farm after serving with the army's Raynolds expedition of 1860. He reached Denver in late April, 1861, talked to Berthoud, and agreed to help him find a gate directly west of Denver, instead of reviewing the roundabout Cherokee Trail up the Cache la Poudre and west over the Continental Divide in southern Wyoming.

Early in May, Berthoud, Bridger and eight other explorers rode up Clear Creek from Golden. At Georgetown, Berthoud despatched Bridger and two companions to South Park over Guanella and Kenosha passes to inspect the Georgia and Breckenridge crossings. Berthoud and the rest prodded their mules up West Clear Creek above Empire to look at two passes, Jones and Vasquez, which appeared to be most unpromising. They had heard of a third gap, said to have been seen from an adjacent mountain by four prospectors the year before, but they could not find it. At last, on May 12, 1861, they left their mules and simply walked up the mountain. As Berthoud said later, "Scrambling, jumping and climbing over snowy cliffs, at eleven A.M. we reached the summit almost exhausted. In about two minutes' walk on the summit we found that by the merest chance we had hit a low spot in the range, and, at our feet, and flowing northwest, was a small stream running about fourteen miles through an open, unbroken park."

The northwest stream was Middle Park's Fraser River. Soon afterwards, from a crest point to the North, Berthoud could trace the course of the east-side stream (present Hoop Creek, named for T. Hoopes of Georgetown) which "started from the low, even and well-defined pass." During the next four days, the explorers blazed a three-mile pack trail to the top at 11,315 feet, and down into the flaring Fraser Valley, so beloved a century later by Dwight D. Eisenhower.[4] And they raised a flag on that triumphant gap, which remains Berthoud Pass today, one of the busiest and most beautiful highway crossings in the West.

The discovery was quite unique. Unlike most Rockies gates, Berthoud Pass showed no signs of having been used before by Indians, buffalo or any other traveling thing. Jim Bridger, returning to Clear Creek after his fruitless South Park mission, was enthusiastic about it and sent a strong recommendation to his Central Overland California employers in Leavenworth. Orders came back hiring both Bridger and Berthoud to lay out a wagon road from Denver all the way to Salt Lake City. The two men set out in July with a survey crew of ten and a pack train of supplies. Berthoud spent most of his time that summer writing travel articles for editor Byers. For example, in the *Rocky Mountain News* of July 12, 1861:

> On up Clear Creek to Berthoud Pass where we camped in a most delicious meadow skirted by a beautiful forest of spruce trees; here the mountain vegetation attains at this altitude an exuberance, richness and a brilliancy of coloring that can nowhere be exceeded. It was almost tropical in profusion, and the air so pure, so brilliant and so exhilarating that we were at an altitude of between eight thousand and nine thousand feet was difficult to believe. After the usual round of camp jokes, stories and songs, sleep visited us with no niggard hand and when *rosy-fingered morn* awoke us we prepared for a bold push down Moses Creek (Fraser River), which in about twelve miles led us down into the Park.

During the next few weeks, Berthoud and Bridger rode along various Ute Indian trails to Utah — "a most excellent way to discover a good road." Their route left Middle Park by Gore Pass to Egeria Park, followed Yampa River drainage to near present Craig on U.S. Route 40, and veered south over Yellowjacket Pass (7300) to White River at present Meeker. The White led them to the Duchesne, the Provo and Captain Stansbury's Timpanogos Canyon to the Mormon capital. On returning in August, they used present Strawberry Pass (which

Berthoud named "C.O.C. Pass" after his express company) to Strawberry and Duchesne rivers, and up White River again — this time to source streams between Pagoda Peak and Trappers Lake, and so on home through Egeria Park and Gore Pass to Middle Park and Berthoud Pass. Berthoud's prose reached an emotional climax in the *Rocky Mountain News* of August 21 as he described Egeria Park at the west end of Gore Pass:

> Imagine an amphitheatre of long, low ridges, covered with elegant evergreens, meandered by clear brawling brooks, interspersed with grassy deep green meadows, gemmed with groups of gay purple, red, blue, white and yellow flowers, and dotted here and there with small groves of quaking asps, whose bluish and whitish foliage, ever in motion, gave a magical effect to the landscape . . . Indeed nature here seemed still so new, so fresh in creation, that we in imagination appeared to be its first human tenants; and that from each poplar grove the wood nymphs, the dryads of antiquity, still remained and peeped at us shyly; indeed the name for this park, suggested by Governor Gilpin, is very appropriate . . . Egeria.[5]

It was a fine exploration of a thousand miles — July 8 to September 19, 1861 — and yet nothing seemed to come of it except a petrified turtle, picked up at Green River, which Berthoud gave to William Byers.[6] Before the winter ended, the Central Overland California decided to shift its Indian-harassed stage and mail line southward from South Pass only as far as Bridger Pass — the new Overland Trail up the South Platte and Cache la Poudre.[7] Congress would soon approve as a war measure a transcontinental railroad, but the Union Pacific's route would be in Wyoming too, by Cheyenne Pass and the Red Desert north of Bridger Pass, rather than Berthoud Pass.

Bad news for Denver. Besides, it was becoming clear, even to an incorrigible Colorado booster like William Byers, that the Pikes Peak gold rush was in the doldrums. The surface gold at Tarryall, Georgia Gulch and Kelley's Bar was gone. The lode stuff around Gregory Gulch and Central City was becoming increasingly hard to extract. Hundreds of miners were leaving the Rockies to fight the Civil War in the East.

That last was ironical. In March, 1862, the Civil War came to the Rockies when General Henry H. Sibley and his Texans captured Santa Fe for the Confederacy and began planning to march on Denver.

AND SO WE RETURN to the first scene of this book, La Glorieta Pass, just about as Coronado saw it — a twenty-mile, looping, easy passage through round piñon hills, narrow at both ends, with the jays still flashing blue among the scrub oak and faded rabbit bush.

Only one Colorado leader foresaw the Battle of La Glorieta Pass. Governor William Gilpin was a visionary so far ahead of his time that we haven't caught up with him yet. One of his more conservative dreams was to build a railroad from Denver, Colorado, to London, England, by bridging Bering Strait, passing through Moscow, and tunneling beneath the English Channel. In 1843, Gilpin had deadheaded to Oregon with Frémont. He barnstormed with Doniphan in the Mexican War. He was so radical that the War Department would not listen to his warning that Jefferson Davis would try to seize Colorado's gold mines to use as collateral for foreign loans.

When he was refused soldiers to stop General Sibley in New Mexico, he made an army of his own, one of the oddest in history. "Gilpin's Lambs" consisted of 1342 gold camp miners, bartenders, lawyers, preachers, con men, shoe clerks, pimps, actors and mule skinners. To raise money to feed them, dress them and supply them with guns bought from Denver pawnshops, he issued personal drafts on the United States Treasury, as Governor Stevens had done at Fort Benton. Not one man in three of this First Regiment of Colorado Volunteer Infantry had ever fired a gun. The army's colonel, John P. Slough, was a Denver lawyer without military experience. The major, the

Reverend John M. Chivington, was presiding elder of the Rocky Mountain District of the Methodist Episcopal Church. He had confined himself heretofore to being reverend.

Such was the tatterdemalion of pedestrians from Denver who tramped across Raton Pass on March 8, 1862, to save the Rockies. A horseman arrived from La Glorieta to report that Sibley's eleven hundred regulars were to leave Santa Fe soon to seize Fort Union, the great United States supply center seventy miles north of the capital. If Fort Union fell, the Rockies would fall too, and California would become a Confederate naval base.

Gilpin's Lambs dropped all their equipment except their blankets and guns and marched ninety-two miles on the double through a raging blizzard to reach Fort Union on March 10. For two weeks they practiced shooting there, and then marched on toward the enemy camp inside La Glorieta Pass near the ruins of Pecos Village. Major Chivington and four hundred and eighteen men scouted along the Santa Fe Trail through the pass on March 26, captured thirty Sibley pickets in a skirmish, and found the well-armed rebels and their big wagon train just beyond Apache Canyon preparing to advance.

The showdown came two days later. Sibley's tough Texans, many of them frightening fellows with yard-wide sombreros, lassos, tomahawks, bowie knives and mounted on mustangs, moved confidently over La Glorieta that morning, red Texas flags flying, cannon-carriers rumbling over the bridges. At 10 A.M. they met Gilpin's Lambs head-on at Pigeon's Ranch near Pecos Village. For several hours the bloody struggle raged — rifle fire, grapeshot, booming cannon, hand-to-hand combat — in that narrow grass-and-cacti passage of the Santa Fe Trail, split by a deep arroyo. In late afternoon neither side could take any more. Colonal Slough ordered a retreat east down the pass a few miles with his fifty dead and sixty-five wounded. The battle had reached a stalemate, which meant a Confederate victory under the circumstances, since the whole town of Santa

Fe was close at hand for the Texans to fall back on. Gilpin's exhausted Lambs, already short of water, had no such resource.

A Confederate victory in effect — except for the work of one Methodist Episcopal presiding elder. The Reverend Major Chivington was a vast bearded man, oracular as Moses, six feet three inches tall and weighing nearly three hundred pounds. He burned inside with a furious wish to win this Battle of La Glorieta Pass for the Union, perhaps because his brother back East had joined the Confederacy. While the Texans had marched noisily east that morning over La Glorieta Pass, he had marched quietly west with four hundred and thirty men, but not on the Santa Fe Trail. His hidden route was through San Cristobal Cañon just to the south, bringing his brigade in sixteen miles to the top of the piñon-cedar hill at the Apache Canyon end of the pass overlooking Sibley's huge supply train of seventy-three heavily-loaded wagons.

The time was 1:30 P.M. For an hour Chivington made plans as he watched the two hundred and fifty unsuspecting guards and teamsters a thousand feet below. Then he lined up his gold campers, gave the charge order and led them down the mountain — sliding, slipping, crashing from piñon to piñon, howling like Blackfeet. Within minutes, some of them seized and spiked the sole cannon while the terrified guards were killed or captured and the teamsters scattered. The next four hours were spent in a frantic orgy of destruction. Chivington was everywhere at once directing crews to get the wagons piled up and fired before the enemy reappeared. In their careless rush, men almost lost their lives as gunpowder exploded, scattering firebrands over the area. Everything which Sibley's army needed to take Denver went up in smoke — half a million dollars worth of ammunition, saddles, subsistence, clothes, baggage, medical supplies, maps, wagons. The tireless Chivington had the six hundred horses and mules corralled and shot in relays, their blood flowing down the arroyo. At nightfall, the job was done and the Major led his weary force up the hill and away from the smoke-filled ruin to rejoin Slough's contingent at daybreak below Pigeon's Ranch.

By then, Colonel William R. Scurry, commanding the Texans, had learned of the disaster to his wagon train, and so had General Sibley himself at his headquarters in Santa Fe. There was no escaping what had to be done. Both recognized that, without armament or transport or medical supplies, the Civil War was over as far as New Mexico and the Rockies and California were concerned, and a bunch of untrained maniacs from Denver had won it, led by an oversized Jehovah. There was nothing for the Texans to do but bury their seventy dead in shallow trenches at La Glorieta Pass, abandon their fifty wounded in Santa Fe, and head for home with all possible speed before Union forces could cut them off.

IN THE SUMMER OF 1862, the heroes of La Glorieta returned to Fairplay and California Gulch, to Central City and Breckenridge and Golden, and all was quite peaceful around Denver. For some weeks, editor Byers injected hopeful notes in his *Rocky Mountain News* columns, only to rise again in wrath during the fall. His complaint this time was far more anguished than it had been when he revealed the perfidy of Charles Baker and his San Juan humbug. The object of his rage concerned the word Bannack, which, it appeared, was the name of the center of new gold diggings to which "disloyal Pikes Peakers" were flocking in an outlandish part of the Rockies far to the north.

14

Continental Tea

THE ORIGINS of the Colorado gold rush were relatively simple. Men heard of a place called Gregory Gulch in virgin wilds and piled in at once by the thousands. By contrast, the Montana rush had a long and complicated development. It was a sort of historical stew which simmered for a decade before it was ready.[1]

One ingredient of the stew was the California forty-niner who wandered all over Oregon and Washington territories through the 1850's hunting for new diggings. Another was the exploration in 1853–1854 of those fourteen Montana passes by Stevens's young men. They spread word of the region's agricultural promise in its charming and accessible valleys — Bitterroot, Big Hole, Beaverhead, Deer Lodge, Three Forks. A third ingredient was Mormon hostility to emigrants after the "Mormon War" of 1857–1858.[2] This hostility created a demand for routes passing north of the Oregon Trail beyond the reach of Mormon wrath.

One man was more than eager to meet the need for a northerly route — our cantankerous friend Frederick W. Lander, whom we met as engineer of the Stevens survey, moving heaven and earth to avoid doing what the Governor asked him to do. Lander's final triumph before quitting his job was his success in failing to find a winter route for Stevens across the Cascade Range in 1854–1855.[3] Lander had only contempt for the Mullan

Pass route which Congress would approve for the army's road from the Fort Benton head of Missouri navigation through the Rockies to Fort Walla Walla and the Columbia. On his way east, he did some exploring on his own and found what he thought was a good cutoff for ox-team travelers which left the Oregon Trail near Fort Hall and Snake River and returned to it at South Pass. In Washington, Lander had connections — political, social, sportive, artistic. His wife was the actress, Jean Margaret Davenport, and he himself was a celebrated athlete. Soon Congress was induced to back his plan for the Rockies part of its proposed "Central Overland Route" from Fort Kearny, Nebraska, to Honey Lake in northern California. The road would be built under the authority of Secretary Jacob Thompson of the Department of the Interior, who practiced none of Stevens's army nonsense, such as making civilian engineers strike their own tents.

Thompson knew nothing about road building and he made Lander his confidante as well as chief engineer of the Central Overland. The choice was good for unexpected reasons. Thompson's main problem was handling Lander's superior, Superintendent William M. F. Magraw, a snorting bull of a Pennsylvanian who was also a power in Democratic politics. Magraw was an irresponsible alcoholic, but a lovable one with many friends, including President Buchanan. When Thompson had to fire him for incompetence, he began causing trouble for the Central Overland and for its chief engineer by libel suits and slanderous talk.

Lander decided to silence him. He challenged Magraw to a duel, but his man refused to face him. Then he beat Magraw up in the lobby of the Willard Hotel before a mixed crowd of Washington socialites. When that didn't work, he beat him up once more in a bloody brawl which occurred outside and inside the Kirkwood Hotel. The hotel manager handed Magraw a gun to use on his unarmed opponent, but Lander heaved a lobby chair at him with such force that he dropped the gun.

The second beating convinced Magraw that slandering Lander was a losing game.

The Lander Cut-Off was built by Mormon labor between June 10 and September 15, 1858. Though Lander had not been able to find Marias Pass for Stevens, he had no trouble finding passes for his own project. He claimed to have found nineteen for the Central Overland.[4] Historically, his 350-mile route from Snake River to South Pass traced all the way back to 1812. During that year, you remember, Robert Stuart and his five Astorians crossed Salt River Range by Sheep Pass, and came within five miles of finding a short way through Wyoming Range to Piney Creek and South Pass before losing their nerve and retreating to Pierre's Hole and Teton Pass.

From South Pass, Lander laid down his road northwest along the base of Wind River Range and west across Green River near present Big Piney, with the summits of Wyoming Peak (11,363) and Lander Peak (11,134) ahead. It ran up Piney Creek and, by a progression of lovely sage hills and lovelier forest uplands, reached a gap which Lander named Thompson Pass (9500), after his doting Secretary of the Interior, just beneath Mount Thompson. The pass linked South Piney to La Barge Creek headwaters. The cutoff continued through lush meadows sprinkled with cranesbill, lupine and sunflowers over what is known as Commissary Ridge and Wagner Pass (9026) to the source of Smiths Fork of Bear River. William H. Wagner was Lander's assistant.

This fragrant part of the Wyoming Range was — and is — a sylvan park of great beauty. From Wagner Pass, Lander's road ran south down the little rock canyon of Smiths Fork on the south side of Wagner Mountain. The Sheep Pass which the Stuart party crossed in 1812 was seven miles away on the north side of Wagner Mountain. At the site of present Smiths Fork Guard Station, the cutoff turned northwest, crossed low piney ridges of the Salt River Range and emerged in Star Valley at the north foot of Salt River Pass (7616). Star Valley, a spacious garden enclosed by a wall of sage mountains, was soon being called Paradise Valley by travelers passing through. Half-way down Salt River northward, at present Auburn, Wyoming, the cutoff rambled northwest from Star Valley across the Gannett Hills, passing south of Grays Lake and north of present Blackfoot River Reservoir to the Oregon Trail junction near Fort Hall.[5]

With his appetite for controversy, Lander was unhappy when nobody criticized his finished work. The cutoff was so popular that thirteen thousand people used it during 1859. He sulked for a time until he found something to scrap about — the army's new competing route from Salt Lake City across Utah to California which Captain James H. Simpson was surveying. Simpson's route, he said, might be shorter than the Central Overland, and useful in pacifying the Mormons, but it was utterly unfit for ox teams. Lander charged that Simpson was cynically guilty of cruelty to animals in promoting such an arid death trap.

Unfortunately for Lander, Simpson was a gentle soul. His response to Lander's outcry gave the muscular engineer no excuse to challenge him to a duel or engage him in hotel-lobby fisticuffs. Simpson announced publicly and profusely that Lander was quite right. Ox-train emigrants, he said, would be wise to go west on the well-watered, grassy, scenic Lander's Cut-Off instead of his bleak Utah desert route.

As LANDER'S CUT-OFF opened in May, 1859, Lieutenant John Mullan, all of twenty-nine years old now, began work on his 633-mile military road from Fort Walla Walla (present Walla Walla, Washington) to Fort Benton through the Montana highlands which he knew so well.[6] We noted that Governor Stevens's soldiers had found gold six years before in the Gold Creek branch of Clark Fork, at Hell Gate, and other places. Lieutenant Mullan spattered his road map with the names of alleged diggings — Nez Perce Gold Mines, Colville Gold Mines,

Prickly Pear Gold Mines, and such. But setting the stage for a Montana gold rush was not among the army's serious aims for the Mullan Road.

These unproven Golcondas were marked on the map mainly to lure settlers to Montana, to fill up the land as part of the solution to the Indian problem. By 1859, Indians throughout the Rockies were organizing to save their hunting grounds — Sioux and Cheyennes east of the Big Horns, Snakes from South Pass to Togwotee Pass in the Wind River Range, the once-gentle Nez Perce west of Stevens Pass.[7] The road's primary purpose was to increase the population of Washington Territory. Soldiers in army camps along the way would cooperate with settlers in controlling the Indians. An important by-product from Governor Stevens's point of view would be to give him full scope to exercise the superior brains which he felt that God had given him.

By early fall of 1859, Mullan's ninety-man building crew and escort of one hundred and forty soldiers had pushed the Mullan Road from Walla Walla northeast around the south end of Coeur d'Alêne Lake to Father Ravalli's Coeur d'Alêne Mission, and had reexamined the several Bitterroot passes to St. Regis River. New ones were found on north branches of the Coeur d'Alêne — Glidden, Cooper and Thompson passes, which would link the future Gem-Burke-Sullivan silver-lead mining area to Clark Fork on the next drainage north of St. Regis River.

Mullan recognized now that the Bitterroot Range was harder to cross than the higher main Rockies at Mullan Pass because of its many streams, much heavier timber, deep winter snows and the delaying tactics of the Nez Perce Indians. He complained that more delay derived from "the erroneous judgments made by F. W. Lander in 1853." He perceived that his road budget of about two hundred dollars a mile would not be half enough to see him through.

The Coeur d'Alêne Pass area presented problems, but these

were met in October when his guide and interpreter, Gustavus Sohon, "found a pass which, probably, is the lowest in the Coeur d'Alêne Range and which, in honor of Mr. Sohon, who made the first topographical map of it in our expedition, I have termed 'Sohon's Pass' . . . It is within half a mile of what is called by Governor Stevens 'Coeur d'Alêne Pass.'" Sohon's Pass became today's St. Regis Pass. The Mullan Road over it was abandoned in modern times with the building of U.S. Route 10 over the adjoining Lookout Pass.

After surviving a ghastly winter at Cantonment Jordan east of Sohon's Pass, Mullan's crew spent the spring rushing pell-mell past "Hellgate Ronde" and Coriacan's Defile and up Clark Fork. The men put the trace across Mullan Pass on July 18, 1860. From there it was continued northeasterly by way of Big and Little Prickly Pear creeks, through Medicine Rock Pass sector to Dearborn River, and past Bird Tail Mountain to Sun River and Fort Benton. On August 2, the Lieutenant declared his seven-year-old dream to be realized. The name Mullan Road was something of a euphemism. Long stretches of it — Sohon's Pass to Mullan Pass, for example — were just the ancient Indian trail cleared of timber and rocks.

DURING THAT SAME SUMMER of 1860, two shallow-draft steamboats puffed from St. Louis all the way up the Missouri to Fort Benton. However, Mullan was not impressed with them for emigrant use, or with any northern wagon route across the Montana plains, because of the Indian unrest. The Mullan Road, he concluded, should connect with some branch of the Oregon Trail arriving at Mullan Pass or Deer Lodge Pass from Fort Laramie or Fort Hall. He hoped to develop such feeders himself, but dropped the idea when he learned that the War Department was assigning Captain William F. Raynolds of the Army Engineers to cover much the same ground, aided by Lieutenant Henry E. Maynadier of the Tenth Infantry.

Captain Raynolds, aged forty, was an unpretentious West

Pointer from Canton, Ohio. He had not asked for the adventurous life of an explorer, but, since it was tossed in his lap, he meant to enjoy it peacefully. His orders were conceived by an army official who pictured the Rockies as about the size of the Green Mountains of Vermont. Raynolds was instructed to explore half a million square miles of wilderness inhabited by angry Indians. In the process, he was to find the best emigrant routes from Fort Laramie north to Fort Benton and the Mullan Road on both sides of the Big Horn Mountains, and from Fort Laramie to the source of the Yellowstone by way of South Pass and Wind River headwaters.

The Captain, who had learned how to handle army impossibles during his long career back East as a topographical officer, dumped the Big Horn part of the orders by calling his trip "an exploration of the Yellowstone." He hired Jim Bridger — Old Gabe — as his guide, and set out on May 10, 1860, from Fort Casper on the North Platte a bit west of Fort Laramie. He knew that he could trust Lieutenant Maynadier and his thirty dragoons to get over a portion of the ground while he covered some of what remained as pleasantly as he could with his tea served promptly each afternoon at five.

After a day or two along the Oregon Trail, Bridger led Captain Raynolds's part of the expedition northwest through Cedar Gap to the same desolate Indian trail down Badwater Creek which we followed to Wind River and Union Pass with Wilson Price Hunt in 1811. Union Pass had no name yet, of course. Old Gabe had not ascended Wind River in fifteen years and he had a desire to see Two Ocean Pass at the Yellowstone's source one last time before retiring. That odd, imperceptible divide where the waters ran both east and west was dear to him because of the glorious view of the Tetons and Jackson Hole, and because he claimed to have discovered it in 1832 — John Colter notwithstanding.

Raynolds was enthusiastic about reaching the Yellowstone, but objected to Bridger's way of getting there — west over the

Continental Divide at the head of the Wind, down Blackrock Creek toward Jackson Lake, and back northeast up Pacific Creek to cross the Divide again at Two Ocean Pass. Why cross the Divide at all, since both Wind and Yellowstone rivers were on the Eastern Slope? Bridger explained that the snow was still too deep for travel, even if trails existed up there in that highest Absaroka Range between Togwotee Pass and Younts Peak where the Yellowstone began.

And, on May 30, they found that even Togwotee Pass was snowbound. Bridger wasted a day searching for the trail to the next gate south of Togwotee (it would be known as Sheridan Pass). When he could not find it, he told Raynolds contritely that he had trouble remembering the landmarks of his youth. There should be still another pass which led to both the Green and the Snake but he feared that he had lost his bearings. Perhaps it was best to return down Wind River and take the long South Pass trail around the range.

Captain Raynolds trudged up a knoll by himself to think it over. Southward, he noticed an easy gap above him and he knew at once that it had to be Bridger's triple divide to the Green (Gulf of California) and to the Snake (Pacific Ocean). Beyond it he saw "a bold conical peak . . . the topographical center of the continent." In a misty-eyed moment of patriotism, he named the mountain Union Peak, the gap Union Pass. Then he filled his canteen with Wind River water (Gulf of Mexico), planning to celebrate the christening with a spot of "Continental Tea" on the far side of Union Pass by adding the Green and Snake to his canteen of Wind. By teatime, he had moved his party through the snow over Union Pass and had encamped it on Fish Creek of Gros Ventre River, a Snake tributary, five miles below the Lake of the Woods. There, Raynolds had his continental tea, but without any Green River water in it after all. The Green was ten miles farther south.

After a good night's rest, Old Gabe knew where he was again and guided the party down the swollen Gros Ventre to

Snake River and Jackson Hole. The trip to Two Ocean Pass and the Yellowstone was given up for lack of time. By June 18, the men crossed to Pierre's Hole by quite a good pack trail over Teton Pass. At the top of the pass, Bridger showed Raynolds a pine tree with the initials "J.M." carved on it, and the dates "July 7, 1833," and "July 11, 1833." Young Joe Meek had put them there on his way to the rendezvous of that year near Captain Bonneville's Fort Nonsense.

A week later, they reached the same modest pass above Henrys Lake which Andrew Henry had crossed southbound from Madison River in 1810. Raynolds wrote in his journal: "The pass is only four miles from and two hundred feet above the lake, and so level that it is difficult to locate the exact spot at which the waters divide . . . I named it Low Pass and deem it to be one of the most remarkable features of the topography of the Rocky Mountains." Crossing this Raynolds Pass was to be his last achievement. Nothing more of note occurred as Bridger took the party down the Madison to Three Forks and then to Fort Benton by way of Smiths Fork of the Missouri, to avoid the rough trail past Great Falls.

As he wended his way home, Raynolds could congratulate himself that he had accomplished his "Exploration of the Yellowstone" with distinction, even though he never managed to lay eyes on the Yellowstone itself.[8]

ALL THESE EVENTS of the 1850's — Stevens's exploration, the army's "Mormon War," the Raynolds expedition, the construction of Lander's Cut-Off and the Mullan Road — stimulated the thin but pervasive trickle of commerce through Montana's low passes, and set the stage for the rush from the Denver area to Bannack which caused editor Byers so much pain. During 1862, hundreds of riding and walking prospectors, and thousands of horses, mules, wagons and cattle followed the Overland Trail over Cache la Poudre and Bridger passes to Fort

Bridger and the Oregon Trail. At Fort Hall, these gold-seekers were joined by men from Salt Lake City, from Sacramento, and from Virginia City, Nevada.

The bleak tent-and-shanty town of Bannack sat in the sage a dozen miles up Grasshopper Creek, a branch of Beaverhead River just below Horse Prairie Creek. Horse Prairie, you recall, was the stream which Lewis and Clark ascended to Lemhi Pass, with Sacajawea trailing after, sucking her fingers for joy. The argonauts closed in on the place by a long circular reconnaissance, though some went directly from Fort Hall on the Medicine Lodge Pass trail. Many visited the already exhausted Salmon River placers first near Sacajawea's old home at the west foot of Lemhi Pass. This involved crossing Bonneville's Lost River Sinks and Gilmore Divide to Lemhi and Salmon rivers. From the Salmon, they panned up the gulches of the Bitterroot Range in Colorado fashion, and down the east slope of the Continental Divide.

Those who crossed by Bannock Pass and Lemhi Pass wound up on Horse Prairie Creek, where all roads led to Bannack town. But some used Big Hole Pass farther north, which put them on another watershed entirely — Moose Creek and Big Hole River. Thereafter, they crossed Gibbons Pass northward to Ross's Hole and Bitterroot River to join prospectors arriving from Orofino and Elk City diggings on the Clearwater by way of those tedious Nez Perce Pass and Lolo Pass trails. At Hell Gate, they met people hurrying along the Mullan Road from Walla Walla and Portland, and continued with them up Clark Fork to Gold Creek.

One branch of Gold Creek was so crowded with "disloyal Pikes Peakers" that it was called Pikes Peak Gulch. But Gold Creek was petering out so the newcomers pressed on up Clark Fork. Several took the Little Blackfoot, inscribed their names on a post atop Mullan Pass and found color in the two Prickly Pear creeks, foreshadowing the boom of 1864 on Last Chance Gulch and the birth of Helena. A majority pushed south through Deer Lodge Valley and over Deer Lodge Pass to the Big Hole, and on up the Beaverhead to Bannack.[9]

They did not stay long. Bannack was the most ephemeral of all ephemeral gold camps. By the spring of 1863, it was falling apart. Many Pikes Peakers began the long haul back to Denver over Medicine Lodge Pass. Others resumed scrambling around Montana's round hills. Six of these struck it really rich in late May some thirty miles up a branch of the Lewis and Clark Philanthropy River — today's Ruby River, which joins the Beaverhead just above the Big Hole. William Byers had still another name for it, "the Stinking Water," which he used with relish when he started to belabor this new threat to Denver's prosperity. The town which arose in the area was called Varina City at first, honoring Jefferson Davis's wife, but Union sentiment forced a compromise name, Virginia City. During its first bizarre year of life, at least ten million dollars worth of pure gold was picked up by fourteen thousand men who swarmed to Alder Gulch and other tributaries of the Stinking Water in that treeless area between the Tobacco Root and Gravelly ranges.

Ten million dollars was an enormous amount of money to be floating around in the wilds four hundred and twenty-five miles from the nearest judge or jail at Walla Walla. The result was an orgy of lawlessness throughout Montana. All the West's professional bad men poured in, along with quite a few amateurs who seemed determined to seize this golden opportunity to see what sin was like. For a time, this criminal mob lived the life of today's television westerns, casing saloons and dance halls for suckers, jumping claims, and brawling over the plump German hurdy-gurdy girls who had arrived from San Francisco for their fair share of the ten million. Virginia City and Bannack vied for the honor of housing the toughest, fastest-drawing hombres. One Virginia City monte player was said to be so tough that the cards clutched in his dead fist after his murder could not be pried loose and were buried with him.

The acting governor of Montana Territory, Thomas F. Meagher, drank to excess like everybody else. He tottered, or fell, into the Missouri River at Fort Benton one night and drowned. Last Chance Gulch, below Mullan Pass, changed its name to Helena, after the town in Minnesota, but pronounced the word Hell-na to suit the environment, instead of the usual way. The crowning glory of this unrestrained society was the dapper Henry Plummer, who was smart enough to get appointed sheriff of Bannack and Virginia City but not smart enough to live long. He and his crew of fifty road agents robbed and murdered travelers by the dozens on the pass roads until the residents became tired of crime and organized the Virginia City Vigilantes. During January, 1864, these secret police strung up Plummer and twenty-four of his gang on a variety of tree limbs. Thereafter, Montana's gold camps quieted down and became almost as respectable as Denver and Central City.

The shift of the gold rush center in 1863 and 1864 from Bannack to Virginia City and on north to Helena called for other pass routes. The eighty-mile Bannack–Virginia City road was changed to reach the Beaverhead by Rattlesnake Creek in place of Grasshopper Creek, approximating today's Bull Creek–Badger Pass road, which connects the Big Hole and Beaverhead valleys. Travelers to Virginia City from Green River and Jackson Hole went by Teton and Raynolds passes to the Madison near present Ennis and over the low hills to Alder Gulch. The Medicine Lodge Pass trail over the Continental Divide from Fort Hall to Bannack was not needed. It resumed its old use as part of the trail to Big Hole Valley and over Gibbons Pass to Bitterroot Valley, Fort Owen and the Mullan Road.[10] Monida Pass took much of the traffic from Fort Hall now. After crossing it, prospectors went up Little Sage Creek from Red Rock River in the Wild Cat Canyon — Clover Divide area. If Bannack was their destination, they descended Blacktail Creek from the canyon to Rattlesnake Creek and the Beaverhead near today's Dillon. Those bound for Virginia City carried on north to Sweetwater Creek and the Stinking Water (Ruby) and so to Alder Gulch.

In 1863, A. J. Oliver operated an express wagon and then a stage from Salt Lake City and Fort Hall over Monida Pass to Bannack and Virginia City. A year later, Ben Holladay, the stagecoach king whose lines served three thousand miles of roads in the mountain west, ran Oliver out of business. For his service from Fort Hall over Monida Pass to Virginia City, Holladay reported buying two hundred and ninety Missouri mules, thirty four-mule Concord coaches and ten freight wagons. He extended the Monida Pass line soon to Helena and honored Montana with main-line rolling stock — splendid six-horse Concord coaches of the latest design, seating seventeen passengers and costing fifteen hundred dollars each.

All this frenetic while, Montana Territory was undergoing transition. Emigrants to the rich and beautiful Gallatin and Bitterroot valleys began to outnumber gold-seekers as the placer diggings approached exhaustion. On the Mullan Road, there were not enough mules to carry all the goods from Oregon, and somebody imported a herd of camels from China to help out. Their peculiar stench so outraged the mules that whole pack trains were demoralized. The camels suffered from sore feet, too. Finally, when a hunter near Sohon's Pass bagged a camel thinking it was a moose, the camel man resigned from the business and turned his herd loose to shift for itself. Some of the camels survived in the wilds for years.[11]

Emigration to Montana across the plains from the East was relatively small for a time because of the distances involved to Virginia City on the Oregon and Overland trails to Fort Hall, and the need to cross the Continental Divide twice, first at Bridger or South Pass and again at Monida or Raynolds Pass. Jim Bridger thought that this rambling route was foolishness, and so did John M. Bozeman, a young Pikes Peaker from Georgia who was also a Bannack pioneer. Both men laid out direct routes to the Gallatin Valley which left the Oregon Trail at points west of Fort Laramie and short of South Pass. To test their routes, each trailmaker led emigrant trains over them during the summer of 1864 — trains large enough to re-pel Indian attacks.

The Bridger train set out some weeks ahead of Bozeman's, passing west of the Big Horns and on north to the Yellow-stone Valley. The old scout had worked up an antipathy of late toward Bozeman Pass, feeling that its heavy animal traffic had caused overgrazing along the road. He wanted the mules and cattle of his train to eat well going over the range, even if the trip took a couple of extra days. Therefore, he left the Yel-lowstone near present Livingston, Montana, ascended Shields River north ten miles and pushed west up Brackett Creek to what we can call Bridger Pass (in Montana) and Bridger Creek, leading down southward through Bridger Canyon to East Gallatin River and the regular Bozeman Pass road. Bridger Pass was one hundred and forty feet higher than Bozeman Pass. The rough trail over was twenty miles longer than the regular road.

In the meantime, John Bozeman took his train across the North Platte at Bridger's new ferry upstream from Fort Laramie and plunged into the hostile heart of the Sioux hunting grounds immediately east of the Big Horns. The Indians threat-ened trouble, but made none that time as the emigrants trailed through the vast rolling plain across Powder River, the Tongue, Little and Bighorn rivers to the Yellowstone and over the ancient gate which Gallatin Valley settlers now began to call Bozeman Pass. The wagons rolled down the west side of the pass to discover Bridger's wagons emerging from Bridger Canyon into the valley. From there, the rival emigrant trains raced from Gallatin River to the Madison and on to Virginia City by Meadow Creek, arriving at about the same time.

The Bozeman Trail was much the shortest of the rival routes. Thousands of emigrants pushed along it to Bozeman Pass in

1865 and 1866, and four army forts were built to protect them from the Indians. Then, on December 21, 1866, the Sioux and Cheyennes expressed their view of this passage through their homeland by killing with arrows and clubs all eighty-one members of Captain Fetterman's scouting party below the benign mass of the Big Horn Mountains. Soon after, the federal government gave back the Powder River region to the Indians as a bribe to induce them not to hamper construction of the Union Pacific Railroad across Wyoming. Without military protection, the Bozeman Trail was unsafe and its career as an emigrant route was suspended for a decade. Its place was filled by the Union Pacific which, in March, 1869, reached Corinne, Utah, only two hundred and forty miles south of Monida Pass and Montana. Thereafter, Monida Pass took most of the Montana traffic. Its reign would last until the 1880's, when the territory would get its own railroads from Chicago and St. Paul through Bozeman, Mullan, Homestake and Marias passes.[12]

WHILE THE LURE OF GOLD was changing the face of Colorado and Montana during the 1860's, nothing of the sort disturbed the austere loneliness of the Canadian Rockies. Though placers were found on the Kootenay west of Crowsnest Pass and on the Upper Columbia below Dr. Hector's Kicking Horse, they were too poor to draw crowds into those beautiful, ice-wrapped ramparts which so few men, red or white, had ever really known. Several parties did cross them, but their objective was the Fraser River gold region, to which some twenty thousand West coast Americans began flocking in 1857. The Fraser River rush was going strong five years later in the Cariboo district far in the north of the new Crown colony of British Columbia.

The Cariboo and its roaring camp of Barkerville were reached in only one practical way — by steamer and stage from Vancouver on the Pacific six hundred miles up the Fraser. However, any one studying a map of British North America could see that, not far from Barkerville, the Fraser began at a

Rockies pass where a branch of the Athabaska River had a source too. At the east foot of this pass was the Hudson's Bay Company post, Jasper House. As we have mentioned, the post had been named for a yellow-headed Missouri trapper of the very early days, Jasper Hawse. The pass, therefore, was called Yellowhead by Englishmen and Tête Jaune by the French. A third name was Leather Pass, since quantities of leather were taken over it as an article of trade.

In the spring of 1862, newspapers in London ran the following advertisement:

British Columbia Overland Transit, via Canada
The British Columbia Transit Company will punctually despatch on the 21st of May, at 12 noon from Glasgow, in the first class and powerful screw steamship United Kingdom . . . a party of first and second class passengers for Quebec, Canada, and over the Grand Trunk Railway . . . to Chicago and St. Paul and via the Red River settlements, in covered wagons, to British Columbia.

This is the speediest, safest and most economical route to the gold diggings. The land transit is through a lovely country unequalled for its beauty and salubrity of climate . . . Through fares £42 from England to British Columbia, saloon berths £5 extra.

Thousands of Britishers checked the ad against their maps of Canada and decided that the offer must be genuine. The six-thousand-mile trip to Barkerville and the pot of gold seemed cheap at twice the price — steamer to Quebec, railroad train to St. Paul, Minnesota, and comfortable covered wagon on good roads along Red and Athabaska rivers to Jasper House, Yellowhead Pass, Fraser River and the Cariboo. The reality was rather different. Of all those would-be Overlanders, only a hundred-odd managed actually to get as far as the plains of western Canada that summer along the chain of Hudson's Bay Company posts. The promised roads did not exist. Instead of the "covered wagons" of the advertisement, they had to travel by ox cart and pack horse. The "salubrity of climate" brought heavy rain, awful heat, mud to the hubs of the carts, swarming bugs, spoiled food and underbrush so thick that it blocked and obliterated the trail.

In mid-August of 1862, the weary argonauts arrived at Jasper House on the Athabaska and found that there was no cleared or marked trail from there over Yellowhead Pass. Barkerville was still four hundred miles farther west, instead of just over the Continental Divide. They could not turn back so late in the season. Though they had no guide, they pushed up the Miette branch of the Athabaska toward Yellowhead — a diversion from the old Athabaska Pass trapper trail which David Thompson had developed to the Columbia in 1811.

They were surprised by the easy grade of the Yellowhead traverse, but the lodgepole forest was thick and they had to hack a path through it for the carts. Their food supply was running short. It happened that the one lady among the Overlanders, Mrs. August Schubert, was far advanced in pregnancy, and had two small children hanging on her skirts and a four-year-old on her back. She maintained energy with a diet of chipmunk, woodpecker, porcupine and skunk.

On August 22, 1862, the party crossed low Yellowhead without knowing it and camped in the pines on Buffalo Dung Lake (today's Yellowhead Lake), which drained into Fraser River. A little farther on they trudged past Moose Lake, too exhausted and dispirited to notice the great isolated tower in the northwest — Mount Robson (12,972), which would be recognized as the highest peak in the Canadian Rockies. They came upon Fraser River proper below Moose Lake, but it was not the broad navigable stream of their dreams. Here the Overlanders split up, as a majority decided to risk their lives running a long series of Fraser River rapids on rafts. Most of these daredevils made it to Fort George and the Cariboo district after eighteen days of miraculous escapes from disaster.

The rest of the party hiked south from the Fraser over a divide to North Thompson River, and rafted down that to Fort

Kamloops and the trail to the Cariboo stage road. As they floated in to Kamloops on October 13, Mrs. Schubert asked for help. A tent was put up for her on shore and she retired into it. Next day she produced a daughter, the first white child born in the interior of British Columbia. Her Shushwap Indian midwife christened the baby "Kamloops," meaning "steelhead trout." But Mrs. Schubert was the conservative type. She changed the name of the girl to Rose.[13]

15

The Rover Boys

As WE HAVE SEEN, Indians and buffalo shared the lower passes, with the handful of trappers who followed up the sparkling streams through the beaver era of the 1820's and 1830's. For twenty years more, Topographical Engineers like Gunnison, Stansbury and Stevens examined new gates, hoping that they would be improvements on South Pass for the thousands of emigrants hurrying anxiously through the Rockies to Utah, Oregon and California before winter trapped them. Then the change came, incredible and complete. In the 1860's and 1870's half a million Americans poured into these same mountains, even filling parts of the high "wastelands" which the earlier emigrants had avoided. A few thousand Indians tried, pathetically and passionately, to resist the tide, but they were washed aside like driftwood.[1] Nothing could stop the push of people who came to find gold and stayed to enjoy a fruitful paradise extending north from the piñon foothills of La Glorieta Pass to the lovely intervales of western Montana.

When the Civil War ended, the word got around nationally that the Rockies were not a wasteland at all. They were benign, solicitous, sheltering, profitable — most of the time. Rockies soil could out-produce Ohio's, by the miracle of cooperative irrigation. The climate was more moderate than Pennsylvania's, with just the right amount of winter cold, summer heat, snow and wind. The wonderful sunlight, the clear, clean air, the soft, wetless rain, the variety of scene, the universal fragrance, the feeling of youthful vitality — these things cured the ailing body and the despairing soul. Beyond each high pass of the Continental Divide were fresh enchantments for any romantic person seeking a fuller life.

Back East, it all sounded too good to be true, and yet something had to lie behind this mass of lyrical hearsay. At last, Congress decided to send out a new crop of experts to examine the Rockies again — for their virtues this time rather than for their evils as a barrier to progress. There were four main groups of them: The United States Geological Exploration of the Fortieth Parallel (War Department, 1867–1872) under Clarence King; Lieutenant George M. Wheeler's United States Geographical Surveys West of the Hundredth Meridian (War Department, 1871–1877); John Wesley Powell's United States Geological and Geographical Survey of the Rocky Mountains (Department of the Interior), the brave staff of which boated down the Colorado in 1869 and 1871; and the United States Geological and Geographical Survey of the Territories (Interior, 1869–1878), directed by the many-sided Ferdinand Vandeveer Hayden. This Hayden Survey was an epic of exploration, so thorough that very little new material has been added from then till now.

The origin of Dr. Hayden's imported front names is obscure. In all other respects he was as American and as unpretentious as a Kansas sunflower. He was born in Massachussetts in 1829, but he grew up on an uncle's Ohio farm, since his father died when he was ten and he couldn't get along with his New England mother. He taught grade school at sixteen, and then obtained a fine education by pestering President Finney of Oberlin College. Finney helped him through Oberlin (1850) and Albany Medical College (1853) to get him off his neck. The exploring bug bit Hayden in 1853 before he could try to practice medicine. During the rest of the decade he roamed the nearer far West, usually as a deadhead with the American

Fur Company up the Missouri, or with a railroad survey crew in Wyoming, or an army group like Captain Raynold's "Yellowstone Expedition" of 1860. He served as a surgeon through the Civil War, taught geology briefly at the University of Pennsylvania, and applied his pestering skill on Congressmen in Washington to get his tiny first funds — five thousand dollars — to begin his monumental Hayden Survey.

He had passed forty by then, which made him much too old to accomplish anything important. His face was ordinary, his body of unremarkable size and shape. His frayed dress coat and tattered felt hat could have belonged to James Whitcomb Riley's hired man. But beneath that undistinguished exterior lay a wild energy, an iron will, great physical endurance, and a quenchless thirst to know nature's secrets — geological, zoological, botanical, biological, ornithological, paleontological.[2] And, in addition to the scientific curiosity, his spirit was animated by a delight in the wonder of outdoors which was as pure as a child's. When he laid out Yellowstone Park in 1871, modern tourism was just beginning. He could guess from his own feelings how millions of visitors would be drawn to that fairyland of bubbling paint pots, rambling geysers, thundering falls and turquoise lakes, with the Atlantic-Pacific Divide curling through the lodgepoles so inconspicuously that nobody could tell on which side he stood. Two years later, Hayden held the same hopes of future fame for Colorado's Mount of the Holy Cross beyond Tennessee Pass, and for the ancient apartment houses of the Cliff Dwellers — today's Mesa Verde National Park, which Father Escalante and his merry men had glimpsed a century before west of Horse Lake Pass.

The commercial possibilities of new terrain interested Hayden deeply. While looking for these around Yellowstone in 1872, he went up Henrys Fork from Fort Hall to the beflowered clearing under Sawtelle Peak at Henrys Lake which Andrew Henry had enjoyed in 1810. Gilman Sawtelle himself, the lake's owner, had Hayden's full attention as he told how he had tried and failed to raise beef because the deer flies descended and the cattle lost weight. As a substitute, he began to raise trout in Henrys Lake. He packed the trout in ice, cut from the lake in winter, and delivered them once a week to the sporting houses of Virginia City over Raynolds Pass. The trout, Mr. Sawtelle intimated, cost the customers almost as much as the girls.

Hayden mapped the Yellowstone region carefully and called Raynolds Pass Madison, or North Pass. His West Pass was Red Rock Pass, and he noted that Targhee Pass (Tahgee, Tyghee or East Pass) was on the old Bannock Trail from Snake River through Yellowstone Park to the Yellowstone and Bighorn valleys. Though impressed by the commercial possibilities of Sawtelle's trout business, he was even more pleased with the passes of the area. He wrote: "The ease with which railroads or wagon roads can be constructed across these great divides is almost incredible to one who has not made them a subject of study." [3]

He continued northward to Fort Ellis at Bozeman town to examine Bozeman and Bridger passes, and also Flathead Pass a few miles north of them, which he described as "the great thoroughfare for the Flathead and Bannock Indians on their way to the buffalo grounds of the *Muscleshell* (Musselshell) River." Early in August of 1872, he made a side trip from Tower Falls in Yellowstone Park to inspect limestone formations said to contain silver beyond Cooke Pass (his Clark's Pass) at the head of Soda Butte Creek — the park's northeast entrance today.

His companion on the side trip was the congenial William Blackmore, an English financier whose brother had just become famous as the author of *Lorna Doone*. Blackmore had invested in the old Sangre de Cristo Grant below Sangre de Cristo Pass, and also in the new town of Colorado Springs and in the Denver and Rio Grande Railroad, both of which were being built by General William J. Palmer of Philadelphia.

Blackmore loved Yellowstone Park as much as Hayden loved it, and he contributed to the cost of the survey there. At Cooke Pass, Hayden did find signs of silver, and he commented on the startling "index finger" shape of Index Peak above it, as John Colter had done in 1808.

THE MAJOR WORK of the Hayden Survey was the mapping of sixty-nine thousand square miles of the Colorado Rockies during the summers of 1873, 1874 and 1875, and that was gratifying to everybody. Denver and Colorado Springs made excellent headquarters. They were extremely civilized towns, and much admired by the hundred or so extremely civilized survey scientists from the East who enjoyed a bath or a ball or an evening of charades now and then. Hayden owned property in Little London — Colorado Springs's nickname — and was often a guest at General Palmer's home near the Garden of the Gods, and at the home of the very-English Margaret Hamp, William Blackmore's sister. Hayden was glad to be able to survey part of Blackmore's Sangre de Cristo land, which soon would provide a right-of-way over La Veta Pass, a variant of Sangre de Cristo Pass, for Palmer's narrow-gauge railroad.

But these were agreeable coincidences, not primary reasons for special treatment. Rock-hunting scientists, like gold-hunting prospectors, found the Colorado Rockies much more interesting than lower parts of the chain because so much of the earth's core lay exposed for inspection, dating back through a thousand million years of assorted zoics. Furthermore, Colorado Territory in the early 1870's was far ahead of Wyoming, Montana and New Mexico in population. This was so even though growth west of the Cochetopa-Tennessee-Gore Pass line of the Western Slope all the way to Utah had been stalled by the Colorado Ute Indians, who were not only well behaved but adroit in holding on to their high, deliciously watered homeland.

By the Treaty of 1868, the United States Senate had given these three thousand five hundred Utes title "forever" to sixteen million acres of Colorado's Western Slope, which was most of it — the White River and Gunnison River valleys, the Elk Range and Charles Baker's dramatic San Juan gold fields.[4] For a while, the Utes were lenient if properly approached, allowing some whites on the Reservation. But then a new gold-silver rush to the San Juan region began in 1871, and this time the patient Utes were less patient. They forbade trespass. To avert a clash, government negotiators induced them, by the usual process of promising compensation which they could not deliver, to release four million acres of the highest San Juans around Baker's Park. Long before this Treaty of 1873 was signed, Coloradans pressed Hayden to map the whole territory. On June 8, 1871, for example, *The Colorado Miner* (Georgetown) declared editorially: "We know of no better way of giving the world a knowledge of our mineral wealth than by having a thorough geological survey."

There was something wonderfully carefree and quixotic about the young men whom Hayden dispatched from his Colorado Springs or Denver office to spend those three summers mapping the land from the highest peaks by triangulation.[5] Their gay spirit recalled that of Father Escalante's companions in 1776. Like the young priests, they plunged into the wilds without the slightest thought of danger. Escalante had felt himself to be armored by his religion, his God, his holy mission to find a route from Santa Fe to California. Hayden's men seemed to be armored by their absorption in the marvels of science. They found things of intense interest at every step and they had no time to be afraid.

Most of them were not yet thirty years of age, and they tried to conceal their youthfulness by wearing ferocious beards. They had been thoroughly educated at places like Harvard and the University of Pennsylvania. Some of them had distinguished antecedents. The geographer Henry Gannett, for whom Wyoming's highest peak would be named, was descended from the Pilgrims of Massachusetts Bay. Albert Charles Peale, the geologist, was a great-grandson of the painter Charles Willson Peale, whose son Titian Peale, you remember, went with Major Long to the Rockies in 1820.

On the whole, they made better mountain men than Major Long and Lieutenant Frémont and some of the other Topographical Engineers. They were neither too timid nor too reckless as they roamed the wilderness, and they appeared to be in better physical condition. They did not shoot their horses accidentally and they had no use for armed escorts, rubber boats, howitzers or guides. They worked in parties of six or eight — a topographer and his assistant, a geologist or two, packers and a cook. Each man rode a mule, and there was a pack train of five or six more mules carrying food, instruments and a Dutch oven. The men seldom unpacked their tents in good weather, preferring bedrolls in the open. They always had an odometer along, for measuring mileage. It was attached to a two-wheel axle by a mule, which was supposed to walk in a straight line. The odometer was their passport when they trespassed on Ute lands. It informed the Utes that they were surveyors, and not settlers, prospectors, politicians, speculators or any other kind of white land-grabber. They had very little trouble with the Utes.

Hayden's Rover Boys could work harder and longer at higher altitudes than many of the earlier explorers. They seemed to get more done with less fuss and fewer mistakes. Most of them made out with less equipment. The notable exception on this score was the survey's phenomenal photographer, William Henry Jackson. His mule, the famous Hypo, was burdened by Jackson's tent darkroom, bath-holder, huge twenty-by-twenty-four camera, wet plates, chemicals, tripod and keg of water for washing plates. Hypo was no mountain goat. He could climb only so high above timberline. From there to the top of a peak or pass, Jackson and his helper had to carry the stuff. Under these nerve-wracking conditions Jackson made pictures which camera men today find quite unbelievably perfect.

During those busy Colorado summers, the survey crews tramped along the humping, curling crest of the Continental Divide from Rabbit Ears Pass in the north to Cumbres Pass on the Colorado–New Mexico border. As a rule, they left headquarters in mid-July, when the streams could be forded after the spring runoff and the snow was melting on even the highest passes. They stayed in the field until late October, unless snow drove them down earlier. They lived for days on end at twelve thousand feet, well above timberline, in the brittle, wind-sighing country of rubble, tarns, ptarmigans and squeaking gopher-like conies, where they could see how the passes linked the streams which had formed them. They named everything that had no name, sometimes putting their own names on their maps, or the names of Eastern scientists whom they admired.[6] When they made it to the top of a peak, they were never too weary to build a rock cairn several feet high as proof that they had been there. Some Hayden cairns still stand, renovated now and then by devoted Colorado Mountain Club members.

In 1873, the topographer Archibald Marvine, aged twenty-five, charted the three trail passes linking Middle and North Parks — Muddy (8772), Troublesome (10,027) and Willow Creek (9683). His imaginative assistant, S. B. Ladd, expressed an intriguing thought. *If* the very low Muddy Pass had been eight hundred feet lower, and *if* Middle Park had been eight hundred feet higher at Gore Canyon of Colorado River near present Kremmling, *then* the Colorado would have been an Eastern Slope waterway, leaving Middle Park through Muddy Pass to join the North Platte in North Park. The combined streams would have made a river almost as large as the Mississippi. Wyoming would have become a corn-and-hog state rivaling Iowa, and people would have voyaged to the Rockies in deluxe steamers, debarking at some Denver-displacing port at the west foot of Berthoud Pass. Ship ahoy!

From Middle Park, Marvine accompanied Dr. Hayden, William Jackson and Hypo on their trip over Tennessee Pass and down Eagle River to confirm the existence of the Mount of the Holy Cross.[7] Then Marvine led his men north by a network of well-worn Ute elk-hunting trails up and over the enchanting meadow-aspen-lodgepole area of the Flattops, known today by all dedicated trout fishermen, on the divide between Colorado and White rivers. They mapped its hills and myriad little blue lakes and crystal streams, including what has become the celebrated Marvine Lake, Marvine Creek and Big and Little Marvine peaks west of Trappers Lake. From the Ute Indian Agency on White River near present Meeker, they followed the Yellowjacket Pass stretch of Captain Berthoud's Denver–Salt Lake stage route and left it to move on north into Wyoming by the government mail road running just west of Bridger Pass to Rawlins and the Union Pacific Railroad.

Other Hayden parties examined the familiar mining camp passes west and southwest of Denver, and toured the new Summitville mining district in southern Colorado and the passes above it which we call Ellwood, Summit, Silver, Railroad and Wolf Creek (U.S. Route 160 crosses Wolf Creek today west of Alamosa). One group mapped the Sangre de Cristos southward from Poncha Pass, noting the new Hayden Pass trail, twenty miles south of Poncha, which shortened the pack train distance by thirty miles from Canon City and Wet Mountain Valley to San Luis Valley and Cochetopa Pass. Hayden Pass was not named for the survey director. The name honored another Hayden, a Texas Creek settler who had pioneered the crossing up Hayden Creek from the Arkansas below Galena Peak and down Hayden Pass Creek into the north end of San Luis Valley. Continuing south below the great Crestone summits which Pike's frostbitten men had known too well, the scientists found a new toll road over Mosca Pass, an indication that the long reign of Sangre de Cristo Pass as the main crossing to San Luis Valley was ending.[8]

Some of the trails of the Utes from their Western Slope valleys to the plains had become prospector trails by 1873. Henry Gannett, Albert Charles Peale, and six helpers took one of these trails to reach the Elk Mountains. Their mules carried them from Denver along the Turkey Creek–Kenosha Summit stage road to South Park, and on the Weston Pass road through the Mosquito Range to the Upper Arkansas seven miles south of California Gulch. From there they rode four miles to Twin Lakes under the tremendous domes of Mount Elbert and Mount Massive, with the Mount of the Holy Cross just out of their sight as the northern anchor of this thick and overwhelming Sawatch Range.

They ascended Lake Creek to its fork where the present Independence Pass road begins its climb up the north branch toward Aspen — its harrowing or winsome climb, depending on how one feels about shelf roads to a no-man's-land twelve thousand feet above the sea. The scientists didn't go that way. They followed the Ute trail up the south fork, a scenic slot walled on the east by ridges of red, orange, yellow and purple shale, and, on the west, by Grizzly Peak (14,000), Garfield Peak (13,800) and Red Mountain· (13,500) — one of many "red mountains" in Colorado's highly oxidized ferrous uplands. Above Peekaboo Gulch, they slogged around the edges of beaver ponds and reached the big cirque under the Continental Divide. Here a steep shale path left their Lake Pass trail to zigzag over Red Mountain Pass (12,200) near the junction of the north-south Sawatch Range and the west-running Elk Range. Of Lake Pass itself (12,226) Henry Gannett wrote: "Upon the summit is a little lake of water from melting snows. On both sides are high walls about a fourth of a mile apart . . . an illustration of the slow wearing away of the crest between the sources of the streams."

Taylor Park spread away below them — a lonely high basin then, even as it is today, for all of the summer sailors on Taylor Reservoir. They observed how Gunnison River tributaries fell into the park's grasslands and forests, tumbling down from the passes of the Elk or Sawatch ranges — Taylor Pass (11,900), linking the park to the Roaring Fork of the Colorado; Cottonwood (12,126), Tincup (12,154) and Williams (11,762) passes, leading from Taylor Park to the Upper Arkansas Valley. The men rode down Red Mountain Creek, to Taylor River, crossed it south of the picturesque red, white and green Italian Mountain, and moved southwest and out of the park along Rock Brook Trail Creek, Spring Creek and Deadman Gulch.

That put them on Cement Creek, which led to the exquisite valley of East River near today's Crested Butte. The valley rose in steep and stunning multicolored slopes toward Pearl Pass (12,715) and Coffee Pot Pass (12,500), Triangle Pass (12,500) and West Maroon (12,400), Schofield (10,-700), Yule (12,200) and Anthracite (10,150). In mapping Schofield Pass, Gannett was impressed by its trachyte, igneous cores, Cretaceous clays and limestones. He was moved too by "the beautiful green lake fed by the melting of the snows," (Emerald Lake), and by the booming waterfall into the Punch Bowl. This last remains a spectacle to four-wheel-drive travelers on the trip from Crested Butte over Schofield and down the twenty-seven-degree grade of Crystal River canyon to Crystal ghost town and to Marble.[9]

Perhaps the greatest adventure of the Hayden Surveys was mapping the gold-silver lands released by the Utes. It began on a "delightfully cool day," in July, 1874, when young Franklin Rhoda and other members of the San Juan Division left Colorado Springs and rode up the new Ute Pass road through the canyon of Fountain Creek. They entered South Park over a second low pass to be named Wilkerson after an English rancher at Badger Mountain, and they followed the centuries-old track over Trout Creek Pass, Poncha Pass and Cochetopa Pass to Los Pinos Ute Agency and Lake Fork of the Gunnison. There was no pleasant Lake City yet. But Lake San Cristobal was on display ("By far the finest of the many little lakes we saw during the Summer") and also the "slumgullion" of Slumgullion Pass ("From the east a rapid mountain stream flows into Lake Fork near . . . which a large mass of yellow volcanic material has been deposited. This slide probably happened not too long ago").[10]

They did not go on southwest at once over Cinnamon Pass to Baker's Park. They rode west instead up Lake Fork's cheerful branch, Henson Creek, and north up Nellie Creek nearly to the top of the great granite landmark, Uncompahgre Peak (14,301), where they tethered their mules to boulders and climbed the last thousand feet of rubble on foot. The view from Uncompahgre Peak was of Charles Baker's San Juan Uplift to the west and southwest. A new vista stretched north for eighty miles — the tortured mesas gashed by the Black Canyon of the Gunnison and, beyond, the Elks running eastward from Mount Sopris (12,823) through the line of fourteen-thousand footers — Capitol Peak, Snowmass, Maroon Bells, Cathedral, Castle — to the end of the range near Lake Pass.

Ada D. Wilson, topographer of the San Juan Division, and Franklin Rhoda took altitudes on Uncompahgre and returned to Henson Creek.[11] They pushed west upstream to what silver miners would name American Flats before 1874 ended — a deathly-still alpine meadow just below what we call Yvonne (12,250) and Engineer (12,800) passes. They forebore to put their mules on the slide down the west side to Mineral Point and the start of Uncompahgre River. Today this brutal slope carries a zigzag trace for four-wheel-drive cars which is as frightful as the west-side shelf of Mosquito Pass from Fairplay to Leadville, or the sliding shelf down the west side of Argentine Pass.

They went back to Lake San Cristobal, crossed Cinnamon Pass to "far-famed Baker's Park," and spent a happy month scrambling about that fascinating cul-de-sac, to the amusement of the pioneer miners of Howardsville, Eureka and Silverton. One of their tasks was to find pass routes which wagons could use for hauling in heavy mining machinery. They knew that the deep and beautiful seventeen-mile canyon of Animas River up from the south was impassable. The Coal Creek Pass–Molas Divide trail around the east side of Sultan Mountain (today's U.S. Route 550 from Durango to Silverton) was scenically splendid but practically useless. The third way in from the south, the Bear Creek trail around the west side of Sultan Mountain, was better than the other two but beset "by bogs, fallen timber and rock-slides."

Wagon road pass prospects on the north were still more discouraging. From Silverton, the scientists went up Mineral Creek and over Red Mountain Pass (11,018) — the present course of the sensational Million Dollar Highway between Silverton and Ouray. The pass itself was not too bad, but, when they struck the awesome box canyon of the Uncompahgre River where U.S. Route 550 shelfs down the cliff to Ouray, Rhoda noted bluntly: "The canyon bars all egress."

Westward? For a week they toiled from Silverton up the south fork of Mineral Creek between Vermilion Peak and Rolling Mountain and over an impossible twelve-thousand-foot pass from Las Animas River to San Miguel River drainage. Rhoda called it "Bear Creek Pass," but it had no relation to present Bear Creek just west of Sultan Mountain and it has no name today. It brought them to Lake Hope and "San Miguel Lake filled with fine trout" — by which Rhoda meant Trout Lake at the north foot of Lizard Head Pass on the present Cortez-Telluride road. They mapped Lizard Head Pass ("Marked by a curious monument of trachyte two hundred and ninety feet high"), climbed Wilson Peak (14,017) and Mount Sneffels (14,150) and went back to Silverton by the same impossible "Bear Creek Pass." [12]

They found a possible pass at last to the east, though not Cinnamon Pass, of which Rhoda wrote: "How the Saguache people ever expect to bring a wagon road up this I cannot see." It was August 18, 1874, when they left Howardsville and ascended Cunningham Gulch, "up which," Rhoda wrote, "a well-marked trail leads over to the Rio Grande. After passing the main bend, which is about two miles east of Howardsville, the side-slopes become steeper and steeper, and finally end altogether in becoming nearly vertical bluffs . . . A number of mines are located high up the slopes wherever they are not too steep to be ascended . . . Near the head of the gulch, the trail is very muddy and badly cut up . . . It now leaves the creek and ascends the east slope. The grade may be appreciated by calling to mind the fact that from the bed of the stream to the pass the rise is about one thousand five hundred feet in one-and-a-half miles. The incessant travel over this trail by miners with their horses, mules and burros keeps it in a bad condition. The really bad part is only a small part of the whole distance. On the summit the ground is gently rolling . . . The elevation of the pass above the sea, as determined by a single reading of the mercurial barometer, is 12,090 feet."

When Rhoda made these Stony Pass notes, the pack-train trail ran a bit south of the Stony Pass (12,594) road which would be built over the Continental Divide in time between Canby and Green Mountains, where the Rio Grande starts its long trip to the Gulf of Mexico. The San Juan pioneers called it Rio Grande Pass in 1874, or Cunningham Pass, after the Chicago promoter of Cunningham Gulch. The distance to it from the supply town of Del Norte in San Luis Valley was ninety miles, past Wagon Wheel Gap, Antelope Park, the mouth of Weminuche Creek below Weminuche Pass, and the mouths of Lost Trail, Pole and Bear creeks. At Lost Trail Creek, wagon cargos from Del Norte were shifted to pack trains for the sixteen-mile climb over Stony Pass to Howardsville.[13]

Rhoda's party examined the easy east-slope trail as far down as Lost Trail Creek, and then entertained themselves by climbing the classic Rio Grande Pyramid (13,838) twelve miles southeast of Stony Pass. They were astonished to find on top a neat ptarmigan's nest of alpine grass, and "a nicely built monu-

ment of stones, which we increased in height to about six feet
. . . The fact that the monument was on the true summit indicated the fact that its builder was something else than a
common miner." Next, they rode over Hunchback Pass (12,-
487), which was eight miles south along the Continental Divide from Stony Pass. They reached it up the Bear Creek fork
of the Rio Grande. From Hunchback, they climbed Mount
Nebo (13,492) for a better view of the valley of Vallecito
Creek, of the marching Grenadier peaks, and of a second
spectacular group "all very steep and rugged, more like needles
than mountains" — today's Needle Range, of course.

Near Nebo's summit, Rhoda's female mule "Bones" almost
tramped on a small grizzly bear which jumped up and scam-
pered off. The appearance of this animal combined with the
appearance of the ptarmigan nest and cairn on Rio Grande
Pyramid caused Rhoda to complain: "It is ever thus: when
you feel you are treading a path never trod by a living thing
before, and your imagination begins to build for itself a
romantic picture, if some such vile worldly thing as a paper
collar or a whisky-bottle does not intrude itself on the sight,
some beastly quadruped needs must break the previous solitude
and scatter your air castle to the winds. To show our utter disgust for all animate things that could not live below this
altitude, we yelled and threw stones after the bear till he finally
was lost to sight far down the mountain-side. In our hate we
even wished he might have been in a position whence we
could have rolled rocks down on him." The incident explains
the naming of Bear Creek and, in the 1890's, of Beartown
silver camp below Hunchback Pass.

Intruders notwithstanding, the San Juan Division ended the
1874 survey season on a high note as the first whites since
James Pattie to describe crossing Weminuche Pass (10,629).
They left Baker's Park for good by the southern Molas Divide
trail in late September. From Animas River at present Durango
they moved east to Los Pinos River (Bayfield) and upstream on

the old Ute trail to the Rio Grande. The weather had not changed much since Pattie's snowy traverse on May 1, 1827. Snow fell on Rhoda and his friends too — for four days — and was, at the top of Weminuche on October 7, "two or three feet deep, which, with our shoes nearly worn out, was very disagreeable. We knew now that winter had commenced and we wanted to get out of the mountains as fast as our mules could carry us. The pass by this route was good, though covered with snow. In the summer it must be very easy and pleasant."

They hurried from Weminuche down to the Rio Grande, on to Wagon Wheel Gap and Del Norte, and across San Luis Valley and Mosca Pass to the plains. On October 19, Dr. Hayden welcomed them back to his survey headquarters in Denver.

WHILE HAYDEN was visiting Colorado's Mount of the Holy Cross in 1873, the Army Corps of Engineers concluded a bit of Wyoming business which Captain Raynolds and Jim Bridger had left undone in 1860. It concerned the rediscovery of Two Ocean Pass and the finding of other gates to Yellowstone Park from the Wind River–Bighorn watershed. The assignment fell to Captain William Albert Jones, a thirty-two-year-old West Pointer from St. Louis who was all get up and go, and none of this tea drinking on duty, continental or otherwise. The Jones party, in contrast to the ragamuffin Hayden Survey crews, was plushly constituted: eighteen scientists, Indian guides and servants; sixty-six pack and saddle mules; eight wagons and a cavalry escort. It convened at Fort Stambaugh, seventeen miles northeast of South Pass, and on June 27 started north on the customary road past Camp Augur (Lander) and Fort Brown (Washakie).[14] It crossed Wind River, the low east end of the Owl Creek Range near Mexican Pass, and on to the Greybull and the Stinking Water (Shoshone) at today's Cody. Jones examined the Indian trial up the Shoshone's south fork to "Stinking Water Pass," which is the present horseback trail from Cody to Dubois over Shoshone Pass (9730). He inspected the lower part of a pretty tributary next, and reported: "I have given Ishawooa River the Indian name of a peculiar shaped rock — a finger-shaped column about three miles up the southwest fork." If he had fully explored this "southwest fork" (Ishawooa Creek) he would have crossed the Absaroka Range into Yellowstone Park at Ishawooa Pass (9870).

The expedition dropped its wagons on July 27 and struggled up the north fork of the Shoshone on the difficult trail through Shoshone Canyon, which every thrilled tourist photographs today as he approaches the Sylvan Pass east entrance to the park. When the trail left the Shoshone's north fork and moved up what is now called Jones Creek into Yellowstone, he took pen in hand and wrote: "The trail leads through a perfectly lovely country of open pine forests, carpeted with long soft grass and the mountain huckleberry. We camped in a spot that was absolutely perfect, having ice-cold water, a broad meadow of thick grass, with dark forests of spruce and pine close around, carpeted with a long grass that makes our camp-bed feel like down." On August 2, they reached Jones Pass (9450), which was six miles north of Sylvan Pass (8559) along the crest of the Absarokas, but very much like it. Jones's reaction was that of the modern Sylvan Pass traveler on U.S. Route 14–20. "After the Indian guides, I was the first to reach the summit of the pass, and, before I knew it, had given vent to a screeching yell, which was taken up with a wild echo by the Indians, for there, seemingly at their feet, and several miles nearer than I had expected was spread out a scene of exceeding beauty — Yellowstone Lake."

The Jones party spent the rest of August, 1873, enjoying the park. Then Jones's Snake Indian guide led the men south up the Yellowstone to its Atlantic Creek source and over Two Ocean Pass to Pacific Creek and Snake River in full glorious view of Jackson Lake and Grand Teton. The Captain had only one last problem now — finding the way from Pacific Creek to Wind River headwaters over what we have been calling Togwotee Pass ever since John Colter's alleged crossing in 1808, though the pass did not have this name, or any name, of its own in September, 1873. To find the pass, Jones felt, was paramount. His whole future required that he succeed where so many before him had failed — Captain Bonneville in the 1830's, Captain Raynolds and Jim Bridger in 1860, even Dr. Hayden in 1871.

And success seemed to depend on how he handled his Indian guide, whose Snake name sounded to him like "Togwotee," which meant "shoots with a spear," and, also, "goes from this place." "Only one Indian in the party," Jones wrote on September 4, "knows the country between here and Wind River, and he seems to be getting proud of the power he has over us and wants to exercise it a little." Togwotee did exercise it by disappearing for that whole day to amuse himself trapping beaver on the Snake. When he returned that night, Jones instructed his soldiers to chain him up and to inform him that he would soon be a resident of the stockade at Camp Brown if he delayed things longer.

The threat worked. Early next day, Togwotee, "cheerful, obedient, contented," took the party from Pacific Creek over to Blackrock Creek and up the Togwotee Pass trail, heavily impeded by underbrush because of disuse in recent years. Two days were spent chopping a steep zigzag path through to the top, which caused Jones to comment: "I am free to confess it seemed about as feasible as to lead the train over a squirrel-trail up a tree." And still he saw virtues in the traverse: "The approaches are quite easy. A railroad could be carried over it without extraordinary expense."

Captain Jones and his crew returned East in October, and Jones went on to achieve the rank of brigadier general and to have a bright career after retirement as owner of a huge oyster plantation on Chesapeake Bay. But the great triumph of his life was his reconnaissance of northwestern Wyoming in 1873, during which he conquered the Absaroka Mountains and became the official discoverer of Shoshone Pass, Ishawooa Creek, Jones Pass and that superb gate to the Tetons, Togwotee Pass.

16

Timberline!

While Hayden's surveyors were playing with lightning on the peaks during the Seventies, the Rockies scene was changing faster than the population could adjust to it — but mostly in Colorado. In the Canadian Rockies, from South Kootenay north to Yellowhead Pass and Mount Robson, white men were still as scarce as in Dr. Hector's time. Montana had a copper boom in its future, but its gold placers were almost exhausted and its agriculture was in the pioneer stage. Although everyone had heard that Wyoming women had won the vote at South Pass City, Americans generally knew as little about Wind River, Togwotee Pass and the charms of Jackson Hole and Grand Teton as they knew about Tibet.

Colorado's mineral wealth, found in ever-increasing amounts along that exposed granite core of the Continental Divide, was a main cause of change and expansion. The several million dollars' worth of gold which had been picked from the gulches near Denver before the Civil War seemed paltry now. Mining men had come to think in terms of a billion-dollar production in terrain stretching from the San Juans and Wet Mountains to Taylor Park of the Upper Gunnison, Elk and Tenmile ranges and on to North Park and the Hahns Peak part of the Sierra Madre north of Rabbit Ears and Buffalo passes. Their huge smelters and other sophisticated plants for extracting metal were built after 1870. The plants required whole towns of workers to run them, and they were served by armies of freight-ers, in contrast to the sluice boxes for catching free gold at Tar-ryall and Buckskin Joe during the burro-train years. It was no wonder that Denver leaders visualized a metropolis of a million people rising in two decades from the hamlet on Cherry Creek.

From this lure of precious metal stemmed other compulsions pulling hordes of newcomers over the passes to new parts of these highest Rockies. Some came to homestead farms and ranches in South and Middle Parks, in San Luis Valley, in the Upper Arkansas, and beyond Gore Pass on Yampa River north of the Ute Indian Reservation. Some were busy supplying all these new-rich mine owners with whatever they wanted wherever their mines were, even far above timberline — every-thing from Steinway pianos and aerial trams to pressed-brick privies and vintage champagne. Hundreds of engineers hiked along the Continental Divide making surveys for railroad tun-nels through the wall. Writers wrote articles and artists drew sketches for magazines to satisfy the curiosity of readers back East about this incredible mountain West.

Most surprising of other compulsions was the rise of tourism on a large scale only a few years behind the post-Civil War growth of Newport, Saratoga Springs, the White Mountains of New Hampshire and the Virginia "Hots." Tourists poured from trains into Denver and Colorado Springs when no proper facilities existed as yet to house them. They made their own paths through the Garden of the Gods and up Pikes Peak, and up Grays Peak from Georgetown. They bathed at Idaho Springs, at the soda springs of Manitou, at Poncha Springs be-low Poncha Pass. They attended fancy dress balls at Twin Lakes. They camped in Estes Park and boated on Grand Lake before either place had a name.

And tourism, as much as anything else, was what finally put roads over that extended nightmare of a barrier, the Front Range, into Middle Park straight west of Denver. In the 1860's the irrepressible William Byers acquired Middle Park's old Ute bathing pool, Hot Sulphur Springs, and worked to make it the one Rocky Mountain spa which fashionable people could not afford to miss. He had reason to be enthusiastic. Hundreds of tourists took the trouble to reach Hot Sulphur by horseback from Georgetown over Captain Berthoud's rugged trail.

Meanwhile, Byers, as we have seen, supported every kind of Middle Park road scheme, starting in 1862 with that of William H. Russell of the Central Overland California and Pikes Peak Express. Russell chose Vasquez Pass (11,655), up West Clear Creek near Berthoud Pass, and did get a road almost to the top from Empire, but could not push it over. Some years later, another ex-C.O.C. executive, John S. Jones, toiled to conquer Jones Pass (12,453), also up West Clear Creek. Jones owned a mill at Empire, and he was a noted freighter who had performed the feat of moving seven loaded wagons over Breckenridge Pass during the 1865–1866 winter of deep snow. He had a ranch on the Colorado River near Hot Sulphur Springs at the lower end of Byers Canyon, and he meant to reach it from Jones Pass by way of Williams Fork River. He built his road over all right, but there is no record that wagons could use it, not even his own.[1]

Berthoud Pass was not entirely neglected. In 1865, the Denver promoter, Bela M. Hughes, surveyed a new route from Salt Lake City eastward across Gore Pass to Middle Park. Hughes was assisted by a troop of one hundred and fifty California volunteers and their twenty-two wagons. When the soldiers reached the west foot of Berthoud Pass (11,313) and faced the problem of hauling the wagons up the Fraser River trail, they resigned from the project. They took the wagons up the easier Ranch Creek trail and over Boulder Pass, which was twelve miles north of Berthoud on the north side of James Peak next to Devil's Thumb Pass. From the broad top of Boulder, they snubbed the wagons on down to Yankee Doodle Lake and South Boulder Creek.

During that same summer, a party of one hundred Mormons

with thirty-nine wagons and teams chose to cross Boulder Pass also on their westward trek from Denver to Salt Lake City. The awful east-side pitch above Yankee Doodle Lake should have daunted them, but there was no daunting Mormons on their way to paradise at Deseret.[2] The wagons were taken apart and carried piece by piece to the top — each man, woman and child having something to carry. As they toiled up, they paused now and then to sing hymns.

To some rail fans today, Boulder Pass is Corona Pass. To road students, it is Rollins Pass. The Gentile who guided the singing Mormons up South Boulder Creek and on to the pass was a forthright, cheerful prospector from Gold Dirt and Buckskin Joe named John Quincy Adams Rollins, aged forty-nine, and almost as broad as he was tall. He was born in New Hampshire at a time when proud Yankees honored President Monroe's Secretary of State by attaching his full name to their sons. Rollins moved west through tumultuous business adventures in Boston, Chicago, St. Louis, Cheyenne and Denver. He made and lost large fortunes in farming, real estate, lumber, cattle, hotels, mining and freighting.

He was about to lose seventy-five thousand dollars more in the Butterfield Stage Company. Another sixty thousand dollars would sink in the South Park salt works below Fairplay and Trout Creek Pass. Salt was used in the 1870's by Denver ore refineries, but it was often cheaper to haul the stuff two thousand miles by rail from Pennsylvania than to freight it a hundred miles over Kenosha Pass. Rollins seemed to play with money as he played billiards — for the pure joy of the game. His joy in billiards reached a peak in 1866 over Brendlinger's Cigar Store at Blake and F Streets, Denver. For thirty-two solid hours he matched cues at eight hundred dollars a game with banker Charles A. Cook. In the end, Cook owed and paid him eleven thousand dollars before falling asleep on the billiard table.

After the Mormons and California Volunteers got their sixty-one wagons over his crossing, Rollins decided that it was time for another business adventure. He would build a forty-mile Rollins Pass road linking his new town of Rollinsville on South Boulder Creek to Hot Sulphur Springs and the Gore Pass road to Salt Lake. Hot Sulphur tourists would use it and, furthermore, Middle Park could certainly stand a second resort — a Rollins stage stop, say, at the junction of the Ranch Creek (Rollins Pass) and Fraser River (Berthoud Pass) trails. Rollins began building in 1866. His progress was so slow that nobody paid much attention for years — not even the rich and complacent merchants of Georgetown on the other side of James Peak. They did not seem to be aware that, lacking their own Berthoud Pass road, Rollins's route would bypass them completely. His new Rollinsville, reached from Denver through Black Hawk and Central City, could become the tourist depot for Middle Park, and also its supply center.

They awoke to reality in June of 1873 when Rollins finished blasting a ledge above Yankee Doodle Lake up the east face to timberline and around the north precipice of Rollins Pass (11,680). The road opened late that summer. It cost forty thousand dollars — twice as much as expected. But to Rollins, spending that kind of money was as easy as playing billiards at eight hundred dollars a game. Besides he enjoyed being the first to penetrate the Continental Divide due west of Denver. The road was not restful, being more nerve-wracking than today's version for standard cars — and today's version from Yankee Doodle Lake to the top has a few equals in the Rockies for making one's hair stand on end.[3]

The Georgetown crowd pretended to ignore Rollins's pioneer trace even as they pulled themselves together, raised twenty-five thousand dollars and formed the Georgetown, Empire and Middle Park Wagon Road Company. The stock books were kept by Thomas Guanella, Georgetown's dealer in exotic groceries who supplied the high-living residents with *champignons au naturel* and *petits pois fins*.[4] In June of 1874, the company hired William Cushman, head of Georgetown's First National Bank, to start construction up Hook Creek from the Jones Pass–Vasquez Pass road five miles above Empire. He made good time on the three-mile grind to the top of Berthoud Pass, partly because the slope had been denuded of its Engelmann spruce to provide timbers for the deepening mines of Clear Creek. The eleven-mile descent down the Middle Park side went well, too, to where Berthoud's pack trail ended and the Hot Sulphur Springs — Salt Lake City road began — the present site of Denver's ski resort, Winter Park. The trees were cut back forty feet on either side and swamps were paved with corduroy.

On November 18, 1874, all of Georgetown gathered at 7 A.M. beneath a banner strung across the front of the First National Bank. Six horses pulled up a new Concord stage of the Colorado Stage Company. The driver was Billy Updike, the daredevil who had scared General Grant almost to death in 1868 on the Golden–Central City run over Guy Hill. Seven Georgetown leaders boarded the coach, and also Mrs. Thomas Guanella in a party dress and picture hat. She rode as far as Empire. At 10:45 A.M., the coach reached the top of Berthoud at timberline and Updike blocked it to let the horses blow. The autumn day was crisply cold but so clear that Updike claimed to see a weasel perched on Byers Peak eight miles away. Then they rolled down to the west foot of the pass at Mr. Grimshaw's home on the willowed banks of the Fraser. Before dark they were drinking toasts to the Berthoud Pass road and having supper in Hot Sulphur Springs.[5] A supper guest was that cheerful John Quincy Adams Rollins. He observed with wry amusement that no toasts were proposed to his Rollins Pass road, even though he had bought a little stock in the Berthoud Pass Company just to help out these Georgetown johnny-come-latelys whom he had beaten to Middle Park by more than a year.

BREECHING THE FRONT RANGE at Berthoud and Rollins Pass, at Jones and Vasquez, was hard enough. Breeching it farther south was impossible, or so it was said by Georgetown residents in the 1860's. The Continental Divide north of Berthoud Pass was awesomely grand as it moved north through the round brown humps of Parry Peak, Mount Bancroft and James Peak — all thirteen-thousand footers. And yet it had a reassuring regularity. South of Berthoud, the Divide was the opposite of reassuring — a topographical bad dream of gale-whipped summits flung about like jackstones and bound together by sharp ridges.

The whole batch of monster mountains dipped near the head of Clear Creek at an unnamed gap, and dipped again a mile farther at the top of Grizzly Gulch — Quail Pass or Irwin Pass, named for the mining pioneer, Dick Irwin. Then came the largest of the monsters, Torreys Peak (14,264) and Grays Peak (14,274), eight miles southwest of Georgetown. Two miles south of Grays Peak was the highest of the binding ridges, and on it, above the source of Leavenworth Creek, was a notch called Sanderson's Pass, relating to the Sanderson stage line family. As Hayden's survey showed, when Sanderson's Pass became Snake River Pass and then Argentine Pass, the notch was 13,132 feet above sea level, highest in the whole two thousand miles of the Continental Divide. It stood 4500 feet above Georgetown — a vertical rise of some hundreds of feet more than that of any other Divide crossing.

Georgetown miners had trudged early to the head of Leavenworth Creek, where a camp, East Argentine, was made on the bleak ptarmigan tundra at twelve thousand feet. Tourists liked to come up the South Clear Creek trail toward Guanella Pass to picnic at Green Lake, or to fork their way steeply up Leavenworth Creek to climb Mount McClellan above East Argentine. The west side of Argentine Pass was a forty-degree rubble pitch. A small, nimble horse could slither down the three-mile trail on its rump to Peru Creek and the future sites of Montezuma and

Chihuahua, near the junction of Peru Creek and Snake River.

We have explained that Snake River has a branch, St. John's Creek, flowing down from Glacier Mountain in the southwest, and from the divide there leading to the North Fork of Swan River. All through the 1860's, Georgia Gulch and Breckenridge miners had found gold and silver on St. John's Creek, and northeast right up to the west foot of Argentine Pass, hardly a dozen miles from Georgetown. But ore could not be carried up that rubble pitch. As we have noted, the distance from the Montezuma-Peru area to the Denver smelters back past Glacier Mountain and south over Georgia Pass to South Park and east over Kenosha Pass was two hundred miles. There was no mining future for Peru Creek.

No future until a pioneer who called himself "Commodore" Stephen Decatur slid down to it from Argentine Pass in 1867. This New Jersey-born Decatur was not the hero of Tripoli. He was really one of the famous Brosses, a brother of Governor William Bross of Illinois, for whom, inexplicably, Mount Bross above Hoosier Pass was named. But he didn't want to be a Bross, or a Williams College alumnus, or any of the other things he actually was, such as the bigamist husband of two white and several Indian wives, and the father of five children, *and* a Mexican War hero. He turned up in Georgetown as Stephen Decatur. When various Bross relatives trailed him there to make him a Bross again, he denied ever having laid eyes on them. He was Stephen Decatur, a man of many missions whose motto, in the words of his biographer, Inez Hunt, was "no orthodoxy, no monogamy, no monotony." He took on his next mission as he took a slug of whiskey or a pretty girl — because he liked the way it felt. His plan was to make Peru Creek the greatest silver district in the Rockies by putting a road over Argentine Pass. The capital of the district would be his own new town, "Silveropolis."

He raised ten thousand dollars for his Georgetown and Snake River Wagon Road Company, the directors of which in-

cluded William Byers, and the Central City promoter, Henry
M. Teller, the future senator. On June 6, 1867, Georgetown's
Colorado Miner reported: "On Monday last, Commodore
Decatur surveyed, staked and laid out a portion of the Georgetown, Argentine and Silveropolis Wagon Road . . . The ascent
is rendered comparatively easy by starting the road from the
head of Rose Street, running thence toward the right hand fork
of Clear Creek, then across the face of the mountain to the
summit of the bench near the left hand fork of Clear Creek."

The Commodore's friend, Joe Watson, did the first building, but the work was so frightening that new crews had to be
hired every few weeks. Even so, the road was pushed up
Leavenworth Creek and above timberline to East Argentine in
1868, and to the cyclonic top of Argentine Pass a year later.
The Commodore loved to utter flowery phrases, but he had to
restrain himself on his road so far. He announced merely: "It's
every bit as safe as Virginia Canyon." That was not a glowing
recommendation. When Walt Whitman traveled the Virginia
Canyon shelf road once from Idaho Springs to Central City he
said, "The only safe way to get to Central is on your hands
and knees — and that's risky."

In the spring of 1870, Decatur's vertiginous trace, barely
wider than a wagon track, was cut diagonally down the west side
of Argentine Pass to Peru Creek, Silveropolis and Chihuahua.
The effort exhausted the company's ten thousand dollars. The
Commodore was beginning to drink quite a lot, and some of
his employers thought that he was spending as much money
for whiskey as for blasting powder. By the time a toll gate was
installed near Waldorf four miles above Georgetown and another gate below Silveropolis, he had to resign from the management, ostensibly to promote Silveropolis (later Decatur)
and to write rhapsodic articles about Peru Creek for the *Colorado Miner.*

It was just as well. The Georgetown and Snake River Wagon
Road became a headache to the succession of owners who tried

to make it pay. Snow blocked Argentine Pass until mid-July and after late September. If Charley Utter crossed out of season with a pack train he was apt to see a mule or two blown off the shelf. The grade required doubling and tripling of wagon teams. Tolls didn't begin to cover the cleanup cost of rock slides. In a few years the company stopped trying to clean up. The road simply stayed blocked until a customer wanted over badly enough to remove the slide himself. For these reasons, the road did little to promote the mines of Montezuma–Peru Creek. By 1877, it was just a very difficult pack train trail most of the time.

Meanwhile, two Snake River pioneers, William and Emerson Webster, of the Montezuma Silver Mining Company, used their leisure to build a freight road which would at least shorten the long Georgia Pass–South Park trek out of the Peru district. From Montezuma they ran their road six miles south up Snake River without too much trouble along the austere red wall of the Continental Divide and over a gap called Handcart Pass (12,108). The gap led to Handcart Gulch and the North Fork of the South Platte River, which flowed down in a few miles to the Denver–South Park road east of Kenosha Pass. What the Webster brothers had done was to eliminate South Park from the route by getting out of their Snake River–Peru Creek pocket on the Denver side of Kenosha.

Handcart Gulch had been prospected in the 1860's by two Norwegians who plodded up there from Canon City, hitched like mules to a cart loaded with their supplies. Their gulch angled off right from the North Fork. It became, above the junction, the lively Hall Valley mining area. Though Hall Valley was managed by genteel Englishmen, it was distinctly on the rough side (one of its camps was called Gouge-Eye). The Englishmen built a reduction plant for their Whale Mine which used some of J. Q. A. Rollins's South Park salt. The Websters changed the name of Handcart Pass to Webster Pass when they opened their freight road over it. In the *Colorado*

Miner of October 19, 1878, Commodore Decatur described the event in his usual vivid prose:

> The blockade on the mining industry of the Snake River mining district has been raised. The Snake River and Hall Valley Wagon Road has been completed. Hipla! Hurrah! Carry the news everywhere! . . . The road just finished is said to be the best and have the easiest grade of any road in the state. There is Joy in the Halls of Montezuma![6]

DECATUR'S ARGENTINE PASS ROAD was a disappointment to Snake River people, who saw that a miracle would have to happen to give them a real stage connection with Georgetown. The miracle did happen, just as the Webster Pass road opened. It had the shape of a fantastic silver boom on the old California Gulch diggings below Tennessee Pass, and the rise of a new metropolis called Leadville. The mining world was stunned in 1878 by evidence that Leadville's mines there on the Upper Arkansas were going to be as rich as Virginia City's Comstock Lode, the wealth of which had built most of San Francisco.

The shortest route on paper from Denver to Leadville was up Clear Creek from Golden past Georgetown, over the Continental Divide to Snake River and Tenmile Creek, and over the Divide once more by Fremont (Tenmile) Pass to the head of the Arkansas. Argentine Pass had failed as a practical stage crossing, but there was that unnamed gap just north of it and Irwin Pass at the head of Clear Creek itself. Captain Berthoud had filed on the gap years earlier as a possible route for the westering continuation of William A. H. Loveland's Colorado Central Railroad which, by 1878, had pushed up Clear Creek from Golden all the way to Georgetown. Loveland, aged fifty-four, was a Massachusetts native who had been wounded at Chapultepec, had mined for gold in California, and had worked futilely to put a canal across Panama for Commodore Vanderbilt. He had arrived at Golden in 1859 with a wagon load of axes and mouse traps, the profits from which started him building railroads and fire-brick plants, and discovering coal mines.

Loveland perceived the glittering advantages of getting the first good road to Leadville's treasure. He set up the Bakerville and Leadville Wagon Road Company during the winter of 1878–1879 (Bakerville, where tourists took off for Grays Peak, was six miles from Georgetown up Clear Creek). He meant to do nothing more until May. However, he changed his plans when Stephen Decatur revealed in March that a "Ten Mile Wagon Road Company" had ten men cutting a road from Bakerville up Grizzly Gulch toward Irwin Pass. Overnight Loveland signed on a hundred employees of his own and ordered them up Clear Creek with teams, dynamite, scoops and chuck wagons to push his "High Line Wagon Road" over the unnamed gap which he now called Loveland Pass. The top was 11,992 feet above sea level —a very high crossing but enough lower than Argentine to allow the road to succeed. Loveland Pass then was as overwhelmingly beautiful and exciting as it is today on that twelve-mile stretch of U.S. Route 6 which hairpins over the Divide between the ski resorts of Loveland Basin and Arapahoe Basin on the Snake River side.

Little snow fell on Loveland Pass during that spring of 1879 to hamper the work. By mid-May, Loveland's hundred men had put the road across. On June 4, fifty wagons were counted descending to Montezuma and the Peru area. S. W. Nott's Georgetown and Leadville stages began running daily past Fiske's Mill above Bakerville and on to Haywood's Halfway House on Snake River, to future Dillon on the Blue, to Frisco and the three-month-old camp of Kokomo on Tenmile Creek and finally over Fremont Pass to Leadville, bursting at the seams with people, optimism and investment capital.

It was all Hipla! Hurrah! to Georgetown residents, who were sure that Loveland's High Line was the most spectacular road on earth. They hadn't seen anything yet.[7]

17

Leadville Fever

THE COLORADO ROCKIES today, highest and broadest of the great chain, are also the most accessible. This paradox flowered after 1878 because absolutely everybody had to get to Leadville, and getting to Leadville meant reaching the center of centers, the inner sanctum, the ultimate hinterland. Leadville stood — and stands — near the tip of the tallest of the three Rocky Mountain pyramids. Its altitude is 10,152 feet above sea level. Its windy valley below Tennessee and Fremont passes is an elbow of Mount Elbert (14,432), whose supreme summit is ten miles from Harrison Avenue. The South Platte, Arkansas and Colorado rivers have sources within that ten-mile radius. The Leadville pyramid is three thousand feet higher than the Yellowstone Park pyramid, where the Missouri, Snake and Green rivers begin.[1] It is a mile higher than Canada's Banff-Jasper pyramid, which contains glacier sources of the Columbia, Fraser, Athabaska and Saskatchewan rivers.

Through the summer and fall of 1878, while William Loveland planned his road over Loveland Pass, every other route to Leadville was jammed with wagons, stages, buggies, carts. There were men pushing wheelbarrows, men riding animals, men and dogs driving herds of cattle, sheep, pigs and goats. Their commotion coated the uplands with a general dust. From Breckenridge and other Blue River camps, and from the Steamboat Springs ranching country west of Gore Pass they scurried up Tenmile Creek and over the Fremont Pass trail, which soon became a rough road. Mexicans and Anglos left Santa Fe and the exhausted placers of the Red River Pass–Elizabethtown–Eagles Nest district north of Taos, and hurried up San Luis Valley and over the Poncha Pass road.

All the roads of the 1860's from the plains through South Park to California Gulch were revived and improved by the Leadville traffic — from Canon City over Currant Creek Pass, from Colorado Springs over Ute and Wilkerson passes, from the advancing ends of the tracks of the Denver and South Park Railroad, which had been pushed up the North Fork of the South Platte by October of 1878, to Bailey's Ranch twenty miles short of Kenosha Pass. The favored wagon crossing of the Mosquito Range out of South Park was Weston Pass which, at 11,945, was only a few feet lower than Loveland, but sheltered by Ptarmigan Peak on the north and by the twin Buffalo Peaks on the south. Weston Pass put the new mob of fortune seekers on the Upper Arkansas in plain sight of their Eldorado at a point above the canyon shelf road which made traveling difficult between Trout Creek Pass and Granite. When snow closed Weston Pass, people took the long way from the South Park salt works over Trout Creek.[2]

Some travelers scorned Weston Pass and crossed, or tried to cross, the highest part of the Mosquitoes directly from Fairplay to Leadville — on the Mosquito Pass trail, or five miles south of it over Horseshoe Pass between Mount Sheridan and Horseshoe Mountain. The California Gulch and Buckskin Joe pioneers of 1860–1867 had walked over Mosquito Pass in emergencies, and always with respect for its whimsies — the midsummer blizzards and forest fires, the fall and spring gales of hurricane force, the sudden sixty-belows of winter when a man could freeze to death if he stopped moving long enough to get his bearings. Life insurance policies of the period stipulated no payoff if the insured met his end on Mosquito Pass. There was a snowbank at the head of North Mosquito Gulch where, through some trick of soil chemistry, the tracks of a transient came out as red as blood. The track-maker considered it to be a reminder of his peril.

The greatest legend of the Mosquitoes, next to that of the dance hall girl, Silverheels,[3] involved the deeds of the Methodist preacher-prospector, the Reverend John L. "Father" Dyer. In her history of Mosquito Pass, Norma L. Flynn has told how Dyer worked through the week and preached on Sundays during August of 1861 in Mosquito town some eleven miles from Fairplay up North Mosquito Gulch. On September 16, he crossed Mosquito Pass for the first time to take over the California Gulch mission. Three years later, he signed on in winter to carry the mail weekly from Buckskin Joe to California Gulch and on down the Upper Arkansas to Granite, a distance of thirty-seven miles. He also carried gold dust to be traded for money.

In his autobiography, Dyer wrote:

> The mail's weight was from twenty-three to twenty-six pounds, with from five to seven pounds of express matter. The carriage was on snowshoes, over an Indian trail that was covered from three to twenty feet of snow. My snowshoes were of the Norway style, from nine to eleven feet in length, and ran well when the snow was just right, but very heavy when they gathered snow. I carried a pole to jar the sticking snow off. Suffice it to say that the winter of 1863 and 1864 was a remarkably hard one, and the spring held on until June, with terrible snow-storms . . . There was no cabin from Mosquito to California Gulch, and no one living between the Gulch and Cache Creek [Granite]. At first I had no company, say the first month. After that I often went at night, as it thawed in the day so that it was impossible to travel, and passengers sought to go with me.[4]

Dyer and his friends had no illusions about Mosquito Pass in the Sixties. The illusions came with the Leadville boom. History shows again and again how people, thrown into an incredible environment, soon take it as a matter of course and begin behaving incredibly themselves. During that frenzied summer of 1878, old Fairplay residents and new residents of California Gulch watched Leadville grow from a few hundred people to six thousand and on toward ten thousand. A few of them stared at that awful Mosquito wall and did some arithmetic. The distance from Leadville to Fairplay on the Mosquito Pass trail was twenty-one miles. It was forty miles by way of Weston; seventy-two by Trout Creek Pass. As they figured the saving in time and distance, and the tolls a Mosquito Pass road could command, the wall seemed to subside until they found themselves pretending that it was no trick to run a road over it.

The wall seemed to subside, even though Hayden's *Atlas of Colorado* had just been published and contained the truth about Mosquito Pass. At 13,188 feet, it was the highest in North America — so high that a man standing wanly and light-headedly on top had an unobstructed view of Mount Sopris and Grand Mesa one hundred miles to the west at the end of the Elks. He could gaze east another hundred miles at Pikes Peak and the Great Plains. By looking both east and west, he could enjoy a superb panorama — the entire width of the main Rockies at their widest part. We have observed that Argentine Pass was the highest Rockies crossing *on* the Continental Divide. Mosquito Pass was forty-eight feet higher still, but *not* on the Divide, which was nine miles north of it as it ran west from Hoosier Pass to Fremont and Tennessee passes before turning south through the Sawatch Range.[5]

The Mosquito Pass Wagon Road Company was incorporated on October 8, 1878, "to promote the industrial interests of the State of Colorado." [6] Its Leadville, Fairplay and Denver directors included H. A. W. Tabor, soon to be known well as Leadville's silver king, and even better as the aging lover of an adolescent beauty named Baby Doe. When skeptics asked these rash promoters how they could succeed when Decatur's Argentine Pass road had failed, they could reply that everything succeeded in Leadville. Besides, the projects were not comparable.

at historic first crossing of a Rockies pass — La Glorieta — in 1540, Coronado's men
d Pecos Pueblo, just as tourists do today. They wrote of it: "A very strong village four
s high . . . The houses do not have doors below, but they use ladders." The ruins date
the pueblo's Spanish mission period. (New Mexico Department of Development photo)

1

t difference does a couple of centuries make? When Taos Spaniards began chasing run-
Indians to the Arkansas at the start of the eighteenth century, the south view from
n Pass was like this — northern New Mexico spreading away dreamily, with mesas and
s rising like isles in a tropical bay. The town is Raton. (New Mexico State Tourist photo)

2

3   Leaving Traveller's Rest and the beautiful Bitterroot Valley in mid-September, Lewis Clark and their thirty companions headed for the Pacific up bright bubbling Lolo (toward Lolo Canyon, Lolo Hot Springs and Lolo Pass. The fall foliage was at its g best. (G. Sohon sketch, *Entrance to the Bitter Root Mountains by the Lou Lou Fork,* 1853, from Pacific Railroad Surveys)

4   As Zebulon Pike's starving men descended Medano Pass behind Sangre de Cristo Range at right, they came upon a strange sight — miles of Sahara-like dunes. Medano Creek be a thin wide sheet of icy water and then vanished in the sand. (National Park Service ph

n David Thompson nearly lost his life crossing Athabaska Pass on a sub-zero day in
ary, 1811, he stood at the north edge of the greatest glacier area in North America, the
mbia Ice Field. This modern view, taken from near Sunwapta Pass and the Banff-Jasper
way, shows Athabaska Glacier, a tiny piece of the Columbia field which has spilled over   **5**
e east side of the Continental Divide. A forty-mile sea of ice intervenes between Athabaska Pass and Athabaska Glacier. (Canadian Pacific photo)

on Price Hunt's motley party of sixty-five Astorians reached the top of Powder River
from Crazy Woman Creek on September 5, 1811, and moved on west down Tensleep
k. It dumped them into the dizzy pitches of Tensleep Canyon in full view of rainbow   **6**
nds — humps of cream and red and gruesome purple sand which mark the east edge of
orn River Valley. (Photo of Powder River Pass highway in Tensleep Canyon from the
Wyoming Travel Commission)

Captain Howard Stansbury hired Jim Bridger himself to take his men through Bridger ▮ which was almost as hard to find in 1850 as it is now. This sketch of Bridger Pass Sta▮ made a dozen years later, when it was on the Overland Trail, shows the bleakness of the approach, in contrast to the forested beauty within the pass itself. (Reprinted by permis of the publishers, The Arthur H. Clark Company, from *The Bozeman Trail*, by Grace ▮ mond Hebard and E. A. Brininstool)

7

Captain Gunnison's artist, R. H. Kern, stretched the facts a little in this quaint versio▮ Sangre de Cristo Pass where "the bold peaks tower loftily above us, whitened by line▮ snow." Today's new U.S. 160 ascends the ravine eastward at right, eliminating the old ▮ way's famous La Veta Pass "mule shoe." The pleasant Pass Creek Pass road to Gardner m▮ left around Kern's central hummock. (From *Exploration and Surveys for the Pacific Railr* *1853*, Denver Public Library Western Collection)

8

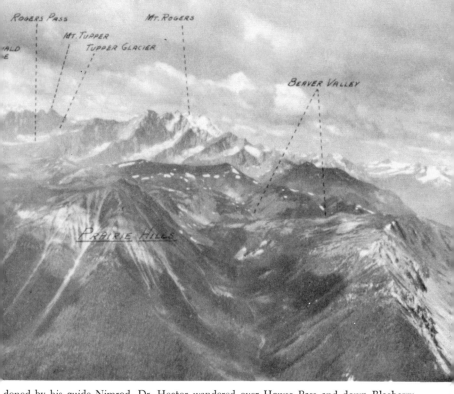

ROGERS PASS MT. ROGERS
MT. TUPPER
...ALD TUPPER GLACIER
...E

BEAVER VALLEY

PRAIRIE HILLS

...doned by his guide Nimrod, Dr. Hector wandered over Howse Pass and down Blaeberry ... to the Columbia, still hoping to find a way west. This mighty part of the Selkirk Range ...vhat he saw before him. Canada would have to wait a century for its transcontinental road over Rogers Pass. (British Columbia Government photo) *9*

... Indiana natives, the prospectors named the crossing Hoosier Pass (hump, right), under ...nt Lincoln — "the highest mountain on earth." Actually, at 14,284, it is only eighth ...st in Colorado. Below them, Montgomery gold camp was springing up at the extreme ...irce of South Platte River. (J. Bien lithograph, 1866, from the Library of Congress) *10*

In 1859, Lieutenant Mullan began building his 633-mile road from Walla Walla, Washington, east to Fort Benton through the Montana Rockies. The Mullan Pass (east side) of Irwin Shope's stagecoach painting was a busy highway in the 1870's. (Photo of painting through the kindness of Montana State Highway Department)

11

Three men are more than enough to start a club in the U.S. In 1862, Nathaniel Pitt Langford (right) and two friends met on top of Mullan Pass to hold Montana's first meeting of "the ancient and honorable institution of Freemasonry." Later Langford became the superintendent of Yellowstone Park. (L. H. Jorud photo of Seltzer painting in the Helena Masonic Lodge No. 3)

12

the whole, Hayden's surveyors made better mountain men than many of the Topographi-
Engineers of an earlier day. Camp scene of 1872 shows, left to right, photographer W.
Jackson; Albert Charles Peale, great-grandson of painter Charles Willson Peale; Dr. Turn-
bull and Packer Dixon. (Jackson photo, U.S.G.S.) **13**

nan Sawtelle's ranch at the south foot of Raynolds Pass looked like this in 1872 when
telle described his Virginia City trout business to F. V. Hayden. Andrew Henry, you
recall, passed this Henrys Lake site in 1810. (W. H. Jackson photo, U.S.G.S.) **14**

From Mount Nebo above Hunchback Pass, the Rhoda party in '73 glimpsed the wildest
most awesomely beautiful part of the high Rockies, the Needle Mountains of the San J
Range south of Silverton. The peak is Mount Eolus (14,086). The 1901 photo was ta
from near Trimble Pass, facing north. Just left of center, a trail runs north past Colum
Lake and through the notch in the ridge, right of center, which is Columbine Pass (12,6
(Whitman Cross photo, U.S.G.S.)

15

Everyone except "Commodore" Stephen Decatur thought that the barrier due west of De
was insurmountable. In 1870, he opened his road from Georgetown to Montezuma over Ar
tine Pass (13,132), the highest C.D. crossing in all the Rockies. The zigzag trail right of ce
is the grade of the old Argentine Central railroad for sightseers to the top of McClo
Mountain (13,423). (United States Geological Survey)

16

The tycoon and billiard expert, John Q. A. Rollins, got his wagon road over Rollins Pass to Middle Park in 1873, a year ahead of the Georgetown crowd building over Berthoud Pass along a route similar to the Berthoud Pass highway shown here. A big ski lodge stands on top now where the parking lot was (right of center). Dr. Thomas Seward Lovering, dean of the United States Geological Survey in Denver, took these remarkable aerial photos in 1928 from 16,000 feet in a rickety old army biplane — and almost fell out of it. (Aerial photos and identification, kindness of Dr. Lovering, U.S.G.S.)

17

Inspired by the Argentine Pass and Berthoud Pass roads, W. A. H. Loveland in 1879 [..] one of his own over Loveland Pass, exactly between the other two passes, aiming to cor[..] the Denver-Leadville transportation business. Today's stupendous Loveland Pass highw[..] takes the same route from Georgetown past Loveland Basin ski resort and the Seven Sist[..] avalanche area (you can count the seven slides almost). To eliminate the slides, the Strai[..] Creek vehicular tunnel will take off just short of them, boring right through the mount[..] for two miles or so to emerge on the Western Slope near Dillon Reservoir. But you will [..] able to drive over Loveland still, praises be. (T. S. Lovering photo, U.S.G.S.)

18

The incredible wagon road from Fairplay to Leadville over Mosquito Pass, 13,188 feet above sea level, opened in 1879 — the highest traverse in North America, then and now. The E. Jump sketch shows teams ascending the east side, struggling around the north slope of London Hill. (E. Jump in *Frank Leslie's Illustrated Newspaper*, May 24, 1879, Library of Congress photo)

19

The Leadville overflow at the start of the 1880's pushed even up the Colorado River's final valley and on up its extremest gulch (center foreground) past Lulu town and over Lulu Pass into North Park. The Trail Ridge road at left is descending from Milner Pass toward Grand Lake after crossing Rocky Mountain National Park. (T. S. Lovering photo, U.S.G.S.)

20

Before the Stony Pass road opened in 1879, the booming Silverton mines were supplied mainly by pack train over Stony and down this hair-raising shelf trail above Cunningham Gulch to Howardsville. The mule in this W. H. Jackson scene of 1875 was the great photographer's famous "Hypo." (United States Geological Survey)

21

The new Stony Pass road was a boon to everybody. Within a month Cunningham Gulc had this bustling aspect, with mines all over Galena Mountain. The Silverton and Grassy Hi toll road (Stony Pass) is shown right of center, disappearing as it climbs into Stony Gulc (Gustave Niegold drawing, 1879, Library of Congress)

Otto Mears's "Rainbow Route" shelf road up above Uncompahgre River and over Re Mountain Pass — today's Million Dollar Highway — had countless ways to torment, delay kill and generally inconvenience travelers. In July, 1888, for instance, an avalanche descende on both the road and the river. The only solution was to dynamite a tunnel through th summer snow. (Library, State Historical Society of Colorado)

ilroads have special enchantment, especially those Colorado lines of the 1880's when no
ilder thought of being sensible. This photograph of Otto Kuhler's fine painting shows a
nver and South Park train climbing from Leadville up Fremont Pass (11,318) beneath
ount Arkansas and Buckeye Peak. The engine is named for Sidney Dillon, president of the
nion Pacific. (Kindness of Otto Kuhler and of Leon Snyder, owner of the painting. Photo
by Knutson-Bowers)

24

mehow General Palmer's narrow-gauge conquered La Veta Pass — the first crossing of real
ckies by rail. This *Harper's Weekly* sketch (September 15, 1877) showed people what
ills they could expect riding around the "mule shoe" and up Dump Mountain to the
. To heighten drama, the artist put in wagons drawn up against Indian attack, though
hting red men were long gone from the La Veta Pass area. (Denver Public Library
Western Collection)

25

By the late 1880's, Hagerman's Colorado Midland trains (left) were groaning up Ute P
from Colorado Springs, bound for Leadville and Aspen. The four per cent grade was se
arated from the old 1872 wagon road (right) by Fountain Creek. Today, U.S. 24 ru
partly over Fountain Creek on a bridge to join the old wagon road at the gap in the upp
center of the picture. (Photo from *Ute Pass: Route of the Blue Sky People*, through th
kindness of the author, Virginia McConnell, and Alan Swallow of Sage Books)

tain Lewis could see these Marias Pass ridges from near Two Medicine Creek after bagg his Blackfoot in 1806. The scene changeth. Now, James J. Hill's streamliners from et Sound clatter over Marias past the Stevens statue and the Roosevelt obelisk and on ast near the scene of the unhappy Lewis contretemps. (Great Northern Railway photo)

28

Modern climbers on Victoria Glacier examine the "Death Trap" slot of Abbot Pass. The Boston alpinist, Philip Stanley Abbot, lost his life near here in 1896 during an attempted first ascent of Mount Lefroy. (Canadian Government Travel Bureau photo)

29 Young Dr. Hector's horse kicked him in the chest in 1858 a bit below this west-side point Kicking Horse Pass. The soaring heights are the President Range, the passes of which we explored in 1901 by the great English conqueror of the Matterhorn, Edward Whympe

(Canadian Pacific photo)

30 This view of the spectacular new road is from the west side of Rogers Pass three miles fro the top facing Mount Sir Donald (10,818). Major A. B. Rogers, the New England ex-sailo is the only Rockies hero to have two major crossings named for him, Rogers Pass in t Selkirks and Rogers Pass in Montana. (British Columbia Government photo)

Decatur had to build fifteen miles of road from Georgetown to Silveropolis. Though the vertical descent on Argentine's west side was a moderate 2300 feet, the descent down to Georgetown was, as we know, an outrageous 4500 feet. By contrast, the Mosquito Pass company was undertaking only six miles of new construction. A good road existed already from Fairplay up North Mosquito Gulch around the north shoulder of London Hill, a glum pile which sat exactly in front of, and three miles east of, the top of the pass. The road ended at Mosquito town near the mill of the rich London Mine, altitude, 11,300 feet. From Mosquito, the rise to the top of the pass was less than two thousand vertical feet. The rise from Leadville's outskirts to the top was about three thousand.

In November, thirty road-builders and their teams moved east from Leadville along Evans Gulch and began switchbacking their way up the dun-colored ridge to the narrow notch in the sky above Bird's Eye Gulch. Everything on the ridge was above timberline. The plans called for two miles of road up the ridge hung on a shelf sixteen feet wide, with a steady grade of eight per cent. As the road climbed, the slope steepened. Near the top it was almost a cliff. When one of the mules shied at a raven and slipped from the shelf, it tumbled half a vertical mile down to Bird's Eye Creek.

Meanwhile, all through an unusually mild winter, a second crew hacked out the east side shelf from Mosquito town three miles up past London Mine to a stretch of alpine flats and a final violent pitch. The top of Mosquito was not much lower than the mountains which circled it — Mosquito Peak, Loveland, Buckskin, Evans, Dyer, Mount Sheridan. In late spring of 1879, the road was finished. By July, one hundred and fifty outfits a day were going through the toll gates — trains of freighters, all sorts of spring wagons pulled by four or five mules, even ponderous six-horse Concord stagecoaches. People gathered at the Leadville foot of the pass to watch the parade, hoping for gory accidents as drivers on the down side whipped their teams and vehicles around the hairpin turns of the lower mile. Unhappily for the spectators, there were no gory accidents, and the sole Mosquito Pass holdup was not very exciting. Though four desperadoes robbed a stage of twenty thousand dollars worth of silver, nobody was killed and the robbers were picked up soon as they slept off a drunk in a Leadville saloon.

The owners of the Mosquito Pass road were pleased when lack of snow allowed them to keep open and collect tolls until mid-December. Even so, income for that first summer of 1879 did not meet expenses and some of them knew that their best season was over. Most of their traffic from June on had been supplied by the Como–Red Hill stations of the Denver and South Park Railroad near Fairplay. By late February of 1880, the railroad had moved on over Trout Creek Pass to Buena Vista on the Upper Arkansas, only thirty-five miles short of California Gulch. General Palmer's Denver and Rio Grande Railroad reached Buena Vista in June from Pueblo and Salida. By August of 1880, trains of both lines were serving Leadville.

The Mosquito Pass road took no more heavy traffic thereafter. Nobody in his right mind would endure four hours of bruising bumps, nervous strain, stifling dust and danger when he could ride the rails. During the brief season of 1880, and again in the summer of 1881, the road was used mostly by thrill-seekers. In 1882, the owners, who had sunk thirty thousand dollars in it, gave up their toll road charter after trying to sell it for ten thousand dollars. Soon, the road fell into disuse and remained so until 1949. In that year, Leadville and Fairplay residents cleaned up the rock slides and bulldozed the mud holes away for their first World's Championship Mosquito Pass Pack Burro Race. This rugged event, in which men and women on foot coax their temperamental little pack animals to hurry along over the range, is held annually in late July between the two towns, and once again spectators gather at the Leadville foot of the rubble slope to watch the parade.[7]

IN 1878, EVERYTHING CONSPIRED, nationally and internationally, to fill up the Leadville mining area.[8] Next year the high little valley had no room for more people. It overflowed like a broken water main in a city street — an eruption of frustrated, too-late prospectors spreading out over the rest of the Colorado Rockies to find other Leadvilles. Today's tourist, driving through the quiet mountains, finds it impossible to imagine how they stirred with bright life in the early 1880's — every inch of them from the lovely parklike valleys up the slopes of the Continental Divide through the pines and spruce and aspen, and on up above timberline two or three thousand feet more to the great red-gray summits of the range.

The men of the Leadville overflow built hundreds of little towns which were miniatures of towns they had left behind in Iowa or Illinois or Ohio or Maine — often bearing their names. They were family towns, composed of husbands and wives, children, pets, schools, churches. There was a curious innocence about them, about their guileless humor and foolish optimism. They were law-abiding and conservative, for all of the wildness of the environment. The dream of their founders was to give them all a happier life, but most of the towns faded and died in a year, and blew away. Only a few have survived as rustling ghost towns, pathetic mementoes of what should have been.

The Leadville overflow washed prospectors northward from California Gulch over Fremont Pass to build the camps of Kokomo and Robinson on Tenmile Creek. Some were swept over what was called Frying Pan Pass — today's Hagerman Pass (12,050) — to Frying Pan River, or over Tennessee Pass and down Eagle River to Battle Mountain. Redcliff was born there and, up Homestake Creek near it, Gold Park and the unbelievable Holy Cross City (11,500), four miles south of Hayden's Mount of the Holy Cross. Kokomo and Robinson residents visited Redcliff often, using a crude road which they cut through the spruce forest over Eagle River Pass (11,000) from Tenmile Creek around the shoulder of Sheep Mountain and down the East Fork of Eagle River. The sixteen-mile road crossed the site of today's survival-training center, Camp Hale. It was much shorter than the wagon road to Redcliff from Kokomo over Fremont and Tennessee passes.

North of Kokomo, the prospectors of 1879 pushed to and beyond the sources of the Colorado River in the northwest corner of present Rocky Mountain National Park, up past Grand Lake and the thick forests of the Never Summer Range. They had no luck at the head of the Colorado itself, or beyond that head at La Poudre Pass, where they found a Cache la Poudre source stream. But some silver and gold were mined on the Colorado fork to the west, which was named Lulu Creek by Benjamin Franklin Burnett, founder of Lulu town. The name honored Burnett's daughter, whom he brought up, presumably, on *Poor Richard's Almanack*.

A road was scraped over the Continental Divide north of Lulu at Lulu Pass (11,400) to Teller City, which was the first and last camp of any importance to lure miners into North Park. Lulu Pass was named Thunder Pass also, because of the rolling music of the Never Summers. Teller City's main ties were with Laramie, Wyoming, though a stage ran twice weekly from Georgetown over Berthoud Pass to Lulu and on over Lulu Pass. Fort Collins traders packed in to Teller City up the Cache la Poudre, over the little divide to Chambers Lake of the Laramie River and across Cameron Pass (10,285) into North Park. The pass had been discovered in 1870 by General Robert Cameron, a neglected Colorado hero who platted the spacious towns of Greeley, Colorado Springs and Fort Collins. In 1882, a toll road was built over Cameron Pass, foreshadowing today's pleasant State Route 14 which rambles amiably across the Medicine Bows from Fort Collins to Walden, capital of North Park.

Gravity being what it is, the big overflow from Leadville

was south downstream. Supply towns for gulch camps of the Sawatch Range sprang up on the north and south sides of Mount Princeton (14,197) — Buena Vista on Cottonwood Creek near the west foot of Trout Creek Pass, and Nathrop and Alpine on Chalk Creek. Other supply towns were Crazy Camp (Maysville), and Junction City (Garfield) where the State Highway Department today parks its snowplows for clearing U.S. Route 50 across Monarch Pass. Both towns were up the South Arkansas from its junction with the main river at Salida near the north foot of Poncha Pass.

This east-side stretch of the Continental Divide along the Sawatch Range has a peculiar topography. Chalk Creek, and the South Arkansas, both delightful, clear, rushing trout streams, are only twelve miles apart as they flow down to the Arkansas from the Continental Divide. Between them rise a company of round peaks, brown in summer, dazzling-white in winter — Antero (14,269), Jones (13,908), Shavano (14,229) and a dozen more. All of the peaks are at least eight miles east of the Divide, separated from it by the south-curving valley of Chalk Creek and the north-curving valley of the South Arkansas. The two valleys head together at a two-mile, above-timberline saddle just east of the Divide called Chalk Creek Pass (12,070).

These little slots of valleys, pressed between the thirteen-thousand-foot wall of the Divide on the west and the Antero-Shavano group on the east, became spotted with gold and silver camps. Some of them were Iron City, St. Elmo, Romley and Hancock along Chalk Creek; Shavano, Babcock and Monarch on branches of the South Arkansas. They were connected by spectacular toll roads and trails. A road ran from St. Elmo and Romley south past the alpine Hancock Lake (11,615) and across Chalk Creek Pass to the Middle Fork of the South Arkansas and on down to Garfield. Another road ran northwest from Maysville as far as Shavano camp. Here a frightening trail ran on up the North Fork of the South Arkansas past Billings Lake and Pride of the West Mine, and zigzagged over Pomeroy Pass (13,050) — eighth highest in the Rockies. This bleak, barren top-of-the-world path continued three miles past Pomeroy Lake and descended Pomeroy Gulch to Chalk Creek at Romley. Travelers from Shavano who disliked such high altitude could climb the Cyclone Creek trail on the east side of Calico Mountain and over Calico Pass — a mere 12,816 feet — to Grizzly Gulch and St. Elmo.

West of the Divide was the tumbled Gunnison country which Hayden's men had reached in 1873 from Twin Lakes up Lake Fork of the Arkansas and across Lake Pass. It had been well combed for gold even that early. Now, in 1879–1880, silver miners poured in by the thousands. Most of them avoided Hayden's steep Lake Pass trail and were too impatient to make the long swing south over Poncha Pass and old Cochetopa. Some explored west from Garfield and from Monarch camp five miles short of the top of present Monarch Pass.[9]

Two miles above Monarch camp, one party scrambled up a small branch of the South Arkansas and crossed the Continental Divide on crusted snow at a point which the Salida novelist, Steve Frazee, has dubbed, somewhat unofficially, *Old* Old Monarch Pass (11,523). On the west side, these pioneers liked the look of a main branch of Gunnison River called Tomichi Creek. As spring reddened the willows, they built White Pine town on its green banks. Tomichi camp was born later three miles upstream, and also Pitkin and Ohio City on Quartz Creek, a Tomichi tributary. In the meantime, a good road was built over Old Old Monarch — in the summer of 1880. By the following May, a stage was crossing it daily from Garfield to Pitkin.

Pitkin was reached easily from White Pine and Tomichi by way of Black Sage Pass (9745), Waunita Hot Springs and Waunita Pass (10,303).[10] For those who liked to do things as dangerously and laboriously as possible, there was a special twelve-mile pass route of many horrors — perhaps the worst shelf trail in the Rockies for man, beast or mountain goat. It started at Tomichi, snaked north above timberline to the icy pond at the headwaters of Tomichi Creek, and then over Tomichi Pass (11,979), on the steep shaly side of Brittle Silver Mountain. From there it plunged out of the stratosphere into Brittle Silver Basin and on down Middle Quartz and Quartz creeks to civilization.

West of Pitkin, Gunnison City, spaciously platted on level rangeland at the junction of Tomichi Creek and the Gunnison itself, was beginning to assume its role as the region's metropolis. Its founders did not care much for Old Old Monarch Pass as a crossing of the Continental Divide from the Arkansas. The solution was to put pressure on Otto Mears to improve the wagon track which he had laid carelessly over Marshall Pass in 1877.

This Mears, a tiny, effervescent, black-eyed, black-bearded man in his late thirties, was probably the most exotic bit of humanity on the Colorado scene. He was born of Jewish parents on a remote Ural steppe of Russia. He was orphaned at the age of two, passed from uncle to uncle, and stuck in the steerage of a steamer at ten to join still another uncle who was alleged to be waiting for him in San Francisco. Neither the uncle nor anybody else met him at the dock, but nothing ever stumped Otto Mears. He brought himself up selling newspapers, learning to speak English and observing how money was made in this new land of opportunity. During the Civil War, he came to Santa Fe with the First California Volunteers and settled at Saguache below Cochetopa Pass in the mid-Sixties. To further his interests as a Saguache merchant and Ute Indian trader he built a toll road over Poncha Pass in 1869, and (with Enos Hotchkiss) the Cochetopa Pass toll road through the Ute Indian Agency and on to Lake City in 1874–1875.

His Marshall Pass road to Gunnison branched from his Poncha Pass road five miles south of Salida and moved west up Poncha Creek to the Continental Divide. Just north of the crossing was the striking summit which would be named Mount Ouray, honoring the last chief of the Utes before most of them were put out of Colorado in 1881. This beautiful Marshall Pass (10,846) had a rather painful history. Hayden's men were not the only government engineers mapping the San Juan area in 1873. Lieutenant Wheeler's army surveyors were there too, and one of them, Lieutenant William L. Marshall, came down with a bad toothache. A Silverton blacksmith offered to yank the tooth with horseshoe pincers. Marshall declined the help with thanks and left for Denver and the nearest dentist on the Cinnamon Pass trail through Lake City. He took with him a packer, Dave Mears — no relation to Otto. The two men rode the fastest mules they could find, and another mule carried their supplies.

When they approached the west foot of Cochetopa Pass, Marshall decided to find a quicker, shorter trail to Denver, eliminating the standard trek over Cochetopa, San Luis Valley and Mosca Pass. His tooth was aching more than ever, but, before the day ended, the travelers struck what would be called Marshall Creek and followed it up to Marshall Pass. Next day they hurried down Poncha Creek to Salida. Soon after, Marshall found himself sitting happily in a Denver dentist's chair. He asserted later that his discovery of Marshall Pass as a therapeutic measure had saved him one hundred and twenty-five miles of trail and four days of misery.[11]

THE RUGGED, PINEY Tomichi Creek–Quartz Creek watersheds of Gunnison drainage are separated from the open Taylor Park part north of it by a very considerable ridge. This ridge is crossed from Pitkin on a narrow, twisting, gravel road over Cumberland Pass to Tincup — the ghost town–turned–resort — and to Taylor Reservoir of Taylor River. Cumberland Pass (12,200) is slightly higher than Independence Pass (12,095), on the Twin Lakes–Aspen road, which is often described as the highest Rockies crossing for standard cars. Above the top of Cumberland, old shaft houses and mills seem about to topple down on the road — vestiges of the Jimmie Mack Mine, Blistered Horn, and so on.

A pack-train trail was cut over Cumberland Pass in 1880, connecting Pitkin and Tincup, but it was not used much until it was promoted to a road two years later. Tincup residents found it cheaper to bring in supplies and haul out ore by pack train over Tincup Pass (12,154) around the south slope of Mount Princeton. The Tincup Pass trail ran up the East Willow branch of Taylor River beyond Mirror Lake and over the Divide to the north fork of Chalk Creek and St. Elmo town. The heaviest Tincup shipments were sent over Cottonwood Pass (12,126) around the north side of Princeton. This Cottonwood trail, closely guarded by Mount Yale (14,194) two miles north of it, became a road in the spring of 1880. A road materialized over Tincup Pass too, with Witowski and Dunbar's Hack Line in operation by October, 1880. But the Cottonwood Pass road was used more between the Upper Arkansas and Taylor Park. Its grades were gentler, as motorists today can observe for themselves.[12]

The dynamics of American capitalism have startled economists for two centuries and they were in good form during those early 1880's in that heart-lifting, sun-cheered square spreading west over the Continental Divide from the Upper Arkansas to the Gunnison–Crested Butte–Aspen area. The railroad crowd laid their tracks almost on a dead run toward Leadville and started spurs to the gulch camps. Each mile of track seemed to create a freshet of grubstake money, propelling prospectors up remoter gulches. Behind them, like gulls in a steamer's wake, came the storekeepers, lawyers, madames, doctors, ministers, assayers, editors, saloon and hotel operators, and also the transport mob — frieghters, stagers, stablemen, horse traders, blacksmiths, veterinarians, road builders, bandits, and all the rest.

A sort of wild race developed to find the hidden treasure, the second Leadville, but everybody had a different idea of where this second Leadville was. From the Arkansas, many miners tramped to Twin Lakes, and on west up the north branch of Lake Creek to a Sawatch traverse called Hunter's Pass, which was below — but not much below — the top of Mount Elbert. Hunter's Pass was a revolting thing to get over, summer or winter, with cliffs to climb on both sides, and a rock-bound top so mournful that even the ravens stayed away. No matter. There was treasure that way because some pioneers had found gold four miles down the west side on July 4, 1879. They had built Independence town there, flecked with spray from the waters of Roaring Fork River. Other pioneers had found traces of silver farther downstream and had built Ute City (Aspen). To all of these, Hunter's Pass was known as Independence Pass (12,095). When Aspen began to show promise in the spring of 1880, Leadville men formed the Twin Lakes and Roaring Fork Toll Company, capitalized at forty thousand dollars. They improved the old Independence Pass trail so that horses could use it, talked of its virtues and collected tolls while raising cash to build the road itself.

The horse trail's virtues were not evident to some that spring. Hamilton S. Wicks reported to the *Leadville Chronicle:*

> We pictured to ourselves a pleasant little canter over the Twin Lakes Toll Road, amidst picturesque beauties of the Continental Divide. OH! witching scenes of foul delusion! . . . I do not wish to, or shall I say aught against the Toll Road Company . . . but I want to say a word to my friend the toughfoot who, out of abundance of his experience, actually believes a trip of fifty to sixty miles over the mountains a very simple and easy matter to accomplish. Do not hereafter speak so glibly about the rapidity with which you accomplish the trip from Leadville to Roaring Fork and return . . . Don't level down whole mountains, and fill up vast chasms of mud; for your simple-minded tenderfoot believes all you say, and when he finds these mountains, and that mud to be toiled over and wallowed through he curses you with imprecations loud and deep.

While the Independence Pass men begged for road funds, the merchants of Buena Vista timbered the snow tunnel at the top of their busy Cottonwood Pass road and praised the Lord for the railroad tracks from Denver at their front door. Though their road was on the long side to the top — seventeen miles up the middle fork of Cottonwood Creek — the length was a blessing, since the vertical climb was 4326 feet. The merchants corduroyed the bogs on Cottonwood's west-side descent to Taylor River, and they were generous with grubstakes to miners who were finding treasure in the north end of Taylor Park above Bowman camp, and over the Elk Range crest on Castle Creek of the Roaring Fork.

The miners crossed the crest by Bowman Pass (12,700) and Difficult Pass (12,400) or some version of what we call Taylor Pass (11,900). Their trail from Taylor Park threaded up through the aspens and boulders along the bright trickle of Taylor River. It was steep but brief — 1800 vertical feet of climb in three miles. Just short of the top was the tiny Taylor Lake and then a three-hundred-foot rubble pitch. In 1880, the gold-silver town of Ashcroft arose at the junction of Express and Castle creeks, five miles down the Aspen side of Taylor Pass. Wagons began crossing, winched up the pitch until switchbacks were cut. Soon stage and freight operators were serving the Ashcroft area and watching developments at Aspen, which the Independence Pass men were striving to reach before the Cottonwood-Taylor route became a habit to the public. The Independence road would be shorter — sixty miles from Leadville to Aspen as against one hundred miles over Cottonwood — if they could build it up those Independence cliffs.

A second rival to the Independence Pass route appeared in 1881, when the Denver and Rio Grande tracks reached Crested Butte, the new coal town below Schofield Pass. These tracks were only twenty-three miles southwest of Ashcroft, thirty-five miles from Aspen. Accordingly, a pack trail was built to connect them, running up Cascade Creek and Middle Brush Creek between Teocalli Mountain and Italian Mountain, which Hayden's men had admired in 1873. The pack trail crossed the great multicolored Elk divide at Pearl Pass (12,715) and fell on down Castle Creek through Ashcroft to the Roaring Fork and Aspen. Within weeks, mule skinners were conducting their teams and wagons over it, though not with ease and gladness. The seventeen-mile ascent north from Crested Butte to the barren, gloomy top was not much worse than very difficult. The real trouble began on the Aspen side — an eighteen-mile torment. The vertical fall was 4915 feet — greater even than Argentine's, though the rate of fall per mile was somewhat less. Nevertheless, by late 1881 the Pearl Pass road was carrying almost as much traffic to Aspen as the road over Cottonwood and Taylor passes.

The success of Pearl Pass disturbed the Cottonwood-Taylor men, but they did not seem to have to fear competition from Independence Pass during the spring of 1881. In their study, "Twin Lakes Toll Road," Don and Jean Griswold have told how construction was stalled some miles from the east foot of the pass. The whole nation was laughing about the crew of impatient Leadville bakers who, road or no road, were trying to move a huge oven over the Independence trail to cash in on the high Aspen market for pies. On March 15, the *Leadville Chronicle* reported in part:

> A sled was purchased, on which the furnace was securely fastened . . . with half a dozen jacks as motive power. The trail soon narrowed to such an extent that the projecting sides of the oven stuck, and it was found necessary to excavate several feet at each side to admit its progress. At night the weary bakers slept in the oven, haunted by the faint aroma of pastry that, like the scent of roses, hung around it still. . . . Meanwhile an unexpected difficulty arose. The spring tide of travel had already set in, and several jack trains were not long in following the bakers' caravan. They were not long in catching up

with it, either, and the awful fact dawned upon them that they could not pass it, but would have to linger in the rear. This filled them with sorrow and disgust, for they were in a hurry, and, like most travelers into a new mining camp, imagined if they didn't get there right away all the land would be staked off, all the trades overcrowded and all the provisions eaten up. So it looked as though three or four rainbows and all their varied hues, particularly blue, had settled on the spot. Then another and another jack train came hurrying up, and stopping at the rear of their unfortunate predecessors, inquired anxiously:

"What's up?"

"A G— D— pie factory is blockading the road!"

"Well, why don't you push the ———— thing off?"

"Can't do it, it's too hell-fired big!"

The oven isn't at Aspen yet, and isn't liable to be before late this week, and the pack trains still accumulate in the rear, until the road for nearly a mile is black with shivering, swearing, howling men.

But the oven crisis, and the realization that Aspen was really the second Leadville which every one had been seeking for two years, caused action in July. Seventy-five toll company men and the whole town of Independence attacked the pass from both sides, pushing it over the top before the August rains began. Pitkin County employees completed the last miles into Aspen in October, and the road was officially opened on November 6, 1881.

Though snow fell heavily a week later, the immense stage and freight traffic which switched to Independence at once from Cottonwood, Taylor and Pearl passes could not be stopped by it. Big sleighs and small cutters replaced wagons and stages. A shovel army scooped out deep trenches across the forty-foot-deep snowbanks. All through that winter, and the next four, the broad, bleak, windy top of Independence presented an eerie spectacle — a solid double line of traffic moving in opposite directions. For summer, the hairpin turns were banked and broadened so that the stagecoaches could descend with the teams at full speed. Well-trained dogs ran ahead of these madly-flying coaches to warn up-coming traffic to get out of the way.

Times do change. Aspen, the world-famous mining camp, be-came Aspen, the world-famous ski resort of today, its transport problems met by the marvels of modern technocracy. And still, no way had been found up to 1964 to keep Inde-pendence Pass open for auto traffic after October 15, as it was kept open in winter from 1881 until railroads reached the Roaring Fork six years later.

THE LEADVILLE OVERFLOW was felt in the San Juans, but these theatrical highlands were booming through the 1870's on their own, spurred by the rivalry of Del Norte town on the Stony Pass trail, and Otto Mears's Saguache town below Cochetopa Pass. Mears's toll road through Cochetopa to Lake City and Lake San Cristobal in 1874–1875 was matched by Del Norte's toll road to the same charming destination. It ran up the Rio Grande past Wagon Wheel Gap as far as Antelope Park and then up Clear Creek and over Cebolla Pass and Slumgullion Pass — approximating today's Spring Creek Pass–Slumgullion Pass road.

As in the Elk and Sawatch ranges, San Juan roads ran wherever miners thought that they had struck it rich. No granite wall was too steep for them to cross, though the winter ava-lanches, which are a characteristic of the region still, ruined their work often. A toll road was pushed up Henson Creek in 1877 from Lake City past Capitol City and the alpine saloon called Rose's Cabin to American Flats. From these wild mead-ows, the road crossed Engineer Mountain at Yvonne Pass (12,250) or nearby Engineer Pass (12,800). Then it fell down the pitch to Uncompahgre headwaters and the rich Mineral Point mines. A road led out of Mineral Point over Denver Pass (12,200) running south to Animas Forks and Silverton. A second road from Lake City was built by Enos Hotchkiss up Lake Fork past the new camps of Sherman and Whitecross and over Cinnamon Pass (12,600) to the Mineral Point–Silverton Road.

When the Ute Indian Agency was moved in 1875 from the west foot of Cochetopa Pass to Uncompahgre River, the ubiquitous Otto Mears built a road to the Uncompahgre from his Saguache–Lake City road. It crossed Cerro Summit and Blue Mesa Summit pretty much as Antoine Robidoux had crossed them in the 1820's, and as U.S. Route 50 crosses them now, from Gunnison past Curecanti Reservoir to Montrose. This Mears road encouraged the growth of Ouray town, which began in a picturesque pocket of rocks under Mount Sneffels as far up the Uncompahgre as a burro could walk. From Ouray, a terrible burro trail was fashioned along the sides of Uncompahgre Canyon for four miles where it split into two terrible trails. One went east five miles more to Mineral Point and Engineer and Denver passes. The other continued south to rich mines which had been found in the late 1870's on both sides of Red Mountain Pass (11,018).

For years thereafter, Ouray residents talked of putting a road up that sheer canyon to Red Mountain Pass so that the town could grow on equal terms with Silverton. Nothing came of the talk until 1882, when Otto Mears took hold of the project, assisted by Fred Walsen of Walsenburg. Mears spent two years blasting his "Rainbow Route" up the canyon at a cost of ten thousand dollars a mile — an unheard-of investment in those days. The shelf which he cut high above the seething Uncompahgre is the same used by today's Million Dollar Highway, so named, they say, because its gravel is gold-bearing. The distance from Ouray to Silverton on this U.S. Route 550 over Red Mountain Pass is twenty-three miles. The drive provides one of the most vivid mining and geological spectacles in the West.[13]

Stony Pass remained the favored gate to Silverton and Baker's Park during the 1870's, in spite of the competition. The one-hundred-and-ten-mile route from Del Norte was the shortest, and it crossed no Ute Indian lands, as the Mears roads did from Saguache to Lake City and Ouray. The route was sociable with towns and ranches for ninety miles along the grassy, green-gold Rio Grande as far as Lost Trail Creek, where the wagon road ended and the twenty-mile pack trail over the Continental Divide began. It was bothersome to have to shift wagon cargos to the backs of mules at Lost Trail Creek, but there were compensations. A big, cheerful road house stood among the Engelmann spruce where the Lost Trail Creek campsite is now at the end of the auto road. Travelers enjoyed spending the night below the blue-red chalk cliffs of the valley's edge, crenellated like the bastions of an English castle.

Beyond, the Stony Pass trail crossed the mean steep Timber Hill past the huge, mossy "robbers' roost" boulder where bandits could be waiting to hold up travelers.[14] The boulder was dotted with bullet holes, though bandits didn't make most of them. Hunters had made them, testing their firearms, just as today's hunters take potshots at highway markers. Six miles beyond Timber Hill, the trail passed the mouth of Bear Creek leading to Hunchback Pass and Franklin Rhoda's intruding bears, and then it crossed Pole Creek and Grassy Hill. Thereafter, it climbed for six more easy miles along the last Deep Creek waters of the Rio Grande to the Divide below Canby and Green Mountains. The top was gloomy, as all high passes seem to be, but women had an affection for it. Baker Park's first girl baby, "the Lily of the San Juans," was born beneath a snowbank up there in 1875 to Mrs. George Webb in luxurious circumstances. Two doctors were in attendance and the mother rested comfortably on a fragrant maternity bower of fir boughs under six wool blankets.

Baker's Park was immediately below the top, and that was the trouble with Stony Pass. During the next two miles, the trail dropped from 12,494 feet above sea level to 11,000. It was an anxious process of inching down, and if a mule began to slip, it was apt to keep going until it hit bottom in Cunningham Gulch. Nevertheless, a surprising number of loaded wagons and large amounts of heavy machinery were slid down that incline through the years. After 1876, professional snubbers waited for clients at the top and snubbed their vehicles down the two miles, using trees for posts at proper intervals. The time came when the snubbers were out of work. A way was found to build a road down to Howardsville by way of Stony Gulch from a point on the Divide which was a mile north of, and a hundred feet higher than, the old summit. And so, in 1879, the Stony Pass road was opened.[15]

Its years of service would be few, like all Colorado toll roads of the 1870's and 1880's, for the railroads had begun their fantastic invasion of the high country. Before the nineteenth century ended, their wonderful whistles, their moaning air pumps, squealing brakes, trails of black smoke and white steam and rapturous tourists on open vestibules would be as common through all the Rockies as bear, deer, elk and moose.[16]

18

The Highest Rails

T HE RAILROADS. Some things — circuses, the Eiffel Tower, zoos, Madame Tussaud's waxworks — always enchant people, and are loved especially in this dull age of computers, hydrogen bombs, jet planes and space ships, all of which should be interesting and somehow are not. Railroads have been loved most of all, and the period when they first crossed the Rocky Mountain region is one that most enchants their fans.

The Union Pacific was the very first, but it was a pallid affair which broke the hearts of ex-Governor John Evans and other Coloradans in 1868 by crossing the Continental Divide in southern Wyoming, where there was nothing higher than the front stoop, instead of being heroic and using Captain Berthoud's 11,313-foot pass. This is no reflection on the U.P.'s great chief engineer, General Grenville M. Dodge. He did his job, and his job was to get tracks from Omaha straight to San Francisco, and to hell with Denver and the scenery. He had begun studying the problem for the army and the government in the late 1850's before there was any Denver, and he had a notion even then that any railroad going west had to use some version of Howard Stansbury's Cheyenne Pass over the Laramie Hills of southern Wyoming, and on over the Continental Divide in the low Wyoming Basin area just north of Bridger Pass.

But he wanted to be fair and thorough. While he was busy

fighting the Civil War, he approved the Union Pacific's act of examining the high Colorado passes — Berthoud and Hoosier, Breckenridge and Webster, Argentine and Quail and Loveland, Jones and Vasquez and Rogers. Berthoud Pass required a three-mile tunnel. The Colorado reports were placed before him and he turned all these high passes down. He had no use either for the route over Antelope Pass on the Wyoming-Colorado border — up the South Platte, Cache la Poudre, Dale Creek, and on down to Laramie River on the west side of the Laramie Hills; or for the long, northerly South Pass route of the Oregon Trail.

So the General decided once and for all on Cheyenne Pass, 8591 feet above sea level, and then over the Divide at 7100 feet or so in the Wyoming Basin.[1] Cheyenne Pass was a little high, but his assistant, James A. Evans, had reported seeing a lower summit, an Evans Pass, south of it through field glasses. The time of Dodge's decision was 1865 as he was winding up army duty chasing Powder River Indians and preparing to take over officially as the U.P.'s chief engineer. He led his cavalrymen homeward along the east side of the Laramie Hills. When he struck the Lodgepole Creek trail to Cheyenne Pass, he left his force on a sudden impulse and ascended the old trail with a few soldiers to hunt for the elusive Evans Pass. Hostile Indians were still around, so he asked his troop to watch for his smoke signals in case they gave him trouble. He wrote later, in part:

We worked south from the Cheyenne Pass and around the head of Crow Creek, when I looked down into the valley there was a band of Indians who had worked themselves in between our party and the trains. . . . I dismounted, and giving our horses to a couple of men with instructions to keep on the west side of the ridge out of sight and gunshot, we took the ridge between Crow Creek and Lone Tree Creek, keeping it and holding the Indians away from us, as our arms were so far-reaching that when they came too near our best shots would reach them. . . . We made signals for our cavalry, but they did not seem to see them. It was getting along in the afternoon, as we worked down this ridge, that I began to discover we were on an apparently very fine approach to the Black [Laramie] Hills, and one of the guides has stated that I said, "If we save our scalps I believe we have found a railroad line over the mountains." About four o'clock the Indians were preparing to take the ridge in our front. The cavalry now saw our signs and soon came to our rescue, and when we reached the valley I was satisfied that the ridge we had followed was one which we could climb with a maximum grade within our charter. . . . As soon as I took charge of the Union Pacific [1866] I wired James A. Evans . . . describing this ridge to him, as I had thoroughly marked it by a lone tree on Lone Tree Creek. . . . He immediately made an examination and discovered a remarkably direct line of only a ninety-foot grade reaching from the summit to the valley of Crow Creek where Cheyenne now stands, and this summit I immediately named for my old commander General Sherman.

Sherman Hill Summit was to be the highest point on the Union Pacific until the line was rerouted some miles south over a crest at 8013 feet in 1903–1904. Sherman Hill Summit is marked still by the big Ames Monument, built in 1882 to honor U.P. backers, a mile off U.S. Route 30. Cheyenne Pass is on the next ridge north. In Utah, General Dodge put his rails through the Wasatch Range by way of Wasatch Divide (6816), Echo Canyon and Weber Canyon, bringing them to Ogden but not to Salt Lake City. This was a disappointment to Brigham Young, who had financed surveys himself so that the U.P. would come to his Mormon capital through Simpson's Timpanagos (Provo) Canyon. The Central Pacific Railroad, which was built east from San Francisco Bay to meet the U.P. at Promontory Point, Utah, crossed the High Sierras by Donner Pass at 7135 feet.

THE OPENING OF THE UNION PACIFIC in 1869 inspired the arrival in Denver a year later of the Denver Pacific Railroad, running south from the U.P. tracks at Cheyenne, and of the Kansas Pacific from Kansas City. Denver's John Evans brought in the Denver Pacific while Golden's watchdog, William A. H. Loveland, looked on in jealous frustration. Loveland, guarding the Clear Creek entrance to the mines of Central City and Georgetown, plotted to thwart Denver with railroads of his own, centered at Golden. The Kansas Pacific was built by a third bundle of energy, General William Jackson Palmer, whose Civil War career as cavalry leader and Union spy had made him almost as famous as Jeb Stuart.

During the next decade or so, these three men would build things up to a dramatic and complicated climax. Railroads and railroad passes were the focus of the action, flickering and uncertain for a time, but sharpening to sunspot intensity after 1878, when the treasures of Leadville, Aspen and the San Juans became the salient fact of Western life. Of the three men, the tall, slender Loveland was the best looking, and also the least sophisticated, even if he had thought of building a Panama canal in his salad days. At the age of forty-four, his ambition was that of a talented merchant whose main interest was the growth of his town, to which he hoped to bring glory by his railroads.

Dr. John Evans, at forty-eight, was already past his prime when he reached Denver to serve Abraham Lincoln as territorial governor. He was an Ohio Quaker who had founded Northwestern University and won honor as a Chicago physician and humanist. Personal tragedy — his first wife and three children had died by 1850 — tended to make him sombre and withdrawn. He was extremely complex. Though of fine intellect, he was vain enough to love raw political power, and acquisitive enough to work hard at piling up property. He was a genius in corporate poker games, while remaining honest in an age when honesty was naive, if not downright stupid. Physically, he was as imposing as the round-shouldered peak above Denver which bears his name, Mount Evans (14,264).

General Palmer, the young one, was a Quaker too, from Philadelphia. He was aged thirty-four, curly-haired, trim, stubborn, small, shyly authoritarian, quite reminiscent of that other Pikes Peak hero, Zebulon Pike. Unlike Loveland and Evans, Palmer was a professional builder of railroads, having been trained by the great engineer of the Pennsylvania, J. Edgar Thomson. In time, he would become as cynical and as realistic as John Evans, but in 1870 he was head over heels in love with a teen-aged Cincinnati debutante named Queen Mellen. For Queen, he bought ten thousand acres of Pikes Peak land and began preparing a Rocky Mountain love nest, a town, Colorado Springs, and a railroad, the Denver and Rio Grande. The railroad was his very own, like Queen, and to make sure no corporate wolf from the East like Jay Gould tried fooling around with it, he made it narrow gauge — tracks three feet wide, instead of the standard four feet eight and a half inches. This gauge symbolized purity and sole possession — a chastity belt, in effect. Besides, the Denver and Rio Grande could be built cheaper that way, with thirty-degree curves and four per cent grades, and that was a point since Palmer could get no federal land grants to help him financially.

Loveland, Evans, Palmer — loyal Coloradans all three. And just where were their paper railroads going? To Utah and California? To South Park? To the San Juans? Loveland and Evans hadn't the vaguest idea. They knew only that their transcontinental hopes were for the far future. Railroads in Colorado had to be paid for by Colorado mining, and mining was not doing much in 1870 from a railroad point of view. The two promoters worked together briefly on a Berthoud Pass scheme and split — partly on the Golden versus Denver issue, and partly because there were still no mines beyond Berthoud.

The handsome Loveland did build fifteen miles of his Colorado Central and Pacific, standard gauge, from Golden to Denver. Then he got Union Pacific backing to push narrow-gauge tracks up Clear Creek, short of Idaho Springs, and up North Clear Creek, short of Central City — twenty odd miles. Those two stations were the ends of his line in 1873. They remained the ends for five years, during which Loveland talked of how his rails would cross Loveland Pass to Stephen Decatur's Silveropolis, say, and then maybe up St. John's Creek past Glacier Mountain to Georgia Gulch, Breckenridge and Hoosier Pass to South Park. En route to California, naturally.

Meanwhile, John Evans made dignified motions about an idea called the Denver, Georgetown and Utah Railway. It would run to Idaho Springs and Georgetown, since Loveland seemed unable to reach them, on the southern loop — up Mount Vernon Canyon and over Floyd Hill (today's U.S. Route 40, more or less). After Georgetown, on to Loveland Pass, Snake River, Tenmile Creek, Fremont Pass, Tennessee Pass, Eagle River, Salt Lake City! Possibly a branch to the San Juans — from Fremont Pass down the Arkansas, over Poncha and Cochetopa passes to Lake City and Cinnamon Pass, and there you were in Silverton. But, by June of 1872, Evans was tired of paper lines. South Park seemed the best place to head for and, in October, he began his real railroad, the Denver, South Park and Pacific. On June 24, 1874, his narrow-gauge tracks reached Morrison, fifteen miles from Denver. At Morrison, Evans ran out of steam. He got no farther along toward South Park and the Pacific until 1877.

Young Palmer married his beautiful Queen, fashioned his Glen Eyrie love nest near the Garden of the Gods, and prodded his Denver and Rio Grande tracks from Denver through Colorado Springs and all the way to El Moro near Raton Pass by April of 1876 — two hundred miles. His destination was El Paso, Texas, by way of the Royal Gorge of the Arkansas, Poncha Pass and the Rio Grande. But first, he had to build from Pueblo past the Spanish Peaks to El Moro's coal fields before the Santa Fe Railroad, approaching from Kansas, snapped them up. At the Spanish Peaks, he noted the heavy wagon traffic over Sangre de Cristo Pass bound for Del Norte, Stony Pass and Silverton. The railroad, he decided, could use that San Juan traffic, and so he scrapped the Poncha Pass route to El Paso.

He would cross to the Rio Grande here rather than at Poncha Pass.

Neither De Anza's Sangre de Cristo Pass trail of 1779 nor Gunnison's road of 1853 suited the General, who chose La Veta Pass — up South Veta Creek from Cucharas River to the top of the range. It was an anxious time, that pioneer construction in the golden fall months of 1876 and the cold spring of 1877. The problems of Palmer's engineers were nothing like the problems he had studied for J. Edgar Thomson in the hills of Pennsylvania. La Veta Pass — 9383 feet above sea level — required the crews to slide the tracks around, and steeply up, a marvelous mule-shoe curve through the pines of Dump Mountain, so named because it looked like the dump in front of a mine. The tracks, climbing two hundred and seventeen feet to the mile, doubled upon themselves as they rose in view of the Spanish Peaks. This would terrify and titillate the tourists and get the railroad talked about, but that was the best you could say for La Veta. It involved fourteen miles of three and four per cent grade, as compared with General Dodge's maximum for the U. P. of less than two per cent. The vertical rise was 2359 feet.

And still, to Palmer's surprise and relief, his narrow-gauge tracks conquered La Veta Pass — the first crossing of real Rocky Mountains by an American railroad — without serious trouble, and ran down the moderate grade of Sangre de Cristo Creek to his new Garland City near Fort Garland. His experiments had worked. He had used fills of plain dirt rather than of stone and they had held up, through the winter snow and spring runoff. His little work cars took the thirty-degree curves at a good clip without wheel wear. The brakes of his twenty-ton locomotives controlled the cars well down grade. A year later, in June of 1878, the Denver and Rio Grande reached the blue mountain stream for which it was partly named, at the company's townsite, Alamosa. Many cottonwoods ("alamos" in

Spanish) shaded this San Luis Valley site, which was thirty miles east of the San Juan supply center, Del Norte.[2]

IN 1878, General Palmer was a sadder, harder, wiser man than he had been in 1870 as Queen Mellen's dewy-eyed husband. The Glen Eyrie love nest had been a failure. Queen just didn't like Colorado or pioneering and she spent much of her time elsewhere. Palmer, after driving his "baby" railroad south almost to Raton Pass, realized now that the Leadville region was the objective of all objectives in the West — not El Paso, Texas, not California, not the San Juans. For this reason, when the Santa Fe Railroad seized Raton Pass in late February, 1878, Palmer let Raton go with hardly a struggle.[3] But, two months later, he fought with all his heart and soul as the Santa Fe started building grade from Canon City through the Royal Gorge of the Arkansas toward Leadville. Exactly two years passed before the General stopped the Santa Fe by winning possession of the Royal Gorge from the United States Supreme Court.

The long suit delayed him, but his Leadville rivals were delayed too. As the stakes rose higher and higher, Loveland got out of his depth and found himself and his Colorado Central to be mere pawns for the Union Pacific and Kansas Pacific and for their shadowy grand master, Jay Gould. This quiet, tuberculous New York blueblood, Palmer's age exactly, had won fame and admiration — in some circles — by wrecking the Erie Railroad back East, and ruining thousands of investors through bribery, stock manipulation and alleged embezzlement. Gould tried to bore into Palmer's Denver and Rio Grande and into Evans's Denver and South Park by threats which Loveland issued for him after the Colorado Central reached Georgetown in 1878. Examples: The Colorado Central would zoom over Loveland Pass and win the race to Leadville with the help of a rig combining the best features of ferris wheel and aerial tram.

If it didn't get there, the Union Pacific would invade Colorado from its main line at Laramie, Wyoming, over Pinkham Pass into North Park, over Muddy Pass into Middle Park, and over Fremont Pass to the big pot of silver. From Leadville, this U. P. would build over Tennessee Pass to join the Southern Pacific, which would come east from Ogden, Utah, to a terminus at — the Mount of the Holy Cross!

Gould's threats had no effect on Palmer and Evans. His real gambit was his capital, which they had to have and which allowed him to put pressure on both of them. Meanwhile, Evans left his Morrison terminus behind and nudged the Denver and South Park up the South Platte Canyon, which the Long expedition of 1820 had refused even to reconnoitre. On May 19, 1879, the tracks reached the top of Kenosha Pass (9950) seventy-six miles from Denver. The top was six hundred feet higher than Palmer's La Veta Pass and so Evans took over the United States altitude record. His narrow-gauge tracks curved five hundred and sixty times. To build a shelf up Platte Canyon, his men worked on tiny platforms high up the walls drilling holes for dynamite. The vertical rise of the road from Denver totaled 4711 feet. The grade to the top was four per cent from the point where the tracks left the North Fork of the South Platte at the start of the Webster Pass toll road. Beyond Kenosha, nothing awful was in the way. Soon, Evans's jaunty trains, gaily painted, diamond-stacked, with their incongruously huge headlights, were chugging through the sage and grass of South Park.

They reached Como at the foot of the Breckenridge Pass wagon road in late June, crossed the Weston Pass toll road in October, skirted John Q. A. Rollins's defunct salt works, and took the short climb to the top of Trout Creek Pass in January, 1880.[4] Two months later, the Denver and South Park was on the Arkansas under Mount Princeton serving Buena Vista town thirty-five miles from Leadville, and its Cottonwood Pass–Taylor Pass wagon lines to Aspen. It fed passengers and freight also to vehicles ascending Chalk Creek toward St. Elmo, Tincup Pass and Taylor Park. And Chalk Creek had a new wagon road which crossed from St. Elmo and Hancock to Pitkin by another of those spectacular Sawatch Range gaps over the Continental Divide, Williams Pass (11,762).[5]

During all that spring of 1880, Palmer was laying *his* rails up the Arkansas toward California Gulch. Only two years before, those rails had been bound due south for Texas. Now they reversed their field at Pueblo and pointed west and north. Though Palmer seemed to be racing the Denver and South Park, that race had been called off by Jay Gould. He had given the Leadville right-of-way to Palmer as a reward for keeping the Sante Fe out of the Rockies in the Royal Gorge fight. Palmer got Leadville. John Evans got the Pitkin-Gunnison country, which had been his first objective anyway.[6] In late July, the Denver and Rio Grande entered Leadville while the Denver and South Park was creeping west from the Arkansas on a shelf above Chalk Creek.[7] The D. & S. P. tracks reached St. Elmo in December. By the following August, 1881, they were at Romley and Hancock, where they paused for quite a while.

The pause was to await completion of an epic project called the Alpine Tunnel which John Evans had been pushing through the Continental Divide since late 1879. Its engineer was James A. Evans, General Dodge's old Union Pacific friend. The engineer's assistant was Robert R. Williams, who promoted the Williams Pass wagon road to aid construction. The tunnel site was beneath a crossing called Altman Pass (12,124), which a stage driver named "Colonel" Henry Altman had found while hunting for a wagon route from St. Elmo to Pitkin. James Evans had begun boring two miles from Romley at an altitude of 11,600 feet. He had assumed that the mountain was solid rock, but it was ninety-five per cent decomposed granite and loose stone, and soused with running water. A large sum had to be spent on twelve-by-twelve California redwood for timbering.

The tunnel was about eighteen hundred feet long, twelve

feet wide and seventeen feet high. It rose to an apex of 11,612 feet and emerged on Middle Quartz Creek drainage near Brittle Silver Basin at the foot of the hair-raising Tomichi Pass trail from White Pine. The apex figure gave the Denver and South Park a new high altitude record for American rails. To reach the tunnel, the railroad climbed 4500 feet vertically in twenty-one miles from the Arkansas. The deep winter snows required the construction of six hundred and fifty feet of west portal snowsheds, one hundred and fifty feet at the east portal. Fortunately, the bore needed no ventilating system. The wind up there blew it clean as a whistle every minute of every day. The total tunnel cost was $242,090 — a sickening charge for a third of a mile of railroad. But John Evans did not have to worry about that. On November 9, 1880, he sold the Denver and South Park to Jay Gould for $2,590,800 and bowed his dignified form out of our passes story.

The Alpine Tunnel was holed through on December 21, 1881, which was the six hundred and ninety-ninth day after James Evans began digging. It was an exercise in heroism, and it did not deserve the troubles which would befall it soon, and keep on befalling it. The first Denver and South Park trains ran through it to the Western Slope camp of Woodstock in June, 1882; to Pitkin in July; and all the way to Gunnison on September 1. That should have been a happy day. It was not. The trains reached Gunnison too late — more than a year after the Denver and Rio Grande arrived there.[8]

THE WEST HAD NEVER SEEN anything like the growth of Palmer's "baby" railroad. Leadville profits provided funds and freed the General from Gould's pressure for the time being. As Robert Athearn wrote in his *Rebel of the Rockies*, Palmer's construction force from 1880 to 1883 was larger than the United States Army. He had forgotten all about El Paso, Texas, and he had no further interest in the Rio Grande, the stream.

What he wanted now was to rule the Colorado Rockies and to control the state's transcontinental destiny.

Hardly had his tracks reached Leadville in July, 1880, before his crews were pushing grade over Fremont Pass (11,320) to Kokomo and Robinson; over Tennessee Pass (10,423) to Redcliff on the Eagle, and to the mouth of F. V. Hayden's Roche Moutonnée Creek. In October, a new batch of transit men filed up the Poncha Pass road from Salida, and west toward Gunnison along the Marshall Pass toll road which Palmer had bought from Otto Mears for thirteen thousand dollars. John Evans complained of perfidy in bitter terms. The General, he pointed out, had promised him never to build to Gunnison to compete with Evans's line. Palmer replied that the promise was made to Evans personally in his role as owner of the Denver and South Park. It was not transferable. It did not go with the railroad which the ex-Governor was about to sell to Jay Gould. Palmer added that he trusted Evans, but he couldn't trust the buccaneer who had wrecked the Erie.

Lieutenant Marshall's toothache traverse, 10,846 feet above sea level, called for four per cent grades and twenty-four degree curves. And yet the Denver and Rio Grande rails wound their way up Poncha Creek with incredible speed. They crossed Marshall Pass on June 21, and descended to Tomichi Creek at the foot of present Monarch Pass in mid-July. The ascent from the Arkansas was somewhat steeper than the west side — 3346 feet of climb in seventeen miles. On August 8, 1881, a Denver and Rio Grande train of two coal cars, a baggage car and two passenger cars rattled into Gunnison with its whistle screaming out the glad news.[9]

So Palmer's rails were in Gunnison, and that was just an item. During the winter and spring of 1880–1881, the General was doing more than putting out wild talk about getting to the San Juans and Silverton. His men were slamming down track south from Alamosa and Antonito, and west into the mountain wilds along the New Mexico border toward the top of

Cumbres Pass (10,022). It was a compromise route, avoiding the 12,594-foot wall of Stony Pass, and the too-long southern detour over ancient Horse Lake Pass. Soon Ernest Ingersoll was describing the Cumbres crossing with the hot prose which characterized America's favorite travel writer. We quote in part from his *The Crest of the Continent:*

> Six miles ahead lay . . . the Toltec Gorge, whose praises could not be overdrawn. . . . Was this king of canyons so great he could afford to risk all rivalry? What noble martello-tower of native lava is that which stands undizzied on the very brink of the precipice? I should like to roll it off and watch it cut a swath through that puny forest and dam up the whole stream. . . . All the road-bed is heaped up or dug out artificially. It is nearly a shelf near the summit. It hugs the wall like a chamois-stalker, creeping stealthily out to the end of and around each spur. . . . In the most secluded nook of the mountains we come upon Phantom Curve, with its company of isolated rocks, tall, grotesque, sunburned. They fill the eye, and in their fantastic resemblance to human shapes, seem to us crumbled images of the days when there were giants, and men of Titanic mold set up mementoes of their brawny heroes. . . . The blank of a tunnel gives one time to think . . . then a gleam of advancing light, and dash out into the sunshine — into the sunshine only? Oh, no, out into the air, — catch your breath, startled beyond self-control! Just west of the tunnel, and close beside the track, the rocks have been levelled into a small smooth space, and here, on the 26th of September, 1881, were celebrated as impressive memorial services for GARFIELD, the noble man and beloved President, then lying dead on his stately catafalque in Cleveland, as were anywhere seen.[10]

The broad top of Cumbres Pass was as stark then as it is now. The thick evergreens had been destroyed in 1878 by a fire so intense that nothing grew up there for half a century, and not much grows today. Cumbres links tributaries of the Rio Grande — Los Pinos River and the Chama. The Continental Divide is some miles farther west. The D. & R. G. crossed it in 1881 at a saddle in the sage almost too low to be noticed, like Escalante's Horse Lake Pass just south of it. The tracks were hurried on west down drainage of the San Juan River and reached Durango in July. A year later they had conquered Animas Canyon, breaking forever the isolation of Charles Baker's Park. Soon cars were carrying passengers forty-five miles up the canyon to Silverton. The passengers were as delighted and as excited as Durango-Silverton passengers are now on the same run up the same canyon in the same cars on the same Denver and Rio Grande Railroad during the line's celebrated summer "trip to yesterday." Tempus, thank heaven, doesn't always fugit.

WHAT NEXT? There really was no very good reason for any more railroads to the mines of Colorado. But the stream generated by Leadville and by Aspen was far from abating, and railroaders did not want to be reasonable. Throughout 1881, Denver and South Park men watched the extension of Palmer's tracks until they couldn't stand it. The main watcher was a seventy-year-old rail expert named Sidney Dillon, president of the U. P., which is to say, a sort of flunky for Jay Gould. But Gould was back East organizing Western Union and running the *New York World*. Dillon was in charge out West, and he liked to keep building, since the D. & S. P. had to buy all its construction materials from the U. P.

Furthermore, mining prospects were bright across Brecken-ridge Pass on Blue River and at Montezuma. From Blue River and Tenmile Creek it was just a step over Fremont Pass to Leadville, where the D. & S. P. could demand its fair share of Palmer's traffic. The Dillon version of Loveland's Colorado Central could be pushed from Georgetown over Loveland Pass and down Snake River to join the D. & S. P. on the Blue at Dillon town. This combination would teach Palmer not to try to steal a whole state from under the nose of Sidney Dillon. It was true that tracks from Como in South Park to Leadville had to cross the Continental Divide twice at an altitude of better than eleven thousand feet. And still there were advantages. The Leadville-Denver distance on that stupendous D. & S. P. roller coaster would be one hundred and fifty miles. The distance on the D. & R. G. was two hundred and eighty miles because Palmer had headed for Texas in the 1870's and never had the good sense to straighten his track.

In the spring of 1882, Dillon yanked his weary chief engineer, James Evans, off Alpine Tunnel which he had just finished, and put him to laying rail from Como toward Breckenridge Pass (11,482). The name was changed to Boreas Pass; Dillon could use fancy language as well as Ernest Ingersoll. The name, Greek for "rude north wind," was an understatement for the constant gales on Boreas Pass. The tracks veered east from Tarryall Creek and then north to gain altitude, joining the old stage road under Boreas Mountain. It was ten miles of moderate grade to the top. In June, Evans's rails crossed Boreas, descending Indiana and Illinois gulches to Breckenridge by September. That drop was not moderate — 1925 feet in eleven miles, which was almost as bad as the D. & S. P.'s drop between Alpine Tunnel and the Arkansas.

Evans had no construction trouble from Breckenridge to Dillon, to Frisco and the outskirts of Kokomo. But here lawyers for the Denver and Rio Grande blocked progress interminably. As a result, the Denver and South Park got no trains over Fremont Pass to Leadville until September 30, 1884. In the interim, Dillon and the U. P. made mankind's last attempt to reach Blue River by rail over Loveland Pass from Georgetown. The tracks were laid only eight miles to the east foot of the pass. But the first three of those miles contained such an inconceivable maze of trestles, bridges, cuts, shelfs and curves between Georgetown and Silver Plume as to constitute one of the greatest of tourist attractions — the Georgetown Loop — from 1882 until the thing was torn down in 1937.

FINALLY, there were the two mavericks of these Colorado mining railroads: James J. Hagerman, the cantankerous invalid;

and Otto Mears, the diminutive transport king of the San Juans.

Hagerman was among the first of many multimillionaires to bring their ailing bodies to Colorado Springs for repairs. In the course of his bedpan routine, he bought an Aspen silver mine, made more millions out of it, and began building a standard-gauge railroad to Aspen via Leadville straight from Pikes Peak. His personal motive was curative. Nothing seemed to improve his health so much as thumbing his nose at his enemies — in this case, the managers of the D. & R. G., who were charging the usual all-the-traffic-would-bear for Aspen ore shipments at their Redcliff railhead west of Leadville and Tennessee Pass.

The Colorado Midland Railway was built to smash the D. & R. G.'s monopoly. It was also an outrageous attempt by an iron-willed man to defy the laws of gravity. After Hagerman had put up seven million dollars of his own and other people's money, his crew started laying track from Colorado Springs up Ute Pass on a granite shelf high above the road. The tracks were rushed across South Park and Trout Creek Pass to reach Leadville by the end of the summer of 1887. From there they pointed due west at Sugar Loaf Mountain and a Continental Divide gap which we call Hagerman Pass (12,050).[11]

The invalid hoped to run his standard-gauge rails over this pass to snatch the American altitude record from the narrow-gauge D. & S. P., which, you recall, had held it for five years with its Alpine Tunnel at 11,612 feet. But crossing Hagerman was impossible. A regiment of rock men spent that summer of 1887 driving a 2196-foot bore under the pass at the 11,500-foot level — a record height, at least, for standard gauge. They built a fine tunnel, but their best efforts were devoted to cultivating the alpine night life of their shanty town among the ptarmigans, Douglass City. This delightful place had no police, no firemen, no churches, no schools and no chamber of commerce. During its brief existence, it won fame as the drunkenest, gamblingest, most lecherous spot in the Rockies, winding up in a blaze of alcoholic glory when the tunnel's powder house blew up.

The dozen miles of Midland track from the Arkansas up to the tunnel entrance under Hagerman Pass had an average grade of 3.24 per cent. From Loch Ivanhoe at the west end, the rails ran forty-two miles down the lovely Frying Pan River to Basalt — an even three per cent grade in a tremendous vertical fall of 4866 feet. At Basalt, the standard-gauge track doubled back east eighteen miles up the Roaring Fork to reach Aspen in late January, 1888. The narrow-gauge rails of the D. & R. G. were there already, having arrived from Redcliff by way of Glenwood Canyon on October 23, 1887. The D. & R. G. board of directors had twiddled its thumbs for a year before building those last eighty miles, waiting for the wild invalid to die of his tuberculosis, or go broke, or explode after indulging once too often in a nose-thumbing tantrum.

Far from dying, Hagerman had pushed his lunatic line through, forcing an immediate reduction of D. & R. G. freight rates. On top of this supreme insult, he sold the Midland two years later to the D. & R. G.'s perennial foe, the Santa Fe.[12]

While Hagerman's tunnel army was living it up at Douglass City, our little ex-Indian trader and former guardian of Cochetopa Pass, Otto Mears, was acting out an old dream. It concerned the laying of track to close the twenty-six mile gap over Red Mountain Pass between the D. & R. G.'s track at Silverton and its track which had just arrived at Ouray from the Marshall Pass–Gunnison–Grand Junction line. Mears had given up several of his pioneer toll roads but he still operated one hundred and seventy miles of them, including the Montrose–Ouray–Silverton–Animas Forks–Mineral Point route and the road to Telluride over Dallas Divide from the Uncompahgre. Though nearing fifty now, and head man of the San Juans, he remained essentially the wide-eyed Russian orphan determined to overcome the buffetings of fate and to rank with such aristocrats as Palmer, John Evans, Hagerman and Jay Gould.

He named his dream the Silverton Railroad and, during the summer of 1888, he forced its right-of-way somehow from Silverton up the Mineral Creek branch of Animas River past Chattanooga and over Red Mountain Pass at a spot which he called Sheridan Pass — a hundred feet above today's U.S. Route 550 traverse at 11,018 feet. In that gorgeous red turmoil of topography beyond the pass, he used turntables and switchbacks to serve camps of Vanderbilt and Yankee Girl, Corkscrew Gulch and Joker Tunnel. But he had to stop building at Albany in Ironton Park. Ouray was eight miles farther north at the foot of the boiling Uncompahgre Canyon. There was just no room in that awesome slot to maneuver, to reduce the seventeen per cent grade of the shelf road which Mears had opened in 1883. He considered an electric or cog line but the cost was too great.

His failure irked him for two years, Mears being Mears, above all else indomitable. He began building what Lucius Beebe has described with felicity as "the futile, transcendently triumphant Rio Grande Southern . . . a masterpiece of evasion." During the year ahead, Mears evaded those eight Uncompahgre Canyon miles by a great westering circle through the San Miguel Range, an entirely different set of mountains. From Durango, the Rio Grande Southern ran west to Dolores River, north to Rico town, and over Lizard Head Pass (10,022) to San Miguel River, Ophir town, Telluride, Dallas Divide (8735) and so to Uncompahgre River at the D. & R. G. depot, Ridgway, ten miles north of Ouray. Rails from Silverton to Ouray at last! Two hundred and seventeen miles of them, combining Rio Grande Southern and D. & R. G. properties. The distance between the two points by wagon road was twenty-six miles. Mears's first train made the Durango-Ridgway run on December 21, 1891. Two years later the "futile, transcendently triumphant" road was bankrupt, and the D. & R. G. took over as receiver. But that was a matter of no importance. Mears had not built the Rio Grande Southern to succeed, but just to show that it could be done.

As every narrow-gauge rail fan will tell you, the Mears lines in the San Juans were the quintessence of this quaintest of railroad forms — charming, irresponsible, unpredictable. Mears's free passes — of various shapes and made of gold, silver and buckskin — became as legendary in Colorado as Silverheels. His Silverton Railroad, a two-hour run, had a luxurious sleeping car, because that was the last thing it needed. The San Juan historian, Josie Moore Crum, has told the story of the sweet young thing boarding the train at Ironton and being asked by the conductor if she were cold on the Sheridan Pass climb. She admitted that she was. The conductor stopped the train, chopped some firewood from beside the track, and had the car's potbellied stove red hot in a jiffy.

The Mears lines deserved the superlatives which their affectionate biographers have heaped upon them, but they were no more unusual than the rest in a construction and operating sense. By 1888, five other rails had reached altitudes higher than the rails of the Silverton Railroad at Sheridan Pass (11,113) — at Alpine Tunnel (11,608), Hagerman Tunnel (11,500), Boreas Pass (11,482) and Fremont Pass (11,320). Two sets of rails crossed Fremont. In 1904, David Moffat's standard-gauge Denver, Northwestern and Pacific would go a little higher even than Alpine Tunnel at Rollins Pass (11,-680).[13]

The Silverton Railroad had bits of very heavy grade — almost seven per cent. But its *average* steepness and that of the Rio Grande Southern from valley to crest were not as great as the east-side grade to Alpine Tunnel, the north-side grade to Boreas Pass, the east-side grade to Marshall Pass and the east-side grade to Kenosha Pass. Furthermore, the tremendous construction problems of the eighteen-mile Silverton were solved elsewhere on a grander scale. General Palmer, for instance, had to lay forty miles of track up the east slope of Cumbres Pass. James J. Hagerman used long shelves and trestles to conquer Sugar Loaf Mountain. Most remarkable of all was the heroic work of James A. Evans in boring Alpine Tunnel through rotten rock. Perhaps it was an act of atonement for his part in building the Union Pacific as unheroically as possible over Sherman Hill at a mere 8235 feet above the sea.

19

Marias Pass, and Kicking Horse Again

WHILE GENERAL PALMER was stealing Colorado passes right
and left for the Denver and Rio Grande, his Denver and
South Park rival, Sidney Dillon, was stealing a couple in Montana Territory for the Union Pacific. Both of them would become major rail crossings of the Continental Divide, but Dillon
laid his tracks so stealthily that nobody paid much attention to
them at the time.

Dillon's road, a narrow gauge, was called the Utah and
Northern, and if ever a carrier was mixed up with the history
of the Rockies it was this one. The Mormons began to build
it in 1869 when the U. P. reached Corinne, Utah, just north
of Ogden. It was a homemade, cooperative affair, serving
Mormon towns in Cache Valley of Bear River and thriving on
transient traffic to non-Mormon Corinne, where a man could
get a drink, or a divorce for two dollars and fifty cents, or otherwise take a breather from Mormon righteousness. Jay Gould
bought the tracks in 1873 because they pointed at the Montana
gold camps four hundred miles north. He handed them over
at cost to the U. P. and to President Dillon two years later. In
1878, Dillon took Captain Edward L. Berthoud away from his
troubles trying to put the Colorado Central over Loveland Pass
and had him survey a Utah and Northern route from Corinne
to Fort Hall and Snake River. The old trapper path, you may
recall, was up Bear River to Soda Springs and a junction with

the Oregon Trail, but Berthoud ran the line a bit to the west — down Marsh Creek and Portneuf River to the Snake.

The Utah and Northern was pure speculation, since Montana's mining was in a doleful state and nothing much else was happening to bring traffic to the U. P. at Corinne. Dillon told his Colorado engineer, Thomas J. Milner, to build cheaply.[1] The locomotive ran at night without headlights, and the fireman's handkerchief was the signal system. From Fort Hall, the tracks ran on north toward the innocuous Continental Divide of the Beaverhead Range along the dusty, dreary old Virginia City stage road through Beaver Canyon. It was the route Lieutenant John Mullan and his men had taken in the winter of 1853–1854 on their return from Fort Hall to Hell Gate and Bitterroot Valley. Dillon chose Red Rock Pass (7056) first for the Divide traverse since it led more directly to Virginia City and to the capital, Helena, stagnating at the foot of Mullan Pass after its Last Chance Gulch years of glory. But mining revived a little in the Butte–Silver Bow area, so Dillon headed for low Monida Pass (6823), in line with the Deer Lodge Pass road over the Divide again to Silver Bow.

The first Utah and Northern train chuffed up to Monida station on the prairie top of Monida Pass on March 9, 1880.[2] There was champagne for the crew and somebody drove the usual silver spike with a telegraph wire stuck to it so that U. P. telegraph operators back in Cheyenne and Omaha could hear the click of the sledgehammer. Seven months later, the line's antique locomotive, still running nights without a headlight, reached the junction of Blacktail Creek and the Beaverhead. It occurred to no one that the ghosts of Lewis and Clark and Sacajawea might be around. The three had had a happy time near this spot in August, 1805, when Sacajawea recognized her home ridge above Lemhi Pass a day's march to the southwest.

The railroaders put up a station on the Beaverhead and named it Dillon, a shack similar to the Dillon station of the

Denver and South Park which was to appear soon, as we have seen, at the junction of Blue River, Snake River and Tenmile Creek in Colorado. Beyond Dillon, the Utah and Northern crossed from the Beaverhead over to and up Big Hole River and over Deer Lodge Pass (5902) to Silver Bow. From there, a short spur ran to Butte, where the first gala train of fifty passengers arrived on December 21, 1881. From Silver Bow, the line was built on north in leisurely fashion down Clark Fork of the Columbia. Its destination was the mouth of Little Blackfoot River and the so-called "worst out of hell" remains of the Mullan Road, which no wagons had used in years to get through the Rockies.[3]

Some people were amused by the wobbly tracks and haphazard operation of the Utah and Northern, but it was not a joke to the crowd involved in that colossus of corporate failures, the Northern Pacific Railroad Company. Lincoln had signed the N. P.'s charter in 1864. Its incorporators included John Charles Frémont and J. Edgar Thomson, General Palmer's mentor. It was to be the Union Pacific of the north, the dazzling realization of Governor Stevens's dream of a road to Puget Sound. It would run from Lake Superior and St. Paul to the Great Falls of the Missouri, up Dearborn River into the delectable forests of the Lewis Range, and over Cadotte Pass where Lieutenant Grover had tried to sleep with eleven sled dogs on a cold January night in 1854. From Cadotte Pass, the tracks would go through Hell Gate to present Missoula, up Coriacan Defile and over Evaro Pass to the Jocko and on to Lake Pend Oreille and the Snake-Columbia junction near Wallula, Washington.

One of the world's great banking firms, Jay Cooke and Company, took over fund raising and, in 1869, sent railroad experts west. They relocated the N. P. up the Yellowstone and over Bozeman and Deer Lodge passes. Two years later, the N. P.'s own experts went at it again. They examined all the gaps in Montana except Marias Pass, which had been marked on every United States map since 1840, even though nobody was saying publicly where it was. The pass field was narrowed to Mullan, Deer Lodge and a new one — Pipestone Pass (6418), reached up Little Pipestone Creek from Jefferson River. The west side of Pipestone Pass fell into Butte town along Blacktail Creek. The N. P. experts ruled that Pipestone was too high and Mullan required a tunnel. So Deer Lodge Pass was the choice, though it would make the railroad forty miles longer.

Meanwhile Jay Cooke's super-salesmen peddled bales of N. P. bonds with the help of inspired pamphlets describing how warm winds from the South Pacific gave Montana a climate resembling that of Tidewater Virginia. People like Lieutenant Grover who had been there in winter laughed at the pamphlets and called the proposed railroad "the banana line." Still, the fund-raising went well until the Jay Cooke outfit, "the Gibralter of American finance," blew up to help start the Panic of 1873, and the Northern Pacific almost blew up too. However, an old-time railroader from Vermont, Frederick Billings, became N. P. president in 1879, glued the broken company together, and soon had crews building grade east from the Snake-Columbia junction and west from Dakota up the Yellowstone toward Bozeman Pass. Another crew occupied Hell Gate to keep Sidney Dillon from running the Utah and Northern down Clark Fork to Bitterroot Valley. By 1879, Dillon and the U. P. controlled Deer Lodge Pass, so Billings erased it from his N. P. plan and substituted Mullan Pass.

The Montana of the early 1880's had its own Jay Gould, with the ruthlessness tempered. His name was Henry Villard, a cultured Bavarian from Speyer on the Rhine. In 1853, he fled from Prussianism to St. Louis and became a reporter whose first stories in English concerned the Lincoln-Douglas debates. He began learning about the Rockies when he covered the Denver–Gregory Gulch rush of 1859 for the *Cincinnati Commercial*. Then he organized a pioneer news syndicate and married the

daughter of William Lloyd Garrison, the abolitionist. Thereafter, as agent for German bondholders, his specialty was
bankrupt railroads — first General Palmer's old Kansas Pacific,
and then Oregon lines which would meet the Northern Pacific
at Wallula, Washington, to make it transcontinental.

Wealthy Americans trusted Villard, partly because of his
friendship with the late Abraham Lincoln, and with the current
Secretary of the Interior, Carl Schurz, whose career as a German expatriate newsman was so much like Villard's. These
millionaires — J. P. Morgan, August Belmont and such — supplied the cash with which Villard bought the Northern Pacific
on the open market in January, 1881. Some months later,
Villard, aged forty-six, replaced the ailing Billings as president.
By then, the N. P. tracks had reached Billings, Montana. From
the west they were approaching Pend Oreille Lake in present
Idaho. The Rockies gap between these track ends was about
six hundred miles long.

President Villard began putting tunnels under Bozeman
and Mullan passes at once, using estimates based on their
presumed lesser costs as compared with the cost of Denver and
South Park's Alpine Tunnel. These estimates turned out to be
badly in error. The Alpine Tunnel line, true enough, involved
awful altitudes and unconscionable miles of extra track to
achieve even an impractical four per cent grade. But the high
Colorado terrain reduced some costs because the bed rock was
right there, exposed or just inches below the soil, ready for
blasting. By contrast, the N. P. men in lower Montana toiled
month after discouraging month far behind schedule making
long cuts through soggy, dangerous dirt and coping with its
whims before they reached rock.

The Mullan Tunnel through the Continental Divide was
finished first — in the early summer of 1883. It was 3875 feet
long with an apex of 5547 feet above sea level (the pass over-
head was about 6000 feet). The three-mile west-side approach
from the Little Blackfoot had a grade of only seventy-four feet

to the mile. The three-mile east-side grade was one hundred and sixteen feet to the mile, the same as that of the Baltimore and Ohio over the hills of West Virginia. The Bozeman Tunnel through the Bridger Range was to be 3610 feet long and its construction was delayed by cave-ins of sticky blue clay around the site of the west portal. Its altitude was 5712 feet, the highest point on the Northern Pacific. Villard got in a frenzy to have his through trains running, so he bypassed the incompleted tunnel by running track two and a half miles over the top at 6020 feet. The bypass had a grade of two hundred and twenty feet per mile — as bad as the grades of those Colorado narrow gauges. By using the bypass, the first Northern Pacific train from St. Paul steamed into Bozeman town on March 21, 1883. Many of those who watched it arrive had never seen an engine before. In June, the rails reached Helena and, on September 8, 1883, those from the east and those from the west came together forty miles west of Mullan Pass on Clark Fork of the Columbia near Garrison station. More champagne, and a gold spike this time.

Henry Villard was pleased to name that station in honor of his father-in-law, William Lloyd Garrison. He was not so pleased when the Bozeman Pass and Mullan Pass tunnel bills were presented for payment and the Northern Pacific found itself to be a bankrupt line and a national scandal once more. He was removed from the presidency just before Bozeman Tunnel was opened in January, 1884. But he was not downcast. Within five years, he was back as chairman of the Northern Pacific board, and full of plans for his next creation, the General Electric Company.

THE NORTHERN PACIFIC was regarded more as a Wall Street poker game with all the cards wild than as a transcontinental railroad to develop the Northwest. The soon-to-be-born Great Northern was exactly the opposite — pure railroad through and through. It was conceived slowly after 1870 in the mind of a large, shaggy, gifted Canadian gentleman named James Jerome Hill, born and bred in Ontario. It acquired, and retains still, a strong Canadian flavor, partly because it crossed the American Rockies where they began looking like Canadian Rockies — those misty pinnacles and precipices, glaciers and thick forests which we met first at Howse Pass in 1807 with David Thompson. The progenitor of the Great Northern, the St. Paul, Minneapolis and Manitoba, was bought for Hill to play with in 1879 by such Canadian stalwarts as Donald Smith (Lord Strathcona), head of Hudson's Bay Company, and George Stephen (Lord Mount Stephen), president of the Bank of Montreal. This Minnesota wheat carrier was planned originally as a north-south road — to tie St. Paul to Winnipeg and the Canadian Pacific Railway, which was being pushed into the Canadian plains.

Then the hardheaded Hill got bigger ideas. He saw that the Northern Pacific was badly built and hopelessly over-capitalized. Using his Minnesota freight profits, he extended his tracks west across North Dakota and northern Montana to Great Falls on the Missouri. There they joined his Montana Central, which carried his trains on up the Missouri to Helena and over the Continental Divide to Butte.[4] By this time, 1888, Butte's copper mines were the wonder of the world, and so were its twelve hundred prostitutes in back of Mercury and Galena Streets.

Booming Butte seemed to be as far west as James Jerome Hill wanted to go. But all the while he had an army of surveyors staking right-of-way for what he would call the Great Northern Railway from eastern Montana to Puget Sound. The head staker was an ex-New England sailor named Major A. B. Rogers whom we will meet more fully in Canada some pages hence. Rogers favored what amounted to the old 1806 trail of Meriwether Lewis from the Great Falls of the Missouri up Dearborn River, but he wanted to cross the Continental Divide a few miles south of Lewis and Clark Pass at a gap known now as Rogers Pass (5609). Rogers considered Marias Pass too, having learned of it from Duncan McDonald, the old Hudson's Bay Company trader who had crossed it from Flathead Lake. Before Rogers could hire McDonald to show him Marias Pass, the old fellow died (in the spring of 1889) and Rogers turned in his incomplete pass findings to James J. Hill and moved off to other work. Meanwhile, Hill was hearing rumors that Marias Pass might be the lowest pass in Montana. He was furious to find that Rogers had done no more for him in the Marias Pass matter than Frederick Lander and Abiel Tinkham had done for Governor Stevens in 1853. The pass was marked right there on the maps, wasn't it? In the late fall of 1889, Hill sent word to his new chief engineer, E. H. Beckler, that his promotion could be rescinded if somebody didn't find Marias Pass before snow fell.

In desperation, Beckler clutched at a straw. He got to a telegraph key and sent for Major Rogers's friend and colleague, a certain John Frank Stevens, who was a member of the Great Northern's staking crew in Spokane, Washington. Stevens was thirty-six, a quiet, modest native of Washington, unrelated to Governor Stevens. He lacked formal engineering training, but he was a first class axman, rodman and instrument handler. Furthermore, he had worked for General Palmer in Colorado on gradients for the Denver and Rio Grande over Tennessee Pass and Fremont Pass, and he had learned about mountains up there. More recently, he had done well surveying for the Canadian Pacific at Kicking Horse Pass.

About December 1, John F. Stevens arrived by rail at Fort Assiniboine near the Havre station of the Great Northern on Milk River, two hundred miles east of the Rockies. From there, he trekked to the Blackfoot Indian Agency one hundred and sixty miles west. This agency was on Badger Creek, thirty-five miles short of where Marias Pass was supposed to be. His outfit consisted of a wagon, a mule, a saddle-horse, snowshoes, a leather jacket and a wool stocking cap. He had an assistant, but the assistant drank so much whiskey to keep up his courage that Stevens fired him and continued alone. His route on the Marias River plain was near that of Meriwether Lewis, George Drewyer and the Fields brothers in 1806. He passed close to the Two Medicine Creek campsite where Reuben Fields stabbed a Blackfoot to death and Lewis shot another.

At the Blackfoot Agency, Stevens found that the Old Marias Pass jinx was still working. The Blackfeet would not guide him to the gap because evil spirits guarded it and the guides did not want to die yet. Stevens had to hire a Flathead half-breed, an outcast who claimed to have no fear of spirits until he arrived with Stevens at the foot of the pass. The date was December 11, 1889. The spot came to be called False Summit because the field men who mapped Stevens's line some months later marked it as being actually the top of the Continental Divide. It was snowing at that False Summit and just about as cold as Colorado's Wet Mountain Valley had been when Pike's men were there in January, 1807.

Stevens's terrified guide refused to advance and settled down in bivouac. Stevens trudged on by himself through deepening snow up the Summit Creek branch of Two Medicine Creek. Darkness was falling among the lodgepoles as he crossed the top on his snowshoes and came to the first trickle of Bear Creek, which had to flow west to the Flathead, Clark Fork and the Pacific. The cold was becoming painful, but Stevens was thrilled by a professional admiration for Marias Pass, which seemed to him to have been formed by nature just to accommodate a railroad. It was virtually straight as a ruler, only five miles long, and with a miraculous grade of about one per cent. The Great Northern deserved such a pass, which meant that he must survive the bitter forty-below-zero night. To make sure of it, he decided to keep vigorously on the move — not even building a fire, by some accounts, which might put him to sleep. So he tramped out a path in the snow a hundred yards long and walked back and forth for several hours until daylight.

Then he hurried down the five miles of Summit Creek to False Summit, retrieved his spooky guide, and was back at the Blackfoot Agency on the twelfth before dark.

All this was in the railroader's line of duty. As Stevens wrote later:

> I made only a verbal report to Mr. Beckler . . . and none whatever to Mr. Hill or anyone else. As soon as the weather permitted early next spring, engineering parties were put in the field and the pass and approaches to it were fully developed, and the outcome was even more favorable than I had reported. The net advantage which the Great Northern obtained by the discovery and adoption of the true Marias Pass were: The saving of more than one hundred miles of distance, much less curvature, and an infinitely better grade line, together with the lowest railway pass in the United States north of New Mexico [5215]. In other words, these advantages put the Great Northern on the map — as being the most economical, from an operating standpoint, of any of the transcontinental Railway lines.

James J. Hill rewarded his assistant engineer by making him "principal assistant engineer," and then promoted him to chief engineer in 1893. But it was not until long after Hill's death that the railroad's publicity man decided to exploit Stevens's adventure as a way of telling the world about the Great Northern. The New York sculptor, Gaetano Cecere, was commissioned to make a heroic bronze statue of the "eminent explorer" in his leather jacket and stocking cap. On July 21, 1925, this statue was unveiled on top of Marias Pass by members of "The Upper Missouri Historical Expedition of the Great Northern Railway" in the presence of assorted celebrities and John Frank Stevens himself.

As Grace Flandrau, the G. N.'s reporter wrote, it was a moving moment when "the enfolding stripes that had enveloped the bronze colossus fluttered aside; and there stood before the spectators the bronze figure of the man who had battled for his life through the storms of that wild winter night in December, and the living man himself, who had accomplished what none of his predecessors had dared. I do not think any of us noticed the tears coursing down Mr. Stevens's cheeks."

If the modest Mr. Stevens wept during the unveiling and ensuing eulogies it was purely from embarrassment. He had never thought that his discovery of Marias Pass for Mr. Beckler was particularly heroic or hazardous, even though it had been pretty chilly up there. Every Rocky Mountain engineer endured such trials as a matter of course.[5] His own remarks chided the eulogists for their "unconscious exaggeration." Much later he was wryly amused to find that posterity would honor him more for a few hours' tribulation on Marias Pass than for his years of toil as head of the Panama Canal Commission and more years directing railroaders in Russia during World War I.

YEARS BEFORE BUILDING the Great Northern, James Jerome Hill was a director and an owner of the Canadian Pacific Railway. This great carrier was planned in the early 1870's, and it was many things to many people. Its promoters regarded it as a chain of British imperialism linking Liverpool to Hong Kong. But nationally it expressed the desire of patriotic Canadians to control their own destiny, free of dependence on either the British Crown or the United States.

The Canadian government hired a Boston contractor, Andrew Onderdonk, to start building from Vancouver eastward up Fraser River along the Yellowhead Pass route of the unhappy Overlanders of 1862. Yellowhead was picked in 1875 for the Rockies crossing after three million dollars had been spent to survey Kicking Horse, Howse, Athabaska, Pine River and even Peace River Pass, which Alexander Mackenzie had used in 1793. The government gave up the job in a few years and turned it over to a syndicate of Canadians, Americans, Englishmen and Frenchmen. One of their first acts in 1881 was to install William Cornelius Van Horne, a protégé of James J. Hill's, as general manager. Van Horne, a thirty-eight-year-old giant, had been born and bred on an Illinois farm and had risen from messenger boy to general manager of the Chicago, Milwaukee and St. Paul Railroad. He was a prodigious eater and was said to digest this consumption by working twenty hours each day, including Sunday. Van Horne started off by discarding the far-north Yellowhead Pass route and hiring our friend Major A. B. Rogers to locate a Rockies passage where prospects for coal, lumber and farming were better than they were around Yellowhead and Jasper House.

The Major, aged fifty-two in 1881, had never mapped mountains before that year, but he had won fame as a locator throughout the Middle West. Besides, James J. Hill had recommended him. He was called the Bishop because he was always calling down God's wrath on some one. An associate, J. H. E. Secretan, described him as "a rough and ready engineer, or rather pathfinder. A short, sharp, snappy little chap with long Dundreary whiskers. He was a master of picturesque profanity, who continually chewed tobacco and was an artist at expectoration. He wore overalls with pockets behind, and he had a plug of tobacco in one pocket and a sea-biscuit in the other, which was his idea of a season's provisions for an engineer. His scientific equipment consisted of a compass and an aneroid slung around his neck." [6]

The Bishop did not have to decide where to cross the Continental Divide. By 1881, everybody agreed that the gap where our brash young Dr. Hector got kicked by a horse in 1858 was the best because of its east approach up fertile Bow Valley and its west end on Columbia River. His problem was the one Hector left unsolved when he reached the Columbia from near Kicking Horse too late to find a second Rockies gate through that subsidiary, but equally splendid Selkirk Range. Captain Palliser, you recall, saw no way to cover those eighty miles west over the Selkirks, and he condemned the two-hundred-mile detour which the Columbia made in flowing north and

then south around them. Canada's Pacific Ocean, he predicted dourly, would continue to be reached through American territory.

Rogers thought not. He went after his Selkirk pass from the
west, leaving Thompson River Valley at Kamloops on April
29, 1881, ascending the beautiful Illecillewaet ("Rushing
Water") Valley from the site of today's Revelstoke resort on
the Columbia. His crew consisted of his nephew, A. L. Rogers,
and ten Indian guides of Catholic persuasion whose wages
would go to their mission if they did not behave. The wilderness was complete — a landscape of lodgepoles rising to the
meadows and warm springs of Albert Canyon. Beyond was
the breathtaking high country of pointed piles of rock and
snow and flowing glaciers, nameless then but bearing names
today like a history of the Canadian Pacific — Bishops Range,
Mount Sir Donald, Mount Shaughnessy, Sir Sandford Range,
Moberly Pass, Mount Rogers, Mount Dawson, and so on.[7]
Late on a mid-May evening, the explorers reached a summit
well above timberline. Later, Rogers's nephew wrote of the discovery of Rogers Pass:

> Crawling along this ridge, very much exhausted, we came to
> a small ledge protected from the wind by a perpendicular rock.
> Here we decided to wait until the crust again formed on the
> snow and the morning light enabled us to travel. At ten o'clock
> it was still twilight, on the peaks, but the valleys below were
> filled with the deepest gloom. We wrapped ourselves in our
> blankets and nibbled at our dry meat and bannock, stamping
> our feet in the snow to keep them from freezing, and taking
> turns at whipping each other with our pack-straps to keep up
> circulation. Only four hours we waited, but it seemed as if
> those four hours outran all time. At two o'clock dawn began to
> glimmer in the east, and as soon as we were able to distinguish
> objects we were only too glad to crawl back to the ridge. Com-
> ing to the foot of the great triangular peak we had named
> Syndicate, we traced the valley to the upper south fork of the
> Illecillewaet, and found that it extended but a short distance
> in a southerly direction, and paralleled the valley on the oppo-

site side of the dividing range through which, we concluded, ran the waters of the Beaver, which emptied into the Columbia on the east side of the Selkirks.

The Rogers party retreated west to Kamloops then, having run out of dry meat and bannock (oatmeal cake). The Major began his Rogers Pass exploration from the east side a year later. In July, 1883, with two white men and three Indians he approached the Selkirks from Kicking Horse Pass by way of the Columbia and Beaver Creek. On the twenty-fourth he went over the pass from the Connaught Creek branch of the Beaver to the source of the Illecillewaet and reported "a line with maximum gradients of 105.6 feet per mile, but in this case I would recommend gradients of 116 feet per mile in order to avoid some points where dangerous snowslides are to be feared. The work through the Selkirks will be very heavy and expensive but I believe that the increased cost will be fully justified by the great saving in distance and in the cost of operation."

Thus, after a century of failure, the great Rocky Mountain obstacle to Canadian nationalism was conquered at Rogers Pass. On November 7, 1885, the last spike of the $150,000,000 Canadian Pacific — Montreal to Vancouver — was driven just west of Kicking Horse, Rogers Pass and Revelstoke. The Bishop held the tie. The ceremony symbolized connecting two Canadian ocean shores in an integrated system which has not been achieved in the United States even yet. General Manager Van Horne decreed that the last spike be an iron one, and he would not permit the blows to be recorded by telegraph. Too many American lines had come to grief soon after their gold and silver spike driving, and Van Horne was superstitious. Perhaps that was wise. The Canadian Pacific has had less trouble through the years than almost any other railroad in the Americas.

WILLIAM VAN HORNE became president of the Canadian Pacific in 1888, and Queen Victoria dubbed the one-time

Illinois farm boy Sir William six years later. By then he was as Canadian as Lord Strathcona himself. He had fallen out with his friend James Hill because the Great Northern had built feeders from its Marias Pass tracks right up to the border to steal business from the South Saskatchewan and from placer camps on the Canadian Kootenay. Since 1863, these camps had centered on Wild Horse Creek, near present Cranbrook. A government trail from Fraser River had been built to them in 1865, continuing eastward up Elk River and over the very low but thickly forested Crowsnest Pass (4453). Van Horne had mapped a C. P. right-of-way over Crowsnest in 1881, but Canadians in those days feared seizure of their West by the United States and the C. P. charter prevented it from putting tracks near the border. One of Van Horne's last acts before retiring from the presidency in 1899 was to have the charter amended and to run a Canadian Pacific branch from Medicine Hat over Crowsnest Pass and the Continental Divide into the Kootenay country.

For his successor, Sir William picked an old friend, Thomas George Shaughnessy, whom he had brought to the Canadian Pacific in 1882 from the Chicago, Milwaukee and St. Paul. Shaughnessy's origins were as humble as Van Horne's — he was the son of a poor Irish immigrant to Milwaukee — but he had a talent for politics, and he became boss of Milwaukee's third ward and then president of the board of aldermen. He had a distaste for the outdoors, particularly in the presence of horses, which he detested. When Van Horne asked him to leave Milwaukee and become the C. P.'s purchasing agent he had to be assured that he would not be required to ride a horse and that his work would be confined to an office. Shaughnessy made a fine president and he was especially good at improving gradients through the Rockies. In 1909, he began spiral tunnels on the west descent of Kicking Horse Pass so that five locomotives would not be needed to get passenger trains through. A thousand men worked two years on the tunnels, which gave the roadbed the shape of a figure eight with the higher loop circling inside Cathedral Mountain and the lower into Mount Ogden. When those remarkable tunnels were done, Shaughnessy directed the boring of a five-mile double-track tunnel through the Selkirks to get out of the way of the avalanches, which hampered train operation on Rogers Pass. Travelers today moving up Connaught Creek on the marvelous Rogers Pass highway can see the C. P. roadbed to the tunnel on its shelf across the lovely valley.

Shaughnessy developed deep cultural interests in his later years, but he never lost his shanty Irish sense of humor. He was knighted by the Duke of York while building his spiral tunnels, and he laughed as loudly as any Canadian when the newspapers called him "Lord Shaughnessy, the Peer that made Milwaukee famous." [8]

20

Les Cols de Canada

THE TRANSCONTINENTAL BUILDERS, Grenville M. Dodge of the U. P., James J. Hill of the Great Northern and William C. Van Horne of the Canadian Pacific, flinched at the mere mention of the word "scenery." To them the horrid syllables implied altitude and the problem of running trains profitably up grades of more than one per cent. But Van Horne changed his mind during the middle 1880's when he perceived that Kicking Horse Pass and Rogers Pass contained a revolutionary potential both for passenger revenue and national prestige.

Van Horne backed into the great discovery of his career — the value of scenery — protesting every inch of the way. He would have liked to whisk his passengers nonstop through the Canadian Rockies so that they would not have to see much of the unexplored uplands which had caused him so much trouble. However, the people had to be fed. Since dining cars were too heavy to be hauled over Kicking Horse and Rogers, Van Horne built small inns for his customers at three points along the Rockies section of the Canadian Pacific. One of these points, at Bow River Falls under Dr. Hector's Mount Rundle, was called Siding 29 — a rather prosaic name for one of the loveliest spots on earth. Lord Strathcona (the C. P.'s Donald A. Smith) changed it to Banff, honoring his hometown in Scotland. A second place for dining was built at Field station, a dozen miles down the west side of Kicking Horse Pass, beneath the monumental dome of Mount Stephen. A third, Glacier House, stood just beyond Rogers Pass near the foot of the vast Illecillewaet Glacier, surrounded by the overwhelming ice spires of the Selkirk Range.

It so happened in these same mid-1880's that devotees of the new international sport of mountain climbing had reached an impasse. They had run out of peaks to conquer, to improve their skill on, to apply their names to. Though they had been scrambling for only twenty years around the cols and seracs of the European Alps, the Caucasus and the New Zealand Alps, it was all routine now, with a tramway planned for Monta Rosa, and cables on Matterhorn, which the great Edward Whymper climbed first in 1865. The high Rockies of Colorado were of no use to these specialists. They lacked the sharp conformation necessary for good rock climbs, and the rainfall to sustain real glaciers for sport on ice and snow fields.[1]

Several frustrated alpinists were passengers by chance on the first through Canadian Pacific trains of 1886 which stopped for meals near Illecillewaet Glacier. They had hardly heard of the Canadian Rockies, and they could scarcely believe what they saw in the Selkirks beyond Rogers Pass. These fantastic pinnacles were virgin terrain and quite properly constructed so that the expert climber had a good chance of killing himself. The train brakemen — there was one on each car to work the hand brake — told them that there were dozens of unexplored Selkirk peaks, and probably even more in the main Rockies stretching along the Continental Divide far north and south of the C. P. tracks at Kicking Horse Pass. There seemed to be enough new mountains to keep them all busy for a generation — the Alpine Club of London, the Swiss Alpine Club, the German crowd, the Austrians, the French, the Italians. Westward ho!

The invasion of alpinists began two summers later, on July 18, 1888, when the Reverend William Spotswood Green and the Reverend H. Swanzy, both of the Royal Geographic Society and secondarily, of the Church of England, turned up at Glacier House — a snug Swiss chalet by now. Mr. Perley, the innkeeper, his bear cub and his big bumbling dog Jeff observed them leaving the train in full panoply of ice-axes, ropes, aneroids, hypsometers, walking-stick guns, sleeping bags, mosquito nets and a small Stirn's camera. During the next few weeks, the two men trekked south into the unknown from the inn with Jeff as their uninvited guide. They inspected Illecillewaet Glacier below the Sir Donald Range, took to ropes and crossed a treacherous glacial col. They were watched by a flock of mountain goats, the long white wool of which, "hanging thick above the knee, gave them the appearance of wearing knicker-bockers."

They named the col Asulkan Pass (7720), "asulkan" being the Shushap Indian word for "mountain goat." The col brought them southward to Geikie Glacier, the Dawson Range and a thrilling view of the beautiful Purity Mountain above Purity Pass. They saw beflowered valleys "like the Engadine" of Switzerland, countless waterfalls, exotic birds and animals. They named the glacier beyond Purity Mountain "Van Horne Neve," since William Van Horne had given them permits to ride free on any Canadian Pacific vehicle, including cabooses and hand-cars. And they named other landmarks — Mount Green, Mount Swanzy, Perley Peak. In August, they concluded their Selkirk Range tour by riding a caboose downstream from Rogers Pass to Illecillewaet station and crossing Corbin Pass to look at Mr. Corbin's mine on the Tangier River side.

The Reverend Green's book on his Canadian adventure, *Among the Selkirk Glaciers,* was published in 1890 and contained sentences like "The dark green forest, rushing streams, purple peaks, silvery ice, a cloudless sky, all combine to form a perfect alpine paradise." Such ecstasy caused a rush of Englishmen and Swiss climbers to Glacier House and Asulkan Pass. A handful of charter members of the Appalachian Mountain

Club of Boston arrived too — pioneers like Professor Charles E. Fay, who would be the first president of the American Alpine Club; Philip S. Abbot, C. S. Thompson, and the Yale undergraduates, W. D. Wilcox and S. E. S. Allen.

These American greenhorns soon tired of the rainy Selkirks and began roaming back from the C. P. tracks in Kicking Horse Pass. They learned the climbing craft rapidly and became the most active group in opening the high Continental Divide country of what we call Banff Park and Jasper Park — some two hundred and fifty miles of it from Mount Assiniboine and Father De Smet's White Man Pass in the south to Mount Robson and Yellowhead Pass in the north. They made headquarters often at Laggen station, the old name for present Lake Louise town. If they could afford it, they lodged in William Van Horne's (and the C. P.'s) magnificent Banff Springs Hotel. This incredible palace in the wilderness was created in 1888 by the American architect, Bruce Price, who gave it French chateau lines as a tribute to the French-Canadian trappers who had used Howse and Athabaska passes in the fur era.

Professor Fay's Americans and the sophisticated English and European climbers of those glad early 1890's around Banff enjoyed a freshness of experience which is rare indeed. No matter where they went, they were apt to be the first white men there. It was all trail work of course — horseback and afoot — and remains so today for the most part. The area has had no big mining boom to pay for the kind of wild roads which have made the higher Colorado Rockies so accessible. These Canadian Rockies, with their deep-cut valleys, low timberline and ice fields are infinitely more rugged besides. At the start, the alpinists roamed without the help of professional guides. Peter Sarbach, the first of the famous Swiss guides to be brought in by the Canadian Pacific, did not arrive until 1897. But there were remarkable amateur guides, who served also as pack-train outfitters. One was the future Boer War hero, Bill Peyto, "picturesque and workman-like," though some of Peyto's clients claimed that his "trusty mare" actually did the guiding. Peyto Lake and Peyto Peak, above today's stunning Banff–Jasper highway near Bow Pass, were named for him.

Another amateur was a former member of the Royal Canadian Mounted Police, Tom Wilson, who had kept Major Rogers from getting lost during his investigations of Kicking Horse Pass for the Canadian Pacific. Wilson was the immortal discoverer of Lake Louise (Lake of Little Fishes) in 1882, and he blazed a trail to it from Laggen which has been followed by millions of tourists since then. Wilson found many other beauty spots, though not as a nature lover. He came across them while hunting for stray horses. Mount Wilson, at the northeast foot of Howse Pass, was named for him. Around Banff, a campfire song about him is a favorite still. The song's last lines read:

> And when he told a fishing tale, you saw the fishes grow
> From mountain trout to giant whales, all swimming in a row;
> And if at times you thought he had a tendency to blow,
> He said he caught the habit from those whales of long ago,
> Like a great Canadian pioneer, all of that olden time.

MANY PAGES BACK, we explained how Professor A. P. Coleman of the University of Toronto found a way to Athabaska Pass, where he demoted the old impostors, Mounts Brown and Hooker, from their entrenched position in the public mind as the highest peaks in all the Rockies. During that July of 1893, Coleman and three companions approached the mountains from Red Deer and Rocky Mountain House up North Saskatchewan and Cline rivers, crossing Cataract Pass (7550) to Brazeau River. Coleman had along two pack horses which he named Brown and Hooker. His third pack horse was a mean, unintelligent beast of such surpassing ugliness that Coleman decided to name something beautiful for him, as compensation. And so we have Pinto Lake south of Cataract Pass below Mount Coleman, and Pinto Pass (7100), linking Cline River and the North Saskatchewan.

The Coleman party had no guide, but a large family of Stoney Indians trailed along with the whites for a week or so, led by Chief Jonas. When the professor asked Jonas for routes, he removed a piece of brown wrapping paper from a ham and drew a map on it. The map showed Coleman how to get from Brazeau River to the Athabaska by a pass and creek which are known still as Jonas Pass (7500) and Jonas Creek. Having reached the Athabaska, Coleman had no great difficulty ascending David Thompson's Whirlpool River along the old trapper trail to Athabaska Pass and the Committee's Punch Bowl.

In that same year of 1893, Tom Wilson and the American, R. L. Barrett, visited Mount Assiniboine (11,870), a terrifying white tooth of a peak not thirty miles south of Banff. It was the highest tower on the Continental Divide south of Kicking Horse Pass, and it reminded everybody of the Matterhorn and Dent Blanche in Switzerland. Wilson took Barrett only as far as the mountain's base, by way of Healy Creek, Simpson Pass (6954) and Assiniboine Pass (7152). Next year, Bill Peyto did the same thing for several Americans, including the youngster, W. D. Wilcox. The party examined the minor glacier passes of the area, Marvel, Wonder and Og, and emerged "black as coal-heavers from our long walk in the burnt timber."

Wilcox returned to Mount Assiniboine five years later with H. G. Bryant, the Arctic explorer from Philadelphia, and the English alpinist, L. J. Steele. Their plan of ascent brought them to near tragedy at the 10,000-foot level. As Wilcox told the story: "They had just come to the top of the last ice slope, when Steele's foothold gave way, and he fell, dragging Bryant after him . . . A projecting rock of considerable size appeared not far below. Steele, with a skilful lunge of his ice-axe, swung round to it and anchored himself in a narrow crevice. No sooner had he come to a stop than Bryant shot over him from above and likewise found safety." Mount Assiniboine was conquered at last in 1902 by Bill Peyto and the Reverend James Outram, a Scots expert, accompanied by the Swiss guides,

Christian Hasler and Christian Bohren. By then a variety of beautiful trails had been developed to reach the mountain, including one up Spray River past the Three Sisters and over White Man Pass to Cross River. A few mountaineers continued up the Spray to its source and then crossed to Kananaskis headwaters, Kananaskis Pass and Palliser River on the western slope.

The most spectacular glacial gap in the Banff region was, and is, Abbot Pass (9598), at the top of Victoria Glacier five miles above Lake Louise. It is an ominous, desolate notch, entirely snow-covered and without a sign of life. In the earliest days, climbers called it the Death Trap because huge blocks of ice were constantly breaking away in summer from the fluid ice hanging over the cliffs above. These cliffs to the north were part of Mount Victoria — at 11,365 feet the highest peak of the Bow Range above Lake Louise. The cliffs on the south side of the notch were part of Mount Lefroy — named for Sir John H. Lefroy of Toronto by Dr. Hector during his Kicking Horse Pass visit in 1858.

Abbot Pass was reached first in 1894 by S. E. S. Allen, but not from the steep, steamy Victoria Glacier. Allen approached from the west side of Kicking Horse, moving up Cataract Brook to that most delicious of pools, Lake O'Hara. He did not actually cross Abbot Pass either that year or the next year, when he climbed up to it from Lake Louise. The first crossing was made by Professor Fay, who found that the falling ice blocks of the Death Trap were not so dangerous after all. Abbot Pass got its name as a result of the first climbing fatality in the Canadian Rockies. Philip Stanley Abbot was probably the ablest and most experienced of all the Boston pioneers in the Canadian Rockies. On August 3, 1896, he and three friends were attempting a first ascent of Mount Lefroy. At the 10,400-foot level, he missed his footing on a routine climb up a chimney of rotten rock. He tumbled nine hundred feet to a plateau of debris where he died some hours later. His companions had to go down to Lake Louise next day for help to bring his body off the mountain. They spent the tragic night of the accident in the gloomy notch which has been known since as Abbot Pass.

Early explorers toward Simpson Pass and Mount Assiniboine preferred to work out of Banff. The Mount Lefroy and Valley of the Ten Peaks crowd hung around the Canadian Pacific's chalet at Lake Louise. Field station, down the west side of Kicking Horse Pass, did not become popular until after 1897, when the celebrated Berlin alpinist, Jean Habel, hiked northward from Field to come upon the glories of Yoho Valley and its circling ice fields and peaks. The word "Yoho" means "wonder" in Stoney. Habel ascended Emerald River to find Emerald Lake, Yoho Pass, and the phenomenal booming Takakkaw Falls. "Takakkaw" is an Indian phrase meaning "it is wonderful," which William Van Horne applied to the falls later. Habel saw something of the vast Waputik Ice Field which fed water to Takakkaw Falls, and of the miniature mountain range rising above Yoho Valley on the west with its astonishing variety of alpine terrain. On his return to Europe, Habel could talk of nothing else, and soon Field was full of alpinists. Among them were the Englishmen, G. P. Baker and Professor J. N. Collie, who went up Amiskwi River from Field and over Baker (Amiskwi) Pass (6545) to Blaeberry River and the Howse Pass trail.

Canadian Pacific officials enhanced the Yoho's charms in 1900 by building good trails to Takakkaw Falls up Yoho River and to Emerald Lake up Emerald River — the trails which are highways today. A scenic route was blazed also over Burgess Pass (7160) between Mount Wapta and Mount Burgess so that visitors could reach Emerald Lake directly from Field. An unexpected development was the appearance of female climbers at Field, including Miss Vaux, a fragile young lady from Philadelphia. Miss Vaux shamed the male experts by tripping gaily up Mount Stephen (10,495), which was supposed to be a very hard climb. The Canadian Pacific, meanwhile, assumed a proprietary interest in the country north of Field by calling it the

President Range, in honor of C. P. President Thomas G. Shaughnessy. The highest peak of the group is still called the President (10,297). The Vice President is two hundred feet lower, to be sure, and separated from the President by a nasty glacial gap called President Pass (9469).

During the summer of 1901, all Canadians and many Americans read in their papers about the Yoho area when the one and only Edward Whymper arrived at Field for an outing of some weeks, accompanied by four Swiss guides. Whymper's alpinist past included climbing Chimborazo (20,500) and Cotopaxi (19,613) in the Andes, as well as the Matterhorn (14,782), but he did not belittle the peaks around Kicking Horse. He claimed that he was getting along in years now — (he was sixty-one), and whatever was high enough for Miss Vaux was high enough for him.

Nevertheless, he and his guides made a first ascent of Mount Collie (10,325) and Mount Des Poilus (10,371), and a first crossing of the treacherous Emerald Pass (8899). Bill Peyto and Tom Wilson took turns showing him the best they had in the President Range by way of President Pass and Kiwetinok Pass, and so on back to Field along the Amiskwi. While Whymper was kept entertained, the Reverend James Outram took two of his Swiss guides northeast from Yoho River above Takakkaw Falls, explored the ice fields and crossed the Continental Divide by Balfour Pass (8400) between Mount Gordon and Mount Balfour. From there they made it safely down Balfour Glacier to Hector Lake and Bow River at a point ten miles upstream from Lake Louise. The Swiss were not very enthusiastic about the terrain from their professional point of view. But they admired the big raspberries, blueberries, black huckleberries and enormous porcupines along the way.

THE GREAT LURE for all the international alpinists was always northward along the Continental Divide from Kicking Horse — it was the same lure that draws Banff visitors today up the majestic highway toward Jasper in the shadow of those beautiful, snow-covered peaks — up Bow River and over Bow Pass to the Mistaya and North Saskatchewan, across barren Sunwapta Pass near Athabaska Glacier to Sunwapta River and the Athabaska.

In 1896, the Americans W. D. Wilcox and R. L. Barrett found a better route to Athabaska River from Sunwapta Pass by way of Wilcox Pass, which took them around the unpleasant muskeg at the foot of Dome and Athabaska glaciers. C. S. Thompson approached the ominous Columbia Ice Field in 1900 by ascending Alexandra River between Mount Bryce and Mount Lyell. He discovered Thompson Pass (6511) from Castleguard River over the Divide to Bush River and the Columbia. Two years later, James Outram led a small party to the top of Mount Columbia, which measured 12,294 feet above sea level. Many geographers were convinced that this mammoth, hard-to-reach ice-capped pile was really the highest in the Canadian Rockies, replacing Mounts Brown and Hooker.

Or was it? In 1898, James McEvoy of the Canadian Geological Survey had declared in favor of that lonely wedge-shaped mountain northwest of Yellowhead Pass, Mount Robson.[2] He estimated that its altitude was 13,700 feet, but he arrived at the figure from quite a distance. Everybody, it seemed, kept at a distance from poor Robson, for reasons as obscure as those which kept explorers out of Marias Pass until John Stevens got there. Though the Yellowhead Pass trail from Jasper House to Kamloops passed within fifteen miles of Robson, no travelers had made the slightest effort to climb it.

This apathy was a disgrace, in the opinion of that demoter of mountains, Professor Coleman of Toronto, who thought it was about time also that Canadian climbers showed these Americans, Europeans and Englishmen a thing or two. In August of 1907, he left Lake Louise with the Reverend George Kinney of Victoria, reaching Yellowhead Pass by way of Pipestone Creek and Pipestone Pass (the Bow River route was too wet), Siffleur

River and North Saskatchewan River, Sunwapta Pass and Wilcox Pass. In mid-September, the Coleman party was at the southwest foot of Robson on Grand Forks (Robson) River, but an early blizzard drove them out of the region. A year later Coleman and Kinney assaulted the mountain from the north side, by way of Moose River, Moose Pass, Smoky River and Robson Pass. They got far up above timberline to 11,500 feet, but heavy snow ruined their chances again. A second handicap was the Reverend Kinney's refusal to climb on Sunday, and Sundays seemed to provide the best climbing weather in that year.

Coleman could not go west in 1909, but Kinney returned in August with a young engineer named Donald Phillips who had never climbed any sort of mountain before. After a period of false starts due to bad weather and the minister's never-on-Sunday policy, the two arrived in triumph on the top. Phillips's barometric calculation of altitude sustained James McEvoy's triangulations, and Mount Robson has held its position ever since as the highest peak in the Canadian Rockies with an official altitude of 12,972 feet. Perhaps it will stay highest forever, but that is what the experts said for three-quarters of a century about Mounts Brown and Hooker.

21

And Then, the Benzine Buggy

W E HAVE SEEN many Rockies passes since Alvarado rode over La Glorieta with the wily Turk in 1540, since De Anza crossed Sangre de Cristo dreaming of empire in 1779, since David Thompson and his Charlotte gazed on the ice fields of the Columbia from Howse Pass in 1807. We were present as Lewis and Clark, Wilson Price Hunt of Trenton, New Jersey, Robert Stuart of Scotland, and John Charles Frémont used gates which speeded the creation of a continental United States. We watched the topographical engineers — Gunnison, Stansbury, Stevens — and England's Captain Palliser seeking crossings to advance their respective nations. After 1859, a million argonauts used a thousand other passes in their wild pursuit of wealth and happiness.

What else could occur to draw people to those quiet, peaceful high places where most of our western rivers begin?

Not one resident in a thousand foresaw the approach of a Rockies millennium in 1901 when two Denver mechanics, W. B. Felker and C. A. Yont, coaxed a Locomobile steam car from Colorado Springs up the Ute Pass road and on nearly to the top of Pikes Peak. Two years later, Dr. H. Nelson Jackson of Burlington, Vermont, drove a twenty-horsepower Winton from San Francisco to New York City in sixty-three days. These were daredevil stunts, sound thinkers agreed, signifying nothing. Benzine buggies might do on the level. But in the Rockies the all-weather, comfortable railroads would continue to monopolize transport now and forever through a handful of passes — Raton and Marshall, Boreas and Bozeman, Marias and Crowsnest, and a few more.

And still people bought cars, and then more cars, in Denver and Colorado Springs, Salt Lake City, Cheyenne, Helena, Calgary. Perhaps the fad spread fast because of the relatively mud-free gravel roads and the wide-open spaces which gave motorists room to control their contraptions with a minumum of damage to pedestrians and livestock. Some drivers seemed determined to test their Reos and Kisselkars, Appersons and Stevens-Duryeas where the danger was greatest. They assaulted the obsolete, washed-out, vegetation-blocked wagon roads of the mining era, hoping to be the first to reach the top of Argentine or Breckenridge or Kenosha Pass by automobile.

As early as 1902, the Colorado Springs mining stock broker, W. W. Price, stunned the community by driving his Winton from Leadville over Tennessee Pass to Glenwood Springs. Even General William Jackson Palmer, who detested cars at first as only a railroad man could, acquired a huge White Steamer in 1906 to trundle him around the Garden of the Gods during his last years. The White Steamer, according to Palmer's chauffeur, Glen Martin, was "a gaudy thing with bright red seats, and larger than any automobile today. It had a flash boiler made with a coil of steel and the firebox was as big as the coach top and you sat on top of the whole thing." Palmer instructed Martin to see what his monster could do with the Ute Pass road. It pounded up the stiff grade with ease. Next, the General tried touring on some of his steep private bridle paths, including the one over Buckhorn Pass above Broadmoor, which constitutes today's Colorado Springs Municipal High Drive. Trees and boulders were in the way, but the General ordered Martin to advance the throttle and push right through them. Though each of his bridle-path rides cost Palmer several hundred dollars for new tires and body repairs, he felt that it had been worth it. He had satisfied his burning desire to see if the old bus could make it over the top of something.

While cars were attacking the Rockies barrier from the east, others went at it beyond the Continental Divide. In his "Early Days of Telluride" (*Colorado Magazine,* January, 1949), L. C. Kinikin of Montrose has described a trip on the old Otto Mears wagon road from Ridgway to Telluride, involving a vertical climb of two thousand feet in ten miles:

John H. Adams purchased one of the first automobiles which came to Montrose, and asked me to accompany him to Montrose to claim it, which I did. This was in the early 1900s. We helped unload the light, no-top machine from the freight car, put in gas and water and oil and drove uptown for demonstration. We picked up two newlyweds, who sat in the back of the car, and starting about the same time we beat the D. & R. G. train to Ridgway! The newlyweds got out, and we started for Telluride in high spirits. The steering gear was on the left outside, and Adams furnished me with a can of powder to extinguish fire in the engine. I was kept so diligently on guard after we started up Dallas Divide — the first car to follow the ox-cart and mule sixes — that I had little time to enjoy the scenery and mechanism under us. About half way up Dallas Divide the radiator went dry, and we had no place to turn, so backed down to the first farm house. We started back up, chugg, chugg, chugging along, till we got on top, when John ran over a boulder too big to negotiate safely and it damaged the oil tank. To repair that took some two or three hours, and the train passed us up there on top of the world. Then we drove down Leopard Creek road very nicely and up from Placerville till we reached the Lime Kiln at Deep Creek, when we got stuck in a mudhole. I walked a half-mile and got a man, a mule and chain, and, in pulling us out of that mudhole the front axle was loosened. It took two or three hours and several feet of bailing wire to fix that, and with several fires extinguished up Key Stone Hill we reached my home in Telluride at midnight.

People were buying cars in the Rockies, but the wave of the future was not clearly visible in 1902 when the Colorado Automobile Club was formed, nor yet in 1905 when the Colorado Good Roads Association began its militant career to put a benzine buggy in every Rockies stable. A plainer hint of what was ahead appeared in 1907, when President Roosevelt backed Gifford Pinchot's scheme to spend twenty-five per cent of National Forest gross income on auto roads in the forest reserves. Since the American Rockies lay mostly inside these forests, motorists dreamed of driving everywhere in the high country on real roads built with federal money. And, if the Forest Service could get funds, why not other federal agencies, and even state governments?

The Colorado Good Roads Association lobbied through a bill in 1909 to create the Colorado Highway Commission. Four years later, the commission received funds of its own and went to work with the Forest Service and with county commissioners to build what is still one of the loveliest of Rockies drives, the forty-two-mile, winding, superbly scenic Wolf Creek Pass auto highway. It would cross the Continental Divide at 10,850 feet above sea level on its westering way from Walsenburg, La Veta Pass, Fort Garland and San Luis Valley toward Durango, Silverton and the new Mesa Verde National Park. It would penetrate glorious forests of Engelmann spruce and aspen, the beauty of which was enhanced by an unusual rainfall averaging forty inches annually.

Wolf Creek Pass lies between Ellwood Pass (11,775), some miles south of it, and the old Ute favorite, Weminuche Pass (10,629), which is northwest of it. It had had no noticeable use before 1913. Travelers from San Luis Valley had no choice up to then but to take the Denver and Rio Grande narrow-gauge from Alamosa over Cumbres Pass to reach Durango. The historic Stony Pass road from Del Norte up the Rio Grande had been all but abandoned. A road did exist over Ellwood Pass to Timber Hill, Ellwood ghost town and Pagosa Springs but it was badly washed in the flood of October, 1911. Besides, its grades were as much as twenty-five per cent.[1]

Other things happened during the construction period (1913–1917) of the Wolf Creek Pass highway to boom Rockies motoring. In 1913, Carl G. Fisher of Detroit's automotive Fisher Brothers, collected four million dollars from auto makers to create the Lincoln Highway, running 3143 miles from New York to San Francisco. The route was about the same as today's Interstate 80, which crosses Wyoming's Laramie Hills at the head of Telephone Canyon between Cheyenne Pass and Sherman Hill Summit, and on over the Continental Divide near the source of Separation Creek west of Rawlins. After Lincoln Highway came the National Old Trails Road, which used Raton Pass on its transcontinental sweep to Los Angeles, and the Pikes Peak Ocean-to-Ocean Highway. This last reached the Front Range at Colorado Springs and bounded over Ute Pass, Wilkerson Pass, Trout Creek Pass and Tennessee Pass — today's charming U.S. Route 24 through Leadville to Grand Junction and Utah.

In 1916, Congress passed the Federal-Aid Road Act to provide funds for state highway departments on a matched-money basis, aided by the Federal Bureau of Public Roads. In another three years, Rocky Mountain motorists began paying, almost with pleasure, state gas taxes of one cent a gallon for road improvement. And all the while, the high country was responding to a special stimulus — Henry Ford's miraculous Model T roadster, which could be bought new for a mere $275. These little light Tin Lizzies, as sturdy and as patient as burros, seemed made for mountain touring, with their high axles, and with forward and reverse pedals ready to help with the braking if need be.

By 1913, Model T's in Montana were scooting over Priest, MacDonald, Pipestone, Bozeman and Monida passes. In Wyoming they crossed Sherman Hill and the wild red Birdseye Pass around Wind River Canyon between Casper and Thermopolis. Model T's made nothing of climbing La Glorieta out of Santa Fe past the ruins of Pecos village. They putt-putted serenely over Palo Flechado out of Taos, and over ancient Raton, cluttered with the artifacts of centuries of travel. In Colorado, they negotiated most of the wagon road passes, including that vertiginous torment, Independence, which hadn't had such excitement since the pie-oven incident.[2]

WHEN WORLD WAR I ENDED, the Rocky Mountain community began a program of frantic road building, using six per cent grades in the main so that no motorist need suffer the indignity of having to shift gears. These first, narrow, unpaved, undulating roads had pleasant names, since we had not yet allowed our lives to degenerate into a numbers game. Colorado's Victory Highway crossed Berthoud Pass and Rabbit Ears Pass on its way from Denver to Salt Lake City. The relocated Berthoud Pass part of the road was sixteen feet wide, cost nearly five hundred thousand dollars, and took five years to complete (1919–1924). In the same period, the Red Mountain Pass wagon road from Ouray to Silverton became the first section of the Million Dollar Highway because it cost that much, or because the gravel was gold-bearing, if you prefer romance. By 1921, cars from Silverton were arriving in Durango on the Million Dollar Highway over what excited passengers called "double hairpin loops." From the heights of Molas Divide and Coalbank Pass, they could gaze east at the wonderful spires of the Needle and Grenadier Mountains which Franklin Rhoda had admired from the opposite side in 1873.

The Hard Pan Triangle Route took Denver's Sunday drivers over Kenosha Pass into South Park to call on Fairplay's celebrity, Prunes the Burro, aged forty. Others visited Rocky Mountain Park, wending warily up the incomplete Fall River road toward Fall River Pass and Milner Pass — the valley-route predecessor of today's Trail Ridge Road across the park to Grand Lake. Adventurers from Fort Collins were driving over Cameron Pass to North Park and Walden town long before that enchanting passage of the Medicine Bow Range was officially opened in 1926.

From Salida on the Arkansas, the Tenderfoot Trail was constructed south across Poncha Pass to San Luis Valley and the Gunbarrel Road to Monte Vista. In 1922, the Bureau of Public Roads acquired $204,450 of Forest Service funds and built the Continental Divide traverse which we have called Old Monarch Pass, as part of its Rainbow Route from Salida to Gunnison and Montrose. Old Monarch Pass was a mile south of "Old Old Monarch Pass," which General Grant had crossed eastbound from Pitkin in 1880. The worst part of the Rainbow Route to build was the deep-gullied stretch away from Gunnison River at Sapinero over Son-of-a-Bitch Hill to Stumpy Creek and on to Cerro Summit. That stretch, you recall, had caused Antoine Robidoux and others much pain too.

The development of roads and of the towns along them in the Colorado Rockies was severely handicapped by capricious weather. Because of the altitude, the high passes were shut down by snow even in summer at times, and they were sure to be closed from mid-October until June. In the fall of 1928, the Highway Department assembled some primitive snowplows at Leadville and surprised itself by keeping Tennessee Pass open all winter — perhaps because it didn't snow much. A year later, the snow problem was dumped in the lap of a strong-minded character named Charles D. Vail, who had just resigned as Denver's Manager of Parks and Improvements to become chief engineer of the Highway Department.

Vail was a railroad man by training, and he believed that superior power was the answer to all resistance. Through the depression years, he tinkered constantly with bigger and stronger snowplows and encouraged employees to learn the secrets of controlling avalanches. As a result, most of his major highway passes were being crossed in any weather by 1939, including those champion snow-catchers of the San Juan Range, Wolf Creek Pass and Red Mountain Pass.

An important exception was Old Monarch Pass, which frustrated Vail's best plans by filling up with snow continually, forcing drivers going west from Salida to take the long way around over Poncha and Cochetopa passes. Residents of the region made strong pleas to put a road over Marshall Pass, which was five hundred feet lower than Old Monarch. But Charles D. Vail was not the kind of public servant who was inclined to follow amateur advice. He found a crossing of his own not much more than a mile south of Old Monarch Pass. Though the Marshall Pass crowd stormed and held mass meetings and wrote letters to editors, the chief engineer held firm, with the support of the Bureau of Public Roads. And so the old Rainbow Route, U.S. Route 50 by then, was relocated over his crossing, following Agate Creek down the west side of the Divide to its junction with the Tomichi. When the new twenty-eight-mile stretch opened in November, 1939, new Highway Department signs appeared on it bearing the words VAIL PASS. To nobody's surprise, unknown partisans of Marshall Pass slopped the signs with black paint overnight. The Highway Department took them down and announced that they had been put up just as a joke at the instigation of a group of contractors who had good reasons to admire the chief engineer. The task of naming the crossing fell to oil companies who called it Agate-Monarch Pass on their highway maps. Soon the maps were marked simply Monarch Pass, and that is the name today.

But the matter of VAIL PASS was not forever dead. In the middle 1930's, engineer Vail transformed the old Loveland Pass road into a sensational above-timberline traverse of great beauty, and then continued U.S. Highway 6 to Dillon and over Gore Range through a gap formed by West Tenmile Creek on the east and Gore Creek on the west. As the road over this brand-new pass neared completion in the summer of 1940, the Highway Department disclosed that the gap had been named in honor of its chief engineer. This time, no rascals got out the black paint. Coloradans generally were ready to recognize Vail's genuine abilities, and the name VAIL PASS marks the spacious crossing still.

Charles Vail died in 1945, but his professional standing rose further five years later during a spectacular test of his Monarch Pass road. On November 23, 1950, a huge bus, driven by a certain Jerry Tobin, left Western State College at Gunnison carrying thirty-one members of the Mountaineers football team and two coaches bound for Canon City to play the last game of the season with Adams State College. The bus ground its ponderous way to the top of Monarch Pass and began the twenty-three-mile winding descent to Salida, a vertical drop of 4262 feet, one of the greatest in the world, for standard highways. Suddenly, Tobin felt his brakes grab and then release, and he noticed on his air gauge that his brake pressure had dropped from one hundred and fifteen pounds to thirty pounds. As the eleven-and-a-half ton vehicle gained speed, the clutch slipped out of second into neutral. Head coach Joe Thomas and several of the larger players tried to push it back into gear. The clutch rod broke off an inch from the floor.

By now the bus was flying downwards at eighty miles an hour or more. However, the heroic driver Tobin discovered that he could slow it down considerably on the wide, banked curves, which engineer Vail had designed. At each one of these many curves, he ordered the players to pile up on the high side, not so much to keep the thing from tipping over but to keep the fenders from bearing down on the tires and cutting them open. Tobin worried also that the daily ore train from the quarry at Monarch might be crossing the track near Garfield. "I guess I was praying then," he said later. But the tracks were clear and the bus went over them at one hundred and ten miles an hour, passing a car on the left in the process while an up-coming car simply piled safely out of the way into the ditch. Then Vail's grade eased, and the highway straightened. By judicious pumping of his brake pedal, Tobin slowed the bus down by degrees and was able to stop it completely on entering Salida.

Incredibly, the danger was over. Tobin had the air brakes

fixed and drove his team on down the Grand Canyon of the Arkansas to Canon City. The players seemed to forget completely their escape from a very gruesome death, for they beat Adams State handily, 35–14. Jerry Tobin's heroism, of course, and Vail's Monarch Pass curves were the reasons why they were able to play at all.

THE BUILDING FRENZY after World War I was far from being confined to Colorado. In 1923, the Canadians built their first auto road over their beautiful, brooding Rockies at Dr. Hector's Vermilion Pass (5416) — today's Banff-Windermere highway. Other Canadian pass roads followed soon — over Kicking Horse and Crowsnest, Yellowhead and Sinclair. Meanwhile, James B. Harkin, first Commissioner of the National Parks of Canada, sought ways unsuccessfully so that cars could cross the Selkirks west of Kicking Horse without boarding the Canadian Pacific or following the Columbia interminably northward around the Great Bend and south again. Harkin had better luck planning a route along the main range from Banff over Bow Pass (6878) to the North Saskatchewan, Athabaska Glacier and Jasper. Work on that thrilling road beneath the Columbia Ice fields began in 1931. It crossed Sunwapta Pass (6675) and proceeded west of Wilcox Mountain instead of east of it over Wilcox Pass. This early version of the present magnificent Banff-Jasper highway was completed in 1940.

Montana's fine road over Marias Pass — all fifty-six miles of it — was inspired in 1917 by some insistent Kalispell motorists who formed the Flathead Motor Club and asked the world what was the point of having the new Glacier National Park if nobody could drive to it from the east across the Continental Divide. The road opened on July 19, 1930, when a crowd assembled on top to hear dignitaries praise the late Theodore Roosevelt for his national forest policies, and name the road the Theodore Roosevelt Highway. They also made appropriate remarks about a pretty ugly obelisk in Roosevelt's memory which cost twenty-five thousand dollars and still stands up there overshadowing the statue of John Frank Stevens in his stocking cap.

Four years later, August 5, 1934, another President Roosevelt, Franklin D., arrived with Mrs. Roosevelt by special Great Northern train at West Glacier, transferred to a Cadillac and headed a party of eighty-eight people in eight cars and six buses on a tour of Glacier National Park. The main attraction was the year-old Going-to-the-Sun Highway, which crossed the Continental Divide by way of Logan Pass between the great towers of Haystack Butte and Oberlin Mountain. The cars carrying the presidential group ascended the majestic grade along the Garden Wall in view of Bird Woman Falls. At the top of Logan, the President stopped briefly to feed the chipmunks and examine the plaque memorializing Stephen T. Mather, founder of the National Park Service. Then the cars moved leisurely down the east slope past Red Eagle Mountain and the blindingly-blue St. Mary Lake and on to Two Medicine Chalet. Here, Blackfoot chieftains, letting bygones be bygones in regards to the murders which had been committed by Meriwether Lewis and Reuben Fields, made Roosevelt a member of the tribe with the title of Long Chief. Mrs. Roosevelt was dubbed Medicine Pipe Woman.

Logan Pass, named for the late Major W. R. Logan, first superintendent of Glacier National Park, had no history before the Going-to-the-Sun Highway was constructed over it. It is only 6654 feet above sea level — a mere 3454 vertical feet above West Glacier thirty-two miles away. Statistically, therefore, it cannot compare with any high pass of Colorado or Wyoming. Nevertheless, it is quite the most beautiful, dramatic and satisfying motor traverse in all the Rocky Mountains.

In contrast to youthful Glacier, Yellowstone National Park had been attracting motorists as early as 1915, which was the first summer that cars were admitted — 958 of them. After World War I, thirty thousand machines were rolling in annually to enter-tain the bears and take advantage of the park's pioneer roads such as the paved Grand Loop, the Old Faithful–West Thumb–Canyon run, and the scenic road through the lodgepoles over Dunraven Pass, which opened in 1921. When the Wyoming State Highway Department was born in 1917, feeding traffic to Yellowstone became one of its first concerns. In consequence, the Yellowstone Highway, bordered with stones painted a gaudy yellow, was blasted through Wind River Canyon in 1922–1924, eliminating the steep traverse of Birdseye Pass which had to be braved up to then by tourists driving from Casper to Cody and the park's Sylvan Pass entrance.

In 1924, that old aristocrat, the Lincoln Highway, was paved from Cheyenne across the Cheyenne Pass area toward Rock Springs. This stimulated the movement of tourists along the west side of the Wind River Range and over The Rim on the new Hoback Canyon road to Jackson Hole, the peerless Tetons, and the park's south entrance. It encouraged use also of the so-called Rocky Mountain Highway from Lander to Jackson Hole over Captain Jones's Togwotee Pass (the spelling was "Twogotee" in the 1920's). From charming Jackson town, a road of steep switchbacks was pushed somehow over old Teton Pass to Victor, Idaho. The grades far exceeded the six per cent standard, and so nobody was eager to go to Victor that way until the grade was improved somewhat in recent years.

Even Wyoming's aloof, serene Big Horn Mountains were opened up to the Model T's and Buicks in the 1920's. The Black and Yellow Trail was constructed from Buffalo south and west in a grand circle of Cloud Peak, over Powder River Pass and down to the weird badlands beyond Tensleep. From the quiet, shady cow town of Sheridan, a second Big Horn highway was built over Baldy Pass near the mysterious Indian Medicine Wheel, to arrive eventually at Lovell amid more multicolored badlands. Somewhat later (1936) a combine of Montana, Wyoming and federal bureaus made a remarkable summer highway from Red Lodge, Montana, southward for sixty-four miles into the Absarokas and over Beartooth Pass (10,940) and Cooke Pass to Yellowstone's northeast entrance. The road has been paved since. Beartooth Pass, over which Chief Joseph and his Nez Perce followers fled in 1877, is Wyoming's highest motor crossing, and one of the most spectacular in the West.

A SECOND WORLD WAR OCCURRED, fought as much by machines as by men. When it ended, the machines found peacetime work in the Rockies — the speeding earth-movers with rubber tires as big as houses, the vast shovels, the tractor-pushers moving a mountain in an eight-hour day, the hot-mixers laying pavement as fast as the trappers of old could walk.

They have built, and are building, some marvelous pass roads. But we seem to take the new roads for granted, perhaps because the machines have made them so easy to build, compared to the toil of men and mules in wagon-road days. We are not properly impressed by the superb trace from Cody up past Shoshone Dam and Lake to Sylvan Pass, or by the gorgeous boulevard through Bozeman Pass, erasing the hairpins of yesteryear, or by the great curves of the Durango-Silverton-Ouray road — no mere Million Dollar Highway now! — or by the imminent Straight Creek tunnel, which will rob motorists soon of the thrills of Loveland Pass. But surely Major Rogers, at least, would be impressed if he could see Montana's new Great Falls–Missoula road over Rogers Pass, or that snowshedded thoroughfare west of Kicking Horse over the other Rogers Pass, conquering the Selkirks, for all of Captain Palliser, to complete Canada's first all-weather transcontinental highway.

Of course we are a-tingle about the astronauts now, flying over the Rockies in six seconds flat every hour or two, making ready so that the rest of us can go touring to the moon almost any Sunday. The dear old wagon-road days! People say that the hills were higher then. But were they really? Some of us find them pretty high still, higher even than where the space ships go. Tell me, do they have sweet-voiced ptarmigans and alpine meadows in the stratosphere? Cutthroat trout lazing in crystal streams? Do they have hillsides of aspen against the dark spruce, aspens blazing gold and orange in the crisp air of September? Will the lift-off from that launching pad send me somewhere better than the top of Mosquito Pass?

Notes

Chapter 1: THE EARLIEST GATES

1. In *New Mexico* of the American Guide Series "palo flechado" is translated "tree shot with arrows." Such an arrow-filled tree was seen once on Palo Flechado Pass.

2. Some students believe that Ulibarri came down Lorencito Canyon, seven miles west of Long's Pass. There are possible routes also just east of Long's by what would be known later as the Chicken Creek road from Brilliant and the Rex–Coal Canyon Road.

Chapter 2: HORSE LAKE AND SANGRE DE CRISTO

1. Many Frenchmen probed toward the Rio Grande in those days. In 1714, Juchereau de St. Denis, founder of Natchitoches, Louisiana, was caught poaching in Texas. In 1718, Bernard de la Harpe explored up Red River and the Arkansas almost to the site of Tulsa, Oklahoma.

Chapter 3: VICTORY AT LEMHI

1. Authorities differ as to what Rockies were seen by the brothers. Francis Parkman and Bernard De Voto favor the Big Horns. Granville Stuart has them at Gate of the Mountains near Helena, Montana, and even up Wind River in Wyoming, where they could have heard about South Pass.

2. This Arctic drainage established by Mackenzie begins at Athabaska Pass far south in British Columbia. From there, Athabaska River flows north into Lake Athabaska near Fort Chipewyan. North of the lake, the stream is called Slave River, the main branch of which is Peace River coming in also from the Rockies. After flowing on north into Great Slave Lake, Slave River becomes Mackenzie River all the rest of the long way to the Arctic.

3. This was the Nootka Sound Convention, signed October 28, 1790, which set up the principle that occupancy determined sovereignty — the principle which would determine ownership of the whole Northwest.

4. As we have seen, Escalante got only as far west as Utah Lake in 1776. Before Mackenzie, the only men to cross the continent north of México (but not in the Rockies) were Cabeza de Vaca and three friends who arrived near the Gulf of California from Florida in April, 1536.

5. They gave up the canoe on July 9.

6. The precise area of Louisiana was flexible. Under the original French ownership, France often defined it as the entire Mississippi drainage west to the unknown Continental Divide, plus everything north of the Rio Grande — Texas, much of New Mexico, and so on. In 1763, Spain accepted possession of the Mississippi drainage only, stating that Texas and New Mexico, plus the Raton Pass region south of the Upper Arkansas, were hers anyway. When France resumed possession in 1800, Napoleon held that the Rio Grande border was valid, and so did Jefferson, for bargaining purposes, when the United States bought Louisiana.

7. Later, Lewis spotted another kind of "jay-bird" — the beautiful camp robber of the spruce uplands which we call Clark's nutcracker. It was the special joy of these men to first see and report also grizzly bears, mule deer, Rocky Mountain goats, black squirrels, sage grouse and salmon trout.

8. In 1855, Mormons arrived from Utah to settle on what they called Lemhi River, after Limhi, a character in their Book of Mormon. Indians drove them out for good three years later, but the name survives for the river and the pass.

9. Bitterroot (Lewisia rediviva) is the fleshy-leaved plant with the rose-red, cactus-like flowers which Captain Lewis discovered in the Lemhi Pass area when he found Sacajawea's people eating the taproot. The name has been applied to the Bitterroot Mountains and Bitterroot River. The blossom is Montana's state flower.

10. Actually, the extreme source of the Missouri River is considered to be Upper Red Rock Lake at Red Rock Pass, 2714 miles from the Missouri-Mississippi junction. Beaverhead River above Horse Prairie Creek is called Red Rock River.

11. The Salmon ("The River of No Return") remains unnavigable for ordinary craft and virtually impassable today in its two-hundred-mile westward plunge through awesome gorges, one of which is a thousand feet deeper than the Grand Canyon of the Colorado.

12. A situation similar to that of Gibbons Pass and Lost Trail Pass exists at Muddy Pass and Rabbit Ears Pass in Colorado.

13. How Lolo Pass got its name is not known. The word is written "Low-Low" on army maps of 1855, which might be a clue as it is quite a low crossing, though by no means the lowest, for the Bitterroots. Some say the word is the Flathead pronunciation of Lawrence, the name of a white pioneer.

14. Also called Bull Creek Pass.

15. An unimproved dirt road is shown on Montana State Highway maps running from State Route 20 up Alice Creek nearly to Lewis and Clark Pass.

16. History-minded motorists can follow the Lewis and Clark Rocky Mountain route easily. From Great Falls, Montana, take U.S. Route 91 to Helena, U.S. 10N to Three Forks, U.S. 10S to State Route 41, south on State Route 41 to Dillon, to Armstead on U.S. 91, and then west by dirt road up Horse Prairie Creek and over Lemhi Pass to Tendoy and Salmon, where U.S. 93 continues north over Lost Trail Pass to Lolo (Lolo Pass is thirty-three miles west of Lolo by gravel road). Lolo is very near the site of Traveller's Rest. West of Lolo Pass, a fine paved highway runs

a bit south of the Lewis and Clark route to Howell, Idaho, and Clearwater River.

Clark's route eastward from Traveller's Rest is approximated by returning up U.S. Route 93 almost to Lost Trail Pass but over Gibbons Pass — or the new Chief Joseph Pass — on to Wisdom, and south up the Big Hole River to Armstead again, north to Three Forks, east on U.S. 10 over Bozeman Pass, and right down the Yellowstone to North Dakota.

For Lewis's east route, take State Route 20 from Missoula over Rogers Pass (near Lewis and Clark Pass) to Great Falls.

Chapter 4: PIKE'S GAP — AND A SHOT IN TIME

1. On February 24, 1808, Secretary of War Henry Dearborn wrote Pike "that although the two exploring expeditions you have performed were not previously ordered by the president of the United States, there were frequent communications on the subject of each between General Wilkinson and this department, of which the president of the United States was from time to time acquainted."

2. The Mississippi trip took place between August 9, 1805, and April 30, 1806. Pike (with Corporal Theodore Miller) reached Cass Lake, a hundred miles short of the Mississippi's actual source at Lake Itaska, which was discovered in July, 1832, by Henry Schoolcraft.

3. President Jefferson and Congress sent Dr. John Sibley exploring up the Red from Natchitoches soon after the Louisiana Purchase of 1803. He was able to ascend only as far as present Shreveport — eighty miles. From October, 1804, to January, 1805, William Dunbar and George Hunter tried to reach the source and wound up on the Washita near Hot Springs, Arkansas. During Pike's Rocky Mountain trip, a government party under Captain Sparks and Thomas Freeman advanced half way — about six hundred miles above its mouth. Red River, meandering, sluggish, full of silt and matted trees in places, had created a difficult terrain. It was not until July 1, 1852, that Captain Randolph B. Marcy and his party found its ultimate headwaters in the Staked Plains of west Texas above Palo Duro Canyon where Charles Goodnight later established his JA Ranch. For this story, see W. Eugene Hollen's *Beyond the Cross Timbers* (University of Oklahoma Press, Norman, Oklahoma, 1955).

4. This news came on October 4, 1806, from French traders at the Pawnee village. Lewis and Clark heard about Pike's expedition earlier, on September 10, as they were descending the Missouri just below the mouth of Platte River.

5. La Lande was one of several brave pioneers in Santa Fe trying to get the Rio Grande Spanish to do business with the United States. Others included the Frenchman, Jacques d'Eglise; Laurent Durocher, a native of Quebec; and the Kentuckian, James Pursley. Real commerce did not begin until the Mexican revolution of 1821.

6. Of this bill, Pike writes in his journal: "The demands which Dr. Robinson had on persons in New Mexico, although legitimate, were in some degree spurious in his hands."

7. Pike first saw the Rockies from a point a few miles east of Las Animas, Colorado, near Beethurst and John Martin Reservoir. Motorists on U.S. Route 50 usually see them from the railroad bridge in Las Animas

itself. The 120 miles is a common limit of Pikes Peak visibility whether west from Las Animas, south from Fort Collins, east from Monarch Pass or north from Raton Pass.

8. Pike was using a Réamur thermometer — zero being thirty-two degrees Fahrenheit, and with eighty units between Réamur zero and boiling.

9. Pike could have climbed the peak if he had kept up Fountain Creek to Ute Pass, and then used the nine-mile Ruxton Creek route to the summit which the Cog Railway follows today. By crossing to Turkey Creek he and his men got themselves blocked behind the extruding mass of Cheyenne Mountain — the worst possible approach.

The most thorough study of Pike's attempt to climb the peak was made more than thirty years ago by the late Dr. Lloyd Shaw, the Colorado Springs educator and square-dance expert. Mrs. Shaw told the author how her husband ascended Little Turkey Creek below Blue Mountain, and then climbed a ravine to the left to the minor ridge where the peak appeared. He named the ridge Miller Mountain after Pike's Private Theodore Miller. According to Mrs. Shaw, Dr. Shaw felt such an affinity to Pike that he could hear him talking to him as he stood on Miller Mountain. He heard Pike's voice again later when he visited the Pike stockade on Conejos River.

10. Elliot Coues, in his presentation of Pike's journals, has the expedition going up Oil Creek rather than Currant Creek, and then over the West Fourmile Creek area by Saddle Mountain to the South Platte. The present author prefers the Currant Creek Pass route, partly because it was the ancient Indian trail from the Arkansas to South Park and partly because it would have been hard for Pike to have negotiated the Helena Canyon part of Oil Creek with horses, or even on foot.

11. The Mosquito Range has no corner on mosquitoes, which bother anglers all over the Rockies, partly because there are so many beaver ponds and irrigation ditches for them to breed in.

12. Pike learned at Santa Fe later that this camp had been visited in 1805 by the wandering Kentuckian, James Purcell, in a group of Comanche and Kiowa Indians.

13. The food shortage was eased when Dr. Robinson and Private Brown shot a couple of Rocky Mountain sheep, an exciting new species.

14. Though not especially wet, the Wet Mountains were so called by Mormon travelers in 1846 who rejoiced, on arrival at Pueblo, to see these green slopes after weeks of aridity on the Santa Fe Trail. The name was not original. The Spaniards had always called them "wet" in their tongue: "Sierra Mojada."

15. Motorists can follow Pike's passes route (December 10, 1806–January 27, 1807) via State Route 9, northwest from U.S. Route 50 near Canon City, over Currant Creek Pass to Hartsel, U.S. 24 over Trout Creek Pass to the tremendous Sawatch Range, south on U.S. 285 to Salida, and down the Grand Canyon of the Arkansas on U.S. 50 to Canon City again (with detour to toll bridge over Royal Gorge, and incline railway into Gorge at point where Pike climbed out). Then to Westcliffe in Wet Mountain Valley (State Route 69), on south to Bradford crossroad (Medano Pass visible to southwest), to Gardner and Malachite (detour to near top of Mosca Pass), over Pass Creek Pass to U.S. 160 at top of La

Veta–Sangre de Cristo passes, and down past Fort Garland and around magnificent Blanca Peak to Great Sand Dunes National Monument.

Pike's stockade on original Conejos River site south from dunes has been carefully reconstructed by the State Historical Society. It can be reached via Alamosa on back road five miles from Sanford.

Chapter 5: TETON TOURISTS

1. Why the 10,500-foot maximum, as a rule? Why no interest in the passes which became today's popular highway crossings, such as Loveland (11,992) and Independence (12,095) in Colorado, Beartooth (10,940) and Snowy Range (10,800) in Wyoming?

Until 1859, when the gold rush started in the Rockies, animals and people looked only for those passes which had good grass and water to sustain them all the way over the crest in any weather — and trees, too, for shelter. Buffalo, the first Rockies tourists, built their pass trails by engineering principles so precise in terms of grade and forage and footing that the Indians could not improve on them. The Utes and Snakes and Flatheads and the rest refused to give a crossing the distinction of a name unless buffalo or horses could use it. White men — explorers, traders, trappers — had the same attitude as Indians.

The maximum trail-pass altitude lowered with timberline, being roughly a thousand feet below that limit of tree growth. Colorado's north-side timberline approaches 11,500 feet, Wyoming's 10,000 feet, Montana's 8500, and so on down to the low 5000-foot timberline which Mackenzie found at Peace River Pass. Timberline can be 500 feet higher on the warmer south slopes. You may recall that Simon Fraser's Summit Lake crossing was 3060 feet. The Lewis and Clark buffalo road over Lemhi was 7373, and Pike's Medano was 9900. Perhaps the highest of the popular old Ute Indian trails was that over Weminuche Pass (10,629), from San Juan River drainage of southwest Colorado to the Upper Rio Grande and San Luis Valley, a shortcut which the Utes preferred to the loop around the southern end of the San Juans by way of Horse Lake Pass. Of course there were some higher passes which the Indians used if necessary. Lake Pass (12,226) seems to have been an emergency route for Ute war parties moving from Gunnison River to the Upper Arkansas. The Utes crossed Georgia Pass (11,598) and Hoosier Pass (11,541) in moving from South Park to Middle Park. One of their trails from Middle Park ran around the slopes of James Peak and past Echo Lake to reach the plains. In Wyoming, the Snakes crossed the Wind River Range at Washakie Pass (11,610). As a rule, though, all the Indians crossed where there was grass.

2. The year 1807 is Lawrence J. Burpee's date in *The Search for the Western Sea*. Bernard De Voto makes it 1808.

3. Thompson did not discover Howse Pass. His North West Company colleague Duncan McGillivray could have gone over it as early as 1800, according to an allusion in Thompson's journal, and several used it after that. There seem to have been two men of similar names in the Northwest fur business. Joseph Howse of Hudson's Bay Company crossed Howse Pass in 1809. Jasper Hawse or House was a towheaded Missourian for whom Yellowhead Pass and Jasper, Alberta, were named later on.

4. Pryor's Gap was named for Lewis and Clark's Sergeant Nathaniel

Pryor. The Shoshone River was called Stinking River in Colter's time, and it stinks to this day below Shoshone Reservoir. The name was changed to Shoshone (Snake) by the Wyoming legislature in 1901 when Cody dude ranchers complained that the original name was bad for business.

5. If Colter did arrive at Two Ocean Pass, he probably did not understand the phenomenon before his eyes. From below Younts Peak (12,165), a rill named Two Ocean Creek falls into a marshy pond full of noisy frogs right at the top of the pass, which is a mile long and a mile wide. One stream flowing from the pond is Atlantic Creek, running seven miles northeast to join the Yellowstone and to wind up in the Gulf of Mexico. The other stream is Pacific Creek, running down west and south from Two Ocean Pass to Snake River near Jackson Lake, and so on to the Pacific. The red-gilled, black-spotted cutthroat trout of the pond thus spend their time between the Eastern and Western slopes of the continent. Easy horseback trails lead to Two Ocean Pass from Yellowstone Park and from Jackson Lake in Grand Teton National Park. However, visitors in the Absarokas are almost as uncommon as they were when Colter did, or didn't discover Two Ocean Pass.

6. The Bighorn River changes its name to Wind River at some point in the canyon eight miles south of Thermopolis, but there is no agreement as to whether that point is at the start, the middle or the end of this Wind River Canyon. The Indians had the Bighorn start at present Riverton where the Popo Agie joins the Wind. As the Orrin H. Bonneys explain in *Guide to the Wyoming Mountains*, Lewis and Clark named the Bighorn after the bighorn (one word) sheep observed at its mouth. For no rational reason, Big Horn Range, Big Horn County and the town of Big Horn are written as two words, Bighorn National Forest as one word, and Big Horn River appears both ways. The Bonneys pronounce the word Popo Agie as Po-poz'-yuh. In Crow language, "Popo" is "head" and "agie" is "waters" — "headwaters."

7. The Henry party could have noted three other Continental Divide passes close to Henrys Lake. Five miles east of it up Targhee and Howard creeks was Targhee Pass (7078), named for a Bannock chief, over which U.S. 20 runs to the west entrance of Yellowstone Park. Seven miles southeast was Reas Pass (6935) — the Union Pacific Railroad crossing to West Yellowstone from Idaho Falls, Idaho. Five miles west was Red Rock Pass (7056), near the extreme source of the Missouri which we mentioned when Sacajawea was guiding the way to Lemhi. If Lewis and Clark had continued up Beaverhead–Red Rock River instead of turning west up Horse Prairie Creek, they would have reached Henrys Lake five years before Henry did. Targhee is often cited as the pass which Henry crossed, and perhaps he did. However, the Raynolds Pass trail to Henrys Lake was almost thirty miles shorter for travelers coming up the Madison, bypassing Madison River Canyon and the prairie beyond it now covered by Hebgen Lake.

8. The *Missouri Gazette* published Williams's letters on August 7 and September 14, 1816.

9. Note for motorists: There is no road anywhere near David Thompson's Howse Pass. The Howse Pass trail takes off from the marvelous Banff-Jasper highway at a point on North Saskatchewan River fifty miles

northwest of Lake Louise. Thompson's Columbia-Kootenay trail is approximated by the highway from Boat Encampment to Donald Station to Cranbrook-Elko and on to Libby, Montana. The closest auto road to Thompson's Athabaska Pass trail is the Banff-Jasper highway fourteen miles southwest of Jasper at the mouth of Whirlpool River.

John Colter's Pryor's Gap is crossed today by the country road south of Billings, Montana, through Pryor, Bowler and Warren, into Wyoming at Frannie, and then Powell. U.S. Route 26–287 sweeps over Togwotee Pass, Dubois to Jackson Lake; State Route 22 over Teton Pass — Jackson to Victor and Pierre's Hole. As noted, U.S. 212 crosses Cooke (Colter) and Beartooth passes — the latter a prime traverse. The Cooke City — Cody road follows Colter's route from Yellowstone Park down Clarks Fork. Bozeman Pass is on Montana's busy U.S. 10 (Interstate 90), Bozeman to Livingston. Good roads cross Andrew Henry's Reynolds, Targhee and Red Rock passes over the Divide from Montana into Idaho. Star Valley makes a nice trip from Jackson by U.S. 26–89 down Snake River Canyon, which cuts off the north ends of Wyoming and Salt River ranges.

You will have to get a horse to ride over Two Ocean and Ishawooa passes in the wild Absaroka Range. The only roads over are U.S. 14 — Cody to Yellowstone Park by Sylvan Pass, and U.S. 212 across Cooke and Beartooth passes from the park to Red Lodge, Montana.

Chapter 6: South Pass: Fruit of Failure

1. Kootenay is spelled Kootenai south of the 49th parallel, the United States–Canada border. Nobody knows why.

2. When David Thompson reached Missoula in 1810 and Ezekiel Williams advanced from Fort Lisa in Montana south to the Arkansas in Colorado late that year, the Rocky Mountains stood discovered at last throughout their two thousand miles. It took two hundred and seventy years to do it.

3. The Canadian Rockies have the only real Rockies glaciers, though small ones exist in Glacier National Park and in the Gannett Peak area of the Wyoming Wind River Range. The Arapaho "glacier" of Colorado's Front Range is a fast-disappearing remnant.

4. The area has American pyramidal counterparts. One surrounds Yellowstone Park and contains sources of the Missouri, the Snake and the Green, as well as Montana's highest peak (Granite, 12,850), and Wyoming's highest (Gannett, 13,785). The highest counterpart of all is the Leadville–Tennessee Pass–Fremont Pass part of Colorado below Mount Elbert (14,431), king of the Rockies, which Pike saw in December, 1806. Near Mount Elbert rise the Arkansas, the South Platte, and four branches of the Colorado — Blue, Eagle, Roaring Fork and Frying Pan.

5. Though Thompson's paper carried an implication that he had explored the Columbia throughout its length, he had not yet seen a stretch of some three hundred miles between Canoe River (today's Boat Encampment, British Columbia) south to near present Kettle Falls, Washington. In October, 1811, he explored this part too. The Columbia starts in Canada, but most of its drainage lies within the United States. Canada's most important West Slope river is the Fraser.

6. It can be argued that the Blackfeet did the United States a favor by keeping traders out of the Upper Missouri country, forcing them to abandon the dream of water transport.

7. Some authorities have Hunt crossing the crest of the Big Horns ten or fifteen miles south of Powder River Pass, which would put him on Canyon Creek, a branch of Tensleep. Others believe that the crossing was made in much lower Big Horn country to the south, west of Kaycee — perhaps on the old Sioux trail from Powder River to Sweetwater drainage by Dull Knife and Fraker passes. But if this had been so, these westbounders would have discovered South Pass.

8. For six miles beyond and south of the top of Union Pass, the Hunt party were crossing an unusual triple divide. A marshy part in the center was made by Fish Creek, running northwest to join Gros Ventre and Snake rivers. Then they climbed three hundred feet to make it over a secondary divide (9253) where Wagon Creek began its four-mile run to join Green River. Today a trail goes down Fish Creek to the Gros Ventre and Jackson and perhaps it existed in 1811, but Hunt's guides did not want to go that way even if it were a shortcut to Teton Pass and Pierre's Hole.

9. The power of environment! Descendants of that same elk herd occupy the same grassland today just above Jackson town, in a 24,000-acre tract, the United States Bureau of Biological Survey Elk and Bird Refuge.

10. The drowning of Antoine Clappine occurred at present Milner, Idaho, in a Snake River rapid which Donald McKenzie called "Caldron Linn," a part-Gaelic phrase meaning "boiling kettle waterfall." Soon afterwards, Hunt gave up the canoes in the tradition of Alexander Mackenzie and Meriwether Lewis. His party did not resume water transport until it reached the Falls of the Columbia, 790 miles west.

11. One story has it that Martin Cass returned to St. Louis to find a rumor circulating that he had been eaten by Hoback, Reznor and Robinson during the winter of 1811–1812. No Hunt Astorian seems actually to have been lost. Pierre Dorion was killed in 1814 by Indians. His wife, Marie l'Aguivoise, won fame that year by surviving the winter in the Blue Mountains alone with her children and making it safely in the spring to Fort Astoria. The total mortality then was three men dead out of the sixty-five who left the Arikara village.

12. This Alexander McKay had been with Mackenzie in 1793 on his epic trip from Peace River to the Pacific.

13. Wilson Price Hunt was not one of the bad-news bearers because he had to stay on and direct affairs at Astoria. When he finally came home in 1814 it was by ship. John Day started back with Robert Stuart, but went insane at the outset and was returned to the fort.

14. Data in files of the Wyoming State Historian's office inform us that Lost Soldier Gap and Creek were named in 1880. A soldier in a survey party which was camping on that creek got lost and broke a window to enter Tom Sun's ranch house for food and shelter, even though the Sun latchstring was out hospitably. Tom Sun said later, "A man who hasn't sense enough to go into a man's home by the door when it is left open for him would get lost anywhere." And so the name.

15. Motorists can follow Hunt's trail across the Big Horns on U.S. 16 from Buffalo, Wyoming, to Tensleep over Powder River Pass, seventy-two

miles — an especially delightful trip because of the range's serenity and the drama of the west-side badlands. From Tensleep a road of sorts runs south up No Wood Creek and over Cottonwood and Sioux passes to Lysite, U.S. 20–26 at Moneta, and then west to Wind River, Riverton, Dubois on U.S. 26–287, and the Union Pass road by which 4WD cars do make it to Green River and Pinedale.

Robert Stuart's ramble from Snake River can be roughly paralleled on U.S. 30N from Pocatello, Idaho, to Montpelier, U.S. 89 north over Salt River Pass to Star Valley, Wyoming, down the Snake on U.S. 26 to Heise, Idaho, and north and east to Pierre's Hole, Victor and Teton Pass. South Pass is on State Route 28 northeast of Farson, Wyoming.

Chapter 7: HELL-BENT FOR TAOS

1. Note for motorists: The Gardner area is a delightful place for a day's ramble in summer. The Pass Creek Pass road parallels roughly the old Spanish Sangre de Cristo highway and actually meets it at the top of the range. Ranch roads run some miles up Oak Creek from Badito Cone.

2. Many years ago, Dr. LeRoy Hafen, the historian, found remains of the walls of the fort near the old Spanish road some seven miles up Oak Creek from Badito. The present author had no such luck in 1961.

3. The Indian population of the Rockies seemed to decrease steadily as the mountain chain ran north, from something like thirty thousand in the Rio Grande area to very few north of present Glacier National Park. The scarcity of game in the Canadian Rockies, the long winters and short summers there, and the frightening noises made by the shiftings and crackings of the glaciers were some of the reasons why red men disliked living in those Rockies, or even visiting them.

4. Many Raton names have special charm. "Chicorica" is said to be a Comanche name for the white-winged doves which used to thrive on Chicorica Creek leading to Manco ("limping") Burro Pass. Una de Gato was lined with black locust bushes, the thorns of which were as sharp as the "claw of a cat." The "chacuaco" of Chacuaco Creek referred to the stream's elder bushes.

5. Pocket gopher students say that the animals do not know how to drink and would have no use for the practice if they did, being strict teetotalers where water is concerned. That is why they thrive in the dry desolation east of the Ratons.

Chapter 8: THE ROARING TWENTIES

1. Antoine would have noted that North Cochetopa Pass was suitable for wheeled vehicles. He did take a small wagon over the pass soon after building his second trading post, Fort Uintah, in 1833, at the junction of Uinta River and White Rocks Creek in northeastern Utah. His first post, Fort Robidoux, was built about 1828 in Ute country on Gunnison River just below the Uncompahgre's mouth — near present Delta. It was Colorado's first and America's second general store west of the Continental Divide, being antedated by Andrew Henry's log cabins (1810) across Reynolds Pass.

2. There is an extremely pleasant gravel road north from Gunnison (forking left from the Almont road) over Ohio Pass, west over Kebler

Pass and then north and northwest past Grand Mesa and Hightower Mountain to emerge at Silt and U.S. Route 6–24 on Colorado River. This road approximates the old Ute trail. Even if you get lost, which is easy, you will enjoy the trip wherever you wind up.

3. You need not wonder why the Mormon Kingdom of Deseret bears so many places named after Ogden and Provo (Provost). The Mormons, who did much of the naming in Utah, had no love for Jim Bridger, and Jim returned the sentiment.

4. In *Jedediah Smith* pages 159–160, Dale Morgan wrote: "It has been said that Ashley was the first white man to undertake the crossing of the Front Range in this latitude. Very likely Chouteau and De Mun preceded him in 1816–1817, since their men penetrated to the Park at the head of the North Platte and gave it a name which long endured, 'The Bull Pen.' "

5. Near the Utah border on this Green River (Wyoming)–Vernal (Utah) road, a left-turn branch leads to Dutch John and Flaming Gorge Reservoir, while Utah Route 44 moves south through fantastic canyons (with a detour to Red Canyon lookout) and rejoins the Flaming Gorge branch before crossing the crest of the Uintas at an altitude of 8100 feet.

6. Pat's Hole (Echo Park) can be reached by car (thirty-eight miles from Jensen, Utah). Any traveler with romance in his soul should go there. The steep dusty road into that deep, lovely canyon was ghastly in 1962, but improvements seemed imminent. Echo Park escaped being drowned out of existence to make another huge storage reservoir because of a national uprising of nature-lovers during the late 1950's.

7. Between 1825 and the collapse of the Rockies beaver boom in 1840 (silk hats became really fashionable the year before), eight rendezvous were held on Green River waters, three on Wind drainage, one on Weber, two at Bear Lake, two at Pierre's Hole on a Snake River branch. The General took his furs back to St. Louis that summer of 1825 over South Pass and then down the Bighorn, Yellowstone and Missouri River as a final test of water transport. It worked out badly. On his last Rockies trip in 1826, he used a pack train on the Platte–Sweetwater–South Pass (Oregon Trail) route.

8. For example, geologist George M. Dawson's report on the Rockies to Canada's Parliament (1886) stated: "The culminating point of the Rocky Mountains is doubtless to be found about the 52nd parallel of north latitude, or between this and the 53rd parallel, where Mounts Brown and Murchison occur, with reputed altitudes of 16,000 and 13,500 feet respectively, and Mount Hooker, also reported to be very lofty."

Chapter 9: SOLDIERS TAKE THE HIGH ROAD

1. Titian Peale's brother, Rembrandt Peale, also made a career of painting George Washington.

2. Joseph Bijeau (or Bessonet) was a trader from the Platte River Pawnee villages who had been trapping the Pikes Peak region for six years. Long named for him Bijou Basin and Bijou Creek, an important branch of the South Platte.

3. In 1963, the old Ute Pass trail could still be followed by 4WD car from the Manitou Incline station as far as Cascade, four miles.

4. The official size of the summit of Pikes Peak is about five acres, according to Al Rogers of the Manitou and Pikes Peak Railway. It is owned by the Broadmoor Hotel, Colorado Springs.

5. Major Fowler would cross this same area eastbound in 1822.

6. The spot is a nice place for a picnic on a summer day, reached by dirt road three miles from U.S. Route 187–189 near Daniel, Wyoming.

7. There is no practical pass at all across the Wind River Range from Union Pass for more than a hundred miles to the South Pass–Christina Pass area. Lowest of the impractical crossings is Jackass Pass (ca. 10,800) just south of Mount Washakie. Indians did use it even though (people said) "only a jackass could be driven through it." Washakie Pass (11,610) was used also. A horse trail runs over Washakie today. Most Wind River passes are high cols, discovered in recent times by climbers. Among them are Glacier Pass (12,900), Indian Pass (12,130), Illinois Pass (11,750) and Angel Pass (11,500). The well-known trail over Green River Pass (10,370) does not cross the Continental Divide.

8. The case for Gannett is made by Orrin H. and Lorraine Bonney in their *Guide to the Wyoming Mountains*. C. G. Coutant, in his *The History of Wyoming*, has stated: "The peak on which Captain Bonneville . . . climbed is thirty-six miles on a direct line west from Lander, and will be found on a map of the State marked Mt. Bonneville." This divide peak, 12,229 feet, is just north of the climbers' Hailey Pass (11,165). Other writers have placed the Captain on Mount Chauvenet (12,280), seven miles short of Hailey Pass and the divide. Chauvenet is reached by trail from North Fork Guard Station of the North Popo Agie.

9. Frémont was of illegitimate birth, though of a most acceptable kind. His mother was the young wife of an aging Virginia aristocrat and his father was a charming young Frenchman who was supposed to be teaching her French. In 1841, Frémont wooed, won and eloped with Senator Benton's seventeen-year-old daughter Jessie, against the Senator's bombastic opposition.

10. Orrin H. Bonney, the Wind River Range expert, has very good reasons in his *Guide to the Wyoming Mountains* for believing that Frémont climbed Mount Woodrow Wilson (13,500) just north of Fremont Peak.

11. That portion of today's Colorado River from its extreme source at La Poudre Pass in the northwest corner of Rocky Mountain National Park to its juncture with Green River in Utah was called Grand River until the name was officially changed in 1921.

12. This road is an interesting way to reach Steamboat Springs for motorists wanting to avoid the usual U.S. Route 40 over Rabbit Ears Pass. It can be reached from Muddy Pass and is rough, roundabout and steep in spots but perfectly safe for standard cars.

13. Frémont was so absorbed in dreams of California glory that he hardly noticed Tennessee Pass. He devoted only a line or two to finding it in his *Memoirs of My Life*. The Ute trail which he followed beyond Tennessee did not wind through Eagle River Canyon to the Colorado River as the Denver and Rio Grande Railroad does today. It shelfed its way harrowingly around Battle Mountain as U.S. Route 24 does, but lower down, and then on to a point below the mouth of Gore Creek where it

left the Eagle and crossed northward to Piney Creek, reaching the Colorado near present State Bridge. From there the Ute trail wound over the Flattop–Trappers Lake region to White River headwaters, and on west to Salt Lake.

In the late fall of 1848, Frémont trailed up the Arkansas as a private citizen to find a railroad route west over Cochetopa Pass. He was a retired colonel now, having been booted out of the army for insubordination in California and reinstated by President Polk. His guide was the ancient, alcoholic trapper, Old Bill Williams, who led his thirty-five men and his mule train from Fort Pueblo over Hardscrabble Pass (9000) into Wet Mountain Valley, and then into San Luis Valley over Mosca Pass. From the sand dunes, Frémont examined Pike's Gap (Medano).

He had crossed passes before in winter to show that they could be used for roads, but in December, 1848, the worst blizzard in memory struck San Luis Valley. Old Bill Williams expected to handle it by working north toward Cochetopa Pass in the sheltering La Garita foothills, instead of taking the blizzard's full force in the open San Luis Valley. Perhaps he had meant to ascend the middle fork of present Carnero Creek and over present Carnero Pass (10,500) to reach Saguache Creek drainage and the Cochetopa Pass road.

However, he followed the Rio Grande too far west, and got his party stalled and snowbound in the Alder Creek–Pool Table Mountain–Wannamaker Creek area well above 11,000 feet northwest of present Del Norte, Colorado. During the weeks of late December, 1848, and January, 1849, eleven men froze or starved to death and the Fourth Frémont expedition had to retreat down Embargo Creek back to the Rio Grande and down it to Taos. William Brandon has written the sad story well in *The Men and the Mountain* (William Morrow & Co., New York, 1955).

Though Old Bill and Frémont had used bad judgment, it was the violence of the blizzard that wrecked the expedition — one of the rare times in Rockies history when experienced mountaineers could not cope with the elements. In normal weather, they would have trailed north down Wannamaker Creek to Saguache Creek in the center of present Saguache Park. From there they would have crossed present Salt House Pass (10,500), southernmost of the several Cochetopa passes. Perhaps Salt House Pass was the "Carnero Pass" mentioned by guides of the 1840's, the name referring to Rocky Mountain sheep ("carnero" in Spanish) which thrived on the grasses of Saguache Park. This Carnero Pass over the Continental Divide was not the same as present Carnero Pass.

Chapter 10: THE NEW MOUNTAIN MEN

1. As we have mentioned, Coronado's army in the year 1540 numbered 320 white men and "several hundred friendly Indians." Governor Valverde's Raton Pass force in 1719 was around a thousand. Governor De Anza chased the Comanches in 1779 with "103 soldiers, 470 colonists and Pueblo Indians."

2. Lieutenant Abert was the son of Colonel John J. Abert, chief of the Topographical Engineers. Quotations are from young Abert's journal, Senate Executive Document 438, 29th Congress, 1st Session.

3. It has been stated that Lieutenant Abert named the great tan tower

above Raton Pass Fisher's Peak, honoring Robert Fisher, who had been a Bent's Fort trader almost since the Bent brothers built the fort in 1832. Abert had met Fisher in the pass and had received helpful information from him. But the name has an additional explanation. In *Trinidad and its Environs*, A. W. McHendrie wrote that the Army of the West camped for the night just above present Trinidad on August 5, 1846. "The next morning, Captain Waldomar Fischer, a German educated as an artillery officer in the Prussian Army, in command of Company B of Major Clark's Battery of Artillery, was deceived by the apparent proximity of the majestic peak that towered above their camping ground, as it now does above the city of Trinidad. Up to that time the eminence had been known as Cimarron or Raton Peak. Not realizing that he was some ten miles distant from and some five or six thousand feet below the summit of this peak, he signified his intention of ascending it before breakfast. He started without breakfast, and did not return until about the middle of the next day, when he announced that he was ready for breakfast. In commemoration of his tenacity of purpose, the commanding officers instructed Lieutenant Emory to mark the peak on the military map 'Fischer's Peak.' It so appears on the original map. Later the German spelling was dropped and the peak has since been known as Fisher's Peak."

Beckwith's army map of 1855 marks the bluff as "Fischer's Peak."

4. One of the six immigrants was a female with whom Stansbury fell in love. His orders said nothing about escorting a female west, but his later report justified her presence as "a fortunate arrangement, since we thereby secured the society of an excellent and intelligent lady who . . . by her cheerfulness and vivacity, beguiled the tedium of many a monotonous and wearisome hour." During every Rockies trek, some woman seemed always on hand beguiling tedium, even before Sacajawea took over the Lewis and Clark expedition.

5. When the fur trade collapsed, Jim Bridger built Fort Bridger in 1842, and opened it to supply emigrants in 1843. It was four hundred miles beyond Fort Laramie, one hundred and fifty miles beyond South Pass. Fort Hall was built by the New Englander, Nat Wyeth, in 1834. He sold it soon to Hudson's Bay Company. Oregon Trail emigrants of the 1840's interpreted the "H.B.C." lettering of the company's red flag to mean "Here Before Christ."

6. At the start of the Civil War, Indian trouble flared on the Oregon Trail over South Pass and so the route was replaced by Stansbury's Bridger Pass route, the famed Overland Trail which lasted through the 1860's until the Union Pacific Railroad was built a bit north of it.

7. The U.S.G.S. altitude of this Cochetopa Pass is given still as 10,032 feet, indicating that it has not been measured since 1853.

8. The most distinguished traveler over Cochetopa Pass in the 1840's was Dr. Marcus Whitman, founder of the famous Presbyterian mission on the Walla Walla River in Oregon. When his superiors sent word to him to close the mission, he hurried east with a single companion in the snowy winter of 1842–1843, taking the southern Gunnison River route from Fort Hall (Idaho) to avoid hostile Sioux on the Oregon Trail. He nearly lost his life, first in the deep snow of Cochetopa, and later beyond Taos trying to get over Raton Pass to Bent's Fort. Somehow he survived, reached Bos-

ton, saved his mission, and was a leading figure in the Great Migration of more than a thousand people to Oregon over the Oregon Trail during 1843.

Chapter 11: THE LAST WILDERNESS

1. The Territory of Oregon was created in 1848, two years after the United States and Great Britain set the boundary at the 49th parallel. Oregon's limits were from the 42nd parallel (California) to the 49th, and west from the Continental Divide to the Pacific (the present states of Oregon, Washington, Idaho and parts of Montana and Wyoming). Washington Territory was carved out of it in 1853, consisting of present Washington and bits of Montana and Idaho west of the Divide and north of the 46th parallel. This new Washington Territory had no population to speak of, since most of the Oregon Trail emigrants had settled in Willamette Valley of Oregon.

2. The American Fur Company built Fort Lewis in 1846 as its upstream trading post and rebuilt it four years later, renaming it Fort Benton, after the Senator. It was about forty miles down the Missouri from present Great Falls, Montana. Fort Benton was the head of navigation for Missouri River steamers from 1859 to 1888.

3. Note no. 18 of "Contributions," v. 10, Historical Society of Montana reads: "There were at least two Cadottes at Fort Benton at this time, a father and son, and the father may have been the Pierre Cadotte for whom Stevens named the pass. Pierre was, no doubt, the man whom Kurz described as the 'best stag hunter in this region. He is a genuine mountaineer . . . unrivaled in the skill of starting, pursuing, approaching, shooting and carving a deer. In other respects he is heedless, wasteful and foolhardy — half Canadian and half Cree.' " Only a trail crosses Cadotte Pass today from Cadotte Creek to the Middle Fork of Dearborn River. The Rogers Pass highway, State Route 20, runs close by it to the south.

4. The Northern Pacific Survey map of 1853 marks the river "St. Regis de Borgia." Today's Deborgia village is on St. Regis River.

5. Squaws of the Bitterroot region seemed to find white men an amusing species. A big event of the 1840's was staged in Jocko Valley by the white trapper, Francois Armintinger, who made a big pile of beads, awls, needles and other feminine trinkets and then called in all Flathead women in the area to run a race on foot for it, winner to get the whole pile. Forty women of all ages entered the contest, which took place over a two-and-a-half-mile track. It was won very easily by the beautiful, slender young wife of Charlie La Moose. This race track was still called "Cours des Femmes" at the time of the Stevens survey.

6. Tinkham's bypass approximated today's back road from Clearwater Junction northward to Salmon Lake and westerly to Placid Lake, Jocko Lake and Arlee on U.S. Route 10A–93 above Evaro Pass.

7. Tinkham called Mullan Pass Flathead Pass.

8. The Nez Perce Pass trail was a more southerly crossing of the rugged Lolo Pass trail country to Clearwater and Snake rivers. Nez Perce Pass (6589) was reached from Fort Owen up South Fork of the Bitterroot and then the west Nez Perce fork of that fork to the top. From there, the trail went down Deep Creek–Selway River to Middle Fork of the Clearwater, or by Red River to South Fork of the Clearwater. The wilder-

ness which it crossed was wild even for those days. Lieutenant Robert Mac-Feely and twenty-six soldiers, who had brought supplies from Walla Walla to Fort Owen in August, 1853, returned west at once by Nez Perce Pass without guide, map or compass. After eight days' work getting up the pass, MacFeely wrote: "For eight days more we continued climbing mountain after mountain, our difficulties increasing as we proceeded; and when after much toil we had attained the summit of one of these mountains, it was only to behold another of still greater altitude rising in advance of us; and so it continued, day after day, until we began to think that there was no limit." Two months later, the indestructible Abiel Tinkham and two others made the same Nez Perce Pass trip on snowshoes through deep snow, each man equipped with "two blankets, tin cup, two pairs of socks and two pairs of mocassins." They were out forty-one days. A back road from Connor, Montana, to Elk City, Idaho, parallels the old Nez Perce trail.

Lieutenant Mullan explored Lolo Pass in September, 1854, on his way to Walla Walla and declared that "the route is thoroughly and utterly impracticable for a railroad." Summing up, the chronology of pass crossings by the Stevens expedition went roughly like this: Lewis and Clark Pass eastbound, Lieutenant Rufus Saxton, September 7, 1853; Nez Perce Pass westbound, Lieutenant Robert MacFeely, about September 12; Musselshell-Missouri divide westbound, Mullan, September 19; Lewis and Clark Pass westbound, F. C. Lander, about September 20; Cadotte Pass westbound, Lieutenant A. J. Donelson with main train, about September 22; Cadotte Pass westbound, Stevens, September 24; Clearwater-Jocko divide westbound, Tinkham, about September 29; Coeur d'Alêne (Stevens) Pass westbound, Stevens, October 10; Marias Pass (to west foot only), Tinkham, October 18; Pitamakan Pass eastbound, Tinkham, October 20; Gibbons Pass southbound, Mullan, about October 25; Mullan Pass westbound, Tinkham, November 10; Bull Creek Pass southbound, Mullan, late November; Medicine Lodge Pass southbound, Mullan, December 9; Monida Pass northbound, Mullan, December 25; Clover Divide northbound, Mullan, December 27; Deer Lodge Pass northbound, Mullan, December 31; Cadotte Pass westbound, Lieutenant Cuvier Grover, January 11, 1854; crossing near Mullan Pass (south fork, Little Blackfoot) eastbound, Mullan, about March 7; Mullan Pass westbound, Mullan, about March 24; Stillwater (Flathead)–Tobacco River (Kootenai) divide northbound, Mullan, April 20; Marias Pass (hill near east foot only), James Doty, June 10; Lookout Pass eastbound, Mullan, June 20; Mullan Pass westbound, James Doty, July 7; Mullan Pass eastbound, James Doty, July 25; Medicine Rock Pass (between present Wilborn and Wolf Creek) eastbound, James Doty, July 26; Lewis and Clark Pass westbound, James Doty, September 12; Lolo Pass westbound, Mullan, September 23; Lookout Pass westbound, James Doty, September 27, 1854.

9. Dr. Hector declared that "the French half-breed was more Indian than white and the Scotch half-breed more white than Indian."

10. The parallel north-south ridges of the Canadian Rockies explain why the old Indian trails over North Kootenay and South Kootenay passes crossed two summits in each case. South Kootenay Pass was, and still is, known also as Boundary Pass. However, there is a trail which crosses to-

day still nearer the boundary, by Akamina Pass (5835). The first American traverse on the Continental Divide south of the border is Brown Pass (6600), perhaps six miles south of Akamina Pass.

11. Dr. Hector wrote: "Here at the west foot of Vermilion Pass is the Vermilion Plain . . . its surface entirely covered with yellow ochre, washed down from the ferruginous shales in the mountains. The Kootanie Indians come to this place sometimes, and we found the remains of a camp and of a large fire which they had used to convert the ochre into the red oxide which they take away to trade to the Indians of the low country . . . as a pigment, calling it vermilion."

Though Hector named Mount Rundle (after an early missionary), the name Banff came later — supplied by Lord Strathcona honoring his birthplace in Scotland. Present Mount Eisenhower, as noted, used to be called Castle Mountain. The Canadians have the good habit of changing place names if they want to. Many Rockies peaks in the United States could have more stimulating and appropriate names.

12. Hector wrote of another kicking horse in his party soon after the accident: "On September 2 after gaining a considerable height we found it necessary to cross the stream, which was boiling and leaping through a narrow channel of pink quartzose rock. It was with much difficulty that we effected a crossing, and then we had much climbing over moss-covered rocks, our horses often sliding and falling. One, an old grey, that was always more clumsy than the others, lost his balance in passing along a ledge, which overhung a precipitous slope about one hundred and fifty feet in height, and down he went, luckily catching sometimes on the trees; at last he came to a temporary pause by falling right on his back, the pack acting as a fender; however, in his endeavors to get up he started down hill again, and at last slid on a dead tree that stuck out at right angles to the slope, balancing himself with his legs dangling on either side of the trunk of the tree in a most comical manner."

13. The passes box score of the Palliser expedition reads: Palliser crossed Kananaskis, North Kootenay and South Kootenay, the last two of which were crossed also by Lieutenant Blakiston. Dr. Hector crossed Vermilion, Beaverfoot, Kicking Horse, Bow, Pipestone and Howse passes. After the expedition, Dr. Hector visited the California gold fields briefly, returned to Scotland and then emigrated permanently to New Zealand, where he became famous as one of the world's best known geologists. He was knighted in 1887.

Chapter 12: OVER THE WALL

1. Starting at the New Mexico–Colorado border just west of Cumbres Pass (10,022), the Continental Divide runs north, west, north and east again for 50, 50, 30 and 100 miles (San Juan Range–Cochetopa Hills); then north 80 miles (Sawatch–Collegiate Range); then east 90 miles from Hoosier to Berthoud Pass (Loveland Pass, section, Front Range); then north 60 miles (Indian and Rocky Mountain Park sections, Front Range); and finally west 40 miles to Rabbit Ears Pass (Rabbit Ears Range).

2. Kenosha Pass was named by homesick prospectors from Kenosha, Wisconsin. Mount Silverheels memorializes a dance hall girl of great beauty and easy virtue who nursed families of the Fairplay area through

a smallpox epidemic, and quietly stole away when the disease ruined her own face and means of livelihood. Earl Hamilton, who gave his name to Hamilton, was a Tarryall pioneer.

3. Somebody reported in the *Rocky Mountain News* of September 22, 1859, that the Garden of the Gods was first called the Garden of Eden because "two rocks there look just like Adam and Eve. This resemblance the writer can not vouch for, never having had the honor of Mrs. Eve's acquaintance."

4. The very beautiful Tarryall route is there still, running north from U.S. Route 24 on an excellent army-improved gravel road a mile west of Lake George. The Tarryall settlement on this road was a Cripple Creek by-product of the 1890's, not the original Tarryall much farther north.

5. You may remember that Frémont avoided the Georgia Pass trail and crossed Hoosier Pass in 1844 rather than run into Arapaho and Ute Indians on the warpath. These tribes were still battling in the area during the 1860's.

6. The mountain was so named because of its question-mark shape and because its gold-bearing mineral put men in a quandary as to what it could be.

7. The average width of this gold-bearing strip was five miles.

8. Colonel William W. Loring, with three hundred men and fifty wagons, left Camp Floyd, near Utah Lake, on July 19, 1858, and arrived at Fort Union, New Mexico, on September 13, after having supplied General A. S. Johnston's "Mormon War" army. Antoine Leroux was the guide and the route east was over Wasatch Pass and along Gunnison's trail to Cochetopa Pass, Taos, Palo Flechado or Osha Pass to Black Lake and Fort Union. LeRoy R. Hafen described the trip in *Colorado Magazine*, March, 1946, expressing a belief that Loring probably crossed North Cochetopa Pass.

9. In later years, some seafaring New Englander noted the splotched-yellow fold which reminded him of slumgullion, the refuse draining from the cutting up of a whale for its blubber. The name was applied to Slumgullion Pass.

10. The road from Lake City to Silverton over Cinnamon Pass is easy for four-wheel-drive cars today and makes an absolutely thrilling trip. People are agitating to convert it into a scenic highway for standard cars.

11. The expert mountaineer, Robert Ormes, becomes poetic just thinking about the remote zigzag Columbine Pass trail linking the Grenadiers and Chicago Basin, heart of the southern Needles. The trail starts at a spot on Animas River called Needleton which can be reached only on the last narrow-gauge passenger train in the United States, the Denver and Rio Grande Western's famous summer run from Durango to Silverton.

12. Charles Baker survived the war only to be killed, reportedly by Indians, while prospecting back in the San Juans during the 1870's.

Chapter 13: Mr. Berthoud, and "Gilpin's Lambs"

1. The first of these routes was from Denver or Golden to Bergen's Ranch (Bergen Park) partly up Mount Vernon Canyon (U.S. Route 40) and south along the line of present Evergreen–Shaffers Crossing–Bailey to the North Fork of the South Platte and on over Kenosha. The second, via

Turkey Creek, was practically today's U.S. 285. The third and shortest crossed the South Platte about three miles above the mouth of Turkey Creek and ran west over Bradford Hill to meet the others near present Conifer Junction. It was called Bradford's Airline Road but it did not last long.

2. These uplands of Grand County in the southern part of Arapaho National Forest contain some of the heaviest and most beautiful forests in the state and are amazingly wild and inaccessible, though only fifty miles or so from Denver. Bottle Pass (11,360) and St. Louis Pass (11,210) are the main trail crossings of Vasquez Mountains. The Williams Fork Range is crossed by the Ptarmigan Pass (11,750) and Ute Pass (9524) trails.

3. In a letter to his friend Major General Winfield Scott, novelist Cooper stated that Berthoud "is of excellent character, is liberally educated, and I make no doubt would prove useful." It was Cooper's idea that Colonel Abert, head of the Topographical Engineers, had the power to employ Berthoud.

4. Fraser River runs through Fraser town, very proud of being "the coldest place in North America," and forever crowing about it.

5. Beautiful and extremely interesting back roads run near Berthoud's entire route today. From U.S. Route 40 six miles beyond Kremmling take the Gore Pass road to Toponas, Oak Creek and Hayden (U.S. 40 again) and Craig. From thence an obscure trace runs south from the airport to Deer Creek, Milk Creek, Yellowjacket Pass and White River at Meeker where State Route 64 leads to Salt Lake City. Coming back through Meeker, you continue east up White River past Buford. The road dwindles, but by bearing northeast and making inquiry you will arrive at Oak Creek once more, and on east over Gore Pass to Kremmling.

The name Gore Pass could have derived originally from its gore, or wedge shape, spreading then to Gore Canyon, Gore Range, Gore Creek and Gore Mountain, which cover the map from Rabbit Ears Pass (Steamboat Springs) south for eighty miles past Colorado River to Tenmile Creek and Vail Pass. Henry Gannett of the Hayden Survey claimed that the name honored George Gore, a Denver gunsmith. But today the name is in memory of a legendary gentleman from Sligo, Ireland, Sir George Gore, who reached St. Louis in 1853, and turned up next spring at Fort Laramie in Wyoming to hunt and to prospect up the North Platte as far as Muddy Pass. He returned to Fort Laramie for the winter of 1854–1855 and hunted for two more years in Wyoming and Montana east of the Big Horn Mountains. His guide for some of his tour was Jim Bridger, who charged thirty dollars a day to put up with Gore's peculiar disposition. He is the hero of many hunting tales and was, supposedly, the real discoverer of gold in the Rockies, but kept quiet about it so as not to spoil the hunting. His luxurious retinue by one account was every sportsman's dream — forty men, one hundred and twelve horses, twelve yoke of oxen, fourteen dogs, six wagons and twenty-one carts full of champagne. At the end of the 1856 hunting season, Sir George agreed to sell his equipage to the American Fur Company factor at Fort Union on the Missouri, but got in a temper at the last minute in a dispute over the price and burned everything up. The evidence is not conclusive that Sir George ever actually arrived in Middle Park from Muddy Pass and North Park to explore or see any of the landmarks which bear his name. Forbes Parkhill has written an excellent account of his career in *The Wildest of the West* (Henry Holt & Co., New York, 1951).

6. The Ute Indian agent had a pack trail built over Berthoud Pass to the annuity distribution station in Middle Park, but that was as far as it got toward being a wagon road in the 1860's. Edward L. Berthoud became Captain Berthoud in the Civil War and then was chief engineer of the Colorado Central Railroad and, later, of the Utah and Northern.

7. This new Overland Trail ran up the South Platte instead of the North Platte, and up the Cache la Poudre to Virginia Dale, the Antelope Pass area, Laramie plains, Rattlesnake Pass, Fort Halleck, Bridger Pass, Fort Bridger and the Echo Canyon route to Salt Lake City.

Chapter 14: CONTINENTAL TEA

1. Montana Territory was carved out of Idaho Territory in 1864, with the capital at Bannack that year, at Virginia City in 1865, and at Helena from 1874 on. Montana became a state in 1889.

2. In 1857, President Buchanan declared the Mormons of Utah to be in rebellion and ordered the Army of the West to control them. Colonel Albert Sidney Johnston wintered the troops at Fort Bridger, having been stopped there by Mormon troops and a lack of provisions. In April, 1858, Buchanan proclaimed a pardon of the Mormons. Johnston led his soldiers to Salt Lake City in July. The Mormons accepted them peacefully, Camp Floyd was established near the Mormon capital and the "Mormon War" — if you could call it a "war," was over.

3. A colleague of Lander's in failing to find Cascade passes for Stevens was Captain George B. McClellan, the future General McClellan who, some said, made an art during the Civil War of doing nothing as elaborately as possible.

4. Lander's engineers explored the mountains thoroughly north of Sublette Cut-Off. Lander's nineteen passes included Cheese, Cliff Creek and Pickle passes and McDougal Gap in the Wyoming Range; and Salt River, Sheep and McDougal passes in the Salt River Range.

5. Motorists can follow Lander's Cut-Off easily from Big Piney, Wyoming, west to Star Valley and west again from Auburn. The map of Caribou National Forest, issued free by the Forest Service, shows the Lander route from Auburn to near Fort Hall, Idaho.

6. This Fort Walla Walla was the army's new post. The Hudson's Bay Company's old Fort Walla Walla was at the junction of the Columbia and the Walla Walla.

7. The Blackfeet who had been so dangerous through the trapper period had degenerated into mere professional horse thieves.

8. Lieutenant Maynadier handled the Yellowstone matter very well. He ascended the Bighorn and Clark Fork to the Yellowstone and west across Bridger Range to the Gallatin by Flathead Pass, which he called Blackfoot Pass, north of Bozeman Pass. He returned to the Yellowstone by way of Bridger Pass, Brackett Creek and Shields River, and descended the Yellowstone this time all the way to meet Raynolds at Fort Union on the Missouri.

9. The copper capital of Butte had its origins in 1864, when some of these Bannack-bound prospectors found color on Silver Bow Creek.

10. Wagons could get over Gibbons Pass if they had to, but freighters hated that steep pitch down the north side to Ross's Hole.

11. The several attempts to use camels in pack trains in the West were begun by Edward F. Beale, who induced the army to import eighty of them for work on the road which he built in 1857 across Arizona from Fort Defiance to the Colorado River. That experiment was not successful either.

12. The Union Pacific put a crimp also in the steamboat business from St. Louis to Fort Benton. Thirty-one boats docked at Benton in 1866. Somebody estimated that two thousand five hundred men and three thousand teams hauled supplies from the boats to the mines that year. By 1870, most of those supplies came over Monida Pass from the U. P. at Corinne. Traffic decreased even on the Mullan Road, which became a pack-train route. John Mullan spent $230,000 on it before finishing it completely for wagons in 1862. Incidentally, poor John Bozeman was killed by Indians on the Bozeman Trail east of Bozeman Pass in 1867.

13. The experiences of the Overlanders gave the Yellowhead Pass route a black eye which has lasted to modern times. At 3717 feet above sea level, Yellowhead Pass is the next-to-lowest gap in all the Rockies (Monkman Pass north of it is 3550). From the enchanting resort town of Jasper, a nondescript gravel road crosses Yellowhead and descends to Mount Robson village sixty miles west. Moose Lake is a pretty sliver of blue water and the mountains are nice, but, on the whole, the lodgepole monotony of the dusty road makes a boring journey. Beyond Mount Robson, some sort of trace continues two hundred and forty miles to Kamloops. Its condition in 1963 must have been almost as bad as when Mrs. Schubert moved her bulging form over it a century before. At least, nobody in Jasper wanted even to talk about it.

In 1863, two young sports from England decided to follow the Overlanders over Yellowhead to the Cariboo just for the fun of it. One of them was Dr. Walter Butler Cheadle, M.A., M.D., *Cantab.*, F.R.G.S., aged twenty-seven. The other was Lord Milton, F.R.G.S., F.E.S.L., F.A.S.L., et cetera, aged about twenty-two. They endured all the trials on the trip that the Overlanders had endured. In addition, Dr. Cheadle found himself going almost crazy trying to cope with Lord Milton's alleged laziness, crabbiness, viciousness, lechery and "symptoms which seemed to be a species of fit," brought on by overdrinking. Near Moose Lake in mid-July, Dr. Cheadle came close to losing his horse, Bucephalus. The animal was found at last on the other side of the Fraser, in sight of a nine-thousand-foot mountain which is still called Bucephalus Peak, five miles south of Yellowhead Pass. Dr. Cheadle's account of this trip — hilarious and apoplectic by turns — is a treat (see Sources).

Chapter 15: THE ROVER BOYS

1. Through the whole nineteenth century, Indian resistance to white men happened often in Rocky Mountain pass areas, beginning in 1810, and again in 1812, when David Thompson's trappers and their Flathead allies battled the Blackfeet in Marias Pass and Cutbank Pass, Mon-

tana. The famous Battle of Pierre's Hole took place on July 17–18, 1832, beyond the west end of Teton Pass in Idaho. The fight was between the Blackfeet and several hundred trappers and Indian allies who had been attending the rendezvous in Pierre's Hole. The trappers were led by Henry Fraeb, Milton and William Sublette, Alexander Sinclair and Nathaniel Wyeth. Twenty-six Blackfeet were killed, and five trappers and seven Indians of the white brigade. Soon after, two white trappers were killed and scalped at the east end of Teton Pass.

Henry Fraeb survived that fight but was killed with two companions in August, 1841. Fraeb was leading twenty-three trappers in a pitched battle against a large party of Cheyennes, Sioux and Arapahos. The battle occurred near the west end of Battle Lake Pass, at the mouth of Battle Creek and Little Snake River. The spot, at today's little community of Battle Creek, Colorado, less than half a mile from the Wyoming line, is a charming picnic objective, by way of the Battle Lake Pass road west over the Continental Divide from Encampment, Wyoming. In July, 1848, the Second Regiment of Missouri Volunteers, on guard duty in northern New Mexico, had a running fight along the high plateau of Cumbres Pass in southern Colorado with a band of Jicarilla Apaches and Muache Utes during which two soldiers and thirty-six Indians were killed. After the 1854 Christmas Eve massacre of Mexican monte players by Muache Utes at Pueblo, Colorado, soldiers under Lieutenant Thomas Fauntleroy caught up with the Muaches in March, 1855, at the east foot of Cochetopa Pass, and harried them over Poncha Pass and on east and far south into Texas. Kit Carson was Fauntleroy's guide.

Captain Alfred Bates and his cavalry unit, assisted by Chief Washakie and a hundred Snake Indians, trailed a Wyoming party of Arapaho plunderers from Wind River up Badwater Creek in July, 1874. They caught them at Cottonwood Pass, on the old Sioux trail which led from the pass down No Wood Creek to Powder River Pass in the Big Horns. Four soldiers and many Indians were killed in this skirmish. Later, November 25, 1776, on the Powder River side of the Big Horns, Colonel Ranald S. Mackenzie and a large force of soldiers and Indian scouts attacked a traveling Cheyenne village under Dull Knife, Roman Nose and Little Wolf and destroyed it. The fight occurred on the Willow Creek branch of the Powder in the Big Horn foothills near Dull Knife and Fraker passes, some ten miles west of present Mayoworth, Wyoming. September 29, 1879, was the day when a handful of Ute Indians murdered their Indian agent, Nathan Meeker, and all his white employees at the White River Ute Agency near present Meeker, Colorado. At the same time, a larger Ute group battled an army rescue force which was rushing up the government road from Rawlins, Wyoming, to rescue the agent. The battle occurred twenty-five miles north of present Meeker just over Yellowjacket Pass on Milk Creek. The Utes won hands down, killing eleven soldiers, wounding forty-three more, and holding the survivors on Milk Creek until reinforcements arrived four days later. The battleground monument at the base of Thornburgh Mountain is reached today by a delightful back road from Meeker. It is well worth a visit.

The greatest of these stories of conflict on passes was the flight of young Chief Joseph and seven hundred of his Nez Perce men, women and children, from the lovely Wallowa Valley of eastern Oregon. Joseph had declined to move his band to Idaho when the government drastically reduced the size of the Nez Perce homeland, which had been given to the tribe "forever" in 1855. The army sent a strong force in June, 1877, to persuade Joseph. His answer was to begin fleeing east across Idaho with his people, their household goods and fifteen hundred Appaloosa horses. Their ultimate objective was the Canadian wilderness. General O. O. Howard and his troops, endowed with youth and the latest in firepower, medicine and food, were beaten time and again as they tried to stop this threadbare mob of shoeless families — near White Bird Canyon on June 29, on the Clearwater's South Fork July 11–12, on Orofino Creek July 17. The fugitives climbed over those rugged Clearwater Mountains to Lolo Pass on the route which Lieutenant Mullan had condemned in 1854 as "thoroughly and utterly impracticable." On the east side of Lolo, young Captain Charles C. Rawn of the Seventh Cavalry built a rat-proof barricade which was sure to stop the Indians. Joseph led his seven hundred, ancients and infants included, around it by a goat path over a cliff. The barricade site is still called Fort Fizzle.

The band slipped on south, a train of anguish moving through the peaceful Bitterroot Valley and over Gibbons Pass. In Big Hole Valley, fifteen miles down from the top, they found Colonel John Gibbon and his troops waiting to accept their surrender. Joseph preferred to fight (the site is today's Big Hole Battlefield National Monument on the Chief Joseph Pass road above Wisdom, Montana). During the two-day struggle (August 8–9), Gibbon lost a howitzer, two thousand rounds of ammunition, and sixty-eight men killed and wounded. The Nez Perce escaped south on the Bannack–Medicine Lodge Pass road, crossed the barrens east to Henrys Lake, and over Targhee Pass into Yellowstone Park.

From Firehole River, they ascended Nez Perce Creek to Mud Volcano and the north end of Yellowstone Lake. Then they went up Pelican Creek over Mirror Plateau to Lamar River, and up Miller Creek to leave the park by crossing the Absarokas at "Papoose Pass" to Papoose Creek and Clarks Fork of the Yellowstone. Some students send them from the park by way of Cache Creek and Crandall Pass to Clarks Fork. They toiled over Beartooth Plateau and Beartooth Pass into Montana, fought the Seventh Cavalry near Billings, escaped north over the Judith Range, and crossed the Missouri east of Fort Benton. On September 29, they pitched camp on Snake Creek near the Bear Paw Mountains. They thought that they had reached Canada and freedom, after a thousand miles of flight from Oregon. But they were fifty miles short of the border. Next day, the Fifth Infantry under Colonel Nelson A. Miles caught up with them. They battled hopelessly for four days before Joseph surrendered. "I am tired," he said to Miles. "My heart is sick and sad. Our chiefs are dead. The little children are freezing. My people have no blankets, no food. I will fight no more forever."

2. At the time of his death in 1887, Dr. Hayden had forty-four genera and species carrying his name.

3. One of Hayden's parties in that same year of 1872 laid out a line for a railroad which the members thought ought to run north to Yellowstone Park from the Union Pacific at Corinne, Utah, around the Pierre's

Hole and north sides of the Tetons. Their proposed line touched at present Idaho Falls, Rexburg and Ashton, Idaho, and ran up Falls River and into the park at Beula Lake and over the low divide to Lewis River, a Snake branch. It must have been a poor idea. Not even a 4WD road ascends Falls River to Beula Lake today.

4. This treaty made the Colorado Utes perhaps the richest per capita Indian land owners in the United States — forty-five hundred acres for each Ute man, woman and child. The 1868 Ute Reservation comprised twenty-five thousand square miles, or about forty per cent of the Colorado Rockies.

5. Hayden's triangulation was part of the process of making contour maps by laying out the region first on paper with the summits of the highest peaks as points of triangles. Pikes Peak was the major triangle point. It could be seen, so that the surveyors' transits could be fixed on it, from most Colorado summits within a hundred miles — Fishers Peak, for instance, at Raton Pass, which was one hundred and twenty-five miles away. These big "primary" triangles were broken down for greater accuracy into dozens of "secondary" triangles, with sides of only ten miles or so. Altitudes were determined by a series of barometric observations, and they did not vary a great deal from official altitudes today. Some of Hayden's peak altitudes, with the modern figures in parenthesis, were: Pikes Peak, 14,147 (14,110); Mount Elbert, 14,351 (14,431); Mount Harvard, 14,375 (14,420); Mount Princeton, 14,200 (14,197); Capitol Peak, 13,997 (14,137); Mount Sneffels, 14,158 (14,150). There is no such thing as an exact altitude. Every so often, the U.S.G.S. issues a new figure promoting or demoting some montane monster. In 1950, Mount Massive was the second highest peak in the Rockies at 14,418, and Mount Harvard was third at 14,399. Since then Harvard has grown twenty-two feet, making it two feet higher than Massive.

6. Hayden Divide, called plain Divide now, at the top of Ute Pass west of Colorado Springs, and Hayden Peak (13,500) near Aspen, Colorado, were named for Dr. Hayden. Mount Daly, next to Capitol Peak in the Elks, honored Judge Charles F. Daly, president of the American Geographical Society, 1864–1899. Rhoda's party named the striking Teocalli Mountain (13,220), above East River and Crested Butte, Colorado, because it resembled the four-sided teocalli temples of Mexico.

7. Hayden and Jackson approached the Mount of the Holy Cross from Eagle River by riding up what is now called Cross Creek. Their name for it was more colorful — Roche Moutonnée Creek, because of the odd sheep-backed boulders in the little valley. Cross Creek can be ascended by car a mile or so today from U.S. Route 24 near Minturn. Its mouth is near the mouth of Two Elk Creek, the upper part of which is at the base of a Vail ski resort chair lift. The army's survival training center, Camp Hale, is farther up the Eagle toward Tennessee Pass. While Hayden was exploring the Eagle, he met two prospectors who were trout fishing and doing well. They told him that they packed the trout in ice and carried them over Tennessee Pass to California Gulch, where they sold them at high prices. They seemed surprised when Hayden replied that he knew of a similar business run by Gilman Sawtelle at Henrys Lake, Idaho. In 1873, travelers descending the Eagle did not go through Glenwood Canyon to

the site of Glenwood Springs in the manner of U.S. 24. They got around the impassable canyon over the low Cottonwood Pass, as motorists can do now by turning south off U.S. 24 at Gypsum.

8. The toll road over Mosca (Robidoux) Pass shortened the distance from the Arkansas to the Rio Grande at Del Norte, the new supply center for Baker's Park. You may recall that trader Antoine Robidoux discovered this advantage in the 1820's when he packed goods from the Arkansas to San Luis Valley and on over Cochetopa Pass.

9. From Crested Butte and Gothic, standard cars can usually make it easily to the top of Schofield Pass, and even down the Crystal River side for three miles before the four-wheel-drive canyon part of the road begins. Now and then somebody tries to go down the canyon in a standard car, gets stuck and bothers the Crystal ghost town summer residents to extricate him. Marble, at the north foot of Schofield Pass, used to be headquarters of the quarries which supplied stone for the Lincoln Memorial in Washington and the Tomb of the Unknown Soldier in Arlington Cemetery.

10. The Rhoda Party arrived at Lake San Cristobal the day after John A. Randolph, a *Harper's Weekly* illustrator, came upon the skeletons of five men at a spot which is now called Cannibal Plateau near the west foot of Slumgullion Pass. It turned out that the five had been eaten during the previous winter by Alfred Packer, who lived on to a ripe age through a series of trials and jail sentences to become one of Colorado's celebrities. Packer escaped hanging because nobody could prove that he had killed the men, and after all, there was no law against eating a dead friend.

11. Thunderstorms on Uncompahgre gave Rhoda and Wilson their first taste of a phenomenon of the San Juans. The tension of electricity made their hair stand on end, stiff as a porcupine's quills. As lightning struck somewhere near them, all the sharp stones gave off the sound of bacon frying and their transit sang like a telegraph key. Incidentally, "Godwin Creek" was their name for today's Henson Creek. Harry Henson and Charles Godwin were pioneer prospectors of the area in 1871.

12. As Rhoda crossed "Bear Creek Pass" he noticed another gap eight miles to the north, but did not investigate it. That gap was Ophir Pass (11,700), which would become in the late 1870's the main wagon route out of Baker's Park to Ophir, Telluride and the other San Miguel silver camps.

13. Today a good gravel road for standard cars runs west up the lovely Rio Grande Valley from U.S. Route 160 at South Fork past Wagon Wheel Gap, Creede, Antelope Park and the north foot of Weminuche Pass as far as Lost Trail Creek at the west end of Rio Grande Reservoir. From there, four-wheel-drive cars can continue at least to the mouth of Pole Creek, six miles from the top of Stony Pass (12,594). Some of them have been going on over the pass in recent years. From Pole Creek, a passable road runs southwesterly up Bear Creek toward Hunchback Pass as far as the ghost camp of Beartown, about four miles.

There is more to this Stony Pass road than trout fishing in the Rio Grande and the pleasure of approaching the source of such a historic stream. Some miles short of Rio Grande Reservoir a well-marked fork runs north and over Spring Creek Pass (10,901) of the Continental Divide and Slumgullion Pass (11,361) to Lake San Cristobal and Lake City, one of the very nicest places in Colorado to spend a quiet night, or week. As motorists drive north toward Spring Creek Pass they should watch to the southwest for a superb view of the romantic little Hermit Lakes, with Rio Grande Pyramid rising in symmetrical splendor behind them.

14. Bryan, now a railroad ghost town near Green River, Wyoming, was the nearest Union Pacific station serving the South Pass gold camps of South Pass City and Atlantic City. Fort Stambaugh was built in 1870 to protect the miners from Indian attack, but it never did much protecting because the South Pass placers were almost exhausted by then. It was abandoned in 1878.

Chapter 16: TIMBERLINE!

1. Vasquez Pass got its name from Vasquez Creek, as Clear Creek was called in the early days, honoring Jim Bridger's old partner, Louis Vasquez. No trace remains of Russell's road. Jones Pass is crossed now from the foot of Berthoud Pass by a fine, narrow, scary four-wheel-drive road used to service the west end of the Jones Pass Tunnel of Denver's water system. The road ends there at the start of Williams Fork River, which joins Colorado River at Parshall. From Jones Pass there are superb views of Vasquez Range peaks, seemingly close enough to touch.

2. The classic example of Mormon persistence was Howard Martin's Handcart Company of five hundred and seventy-six English emigrants to Salt Lake City, who tried to cross the plains and South Pass in 1856 pushing carts containing all their worldly goods. They got caught in November blizzards and more than one hundred froze to death before they were rescued by a wagon brigade from Deseret.

3. The summer-only Rollins Pass gravel road runs from Rollinsville past East Portal of Moffat Tunnel and Yankee Doodle Lake, over the top across a couple of shaky old railroad trestles and on down the easy west side to U.S. Route 40 near the west foot of Berthoud Pass at Hideaway. The trip is quite an experience.

4. Today's Guanella Pass (11,750) was named for Byron Guanella, Clear Creek County road supervisor and a descendant of Thomas Guanella. Byron Guanella built the charming twenty-two mile back road from Georgetown south up South Clear Creek past Green Lake and over the pass to Duck Lake, Geneva Creek and Grant, where it joins U.S. Route 285 east of Kenosha Pass. The Guanella family has lived at Empire in recent times.

5. In those days, the wagon road entered Hot Sulphur Springs by way of the shortcut over Cottonwood Pass (8904). This easy, nine-mile shortcut exists still off U.S. Route 40, bypassing Granby.

6. When the Webster Pass road was finished, the Websters considered but rejected a plan to build a road from Hall Valley to Georgetown, starting at Hepburn's Ranch on the North Fork and using the Hepburn Pass trail to Geneva Creek and Guanella Pass. The road would have approximated today's Geneva Park trail on the five-mile stretch to Geneva Creek from the North Fork of the South Platte. The Webster Pass road served for a dozen years or more as the popular freight route into the Montezuma–Peru area. Today an easy four-wheel-drive road from Montezuma runs to the top of the pass — almost easy enough for small standard cars.

But be sure to stop well short of the top! There is no guard rail or sign up there and, exactly at the top, the old road has fallen away and before you is virtually a cliff, or at least a sixty per cent slope, dropping several hundred feet.

7. And what of Stephen Decatur? He lost his reporting job on the *Colorado Miner* and drifted off to live next door to a saloon in the silver camp of Rosita in the Wet Mountains. There the several-times bigamist seems to have become a justice of the peace who made a living marrying people. He died in 1888.

Chapter 17: LEADVILLE FEVER

1. Our "Yellowstone Park pyramid" includes Union Pass and its source stream of Green River sixty miles south of the park proper.

2. The Weston Pass summer road today is steep in places and dusty, but it is perfectly all right for standard cars. It leaves U.S. Route 285 south of Fairplay and runs twenty-eight miles to U.S. 24 south of Leadville. Superb views of the Collegiate part of the Sawatch Range from top.

3. For a little more on Silverheels, see Note 2, Chapter 12.

4. A small stone marker at the top of Mosquito Pass reads:

1812–1901
J. L. "FATHER" DYER
METHODIST PREACHER
AUTHOR
CARRIED MAIL AND GOLD
OVER THIS PASS 1864
"THE SNOWSHOE ITINERANT"

5. It is often assumed that everything "highest" in the Rockies has to be on the Continental Divide, but this is not true by a long shot. A number of peaks and passes in the Elk, San Miguel and Sangre de Cristo ranges, for instance, are nowhere near the Divide but they can hold their own with the rest.

6. Colorado Territory became a state in 1876. Montana was admitted to statehood in 1889, Idaho and Wyoming in 1890, New Mexico in 1912. British Columbia, a Crown colony since 1858, was admitted to the Canadian Union in 1871, Alberta in 1905.

7. The Leadville–Fairplay burro race is run over a twenty-three-mile course around the south side of London Hill and down South Mosquito Creek instead of the north-side route of the old toll road. The latter-day sourdoughs and their burros enter the race for cash prizes from all over the West. The winning time is usually about four hours — slower than that of the old stagecoaches. A burro, if you don't know, is just a western donkey, or, if you like, an ass, jackass, or jack. Mosquito Pass can be crossed in 4WD cars today either by the south or north route, though the south is roughest. Standard cars go over from east to west now and then (North London Mine side) on a dare.

8. The Leadville discoveries coincided with the desire of Europeans to invest large amounts of money which they did not know what to do with. As we shall see, two railroads from Denver were feeling their way into

the mountains. And it was clear to many people that the Ute Indians would soon be driven off their twelve million acres of Western Slope reservation by the pressure of the whites.

9. Monarch today is a quarry which supplies limestone to the steel mill in Pueblo.

10. "Tomichi" stands for "hot water" in the Ute language. The area abounds in thermal springs and people still go swimming in the old pool at Waunita Hot Springs. Tomichi town had a few days of world fame in July, 1881, when a disappointed office-seeker, Charles J. Guiteau, assassinated President Garfield in a Washington railroad station. Guiteau's divorced wife ran a restaurant in Tomichi and her father had a barber shop there.

11. Lieutenant, later General, Marshall was born in Maysville, Kentucky, and it is said that Maysville town on the Monarch Pass road was so named to please Marshall. Some students assert that Mears Junction, a station in Poncha Pass on the later Marshall Pass line of the Denver and Rio Grande Railroad, was named for Dave Mears, Marshall's packer, rather than for Otto Mears.

Marshall Pass seems to have been the first high crossing of the Continental Divide to be used by a world celebrity. In July, 1880, General (and ex-President) Ulysses S. Grant rode over Marshall Pass from Salida in a four-horse Barlow and Sanderson stagecoach to visit Irwin and other camps on Slate and Coal creeks and Oh-Be-Joyful-Gulch near Schofield Pass, and also Pitkin. The story is that the General insisted on driving the team part of the way himself. He returned from Pitkin to Salida over Old Old Monarch Pass.

12. The Forest Service opened a splendid summer road for standard cars over Cottonwood Pass in 1960 — thirty-two miles from Buena Vista to Taylor Reservoir in Taylor Park. From St. Elmo, a narrow road runs six miles to the top of Tincup Pass. The west side down toward Tincup as far as Mirror Lake (four miles) was a rough 4WD trace in 1964. It was entirely unsuitable for standard cars.

13. David Lavender, the distinguished historian of the West, has written a thrilling novel based in part on the building of Mears's Ouray–Silverton road — *Red Mountain* (Doubleday & Co., Garden City, New York, 1963).

14. When the author went past the big gray Timber Hill boulder in the early 1960's, the dramatic bullet holes were still there, and so was this undramatic poem, in faded white paint:

> BUY YOUR PILLS
> AT THE CITY DRUG STORE
> CHARGE THEM UP
> AND BUY SOME MORE
> P. O. DEL NORTE

15. In comparing the difficulty of Rocky Mountain pass roads, mere altitude above sea level can be deceptive. We record below some of these roads in order of steepness, based on vertical rise. These arbitrary figures, of course, are by no means the last word.

Engineer Pass, San Juans (12,800) — From Ouray to top of pass, vertical rise of 5000 feet in ten miles, 4WD.

Pearl Pass, Elk Range (12,715) — From Ashcroft to top of pass, 3215 feet in seven miles, 4WD.

Yvonne Pass, the usual route over Engineer Mountain (12,250) — From Ouray to top of pass, 4500 feet in ten miles, 4WD.

Argentine Pass (13,182) — From Georgetown to top of pass, 4500 feet in twelve miles, 4WD.

Cinnamon Pass (12,600) — From Sherman ghost town to top of pass (east side), 3052 feet in nine miles, 4WD.

Cumberland Pass (12,200) — From Pitkin to top of pass, 3000 feet in twelve miles.

Mosquito Pass (13,180) — From Alma to the top, 2880 feet in ten miles, 4WD.

Cottonwood Pass (12,126) — From Buena Vista to top, 4326 feet in twenty miles.

Independence Pass (12,095) — From Aspen to top, 4245 feet in twenty miles.

Tincup Pass (12,154) — From Arkansas Valley to top, 4754 feet in twenty-three miles.

Trail Ridge Road, Rocky Mountain National Park (highest through highway in United States) (12,183 at high point) — From Estes Park to highest point, 4683 feet in twenty-five miles.

The vertical rise of a few passes in lower regions follow:

Teton Pass, through the Tetons of Wyoming (8429) — From Wilson, road climbs 2349 feet to top in 6.3 miles.

Logan Pass, Glacier National Park, Montana (6654) — From Lake McDonald to top, 3487 feet in twenty-three miles.

Kicking Horse Pass, Canadian Rockies (5339) — From Lake Louise, to top, 288 feet in six miles.

Tioga Pass, one of the most dramatic highway passes in the California Sierras (9941) — From Lee Vining, Nevada, to top, 2941 feet in seventeen miles.

16. The railroads were the main factor in putting the picturesque toll roads out of business, but they were in bad shape anyhow. Very few of them made a profit even in their best years because tolls collected from users alone could not cover terrific maintenance costs, especially in winter. It is believed that the Webster Pass road did make money for a dozen years, whereas the popular Weston Pass toll road had three owners, each of which went bankrupt. The promising Berthoud Pass toll road, which cost twenty-five thousand dollars, was bought for seven thousand dollars in 1891 at a sheriff's sale by the Georgetown tycoon, William A. Hamill, who tried to make it pay by improving the Blue Hill pitch on the east side. That did little good and the state took over the road from Hamill. The Cottonwood Pass toll road, operated by the Jules brothers, reverted to Chaffee County soon after the Independence Pass road opened in 1882.

Chapter 18: THE HIGHEST RAILS

1. The point where the U. P. crossed the Continental Divide was known as Separation (7107) or "Dodge's Pass." It was, and is, just beyond Separation Creek, twenty-nine miles west of present Rawlins, Wyoming.

2. In 1890, when David Moffat was head of the D. & R. G., he changed the railroad's route west of La Veta town to cross the Sangre de Cristo Range at Wagon Creek Pass (9100) ten miles south of La Veta Pass. His intent was to save fifty miles on the La Veta town–Alamosa run. In addition, Wagon Creek Pass was nearly three hundred feet lower than La Veta Pass. The name Wagon Creek Pass was changed to Veta Pass, causing confusion with La Veta Pass. The old La Veta Pass grade became a wagon road, and then the modern highway, U.S. Route 160. In 1963, the romantic three-mile mule shoe part of this highway was replaced by an easier, straighter, duller route over La Veta Pass.

3. The Santa Fe's chief engineer, A. A. Robinson, took possession of Raton Pass by getting there with a handful of transients about thirty minutes sooner than James A. McMurtrie, the D. & R. G's chief engineer. In 1865–1866, the old frontiersman, Richens L. ("Uncle Dick") Wooton, had built a good twenty-seven mile toll road over the pass, replacing the makeshift wagon roads which had been used since the 1830's. He operated it profitably until the Santa Fe got its grade over the pass in the fall of 1878, and then he sold his toll road to the railroad company. Wooton's toll gate stood at the present ranch home which the Don Berg family has occupied since 1910. I am grateful to Mr. J. E. Eisemann, chief engineer of the Santa Fe, who wrote to me in September, 1959, explaining that the original track went over the top of the pass by means of a switchback for some months at an elevation of about 7800 feet above sea level until a tunnel was opened at 7589 feet on September 7, 1879. The maximum steep grade of one hundred and ninety-five feet per mile required helper and pusher service between Trinidad and Raton, with traffic moving very slowly. To speed up operations, this stretch was double tracked between the years 1900 and 1906 except through the single-track tunnel. In 1908 a second tunnel was completed, and from then until 1949 the old tunnel carried eastbound traffic and the new tunnel carried westbound traffic. In 1949, the eastbound tunnel was abandoned and in 1953 it was plugged. Traffic now passes in both directions through the newer Raton Pass tunnel.

4. Trout Creek used to have plenty of trout in it and Trout Creek Pass was well timbered, but much of the timber was stripped off when the railroads came, wrecking the drainage system and making Trout Creek a sterile flash-flood stream.

5. Today's Williams Pass road, a most interesting 4WD route from St. Elmo and Hancock to Pitkin, crosses the Continental Divide about two miles south of the old Williams Pass road. From Brittle Silver Basin to Pitkin the new road runs more or less on the right-of-way of the Denver and South Park Railroad.

6. The agreement stipulated that the two railroads could use each other's tracks for a three year period. Even so, the Denver and Rio Grande handled more than seventy per cent of the Leadville business.

7. The D. & S. P. shelf is there still, with a good auto road on it from

U.S. Route 285 at Nathrop — alluring, happily wooded, unspeakably scenic, and Chalk Creek below in cool blue curves of beaver ponds and fast trout water.

8. On March 10, 1884, a train pounding down out of the west portal of Alpine Tunnel past the Palisades started a snowslide which wiped out Woodstock village, killing thirteen people. Next winter, heavy snow at Alpine closed the tunnel for months. Three years later, the tunnel caved in and the Denver and South Park was sold at auction (to the U. P.) for three million dollars. Hancock became the west terminus of this Gunnison division until the tunnel could be opened again in 1895. Fifteen years later, in 1910, the Gunnison division and the tunnel closed for good. The rest of the Denver and South Park line was abandoned in 1937.

9. This Gunnison section of the D. & R. G. was pushed on over Cerro Summit (7909) to Montrose and Grand Junction during 1882 to join Palmer's Rio Grande Western Railway, which was completed to Salt Lake City in 1883 by way of Soldier Summit (7440) through the Wasatch Range.

10. In recent years, the Rocky Mountain Railroad Club (Denver) has organized a round trip in late May for railroad fans over the wonderful old tracks from Alamosa to Durango using most of what remains of the D. & R. G.'s narrow-gauge passenger cars and locomotives. The train always stops at the Garfield plaque, and everyone climbs out to look at it, as in the days of Ernest Ingersoll. The plaque reads: "In Memoriam. James Abram Garfield, President of the United States, died September 19, 1881, Mourned By All The People. Erected by Members of the National Association of General Passenger and Ticket Agents, who held Memorial Burial Services on this spot, September 26, 1881." Cumbres Pass is crossed also by a splendid summer gravel road from Chama, New Mexico, to Antonito, Colorado.

11. The beautiful Hagerman Peak (13,056) in the Elk Range near Aspen was not named for James J. Hagerman, but for his alpinist son, Percy, who was distinguished also because he was a member of *both* the Cornell and Yale crews around 1890.

12. The 2196-foot Hagerman Tunnel was too high to permit trains to cope with winter up there, and it was replaced in 1893 by the 9394-foot Busk-Ivanhoe Tunnel, reached at the 10,700-foot level. Even this was too high. For instance, snow blockaded the Colorado Midland at the tunnel from January 27 to April 14, 1899 — a period of seventy-eight days. Albert E. Carlton, the Cripple Creek tycoon, bought the Midland in 1917, and junked most of it soon after World War I. He changed the name of the lower bore to Carlton Tunnel and operated it for many years as an automobile tunnel in connection with the old Midland road bed, which was converted into an auto road. It is a nice drive from Leadville today by way of Turquoise Lake to Carlton Tunnel, which is used now as part of a private water scheme. The Department of the Interior's vast Frying Pan–Arkansas River diversion project calls for construction of a water tunnel very near to Carlton Tunnel. The latter could not be used for the diversion purpose because its grade runs the wrong way — east to west instead of the required west to east. Hagerman Pass is crossed these days by 4WD caravans led by the Leadville Lions Club.

13. The Denver mining magnate, David Moffat, planned the standard-gauge Denver, Northwestern and Pacific Railway to give Denver a direct route to Salt Lake City and to open Middle Park and Yampa Valley to settlement. The climb from Denver to the top of Rollins Pass at Corona station involved thirty-one short tunnels, two miles of snowsheds, four per cent grades and locomotives capable of hauling against ninety-mile-an-hour gales. Moffat's road reached Steamboat Springs, Colorado, on December 13, 1908, by way of the Colorado River route through Gore Canyon, which Frémont had seen in June, 1844, on his way from Muddy Pass to Hoosier Pass. Some say that Moffat should have put his rails over Gore Pass. He died in 1911, having spent his entire fortune of eleven million dollars on his road which was extended to Craig, Colorado, in 1913, two hundred and fifty-four miles from Denver. It never got any farther, though the name was changed to the Denver and Salt Lake after Moffat's death. The 6.2 mile Moffat Tunnel was built 1922–1927 under James Peak at the 9094-foot level to eliminate the Rollins Pass crossing. It was created largely through the efforts of William G. Evans, John Evans's son. It is the second longest in the United States, being exceeded by the Great Northern's Cascade Tunnel, 7.79 miles. The old Rollins Pass line continued to run in summer until 1937. The road bed became an auto road in the late 1950's. In 1934, the tracks of the Denver and Salt Lake were linked to those of the Denver and Rio Grande by the Dotsero Cutoff, which put the D. & R. G. on a direct Moffat Tunnel line to Salt Lake City. It reduced the distance from Denver by 176 miles, and straightened General Palmer's once-Texas-bound tracks at last. The Denver and Salt Lake still runs to Craig as part of the D. & R. G. system.

To summarize successive holders of the American altitude record for through railroads:

Union Pacific, 1868, Sherman Hill Summit (8235).
Denver and Rio Grande, December, 1876, La Veta Pass (9383).
Denver and South Park, May 19, 1879, Kenosha Pass (9950).
Denver and Rio Grande, April, 1881, Fremont Pass (11,318).
Denver and South Park, holed through Alpine Tunnel (11,612), December 21, 1881. First trains ran through tunnel, spring, 1882.
Colorado Midland, fall, 1887, Hagerman Tunnel (11,528). Highest standard-gauge tracks. Tunnel abandoned for the lower Busk–Ivanhoe Tunnel (10,944), 1893. Record resumed then by Denver and South Park Alpine Tunnel.
Denver, Northwestern and Pacific, standard-gauge, 1904, Rollins Pass (11,680). Highest American tracks of any gauge until route was abandoned in 1937.
Starting in 1937, the D. & R. G. narrow-gauge over Marshall Pass (10,846) was highest until *its* abandonment in 1955, when the highest American tracks became those of the standard-gauge D. & R. G. over Tennessee Pass (10,424).

NOTE: The nine-mile Pikes Peak cog railroad, built in 1890, still operates to the top of Pikes Peak (14,110). The Argentine Central narrow-gauge, 16 miles, was built in 1905–1906 from Silver Plume to near the top (13,115 feet) of McClellan Mountain. It closed down in 1921.

Chapter 19: MARIAS PASS, AND KICKING HORSE AGAIN

1. Thomas J. Milner later became chief engineer for the Denver street-car system. Milner Pass, which Trail Ridge Road uses across Rocky Mountain National Park, was named for him.

2. The Utah and Northern's train dispatcher coined the word "Monida" as the name of the station at the top of the pass which marked the Montana–Idaho boundary. The word is formed by the first three letters of each territory's name, and so the crossing became Monida Pass.

3. The Utah and Northern ended permanently at Garrison on the Little Blackfoot. In 1889, it was standard-gauged and became a part of the Oregon Short Line running from Corinne, Utah, to Portland, Oregon.

4. The Northern Pacific built into Butte much earlier, the first train arriving on July 4, 1883. The tracks ran up Big Pipestone Creek, over Homestake Pass (6356), and down Homestake Creek on the Butte side of the Continental Divide. The electrified Chicago, Milwaukee and St. Paul arrived in Butte about 1909 by way of a 2290-foot tunnel under Pipestone Pass (6418).

5. In 1875, the Canadian Pacific engineer, E. W. Jarvis, and a few companions were looking for Robson Pass from Smoky River to the Fraser. They traveled on snowshoes for nine hundred miles with the temperature averaging thirty-nine degrees below zero for twenty consecutive days.

6. This description is stolen from John Murray Gibbon's excellent *Steel of Empire*, page 215.

7. Mount Sir Donald was named for Donald A. Smith (Lord Strathcona) prime mover of the early Canadian Pacific. Sir Sandford Fleming was chief of the government surveys for the C. P. in the 1870's. Walter Moberly was a famous Canadian explorer whose assistant, Albert Perry, had proved the existence of a pass up Illecillewaet River in 1866. Dr. George M. Dawson of the Canadian Geological Survey explored the Selkirks and the Canadian Rockies proper during the 1870's and early 1880's. Incidentally, Mount Sir Donald was called Syndicate Peak at first, in honor of the syndicate of men who took over the C. P. from the Canadian government.

8. Two railroads, the Canadian Northern from Edmonton to Vancouver, and the Grand Trunk Pacific from Edmonton to Prince Rupert, ran their tracks side by side through Yellowhead Pass in 1914–1915. The Canadian Northern was nationalized in 1918, the Grand Trunk Pacific in 1923, both lines becoming part of today's Canadian National Railways.

Chapter 20: LES COLS DE CANADA

1. A handful of alpinists began finding good sport in the glacier area of the Wind River Range, Wyoming, from 1900 on, and also in the Tetons, though the remnant glaciers of Wyoming are extremely modest affairs. The climbing regions of the state are described thoroughly by Orrin H. and Lorraine Bonney in their excellent *Guide to the Wyoming Mountains and Wilderness Areas* (Sage Books, Denver, Colorado, 1960).

2. The author would be glad to know for whom Mount Robson was

named. There was a packer around Banff named Jack Robson in the 1890's, but the peak carried the Robson name at least as early as Dr. Hector's time (1858).

Chapter 21: AND THEN, THE BENZINE BUGGY

1. This Ellwood Pass road was built in 1878 by soldiers. It ran from Fort Garland to the Rio Grande, up Alamosa Creek and over the divide to the army's new Fort Lewis at Pagosa Springs. The fort was established to restrain the southern Utes of the San Juan River country, but it restrained the wrong Utes. It was the White River band in northwest Colorado who murdered agent Nathan Meeker and his staff a year later. The Ellwood Pass road, east side, could be ascended from Jasper by ordinary car almost to the top in 1963.

2. The Colorado State Highway map of 1916 shows auto roads over these passes: Raton, La Veta, Cucharas, Wolf Creek, Ellwood, Red Mountain (San Juans), Molas Divide, Stony, North Cochetopa, Cerro Summit, Old Monarch, Independence, Tennessee, Kenosha, Ute (El Paso), Berthoud, Rabbit Ears, Gore, Cameron, Fall River, Muddy and McClure. The last mentioned McClure, from Crested Butte over to Crystal River and Carbondale, is quite a crossing still and must have been a real hair-raiser fifty years ago.

Sources

Chapter 1: THE EARLIEST GATES

CORONADO: *The Coronado Expedition,* by G. P. Winship, 14th Report, U. S. Bureau of Ethnology (1896); *Great River,* by Paul Horgan, Book I (Rinehart and Co., New York, 1954); *Narratives of the Coronado Expedition, 1540–1542,* edited by George P. Hammond and Agapito Rey (University of New Mexico Press, Albuquerque, 1940).

APACHES: *Indians of the High Plains,* by George E. Hyde, Chapter I, "The Early Apaches" (University of Oklahoma Press, Norman, 1959).

SPANISH EXPEDITIONS: "Origin of the Name of the Purgatoire River," by A. W. McHendrie, *Colorado Magazine* of the State Historical Society of Colorado, Denver, Vol. V, No. 1, pages 18–22; "Spanish Expeditions into Colorado," by Alfred Barnaby Thomas, *Colorado Magazine,* November, 1924; "Journal of the Vargas Expedition into Colorado, 1694," *Colorado Magazine,* Vol. XVI, May 1939; *The Leading Facts of New Mexican History,* by Ralph Emerson Twitchell, Vols. I and II, (Torch Press, Cedar Rapids, Iowa, 1911); *After Coronado,* by Alfred Barnaby Thomas (University of Oklahoma Press, Norman, 1935).

RATON PASS: *Records and Maps of the Old Santa Fe Trail,* by Kenyon Riddle (Raton Daily Range, Raton, New Mexico, 1949).

Chapter 2: HORSE LAKE AND SANGRE DE CRISTO

ESCALANTE: "Pageant in the Wilderness," by Herbert E. Bolton, *Utah Historical Quarterly,* Vol. XVIII (Utah State Historical Society, Salt Lake City, 1950).

SPANISH TRAIL: *Old Spanish Trail,* by LeRoy R. and Ann W. Hafen (Arthur H. Clark Co., Glendale, Calif., 1954); *San Juan Silver* by Arthur W. Munroe (Durango, Colo., publisher not given, 1950).

DE ANZA: *Forgotten Frontiers,* a study of the Spanish Indian Policy of Don Bautista de Anza, Governor of New Mexico, 1777–1787, translated and annotated by Alfred Barnaby Thomas (University of Oklahoma Press, Norman, 1932).

Chapter 3: VICTORY AT LEMHI

BEAVER HISTORY: *The Westward Crossings*, by Jeannette Mirsky, p. 115 (Alfred A. Knopf, New York, 1946).

LA VÉRENDRYES: *Forty Years on the Frontier*, by Granville Stuart (Arthur H. Clark Co., Cleveland, 1925).

ALEXANDER MACKENZIE: *The Search for the Western Sea*, by Lawrence J. Burpee (Alston Rivers, Ltd., London, 1908).

LEWIS AND CLARK EXPEDITION: *History of the Expedition Under the Command of Captains Lewis and Clark*, edited by Nicholas Biddle (Philadelphia, 1814); *The Journals of Lewis and Clark*, with commentary by Bernard De Voto and fine maps (Houghton Mifflin Co., Boston, 1953).

Chapter 4: PIKE'S GAP — AND A SHOT IN TIME

WILKINSON INTRIGUES: Dr. Isaac Joslin Cox, *Encyclopaedia Britannica*, 14th Edition, Vol. XXIII, pages 604–605.

PIKE'S MISSISSIPPI TRIP: *Upper Mississippi*, by Walter Havighurst, pages 42–56 (Rinehart, New York, 1944).

ROCKIES EXPEDITION: *The Expeditions of Zebulon Montgomery Pike*, by Elliott Coues (Francis P. Harper, New York, 1895); *The Lost Pathfinder*, by W. Eugene Hollon (University of Oklahoma Press, Norman, 1949).

Chapter 5: TETON TOURISTS

DAVID THOMPSON: *Land of Giants*, by David Lavender (Doubleday & Co., Garden City, New York, 1958).

JOHN COLTER: *John Colter*, by Burton Harris (Charles Scribner's Sons, New York, 1952); *The Story of Man in Yellowstone* (Yellowstone Library and Museum Association, Yellowstone Park, Wyoming, 1956). *Guide to the Wyoming Mountains*, by Orrin H. and Lorraine Bonney (Sage Books, Denver, 1960). The first two of these books debate the question as to whether the spot called Colter's Hell by the trappers was in Yellowstone Park or near Cody, Wyoming.

OREGON QUESTION: *The Course of Empire*, by Bernard De Voto, pages 534–539 (Houghton Mifflin Company, Boston, 1952).

Chapter 6: SOUTH PASS: FRUIT OF FAILURE

MARIAS PASS: "Earliest Glacier," by Dr. Ralph L. Beals, an article appearing in *Glorious Glacier*, a pamphlet of the Montana Heritage Series, No. 9, page 5.

ATHABASKA PASS: David Lavender's *Land of Giants* cited above.

THE ASTORIANS: The Discovery of the Oregon Trail, edited by Philip Ashton Rollins (Charles Scribner's Sons, New York, 1935). This fine work contains Wilson Price Hunt's diaries and a copy of Robert Stuart's original manuscript.

Chapter 7: HELL-BENT FOR TAOS

FINAN MCDONALD TRIP: *Jedediah Smith and the Opening of the West*, by Dale Morgan, pages 122–125 (Bobbs-Merrill Co., New York, 1958).

NEW MEXICO REPORT: "An Anonymous Description of New Mexico,

1818," edited by Alfred B. Thomas, *Southwestern Historical Quarterly,* July, 1929, pages 50–74, including Melgares report also.

WILLIAM BECKNELL: *The Santa Fe Trail,* by Robert L. Duffus (Longmans, Green and Co., London, 1930).

JACOB FOWLER: *The Journal of Jacob Fowler, 1821–22,* edited with notes by Elliott Coues (Francis P. Harper, New York, 1898).

Chapter 8: THE ROARING TWENTIES

JAMES OHIO PATTIE: *Personal Narrative, Early Western Travels* series, Vol. XVIII (Arthur H. Clark Co., Cleveland, 1905).

COCHETOPA PASS, ANTOINE ROBIDOUX: *Old Spanish Trail,* cited Chapter 2, pages 94–95; *Antoine Robidoux — 1794–1860,* by William Swilling Wallace (Glen Dawson, Los Angeles, 1953).

CLYMAN QUOTATION: *Jedediah Smith,* by Dale L. Morgan, cited Chapter 7, page 84.

WILLIAM ASHLEY: *Notes on General Ashley, the Overland Trail and South Pass,* by Donald McKay Frost, with excellent map by Dr. Edwin Raisz (*Barre Gazette,* Barre, Mass., 1960).

BEAN-SINCLAIR PARTY: "The Bean-Sinclair Party of Rocky Mountain Trappers," by LeRoy R. Hafen, *Colorado Magazine,* July 1954, pages 130–132 (State Historical Society of Colorado, Denver).

JOE MEEK: *The River of the West,* by Frances Fuller Victor (R. W. Bliss & Co., Hartford, Conn., 1870).

MOUNTS HOOKER AND BROWN: *Climbs and Exploration in the Canadian Rockies,* by Hugh E. M. Stutfield and J. Norman Collie, Chapter 4 (Longmans, Green & Co., London, 1903).

Chapter 9: SOLDIERS TAKE THE HIGH ROAD

LONG EXPEDITION: *Account of Expedition from Pittsburgh to the Rocky Mountains, 1819–20. By order of John C. Calhoun, Secretary of War, under Major S. H. Long,* by Dr. Edwin James. The report, printed in London originally in 1823, is found in *Early Western Travels, 1748–1846,* Vol. XV, by Reuben Gold Thwaites (Arthur H. Clark Co., Cleveland, 1905).

GEORGE C. SIBLEY: *The Road to Santa Fe,* by Kate L. Gregg (Albuquerque, 1952).

BONNEVILLE: *The Adventures of Captain Bonneville, U.S.A.,* digested from his journal by Washington Irving (University of Oklahoma Press, Norman, 1961). Irving titled the two-volume book *The Rocky Mountains* when it was first published in 1837.

TOPOGRAPHICAL ENGINEERS: *Army Exploration in the American West, 1803–1863,* by William H. Goetzmann (Yale University Press, New Haven, 1959). A superb and enlightening study of an important subject.

FRÉMONT: *Frémont: Pathmarker of the West* by Allan Nevins (Longmans, Green and Co., London, 1955); *Report of the Exploring Expedition to the Rocky Mountains in the year 1842 and to Oregon and North California in the years 1843-44,* by Brevet Captain J. C. Frémont (Gales and Seaton, Washington, 1845); *Memoirs of My Life,* by John C. Frémont (Belford, Clarke and Co., Chicago, 1887).

Chapter 10:   THE NEW MOUNTAIN MEN

KEARNY'S ARMY OF THE WEST: Lieutenant Abert's journal is in Senate Executive Document No. 438, 29th Congress, 1st Session.

RATON PASS: Naming of pass is from "Trinidad and its Environs," by A. W. McHendrie, *Colorado Magazine*, Sept., 1929 (State Historical Society of Colorado, Denver).

STANSBURY EXPEDITION: Quotes and data are found in *Exploration and Survey of the Valley of the Great Salt Lake of Utah, including a Reconnaissance of a New Route through the Rocky Mountains*, by Howard Stansbury, Captain, Corps of Topographical Engineers, Executive Document No. 3, Special Session, March, 1951, U.S. Senate.

GUNNISON EXPEDITION: *Journey Through the Rocky Mountains and the Humboldt Mountains to the Pacific Ocean*, by Jacob H. Schiel (University of Oklahoma Press, 1959); "Report of Lt. E. G. Beckwith, Third Artillery," in *Reports of Explorations and Surveys to Ascertain the most Practicable and Economical Route for a Railroad from the Mississippi River to the Pacific Ocean made under the Direction of the Secretary of War in 1853–54*, Vol. I, House of Representatives, 33rd Congress, 2nd Session, Executive Document No. 91. These reports in eleven huge volumes are of priceless historical value.

Chapter 11:   THE LAST WILDERNESS

STEVENS: *The Life of Isaac Ingalls Stevens* by his son Hazard Stevens, 2 vols. (Houghton Mifflin Co., Boston and New York, 1901).

DE SMET: *Father De Smet's Life and Travels Among the North American Indians*, by Hiram M. Chittenden and Alfred T. Richardson, 4 vols. (Francis P. Harper, New York, 1905).

NORTHERN PACIFIC RAILROAD SURVEY: All facts on the Stevens expedition and quoted passages are taken from *Reports of Explorations and Surveys to Ascertain the most Practicable and Economical Route for a Railroad from the Mississippi River to the Pacific Ocean*, Vol. I, House of Representatives, 33rd Congress, 2nd Session, Executive Document No. 91. The Governor's own report in this volume is titled, "Report of Explorations for a Route for the Pacific Railroad near the 47th and 49th parallels of North Latitude from St. Paul to Puget Sound." Maps of routes taken by the various Stevens parties are found in Volume VIII.

PALLISER EXPEDITION: The movements of Palliser and Dr. Hector and bits of quoted narrative have been taken from *The Journals, Detailed Reports and Observations Relative to the Exploration by Captain Palliser of that Portion of British North America which, in latitude, lies between the British Boundary Line and the Height of Land or Watershed of the Northern or Frozen Ocean Respectively and, in Longitude, Between the Western Shore of Lake Superior and the Pacific Ocean During the Years 1857, 1858, 1859 and 1860. Presented to both Houses of Parliament (London) 19th May 1863*.

Chapter 12:   OVER THE WALL

GOLD RUSH CHRONOLOGY: Files of *Rocky Mountain Weekly News*, April, 1859–April, 1866.

COLORADO GOLD CAMPS: *Stampede to Timberline,* by Muriel Sibell Wolle (University of Colorado, Boulder, 1949); *Guide to the Colorado Ghost Towns and Mining Camps,* by Perry Eberhart (Sage Books, Denver, 1959); *Early Mining Camps of South Park,* by Norma L. Flynn (privately published, 1952); *Mining in Colorado,* by Charles W. Henderson, U.S.G.S. Professional Paper 138, Department of the Interior (Government Printing Office, Washington, D.C., 1926).

CHARLES BAKER AND SAN JUANS: Articles in *Colorado Magazine,* volumes V, VI, VII, IX, XI, XVII, XIX, and XXII.

SAN JUAN MOUNTAINS: *Guide to the Colorado Mountains,* by Robert M. Ormes (Sage Books, Denver, 1952).

WILLIAM N. BYERS: *The First Hundred Years,* by Robert L. Perkin (Doubleday & Co., Garden City, New York, 1959). A fine history of Denver and the *Rocky Mountain News.*

COLORADO ROADS OF 1860's: Derived from the superb *Atlas of Colorado,* by F. V. Hayden (Jules Bien, Lith., U.S. Geological and Geographical Surveys of the Territories, 1877).

Chapter 13: MR. BERTHOUD, AND "GILPIN'S LAMBS"

TOLL ROADS: "The Mission of Colorado Toll Roads," by Arthur Ridgway, *Colorado Magazine,* Volume IX.

E. L. BERTHOUD, BERTHOUD PASS: *History of Clear Creek and Boulder Valleys,* by W. B. Vickers (O. L. Baskin & Co., Chicago, 1880); LeRoy R. Hafen on the discovery of Berthoud Pass, *Colorado Magazine,* March, 1926.

GLORIETA PASS BATTLE: *Colorado Volunteers in the Civil War; the New Mexico Campaign of 1862,* by William Clarke Whitford (The State Historical and Natural History Society, Denver, 1906).

Chapter 14: CONTINENTAL TEA

LANDER'S CUT-OFF: *Reports of F. W. Lander, Superintendent of the Fort Kearny, South Pass and Honey Lake Wagon Road,* with maps, House of Representatives, 36th Congress, 2nd Session, Executive Document No. 64 (Serial 1100); *Wagon Roads West,* by W. Turrentine Jackson (University of California Press, Berkeley and Los Angeles, 1952).

MULLAN ROAD: *Military Road from Fort Benton to Fort Walla Walla: The Report of Lt. Mullan,* with maps, House of Representatives, 36th Congress, 2nd Session, 1860–1861, Executive Document No. 44 (Serial 1099); *Report on the Construction of a Military Road from Fort Walla Walla to Fort Benton,* U.S. Senate, 37th Congress, 3rd Session (1862–1863), Executive Document No. 43 (Serial 1149); *Wagon Road from Niobrara to Virginia City,* James A. Sawyers, House of Representatives, 39th Congress, 1st Session, 1865–1866, Executive Document No. 58 (Serial 1256).

RAYNOLDS EXPEDITION: *Preliminary Report on the Yellowstone Expedition,* U.S. Senate, 36th Congress, 2nd Session, 1860–1861, Executive Document No. 1 (Serial 1079); *Report of Brevet Brigadier General W. F. Raynolds on the Exploration of the Yellowstone,* with map, U.S. Senate, 40th Congress, 1st Session, 1867–1868, Executive Document No. 77 (Serial 1317).

MONTANA GOLD RUSH: *The Bonanza Trail,* by Muriel Sibell Wolle (Indiana University Press, Bloomington, Indiana, 1953); "Journal of N. H. Webster," *Contributions to the Historical Society of Montana*, Vol. III (Helena State Publishing Co.); "A Historial Sketch of Deer Lodge County, Valley and City," by Granville Stuart, *Contributions to the Historical Society of Montana*, Vol. II; *Gold Camp*, by Larry Barsness (Hastings House, New York, 1962); *The Vigilantes of Montana*, by Prof. Thomas J. Dimsdale (University of Oklahoma Press, Norman, Okla., 1953); *Vigilante Days and Ways*, by N. P. Langford (The University Press, Missoula, Montana, 1957); *Ben Holladay, the Stagecoach King*, by J. V. Frederick (Arthur H. Clark Co., Glendale, Calif., 1940).

BOZEMAN TRAIL, BRIDGER TRAIL: *The Bozeman Trail*, by Grace Raymond Hebard and E. A. Brininstool (Arthur H. Clark Co., Cleveland, 1922); "A Historical Sketch of Bozeman, Gallatin Valley and Bozeman Pass," by Peter Koch, *Contributions to the Historical Society of Montana*, Vol. II.

YELLOWHEAD PASS: *The Fraser*, by Bruce Hutchison (Clarke, Irwin & Co., Toronto, 1950); *Cheadle's Journal of a Trip Across Canada, 1862–63*, with introduction and notes by A. G. Doughty and Gustave Lanctot (Graphic Publishers, Ltd., Ottawa, Canada, undated); *An Expedition across the Rocky Mountains into British Columbia by the Yellow Head or Leather Pass*, by Viscount Milton and W. B. Cheadle, printed for private circulation (Petter and Galpin, Ludgate Hill, London, undated).

Chapter 15: THE ROVER BOYS

DR. F. V. HAYDEN: Article by C. A. White, National Academy of Sciences *Biographical Memoirs*, Vol. III, 1895; Hayden obituary, *American Journal of Science*, Vol. 135, page 179; *Annual Report* of the Smithsonian Institution, 1904, page 585.

HAYDEN SURVEYS: *Great Surveys of the American West*, by Richard A. Bartlett (University of Oklahoma Press, Norman, Oklahoma, 1962), an excellent presentation of the work of Hayden, as well as of Wheeler, Powell and Clarence King; *Annual Reports* of the United States Geological and Geographical Survey of the Territories, 1868–1883 (Government Printing Office, Washington, D.C.). All quotes of reports by Hayden's men are found in these fascinating volumes, particularly for the years 1871 and 1872 (Yellowstone) and 1873–1875 (Colorado); *Geological and Geographical Atlas of Colorado*, by F. V. Hayden (Julius Bien, Lith., Department of the Interior, 1877).

WILLIAM H. JACKSON: *Picture Maker of the Old West*, by Clarence S. Jackson (Charles Scribner's Sons, New York, 1947).

CAPTAIN WILLIAM A. JONES EXPEDITION: *Report Upon the Reconnaissance of Northwestern Wyoming made in the Summer of 1873, Seeking a Wagon Road from the Union Pacific Railroad to Yellowstone National Park*, by William A. Jones, Captain of Engineers, U.S.A., House Executive Document No. 285, 43rd Congress, 1st Session.

Chapter 16: TIMBERLINE!

A. S. WESTON AND WESTON PASS: *The Carbonate Camp Called Leadville*, by Don L. and Jean Harvey Griswold (University of Denver Press, Denver, 1951).

HOT SULPHUR SPRINGS AND WILLIAM BYERS: *The First Hundred Years,* by Robert L. Perkin (Doubleday & Co., Garden City, N. Y., 1959).

ROLLINS PASS: "John Q. A. Rollins, Colorado Builder," by John Q. A. Rollins, Jr., *Colorado Magazine,* Vol. XVI, No. 3, May, 1939.

BERTHOUD PASS: "The First Stage Coach over Berthoud Pass," paper by Dan Tomlinson, aged 16, Idaho Springs High School, submitted for the 1963 Colorado Day Essay Contest of the Central City Opera House Association; *Gulch of Gold,* by Caroline Bancroft (Sage Books, Denver, 1958).

ARGENTINE PASS–LOVELAND PASS: *The Colorado Weekly Miner* (Georgetown) from 1867 to 1879; *Silver Town,* by John Willard Horner (Caxton Printers, Caldwell, Idaho, 1950).

MONTEZUMA AREA, WEBSTER PASS: "Montezuma and Her Neighbors," by Verna (Mrs. Leland) Sharp, *Colorado Magazine,* Vol. XXXIII, No. 1, January, 1956.

COMMODORE STEPHEN DECATUR: *To Colorado's Restless Ghosts,* by Inez Hunt and Wanetta W. Draper, Chapter I (Sage Books, Denver, 1960).

Chapter 17: LEADVILLE FEVER

LEADVILLE, ETC.: *Stampede to Timberline,* by Muriel Sibell Wolle (Artcraft Press, Denver, 1949); *Colorado's Century of "Cities"* by Don and Jean Griswold, with Fred and Jo Mazzulla (Denver, 1958); *Guide to the Colorado Ghost Towns and Mining Camps,* by Perry Eberhart (Sage Books, Denver, 1959); "Word from the West: John J. Vandemoer Reporting," by Don Bloch and Herbert Vandemoer, *Denver Westerners Roundup Magazine,* January, 1959.

MOSQUITO PASS: "History of the Famous Mosquito Pass," by Norma L. Flynn, *The Denver Westerners Brand Book,* Volume XIV, 1958 (Johnson Publishing Co., Boulder, Colo., 1959); *The Snow-Shoe Itinerant,* by the Reverend John L. Dyer (Cranston & Stowe, Cincinnati, 1891).

GUNNISON REGION: *Gunnison Country,* by Betty Wallace (Sage Books, Denver, 1960).

MARSHALL PASS: "The Godfather of Marshall Pass," by General William L. Marshall, *Trail Magazine,* Society of Sons of Colorado, Volume XIII, No. 4, September, 1920.

INDEPENDENCE PASS: "Independence Pass and the Twin Lakes Toll Road," by Don and Jean Griswold, *The Denver Westerners Brand Book,* Volume XV, 1959 (Johnson Publishing Co., 1960).

ASPEN AREA: *Roaring Fork Valley,* by Len Shoemaker (Sage Books, Denver, 1958); *Famous Aspen,* by Caroline Bancroft (Golden Press, Denver, 1954); "Ashcroft," by Carroll H. Coberly, *Colorado Magazine,* Volume XXXVII, No. 2, April, 1960; "Aspen: An Argonaut of the Roaring Fork," by C. S. Thomas, *Colorado Magazine,* Volume VII, No. 4, November, 1930.

SAN JUANS: "Toll Roads in Southwestern Colorado," by D. H. Cummins, *Colorado Magazine,* Volume XXIX, No. 2, April, 1952.

Chapter 18: THE HIGHEST RAILS

GENERAL: *The Story of American Railroads,* by Stewart H. Holbrook (Crown Publishers, New York, 1947).

UNION PACIFIC: *The First Transcontinental Railroad*, by John D. Galloway (Simmons-Boardman, New York, 1950); *How We Built the Union Pacific Railroad*, by Major General Grenville M. Dodge (collection of papers, publisher unknown).

DENVER AND RIO GRANDE: *Rio Grande, Mainline of the Rockies*, by Lucius Beebe and Charles Clegg (Howell-North, Berkeley, Calif., 1962); *Rebel of the Rockies*, by Robert G. Athearn (Yale University Press, New Haven, 1962); *The Crest of the Continent*, by Ernest Ingersoll (R. R. Donnelley & Sons, Chicago, 1885).

DENVER AND SOUTH PARK: *Denver, South Park & Pacific*, by M. C. Poor (World Press, Denver, 1949). This book is the great classic of Rocky Mountain railroads.

OTTO MEARS, SILVERTON RAILROAD, RIO GRANDE SOUTHERN, SILVERTON NORTHERN: *Narrow Gauge in the Rockies*, by Lucius Beebe and Charles Clegg (Howell-North, Berkeley, California, 1958); *Three Little Lines*, by Josie Moore Crum (*Durango Herald-News*, Durango, Colo., 1960); *The Rio Grande Southern Story*, by Josie Moore Crum (Railroadiana, Durango, Colo., 1955).

COLORADO MIDLAND: "How Hagerman Sold the Midland," by John J. Lipsey, *The Denver Westerners Brand Book*, 1956 (Johnson Publishing Co., Boulder, Colo., 1957); "J. J. Hagerman," by John J. Lipsey, *The Denver Westerners Brand Book*, 1954 (Johnson Publishing Co., Boulder, Colo., 1955).

DENVER, NORTHWESTERN AND PACIFIC, ROLLINS PASS, MOFFAT TUNNEL: *The Moffat Tunnel of Colorado*, by Edgar C. McMechen, 2 vols. (Wahlgreen Publishing Co., Denver, 1927).

Chapter 19: MARIAS PASS, AND KICKING HORSE AGAIN

UTAH AND NORTHERN RAILROAD: *Intermountain Railroads*, by Merrill D. Beal (Caxton Printers, Caldwell, Idaho, 1962).

NORTHERN PACIFIC: *History of Montana, 1739–1885*, by M. A. Leeson (Warner, Beers & Co., Chicago, 1885); *History of the Northern Pacific Railroad*, by Eugene V. Smalley (G. P. Putnam's Sons, New York, 1883).

GREAT NORTHERN: *The Life of James J. Hill*, by Joseph Gilpin Pyle, 2 vols. (Peter Smith, New York, 1936); *The Story of Marias Pass*, by Grace Flandrau, undated pamphlet, "compliments of Great Northern Railway."

CANADIAN PACIFIC: *A History of Transportation in Canada*, by G. P. de T. Glazebrook (The Ryerson Press, Toronto, Canada, 1938); *Steel of Empire*, by John Murray Gibbon (Bobbs-Merrill Co., Indianapolis, 1935); *The Making of a Great Canadian Railway*, by Frederick A. Talbot (J. B. Lippincott Co., Philadelphia, 1912).

Chapter 20: LES COLS DE CANADA

THE CANADIAN ROCKIES: *The Canadian Rockies*, by A. P. Coleman (Charles Scribner's Sons, New York, 1911); *Mountaineering and Exploration in the Selkirks*, by Howard Palmer (G. P. Putnam's Sons, New York and London, 1914); *Among the Selkirk Glaciers*, by W. S. Green (Macmillan and Co., London, 1890); *In the Heart of the Canadian Rockies*, by James Outram (Macmillan Company, New York, 1905); *Among the*

Canadian Alps, by Lawrence J. Burpee (John Lane Company, New York); *Climbs and Exploration in the Canadian Rockies*, by Hugh E. M. Stutfield and J. Norman Collie (Longmans, Green & Co., London, 1903).

Chapter 21: AND THEN, THE BENZINE BUGGY

EARLY CARS: *Historic American Highways* (American Association of State Highway Officials, Washington, D.C., 1953); *Ute Pass; Route of the Blue Sky People*, by Virginia McConnell (Sage Books, Denver, 1963); "Early Days of Telluride," by L. C. Kinikin, *Colorado Magazine*, Vol. XXI, No. 1, Jan., 1949.

EARLY AUTO ROADS: "Colorado's First Highway Commission," by Frank Merchant, *Colorado Magazine*, Vol. XXXII, No. 1, Jan., 1955; *Paths of Progress* (undated pamphlet of the Colorado Department of Highways); *The Banff-Jasper Highway*, by M. B. Williams (H. R. Larson Publishing Co., Vancouver, B.C., 1948); *Colorado Highways*, a magazine published by the Colorado Department of Highways, all issues from 1919 to 1931; article on road history of Marias Pass, *Great Falls* (Mont.) *Tribune*, October 25, 1931; *A History of Transportation in Canada*, by G. P. de T. Glazebrook (The Ryerson Press, Toronto, 1938).

Acknowledgments

MOST OF THE RESEARCH for this book was done in the spacious new Charles Leaming Tutt Library at Colorado College in Colorado Springs. I am grateful for the friendship of past President Louis T. Benezet, and his successor, Lloyd E. Worner, and for the help I have received from the Tutt Library staff under Dr. Ellsworth Mason. I am in debt deeply to Miss Joan Shinew, Miss Reta Ridings, Miss Joan Erikson, Miss Esther Burch, Miss Grace Berger, Miss Eunice Toussaint and Mrs. Agnes Watson. I have been aided constantly by Robert M. Ormes, the college's mountaineer, and by its authority on gems and geology, Dr. Richard M. Pearl. If Tutt Library lacked what I needed, I found it at Colorado Springs Public Library, where I was assisted by Mrs. Margaret Reid, Mrs. Lora Light, Miss Edith Kearney and Mrs. Russell De Fries. Often I visited the fine Western Collection of the Denver Public Library, where I imposed on Mrs. Alys Freeze, Mrs. Opal Harber, Mrs. Mary Hanley, Jim Davis, Jack Joyce and Mrs. Hazel Lundberg.

I give thanks to Dr. James Grafton Rogers of the State Historical Society of Colorado, who has been demanding a passes book for these many years. The society has loaned me the wide knowledge of Mrs. Agnes Wright Spring and Maurice Frink. In Cheyenne, Wyoming, I had the support of Miss Lola Homsher at the State Museum, and of Mrs. Katherine Halverson, of the Wyoming State Archives. At Montana's State

Museum in Helena, I was lucky to be helped by Miss Mary K. Dempsey, Research Director of the Historical Society of Montana. In Missoula, I relied on Dorothy M. Johnson and the Montana State University Library. At the fine U.S.G.S. map center in Denver, I had Al Abbott to solve topographical problems, and Mrs. Ruth Alley to find pass photos. I spent instructive hours at the Denver U.S.G.S. with Francis Rizzari and Dr. T. S. Lovering. From Washington, D.C., William H. Heers and W. C. Dawson sent me data from the U.S.G.S. Library, Department of the Interior. Mrs. George W. Goddard ran errands for me in Washington. Princeton's Professor R. R. Palmer wrote me about the passes of world history. George Shea, the *Wall Street Journal* analyst, made suggestions on the nation's economic past. Director Charles B. Hitchcock of the American Geographical Society gave me advice on his specialty.

During and after the tour of the Canadian Rockies which my wife and I made in 1962, I had the help of Frank Perrin of the Great Northern Railway; of J. A. Carman, publicity director of the Canadian Travel Bureau; of M. T. Miard, Deputy Minister, R. J. Baines and Peter Elkington, all of the Department of Highways, Victoria, B.C.; of H. E. Martin, director of publicity for Alberta's Department of Industry and Development; of Air Marshal C. Roy Slemon and Squadron Leader Lewis Lomas, Canadian officials at NORAD in Colorado Springs, who secured superb maps for me; and Pierre Brunet, Assistant Dominion Archivist, Ottawa.

For years I have been encouraged by Joseph N. Hessel, Assistant Regional Forester, Rocky Mountain Region, for the Forest Service. I am grateful to Rangers Thomas E. Forister, John T. Minow, Wallace Johnson and Mark Ratliff of Rio Grande National Forest; Martin Jetley and Eldon G. Lucas, Gunnison N. F.; Lewis A. Cummings and Jack O. Booth, San Isabel N. F.; Ray Johnson, Pike N. F.; and Ed Ekstrom, Carson N. F. In Alberta, Canada, J. F. Hogan, Forest Supervisor of Crowsnest Forest, spent part of a holiday Saturday telling me of old pass trails in that southern part of the Canadian Rockies.

Mark Watrous, the distinguished chief engineer of Colorado's Department of Highways, recalled pass road experiences for me. The department's librarian, Miss Myrtle Swenson, searched out facts, and so did Wallis M. Reef and Tony Kahm. More history came from Paul Harrison, a life-long student of Colorado toll roads. At the Wyoming State Highway Department, Jack Russell gave me much time and the department sent along a full set of county maps. Frank Norris, of the Wyoming Travel Commission, supplied photos. In Helena, I talked at length with George Sime, director of public relations, Montana Highway Department, and with Ernest Neave. Dix C. Shevalier, of the Montana Power Company, gave me railroad material. Miss Ginger Evans, assistant to T. B. White, chief engineer, New Mexico State Highway Commission, found facts on Palo Flechado Pass, as did Mrs. Toni Tarleton, Harwood Foundation, Taos. J. E. Eisemann, chief engineer, Santa Fe Railroad, explained to me how the line gets over Raton and La Glorieta passes. Edward F. Taylor, of the American Snowblast Corporation in Denver, gave me snow removal material and pictures. I prize my Aero Relief Map of the United States from Aero Service Corporation, Philadelphia, and my map of Jeep roads in the San Juans, made by the Telluride Jeep Club 50. I had some exciting hours in the spring of 1963 when Fred Rice, Dick Eflin and Kolbet Schrichte of Crested Butte Ski Area, Ltd., flew me over some of the very highest Rockies to look at a dozen passes from the air.

Mrs. Thelma Gatchell Condit of Gatchell Museum, Buffalo, Wyoming, showed me the whereabouts of Dull Knife Pass. Mrs. Norris Graves of Barnum pointed out the site of the Dull Knife Battlefield of 1876. I was brought up to date on Cochetopa Pass roads by Sheriff Donald E. Zimmer and Mrs.

Mabel Redhead, both of Saguache, Colorado. I learned things from Clyde and Chloe Edmonson, authors of *Mountain Passes* (Estey Printing Co., Boulder, Colorado, 1963), and from Robert L. Brown, who wrote the excellent *Jeep Trails to Colorado Ghost Towns* (Caxton Printers, Caldwell, Idaho, 1963).

I have been blessed by help from a host of friends: Fred Mazzulla, the Denver rare photo sleuth; Thomas Hornsby Ferril, who has written wonderful things about the Denver and South Park Railroad and who permits me to quote the Hardscrabble Pass part of his poem, "Report of My Strange Encounter With Lily Bull-Domingo"; the Kenneth Englerts, Bruce and Elaine Sommers, the Ray Colwells, the John J. Lipseys, Paul Goss, all of Colorado Springs; Mrs. Alex (Ruth Marie) Colville of Del Norte, who recalled crossing Weminuche and Ellwood passes; Mrs. Nora Watson and Mrs. Hal Russell of the Stonewall (Colorado) area; Ward Darley, retired ranger of Monte Vista, Colorado; Mrs. Leland (Verna) Sharp, of Montezuma, Colorado, an expert on Argentine and Webster passes; Betty Kutzled of Leadville; Mr. and Mrs. Walter Balliger of Durango, students of the San Juans; Josie Moore Crum, the Otto Mears authority; the Arthur Ballentines and Gene Perkin of the *Durango-Cortez Herald*, who know the Grenadiers country beyond Columbine Pass; Robert Tripp, of Dubois, Wyoming, who hauled me to the top of Union and Sheridan passes; the indestructible Caroline Bancroft of Denver, who conquered Georgia Pass; Salida's Jeep-wrangling novelist, Steve Frazee; the historian, David Lavender, who grew up near Imogene Pass; Grace R. Pratt, of Coeur d'Alêne, Idaho; Jack Goodman of the *New York Times*, my Utah passes expert; the well-known conservationist, Arthur L. Carhart, who tries to keep me straight on Sangre de Cristo passes; and Nelson R. Burr, of Washington, D.C., who found many old pass drawings for me.

I am truly grateful to those expert writers of Western history,

David Lavender and Jay Monaghan, for putting my manuscript through their critical wringer and squeezing out some of my more glaring errors. Those that remain are my own, and I beg the reader's forgiveness for them. Finally, I am grateful to Allan Reginald (Mike) Sedman, of Joe and Edna Scanlan's Garage, Colorado Springs, for keeping our '49 Jeep from breaking down in some remote place. I refuse to try to thank adequately my typist, Maxine Whitworth, or my beloved wife, Edna Jane, who usually drove the Jeep and caught the trout for supper.

A Roster of Passes

Note: CD = Continental Divide
4WD = Four-wheel-drive car

Passes lacking "standard car" or "4WD" designation have to be crossed on foot or on horseback.

Passes of the Canadian Rockies
and Selkirk Range

ABBOT PASS (9598), CD — Lake Louise–Kicking Horse area. From Lake Louise, climber's trail up Victoria Glacier crosses "Death Trap" pass to Lake O'Hara. Bow–Columbia drainages. Named for Philip Stanley Abbot of Boston who lost his life August 3, 1896, on nearby Mount Lefroy (11,230).

AKAMINA PASS (5835), CD — Waterton Lakes area. From Waterton Park, road runs beside Cameron Creek to top of pass below Mt. Rowe (7968). Trail descends west side down Akamina Brook to Flathead River. Flathead (Kootenay)–Waterton (South Saskatchewan) drainages. First pass north of border.

ALLENBY PASS (ca. 7300) — Banff area, south. On Brewster Creek trail from Bow River to Assiniboine Pass.

AMISKWI PASS (6545) — Field–Kicking Horse area, north. Trail runs up Amiskwi River and over pass to Blaeberry River and Howse Pass trail. Columbia River drainage. Also called Baker Pass, for G. P. Baker of Boston. Amiskwi: Cree for "beaver."

ASSINIBOINE PASS (7152), CD — Banff area, south. Trail from Banff runs up Brewster Creek over Allenby Pass to Assiniboine Pass. Reached also up Bryant Creek from Spray Reservoir road end. Bow–Kootenay drainages. Named for the Indian tribe.

ASTORIA PASS (ca. 7300) — Jasper area, south. Pass links Portal Creek–Maccarib Pass to Astoria River. Athabaska drainage. The name memorializes John Jacob Astor.

ASULKAN PASS (7720) — Glacier–Rogers Pass area, Selkirk Range. This climber's pass links Asulkan and Geikie glaciers. Asulkan: Shuswap for "mountain goat."

ATHABASKA PASS (5724), CD — Jasper area, south. From road (fifteen miles south of Jasper), historic old trapper trail moves up Whirlpool River to the Committee's Punch Bowl at top of pass, twenty miles, between Mount Brown (9156) on west and Mount Hooker (10,782) on east. West-side trail descent down Wood River to Columbia River at

David Thompson's Boat Encampment, thirty-five miles. Athabaska–Columbia drainages. Used by Thompson, 1811. Surveyed 1872 by Walter Moberly for possible Canadian Pacific Railway. Has been called Boat Encampment Pass.

BAKER PASS: See Amiskwi Pass.

BALFOUR PASS (8400), CD — Yoho–Kicking Horse area, north. This medial moraine traverse links Balfour and Diableret glaciers between Mt. Balfour (10,741) and Mt. Olive (10,270). South Saskatchewan–Columbia drainages. First crossed, 1901. John Hutton Balfour was a Scottish botanist.

BALL PASS (7300), CD — Banff area, due west. From Bow River road, trail runs up Redearth–Haiduk creeks to pass. West-side trail descends Hawk Creek–Vermilion River to highway. Bow–Kootenay drainages. John Ball was Under-Secretary of State for the Colonies, 1855–1857.

BALU PASS (6691) — Glacier–Rogers Pass area, northwest, Selkirk Range. Trail from Illecillewaet River branch crosses pass to Connaught Creek branch under Cheops Mountain. Columbia drainage.

BEAVERFOOT PASS (ca. 6000) — Leanchoil–Field–Kicking Horse area, south. From highway, trail ascends Beaverfoot River and over pass to Kootenay River sources. Shown on Palliser map, 1863.

BESS PASS (5330), CD — Mount Robson area north, between Mount Bess and Whiteshield Mountain, south of Chown Glacier. From Smoky River, trail crosses pass, returning over CD by Jackpine Pass and down Jackpine River to Smoky River again. Smoky River (Peace)–Holmes River (Fraser) drainages.

BIDDLE PASS (ca. 8500) — Yoho–Kicking Horse area, south. Pass is just south of Lake McArthur near Mt. Biddle (10,888). Columbia drainage. M. Biddle was an early climber.

BOAT ENCAMPMENT PASS: Same as Athabaska Pass.

BOOM LAKE PASS: See Consolation Pass.

BOULDER PASS (7571) — Lake Louise area, north. From Bow River trail runs up Baker Creek to Baker Lake and Boulder Pass at Ptarmigan Lake, and down Coral Creek to Bow River again. A popular ski area.

BOUNDARY PASS: See South Kootenay Pass.

BOW PASS (6878) — Lake Louise area, north. Banff–Jasper highway runs up Bow River and over pass between Observation Peak (10,214) and Cirque Peak (9768), and down Mistaya River on north side to Howse and North Saskatchewan rivers below Howse Pass. Dr. James Hector crossed Bow Pass in 1858, calling it Little Fork River Pass. So named because wood of trees along river was suitable for making bows. Also because of its bow shape.

BRITISH KOOTANIE PASS: Early English name for North Kootenay Pass.

BRUINS PASS (8160) — Glacier–Rogers Pass area, northwest, Selkirk Range. A glacier crossing, Beaver River drainage.

BURGESS PASS (7160) — Field area, north. From fine Burgess Pass trail, excellent views of President Range, Emerald Lake. Named for A. M. Burgess, a Deputy Minister of the Interior.

BUSH PASS (7860), CD — Howse Pass–Freshfield Glacier area, west.

From Howse Pass, trail forks west up Forbes Brook to pass. West descent by Bush River to Columbia. North Saskatchewan–Columbia drainage. First explored, 1902.

BYNG PASS: See Snake Indian Pass.

CAMPUS PASS (8000) — Jasper–Mount Edith Cavell area. Pass is reached up Campus Creek under Chevron Mountain. Astoria–Athabaska drainage.

CANOE PASS (6722), CD — Near Athabaska Pass and source of Whirlpool River between Mallard Peak (9330) and Mount Brown (9156). Athabaska–Columbia drainage.

CARCAJOU PASS (5120), CD — Mount Robson area, north. From Smoky River, trail ascends Carcajou Creek to pass north of Whitehorn Mountain Glacier. Holmes River (Fraser) drainage on B. C. side.

CATARACT PASS (ca. 7550) — Sunwapta Pass area, east. Pass is just off CD, linking Cline and Brazeau River sources, North Saskatchewan drainage.

CENTRE PASS (6440), CD — Yellowhead Pass area. Part of Miette Pass. Trail from Yellowhead Pass runs up Miette River and over pass and near crest by Grant Pass to Colonel Pass, Colonel Creek, Moose River and Yellowhead Pass road at Rainbow Canyon. Miette (Athabaska)–Moose (Fraser) drainage.

CITADEL PASS (ca. 8200), CD — Banff area, southwest. From top of Healy Creek near Simpson Pass, trail runs south along CD to Citadel Pass and down Simpson River to Vermilion River. Bow–Kootenay drainages.

CLEARWATER PASS (7900) — Lake Louise area, north. From north side (Siffleur River) of Pipestone Pass, trail crosses Clearwater Pass to Clearwater Lake and River. North Saskatchewan drainage.

CLINE PASS (9370) — Sunwapta Pass area, east. High crossing near Mount Stewart (10,871), linking Cline and Brazeau rivers northeast of Cataract Pass. North Saskatchewan drainage. "Old Cline" was the Jasper horse trader who used Cline Pass in his trips from Jasper House to what was called Kootenay Plain at the *east* foot of Howse Pass.

COLONEL PASS (6135), CD — Mount Robson–Yellowhead Pass area. Miette Pass–Grant Pass trail crosses Colonel Pass and descends Colonel Creek–Moose River to Yellowhead Pass road at Rainbow Canyon. Snaring River (Athabaska)–Moose River (Fraser) drainages.

CONSOLATION PASS (8310) — Lake Louise area, south. Pass links source of Boom Creek and Boom Lake to Consolation Valley and Moraine Lake. Bow River drainage. Has been called Boom Lake Pass.

CORBIN PASS (7083) — Glacier–Rogers Pass area, west, Selkirk Range. From Illecillewaet community, trail crosses pass between Illecillewaet and Tangier rivers, into 1880's mining area. Named for mine owner.

COUGAR PASS (ca. 7100) — Glacier–Rogers Pass area, west, Selkirk Range. Pass links Cougar Creek and Illecillewaet branch. Columbia drainage.

CROWSNEST PASS (4453), CD — Near Coleman, fifty miles north of United States border. Highway crosses this easy pass south of Crowsnest Mountain (9138), a rakish pile tilted at a comical angle like any crow's careless home. Highway runs from Pincher west to Elko, ninety-five miles. Pass is used also by coal-carrying branch of Canadian Pacific. A superb sweep of mountains surrounds pass and Crowsnest town on top. This is the lowest of Rocky Mountain passes south of Yellowhead Pass (3717). Called Crow Nest Pass on George M. Dawson map of 1886. Because of heavy timber, pass was not popular with Indians. Original trail was not cut through until 1880's up Crowsnest River and down west side by Elk River branch to wide Kootenay Valley.

DEADMAN PASS (5500), CD — Crowsnest Pass area, north. Oil Company seismic line crosses this old pack trail from Allison Creek (Crowsnest River) to Alexander Creek (Flathead River). South Saskatchewan–Columbia drainages.

DECEPTION PASS (8000) — Lake Louise area, north. From Boulder Pass and Ptarmigan Lake, trail runs north over Deception Pass and down Skoki and Little Pipestone creeks to Pipestone River. Ski country.

DENNIS PASS (7418) — Just south of Field under Mount Dennis and just west of associated Duchesnay Pass. Named for the late Colonel J. Stoughton Dennis, Surveyor-General of Canada.

DOLOMITE PASS (8100) — Lake Louise area, north, between Cirque Peak (9768) and Dolomite Peak (9828). From Lake Helen above Bow River trail runs over pass to Lake Alice and down Dolomite Creek to Siffleur River and North Saskatchewan.

DONKIN PASS (8606) — Glacier–Rogers Pass area, south, Selkirk Range. This wild ice-axe climber's pass for experts links Donkin Glacier and Mitre Creek. Incompappleux (Columbia) drainage. Named for English Alpine Club member who perished in the Caucasus in 1888.

DUCHESNAY PASS (8747) — Near Field, south. In triangle of Mount Dennis (8336), Mount Duchesnay (9602) and Mount Odaray (10,175) of Cataract Brook–Boulder Creek drainage. Duchesnay was first crossed in 1902 and was named for E. J. Duchesnay, early engineer and trail maker.

EDITH–NORQUAY PASS (ca. 7500) — Just out of Banff, northwest. From Stoney Squaw Mountain road end, trail crosses pass to Fortymile Creek, Bow drainage. Pass is between Mount Edith (8380) and Mount Norquay (8275). "Edith" was Mrs. Edith Cox Orde, a Banff visitor in 1886. John Norquay was a premier of Manitoba.

ELK PASS (ca. 7000), CD — Mount Joffre area, Elk Mountains, fifty air miles south of Banff. Elk River (Kootenay)–Kananaskis River (Bow) drainages.

ELYSIUM PASS (ca. 7400) — Jasper–Yellowhead Pass area, just north of Geikie town. Pass is between Elysium Mountain and Mount McKean. Athabaska drainage.

EMERALD PASS (8899) — Field–Kicking Horse Pass area, north, President Range. Pass lies two miles southwest of President Pass near Michael Peak. The great Edward Whymper and Christian Kucker made this dangerous glacier traverse first in 1901.

FATIGUE PASS (ca. 8200), CD — Banff area, southwest. From Bow River, trail runs up Brewster and Fatigue creeks to top of pass just south of. Citadel Pass, and down Simpson River on west side to Vermilion River. Bow–Kootenay drainages.

FERRO PASS (*ca.* 7400) — Banff area, south, Assiniboine group. Pass between Nestor and Indian peaks links Surprise Creek (Simpson River) and Mitchell–Cross rivers. Kootenay drainage.

FLAT CREEK PASS (4910) — Glacier–Rogers Pass area, southwest, Selkirk Range. From Flat Creek settlement on Illecillewaet River, trail runs up Flat Creek to pass and down Slick Creek to Incompleux River. Columbia drainage.

FORDING RIVER PASS (*ca.* 7000), CD — In Highwood Range near Mount Armstrong (9161), seventy-five miles south of Banff. Pass links Fording River (Kootenay–Columbia) and Highwood River (South Saskatchewan).

FORTRESS PASS (*ca.* 5300), CD — Sunwapta Pass area. From Banff-Jasper highway, trail runs up Athabaska River and Cheba River to pass. On west side trail runs along beautiful Fortress Lake to Wood River. Athabaska–Columbia drainages. A sensationally scenic route.

FRASER PASS (6500) — Athabaska Pass area, north. Pass is near Beacon Peak just west of CD at extreme Fraser River source. Baker Creek–Canoe River drainage on south side.

GIBBON PASS (*ca.* 7200) — Banff area, west, Mount Ball group. Pass is on Redearth–Twin Lakes loop from Bow River. Named for J. M. Gibbon, author and trail rider.

GLACIER PASS (*ca.* 8000) — Extreme north edge, Jasper National Park, forty-five air miles north of Yellowhead Pass on the Ancient Wall below Noonday Peak. Mowitch Creek (Snake Indian River)–South Sulphur River (Smoky) drainages.

GRANT PASS (6355), CD — Yellowhead Pass area, northwest. From Miette Pass sector, trail crosses Grant Pass between glaciers under Mount Machray (9020), and then crosses Colonel Pass, descending Colonel Creek–Moose River to Yellowhead Pass road at Rainbow Canyon. Snaring River (Athabaska)–Grant Brook (Fraser) drainages.

GRAVE CREEK PASS: See South Kootenie Pass under Montana passes.

HEALY PASS (7500) — Banff area, southwest. Between Redearth and Simpson passes, though not on CD. Trail up Redearth and Pharoah creeks crosses pass to Healy Creek. Bow River drainage. Named for a mining man, Captain J. J. Healy, who found copper in the region.

HECTOR PASS: See Kicking Horse Pass.

HIGHWOOD PASS (*ca.* 8000) — Near but east of CD, some fifty miles southeast of Banff, Misty-Highwood ranges. Pass links Pocaterra Creek (Kananaskis River) and Storm Creek (Highwood River). Bow drainage. A fine gravel road, Coleman to Kananaskis and Banff–Calgary highway, crosses Highwood Pass amid dramatic cathedral peaks. The George Dawson surveying party went over it in July, 1884, when four inches of snow fell.

HOWSE PASS (5000), CD — Forty air miles northwest of Kicking Horse, Waputik Range. From Banff–Jasper highway, easy trail runs south fifteen miles up Howse River and Conway Creek to pass west of Howse Peak (10,800). South-side trail descent down steep, narrow Blaeberry River to Columbia, about forty miles. From Howse Pass north, CD is continuous ice fields — Waputik, Wapta, Freshfield, Lyell–Forbes, Columbia, Chaba–Clemenceau, and finally Hooker, near Athabaska Pass. David Thompson used Howse in 1807 and called it Saskatchewan Pass or Mountain Portage. It was named for Joseph Howse, of Hudson's Bay Company. Dr. James Hector's party crossed it without a guide in 1859.

HURD PASS (*ca.* 8500) — Field area, south, Ottertail group. High snow pass is between Mount Vaux (10,891) and Mount Hurd (9275). Ottertail–Kicking Horse drainage.

ILLECILLEWAET PASS (5760) — Glacier–Rogers Pass area, south, Selkirk Range. Crossing near Illecillewaet Glacier.

INDIAN PASS (*ca.* 8000) — Jasper area, southwest, Trident Range. Pass links Muhigan and Whistler creeks north of Manx Peak (9987). Athabaska drainage.

JACKPINE PASS (6694), CD — Mount Robson area, north, below Chown Glacier. Bess Pass trail crosses CD from Smoky River, recrosses at Jackpine Pass and descends Jackpine River to Smoky River again. Peace–Fraser drainages.

JACQUES PASS (*ca.* 5800) — Near Jasper, northeast. Pass is on Merlin Pass–Jacques Lake trail south of Jasper Lake. Athabaska drainage.

JAMES PASS (*ca.* 7500) — Wapiti Mountain area fifty miles north and a bit east of Banff. Pass trail links Red Deer and James rivers. Red Deer–South Saskatchewan drainage.

JONAS PASS (*ca.* 7500) — Sunwapta Pass area south of Jasper. From Maligne Lake, Maligne River trail runs south over pass to Brazeau River and Nigel Pass. North Saskatchewan–Athabaska drainage. Named for the Stoney Indian chief named Jonas, who helped Professor Coleman get to Athabaska Pass in 1893.

KANANASKIS PASS (*ca.* 7200), CD — Some forty air miles south of Banff and two miles northeast of Mount McHarg (9476). Ancient trail over pass links Upper Kananaskis Lake of Kananaskis River and Palliser River. Bow (South Saskatchewan)–Palliser (Kootenay–Columbia) drainages. Captain Palliser crossed pass westbound in 1858 and named it for a legendary Cree Indian who recovered miraculously from the blow of an axe.

KICKING HORSE PASS (5339), CD — Lake Louise–Field area, Banff–Yoho national parks. Crossed by spectacular new Trans–Canada Highway and by Canadian Pacific Railroad (main line) from Banff west to Vancouver. Railroad uses its famous two spiral tunnels near Yoho (1909) reducing former grade from 4.5% to 2.2%. Pass links Bath Creek (Bow–South Saskatchewan) and Wapta Lake–Kicking Horse River (Columbia). With its Upper and Lower Canyons, Kicking Horse is the most beautiful of the four Canadian Rockies CD road crossings. From the south these four are Crowsnest (4453), Vermillion (5416), Kicking Horse and Yellowhead (3717). Dr. Hector discovered it in 1858, named it when he was kicked in the chest by his horse and crossed it eastbound. It has been called Hector Pass. The west descent ends in a steep shelf pitch down to Golden on the forested Columbia River. The east descent is nothing at all — 288 vertical feet in six miles from the top to Lake Louise.

KIMPTON PASS (8609) — Kootenay National Park, seven miles southeast of Radium Hot Springs. From Banff–Windermere highway, trail runs four miles up Kimpton Creek to pass and descends Shushwap Creek on other side. Columbia drainage.

KIWETINOK PASS (8000) — Field area, north, President Range. Pass links Kiwetinok River (Amiskiwi) and Little Yoho River between Kiwetinok Peak (9522) and Mount Kerr (9394). Kicking Horse drainage. Edward Whymper crossed it in 1901. Kiwetinok: Cree for "north side."

KOOTANIE PASS: Captain Palliser's name for North Kootenay Pass.

LEATHER PASS: See Yellowhead Pass.

LITTLE FORK RIVER PASS: Dr. Hector's name for Bow Pass in 1858.

LUXOR PASS (*ca.* 8300) — Radium Hot Springs area, north, Brisco Range, Kootenay National Park. From highway near Luxor, trail runs up Luxor Creek to pass and down to Banff–Windermere highway on east side. Columbia drainage.

MCARTHUR PASS (*ca.* 7300) — Kicking Horse Pass area. From Hector just west of Kicking Horse summit, trail runs south of Cataract Brook past lovely Lake O'Hara to pass and down McArthur Creek–Ottertail River to Kicking Horse highway again. Columbia drainage. Named for J. J. McArthur, of the Dominion Land Survey.

MACCARIB PASS (7000) — Jasper area, southwest, Jasper National Park. Pass is on Tonquin Pass trail and links Portal and Maccarib creeks. Athabaska drainage.

MACKENZIE DIVIDE (3000), CD — Spot where Alexander Mackenzie crossed to Pacific drainage on his epic transcontinental trip in 1793. Divide is fifty-five air miles northeast of Prince George, B. C., and eighteen miles west and a little south of Monkman Pass. It is an 800-yard level stretch between two lakes at extreme headwaters of Parsnip River and Jones Creek–McGregor River. Peace (Arctic)–Fraser (Pacific) drainages.

MARMOT PASS (7800) — Jasper area, southwest, Trident Range, Jasper National Park. From Jasper road, Whistler Creek trail crosses pass to Circus Valley and Portal Creek under Marmot Mountain (8557). Athabaska drainage.

MARVEL PASS (7050), CD — Banff area, south, Assiniboine group, three miles east of Mount Eon (10,860). From Spray Reservoir, trail runs up Marvel Creek past Marvel Lake to pass. Aurora Creek and Mitchell–Cross rivers on west side. Bow–Kootenay drainage.

MERLIN PASS (*ca.* 7000) — Jasper area, northeast, under Mount Merlin. On Jasper Lake–Jacques Lake trail. Nushan Creek–Rocky River drainages. (Athabaska).

MIDDLE KOOTENAY PASS (6355), CD — South of Crowsnest Pass. Pass links west branch, Castle River (Oldman) and Pass Creek (Flathead) near Mount Haig (8565). South Saskatchewan–Columbia drainages.

MIETTE PASS: See South Pass, Centre Pass, North Pass.

MISKO PASS (*ca.* 7500) — Vermilion Pass area, Kootenay National Forest. Pass connects source of Misko Creek to Tokumm Creek drainage. It is reached by trail from Banff–Windermere highway. Kootenay–Columbia drainage.

MOAT PASS (6380), CD — Jasper area, southwest. Pass is at Moat Lake just south of Tonquin Pass. Athabaska–Fraser drainages.

MOBERLY PASS (5825) — Donald Station area, northwest, near

Mount Sir Sandford (11,590), Selkirk Range. Pass links Gold River and Gold Stream. Columbia drainage. Named for the explorer Walter Moberly, who discovered it in 1871 while seeking railroad routes.

MONKMAN PASS (3550), CD — Summit Lake area, east. From Redwillow River (Alberta) road end, trail crosses pass to Herrick Creek–McGregor River and Hansard, B. C. Kinuseo Creek (Smoky River)–McGregor (Fraser) drainage. Alexander Mackenzie crossed CD eighteen miles west and a little south of Monkman Pass in 1793.

MOOSE PASS (6570), CD — Mount Robson area. From Robson Pass trail, a trail ascends Calumet Creek to Moose Pass between glaciers and then down Moose River headwaters to Yellowhead Pass road at Rainbow Canyon. Athabaska–Fraser drainages.

MORKILL PASS (5434), CD — In Wilderness Provincial Park (east side) just northwest of Jasper National Park near Mount De Veber and Jackpine Pass. Morkill Pass links Morkill River and Muddywater River. Smoky River–Fraser drainages.

MOUNTAIN PORTAGE: David Thompson's name in 1807 for Howse Pass.

NIGEL PASS (7225) — Sunwapta Pass area, northeast. From Banff–Jasper highway south of Sunwapta Pass, trail runs up Nigel Creek to pass and down Brazeau River on northeast side to Jonas Pass trail. North Saskatchewan drainage.

NORTH FORK PASS (6537), CD — North of Crowsnest Pass. Pack trail and seismic line from Maycroft road crosses grassy open pass to Elk River. Oldman River (South Saskatchewan)–Elk River (Kootenay–Columbia) drainages. A favorite Cree Indian traverse marked by Cree cairns. "Old Man's Playground" from which Oldman River got its name is on pass trail. The George M. Dawson party crossed pass in 1884.

NORTH KOOTENAY PASS (6774), CD — South of Crowsnest Pass. Pack trail over this bare traverse between peaks links Carbondale–Castle–Oldman rivers with Squaw Creek–Flathead River. South Saskatchewan–Columbia drainage. Called North Kootenie Pass on George M. Dawson 1886 map. Captain John Palliser crossed eastbound in 1858. There is a second summit (6850) of North Kootenay Pass over the McDonald range. The westering trail of this second summit crosses from a source of Flathead River and descends the other side by Wigwam River drainage to Elk River and the Kootenay.

NORTH PASS (7010), CD — Yellowhead Pass area. North Pass, part of Miette Pass, is just south of Mount McCord (8240) on saddle above Miette Pass trail. Athabaska–Fraser drainages.

ODARAY PASS (ca. 8000) — Field–Kicking Horse area. Pass is one mile south of Duchesnay Pass between Mount Duchesnay (9602) and, east, Mount Odaray (10,175) of McArthur Creek (Ottertail)–Cataract Brook (Kicking Horse) drainages. Odaray: Stoney Indian for "very brushy."

OG PASS (ca. 8000), CD — Banff area, south, Assiniboine group. From Bryant Creek and Spray Reservoir, trail crosses pass to Og Lake and Simpson River Valley. Bow–Kootenay drainage.

OPABIN PASS (8460) — Lake Louise–Ten Peaks area. Pass is west of CD two miles south of Abbot Pass between Mount Hungabee (11,457) and Mount Biddle (10,888). Tokumm Creek (Vermilion–Kootenay)–

Cataract Brook (Kicking Horse–Columbia) drainage. Opabin: Cree for "snowy."

OTTERTAIL PASS (7200) — Vermilion Pass area. From Banff–Windermere highway west of Vermilion Pass, trail runs up Ochre Creek, over pass and down Ottertail River to Kicking Horse near Field. Kootenay–Columbia drainage.

OTTO PASS (6960) — Field area, north. Pass links Otto Creek (Amiskwi River) and Martin Creek (Blaeberry River). Columbia drainage.

PALLISER PASS (7000), CD — Thirty-five air miles south of Banff. From Spray Reservoir road end, trail runs up Spray River to pass near Belgium Lake below Mount Sir Douglas (11,174). Palliser River is on west side. Bow–Kootenay drainage. Named for Captain John Palliser, head of the 1857–1858 British North American Exploring expedition which included Dr. James Hector.

PINE RIVER PASS (2850) — Murray Range, northern Alberta, on John Hart Highway (Prince George–Dawson Creek, 257 miles). Pine River–Misinchinka River (Peace) drainage. Most northerly Rockies pass listed in this book. Highway built 1954. Pass, at Azouzetta Lake, is east of CD.

PINTO PASS: See Sunset Pass.

PIPESTONE PASS (8036) — Lake Louise area, north. From Lake Louise town, trail runs up Pipestone River to top of pass and down Siffleur River on north side to North Saskatchewan. River was named for its fine-grained gray-blue argillite used by Indians in making pipes. Dr. Hector crossed Pipestone Pass northbound in 1859. It was always a popular route to the North Saskatchewan because of Bow River's bogs and overflowing.

POBOKTAN PASS (ca. 8200) — Sunwapta Pass area, northeast beyond Jonas Pass. From Banff–Jasper highway and Sunwapta River, telephone line runs up Poboktan Creek and over pass to Brazeau Lake and River. Athabaska–North Saskatchewan drainage. Professor A. P. Coleman observed Poboktan in 1893.

PRESIDENT PASS (9469) — Field area, north, President Range. This glacier pass lies between the Vice President (10,059) and the President (10,297). Kicking Horse River watershed. The President was Lord Thomas Shaughnessy, a Canadian Pacific official.

PTOLEMY PASS (5618), CD — Crowsnest Pass area, fifth pass north of United States border. Pack trail runs up Ptolemy Creek–Glacier Creek (Crowsnest River) to top of pass and down west side by branch of Flathead River. South Saskatchewan–Columbia drainage.

PURITY PASS (ca. 8200) — Glacier–Rogers Pass area, south, Selkirk Range. Pass connects Purity and Odin glaciers. Columbia drainage. Purity Mountain (10,467) above it is regarded by many as one of the most beautiful peaks in the Canadian Rockies.

RACEHORSE PASS (7000), CD — North of Crowsnest Pass. Racehorse links south fork of Racehorse Creek (Oldman River) and Alexander Creek (Flathead River). South Saskatchewan–Columbia drainages.

REDEARTH PASS (7966), CD — Banff area, westerly, south end of Ball Mountain group. From Banff–Jasper highway at Massive, trail runs up Redearth and Pharoah creeks past Pharoah Peaks to pass. West-side drainage is Verdant Creek–Simpson River.

RED PASS (7000) — Yellowhead Pass area, west. Pass is just north of Red Pass community, Yellowhead Pass road.

ROBSON PASS (5417), CD — Mount Robson area. From Yellowhead Pass road near Alpland, trail runs up Robson River on west side of Mount Robson (12,972) past Valley of a Thousand Falls and Berg Lake to pass. North-side trail runs down Smoky River. Fraser (Pacific)–Peace River (Arctic) drainages.

ROGERS PASS (4341) — Glacier area, Selkirk Range, Glacier National Park. From Donald Bridge on north-flowing Columbia River, new magnificent Trans-Canada Highway winds westerly over Dogtooth Mountains to join Canadian Pacific Railway and move up Beaver River and over the main Selkirk Range. The highway leaves the C. P. at the start of the five-mile Connaught Railway Tunnel and goes over the easy pass to Glacier at the tunnel's west portal. Then it winds down Illecillewaet River to the resort town of Revelstoke on the south-flowing Columbia. The total distance from Donald Bridge is eighty-five miles. This great pass road, completing Canada's first direct all-weather transcontinental thoroughfare, was opened on July 30, 1962. Before then, motorists had to get around the massive Selkirk Range from Donald to Revelstoke by following the Big Bend of the Columbia — a rough, dusty, summer-only road 180 miles long. In winter, they had to load their automobiles on C. P. freight cars. Originally and briefly, the railroad avoided the Selkirks by following the Big Bend. Then the line was put over the top of Rogers Pass until avalanches forced the building of the Connaught Tunnel in 1912. One avalanche in 1902 completely destroyed the C. P. R. Rogers Pass roundhouse. A dramatic feature of the new highway is the series of cement snowsheds guarding the right-of-way from the annual Selkirk Range snowfall of four hundred inches — nearly as heavy as the Wolf Creek Pass snowfall in Colorado. The longest shed, 1200 feet, is at the famed Lanark slide area. It is made of reinforced concrete and steel, precast and assembled on site. Rogers Pass was surveyed first in 1866 by Albert Perry, an assistant of Walter Moberly, the engineer-explorer, and surveyed again by Major A. B. Rogers in 1882–1883.

SAGE PASS (ca. 7900), CD — Waterton Lakes Park area. From Waterton Park, a road and then a trail ascends Blakiston and Bauerman brooks past Twin Lakes to top of crossing and down Sage Creek to Flathead River. South Saskatchewan–Kootenay (Columbia) drainage.

SASKATCHEWAN PASS: David Thompson's name (1807) for Howse Pass.

SENTINEL PASS (8566) — Lake Louise–Ten Peaks area. From Moraine Lake, popular trail runs through Larch Valley to top of pass between Pinnacle Mountain (10,072) and Mount Temple (11,636), and so on down to Paradise Valley and Lake Louise. Bow River drainage.

SHOVEL PASS (ca. 7350) — Near ski area cabin twelve miles southeast of Jasper under Curator Mountain (8604). Athabaska drainage.

SHUSHWAP PASS: Stoney Indian name for Sinclair Pass.

SILVERTIP PASS (8500) — Donald Station area, thirty-two air miles northwest, Selkirk Range. Glacier traverse, Mount Sir Sandford Glacier.

SIMPSON PASS (6954), CD — Banff area, southwest, Ball Mountain group. From Bow River west of Banff, trail runs up Healy Creek to top of pass and down Simpson River to the Kootenay. Named for Sir George Simpson, Hudson's Bay Company head, who crossed it in 1841 during his round-the-world trip. Redearth and Healy passes are close by.

SINCLAIR PASS (4875) — This ancient crossing of the Stanford Range which separates the Columbia and Kootenay rivers is on Banff–Windermere highway six miles northeast of Radium Hot Springs. Sinclair Creek (Columbia)–Swede Creek (Kootenay) drainage. The Sinclair Pass trail was the westward continuation of the White Man Pass trail across the CD, and consequently was in the "second summit" category of the two North Kootenay passes and the two South Kootenay passes, both of which resulted from the peculiar parallel-ridge conformation of the Canadian Rockies. It appears that Sinclair Pass was named for the half-breed mountain man, James Sinclair, who told Captain Palliser about it when the latter was touring the western United States in 1848 long before the Palliser expedition of 1857–1858. But Palliser never did find Sinclair Pass.

SNAKE INDIAN PASS (6625) — Jasper National Park, north. Trail and telephone line ascend Snake Indian River and over pass near Snake Indian Mountain (9608) to Twintree Creek and Smoky River. Athabaska (Peace) drainage. Adjoins Byng Pass.

SNOWBIRD PASS (ca. 7000) — Mount Robson area just east of Robson Glacier under Titkana Peak.

SOUTHESK PASS (ca. 7300) — Southeast of Jasper. Pass trail links Southesk River (Cairn–Brazeau) to Medicine-tent River (Rocky River). North Saskatchewan (Athabaska) drainage. Named for Lord Southesk, who crossed pass in late 1850's.

SOUTH KOOTENAY PASS (6903), CD — Near Waterton Lakes Park. From Waterton Park, auto road ascends Blakiston Brook to campground, where Lone Brook trail, once a wagon road, leads to top of pass under Lone Mountain (7950) and continues down Sage Creek to Flathead River. Waterton River (South Saskatchewan)–Flathead (Kootenay) drainages. South Kootenay Pass was the eastern end of the United States–Canada boundary survey of 1861 which started on the Pacific coast. It was the west end of the George M. Dawson boundary survey in 1874. Dawson called it South Kootenie or Boundary Pass and put its altitude at 7100 feet. For the westward continuation of this South Kootenay Pass trail, see the listing South Kootenie Pass under Montana passes.

SOUTH PASS (6850), CD — Yellowhead Pass area, north. Pass, part of Miette Pass, is northeast of Razorback Mountain (8548). Miette River (Athabaska)–Grant Brook (Fraser) drainages.

SPRAY PASS (6275), CD — Banff area, south, Assiniboine–King Albert sector. From Spray Reservoir road end, trail runs up Spray River to pass near Leman Lake and Mount Leman (8956). Albert and Palliser rivers form west-side drainage.

SUMMIT LAKE DIVIDE (2315), CD — Twenty-eight miles north of Prince George, British Columbia, on far-north John Hart Highway. This divide links Summit Lake headwaters of Crooked River (Peace) to Fraser River (Pacific). Summit Lake Divide was crossed by Simon Fraser in 1806.

SUNDANCE PASS (6200) — Five miles south of Banff. Sundance Creek–Spray River drainages.

SUNSET PASS (ca. 7100) — Sunwapta Pass area, southeast. From

Banff–Jasper highway near North Saskatchewan, marked trail runs northeast to pass and Pinto Lake beyond, and on down Cline River to North Saskatchewan again. Sometimes called Pinto Pass, after Professor Coleman's ugly pack horse of 1893. There is a lookout atop Sunset Pass, and a youth hostel at the west foot. The peak above is Mount Coleman (10,262).

SUNWAPTA PASS (6675) — On Banff–Jasper highway which ascends North Saskatchewan River to its extreme headwaters and then crosses pass, descending Sunwapta River past the sensational Athabaska Glacier with its parking areas and unique glacier-scooting buses for tourists. This new road was officially opened on August 3, 1961. Sunwapta Pass separates waters of the North Saskatchewan flowing into Hudson Bay and those of Athabaska River flowing into the Arctic. The beautiful Mount Athabaska (11,452) rises above it.

TENT PASS (4900), CD — Near Tent Mountain coal mines just south of Crowsnest Pass. Tent, crossed by oil company seismic line, is sixth pass north of United States border. Crowsnest River (South Saskatchewan)–Flathead River (Columbia) drainage.

TÊTE JAUNE: French–Canadian name for Yellowhead Pass.

THOMPSON PASS (6511), CD — Sunwapta Pass area, south. From Banff–Jasper highway, trail runs west up Alexandra and Castleguard rivers and Watchman Creek to pass. West descent to Columbia down north branch of Rice Brook and Bush River. Spectacular pass near glaciers is overshadowed by Mount Forbes (11,902) and Mount Lyell (11,495). Named for alpinist C. S. Thompson, who crossed it in 1900.

TONQUIN PASS (6390), CD — Jasper area, southwest. From Banff–Jasper highway, trails go up Portal Creek (Maccarib Pass) and up Astoria River through Tonquin Valley past Amethyst Lakes to pass. West-side descent down Tonquin Creek to Fraser River. Athabaska–Fraser drainages. Fine views of Mount Edith Cavell (11,033) from trail. John Jacob Astor's ship to Astoria was named Tonquin.

TORNADO PASS (7200), CD — Twenty-five air miles north of Crowsnest Pass under Tornado Mountain (10,169). Pass links Dutch Creek (Oldman River) and Line Creek (Flathead).

UPRIGHT PASS (6470), CD — Yellowhead Pass area, north. Pass between glaciers links Snaring River (Athabaska) headwaters to Upright Creek–Moose River (Fraser).

VERDANT PASS (7000) — Jasper area, southwest of Mount Edith Cavell (11,033). Pass runs from Verdant Creek (Astoria River) over crest to a branch of Whirlpool River. Athabaska drainage.

VERMILION PASS (5416), CD — Bow Mountain group. From Banff, Banff–Windermere highway runs up Altrude Creek from Bow River to gentle pass between Storm Mountain (10,372) on the south and Boom Mountain (9047). Road on west side descends along Vermilion River (Kootenay) and then crosses Sinclair Pass to Radium Hot Springs and the Columbia. Dr. Hector crossed Vermilion August 20, 1858. Name derives from ochre deposits of chalybeate springs, six miles west of summit.

VISTA PASSAGE (6834), CD — Very near and above Tonquin Pass southwest of Jasper. From Yellowhead Pass road at Geikie, trail runs up Meadow Creek to crossing. West descent down Tonquin Creek to Fraser

River. Athabaska–Fraser drainage. This is the sole use of the word "passage" in the Rockies, meaning "pass."

WAPITI PASS (4439), CD — In north country sixteen miles southeast of Monkman Pass. Links Wapiti River sources (Smoky–Peace) to Herrick Creek (McGregor–Fraser).

WASTACH PASS (8346) — Lake Louise–Ten Peaks area, southwest. Pass is just west of Eiffel Peak (10,101). Bow drainage. Wastach: Indian word for "beautiful."

WENKCHEMNA PASS (8531), CD — Lake Louise–Ten Peaks area. From Moraine Lake road end, trail crosses Wenkchemna Glacier to top of pass near Neptuak Mountain (10,617). Bow River drainage. First crossed in 1894 by S.E.S. Allen, pioneer alpinist. Wenkchemna: Stoney Indian for "ten."

WHIRLPOOL PASS (5936), CD — North of Athabaska Pass. Trail runs up Middle Whirlpool River from old Athabaska Pass trail to pass. Baker Creek–Canoe River drainage on west side. Athabaska–Columbia watersheds.

WHISTLERS PASS (ca. 7500) — Jasper area, southwest. Pass links Whistlers and Crescent creeks. Athabaska drainage. Whistlers are marmots.

WHITE MAN PASS (7112), CD — Thirty miles south of Banff, Mount Assiniboine area. From Spray Reservoir road end, picturesque trail winds up Spray River and White Man Creek (many waterfalls, good fishing) to top of pass. West descent is down Cross River to Kootenay. Bow–Kootenay drainages. Father De Smet went over pass in 1845, and put up a cross on top. This caused it to be called Tsha-kooap-te-ha-wapta, a Stoney Indian word meaning "erecting cross." The White Man Pass name may derive from the fact that a party of emigrants crossed it in 1841.

WILCOX PASS (7660), CD — Sunwapta Pass area, northeast. From Banff–Jasper highway, trail runs east of Wilcox Peak (9463), crosses pass and then rejoins highway. Named for the American climber, Walter D. Wilcox, who went over it in 1896.

WOLVERINE PASS (ca. 9500) — Vermilion Pass area, west. From Banff–Windermere highway, trail ascends Ochre–Tumbling creeks to top of pass between Mount Drysdale and Mount Gray. Descent down Dainard Creek to Beaverfoot Pass trail. Kootenay–Columbia drainages.

WONDER PASS (ca. 8000), CD — Banff area, south, Assiniboine group. Trail from Marvel Lake (Spray River) crosses pass to Sunburst Valley and Mitchell–Cross rivers on west side. Bow–Kootenay drainages.

YELLOWHEAD PASS (3717), CD — Jasper–Mount Robson area. From Jasper, country road uses old railroad grade mostly up Miette River through pine woods over traverse past Yellowhead and Moose lakes and down Fraser River to Mount Robson village, fifty-seven miles. Good views of the highest peak in Canadian Rockies, Mount Robson (12,972), rising in lonely grandeur. Tourists seldom reach Robson because of the narrow, dusty road. Beyond the mountain, the road continues south, getting worse and worse, to meet the Trans-Canada Highway at Kamloops, 299 miles from Jasper. The Canadian National Railway main line also crosses Yellowhead and divides near Tête Jaune, one line bound for Vancouver, the other for Prince Rupert. Two railroads crossed originally. The Grand Trunk

Pacific from Edmonton was completed over Yellowhead to Prince Rupert in 1914. At about the same time, the Canadian Northern from Edmonton was built across and on to Vancouver. They merged gradually into the Canadian National system after 1918. Yellowhead is the second lowest CD pass (after Monkman) in all the Rockies. It was named for the yellow-haired Jasper Hawes, an American trader of the 1820's at Jasper House. It was often called Leather Pass because much leather was taken west over it for the Indian trade in New Caledonia.

YOHO PASS (6030) — Field area, north, President Range, Yoho National Park. From Yoho River road end, very scenic trail runs past Yoho Lake and over pass to Emerald Lake road end. Kicking Horse drainage. Yoho: Cree for "wonder."

Colorado Passes

ABAJA PASS: This seems to be La Veta Pass. The *Rocky Mountain News* (December 27, 1872) reported: "Up this stream (Cucharas) the narrow-gauge is being located, and over the Abaja Pass near its headwaters into San Luis Valley." Abaja: Spanish for "low."

AGATE PASS, AGATE–MONARCH PASS: See Monarch Pass.

ALICANTE PASS: David Moffat's railroad survey name for Fremont Pass, 1891, derived from Alicante Mine.

ALPINE PASS: See Altman's Pass and Tincup Pass.

ALTMAN'S PASS (12,000), CD — Elmo–Tincup Pass area, Sawatch Range. From St. Elmo and Romley, dim ruined wagon road crosses spectacular pass from Chalk Creek (Arkansas) to Quartz Creek (Gunnison) drainage. Alpine Tunnel (11,612) of Denver and South Park Railroad was built beneath Altman's Pass in 1881. Today both ends of tunnel can be reached from Williams Pass 4WD road. Altman's Pass was named for "Colonel" Henry Altman, early stage operator. It was called Alpine Pass because of Alpine Tunnel in 1880's, though Alpine Pass is actually a second name for Tincup Pass. In March, 1884, a snowslide wiped out Woodstock village at west foot of Altman's Pass.

ANDREWS PASS (11,960), CD — Rocky Mountain National Park, Andrews Glacier (South Platte)–North Inlet Creek (Colorado) drainages. Alva Adams Water Diversion Tunnel pierces CD under this pass.

ANGEL PASS (12,200) — Crested Butte area, ten miles northwest and just south of Treasury Mountain (13,442). Trail from Kebler Pass road winds through Ruby Range over Daisy and Angel passes and down Anthracite Creek to road again. Gunnison River drainage.

ANTELOPE PASS (7899) — Kremmling area, northeast. From U.S. Route 40, six miles north of Kremmling, 4WD private road runs eastward over pass to Troublesome Creek road, ten miles. Muddy–Troublesome Creek drainages.

ANTHRACITE PASS (10,150) — Crested Butte–Marble area, Elk Range. From Marble, trail runs south over pass and down North Anthracite Creek to Kebler Pass road. Yule Creek (Colorado)–North Anthracite Creek (Gunnison) drainages. Named for coal in area.

APISHAPA PASS (11,005) — Walsenburg area, Sangre de Cristo Range. From U.S. Route 85–87 at Aguilar, good forest road crosses pass to Cucharas Pass road, thirty-seven miles. Apishapa–Cucharas drainages (Arkansas). Fine close-up views, Spanish Peaks. Apishapa: Apache for "stinking water." Called Fish Pass in 1880's, and Cordova Pass later, honoring J. J. Cordova, commissioner of Las Animas County, to whom road was dedicated in 1935.

ARAPAHO PASS (11,905), CD — Nederland area, northwest. From Fourth of July campground, trail crosses pass and down west side to beautiful Monarch Lake. Boulder Creek (South Platte)–Arapaho Creek (Colorado) drainages. Trail was a minor wagon road in 1900. Also called Caribou Pass.

ARAPAHO PASS (9175), CD — Just east of Muddy Pass. From U.S. Route 40, easy trail runs northeast over pass to State Route 14, ten miles. Arapaho Creek–Diamond Creek drainages.

ARGENTINE PASS (13,132), CD — Georgetown area, southwest. From Waldorf Mine above Georgetown, 4WD road runs to top, steep and rough in spots but the view is magnificent beyond belief. Rock-slid west side down to Peru impassable. Clear Creek (South Platte)–Peru Creek (Colorado) drainages. This historic old mining camp road crossing was called Sanderson Pass in 1860's, often Snake River Pass in 1870's. It is the highest CD road crossing in all the Rockies. The Mosquito Pass road (not CD) is fifty-odd feet higher.

ARKANSAS DIVIDE: See Black Forest Divide.

ARKANSAS PASS: Alternate name in 1860's for Tennessee Pass.

AVALANCHE PASS (11,500) — Redstone–Marble area, Elk Range. From Redstone, trail ascends Avalanche Creek and crosses pass to Carbonate Creek and on down to Marble. Leads also to north fork of Lost Trail Creek and to Capitol Peak–Hagerman Peak country. Crystal River (Colorado) drainage. Hayden's surveyors visited here in 1873. Pass named because of wet-earth avalanches keeping mountainsides clear.

BAKER PASS (11,252), CD — Grand Lake area, north, Never Summer Range. From highway twelve miles north of Grand Lake, trail runs over pass to North Park. Baker Gulch (Colorado)–Michigan River (North Platte) drainages. Probably named for Jim Baker, Colorado mountain man.

BARLOW CREEK PASS (11,565) — Rico area east, La Plata Range. From U.S. Route 550 at Columbine Lake, good narrow road runs through Hermosa Park and becomes 4WD road running over pass just north of Hermosa Mountain and down Barlow Creek to highway between Rico and Lizard Head Pass. From this 4WD road, east side, another 4WD road takes off left up Hotel Draw and over top at Scotch Creek Pass and on down Scotch Creek to Rico. Hermosa Creek (Animas)–Barlow Creek (Dolores) are the drainages for Barlow Creek Pass, which is also called Hermosa Mountain Pass and is marked Bolam Pass on some county maps. George Barlow was a Rico pioneer.

BATH: Rail stop at top of Trout Creek Pass.

BAXTER PASS (8437) — Grand Junction area, northwest. From U.S. Route 50 at Mack, west of Grand Junction, scenic back road crosses pass over beautiful Book Cliffs to Rangely, eighty-two miles, or to Bonanza, Utah. West Salt Creek–Evacuation Creek drainages. The road used to be the right-of-way of the fantastic Uintah Railway or "the Gilsonite Road," the first fifty-three miles of which were built over the pass in 1905 from Mack to Dragon, Utah, according to Lucius Beebe and Charles Clegg in their *Narrow Gauge in the Rockies*. The railroad gave up the ghost on May 17, 1939, and the tracks were sold for scrap a month later. In its heydey of hauling the gilsonite used in asphalt, paints, roofing and printer's ink, the line was famous because of its incredible constant grade of seven and a half per cent for a full five miles south of Baxter Pass. Today a pipeline from Bonanza, Utah, to Mack transports gilsonite over the pass. Charles O. Baxter, for whom it was named, was one of the incorporators of the Uintah Railway.

BEAR CREEK PASS (*ca.* 12,050) — Silverton area, west. Name used by Hayden's surveyors in 1874 for trail crossing linking headwaters of present south fork of Mineral Creek and headwaters of San Miguel River below San Miguel Peak (13,700). Today a trail extends from south fork road end over pass and down San Miguel past San Miguel Lake to Trout Lake and State Route 145 near Ophir. Animas–San Miguel drainages.

BECKWITH PASS (9900) — Crested Butte–Kebler Pass area, Elk Range. From road west of Kebler wilderness trail runs south over Beckwith Pass into Gunnison State Game Refuge of West Elks. Gunnison drainage. Named for Lieutenant E. G. Beckwith of Gunnison expedition, 1853.

BERTHOUD PASS (11,313), CD — Georgetown area. U.S. Route 40, a wide, spectacular highway, runs over pass, Empire to Fraser, thirty miles. Fine lodge and restaurant on top. West Clear Creek (South Platte)–Fraser (Colorado) drainages. Named for Captain Edward L. Berthoud, who discovered it in 1861.

BIGELOW DIVIDE (9350) — Rye area, northwest, Wet Mountains. Good road from Rye and San Isabel crosses divide on way to Hardscrabble road and Westcliffe. St. Charles River–Bigelow Creek (Arkansas) drainages.

BIG HORN PASS (11,300), CD — Wolf Creek Pass area, northwest, San Juan Range. Obscure pass near sources of Goose Creek (Rio Grande) and Beaver Creek (San Juan River).

BLACK FOREST DIVIDE (7340) — Colorado Springs area, north. Crossed by four-lane Interstate 25, Colorado Springs to Denver. Monument Creek (Arkansas)–Plum Creek (South Platte) drainages. This highway runs east of old road through Palmer Lake, west of 1840's trapper trail, Bent's Fort to Fort St. Vrain. Major Stephen Long mentioned divide in 1820. Has been called Arkansas Divide, Palmer Lake Divide, Colorado Divide and Lake Pass. The top of the divide (Monument Hill) is notorious for sudden snows and hails, winter and summer.

BLACK SAGE PASS (9745) — Monarch Pass area, northwest. From Tomichi Creek road at foot of Old Monarch Pass, good road runs west over easy pass to Waunita Hot Springs, as part of charming drive on to Pitkin over Waunita Pass, and then over Cumberland Pass. Hot Springs–Tomichi creeks (Gunnison) drainages.

BLOWOUT PASS (11,800) — Wolf Creek Pass area, south, San Juan Range. From Jasper on Ellwood Pass road, rough 4WD road ascends Spring Creek north to top, four miles. From top, it is hike of one mile to fine fishing on Bennett Creek. Rio Grande drainage. Wild scenery in this old "blowout" mining region.

BLUE LAKE PASS (12,800) — Ouray area, west. From Camp Bird Mine above Ouray, 4WD road climbs four and a half miles through Sneffels to Yankee Boy Mine, and then trail five miles to top. The thirteen-mile descent down east fork, Dallas Creek, past Blue Lakes to State Route 62 is part trail, part road. Uncompahgre (Gunnison) drainage. Members of Telluride Jeep Club 50 have crossed this pass.

BLUE MESA SUMMIT (*ca.* 9000) — Gunnison area, west. From near Sapinero, U.S. Route 50, relocated around Curecanti Reservoir, ascends Big Blue Creek drainage to top of Blue Mesa and down Little Cimarron Creek to Cimarron. Gunnison drainage. This is the Son-of-a-Bitch Hill of old.

BOLAM PASS: See Barlow Creek Pass.

BONITO PASS (11,300), CD — Wolf Creek Pass area, San Juan Range. From U.S. Route 160, east side of Wolf Creek, good horseback trail leads fifteen miles up Pass Creek to Bonito Pass, where it joins Continental Divide Trail along crest southeast two miles to Summit Pass, and one mile more to Ellwood Pass, Pass Creek (Rio Grande)–East Fork, San Juan River (Colorado) drainages. Bonito: Spanish for "pretty."

BOREAS PASS (11,482), CD — Hoosier Pass area. From Como near U.S. Route 285, good summer road, built by army engineers for training, climbs twelve miles to top and descends ten miles to Breckenridge. Former spectacular roadbed of Denver and South Park Railroad. South-side drainage is North Tarryall Creek (South Platte). North side is combination of Indiana Creek and Illinois Gulch flowing into Blue River. A splendid drive. Has been called Hamilton Pass, Breckenridge Pass and Tarryall Pass.

BOTTLE PASS (11,360) — Berthoud Pass area, northwest. Vasquez Range. From U.S. Route 40 at Fraser, good road ascends St. Louis Creek to campground, and then 4WD road goes up West St. Louis Creek to pass. Horseback trail beyond, winding partly down Bonham Creek to Williams Fork River road. St. Louis Creek–Bonham Creek (Colorado) drainage. Unusual stands of large evergreens. Has been called Hunters' Pass.

BOULDER GRAND PASS (12,061), CD — Rocky Mountain National Park. Pass is just north of Isolation Peak, west of Tanima Peak, on south slope of Mount Alice (13,310).

BOULDER PASS: See Rollins Pass, Devil's Thumb Pass.

BOWEN PASS (*ca.* 11,500), CD — Grand Lake area, northwest, and just west of Baker Pass. Trail ascends Bowen Gulch from U.S. Route 34 and crosses pass into North Park to the Illinois River road end. Bowen Gulch (Colorado)–Illinois River (North Platte) drainages.

BOWMAN PASS (12,700) — Taylor Pass area, east, Elk Range. From old Bowman ghost town, trail ascends Bowman Creek to 4WD ridge road, which extends from Lincoln Gulch and Gold Hill to top of Taylor Pass. Gunnison–Roaring Fork (Colorado) drainages. Named for early prospector, John Bowman.

BREAKNECK PASS (10,900) — Fairplay area, southwest. This sheep drive trail over Sheep Creek–High Creek divide runs twelve miles through "tapestry" hills from road ends off U.S. Route 285. Brown's Pass is two miles north of Breakneck, which has been called Warmsprings Pass.

BRECKENRIDGE PASS: See Boreas Pass.

BROWN'S PASS (11,347), CD — Buena Vista–Cottonwood Pass

area, Collegiate Group, Sawatch Range. From Cottonwood Pass road, trail runs around west side of Mount Yale (14,194) up north fork of Denny Creek four miles to top. Trail descends west side past Brown's Cabin in six miles to Texas Creek road and Taylor Reservoir. Arkansas–Gunnison drainage. Brown's Pass is eight miles northwest of Mount Princeton (14,197), seven miles southwest of Mount Harvard (14,420), and six miles from Mount Columbia (14,071). The naming of this so-called Collegiate Group of Sawatch Range 14,000-footers had its origin in 1864 when Professor J. D. Whitney of Harvard, leader of the California Geologic Survey, determined that California's Mount Whitney (14,495) in the High Sierras was the highest peak in the United States, excluding Alaska. Whitney had nagging doubts, though, and brought a group of students and teachers from his new Mining School at Harvard to the Sawatch Range during the summer of 1869 to measure its peaks, all of which turned out to be lower than Mount Whitney. In the process, Professor Whitney gave the name Harvard to the highest of the Collegiate Group and called another Yale because he had graduated from Yale University in 1839. Among the youngsters in the party were A. R. Marvine and Henry Gannett, who became stars of the Hayden Surveys a few years later. Henry Gannett named Mount Princeton in that later period. Mount Columbia was named in 1916 by Roger Toll of the Colorado Mountain Club. The naming of the Collegiates has been told in full by John L. Jerome Hart, "Fourteen Thousand Feet," *Trail and Timberline* Supplement, June, 1925, Denver.

BROWN'S PASS (11,000) — Fairplay area, southwest, Mosquito Range. A sheep-drive crossing two miles north of Breakneck Pass.

BUCHANAN PASS (11,704), CD — Nederland area, northwest. From the Middle St. Vrain Creek lumber road out of Ward, trail goes to top and down west side to Monarch Lake. Middle St. Vrain (South Platte)–Cascade Creek (Colorado) drainages. This trail was shown as wagon road on Nell's maps, 1899–1907. Pass was named for President James Buchanan, who signed bill çreating Colorado Territory on February 28, 1861. It was surveyed once for railroad.

BUCKHORN PASS (7700) — On Colorado Springs Municipal High Drive, gift of General William J. Palmer, reached from North Cheyenne Canyon road. Fountain Creek (Arkansas) drainage.

BUCKSKIN PASS (12,000) — Aspen area, southwest Elk Range. Fine hiking trail crosses divide from Willow Lake five miles west to Snowmass Lake. Willow Lake is reached up Willow Creek from Maroon Creek road out of Aspen. Buckskin Pass, in Maroon-Snowmass Wilderness Area, was named by Ranger Len Shoemaker of White River National Forest, honoring Percy Hagerman's buckskin pack horse which kept falling off the pass trail. Shoemaker laid out the trail in 1922. Roaring Fork (Colorado) drainage.

BUFFALO PASS (10,200), CD — Steamboat Springs area east, Sierra Madre Range. From Steamboat Springs, back road, improved in 1958, ascends Soda and Spring Creek drainages to top near Summit Lake. Descent into North Park is somewhat steep to Grizzly Creek Ranger Guard Station. North Platte–Yampa River (Colorado) watersheds. From 1890 to 1920, this Buffalo Pass road was the main route from North Park to Steamboat.

BUFFALO PASS (11,000) — Buena Vista area, east, Mosquito Range. From Rough and Tumble Creek (Weston Pass road) trail runs through Buffalo Meadows around west side of Buffalo Peaks to pass and down Fourmile Creek trail and road to Buena Vista. South Platte–Arkansas drainages.

CALICO PASS (12,816) — St. Elmo area, south, Sawatch Range. From St. Elmo, trail ascends Grizzly Gulch, over ridge on east side of Calico Peak (13,100) and down Cyclone Creek to Shavano ghost town and North Fork of South Arkansas.

CAMERON PASS (10,285) — Fort Collins area, west, Medicine Bow Range. From Fort Collins, State Route 14 winds west and over pass to North Park and Walden, one hundred miles. Joe Wright Creek (Cache la Poudre)–Michigan River (North Platte) drainages. Wagon road from late 1870's and motor road since 1926. Named for General Robert A. Cameron, the town builder who helped lay out Greeley, Colorado Springs and Fort Collins.

CARIBOU PASS: See Arapaho Pass.

CARNERO PASS (10,500) — Saguache area, south, Cochetopa Hills. From La Garita, attractive back road winds north over pass to Cochetopa Pass road. Carnero Creek–Saguache Creek drainages. Carnero: Spanish for "sheep."

CARNERO PASS: Name used in 1840's for CD Salt House Pass from Gunnison country to Saguache Park.

CASTLE PASS (11,000) — Crested Butte area, southwest, West Elk Range. From Ohio Creek road, horseback trail runs west up North Castle Creek to pass and down west side in Gunnison State Game Refuge by Robinson and Coal creeks to Anthracite Creek and Kebler Pass road. Gunnison (Colorado) drainage. Named for "the Castles" rock formation.

CAT CREEK GAP (7200) — Pagosa Springs area, southwest. From U.S. Route 160, road runs south through Southern Ute Indian Reservation over gap to Pagosa Junction. San Juan drainage.

CEBOLLA PASS (11,800) — Lake City area, southeast, San Juan Range. Old road of 1870's from Antelope Park on Rio Grande used this pass on way to Slumgullion Pass and Lake San Cristobal. Examined 1873 by Lieutenant E. H. Ruffner in his Reconnaissance of Ute Country. Cebolla: Spanish for "onion."

CELESTE PASS: See Stunner Pass.

CERRO SUMMIT (7909) — Montrose area, east. U.S. Route 50 crosses this ridge on Montrose–Gunnison run. This route has been used at least from 18th century to avoid Black Canyon of the Gunnison. Gunnison–Uncompahgre drainages. Cerro: Spanish for "ridge."

CHALK CREEK PASS (12,070) — St. Elmo area, south, Sawatch Range. From Hancock road end, 4WD road ascends Chalk Creek and becomes trail past Hancock Lake to wild top of pass and down Middle Fork of South Arkansas to 4WD road and U.S. Route 50 at Garfield. Chalk Creek–South Arkansas drainages.

CHAPIN PASS (12,200) — Rocky Mountain National Park. Pass is saddle leading from near source of Fall River to headwaters of Chapin Creek, a branch of Cache la Poudre River. South Platte watershed.

CHICAGO BASIN PASS: See Columbine Pass (Durango).

CIMARRON PASS: See Raton Pass, Trinchera Pass.

CINNAMON PASS (12,600) — Silverton area, northeast, San Juan Range. From Silverton, road runs to Animas Forks, where splendid 4WD road ascends Cinnamon Creek three miles to spectacular top and descends Lake Fork of Gunnison twenty-six miles past Whitecross and Sherman ghost towns to Lake San Cristobal and Lake City. Lake Fork (Gunnison)–Cinnamon Creek (Animas River) drainages. One of finest 4WD trips in Rockies. Named for cinnamon-colored meadows at top.

COALBANK PASS (10,664) — Durango–Silverton area, San Juan Range. U.S. Route 550, the Million Dollar Highway, runs north from Durango up Coalbank Hill and over pass below Engineer Mountain (12,972). Molas Divide is eight miles farther north. Las Animas (Colorado) watershed. Magnificent scenery.

COCHETOPA PASS (10,032), CD — Saguache area, west, Cochetopa Hills. This low spot, used now by a secondary road from Saguache to Gunnison, was the original ancient Indian and buffalo trail linking San Luis Valley to the Gunnison country. Otto Mears's toll road to the first Los Pinos Ute Agency reached the pass by way of Luders Creek two miles south of present road route. The new, shorter Saguache–Gunnison road uses North Cochetopa Pass, and so did the wagon road built in the middle 1870's when Gunnison town was founded. Cochetopa: Indian for "pass of the buffalo."

COFFEE POT PASS (12,500) — Crested Butte area, northeast, Elk Range. Old prospector trail, dating from 1879, runs from East River near Crested Butte up Cascade Creek and Middle Brush Creek over pass and down Conundrum Creek to Highland and Aspen. Retired Ranger Len Shoemaker has reported that pass trail is on east side of Triangle Peak. The Triangle Pass trail is on the west side. Coffee Pot Pass was named for coffee pot left there by Hayden Survey men in 1873.

COLORADO DIVIDE: Hayden Survey name for Black Forest Divide.

COLUMBINE PASS (12,600) — Durango area, northeast, Needle Mountains, San Juan Range. A wild, beautiful and rugged trail from the D. & R. G. station, Needleton, goes up Needle Creek to pass and down Johnsons Creek–Vallecito Creek to Vallecito Reservoir. Pass is in center of stupendous mountain group. Also called Chicago Basin Pass.

COLUMBINE PASS (8500) — Montrose area, Uncompahgre Plateau. On roads from Delta or Montrose to Naturita. Uncompahgre–San Miguel (Colorado) drainages. From Montrose to pass, road follows Uncompahgre Plateau crest for sixteen miles.

COMANCHE PASS (12,000) — Westcliffe area, southwest, Sangre de Cristo Range. Ranger Jack Booth explains that Comanche Pass is crossed by horseback from road end out of Westcliffe up Hiltman Creek to Comanche Lake and down San Luis Valley side by middle fork, North Crestone Creek, to Crestone. For Comanche Pass–Venable Pass trail see Venable Pass. Comanches used to contest this Wet Mountain Valley area with the Utes.

CONUNDRUM PASS (12,300) — Aspen area, southwest, Elk Range.

From near top of Triangle Pass, north side, Conundrum Trail runs over pass westerly and drops northward below East Maroon Pass to Maroon Creek road. Conundrum Creek–Maroon Creek (Roaring Fork) drainages. This pass, as described locally, does not cross Elk Range crest. However, the crest passes, Triangle and Coffee Pot, are sometimes called Conundrum Pass.

CONY PASS (12,410), CD — Rocky Mountain National Park. Pass is at top of Cony Creek (branch of North St. Vrain), west of Allens Park. Conies are the rabbits of the high country.

CORDOVA PASS: See Apishapa Pass.

CORONA PASS: Railroad name for Rollins Pass. According to Edward T. Bollinger in *Rails That Climb*, it was selected by Joe Culbertson for Time Card Number One, designating the Moffat Line station at the top of the pass. See Rollins Pass also.

COTTONWOOD PASS (12,126), CD — Buena Vista area, west, Sawatch Range. Superb gravel road climbs 4326 feet in twenty miles from Buena Vista to top. Descent of 2618 vertical feet in twelve miles to Taylor Reservoir road. Middle fork of Cottonwood Creek (Arkansas)–Texas Creek (Gunnison) drainages. Present summer road, following old wagon road, was opened by Forest Service and counties concerned in September, 1959. Tremendous scenery.

COTTONWOOD PASS (8904) — A nine-mile shortcut off U.S. Route 40, bypassing Granby, crosses this low pass on way to Hot Sulphur Springs. This was part of the old stage route from Denver to Middle Park over Berthoud Pass from 1874 on.

COTTONWOOD PASS (8300) — Glenwood Springs area. From U.S. Route 24 at Gypsum, back road takes off southwesterly to arrive at Cattle Creek community and then Glenwood Springs, thus bypassing Glenwood Canyon. Before U.S. 24 was put through Glenwood Canyon in 1937, this Cottonwood Pass road was widely used.

CRYSTAL PASS: See Schofield Pass.

CUCHARAS PASS (9994) — Walsenburg area, southwest, Sangre de Cristo Range. State Route 12, a bit narrow and steep in spots, crosses pass on run from Stonewall to La Veta, thirty-three miles. Purgatoire-Huerfano drainages. From top of pass, the Apishapa Pass road branches off easterly. Cucharas Pass is the place to go to see the Spanish Peaks from the west. Cucharas: Spanish for "spoon."

CUMBERLAND PASS (12,200) — Tincup Pass area, southwest, Sawatch Range. Good, narrow, twisty summer road runs from Tincup, mining town turned resort, south to Pitkin. Willow Creek–Quartz Creek (Gunnison) drainages. Pass is two miles west of CD. One of the great circular high drives of the Rockies for standard cars runs from Buena Vista over Cottonwood, Cumberland, Wuanita, Black Sage and Old Monarch passes and then back to Buena Vista. It takes time, though.

CUMBRES PASS (10,022) — Wolf Creek Pass area, south, San Juan Range. State Route 17, a splendid, thrilling, twisty gravel road, ignored by average tourist, crosses pass from Chama, New Mexico to Antonito, Colorado, fifty-one miles, summer only. The route includes interesting La Manga Pass (10,230). Magnificent scenery, with fascinating views of Denver and Rio Grand narrow-gauge curling above and below road. The large areas of grassland on top were caused by the Osier Mountain timber fire (1879) when 26,000 forest acres were destroyed. The heat was so intense that plant reproduction is still retarded. Cumbres Pass is on the divide between the Wolf Creek Branch of Chama River and the Los Pinos River branch of the Rio Grande. The Chama is a Rio Grande branch too and so the pass is entirely within the Rio Grande watershed. The CD, marked by Chama Peak, runs about eleven miles west of Cumbres Pass. Present highway dates from 1920's, railroad from 1880. Cumbres: Spanish for "crests."

CUNNINGHAM PASS: A Hayden Survey party name for Stony Pass, 1873.

CURECANTI PASS (10,600) — Gunnison area, west, West Elk Range. Summer horse trail used by stock men ascends Curecanti Creek from road end to pass. On north side, trail goes down Coal Creek to Kebler Pass road at Anthracite Creek. Curecanti Creek–Anthracite Creek drainages. Curecanti was a popular Ute sub-chief of the 1870's who happened to be a twin.

CURRANT CREEK PASS (9300) — Colorado Springs area, southwest, West Pikes Peak country. From Parkdale (U.S. Route 50) just west of Canon City, good road runs over pass to Hartsel in South Park, sixty miles. Road dates from 1859 and follows ancient Indian and game trail to South Park from the Arkansas.

DAISY PASS (11,500) — Crested Butte area, west, Ruby Range. Summer trail crosses pass in rugged rimrock terrain six miles north of Kebler Pass. Slate Creek drainage.

DALLAS DIVIDE (8735) — Ouray area, northwest. State Route 62 leaves U.S. Route 550 at Ridgway and runs up to enchanting Telluride by way of divide, forty miles. Dallas Creek (Uncompahgre)–Leopard Creek (San Miguel) drainages. This beautiful road was built originally in the 1880's by Otto Mears. Dallas Divide, named for George M. Dallas, United States Vice President, 1845–1849, has been called Leopard Creek Divide.

DEAD MAN HILL DIVIDE (10,288) — Fort Collins area, northwest. From Red Feather Lakes resort, good road runs through lodgepole and aspen over divide to the splendid Laramie River Valley, with fine views of the Never Summer Range to the south. North Fork, Cache la Poudre–Laramie River drainages. General William Ashley crossed to the Laramie in this vicinity in February, 1825.

DENVER PASS (12,200) — Ouray area, southeast, San Juan Range. From Animas Forks above Silverton, 4WD road continues up North Fork past Denver Bridge and Denver Hill to top of pass beyond London Mine and descends to Mineral Point ghost town and on down Mineral Creek to U.S. Route 550 above Ouray. Animas River–Mineral Creek (Uncompahgre) drainages. Overwhelmingly spectacular country and center for 4WD trips from Ouray and Silverton over Engineer, Yvonne and Cinnamon passes to Lake City.

DENVER PASS (12,920) — Ouray area southeast, San Juan Range. From Denver Bridge near Mineral Point, trail crosses range to Hurricane Basin and Schafer Gulch to meet Yvonne Pass road above Rose's Cabin. Animas River (Colorado)–Henson Creek (Gunnison) drainages. Pass shown on U.S.G.S. Handies Peak Quad.

DEVIL'S THUMB PASS (11,700), CD — Nederland area, west, Front Range. Fair 4WD road, partly in creek, runs from Eldora up Jasper Creek to Jasper Lake and then steep trail to top. Trail down west side reaches road east of Fraser. Middle fork of Boulder Creek (South Platte)–Ranch Creek and Cabin Creek (Colorado) drainages. David Moffat surveyed pass for railroad in 1902. Named for distinctive thumb of rock sticking up above skyline near pass and visible from far away.

DIFFICULT PASS (12,400) — Aspen area, south, Elk Range. Pass reached by 4WD from top of Taylor Pass northeasterly and around east summit of Gold Hill, three miles. From top, old wagon road trail descends Difficult Creek to Roaring Fork road above Aspen. Trail was noted by Hayden men, 1873–1874.

DIVIDE: See Ute Pass, Colorado Springs area.

DOUGLAS PASS (8268) — From Loma on U.S. Route 6–50 west of Grand Junction, gravel road, steep and winding in spots, crosses Roan Plateau northward by this pass where Ute pictographs have been seen. Distance from Loma to Rangely is seventy-five miles. Salt Creek (Colorado River)–Douglas Creek (White River) drainages. Father Escalante used this crossing September 8, 1776. Road dates from 1884. Named for White River Ute Chief Douglas, whose men murdered Indian agent Nathan Meeker and his staff near present Meeker town in September, 1879.

EAGLE PASS (11,700) — Durango area, northwest, La Plata Range. From Hesperus on U.S. Route 160 west of Durango, road runs north to La Plata. From there, 4WD trail continues easterly up Lewis Creek and over pass just south of Lewis Mountain to Junction Creek drainage and on down southeasterly to Durango. Near La Plata, the 4WD road running north goes to Cumberland basin and Kennebec Pass. This is all old mining country.

EAGLE RIVER PASS (11,000) — Tennessee Pass area, northeast. From booming Kokomo and Robinson mining camps, shortcut trail in 1870's ran south of Sheep Mountain and down East Fork, Eagle River, to Redcliff.

EAST MAROON PASS (11,800) — Crested Butte area, northeast, Elk Range. From Gothic, popular horseback trail (old Gothic–Aspen wagon road) ascends Cooper Creek past Cooper Lake to top and down East Maroon Creek to Maroon Creek road and Aspen. Gunnison–Roaring Fork drainages. North side of pass is in beautiful Maroon–Snowmass Wild area (no motors).

EAST PASS: Lieutenant E. H. Ruffner's name for Spring Creek Pass, 1873.

EAST RIVER PASS: See Schofield Pass.

ELECTRIC PASS (13,200) — Aspen area, southwest. From end of Ashcroft road out of Aspen at Pine Creek, Panorama Horseback Trail (very steep and beautiful) runs west past Cathedral Lake, over high pass to American Lake and on down to Conundrum Creek trail in Maroon–Snowmass Wild area. Roaring Fork drainage. Miners used trail in 1880's. Pass was named by Ranger Len Shoemaker in 1920's after escaping severe electric shock on Electric Peak during storm.

ELKHEAD PASS (13,200) — Buena Vista area, northwest, Sawatch Range, Collegiate Group. From Clear Creek road at old Vicksburg ghost town, fine hiking trail with ruins and waterfalls ascends Missouri Creek to pass on east side of Missouri Mountain (14,067) and down Pine Creek to U.S. Route 24, nineteen miles. Trail passes around Mount Belford (14,196) and Mount Oxford (14,153) with Mount Harvard (14,420) and Mount Columbia (14,071) just to the southeast. A perfect way to meet the Ivy League of 14,000-footers. Arkansas drainage.

ELKHORN PASS: Common name for Gore Pass in 1860's.

ELLWOOD PASS (11,775), CD — Wolf Creek Pass area, south, San Juan Range. From Stunner, good 4WD road (passable even by regular car) ascends Alamosa Creek to Pass-Me-By Mine and Schinzel Meadow to top. Padlocked gate prevents passage by 4WD down west side along East Fork, San Juan River, to Sand Creek campground and U.S. Route 160. Ellwood ghost town, said to be Archuleta County's first P. O. (1882), was just over the top of the pass on the west side. Though high, Ellwood Pass has a peculiarly peaceful and pastoral aspect, with sheep all over the place in summer, their bells tinkling. It was named in 1879 by a prospector, T. L. Woodvale (L-wood).

EMPIRE PASS: See Union Pass under Colorado Passes.

ENGINEER PASS (12,800) — Ouray area, southeast, San Juan Range. You can call this a pass if you want to but it seems like just going over Engineer Mountain by a 4WD cutoff from the somewhat less frightening Yvonne Pass 4WD road which swings around the shoulder of the mountain just north of it. These two unique 4WD roads take you from U.S. Route 550 near Ouray up the Uncompahgre and Mineral Creek to Mineral Point, over Engineer to American Flats, and down Henson Creek past Rose's Cabin and the ghost town of Capitol City to Lake City. Mineral Creek (Uncompahgre)–Henson Creek (Lake Fork of the Gunnison) drainages. Colorado watershed.

FALL CREEK PASS (12,500) — Tennessee Pass area, northwest, Sawatch Range. Rugged high trail starts at end of Tigiwon road near U.S. Route 24 and runs up Notch Mountain Creek and Fall Creek eight miles to pass, below and south of Mount of the Holy Cross (13,996). Trail descends then past Seven Sisters and Hunky Dory Lake to Holy Cross City (ghost town) and on down French Creek to Homestake Creek road at Gold Park. Pass is inside Camp Hale United States Military Reservation. Eagle River drainage, Colorado watershed.

FALL RIVER PASS (11,796) — Rocky Mountain National Park. Top, a mile west of Chapin Pass, is now a museum-lunch area on Trail Ridge Road. Formerly it was on the old Fall River road across Rocky Mountain National Park which ran upstream instead of along ridge between Fall River and Forest Canyon Creek. Trail Ridge Road's highest point (12,183) is near Iceberg Lake, making it the highest federal highway in the United States. Old Fall River Pass road was opened in September, 1918. Cache la Poudre–Big Thompson drainages, South Platte watershed.

FANCY PASS (11,550) — Tennessee Pass area, northwest, Sawatch Range. From Holy Cross City, high, spectacular rugged 4WD road crosses saddle to Fancy Lake and on down Fancy Creek to Gold Park ghost town at junction of French Creek and Homestake Creek. This fascinating old mining area is reached from U.S. Route 24 up Homestake Creek. Eagle River drainage, Colorado watershed.

FISH PASS: See Apishapa Pass.

FLY PASS: See Mosca Pass.

FOREST CANYON PASS (*ca.* 11,500) — Rocky Mountain National Park just east of Milner Pass.

FREMONT PASS (11,318), CD — Tennessee Pass area. State Route 91 crosses pass, Leadville to Dillon. Top is occupied by world's largest molybdenum mine — Bartlett Mountain in other words — belonging to American Metal Climax Company. This chromium group metal is used with carbon to form steel-like alloys. Two narrow-gauge railroads, Denver and Rio Grande and Denver and South Park, were built over pass in 1880's. Also called Tenmile Pass, Alicante Pass. Alicante Mine was just south of summit near present Climax. East Fork, Arkansas River–Tenmile Creek (Blue) drainage. Arkansas–Colorado watersheds. Named for John Charles Frémont, who never crossed it but did cross Hoosier Pass to the east on his return from California in 1844, and Tennessee Pass to the west on his way to California in 1845.

FRENCH PASS (12,057), CD — Boreas Pass area, east, Front Range. Trail branches off left from Georgia Pass 4WD road and runs northwest up French Creek to top, descending French Gulch to Breckenridge. Roads from U.S. Route 285 to French and Georgia Pass trails start near Jefferson. Named in early 1860's for French Pete, French–Canadian in French Gulch. Michigan Creek–Blue River drainages, South Platte–Colorado watersheds.

FRYING PAN PASS: Hayden Survey name in 1873 for Hagerman Pass.

GEORGIA PASS (11,598), CD — Boreas Pass area, east. From end of Jefferson–Michigan Creek road, 4WD road runs north to top (left fork near top to avoid caved-in old wagon road). Hard-to-find sidling descent (bear left) goes down South Fork, Swan River, to Tiger ghost town and old Georgia Gulch–American Gulch mining area. Spectacular views at top of South Park and closeup summit of Mount Guyot (13,370).

GOLDEN GATE PASS (*ca.* 8400) — On historic old Golden Gate Canyon road from Golden to Central City via Guy Hill and Guy Gulch. Clear Creek drainage.

GOOD PASS: King Survey name for Willow Creek Pass, 1870's.

GORE PASS (9527) — Kremmling area, northwest, Gore Range. From U.S. Route 40, State Route 84 forks west and over pass to Toponas in beautiful Egeria Park. Formerly the main route from Middle Park to Yampa River Valley, now replaced by Rabbit Ears Pass route. The name recalls the fabulous English sportsman of the 1850's, Sir George Gore, who is said to have hunted in the region.

GOTHIC PASS: Early-day name for Schofield Pass.

GRANITE PASS (11,905) — Rocky Mountain National Park. On trail from north slope, Longs Peak, to Bear Lake road end. Alpine Brook–Glacier Creek drainages. South Platte watershed.

GRASSY GAP (7050) — Steamboat Springs area, Gore Range. On ancient trail from Middle Park (Gore Pass) to Yampa (Bear) River through Oak Creek and Twenty Mile Park. Good back road. Grassy Creek–Fish Creek drainages. Colorado watershed.

GRIZZLY PASS (13,093), CD — Georgetown area, Front Range.

From Loveland Pass highway, road and then trail ascends Quail Creek and Grizzly Gulch to end short of high pass. Surveyed for various roads and railroads in 1880's and 1890's, but nothing ever got over it. Also called Quail Pass, Irwin Pass. Clear Creek–Blue River drainages. South Platte–Colorado watersheds.

GUANELLA PASS (11,500) — Georgetown area, Front Range. From Georgetown, a most pleasant back road ascends South Clear Creek to pass and down Duck and Geneva creeks to Grant at U.S. Route 285. Fine views of CD west. There is a ski area near top, reached in winter from Grant. South Platte watershed. Named for the old Guanella family of Georgetown. Road was built by Byron Guanella of Empire.

GUNNISON'S PASS: See Poncha Pass.

GUNSHOT PASS: See Gunsight Pass.

GUNSIGHT PASS (8332) — Rabbit Ears Pass area, east. Pass reached on private trail from U.S. Route 40 ten miles north of Kremmling. Muddy Creek–Troublesome drainages, Colorado watershed.

GYPSUM GAP (6000) — Montrose area, west, Uncompahgre Plateau. Gap is west of Gladel on sixty-two-mile back road, Dove Creek to Naturita. Disappointment–Gypsum Creek drainages of Dolores River, Colorado watershed. Father Escalante and friends passed near Gypsum Gap on way from Dolores to Uncompahgre River in 1776.

HAGERMAN PASS (12,050), CD — Leadville area, west, Sawatch Range. Wide scenic road from Leadville ascends south fork of Lake Fork of Arkansas past Turquoise Lake to Carlton Tunnel entrance at 10,944 feet, now used by private water company for diversion, beneath pass. This tunnel, first called the Busk-Ivanhoe Tunnel, was built for the Colorado Midland Railroad, replacing Hagerman Tunnel higher up at 11,528 feet. James J. Hagerman was head of the road, the highest standard-gauge carrier in the United States during its Hagerman Tunnel period. The zigzagging caved-in roadbed can still be seen above the Carlton Tunnel entrance. In 1917, Albert E. Carlton, the Colorado Springs mining man, bought the Colorado Midland, dismantled it, and opened the renamed Carlton Tunnel in 1924 for cars running on the roadbed from Leadville to Basalt. The tunnel was closed finally in the mid-1930's. For some reason it was always misspelled on maps, "Carleton Tunnel." Before the Colorado Midland was built in 1887, a foot trail ran over the pass. Today, a restricted passage has been made for equipment in construction of the Frying Pan Water Diversion project and Denver–Grand Junction power line. This passage can be used by 4WD cars. On the west side, fair road runs almost from Carlton Tunnel entrance down Frying Pan to Basalt. Arkansas-Colorado drainages.

HALFMOON PASS (12,400) — Creede area, northeast, San Juan Range. Pass is reached by horseback in utter wilderness from Creede up Wheeler Monument–Famous Creek trail. On east side, trail descends south fork, Saguache Creek, to Sky City ghost town. Wheeler National Monument of strange rock forms, abandoned through lack of patronage, is two miles south of Halfmoon Pass, named for high, broad half-moon in high ridge as seen from north. Rio Grande–Saguache Creek drainages.

HALFMOON PASS (11,551) — Tennessee Pass area, northwest, Sawatch Range. Trail over pass runs from Notch Mountain Creek (Fall

Creek Pass trail) to East Cross Creek on north side of Mount of the Holy Cross. Eagle River drainage, Colorado watershed.

HALFMOON PASS (10,300) — Leadville area, southwest. Old stock driveway crosses this saddle between Mount Elbert and Mount Massive. Reached from Halfmoon Creek road end southwest of Malta. Arkansas watershed.

HAMILTON PASS: One of Hayden's names for Breckenridge (Boreas) Pass.

HANCOCK PASS: See Williams Pass, new.

HANDCART PASS: See Webster Pass.

HANKINS PASS (10,000) — Colorado Springs area, northwest. Tarryall Mountains. Hiking trail crosses pass from Tarryall Dude Ranch to Cheesman Lake. Tarryall River–Lost Park Creek drainages, South Platte watershed.

HARDSCRABBLE PASS (9000) — Westcliffe area, east, Wet Mountains. Good road, State Route 96, runs from Wetmore over this ancient crossing to Westcliffe. Hardscrabble Creek–Oak Creek drainages, Arkansas watershed. Road served Querida and Rosita mining camps of 1870's–1880's.

Of this pass the great Colorado poet, Thomas Hornsby Ferril, has written in part:

> I stopped my car
> On the hump of Hardscrabble Pass up Hardscrabble Creek
> To stare across the blue Wet Mountain Valley
> And listen to the far-off sawtooth snag
> Of the Sangre de Cristo Mountains ripping slabs
> Of purple from the sky and letting them fall
> All purple over purple long ago.

HARTMAN DIVIDE (8500) — Kremmling area, southwest. From near Kremmling, quite scary shelf road crosses this divide on way to State Bridge and Wolcott. Slippery if wet. Colorado watershed.

HARVEY GAP (6400) — Glenwood Springs–Rifle area. On south side of Harvey Gap Reservoir, north from U.S. Route 6 at Silt.

HAYDEN DIVIDE: See Ute Pass, Colorado Springs area.

HAYDEN PASS (10,780) — Poncha Pass area, southeast, Sangre de Cristo Range. From Coaldale on U.S. Route 50, good 4WD road runs over pass to Villa Grove at extreme north end, San Luis Valley. Hayden Creek (Arkansas)–Hayden Pass Creek (San Luis Creek) drainages. A popular 1880's wagon road connected the Wet Mountain mining camps to the Bonanza area west of Villa Grove by means of this pass. Named for a Texas Creek settler.

HEPBURN'S PASS (10,700) — Kenosha Pass area, north. From Hall Valley on old Webster Pass road, the Geneva Park trail cuts across at or near this pass to Geneva Creek and the Grant–Guanella Pass road. North Fork of South Platte–Geneva Creek drainages. Charley Hepburn's Ranch was a popular Hall Valley stopping place in 1880's.

HERMOSA MOUNTAIN PASS: See Barlow Creek Pass.

HILLTOP: Railroader's name for top of Trout Creek Pass.

HOODOO GAP (10,200) — Crested Butte area, southwest, West Elk

Range. Gap is at head of Hoodoo Creek two miles south of Mount Gunnison and two miles northeast of Minnesota Pass. North Fork, Gunnison River drainage.

HOOSIER PASS (11,541), CD — Division point between Sawatch and Front ranges. From Alma, State Route 9 runs north over pass and down Blue River to Breckenridge, nineteen miles. South Platte (source)–Blue River (source) drainages, South Platte–Colorado watersheds. A historic and delightful drive past Mount Lincoln (14,284) and Quandary Peak (14,252) on west, Mount Silverheels (13,835) on east. John Charles Frémont crossed it June 22, 1844, and homesick Indiana prospectors named it about 1860.

HOOSIER PASS (10,315) — Colorado Springs area, on Pikes Peak. From Cripple Creek town, road runs up past Mollie Kathleen mine and over Hoosier Pass to ghost towns of Altman and Grassy. West Beaver Creek–Cripple Creek drainages, Arkansas watershed. The Short Line Railroad had station at Hoosier Pass in 1900's.

HORSESHOE PASS (*ca.* 13,000) — On Mosquito Range crest six miles south of Mosquito Pass. Hardy hikers used it in 1880's on shortcut route from Twin Lakes to Fairplay by Union Gulch road and up Empire Gulch over top to Horseshoe Lake just south of Mount Sheridan (13,700). Arkansas–South Platte watersheds. Named for striking horseshoe of Horseshoe Mountain (13,902).

HUNCHBACK PASS (12,487), CD — Stony Pass area, San Juan Range. From Pole Creek–Bear Creek junction of 4WD Stony Pass road west of Rio Grande Reservoir, 4WD road ascends Bear Creek to Beartown ghost town and then foot trail to top of pass and down Vallecito Creek to Vallecito Reservoir Road and Bayfield. Bear Creek–Vallecito Creek drainages, Rio Grande–San Juan River (Colorado) watersheds. A wild gateway to spectacular Grenadier and Needle Mountains. Hayden's men crossed it in 1870's.

HUNTERS' PASS: See Independence Pass, Bottle Pass.

ICEBERG PASS (11,827) — Rocky Mountain National Park. Clyde and Chloe Edmondson, in their *Mountain Passes*, point out that Trail Ridge Road *dips* rather than rises to cross this pass near Iceberg Lake.

ILLINOIS PASS (10,000), CD — Willow Creek Pass area, Rabbit Ears Range. From Middle Park side of Willow Creek Pass, road and then trail runs over pass to Willow Creek Pass road again in North Park near Rand. Willow Creek–Jack Creek drainages, Colorado–North Platte watersheds.

IMOGENE PASS (13,114) — Ouray area, southwest, San Juan Range. I turn this matter over to my old friend David Lavender who grew up in Telluride and wrote a fine book about it, *One Man's West*. "Imogene Pass is confusing. The main trail went from Camp Bird Mine above Ouray through Imogene Basin and crossed at close to 13,000 feet (if memory serves) into Savage Basin and thence via the Tomboy Mine to Telluride. At the top you could also go on south to Red Mountain Pass and Silverton, or swing into Ingram Basin and so down to Telluride. One of the early and most dramatic high-tension electric lines crossed in the area. The Imogene trail got some notoriety in 1901 when Smuggler Mine strikebreakers were run out of the region by it. The pass divides Canyon Creek and Savage Creek drainages, Colorado watershed. Some 4WDs are getting across eastward these days by the Ingram Basin route past the beautiful Bridal Veil Falls. Imogene was somebody's girl, probably."

INDEPENDENCE PASS (12,095), CD — Aspen area, east, Sawatch Range. Wide, dusty, sometimes rough but always dramatic road runs from U.S. Route 24 and Twin Lakes to eerie top well above timberline. Descent to Aspen is steeper, with a scary, narrow shelf sector. Passing through tremendous peaks, Independence is the third highest summer road for standard cars in the Rockies, after Cumberland Pass road (12,200), and Trail Ridge Road (12,183), both in Colorado also. Superb scenery — Elk Mountains west, Sawatch Range all around. First crude road went over in 1881. From Buena Vista, this pass route is 120 miles shorter to Aspen than U.S. 24 over Tennessee Pass to Glenwood Springs and then back to Aspen. Named for Independence ghost town on west side, begun July 4, 1879. Called Hunters' Pass before that. Lake Creek–Roaring Fork drainages, Arkansas–Colorado watersheds.

INDIAN CAMP PASS (9175) — Glenwood Springs area, Flattop country. From end of Deep Lake Road (reached from U.S. Route 24 at Dotsero), hunters' trail crosses pass and runs down to road end, South Fork, White River. Colorado watershed. Pass was on old Ute route from Colorado River to White River.

INDIAN CREEK PASS (9775) — La Veta Pass area, Sangre de Cristo Range. From East Indian Creek road end southwest of La Veta town, trail runs over pass and down West Indian Creek on private land into San Luis Valley. Cucharas River–Rio Grande drainages. Pass is just south of D. & R. G.'s Veta Pass.

IRWIN PASS: Another name for Grizzly Pass. Richard Irwin, with William A. Hamill and Eben Smith, planned Georgetown–Breckenridge wagon road over this pass in 1867.

JACK'S CABIN PASS (9000) — Crested Butte area, east. Good road runs over pass from Taylor Reservoir road west to Jack's Cabin on Crested Butte road. East River–Taylor River (Gunnison) drainages.

JEFFERSON PASS: Occasional name in 1860's for Georgia Pass.

JONES PASS (12,453), CD — Berthoud Pass area, Front Range. From U.S. Route 40 at east foot of Berthoud Pass, good 4WD road twists and climbs past ghost towns to spectacular top. West descent reaches Bobtail Mine near Williams Fork River, three miles, where road ends. It is used to service Jones Pass Tunnel of Denver water system through CD. Vasquez Pass is five miles northeast of Jones along curving crest. West Clear Creek–Williams Fork River drainages, South Platte–Colorado watersheds. Named for the early Empire mill tycoon and road promoter, John S. Jones.

KEBLER PASS (10,000) — Crested Butte area, west, Ruby Range, Elk Mountains. From Crested Butte, State Route 135 runs up Coal Creek on old D. & R. G. grade to pass near Ruby–Irwin ghost towns and on west forty-three miles more to Paonia and the North Fork (Gunnison) fruit county. Connecting back roads run from Kebler road south over Ohio Pass to Gunnison, north over McClure Pass to Carbonadale and Aspen. Gunnison–Colorado watershed. Pass named for J. A. Kebler, associate of the Redstone coal magnate, John C. Osgood.

KENNEBEC PASS (12,000) — Durango area, northwest, La Plata

Range. From U.S. Route 160 at Hesperus, road runs north through La Plata Canyon to La Plata ghost town, where 4WD road continues north (an east road goes to Eagle Pass) to multicolored flagstones at Kennebec Pass and Cumberland Basin. Here 4WD routes to various diggings run in all directions. One of them westerly is the Bear Creek Trail to Rico–Lizard Head Pass highway. La Plata River–Dolores River drainages.

KENOSHA PASS (9950) — From Denver, U.S. Route 285 crosses pass into South Park, paralleling historic gold rush route from 1860 on. Named for Kenosha, Wisconsin, home of Clark Herbert, a Kenosha Pass stage driver, according to J. Frank Dawson in his *Place Names in Colorado*. Pass was called Kenosha Hill or Kenosha Summit in mining days.

LAKE PASS: See Black Forest Divide.

LAKE PASS (12,226), CD — Independence Pass area, south, Sawatch Range. From Twin Lakes town and Independence Pass road, rough, steep, badly sidling 4WD road runs up south fork of Lake Creek to top of pass in tremendous cirque. Descent by foot trail only down west side to Taylor Reservoir and ghost towns of Pieplant and Dorchester. Same 4WD road up south fork leads also to near top of a Red Mountain Pass. Lake Creek–Red Mountain Creek (Gunnison) drainages, Arkansas–Colorado watersheds. Ute trail crossed Lake Pass, and wagon road from 1882–1900.

LA MANGA PASS (10,230) — On stunning Cumbres Pass road, State Route 17, Chama, New Mexico, to Antonito, Colorado. Los Pinos River–Conejos River drainages. See Cumbres Pass. La Manga: Spanish for "sleeve."

LA POUDRE PASS (10,192), CD — Grand Lake area, north, Never Summer Range, Medicine Bow Mountains. From Cameron Pass road near Chambers Lake, rough service road runs past Long Draw Reservoir almost to top of pass, sixteen miles. Trail descends south side past Lulu City ghost town to foot of Milner Pass on U.S. Route 34, five miles. This remarkable La Poudre crossing marks the extreme headwaters of both the Cache la Poudre River and Colorado River. During Lulu City boom, 1879–1881, Fort Collins stage arrived there thrice weekly by way of La Poudre Pass wagon road.

LA SALLE PASS (9733) — Pikes Peak area, west. From west foot of Wilkerson Pass in South Park, most pleasant back road runs north and east from U.S. Route 24 past Martland Peak through aspen and pine over pass to Thorpe Gulch and upper road to Tarryall River. South Platte–Tarryall drainage. From near pass, Forest Service road climbs Badger Mountain to lookout, four miles. La Salle Pass was on a main route to South Park in the 1860's.

LA VETA PASS (9383) — Sangre de Cristo Range. From Walsenburg, U.S. Route 160 runs west over pass to Fort Garland in San Luis Valley, fifty miles. South La Veta Creek (Cucharas)–Sangre de Cristo Creek (Rio Grande) drainages. Former roadbed, Denver and Rio Grande Railroad, including recently abandoned "Muleshoe" around Dump Mountain. New five-mile section runs straight to top from east foot — easier but less picturesque and historic. Railroad now crosses range at another pass (Veta) eight miles south. Travelers should visit San Francisco Fort Museum (1862) at La Veta town, east side (short detour), and Old Fort Garland on west side (1858). La Veta Pass is the modern equivalent of Sangre de Cristo Pass, used from Spanish times, the road of which is the same as the La Veta highway on the west side. Veta: Spanish for "vein," referring to coal, et cetera, in area.

LEOPARD CREEK DIVIDE: See Dallas Divide.

LEROUX PASS: See Cochetopa Pass.

LIZARD HEAD PASS (10,222) — Rico–Telluride area, San Miguel Range. From Rico, State Route 145 climbs in thirteen easy miles to top and descends more steeply to Rico in five miles. Pass marks extreme headwaters of Dolores River (south) and San Miguel River, both tributaries of the Colorado, and the San Miguel Range is centered on this division. A trail crossed it at least as early as 1833, a wagon road in the 1870's, and the Rio Grande Southern Railroad in the 1890's — Dolores to Telluride to Ridgway, marked by snowsheds at the top and the celebrated Ophir Trestle a bit north of the pass. Lizard Head Peak (13,156), said to be the toughest climb in Colorado, was conquered in 1920 by Albert Ellingwood. Lizard Head name derives from peak's odd shape.

LONG DRAW PASS: See La Poudre Pass.

LONG'S PASS: Early name for Ute Pass, Colorado Springs area.

LOS PINOS PASS (11,100) — Cochetopa Pass area, southwest, San Juan Range. From Cochetopa Pass road, pleasant lonely lane runs southward past old Los Pinos Ute Agency over pass and then over Slumgullion Pass to Lake City, sixty miles. Wooded hills are lovely and fishing is good. Los Pinos Creek–Cathedral Creek drainages, Gunnison–Colorado watershed.

LOST MAN PASS (12,350), CD — Independence Pass area, Sawatch Range. Trail from Independence Pass road just below Independence ghost town runs north up Lost Man Creek to Lost Man Lake and pass, six miles. Descent to highway again, four miles. Pass links Roaring Fork drainage but is practically on CD crest four miles north of Independence. Retired Ranger Len Shoemaker reports that name resulted because Billy Koch took wrong branch of Roaring Fork on way from Aspen to Leadville.

LOU CREEK PASS (10,260) — Ouray area, northeast, San Juan Range. From U.S. Route 550 near Colona, road ascends Deer Creek or Cow Creek drainage and becomes Lou Creek trail over pass to Cimarron Creek road, which runs down to U.S. 50. Lou Creek (Uncompahgre)–Cimarron Creek (Gunnison) drainages, Colorado watershed. Pass is between Owl Creek and Monument passes.

LOVELAND PASS (11,992), CD — Georgetown area, west, Front Range. Magnificent highway, U.S. Route 6, winds up easy grades sixteen miles from Georgetown past Loveland Ski Area to spectacular summit and past Arapaho Ski Area on descent to Dillon Reservoir. This road is being bypassed by Interstate 70 through Straight Creek Tunnel starting at Loveland Ski Area but will continue in service. Clear Creek–North Fork, Snake River drainages, South Platte–Colorado watersheds. One of the most beautiful of high roads, dating from late 1870's in various forms.

LULU PASS (11,400), CD — Grand Lake area, north, Never Summer Range. From U.S. Route 34 at west foot of Milner Pass, trail runs north seven miles to top past Lulu ghost town. Eight-mile trail descent into North Park brings you to Silver Creek road or Cameron Pass road. Lulu Creek–Silver Creek drainages, Colorado–North Platte watersheds. Named for Lulu Burnett, daughter of founder of Lulu City (1879), Benjamin Franklin Burnett. Also called Thunder Pass.

LYNX PASS (8960) — Gore Pass area, Gore Range. From Gore Pass road nine miles west of top, pleasant back road runs over Lynx Pass and on to Phippsburg, thirty-two miles. Triple drainage: Toponas and Little Rock Creek (Colorado) and Morrison Creek (Yampa). The lynx is called a bobcat in Colorado.

MCCLURE'S PASS (9500) — Crested Butte area, northwest, Elk Range. From Kebler Pass road, fair road (slippery when wet) crosses pass and descends in steep hairpins to Crystal River and Marble–Redstone–Carbondale road. Gunnison–Crystal River drainages, Colorado watershed. This old-timer was rebuilt for cars in 1940's. Named for Thomas McClure, a developer of the Red McClure potato.

MANZANERES PASS (9800) — La Veta Pass area northwest, Sangre de Cristo Range. From Placer Creek mouth, west side of La Veta Pass (U.S. Route 160), 1880's wagon road ran up Placer Creek seven miles to pass and then six miles down north side to Point of Rocks and Malachite. Placer Creek–Huerfano drainages, Rio Grande–Arkansas watershed. Named for J. M. Manzaneres of Walsenburg.

MARCELLINA PASS (10,325) — Crested Butte area, west, Ruby Range, Elk Mountains. Pass is on easy, scenic State Route 135, six miles west of Kebler Pass, on divide between Anthracite Creek branches (Gunnison).

MARSHALL PASS (10,846), CD — Between Cochetopa and Monarch passes near Ouray Peak (13,955) at start of Sawatch Range. From U.S. Route 285 in Poncha Pass, good road (former Denver and Rio Grande narrow-gauge roadbed) winds to top and descends west side to Sargents (U.S. 50). Road is quite apt to have spots on west side which are impassable except for 4WDs. Poncha Creek–Marshall Creek (Gunnison) drainages, Arkansas–Colorado watersheds. A fascinating trip for narrow-gauge fans, with water tanks, collapsed snowsheds, turntables, brick privies and other rail relics everywhere. Named for Lieutenant William L. Marshall of the army's Wheeler Survey, who discovered it in 1873 while hurrying to Denver from Baker's Park to see a dentist.

MEADOW PASS (10,200) — Wolf Creek Pass area, east. From three miles above South Fork Ranger Station, trail runs up a creek past and east of Grouse and Cattle Mountains and over Meadow Pass to Park Creek. Rio Grande watershed.

MEDANO PASS (9900) — La Veta Pass area, northwest, Sangre de Cristo Range. From Bradford, a bare spot on Westcliffe–Gardner road, 4WD trail winds through ranches and up very steep, very rough slope to woody top of pass, twelve miles, descending Medano Creek (good fishing) on west side ten miles to Great Sand Dunes National Monument. Lowest three miles is *on* Medano Creek as it runs, visibly at first, through thick sand and then disappears. Sand stretch passable only in low-low gear with some air let out of tires. Bluff Creek–Muddy Creek–Huerfano drainage, east side, Medano on west. Zebulon Pike and his men crossed Medano in January, 1807. Also called Modenos Pass, Sandhill Pass, Sandy Hill Pass, Pike's Gap, Williams Pass (after Old Bill Williams). Medano: Spanish for "sand dune."

MIDDLE PARK PASS: Occasional named used in 1870's for Willow Creek Pass.

MILNER PASS (10,759), CD — Rocky Mountain National Park. Famous Trail Ridge Road (U.S. Route 34) follows old Indian ridge trail more or less from Estes Park over Fall River and Milner passes to Grand Lake, sixty-seven miles. A beautiful, thrilling trip, reaching highest point (12,183) on any United States federal highway. Fall River (South Platte)–Colorado drainages. T. J. Milner was a prominent Colorado railroad and streetcar engineer.

MINNESOTA PASS (9993) — Crested Butte area, southwest, West Elk Range. Summer cattle drive and horse trail runs six miles south up east fork of Minnesota Creek to top of pass and on over Curecanti Pass toward Gunnison River. Minnesota Creek is ascended by road out of Paonia. Gunnison drainages.

MOLAS DIVIDE (10,902) — Silverton area, south, San Juan Range. Divide is crossed by spectacular Durango–Silverton part of Million Dollar Highway, U.S. Route 550. Lime Creek–Animas River drainages, Colorado watershed. Named for moles in moist ground of Molas Lake.

MONARCH PASS (11,312), CD — Sawatch Range. Splendid highway, U.S. Route 50, crosses this beautiful pass from Salida to Gunnison. South Arkansas River–Agate Creek (Gunnison) drainages, Arkansas–Colorado watersheds. Present route (1939) replaced Old Monarch Pass route (1922) which in turn had replaced Old Old Monarch Pass wagon road of 1880. The name Monarch derived from the 1880's Monarch mining camp in the pass near the present east-side limestone quarry.

MONUMENT PASS (11,006) — Ouray area, northeast, San Juan Range. Trail from Deer Creek road runs a mile below west side of this trail-less pass on way to Lou Creek and Owl Creek passes. Deer Creek (Uncompahgre)–Cimarron Creek (Gunnison).

MONTEZUMA PASS: David H. Moffat's name for Webster Pass when he surveyed it for a railroad in early 1890's.

MOSCA PASS (9713) — La Veta Pass area, northwest. Good 4WD road from Red Wing west of Gardner climbs ten miles through huge alpine valley of Huerfano to aspen-pine top. After two miles of west-side descent, old wagon road, which used to run down to sand dunes at Great Sand Dunes National Monument, is blocked. May Creek (Huerfano)–Mosca Creek drainages. Like Sangre de Cristo Pass, Mosca Pass has had a lively history since eighteenth century, and comes up frequently still in plans for a shortcut highway from Alamosa to Pueblo. Mosca: Spanish for "fly." Also called Fly Pass, and Roubideau's Pass, after the trader Antoine Robidoux, who was taking wagons over it at a very early period.

MOSQUITO PASS (13,188) — Mosquito Range. From State Route 9, 4.4 miles northwest of Fairplay, road forks left past Park City ghost town to South London Mine, eight miles, where 4WD road over pass starts. Very steep climb then for 1.5 miles to American Flats, 1.7 miles across Flats, and final steep brief climb to top. Descent on high frightening shelf down ridge to Leadville road, four miles. From east side, pass can be reached more easily by forking right to North London Mine, and on up to American Flats. Both steep rough 4WD roads go around London Hill (13,160) — some hill! Mosquito Creek (South Platte)–Evans Gulch (Arkansas) drainages. This pass, crossed by a mining camp road in 1880's, is the highest for 4WDs in North America, and one of the most thrilling in the Rockies, with views from the top as far as Mount Sopris — last Rockies peak to the west — and Pikes Peak, at the east edge of the chain. It is nine miles south of CD and thus does not compete with Argentine Pass (13,132), the highest Rockies CD pass. Mosquito Pass, scene of annual Leadville–Fairplay burro race in late July, is used by 4WD from mid-July to mid-September. Some standard cars have crossed it, east to west, via North London Mine. A telephone line was built over it in 1889–1890 and some of the poles are still there, dangling out precariously over the steep slope of the west side.

MUDDY CREEK PASS (8600) — Gore Pass area, northwest. Back road runs from Wolcott–State Bridge road east up Muddy Creek and over pass to Piney Creek and State Bridge road again, fifteen miles. Colorado drainage.

MUDDY CREEK PASS: Lieutenant E. H. Ruffner's name in 1873 for Promontory Divide.

MUDDY PASS (8772), CD — Rabbit Ears Range. From Kremmling, U.S. Route 40 runs to top of pass, from whence secondary road descends into North Park and on north to Walden, while U.S. 40 heads west over Rabbit Ears Pass to Steamboat Springs. Muddy is the lowest CD pass in Colorado. John Charles Frémont crossed it on June 17, 1844. Muddy Creek–Grizzly Creek drainages, Colorado–North Platte watersheds.

MUMMY PASS (11,200) — Rocky Mountain Park, Mummy Range. Pass is on a triple divide formed by drainages of Cascade Creek, South Fork of Cache la Poudre and North Fork, Big Thompson River.

MUSIC PASS (11,800) — Westcliffe area, southwest, Sangre de Cristo Range. Can be crossed by very rough, dangerous 4WD trail (dim) from ranch road end (Hudson Creek) south of Westcliffe and down Sand Creek to San Luis Valley, twenty miles and more. Fine cutthroat trout fishing on hard-to-find Sand Creek Lakes, west side. Named for alleged sighing sound of winds in dunes below, or in caves near pass. The Music Pass of Hayden's 1877 Atlas of Colorado is actually Medano Pass.

NAPOLEON PASS (12,055) — St. Elmo–Tincup Pass area, west, Sawatch Range. Rugged trail from near south foot of Cumberland Pass road runs north up branch of North Quartz Creek over pass and down Middle Willow Creek to Gold Cup Republic Mine road near Tincup. Trail passes under Fitzpatrick Peak (13,124), one half-mile west of CD. Gunnison drainage.

NEW YORK PASS (13,100) — Taylor Pass area, east, Elk Range. From Dorchester ghost town, rugged trail runs eight miles north up Tellurium Creek to top. Descent down New York Gulch to Lincoln Creek road. 4WDs out of Aspen cover some of this area via Lincoln Creek, New York Gulch, Gold Hill and Taylor Pass back to Aspen. Tellurium Creek (Gunnison)–Lincoln Creek (Roaring Fork) drainages.

NINE MILE GAP (7494) — Meeker area, north, Danforth Hills. From Meeker, State Route thirteen runs over gap toward Craig. Curtis Creek (White River)–Good Spring Creek (Yampa) drainages.

NORTH COCHETOPA PASS (10,200), CD — Cochetopa Pass area, one of several ancient crossings in low Cochetopa Hills. A new, shorter, road from Saguache goes over pass to U.S. Route 50 near Parlin, approximating stage route of 1870's. North Cochetopa is also called West Pass Creek Pass.

OHIO PASS (10,033) — Crested Butte area, southwest, West Elk Range. From Gunnison, country road of unusual charm ascends Ohio Creek past Ohio Peak (12,251) and over top to Kebler Pass road, twenty-six miles. Stages ran over this road daily in 1880's to Irwin. On north side of pass, road briefly follows bed of railroad, which ran from Crested Butte to Floresta. Ohio Creek–Anthracite Creek drainages, Gunnison watershed.

OLD MONARCH PASS (11,375), CD — Sawatch Range. From U.S. Route 50, one mile below east side of Monarch Pass, this delightful summer road crosses CD and descends by scenic switchbacks to Tomichi Creek road. Road was main highway from Salida to Gunnison, 1922–1939. South Arkansas–Tomichi Creek (Gunnison) drainages, Arkansas–Colorado watersheds.

OLD OLD MONARCH PASS (11,523), CD — Sawatch Range. This oldest of Monarch Pass roads (4WDs only) takes off two miles short of top of present Monarch Pass, east side, crosses divide and then joins Old Monarch Pass road down the west side.

OPHIR PASS (11,700) — Silverton area, northwest, San Juan Range. From U.S. Route 550, five miles from top of Red Mountain Pass, Silverton side, popular and thrilling 4WD road runs four and a half miles west to top. Steeper west side descent to Ophir ghost town, also four and a half miles. Mineral Creek (Animas River)–San Miguel River drainages, Colorado watershed. Ophir was the Biblical site of King Solomon's mines.

OWL CREEK PASS (10,120) — Ouray area, northeast, San Juan Range. From U.S. Route 550 near Ridgway, fair back road crosses pass easterly by Cow Creek drainage and descends on east side along Cimarron Creek to U.S. Route 50 and Cimarron. Owl Creek–Cow Creek (Uncompahgre) and Cimarron Creek (Gunnison) drainages, Colorado watershed.

PALMER LAKE DIVIDE: See Black Forest Divide.

PASS CREEK PASS (9400) — La Veta Pass area, just north, Sangre de Cristo Range. From Gardner, good back road ascends to join U.S. Route 160 near top of La Veta Pass, which is also very near the top of historic Sangre de Cristo Pass. Pass Creek (Huerfano)–Sangre de Cristo Creek drainages, Arkansas–Rio Grande watersheds.

PASS OF THE RIO DEL NORTE: See Spring Creek Pass.

PAWNEE PASS (12,541), CD — Nederland area, northwest, Front Range, six miles north of Arapaho Pass. Robert Ormes's *Guide to the Colorado Mountains* describes eleven-mile trail "Breadline" from end of Ward road west over Pawnee Pass and down Cascade Creek to Monarch Lake. St. Vrain Creek (South Platte)–Colorado watersheds.

PEARL PASS (12,715) — Crested Butte area, northeast, Elk Range. Long, steep, 4WD road runs from East River road near Crested Butte up Brush and East Brush Creeks to spectacular top, and then down Castle Creek to Ashcroft ghost town. This former wagon road, one of worst in Elks, opened September 7, 1882, but did not last long, reverting to a jack trail by 1885.

PENNOCK PASS (9100) — Fort Collins area, west, Medicine Bows. Pass is crossed by pleasant Buckhorn Creek road from Masonville to Colorado State Forestry Campsite, twenty-nine miles. Big Thompson–Cache la Poudre drainage, South Platte watershed. Probably named for the pioneer, Taylor Pennock.

PIEDRA PASS (11,500), CD — Creede area, southwest, San Juan Range. From Antelope Park on Creede–Lake City road, old wagon road trail runs southward up South River (Red Mountain Creek), through Spar City ghost town fourteen miles to top. Several trails go down south side to wind up at Pagosa Springs and U.S. Route 160. South River (Rio Grande)–Piedra River (San Juan) drainages.

PIKE'S GAP: See Medano Pass.

PINKHAM PASS (8649) — Walden–North Park area. From Walden, State Route 127 and roadbed of Laramie, North Park and Western Railway (U. P.) run north up Pinkham Creek and over pass and down Laramie River drainage to Laramie (road is State Route 230 in Wyoming). After 1878, the U. P. threatened often to extend this railroad over Muddy Creek or Willow Creek passes and on to junction at Dillon with Denver and South Park, which was supposed to connect with the Colorado Central at Georgetown via Loveland Pass.

POMEROY PASS (13,050) — St. Elmo area, south, Sawatch Range. From Pomeroy Gulch up Chalk Creek out of St. Elmo, Pomeroy Lake trail runs steeply over pass around east side of Pomeroy Mountain (13,132) and down North Fork, South Arkansas, to Shavano ghost town, seven miles. Shavano is at top of 4WD road from Maysville and U.S. Route 50. Arkansas watershed.

PONCHA PASS (9011) — Salida area, south, dividing Sangre de Cristo and Sawatch ranges. U.S. Route 285 runs over pass from Salida–Poncha Springs south to Villa Grove and north end of San Luis Valley. Marshall Pass road comes into it from west five miles from Poncha Springs. Poncha: Spanish for "mild." Some say word is a corruption of Ute word for a tobacco plant grown in pass. Also called Gunnison's Pass (Lieutenant Beckwith, 1853), and Puncho Pass (Franklin Rhoda, 1874).

PRAIRIE DIVIDE (7905) — Fort Collins area, northwest. From Livermore and Alford, road runs northwest up north fork of Rabbit Creek and over divide to Black Mountain School, thirty miles. Cache La Poudre drainage.

PROMONTORY DIVIDE (9275) — Westcliffe area, south, Wet Mountain Valley. From Westcliffe, State Route 69 runs south over sandy divide to Gardner, thirty-three miles. A few miles south of divide, road passes Bradford bare spot where Medano Pass 4WD trail comes in from west. Grape Creek (Arkansas)–Muddy Creek (Huerfano) drainages. The Pike party crossed this divide on January 24, 1807, on way to Medano Pass and San Luis Valley.

PTARMIGAN PASS (11,750) — Dillon area, northeast, Williams Fork Mountains. From near relocated Dillon and Straight Creek Tunnel highway, this old Indian trail runs northeast to pass and down to South Fork, Williams River, seven miles. Blue River–Williams River drainage, Colorado watershed.

PTARMIGAN PASS (12,200), CD — Rocky Mountain National Park in wild area near Hallett Peak and Tyndall Glacier. Glacier Creek (Big Thompson)–North Inlet Creek (Colorado) drainages.

PUERTO DE LOS CIBOLAS: Eighteen-century Spanish name for Cochetopa Pass.

QUAIL PASS: See Grizzly Pass.

RABBIT EARS PASS: (9680), CD — Steamboat Springs area, east, Rabbit Ears Range. From Middle Park, U.S. Route 40 runs north from the Western Slope to top of Muddy Pass and then west four miles barely on the Eastern Slope a few hundred feet below CD to cross to the Western Slope again at Rabbit Ears. Colorado–North Platte drainages. Named for famous ears of Rabbit Ears Peak two miles north of pass.

RAILROAD PASS (*ca.* 11,100), CD — Wolf Creek Pass area, southeast, San Juan Range. Game and stock trails cross this easy pass from South Fork, Rio Grande, to Silver Creek and San Juan River.

RATON PASS (7888) — Raton Mountains. Perhaps the most versatile of Rockies passes, with the longest recorded history after La Glorieta. It is crossed from Trinidad to Raton town, New Mexico, by sweeping Interstate 25 and the Santa Fe Railroad's main passenger line. "Uncle Dick" Wooten's old toll road (1865–1878) crossed just west of these and so did a variety of old Spanish trails, trapper trails and the makeshift road used by General Stephen Kearny's conquering Army of the West in 1846. Raton Creek (Purgatoire)–Canadian River drainages, Arkansas watershed. Raton: Spanish for "pack rat." Called Cimarron Pass by General W. J. Palmer, 1867. A chair lift on top carries tourists still higher. Towering eminence above pass is Fishers Peak (9586).

RED DIRT PASS (11,520), CD — Steamboat Springs area, north, Sierra Madre (Park) Range. This obscure pass is one and a half miles north of Ute Pass. North Platte–Yampa drainages.

RED HILL PASS (9993) — Kenosha Pass area, west. Crossed by U.S. Route 285 near Como between Jefferson and Fairplay. Tarryall–South Platte drainages.

RED MOUNTAIN PASS (12,200), CD — Independence Pass area, south, Sawatch–Elk Mountains juncture. From the stark cirque near top of Lake Pass, a rugged trail leaves Lake Pass 4WD road to run south and west around Red Mountain and steeply down the other side to Ruby ghost town and Lincoln Gulch road to Independence Pass road. Trail at crest marks start of Elk Range divide as well as CD. In 1870's–1880's, this cirque was hub of miners' routes to Ruby and Lincoln Gulch, or over Lake Pass to Dorchester and Bowman. Lincoln Gulch (Roaring Fork)–Lake Creek (Arkansas) drainages, Colorado–Arkansas watersheds. Hayden called it Red Rock Pass in 1873.

RED MOUNTAIN PASS (11,018) — San Juan Range. Million Dollar Highway (U.S. Route 550) from Ouray to Silverton crosses this spectacular pass on one of the most unforgettable drives in the Rocky Mountains. Otto Mears's Silverton Railroad crossed same crest (Sheridan Pass) at 11,650 feet from Silverton north as far as Ironton. Route is a fearsome avalanche area in winter. On July 6, 1888, a summer avalanche occurred and a tunnel was blasted through it for wagon traffic. Red Mountain Creek (Uncompahgre)–Mineral Creek (Animas River) drainages, Colorado watershed.

RED ROCK PASS: See Red Mountain Pass, Independence Pass area.

RIO GRANDE PASS: See Stony Pass.

ROARING FORK PASS: See Taylor Pass.

ROCK CREEK TRAIL PASS (10,600) — Kenosha Pass, south, Tarryall Mountains. From Rock Creek road southeast of Jefferson, trail runs around north side of North Tarryall Peak (11,300) to south fork of Lost Park Creek and Lost Park. South Platte drainage.

ROGERS PASS (11,925), CD — Berthoud Pass area, north, Front Range. From near East Portal, Moffat Tunnel, trail crosses pass and down to near Winter Park and U.S. Route 40, ten miles. South Boulder Creek (South Platte)–Fraser River (Colorado) drainages. Named for Andrew N. Rogers, early engineer-mayor of Central City, who proposed a Moffat-like tunnel beneath James Peak as early as 1867. Also called South Boulder Pass.

ROLLINS PASS (11,680), CD — Berthoud Pass area, north, Front Range. From Rollinsville, via Tolland, unique, breathtaking road winds above Moffat Tunnel, East Portal, around north shoulder of James Peak (13,260) and over high trestles of old Moffat Railroad to broad top and down gentle west side to U.S. Route 40 near Hideaway, thirty-four miles. Jenny Creek (Boulder Creek)–Ranch Creek (Colorado) drainages. Shelf road on east side above Yankee Doodle Lake is the last place on earth for timid drivers, for this part of the trace is widely regarded as one of the scariest stretches in the West. Railroad crossed pass in 1904. Corona station and extensive snowsheds were built on top. Moffat Tunnel, 6.2 miles long and second longest railroad bore in United States, was completed in 1927 at 9094 feet. Present road was opened in 1956. Named for John Q. A. Rollins, founder of Rollinsville, who put first wagon road over pass to Middle Park in 1873. Also called Boulder Pass, Corona Pass.

ROUBIDEAU'S (Robidoux's) PASS: See Mosca Pass.

ST. LOUIS PASS (11,210) — Berthoud Pass area, west, Williams Fork Mountains. From Fraser, good road runs eight miles to end, and then four-mile trail up St. Louis Creek to top. Trail descent south side to Williams Fork River road, eight miles. Colorado River drainage. This surprisingly rugged wilderness area so near Denver has splendid stands of big spruce trees.

SALT HOUSE PASS (10,500), CD — Cochetopa Pass area, south, Cochetopa Hills. From the west side of Cochetopa Pass (Cochetopa Pass road), a back road proceeds south across Lost Creek, Texas Creek and Mexican Joe Creek, and over low CD to Stone Cellar Guard Station and Sky City ghost town in charming, remote Saguache Park. From Sky City, horseback trail goes twelve miles farther south to Halfmoon Pass (12,400). Salt House Pass gets its name from actual salt house on top for storing livestock salt.

SAND CREEK PASS (9000) — Medicine Bow area, six miles south of Wyoming line. Back road crosses this low pass by which a ditch once carried water from Laramie River to South Platte via Sheep Creek. Sand Creek (South Platte)–Laramie River (North Platte) drainages.

SANDERSON PASS: Early name for Argentine Pass.

SANDHILL PASS: See Medano Pass.

SAN FRANCISCO PASS (8200) — Raton Pass area, east. From Raton, New Mexico, and Sugarite, dirt road runs fifteen miles up Chicorica Creek to end on Barilla Mesa, where rough trail crosses pass to road on north side running down San Francisco Creek eight miles to Barela, Colorado. Chicorica Creek (Canadian)–San Francisco Creek (Purgatoire) drainages, Arkansas watershed. San Francisco Creek was called Ahogadero Creek originally, relating to fact that nine hundred sheep drowned in it during flood in 1849. The name was changed thereafter because it was a bad omen.

SAN FRANCISCO PASS (9500) — Raton Pass area, west. From Tercio road south of Stonewall, private road crosses pass toward Costilla Pass and Costilla, New Mexico. Bonito Canyon (Purgatoire)–Vermejo River (Canadian) drainages. Pass used to be part of old stage road to San Luis Valley.

SAN FRANCISCO PASS (8560) — Raton Pass area, west. From Stonewall, unmarked private 4WD trail, very difficult to follow, winds over Sangre de Cristo Range to San Luis Valley, fifty miles. This route has been suggested for public road. Vermejo River (Canadian)–San Francisco Creek (Rio Grande) drainages.

SANGRE DE CRISTO PASS (9459) — La Veta Pass area, adjacent, Sangre de Cristo Range. From Oak Creek road near Badito, historic old Spanish road ascended South Oak Creek on east side of Sheep Mountain to top, adjoining top of La Veta Pass. This road continued down west side to San Luis Valley much as U.S. Route 160 does now. South Oak Creek (Huerfano)–Sangre de Cristo Creek (Rio Grande) drainages, Arkansas–Rio Grande watersheds. Sangre de Cristo: Spanish for "blood of Christ," referring to sunrise and sunset hues on mountains.

SAN LUIS PASS (*ca.* 12,000), CD — Creede area, San Juan Range. From Creede, rugged trail runs north up West Willow Creek to pass beneath San Luis Peak (14,149). Descent on north side is partly down Spring Creek to the Los Pinos Pass road. Rio Grande–Colorado watersheds.

SAWATCH or SAGUACHE PASS: See Cochetopa Pass.

SCHOFIELD PASS (10,700) — Crested Butte area, north, Elk Range. From Gothic ghost town–resort, good road crosses pass beyond Lake Emerald and on for four miles more to start of very steep, often impassable 4WD road down Crystal River Canyon to fascinating Crystal ghost town, five miles. This 4WD road has twenty-seven-degree grades and bridge problems. Beyond Crystal, a steep and rugged shelf road continues six miles to Marble and the road to Carbondale. East River (Gunnison)–Crystal River (Roaring Fork) drainages, Colorado watershed. Very beautiful terrain around Gothic. The trail to West Maroon Pass (12,400) starts from Schofield Pass road one mile north of top. Named for Judge B. F. Schofield, founder of Schofield town near pass, 1879. Has been called Gothic Pass.

SCOTCH CREEK PASS (10,423) — Rico area east, La Plata Range. From Rico, 4WD road ascends Scotch Creek to pass and down Hotel Draw on east side of Barlow Creek Pass road on Hermosa Creek, and so on to U.S. Route 550 at Columbine Lake north of Durango. Regular cars can negotiate much of east side. Scotch Creek (Dolores River)–Hermosa Creek (Animas River) drainages, Colorado watershed.

SHERIDAN PASS (11,650) — Otto Mears's name for point where his Silverton Railroad crossed Red Mountain Pass area above Silverton.

SHRINE PASS (11,050) — Tennessee Pass area, northeast, Gore Range. From near top of Vail Pass (Interstate 70), east side, pleasant Forest Service road runs northwest and then southwest over high timber-and-grasslands to Redcliff and U.S. Route 24, thirteen miles. Excellent view from road of Mount of the Holy Cross (13,996) to southwest, one of its white snow arms missing these days because of a rock slide. West Tenmile (Blue River)–Turkey Creek (Eagle River) drainage, Colorado watershed. For something like a half century before the Vail Pass highway was built in 1940, this road was the shortest (and roughest) way from Denver to Glenwood Springs and Grand Junction. In 1923, it was named officially the Holy Cross Trail.

SILVER PASS (10,900), CD — Wolf Creek Pass area, south, San Juan Range. Just southeast of Railroad Pass. Pass Creek (Rio Grande)–Silver Creek (San Juan River) drainages.

SIMPSON PARK PASS (8300) — Meeker area, east, Flattop Mountains. Occasional name of old Indian crossing on trail from Williams River (Yampa) to White River just south of Pagoda Peak and north of Trappers Lake. It led to Simpson Park, site of the first White River Ute Agency.

SKULL CREEK PASS (8232) — Extreme northwest Colorado. From Skull Creek settlement on U.S. Route 40, twenty-two miles east of Artesia, road runs north six miles up Skull Creek and over pass to ranches under Red Rock Peak. Skull Creek–Wolf Creek drainages. Lizard Canyon in area has shown evidences of prehistoric Basket Maker culture.

SLUMGULLION PASS (11,361) — Lake City area, southeast, San Juan Range. From Lake City, State Route 149 crosses pass on way to Creede by way of Spring Creek Pass (10,898), fifty-five miles. Lake Fork, Gunnison River–Mill Creek (Cebolla) drainages, Colorado watershed. Fine view of lovely Lake San Cristobal from top. Named by New England pioneers for big slide on west side resembling slumgullion, the multicolored refuse from a butchered whale.

SNAKE RIVER PASS: See Argentine Pass.

SOUTH BOULDER PASS: See Rogers Pass.

SPRAGUE PASS (11,780), CD — Rocky Mountain National Park. Pass is crossed by twenty-mile trail from Moraine Park to Grand Lake past Sprague Glacier. Spruce Canyon (Big Thompson)–Tonahutu Creek (Colorado) drainages.

SPRING CREEK PASS (10,898), CD — Lake City area, southeast, San Juan Range. From Lake City, State Route 149 crosses Slumgullion Pass and then Spring Creek Pass to Rio Grande and Creede. Cebolla Creek (Gunnison)–Spring Creek (Rio Grande) drainages, Colorado–Rio Grande watersheds. From road on south side of Spring Creek Pass there is a beautiful slot view southwest, of Hermit Lakes and Rio Grande Pyramid (13,838). Some version of Spring Creek Pass was used by Old Bill Williams, Antoine Leroux and other Taos trappers and recommended by some as the shortest summer route crossing from Taos to the Gunnison country. It is called Pass of the Rio del Norte (Rio Grande) on the R. H. Kern army map of 1851. It was referred to occasionally as Summer Pass.

SQUAW PASS (11,300), CD — Weminuche Pass area, southeast, San Juan Range. From east end of Rio Grande (Farmers Union) Reservoir road, horseback trail runs south over pass to back road leading to Pagosa Springs, Squaw Creek (Rio Grande)–Williams Creek (Piedra River) drainages, Rio Grande–Colorado watersheds. Pass is next traverse east of the old Ute crossing, Weminuche Pass.

SQUAW PASS (9807) — Denver area, southwest, Front Range. Pass is on Bergen Park–Echo Lake Road on way to top of Mount Evans (14,260). Clear Creek–Bear Creek drainages.

STILLWATER PASS (10,500) — Granby area, Middle Park. From near Stillwater, on U.S. Route 34 just north of Granby, trail runs through Pony Park and over pass under Porphyry Peaks to Lake Solitaire (Lost Lake) and the end of the Willow Creek back road. Stillwater Creek–Willow drainages.

STONEMAN PASS (12,400), CD — Rocky Mountain National Park just west of Longs Peak (McHenry's Peak Quad).

STONY PASS (12,594), CD — Silverton area, northeast, San Juan Range. From Cunningham Gulch above Howardsville, 4WD road, fashioned recently from horseback trail, crosses rugged pass to extreme headwaters of Rio Grande River and on down to west end of Rio Grande (Farmers Union) Reservoir and Lost Trail Creek campground where regular road begins to Del Norte. Cunningham Gulch (Animas River)–Rio Grande drainages, Colorado–Rio Grande watersheds. This was the historic main route to the San Juans until the D. & R. G. reached Silverton in 1882. At Pole Creek on east side, a 4WD road branches left, southeast, to Beartown ghost camp and then, by trail only, to Hunchback Pass. Fine fishing everywhere.

STORM PASS (10,300) — Rocky Mountain National Park. Crossed by trail from near Longs Peak Lodge northwest under Battle Mountain to Wind River from Inn Brook.

STUNNER PASS (10,500) — Wolf Creek Pass area, south, San Juan Range. From Platoro, up Conejos River from Antonito, road runs over pass to Jasper ghost town and Ellwood Pass road, twelve miles. Pass is on divide between Conejos River and Alamosa Creek, both Rio Grande tributaries. The Stunner area, full of anglers these days, boomed in the 1880's but never lived up to its name. Stunner Pass is called Celeste Pass on some maps.

SUGARITE PASS: See San Francisco Pass east of Raton.

SUMMER PASS: See Spring Creek Pass.

SUMMIT PASS (11,775), CD — Wolf Creek Pass area, southeast, San Juan Range. Pass adjoins Ellwood Pass on north and is connected to it by the Continental Divide hiking trail from Wolf Creek Pass. In late 1870's, a road ran from Summitville over Summit Pass to join Ellwood Pass road on west side. It was washed out during a three-day rain in October, 1911, according to Ward Darley of Monte Vista. Park Creek (Rio Grande)–Ellwood Creek (San Juan River) drainages.

SWAMPY PASS (10,100) — Crested Butte area, southwest, West Elk Range. From Ohio Pass road, cattle trail runs over Swampy Pass and on north over Beckwith Pass to Kebler Pass road, fifteen miles. Pass Creek–Cliff Creek (Gunnison River) drainage.

SWAN RIVER PASS: See Georgia Pass.

TARRYALL PASS: See Boreas Pass.

TAYLOR PASS (11,900) — Aspen area, south, Elk Range. From Ashcroft ghost town up Castle Creek and Express Creek south of Aspen, steep

4WD road runs spectacularly to top of pass, six miles. Descending 4WD trail on Taylor Park side goes by beautiful little Taylor Lake near top and on down Taylor River to Dorchester ghost town, four miles (may be very rough and steep in spots, requiring a little road building). One of finest of 4WD trips in Rockies, with side trips at top along crest. A second obscure "Taylor Pass" is said to exist five miles west just short of Pearl Pass. The main Taylor Pass, in conjunction with Cottonwood Pass out of Buena Vista, was used as part of the principal road to Aspen and Ashcroft from 1879 until the Independence Pass road was opened in November, 1881. Castle Creek and Express Creek (Roaring Fork)–Taylor River (Gunnison) drainages, Colorado watershed. Named for Jim Taylor who, with Fred Lottis, pioneered the Taylor Park mining region.

TEMPLETON GAP (6200) — Colorado Springs area. Gap, three and one half miles from north edge of Colorado Springs, is crossed by Templeton Gap road to Black Forest. Named for early settler, Henry S. Templeton.

TENMILE PASS: See Fremont Pass.

TENNESSEE PASS (10,424), CD — Sawatch Range. From Leadville, U.S. Route 24 climbs serenely a mere 272 feet (Leadville is that high!) in ten miles to top of Tennessee. The highway descends the west side to Redcliff, 1826 vertical feet in twelve and one half miles. Tennessee Creek (Arkansas)–Eagle River (Colorado) drainages. Pass was reported first by John Charles Frémont in 1845 on his way to California. Denver and Rio Grande Railroad put tunnel below it when it changed from narrow to standard gauge in 1890. A larger, 2500-foot tunnel with an apex altitude of 10,242 feet was completed in 1945 — the highest mainline railroad passage in the United States. Tennessee was the first CD highway pass in Colorado to be kept open all winter (1928). On top, a magnificent granite memorial contains the names of 993 members of the Tenth Mountain Division killed in action in the Italian theater during World War II. The division was trained at Camp Hale, on the west side of Tennessee Pass. Living members of the Division contributed twelve thousand dollars for the memorial, which was unveiled on May 30, 1959. Efforts to rename the pass Tenth Mountain Pass have not succeeded as yet. Homesick prospectors gave the pass its Tennessee name in the 1860's.

TENTH MOUNTAIN PASS: See Tennessee Pass.

THUNDER PASS: See Lulu Pass.

TIMBERLINE PASS (11,484), CD — Rocky Mountain National Park. Just north of Sprague Pass and Sprague Glacier.

TINCUP PASS (12,154), CD — St. Elmo area, west, Sawatch Range. From St. Elmo, good 4WD road (cars can go as far as top) crosses pass and descends to Mirror Lake down rough west side and on to Tincup ghost town–resort. Regular cars from Tincup reach Mirror Lake easily. North fork of Chalk Creek (Arkansas)–Willow Creek (Gunnison) drainages, Arkansas–Colorado watersheds. Road dates from early 1880's. A marvelous one-day circle 4WD trip from St. Elmo runs over Tincup Pass to Tincup, south over Cumberland Pass, and back again to St. Elmo over (new) Williams Pass. Town name derived from act of Fred Lottis, early prospector, who used a tincup to test gravel for color. Also called Alpine Pass.

TOMICHI PASS (11,979) — Monarch Pass area, north, Sawatch Range. From Tomichi town (wiped out by avalanche in 1899), terrifying wagon road shelved its way north over pass to Williams Pass road, six miles. Tomichi Creek–Quartz Creek (Gunnison) drainages. Today, 4WD travelers from Pitkin can see this Tomichi Pass trail to the south as they head east toward (new) Williams Pass. Tomichi: Indian word for "hot water."

TREASURE PASS (11,610), CD — Just south of Wolf Creek Pass, San Juan Range. Reached from Wolf Creek by Continental Divide Trail, one and a half miles.

TRIANGLE PASS (12,500) — Crested Butte area, northeast, Elk Range. From Gothic, East Maroon Trail up Copper Creek has steep branch to right to Triangle Pass, and then down Conundrum Creek past hot springs to Ashcroft–Aspen road. Copper Creek (East River)–Conundrum Creek (Roaring Fork) drainages. Sometimes called Conundrum Pass.

TRIMBLE PASS (12,800) — Durango area, northeast, Needle Mountains, San Juan Range. Pass is reached from Columbine Pass trail in wild country on south side of Florida Mountain (13,076) at Little Lake. Named for Frank Trimble, pioneer rancher.

TRINCHERA PASS (6000) — Raton Pass area, east. On road from Folsom, New Mexico, to Trinchera, Colorado, by way of State Route 72 east and thence north, instead of straight north from Folsom to Branson. Cimarron River (Arkansas)–Trinchera Creek (Purgatoire) drainages, Arkansas watershed. Charles Goodnight laid out cattle trail over Trinchera in 1867 to avoid paying toll on "Uncle Dick" Wooten's toll road over Raton Pass. Also called Cimarron Pass. Trinchera: Spanish for "ditch."

TROUBLESOME PASS (10,027), CD — Kremmling area, Rabbit Ears Range. From Troublesome Creek road north from U.S. Route 40 at Troublesome, logging road runs to top of this typically low Rabbit Ears Range pass up East Fork, Troublesome Creek, and Haystack Creek. In North Park, road descends Willow Creek to Willow Creek Pass road near Rand. Colorado–North Platte watersheds.

TROUT CREEK PASS (9346) — Mosquito Range. From Antero Junction at west edge of South Park, U.S. Route 24–285 crosses pass to Arkansas and stunning views of Collegiate Range of Sawatch Mountains — Mount Princeton (14,197) dead ahead, and Mount Yale (14,194) and Mount Harvard (14,420), right (see Brown's Pass for Collegiate history). Salt Creek (South Platte)–Trout Creek (Arkansas) drainages. Denver and South Park and Colorado Midland railroads were built over it during 1880's. It was an ancient trail pass when Pike crossed it in 1806.

TWIN CREEK PASS (8600) — West of Pikes Peak. From U.S. Route 24 at Florissant, road runs south of Grape Creek (one of Twin Creeks) and over pass to Hay Creek and junction with Cripple Creek road. South Platte–Arkansas drainages.

TWIN THUMBS PASS (13,100) — Durango area, northeast, Needle Mountains, San Juan Range. Robert M. Ormes reports that this obscure and rugged traverse is reached from the Needle Creek trail end in Chicago Basin by moving north to Twin Lakes and crossing pass northwest under Mount Eolus (14,079) to Ruby Creek drainage. An utter wilderness.

UNION PASS (8640) — Though only two miles long, the little shelf road from U.S. Route 6 near Georgetown over Union Pass to Empire is a terror, and apt to be rockslid or otherwise impassable. Also called Empire Pass.

UTE PASS (9183) — Colorado Springs area, Front Range. From Manitou Springs, U.S. Route 24 runs up through canyon of Fountain Creek to Divide town and on to South Park. Triple drainage: Fountain Creek (Arkansas)–Twin Creek (South Platte)–Oil Creek (Arkansas). Before 1872, road avoided Fountain Creek canyon by using old Ute trail over ridges half a mile or so south of present highway. This Ute Pass, fifth oldest in our chronology, is exceedingly beautiful, first in its four-mile canyon stage, and then in its passage around the north and most photogenic side of Pikes Peak. The abandoned roadbed of the Colorado Midland Railway (1887) can be seen cut in the cliff high above the road. The pass is unique in the Rockies, being a continuous resort through most of its twenty-three-mile length, comprising the substantial communities of Cascade, Chipita Park, Green Mountain Falls, Crystola, Woodland Park and Divide. Their lively, gay history since the 1880's has been charmingly told by Virginia McConnell in her 1963 book *Ute Pass: Route of the Blue Sky People*. Top of pass is called Divide and Hayden Divide.

UTE PASS (9524) — Dillon area, north, Williams Fork Mountains. From State Route 9, fifteen miles north of Dillon, trail crosses pass to Williams Fork River road, eleven miles. Williams Fork–Blue River drainages, Colorado watershed. Ancient Indian route.

UTE PASS (11,100), CD — Steamboat Springs area, north, Sierra Madre Range. From Elk River road out of Steamboat, trail crosses pass to Ute Creek in North Park and Boettcher Lake (private). Yampa–North Platte drainages.

UTE PASS (9869) — Cameron Pass area, north, Medicine Bow Range. From Brownlee, in North Park north of Walden, road and 4WD trail run east over pass to Laramie River road, twenty-five miles. North Platte–Laramie drainages.

UTE PASS (7300) — From Durango, back road runs up Spring Creek eastward and over pass to Florida River and on to Vallecito Reservoir. Animas–Florida (San Juan) drainages.

VAIL PASS (10,554) — Tennessee Pass area, north, Gore Range. Interstate 70 crosses spacious pass from Dillon and Frisco west to junction with U.S. Route 24 and Eagle River. West Tenmile (Blue River)–Gore Creek drainages, Colorado River watershed. The elaborate Vail Ski Area, opened in 1962, is on west side. This pass had no particular use before highway first went over it in 1940. Named for Charles D. Vail, chief engineer of Colorado Department of Highways, who died January 9, 1945.

VASQUEZ PASS (11,655), CD — Berthoud Pass area, adjoining, Front Range. Pass can be reached by hiking from near top of Jones Pass 4WD road, east side, one mile north. Descent down Vasquez Creek to Hideaway, ten miles. West Clear Creek (South Platte)–Vasquez Creek (Fraser River) drainages. Very strange water business has been going on since the mid-1950's in this area. Water from Williams Fork River of the Western Slope has been flowing to the Eastern Slope through Jones Pass Tunnel, back to the Western Slope by the 18,000-foot Vasquez Tunnel beneath Vasquez Pass, and then back to the Eastern Slope once more through Moffat Tunnel for use by Denver's residents. Problems of storage and contamination cause this switching back and forth through the CD. Vasquez Pass bears the name of the mountain man, Louis Vasquez, who built a trading post near Denver in the 1830's. Clear Creek was called Vasquez Creek originally.

VENABLE PASS (12,000) — Westcliffe area, southwest, Sangre de Cristo Range. Ranger Jack Booth explains that Venable Pass is crossed by horseback from road end southwest of Westcliffe up Venable Creek and over crest between Venable Peak and Eureka Mountain. The trail descends down north fork of North Crestone Creek to Crestone in San Luis Valley. From pass, a breathtaking foot trail runs south by way of Phantom Terrace to Comanche Pass. The mysterious Marble Cave is near the east foot of Venable Pass.

VETA PASS (9100) — La Veta Pass area, south, Sangre de Cristo Range. The Denver and Rio Grande Railroad has been crossing this pass since early 1890's from La Veta town. Trains crossed La Veta Pass before that, heavily publicizing La Veta's scenic joys for tourists. The new crossing, which had a perfectly good name, Wagon Creek Pass, was renamed Veta Pass, therefore, to somewhat conceal the fact that the more thrilling La Veta Pass was no longer on the railroad's route. Or so it would seem. Confusion over the similar names has reigned ever since. Indian Creek (Cucharas)–Wagon Creek (Sangre de Cristo Creek) drainages, Arkansas–Rio Grande watersheds.

VICTOR PASS (10,202) — Colorado Springs area, southwest, Front Range. Road from Victor in Cripple Creek mining district runs four miles north over pass beneath Bull Cliffs to Cameron ghost town. Grassy Creek–Wilson Creek (Arkansas) drainages.

WAGON CREEK PASS: See Veta Pass.

WARMSPRINGS PASS: See Breakneck Pass.

WAUNITA PASS (10,303) — Monarch Pass area, northwest. From the faded old resort of Waunita Hot Springs (nice pool), road runs north through pleasant woods and over pass to Pitkin, nine miles. Hot Spring Creek (Tomichi)–Quartz Creek (Gunnison) drainages.

WEBSTER PASS (12,108), CD — Argentine Pass area, south, Front Range. From Montezuma, road for 4WDs and small standard cars ascends Deer Creek southward to top, where it ends abruptly and without warning at an impossible downslope where old wagon road used to be. At foot of slope, old road picks up to carry on down Hall Valley to U.S. Route 285 at Webster. Handcart Gulch (South Platte)–Deer Creek (Snake River) drainages. Named for William and Emerson Webster who built this very popular road in 1878. Also called Handcart Pass, Montezuma Pass.

WEMINUCHE PASS (10,629), CD — Creede area, southwest, San Juan Range. A horse trail from Rio Grande Reservoir crosses this open, grassy pass, so beloved by the Utes in times gone by, and continues down Los Pinos River drainage to civilization at Vallecito Reservoir, or at Pagosa Springs. Weminuche Creek (Rio Grande)–Los Pinos River (San Juan) drainages, Rio Grande–Colorado watersheds. A great place for Indian artifacts.

WEST MAROON PASS (12,400) — Aspen area, southwest, Elk Range. From Maroon Lake, trail crosses pass and runs westerly to join Schofield Pass road on *north* side of Schofield Pass. Maroon Creek (Roaring Fork)–

Crystal River drainages. Maroon Peak, Maroon Bells, Hagerman Peak and Snowmass Mountain appear in a line northwest of pass. Note that West Maroon is not on the crest of the Elks, though East Maroon Pass is.

WESTON PASS (11,945) — Mosquito Range north of Trout Creek Pass. Interesting gravel road, steep in spots but passable, runs from U.S. Route 285 (at point half way between Fairplay and Antero Junction) over pass and down west side to U.S. 24 south of Leadville. South Fork of South Platte–Union Creek (Arkansas) drainages. From the 1860's on, this was the most popular route from South Park to California Gulch (Leadville). Named for Algernon S. Weston, a California Gulch pioneer who owned Weston Ranch on west side of pass. Campsites and good fishing, east side.

WEST PASS CREEK PASS: See North Cochetopa Pass.

WHISKEY CREEK PASS (12,802) — La Veta Pass area, south, Sangre de Cristo Range. A private trail crosses pass from Cucharas Pass road to road end on Culebra Creek east of San Luis in San Luis Valley. Whiskey Creek (Purgatoire)–Culebra Creek (Rio Grande) drainages. In 1937, a road was planned over from San Luis to Stonewall, with tunnel under pass at 12,207 feet. Tunnel and road were not completed. Whiskey Creek Pass — also called Culebra Pass — is highest in Sangre de Cristos.

WILKERSON PASS (9524) — Colorado Springs area, west. U.S. Route 24 crosses pass from Lake George into South Park. South Platte drainage. Named for pioneer rancher of Badger Mountain area.

WILLIAMS PASS, new (11,762), CD — St. Elmo area, southwest. From Hancock ghost town near Stonewall Mine, up Chalk Creek from St. Elmo, late-vintage 4WD road moves west over this Williams Pass, down west side to Denver and South Park abandoned right-of-way, and on down on the road bed most of the way to Pitkin. A stupendous trip. Steve Frazee, the novelist, explains that the original Williams Pass wagon road ran a bit northwest of the 4WD road. Pass was named for Robert R. Williams, assistant engineer of the Denver and South Park Railroad. It has been called Hancock Pass. Chalk Creek (Arkansas)–Quartz Creek (Gunnison) drainages.

WILLIAMS PASS: See Medano Pass, Spring Creek Pass.

WILLOW CREEK PASS (9683), CD — Rabbit Ears Range. From Granby in Middle Park, State Route 125 runs north over pass into North Park and on to Walden. Willow Creek (Colorado)–Illinois River (North Platte) drainages. This route was a popular Indian trail before becoming a road in 1902.

WINDY PASS (9976) — Wolf Creek Pass area, San Juan Range. From marker on U.S. 160, west side of Wolf Creek Pass, pack trail runs five miles over pass to East Fork, San Juan River and Ellwood Pass road.

WOLF CREEK PASS (10,850), CD — San Juan Range, U.S. Route 160 sweeps majestically over pass from South Fork to Pagosa Springs, forty-two miles. South Fork and Pass Creek (Rio Grande)–Wolf Creek (San Juan) drainages. One of the loveliest of pass highways, especially as it descends west side above the beautiful pastures of At Last Ranch. Wolf Creek's heavy snowfall makes it exciting and sometimes dangerous in winter. Highway dates from 1916–1917.

YELLOWJACKET PASS (7300) — Meeker area, north, Danforth

Hills. From near Meeker, an agreeable back road forks right from State Route 13, crosses pass, and rejoins 13 near Hamilton. On north side, a stone monument above Milk Creek marks site where, on September 29, 1879, Ute Indians ambushed an army rescue force trying to reach Indian agent Nathan Meeker twenty-five miles away. The troops never did get to the agency, and Meeker and his staff were killed. Coal Creek (White River)–Milk Creek (Yampa River) drainages. Pass was on government road from Rawlins, Wyoming, to White River Ute Agency near present Meeker.

YELLOWJACKET PASS (7500) — Gore Range. Back road just east of Oak Creek crosses pass below Blacktail Mountain on way north to Steamboat Springs, Yampa River drainage.

YELLOWJACKET PASS (7700) — Durango area, east. U.S. Route 160 crosses this inconspicuous pass just east of Bayfield. Squaw-Yellowjacket creeks (Piedra River)–Hayden–Beaver creeks (Los Pinos River) drainages.

YULE PASS (12,200) — Crested Butte area, Elk Range. Pass is saddle between Slate Creek–Yule Creek headwaters south of Treasure Mountain (13,491). Named for George Yule, discoverer of marble deposit in Marble area from which Lincoln Memorial and other American public buildings were made.

YVONNE PASS (12,250) — Ouray area, southeast, San Juan Range. From Mineral Point ghost town reached out of Ouray, a thrilling 4WD road switchbacks over multicolored Engineer Mountain to old American Flats mining area and vast summer sheep pastures on way to Rose's Cabin and Henson Creek. Total distance, Ouray to Lake City via Yvonne Pass 4WD road, thirty-five miles. Mineral Creek (Uncompahgre River)–Henson Creek (Gunnison River) drainages. The mining era in this tense, eerie region began in the early 1870's.

Montana Passes

(Including those on the Montana-Idaho border)

AENEAS PASS (6000) — Bigfork (Flathead Lake) area, southeast, Swan Range near Mount Aeneas (7530). Old Blackfoot trail crossed this pass between Swan River and South Fork, Flathead River (Hungry Horse Reservoir). Columbia watershed. Named for a Kootenai chief.

AHERN PASS (7010), CD — Glacier National Park, north. From Belly River, a dramatic trail zigzags over Ahern Glacier to cirque pass. Ahern Creek–Mineral Creek drains west side. Belly River (Oldman–South Saskatchewan–Hudson Bay) and McDonald Creek (Middle Fork, Flathead–Columbia) watersheds. Named for Lieutenant George P. Ahern who crossed it in August, 1890, with a detachment of Negro soldiers from the 25th U.S. Infantry.

BADGER PASS (6642) — Dillon area, south end, Pioneer Mountains. From Jackson in Big Hole Valley, road crosses Badger Pass north of Bannack ghost town and down Rattlesnake Gulch to Dillon. Pass is reached also north from Bannack up Taylor Creek road. Beaverhead–Missouri drainage.

BADGER PASS (6700), CD — Marias Pass area, next gap south. From Swift Reservoir, trail runs up North Fork, Birch Creek, and over pass to Strawberry Creek, Gooseberry Park and Middle Fork, Flathead River. Missouri–Columbia watersheds.

BANNACK PASS: Variant spelling of Bannock Pass.

BANNOCK PASS (7484), CD — Due north of Leadore, Idaho, Beaverhead Mountains of Bitterroot Range. From Leadore, good road follows ancient trail up Canyon Creek and down Divide–Horse Prairie creeks to the Lemhi Pass road and Armstead, Montana. Lemhi River (Columbia)–Beaverhead (Missouri) drainages. Bannock: Shoshonean word indicating "tuft of hair thrown from forehead." One of the oddest railroads in the United States, the Gilmore and Pittsburgh, was built over Bannock Pass (seventy-five foot tunnel near top) in 1910 from Armstead fifty-five miles to Leadore, where a nineteen-mile leg ran south to Gilmore, and a forty-five-mile leg went north to Salmon, Idaho. According to its able biographer, Thomas T. Taber, whose manuscript is at the State Museum Library in Helena, "for all practical purposes the railroad started from nowhere, traversed through nothing and ended up nowhere." It hauled cattle, sheep and feed at a loss for thirty years, closing down finally on May 1, 1939. The tracks were torn up in late 1940. It was built ostensibly by Pittsburgh businessmen, but actually by Northern Pacific Railway officials, who seemed to have some vague idea of running the N. P.'s main line some day from the Bozeman area southwestwardly to Armstead and over Bannock Pass and then down the Salmon River to the Snake and Columbia rivers and on to Portland, thereby avoiding all the rough Montana–Idaho country west of Mullan Pass. It was a costly $6,000,000 dream which began and ended with the Gilmore and Pittsburgh.

BANNOCK PASS: Occasional name for Medicine Lodge Pass.

BATTLE RIDGE PASS (6268) — Bozeman Pass area, north, Bridger Range. The Bridger Canyon road out of Bozeman leads to Brackett Creek and pass at Battle Ridge Campground before descending Cache Creek to Sedan. Shields River (Yellowstone–Missouri) drainage. Battle Ridge was a favorite with Indians for hunting antelope. They did so much shooting there that "it sounded like a battle going on."

BIG GAP: Early name (1860's) for Marias Pass, east end.

BIG HOLE PASS (7236), CD — Lost Trail pass area, southeast, Bitterroot Range. From Gibbonsville, Idaho, road runs up Dahlonega Creek eight miles to top (fine views west toward Oregon). East descent down Ruby–Swamp–Moose creeks to Big Hole River and Wisdom, Montana. Columbia–Missouri watersheds.

BIG HOLE PASS (7357) — Near Jackson, Montana. From Jackson, road ascends Bull Creek over pass to Divide Creek–Grasshopper Creek ranchlands and Bannack ghost town. Same road leads also to Badger Pass and Dillon. Jefferson River (Missouri) watershed. Also called Bull Creek Pass.

BITTERROOT PASS (ca. 8200) — Sula area, northeast (Anaconda Wilderness). From Sula road end, trail runs up East Fork, Bitterroot River, to pass just west of West Pintlar Peak and CD. It descends north side by Copper Creek or middle fork of Rock Creek to Philipsburg-bound road. Clark Fork (Columbia) drainage. Very wild country.

BLACKFOOT PASS: Early name of Cadotte Pass, Lewis and Clark Pass.

BLODGETT PASS (*ca.* 6800) — Hamilton area, Bitterroot Range. From near Hamilton, scenic trail ascends Blodgett Creek to pass under Blodgett Mountain, descending on west side partly by Big Sand Creek to Powell–Elk Summit road in Selway–Bitterroot Wilderness area. Bitterroot (Clark Fork)–Lochsa (Clearwater) watersheds. General John Gibbon had a gunner named Joseph Blodgett who was a packer in area in 1862 living on Blodgett Creek. Lyman J. Blodgett settled at the mouth of Blodgett Canyon in 1871.

BLOODY DICK DIVIDE: See Goldstone Pass.

BOZEMAN PASS (6002) — From Bozeman, Interstate 90 ascends beautiful canyon into busy lush open country at top of this historic crossing, which divides the Bridger Range from the Absaroka–Gallatin uplands. The east-side descent through hay meadows and evergreen stands is down Billman Creek to Yellowstone River and Livingston. Missouri watershed. The Northern Pacific Railway goes under top of pass in 3610-foot tunnel at an altitude of 5712 feet, the highest point on the transcontinental line. In earlier days the wagon road went up east grade in switchbacks. Named for John M. Bozeman, builder of the Bozeman trail for immigrants and gold-seekers in the 1860's. Has been called Sacajawea Pass.

BRIDGER PASS (6139) — Just north of Bozeman Pass. From Bozeman town, Bridger Canyon Road ascends Bridger Creek and crosses pass to Brackett Creek leading to Clydepark and Shields River. Missouri watershed. Jim Bridger laid out trail using this pass in 1864, in competition with John Bozeman's trail over Bozeman Pass. F. V. Hayden called it Union Pass in 1872, but it is marked Bridger's Pass on the Rand McNally *Business Atlas* of 1876.

BROWN PASS (6600), CD — Glacier National Park, Livingstone Range. Trail and phone line cross this pass linking Bowman Creek (Flathead) and Olson Creek (Waterton) headwaters below Thunderbird Glacier and Logan Falls. This is the first CD pass south of Canadian border. Canada's first pass, Akamina (5835), is six miles north of Brown. May have been named for Louis Brown, a Flathead squawman.

BULL CREEK PASS: See Big Hole Pass.

BULL OF THE WOODS PASS: See Daisy Pass.

BUNYAN PASS (*ca.* 8250) — Augusta area, west. Pass links South Fork of North Fork of Sun River and Straight (Todd) Creek. Missouri watershed.

CADOTTE PASS (6044), CD — Helena area, north. From Middle Fork, Dearborn River, trail crosses pass and loops down to Cadotte Creek–Blackfoot River. Missouri–Columbia watersheds. This ancient traverse, called Blackfoot Pass, was renamed for the French–Canadian guide, Pierre Cadotte, with Governor Stevens's Northern Pacific Railroad Survey of 1853.

CAMP CREEK PASS (7000), CD — Augusta area, northwest. From

Gibson Lake, trail runs up Sun River, West Fork, and Lost Fork of Ahorn Creek to pass and down Camp Creek–Danaher Creek to South Fork, Flathead River. Missouri–Columbia watersheds.

CAMP PASS (7000) — Ovando area (State Route 20), north. Pass links Falls–Monture creeks and Lake Creek–Kleinschmidt Flat. Blackfoot (Columbia) watershed.

CHAMPION PASS (ca. 8000), CD — Butte area, north. From Basin, road runs up branches of Boulder River to Gospel Hill and over pass near Champion Mine, descending Peterson Creek to Deerlodge town. Missouri–Clark Fork (Columbia) watersheds. Handsome scenery.

CHIEF JOSEPH PASS (ca. 6900) — Montana's newest named crossing (1963), honoring the great Nez Perce leader, Chief Joseph. From Big Hole Battlefield National Monument, where Chief Joseph and his people defeated Colonel Gibbon's soldiers in 1877, new highway deserts old Gibbons Pass route, ascending Chief Joseph Creek instead to Chief Joseph Pass and a junction with U.S. Route 93 and Lost Trail Pass.

CLARK'S PASS: Occasional name in 1850's (honoring William Clark) for Gibbons Pass. In 1872, F. V. Hayden used the name Clark's Pass for what became Cooke Pass.

CLOVER DIVIDE (7400) — Dillon area, Snowcrest Range. From Lima Reservoir, road crosses divide and descends northwest to Dillon. Clover Creek (Red Rock River)–West Fork, Blacktail Creek (Beaverhead) drainages. Lieutenant John Mullan crossed this divide northbound after using Monida Pass in winter of 1853–1854.

COEUR D'ALÈNE PASS: As shown on Rand McNally's map of 1876, this name covers both St. Regis and Lookout Pass. Various Stevens parties used it in 1853–1854. Also called Stevens Pass.

COLTER PASS: See Cooke Pass.

COOKE PASS (8066) — Near northeast entrance, Yellowstone Park, Absaroka Mountains. This low pass is on the beautiful Beartooth Pass highway (U.S. Route 12) two miles east of Cooke town. Clarks Fork–Soda Butte Creek (Yellowstone) drainages. It has been called Colter Pass, after John Colter who crossed over it or near it in 1808. Also Clark's Pass (Hayden). Cooke, the mining-town-turned-resort, was named for Jay Cooke, Jr., son of the financier. Young Cooke had mining claims in the area. The Cooke City highway from Yellowstone Park was built in the early 1920's.

COOPER PASS (5200) — Wallace–Burke, Idaho, mining area. From Thompson Falls, road ascends Gulch and Cooper creeks to pass and down Canyon Creek on west side to Burke and Wallace. Clark Fork–Coeur d'Alène (Columbia) watershed.

CORIACAN DEFILE (ca. 4000) — Top is called Evaro Pass. From Missoula, U.S. Route 10A runs up colorful Coriacan gorge to three-mile-wide pass and descends Jocko River on north side to Ravalli town and Flathead River. Clark Fork drainage. Evaro is said to have been a French count who visited area in early days. Northern Pacific Railway uses this same ancient route which bypasses a big bend in Clark Fork. Koriaka was a Kanakee Sandwich Islander (Hawaiian) who was killed by Blackfeet while trapping on the Jocko for Hudson's Bay Company. It was not strange for a Hawaiian to be trapping in Montana. The standard sea route from the Isthmus of Panama to Columbia River for Americans and English-men was via the Sandwich Islands. The trapping brigades often picked up employees there. In the 1860's, one of Lieutenant John Mullan's soldiers with the grand Irish name of The O'Keefe started The O'Keefe Ranch below Coriacan Defile. It is still going.

CUTAWAY PASS (*ca.* 9000), CD — Georgetown Lake area west of Anaconda. From East Fork Reservoir road, trail runs south up Rock Creek and over pass, descending the west fork of La Marche Creek to Big Hole River road. Clark Fork (Columbia)–Big Hole (Missouri) watersheds.

CUT BANK PASS: See Pitamakan Pass.

CUT BANK PASS (7800), CD — Glacier National Park. From Two Medicine Lake road, trail ascends Dry Fork to pass, the north wall of which drops sheer to Pitamakan Lake. A trail continues north on crest to Pitamakan, which was the original "Cut Bank Pass" of the Blackfeet Indians. A new trail from Cut Bank Pass runs south to Dawson Pass.

DAISY CREEK PASS (*ca.* 5000) — Seven miles southwest of Thompson Falls. Pass links Wilkes Creek (Clark Fork) and Packer Creek (St. Regis River) drainages. Columbia watershed.

DAISY PASS (9712) — Three miles north of Cooke City. Mining road ascends Miller Creek and over pass to headwaters of Stillwater River. Bull of the Woods Pass is close by Daisy to the southwest. Yellowstone watershed.

DAWSON PASS (7500), CD — Glacier National Park. From Two Medicine Lake road end, trail runs through beflowered Bighorn Basin to pass and down Nyack Creek to Middle Fork, Flathead River. Missouri–Columbia drainages. Pass was named for Thomas Dawson (Little Chief), son of Major Andrew Dawson, an American Fur Company trader.

DEADMAN PASS (*ca.* 9800) — Just off CD nine miles southwest of Bannock Pass, Bitterroot Range. Pass links Horse Prairie Creek headwaters with Medicine Lodge Creek, both draining into Beaverhead River (Missouri).

DEARBORN PASS (7100), CD — Eight miles northwest of Lewis and Clark Pass. Trail runs up Dearborn River and west to its extreme headwater under Scapegoat Mountain (9185). West descent down trail network, North Fork, Blackfoot River, to State Route 20 and Lincoln. Missouri–Columbia watersheds. Named by Lewis and Clark for Henry Dearborn, Thomas Jefferson's Secretary of War.

DEER LODGE PASS (5902), CD — Butte area, southwest, Anaconda Range. From Butte, U.S. Route 91 runs up Clark Fork branch in open country to imperceptible pass and down broad Divide Creek Valley to Big Hole River. Missouri–Columbia watersheds. Union Pacific Railroad (Utah and Northern) crossed this pass to Butte in 1881. Name is derived from tipi-shaped mound of deer-attracting salty deposits formed by hot springs in upper part of Deer Lodge Valley.

DEFILE OF CORACAH, or CORICAN: See Coriacan Defile.

DUCK CREEK PASS (7515) — Townsend area, northwest, Big Belt Mountains. From Canyon Ferry Lake, road runs up Duck Creek to pass and down east side along Gipsy and Birch Creek to Smith River. Missouri watershed.

EAST FORK PASS (*ca.* 6170) — Saltese area, north, Coeur d'Alêne

Mountains. From St. Regis River, East Fork trail crosses pass toward Prospect Creek and Clark Fork. Near Taft Summit and Tarbox Hill. Columbia watershed.

EAST PASS: See Targhee Pass.

ECHO PASS (7500) — Ovando area, northeast, in Cooper's Lake–Kleinschmidt Flat mining area. Echo Pass, just northwest of Echo Mountain, links east fork, Landers Fork (Blackfoot River) and North Fork, Blackfoot. Near Windy Pass.

ELK PARK PASS (6374), CD — Butte area, north. From Basin, U.S. Route 91 runs up Bison Creek of Boulder River and over pass to Butte, partly down Yankee Doodle Creek drainage. Missouri–Columbia watersheds. Great Northern Railway uses this pass also.

ELK PASS (6000) — Augusta area. From Elk Creek road end, lumber trail crosses pass to Smith Creek road end. Sun River (Missouri) drainage.

ENEAS (AENEAS) PASS: Occasional name in 1860's for the west end of Marias Pass, honoring a Kootenai chief.

EVARO PASS: See Coriacan Defile.

EXPEDITION PASS (10,000) — Raynolds Pass–Quake Lake area, north. From near State Route 287 on Madison River, pack trail runs up Moose Creek to pass and down Sentinel Creek (many lakes here) on east side to Beaver Creek road end. Missouri watershed.

FALSE MARIAS PASS: See Pitamakan Pass.

FALSE SUMMIT: See Marias Pass.

FATHER'S DEFILE: Alternate name for Medicine Lodge Pass after Father De Smet crossed it in 1841.

FIREBRAND PASS (7150), CD — Glacier National Park. From Glacier Park, trail runs west by Squaw Mountain and up Railroad Creek drainage to pass under Red Crow Mountain. West descent down Ole Creek (Middle Fork, Flathead River). Missouri–Columbia drainage. Named for firebrand blown through pass, causing disastrous forest fire.

FLATHEAD DIVIDE (ca. 5400) — Ovando–Monture area, Flathead Range. From Dry Fork of North Fork, Blackfoot River, trail reaches divide, descending by Danaher Creek branch to South Fork, Flathead River. Columbia watershed.

FLATHEAD PASS (6770) — Bozeman area, north, Bridger Range. From Menard, road runs up Pass Creek and over pass, descending south fork of Flathead Creek on east side to Shields River and U.S. Route 89 at Wilsall. Gallatin–Yellowstone (Missouri) drainages. Lieutenant Maynadier of Raynold's expedition crossed it westbound in 1860. F. V. Hayden wrote of it in 1872; "Flathead Pass is the great thoroughfare for the Flathead and Bannack Indians on their way to buffalo grounds of the Muscleshell [Musselshell] River, etc. The Sioux went through it on their raids to the Gallatin Valley."

FLATHEAD PASS: Abiel Tinkham's name for Mullan Pass in 1853.

FLATHEAD PASS: Name applied to present Pitamakan Pass on Montana map of Rand McNally's Business Atlas, 1876.

FLESHER PASS (6350), CD — Helena area, northwest. From Canyon Creek and Wilborn, good road runs north up Canyon Creek and over pass to Wilbur Creek–Blackfoot River and then to State Route 20 below

Rogers Pass. Missouri–Columbia drainage. Flesher is said to have been an early settler. The road (1963) is about to be considerably improved.

GATEWAY PASS (*ca.* 7505), CD — Marias Pass area, twenty-seven miles southwest along crest. Pass links Middle Fork, Birch Creek, and Gateway Creek–Middle Fork, Flathead River. Missouri–Columbia watersheds. Named passes on CD between Gateway and Marias are Badger and Muskrat.

GIBBONS PASS (6982), CD — Bitterroot Range. Historic old road over this pass from Bitterroot Valley to Big Hole Valley, always a headache to teamsters from the late 1850's, has just been abandoned (1963) by the Montana State Highway Department in favor of a highway from Big Hole Battlefield National Monument over the new Chief Joseph Pass to U.S. Route 93 and Lost Trail Pass. The old Gibbons Pass road leaves U.S. 93 four miles south of Sula, crosses Gibbons Pass and descends Prairie and Trail creeks and on to Big Hole River at Wisdom. Named for General John Gibbon whose soldiers were badly beaten at southeast foot of pass in 1877 by Chief Joseph, Nez Perce warriors, women, children, old men and dogs.

GILMORE DIVIDE (*ca.* 7000) — Leadore (Idaho) area. State Route 28 ascends Birch Creek to divide and descends Lemhi River to Leadore. Birch Creek disappears near Lost River Sinks. An ancient route from Snake River to Salmon River.

GLIDDEN PASS (5765) — Wallace–Burke (Idaho) mining area, Bitterroot Range. From Cooper Pass road, Idaho side, a road goes to top of Glidden Pass, descending Glidden Gulch (Prospect Creek) to Thompson Pass road. Coeur d'Alêne–Clark Fork drainages. Named for S. S. Glidden, who owned the Tiger Mine at Burke in 1892. Muriel Sibell Wolle has reported that an 1884 sign on Glidden Pass beside a noose rope read: "This is for the first Chinaman who crosses this pass into Idaho." In its 1890's heyday, Glidden was the main pass across the Bitterroots from Thompson Falls to the placer diggings at Murray.

GOLDSTONE PASS (*ca.* 9000), CD — North of Lemhi Pass, Bitterroot Range. From State Route 28 near Baker, Idaho, trail runs up Pratt Creek under Goldstone Mountain (9892) to Goldstone Mine and pass where road descends near Bloody Dick Creek and south to Lemhi Pass road. Descent can be made north also to Skinner Lake, Dark Horse Creek and Big Hole River. Missouri–Columbia drainage. Goldstone Pass is near Bloody Dick Divide, named for an Englishman named Richards who settled on Bloody Dick Creek. His principal adjective was "bloody."

GORDON PASS (*ca.* 7900) — Seeley Lake area, Swan Range. Trail up Gordon Creek and Lick Creek from South Fork, Flathead River, crosses pass at Little Carmine Peak and descends Holland Creek past Holland Lake to Swan River. Columbia drainage. Pass was named for a Dr. Gordon of Great Falls.

GRANITE PASS (6400) — Adjoins Lolo Pass on north, Bitterroot Range. From new Lewis and Clark Highway at Lolo Pass, road runs northwest along crest a few miles to Granite Pass and ends on Crooked Fork of Lochsa River. Pass links Granite Creek (Bitterroot River) trail and Crooked Fork. Columbia watershed.

GRAVE CREEK PASS: See South Kootenie Pass.

GREENHORN PASS (6200) — At top of Greenhorn Gulch just north of Mullan Pass.

GUNSIGHT PASS (7000), CD — Glacier National Park. From Going-to-the-Sun Chalet, Gunsight Trail, a great favorite, ascends St. Mary River past Florence Falls and Gunsight Lake to spectacular pass. South trail descends past rock-bound Lake Ellen Wilson and Lincoln Lake to Lincoln Creek and Middle Fork, Flathead River. St. Mary River (Oldman–South Saskatchewan)–Columbia drainage. Also called Lincoln Pass. Named in 1891 by George Bird Grinnell for its resemblance to the rear sight of a rifle.

HELL GATE PASS (*ca.* 5800) — Deer Lodge area. Shortcut road from Deer Lodge northwest to Elliston is said to cross this Hell Gate Pass. Clark Fork–Little Blackfoot drainages. But in his report of 1861, John Mullan uses this Hell Gate name referring to a pass on the CD at the extreme head of Little Blackfoot River south of present MacDonald Pass. On Mullan's maps, the term "Hell Gate Passes" seems to refer to all the passes reached by the Little Blackfoot and its tributaries, including his own Mullan Pass. And then there is plain Hell Gate, meaning the canyon passage of Clark Fork River just east of Missoula.

HENRY'S PASS: Not precisely identified CD crossing just south of Raynold's Pass mentioned by F. V. Hayden (1872), who called it South Pass also. Perhaps Henry's Pass is today's Reas Pass.

HIMES PASS (5500) — Thompson Falls area, twenty-two miles north, Cabinet Mountains. Pass links Himes Creek and Fisher River of the Kootenai. Clark Fork–Columbia drainages.

HOMESTAKE PASS (6356), CD — Butte area, southeast. From Whitehall and U.S. Route 10S, back road has been running up Pipestone Creek and along Homestake Creek over pass for descent to Butte. Northern Pacific Railway follows a similar, more winding route. In 1963, the Montana Highway Department had plans ready to put Interstate 90 over Homestake Pass to Butte rather than over Pipestone Pass used by U.S. 10S. Homestake received its name in the 1870's from a man named Spencer who made a small stake near the pass between Miners Gulch and Niles Gulch.

HORSE CREEK PASS (*ca.* 6500) — Lost Trail Pass area, southwest, Beaverhead Mountains, Bitterroot Range. From Alta, back road runs south up West Fork, Bitterroot River, and Beaver Creek to Idaho border at pass, beyond which road ends at a trail descending west side by Horse Creek trail to Salmon River. Columbia watershed.

HORSE THIEF PASS: See Swiftcurrent Pass.

INSPIRATION PASS (7150) — Swan Lake area, ten miles southeast, Swan Range. From Goat Creek Station of Swan River State Forest, trail runs up to pass and down east side to Bunker Creek–South Fork, Flathead River. Columbia watershed.

INUYA PASS (6200) — Kalispell area, north, Whitefish Range. From North Fork, Flathead River, trail ascends Whale Creek and Inuya Creek to pass west of Mount Thompson Seton. North descent down Yakinikak Creek to road and Flathead River again. Columbia watershed.

JEFFERSON PASS (6900), CD — Glacier National Park, Livingstone

Range. This tremendous traverse below Carter Glacier links Bowman Creek (Flathead) and Valentine Creek (Waterton). Columbia–South Saskatchewan watersheds. Said to have been named for an early prospector and hunter of the region, Thomas Jefferson.

KING'S HILL PASS (7389) — Little Belt Mountains. From Great Falls, U.S. Route 89, a fine scenic highway runs south through alpine fur and spruce groves over pass to White Sulphur Springs and Livingston. Pass links Sawmill–Belt creeks and Lamb Creek–Sheep Creek–Smith River. Missouri watershed.

KOOTENAI PASS (5600), CD — Glacier National Park. Pass links Continental Creek (McDonald Creek) and Waterton River. Columbia–South Saskatchewan–Hudson Bay watersheds.

LARCH HILL PASS (7676), CD — Northwest of Augusta and Gibson Lake in Bob Marshall Wilderness Area. From Mosse Creek of North Fork of Sun River, crest trail reaches pass south of Larch Hill and joins trails on west side running south to White River and north to Wall Creek–Spotted Bear River. Near Spotted Bear Pass. Missouri–Columbia watersheds.

LEMHI PASS (7373), CD — This famous and still obscure crossing is reached from State Route 28 at Tendoy, Idaho, by a good, steep, narrow, interesting back road winding up Agency Creek past Copper Queen Mine, Sacajawea Memorial Camp and Sacajawea Spring to top, thirteen miles, marked by a cattle gate into Montana. Descent down Trail–Horse Prairie creeks into bleakly beautiful Beaverhead Valley and U.S. Route 91 at Armstead. Here Horse Prairie Creek and Red Rock River join to form Beaverhead River. Columbia–Missouri drainage. Meriwether Lewis crossed this pass August 12, 1805. William Clark and Sacajawea followed soon after. It was called Middle Pass in 1850's and it is marked Lewis and Clark Pass on some gas company maps today, though Lewis and Clark Pass is far north and east of Lemhi. Name is a corruption of Limhi, a character in the Book of Mormon.

LEWIS AND CLARK PASS (6323), CD — Helena area, northwest, and just north of State Route 20 and Rogers Pass. From State Route 20, some eight miles east of Lincoln, a marker points north to Lewis and Clark Pass. A pleasant road ascends Alice Creek north ten miles, but it ends at Alice Creek Guard Station short of the pass, which is reached a mile or so farther along on a trail. Perhaps 4WDs could make it over the historic traverse which, it would seem, deserves a good road all the way in, and a picnic area. The pass links Alice Creek of Blackfoot River and Green Creek, which flows into Middle Fork, Dearborn River. Meriwether Lewis and his men crossed it in 1806 on their homeward way. In 1853, Frederick W. Lander called it Lewis's Pass in one place and Railroad Pass in another.

LEWIS AND CLARK PASS: Incorrectly applied to Lemhi Pass at times.

LIMESTONE PASS (7100) — Ovando–Monture area, north, from State Route 20. From Monture Creek, trail forks right to pass and down north side by branch of Limestone Creek–Danaher Creek. Blackfoot–South Fork, Flathead drainages, Columbia watershed.

LION CREEK PASS (ca. 8000) — Swan Lake area, twenty miles southeast near Swan Peak and Glacier. From Swan River road, trail ascends Lion

Creek and over pass to Palisade Creek–Little Salmon River and South Fork, Flathead River. Columbia watershed.

LINCOLN PASS: See Gunsight Pass.

LITTLE BLACKFOOT PASS: Alternate name for Mullan Pass in 1850's.

LOGAN PASS (6654), CD — From West Glacier, the inconceivably beautiful Going-to-the-Sun Highway runs past blue Lake McDonald and up McDonald Creek to the Garden Wall shelf, which carries it ten miles to the pass by an easy six per cent grade. This may be the loveliest mountain crossing for automobiles in the Rockies — for all of such exciting roads as those over Red Mountain Pass and Wolf Creek Pass in Colorado, and Beartooth Pass and Snowy Range Pass in Wyoming. The east-side descent to St. Mary Lake is just as thrilling. St. Mary River (Oldman–South Saskatchewan–Hudson Bay)–Middle Fork, Flathead River (Columbia) drainages. The Logan Pass road was opened for through traffic on July 13, 1933.

LOLO PASS (5187) — Missoula area, southwest, Bitterroot Range. From U.S. Route 93 at Lolo, the fine new (1962) Lewis and Clark Highway ascends Lolo Creek past Lolo Hot Springs (nice pool) and "Fort Fizzle" to pleasant forested pass, and descends Pack and Crooked Fork creeks to Lochsa River on its way to the Clearwater and Orofino, Idaho. Columbia watershed. Lewis and Clark crossed the pass westbound on September 13, 1805; eastbound on June 29, 1806. The Northern Pacific Railway built twenty miles of grade in 1909 with the idea of putting its main line over the pass, and then abandoned the scheme. The mysterious word "Lolo" is "Lou-Lou" on Lieutenant G. K. Warren's 1857 map. Some say the word means simply "Low-Low" since the traverse *is* low. Others claim it is a Flathead version of "Lawrence," a pioneer Bitterroot trapper. Others assert that "Lolo" means "muddy water" in Nez Perce, though that kind of water is not characteristic of Lolo Pass streams. Has been called Northern Nez Perce Pass.

LONE TREE PASS (*ca.* 8000) — Ravalli area, east, Mission Range. Pass links Swan River (South Fork, Flathead) on east below Panoramic Peak with Ashley Creek (Flathead) on west. Columbia watershed.

LOOKOUT PASS (4738) — Wallace (Idaho) area, Bitterroot Range. From Missoula, U.S. Route 10 runs west, up St. Regis River and over this low pass, descending Coeur d'Alêne River to Wallace, en route to Spokane. Columbia watershed. Northern Pacific Railroad uses same crossing.

LOST HORSE CREEK PASS (*ca.* 6750) — Hamilton area, west, Bitterroot Range. From U.S. Route 93, phone line and trail ascends Lost Horse Creek to Twin Lakes and pass where several west-side trails meet, including Moose Creek trail. Columbia watershed. The name derives from the 1881 incident when prospectors tried to ford the creek in high water and one horse drowned.

LOST TRAIL PASS (6951) — Bitterroot Range. From North Fork, Idaho, U.S. Route 93 winds up picturesque North Fork of Salmon River and then Moose Creek through evergreens to top of pass and down Camp Creek to Sula and the lush Bitterroot Valley. Columbia River drainage. Pass is only a few hundred feet west of CD, which is actually crossed by the nearby Chief Joseph Pass highway leading to Big Hole Battlefield

National Monument and the historic old Gibbons Pass road. The Lost Trail highway is of modern origin.

LOW PASS: Captain William F. Raynolds's name for Raynolds Pass.

LULU PASS (9718) — Just north of Cooke City and Daisy Pass. Mining road runs over this traverse to reach Glengarry Mines under Scotch Bonnet Mountain (10,382).

MACDONALD PASS (6323), CD — Helena area, west. From Helena, U.S. Route 12 winds up pebbly Tenmile Creek through evergreens and over the open top of the pass, descending Little Blackfoot River into the pastoral Clark Fork Valley. Missouri–Columbia watersheds. Just south of Mullan and Priest passes. The original ten-mile toll was built in 1870 by E. M. "Lige" Dunphy and managed by Alexander MacDonald until 1876, when MacDonald became owner as well as manager. In 1883, MacDonald sold the road to David H. Gilmore. Three six-horse stages crossed the pass daily in the 1880's on the Helena–Deer Lodge run. One of the great days for MacDonald Pass occurred during the summer of 1911, when old James J. Hill, creator of the Great Northern, offered $10,000 to anybody who would fly an airplane from the State Fair Grounds at Helena across the Continental Divide. A stunt flyer named Cromwell Dixon did the job, using Mullan Pass one way and MacDonald the other. But poor Dixon did not get much pleasure out of his $10,000. A few days later, while he was stunting at the Spokane Fair, his plane crashed and he was killed. For unknown reasons, MacDonald Pass is almost universally misspelled McDonald Pass on maps. Highway Department plans (1963) call for a four-lane road over the pass during the next few years.

MADISON PASS: Hayden's occasional name for Raynolds Pass.

MARIAS PASS (5215) — Just south of Glacier National Park. From East Glacier Park, U.S. Route 2 runs up this easy, handsome, wooded pass along Summit Creek to the Theodore Roosevelt obelisk and John Frank Stevens statue on top, ten miles. Descent to West Glacier is along Bear Creek and Middle Fork, Flathead River, forty-six miles, with fine glimpses to the north of Glacier Park summits. Marias Pass links Summit Creek–Two Medicine Creek–Marias River of the Missouri watershed to Flathead River–Clark Fork of Columbia drainage. Marias River was named in 1805 by Meriwether Lewis for the girl he hoped to marry, his cousin, Miss Maria Wood, who later married a man named Clarkson. The pass is shown on many early maps, including Lieutenant G. K. Warren's (1857). It is called True Maria's Pass on the Raynolds expedition map of 1860. Rand McNally's *Business Atlas*, 1876, has a spot marked Marias Pass, though the spot is imprecisely located. It has been called also Big Gap, and Eneas Pass. The site at the east foot of the pass known as False Summit was judged incorrectly to be the top by a party of engineers in 1890 as they mapped the grade which the Great Northern Railway was about to use. Marias Pass is the lowest CD crossing in the American Rockies.

MEDICINE LODGE PASS (7650), CD — Next gap west of Monida Pass, Beaverhead Mountains. From Dubois, Idaho, back road runs up Medicine Lodge Creek to pass and down Sheep Creek to Dell, Montana, and Red Rock River (U.S. Route 91). Beaverhead (Missouri)–Snake (Columbia) watersheds. From near top of pass, 4WD road runs southwest along crest and down south side into Nicholia Creek country. This ancient crossing was named for a sixty-foot-high medicine lodge said to have been built in the area by Blackfeet Indians in which to make medicine to help them in battle. It was called Father's Defile by some after Father De Smet crossed it in 1841.

MEDICINE ROCK PASS (*ca.* 6000) — Wilborn–Wolf Creek area. Mentioned by James Doty who crossed it on July 26, 1854, en route from Mullan Pass northeast toward Dearborn River and Fort Benton.

MIDDLE PASS: See Lemhi Pass.

MINTON CREEK PASS (4053) — Trout Creek–Larchwood community, twenty-four miles downstream on U.S. Route 10A from Thompson Falls. From Larchwood, road runs south to Minton Creek trail, which crosses pass and descends south fork of Marten Creek to U.S. 10A again. Clark Fork (Columbia) watershed.

MONIDA PASS (6823), CD — From Idaho Falls, Idaho, U.S. Route 91 ascends Beaver Creek northward to low, unexciting pass and town, the latter a former stage stop on trail from Salt Lake City to the Montana gold camps, and later a station on the Utah and Northern Railroad. On the north side, the highway descends Red Rock River to Dillon, Montana. Snake–Columbia and Missouri watersheds. The pass seemed to have no name in its stagecoach days, even if it was the main crossing into Montana. When the railroad was built over it in 1880, a train dispatcher named the pass station Monida, combining parts of the names of Idaho and Montana since it stood on the border.

MONTGOMERY PASS (*ca.* 7500) — Helena area, twelve miles southeast. Trail links Antelope Creek and east fork, McClellan Creek–Prickly Pear Creek. Missouri watershed.

MOON PASS (4964) — Mullan (Idaho) area, five miles southwest. Pass links Placer Creek (Coeur d'Alène) and North Fork, St. Joe River. Columbia watershed.

MULLAN PASS (6000), CD — Helena area, northwest. Good road and Northern Pacific Railway both run from Helena through Austin over this celebrated gap, descending Dog Creek branch of Little Blackfoot River to meet MacDonald Pass highway, U.S. Route 12. Missouri–Columbia watersheds. Mullan Pass was marked Hell Gate Pass on some maps of 1850's and 1860's. It was named for its discoverer, Lieutenant John Mullan (1853), who built the Mullan Military Road — Fort Benton to Walla Walla, Washington — over it in the late 1850's. In 1882, the Northern Pacific pushed its 3850-foot tunnel under the pass at an altitude of 5547 feet above sea level, reducing somewhat the east-side grade advantage which the Great Northern would have later by crossing the lower Marias Pass. There is no west-side advantage, as both lines have a vertical drop of about 2000 feet in their respective runs to Missoula and Belton. In 1887, part of Mullan Tunnel caved in and, during the weeks of repairs, an army of wagons carted freight and passengers over the top. Today, a rustic Masonic lodge with three stations, log seats and a stone altar occupies the top of the pass, memorializing the start of the Masonic movement in Montana at that spot during the summer of 1862 by Nathaniel P. Langford and three companions. Langford, one of Hayden's surveyors later on, came to Montana with the ill-fated Captain Fisk expedition planning a wagon road from St. Paul to Fort Benton. He was the first superintendent of Yellowstone Park.

MUSKRAT PASS (6000), CD — Between Marias Pass and Badger Pass south of it. From North and South Badger creeks, trails reach pass by Muskrat Creek and descend Cox Creek to Middle Fork, Flathead River, or recross divide near Beaver Lake to the Badger Pass trail. Missouri–Columbia watersheds.

NEZ PERCE PASS (6589) — Lost Trail Pass area, west, Bitterroot Range. From U.S. Route 93 at Connor (Montana), a poor but interesting road ascends the old Indian trail along Nez Perce Fork, Bitterroot River to pass, and down Deep Creek–Selway River to Middle Fork of the Clearwater. Columbia watershed. Also called Southern Nez Perce Pass.

NORTHERN NEZ PERCE PASS: Same as Lolo Pass.

NORTH PASS: Hayden's name for Raynolds Pass (1872).

NORTH PASS: During the trapper period, "North Pass" might mean Targhee Pass. On J. H. Young's 1850 map of the United States, the name was applied to Lewis and Clark Pass.

OBSERVATION PASS (7595), CD — Augusta–Gibson Lake area, southwest. From South Fork of North Fork of Sun River, wilderness trail runs over pass and down Danaher–Rapid Creek to the South Fork, Flathead River. Columbia–Missouri watershed.

OLD FLATHEAD PASS: The Montana historian, M. A. Leeson, used this name in 1885, meaning Pitamakan Pass.

PIEGAN PASS (7810) — Glacier National Park. From Logan Pass highway, a popular spruce-and-fir trail ascends Siyeh Creek and branches left off Siyeh Pass trail to Piegan Pass before descending at great length down Cataract Creek to Lake Josephine and Many Glacier Chalet. St. Mary River (Oldman–South Saskatchewan)–Hudson Bay drainage.

PINE CREEK PASS (*ca.* 7200) — Victor, Idaho, area, southwest. From Victor, a fine new road, Idaho State Route 31, runs south up Little Pine Creek, over pass, and down Pine Creek to Swan Valley and Snake River, twenty-one miles. Snake River–Teton River drainages.

PINTLAR PASS (8500), CD — Georgetown Lake area, south, Anaconda–Pintlar Wilderness between East and West Pintlar peaks. From Rock Creek road, trail ascends Middle Fork and over pass to Big Hole River road (State Route 43). Near Bitterroot Pass. Pintlar is said to have been named for an early miner-settler, Charles Pintler or Pinter.

PIPESTONE PASS (6418), CD — Butte area, southeast, Highland Mountains. From Whitehall at U.S. Route 10S, highway winds up Little Pipestone Creek to forested top of pass and down hairpins of steeper west side along Blacktail Creek to the astonishing copper camp of Butte. Jefferson River (Missouri)–Clark Fork (Columbia) drainages. The Chicago, Milwaukee and St. Paul Railroad put its line under the pass through a 2290-foot tunnel about 1909 on its way across Montana and through the Bitterroots in another tunnel under St. Paul Pass. At that time, the Northern Pacific controlled the state's coal fields but the Montana Power Company had plenty of hydro-electric power. As a result, the Milwaukee Road was electrified all the way through the Rockies — a unique and successful experiment. Electric locomotives still haul the Milwaukee's freights, though passenger trains are hauled by diesels. The Northern Pacific to Butte crosses the CD five miles north of Pipestone by Homestake Pass (6356). The Butte-serving Great Northern crosses eight miles north of Homestake by Elk Park Pass (6374). Motor traffic on U.S. 10S over Pipestone may be reduced greatly if Interstate 90 is built over Homestake Pass as planned in 1963. Pipestone Pass, crossed by a road from the 1870's on, got its name from Pipestone Hot Springs nearby, where a ledge supplied pipe material to the Indians.

PITAMAKAN PASS (7861), CD — Glacier National Park. From Two Medicine Lake (reached by road from Glacier Park town near southeast corner of park) trail runs up Dry Fork past Cut Bank Pass. West-trail descent is down Nyack Creek (Middle Fork, Flathead River). Missouri–Columbia watersheds. Pitamakan is the popular Indian Cut Bank Pass of history. It has had a variety of other names including False Marias Pass, alluding to Abiel Tinkham's mistaken idea that it was Marias Pass when he crossed it in 1853. The Raynolds expedition map of 1860 called it Marias Pass. Rand McNally's Business Atlas, 1876, marked it Flathead Pass. It was named for a wonderful Indian maiden, Pitamakan, or Running Eagle, who was known variously as "the Blackfoot Amazon," "the Blackfoot Joan of Arc," or — not quite so laudatory — "the Weasel Woman." Pitamakan wore male attire and led her warriors in raids in the Flathead country, but her great distinction was her skill as a horse thief. As a young girl, she announced that she would wed any man who would steal more horses on a given night than she could. No man ever did, so she never married. She died about 1850.

PORCUPINE PASS (5658) — Thompson Falls area, northwest, Bitterroot Range. From Tuscor community, some twenty-five miles downstream from Thompson Falls, a road leaves U.S. Route 10A and becomes a trail ascending South Fork Creek to pass. The trail runs thence along crest to come down ridge between Rampike and Cabin creeks. Clark Fork–Coeur d'Alêne watersheds.

PRIEST PASS (6000), CD — Helena area, northwest. From MacDonald Pass highway, road forks right up Spring Creek and over gentle pass in grassy setting. On west descent, road meets Mullan Pass road along Dog Creek of the Little Blackfoot. Missouri–Columbia drainage. Valentine Priest, who was about to die of tuberculosis, came to Virginia City from the East with one of Jim Bridger's eighty-wagon trains in 1864. He recovered soon, returned East, broke down again in 1869, and came back to settle permanently on Grizzly Gulch just southwest of Helena. In the late 1870's, he kept the MacDonald Pass toll gate for Alexander MacDonald and decided that he could build an easier toll road crossing of the CD. The result, in 1879, was his road over Priest Pass, which actually was easier as well as three hundred feet lower. Thereafter, until well into the motor age, Priest Pass was the most popular traverse west of Helena.

PRYOR'S GAP (4640) — Billings area, south. From Pryor, Montana, a back road runs near the late Will James's ranch and through gap toward Wyoming border south of Warren. Named for Lewis and Clark's Sergeant Nathaniel Pryor. This old Crow Indian route is Beckwourth's Bad Pass.

PYRAMID PASS (7000) — Seeley Lake area north of Clearwater Junction and U.S. Route 10 Flathead Range. From Morrell Creek road end, Trail Creek trail crosses pass and descends Youngs Creek branch to South Fork, Flathead River. Clearwater (Blackfoot)–Flathead drainages, Columbia watershed.

RAILROAD PASS: F. W. Lander's name for Lewis and Clark Pass, 1853.

RAYNOLDS PASS (7400), CD — Henrys Lake (Idaho) area, north. From near Henrys Lake, good road ascends Timber Creek briefly and over easy pass to Missouri Flats and junction with Montana State Route 1 at Madison River below Quake Lake. Missouri–Columbia watersheds. Pass is next crossing westerly from Targhee Pass. The early trappers, after Andrew Henry's first crossing in 1810, could have used either Raynolds Pass or Targhee Pass when they spoke of moving "through the North Pass to Missouri Lake in which rises the Madison Fork of the Missouri River." Raynolds Pass had no special name until Captain William F. Raynolds crossed it with Jim Bridger and reported on it in 1860. Has been called Sawtelle Pass.

REAS PASS (6935), CD — Raynolds Pass area, southeast. The Union Pacific Railroad from Idaho Falls crosses this forested pass, partly up Thirsty Creek of Henrys Fork and down a Madison River branch to West Yellowstone, Mont.

RED EAGLE PASS (6800), CD — Glacier National Park. From Red Eagle Lake, trail runs up Red Eagle Creek to Red Eagle Glacier and pass. South descent by Nyack Creek to Middle Fork, Flathead River. St. Mary River (Oldman–South Saskatchewan) and Columbia watersheds. Named in 1887 by George Bird Grinnel for his friend Chief Red Eagle of the Blackfoot tribe.

REDGAP PASS (7610) — Glacier National Park. From Elizabeth Lake, a trail ascends Redgap Creek to pass and down south and east along Kennedy Creek to St. Mary River. South Saskatchewan watershed.

RED ROCK PASS (7056), CD — Ravnolds Pass area, west, Henrys Lake Mountains. From Henrys Lake, Idaho, good road crosses pass and descends Red Rock River headwaters, the extreme source of the Missouri River, to join U.S. Route 15 on way to Dillon, Montana. Missouri–Columbia watersheds. Hayden's men called it West Pass (1872).

ROGERS PASS (5609), CD — Helena area, northwest. New State Route 20 (1957) crosses pass on way from Great Falls to Missoula by Middle Fork, Dearborn River, and down Pass Creek and Cadotte Creek to Blackfoot River. Missouri–Columbia drainages. The pass was named for the famous American engineer, Major A. B. Rogers, who surveyed it in 1887 while seeking a low crossing of the CD for James J. Hill's Great Northern Railroad. Hill preferred Marias Pass, which was about four hundred feet lower. In 1882, Major Rogers selected a traverse of the Selkirk Range in Canada for the Canadian Pacific which is known now as Rogers Pass also.

ROSS PASS (7600) — Bozeman Pass area, north, Bridger Range. Pass links middle fork of Bridger Creek (Yellowstone) and Ross Creek (Gallatin). Missouri watershed.

SACAJAWEA PASS: Occasional name for Bozeman Pass.

ST. PAUL PASS (*ca.* 5163) — Wallace (Idaho) area, southeast. From U.S. Route 10 short of Lookout Pass (east side), back road winds up St. Regis River branch called Rainy Creek to St. Paul Pass and descends Cliff Creek and Loop Creek to North Fork, St. Joe River. Columbia watershed. Chicago, Milwaukee and St. Paul Railroad moves beneath this pass through an 8771-foot tunnel built in 1908.

ST. REGIS PASS (*ca.* 5000) — Wallace (Idaho) area, east, Bitterroot Range. The main Missoula–Spokane highway used to cross this pass instead of Lookout Pass a mile away, which is used now by U.S. Route 10. St. Regis River and Coeur d'Alêne River drainages, Columbia watershed. Governor Isaac Stevens called this general low area Coeur d'Alêne Pass in 1853. When John Mullan built the Mullan Road in 1859–1861, he put it over St. Regis Pass, which he renamed Sohon Pass in honor of his guide and interpreter, Gustavus Sohon — apparently a man of many parts because he was Mullan's artist, too. Father De Smet named the pass St. Regis in 1841.

SAWTELLE PASS: Occasional name for Raynolds Pass in 1870's. Gilman Sawtelle was a rancher at Henrys Lake, but the black flies bothered his stock so much that he took to raising trout for the sporting house trade in Virginia City.

SILVER BUTTE PASS (4258) — Thompson Falls area, north, Cabinet Mountains near Himes Pass. From Vermilion River (U.S. Route 10A near Trout Creek), road ascends West Fork to pass and descends Silver Butte Fisher River to U.S. 2 south of Libby. Kootenai–Clark Fork drainages, Columbia watershed.

SIYEH PASS (8110) — Glacier National Park. From Going-to-the-Sun Chalet, trail leads to pass in seven miles by Baring Creek and Sexton Glacier. It descends to Logan Pass highway through Preston Park down Siyeh Creek. St. Mary River–South Saskatchewan watershed.

SKALKAHO PASS (7258) — Hamilton area, east, Sapphire Range. From near Hamilton, fascinating road ascends Daly Creek past the magnificent Skalkaho Falls (superb views west of Bitterroot Range at its best), and on down north fork of Rock Creek to U.S. Route 10A at Porters Corners, fifty-five miles. Columbia watershed. Skalkaho: Flathead word meaning "many trails." In 1853, on his trip from Bitterroot Valley to Fort Hall, Lieutenant John Mullan recorded it as "Sharkahole Creek."

SMITH CREEK PASS (*ca.* 8000) — Swan Lake area, south, Swan Range. Trail from near Condon Ranger Station runs up Smith Creek of Swan River to pass and down Little Salmon River to South Fork, Flathead River. Columbia drainage.

SOHON PASS: See St. Regis Pass.

SOUTHERN NEZ PERCE PASS: See Nez Perce Pass.

SOUTHERN PASS: Name used on Lewis and Clark map, published in 1814 with the history of the expedition, meaning Targhee Pass. Later, the phrase referred to South Pass in Wyoming.

SOUTH KOOTENIE PASS (5119) — Kalispell area, north, Whitefish Range just north of Inuya Pass. From Tobacco River of the Kootenai, ancient Indian trail runs east up Grave Creek and Lewis Creek to pass and descends Nokio Creek and Yakinikak Creek to North Fork, Flathead River. This pass is marked and spelled thus on George M. Dawson's Canadian map of 1886. Also called Grave Creek Pass. The Indian trail continued easterly from Flathead River into Canada and over the Canadian South Kootenay (or Boundary) Pass to Waterton Lakes. Kootenai Indians were using it regularly on their buffalo hunts to the plains as late as 1880.

SPOTTED BEAR PASS (8722), CD — Northwest of Augusta and Gibson Lake in Bob Marshall Wilderness Area. From North Fork, Sun River, and Gates Park, trail runs up Rock Creek to pass near Larch Hill Pass. Trail descends north side along Spotted Bear River to South Fork, Flathead River, and Spotted Bear Ranger Station. Missouri–Columbia watersheds.

SQUAW PASS (7262), CD — Raynolds Pass area, west. Pass links Duck Creek (Henrys Lake–Snake River) and Red Rock River (extreme headwater, Missouri River). Missouri–Columbia watersheds. Name derives from fact that Bannock Indians camped often between the mouth of Squaw Creek (large) and Papoose Creek (small).

SQUAW PASS (ca. 6800) — Cabinet Mountains. Pass under Cube Iron Mountain is crossed by trail from Thompson Falls and Mount Silcox Lookout to Porcupine Lake, Four Lakes Creek and West Fork, Thompson River. Clark Fork (Columbia) drainage. Longer trail continues north from pass to Vermilion River.

STEMPLE PASS (6349), CD — Helena area, northwest. From Canyon Creek and Wilborn, road forks left from Flesher Pass road up Virginia Creek to top of pass and abandoned mine shaft and down north fork of Poorman Creek to Lincoln and State Route 20 on Blackfoot River. Named for J. A. Stemple, who located the Stemple Mining District.

STONEY INDIAN PASS (7310) — Glacier National Park, Livingstone Range. From Waterton River, trail ascends Pass Creek to Stoney Indian Lake and Pass. South descent to Mokowanis and Belly rivers. South Saskatchewan (Hudson Bay) drainage. Tremendous scenery.

SUNDANCE PASS (11,040) — Cooke City area, north, Beartooth Plateau–Granite Peak region. From U.S. Route 12 south of Red Lodge, a long, entrancing and rugged trail ascends Lake Fork of Rock Creek past Lost Lake and September Morn Lakes, climbing steeply then to Sundance Pass and descending as steeply past Sundance Lake to west fork of Rock Creek and Red Lodge road. Rock Creek flows into Clarks Fork of the Yellowstone. Missouri watershed. Sundance is Montana's highest trail pass.

SUN RIVER PASS (6000), CD — Marias Pass area, south. Trail runs up North Fork, Sun River, to pass at its extreme headwaters, and down west side along Bowl Creek to Middle Fork, Flathead River. Missouri–Columbia watersheds.

SURPRISE PASS (6000) — Glacier National Park. Nyack Creek trail crosses pass to Martha's Basin and Coal Creek (Middle Fork, Flathead River). Columbia watershed.

SWIFTCURRENT PASS (7175), CD — Glacier National Park. From the big curve in Going-to-the-Sun (Logan Pass) Highway, important trail runs over pass to Swiftcurrent Creek and several lakes, and then to Many Glacier Chalet and Lake Sherburne. St. Mary (South Saskatchewan–Hudson Bay)–McDonald Creek (Middle Fork, Flathead–Columbia) watersheds. Formerly called Horse Thief Pass.

SWITCHBACK PASS (7768) — Marias Pass area, south, near but not on CD. From Spotted Bear River, trail runs up East Fork, Pentagon Creek, to pass. Various trails descend from pass by Basin Creek and Clack Creek to Middle Fork, Flathead River.

TARGHEE PASS (7078) — From Henrys Lake, Idaho, U.S. Route 20–191 ascends Targhee Creek and Howard Creek to this very old traverse amid lodgepole pines and descends Denny Creek–South Fork of Madison River toward West Yellowstone, Montana. Columbia–Missouri watersheds. Pass was named for Chief Tyghee of the Bannocks, who died in the early 1870's. It was on the main Bannock trail from the Snake River country to Gallatin Valley. In 1872 Hayden's surveyors called it Tahgee Pass, Tyghee Pass and East Pass and recommended it for a railroad from Salt Lake City to Yellowstone Park.

TEN MILE PASS: Rand McNally's *Business Atlas* (1876) name for MacDonald Pass.

TETON PASS (7775), CD — Marias Pass area, south. From West Fork, Teton River, trail crosses pass and descends Bowl Creek near Sun River Pass to Gooseberry Park and Middle Fork, Flathead River. Missouri–Columbia watersheds.

THEODORE ROOSEVELT PASS: Same as Marias Pass.

THERRIAULT PASS (7245) — Eureka area (U.S. Route 93, extreme northern Montana). From Therriault Lakes of Wigwam River (Elk), trail crosses pass and descends Griffin Creek drainage to Tobacco River road. Kootenai (Columbia) watershed. Named for operator of first Thompson Falls–Murray stage.

THOMPSON PASS (4859) — Bitterroot Range. From Thompson Falls, road ascends Prospect Creek and over pass to Prichard Creek and Murray, Idaho. Clark Fork–Coeur d'Alêne drainages, Columbia watershed. Named for the great English explorer of the early 1800's, David Thompson, who considered this region his home.

TRIPLE DIVIDE (*ca.* 8500), CD — Augusta–Gibson Lake area, southwest. Divide is five miles south of Observation Pass at headwaters of South Fork of North Fork of Sun River, Rapid Creek of South Fork of Flathead River, and Dry Fork of North Fork, Blackfoot River. Missouri–Columbia watersheds.

TRUE MARIAS PASS: Name used for Marias Pass on Raynolds expedition map of 1859–1860.

TWO MEDICINE PASS (7675), CD — Glacier National Park, southeast. From Two Medicine Lake, old Indian trail ascends Paradise Creek right fork past Cobalt Lake and along crest to pass above Paradise Lake. Sublime country. West descent is down Park Creek (Middle Fork, Flathead River). Missouri–Columbia watersheds. In olden time, two bands of Blackfoot Indians turned up at lake simultaneously for their separate medicine lodge ceremonies. They decided to hold the rites together — thus the name.

UNION PASS: Hayden's name for Bridger Pass (Montana), 1872.

WELCOME PASS (7165) — Augusta area, southwest, near Scapegoat Mountain. Dearborn River trail forks up Welcome Creek to pass and descends Jakie and Smith creeks to the Augusta road. Dearborn–Sun (Missouri) drainages.

WEST PASS: See Red Rock Pass.

WHITE RIVER PASS (7592), CD — Augusta–Gibson Lake area. From Gibson Lake, trail runs up Sun River, West Fork, and Indian Creek to pass and down west side along South Fork, White River, to South Fork, Flathead River, and Big Salmon Lake. Missouri–Columbia watersheds.

WINDY PASS (9368) — Bozeman area, south, Gallatin Range. From Portal Creek of Gallatin River road end off U.S. Route 191, trail ascends to pass and down Big Creek of Yellowstone River to Big Creek road. Missouri drainage.

WINDY PASS (7000) — Ovando–Lincoln area, northeast. Pass links East Fork, Landers Fork, and North Fork of Blackfoot River by way of McDermott Creek. Blackfoot river drainages, Columbia watershed. Pass is in Kleinschmidt Flat–Cooper's Lake mining country.

YOUNGS PASS (7300) — Ovando area, north, Flathead Range. From Ovando, trail runs up Monture Creek and then Lodgepole Creek to pass, descending Jenny and Youngs creeks to South Fork, Flathead River. Blackfoot–Flathead drainages, Columbia watershed. Named for old-time settler, Charles "Kid" Young.

Northern New Mexico Passes

AMORY PASS: See Emery Gap.

APACHE PASS (9300) — Taos area, Carson N. F., two and a half miles south of Palo Flechado Pass, 4WD trail. Cieneguilla Creek (Canadian)–Fernando de Taos Creek (Rio Grande). United States Army used it some in 1850's.

APACHE PASS: Canoncito part of La Glorieta Pass.

BOBCAT PASS: See Red River Pass.

COSTILLA PASS (10,100) — Costilla area, 4WD trail, much of it private, from Costilla to Stonewall, Colorado, via San Francisco Pass in Colorado. Vermejo River (Canadian)–Costilla Creek (Rio Grande). Former stage road. Prospective D. & R. G. route, 1871. Costilla: Spanish for "Rib."

COSTILLA PASS (9700) — Costilla area, 4WD trail from Red River Pass road north to Comanche Creek. Moreno Creek (Canadian)–Comanche Creek (Rio Grande). Road from at least 1878.

EMERY GAP (ca. 8000) — Raton–Folsom area east of Johnson Mesa. Una de Gato Creek (Canadian)–Purgatoire River (Arkansas). Named for Madison Emery, early settler of Folsom neighborhood.

FOWLER PASS (9189) — Cimarron area of old Maxwell Grant, now Philmont Scout Camp. Road crosses pass, Bonito Creek–Urraca Creek. Named for Major Jacob Fowler, 1820's pioneer.

HOLMAN HILL SUMMIT (9041) — Mora area, all-weather State Route 3, Mora–Taos, forty-seven miles. Mora River (Pecos)–Rio Pueblo (Rio Grande).

HORSE LAKE PASS (7675), CD — Chama area, reached on back roads from U.S. Route 84 at Park View. Park View–Dulce, thirty-five miles. Horse Lake Creek (Chama)–Amargo River (San Juan). Used from 1760's.

KEARNY'S GAP: See Las Vegas Pass.

LA GLORIETA PASS (7500) — Santa Fe area, Santa Fe N. F., U.S. Route 84–85, paved, all-weather, Santa Fe–Las Vegas, eighty miles. Pecos River branch–Galisteo Creek (Rio Grande). Short detour to Old Pecos Pueblo State Monument. West end is Apache Pass. La Glorieta: "Hub" in Spanish. The Santa Fe Railroad crosses pass at 7445 feet, with a westside grade (the steeper side) of 158 feet per mile.

LAS VEGAS PASS (6400) — Defile just south of Las Vegas used by Kearny's Army of the West, August 15, 1846.

LONG'S PASS (8040): Raton area, fifteen miles west of Raton Pass, crossed by private road from Sopris, Colorado, Canadian–Purgatoire (Arkansas). Near Chicken Creek and Rex-Coal Canyon roads over Ratons. *Not* named for Stephen Long.

MANCO BURRO PASS (7762) — Raton area, State Route 72 runs to Yankee and over Manco Burro to Bell in fascinating Johnson Mesa country. East fork, Chicorica Creek (Canadian)–Rathbun Creek. From Bell, road runs into Colorado over Trinchera Pass. Manco: Spanish for "lame."

MILLS PASS (9752) — Elizabethtown area, old Maxwell Grant. Road crosses pass in loop northeast from Elizabethtown. North Moreno Creek. Called Ponil Pass in 1878.

OLD TAOS PASS: See Palo Flechado Pass.

OSHA PASS (9800) — Taos area, Carson N. F., trail nine miles south of Palo Flechado Pass. Cieneguilla Creek (Canadian)–Fernando de Taos Creek (Rio Grande).

PALO FLECHADO PASS (9107) — Taos area, Carson N. F., U.S. Route 64, paved, all-weather, Cimarron–Taos, sixty miles. Cimarron Creek (Canadian)–Fernando de Taos Creek (Rio Grande). Also called Taos Pass, Old Taos Pass. Palo Flechado: "Arrow-shaped trees" in Spanish. This ancient route also called Taos Pass, Old Taos Pass.

PONIL PASS: See Mills Pass.

RATON PASS: See under Colorado Passes.

RED RIVER PASS (9852) — Taos area, Sangre de Cristos, Carson N. F., State Route 38, much of it paved, runs from Eagle Nest (U.S. Route 64) over scenic pass with steep, narrow, hairpin shelf west side. Moreno Creek (Canadian)–Red River (Rio Grande). Highest pass road in New Mexico and part of circle trip (with Palo Flechado Pass road) from Taos. New road will cross Bobcat Pass instead of Red River Pass just north. Road dates from mining boom starting 1867.

RED RIVER PASS (9200) — Stonewall (Colorado) area, Sangre de Cristos, old Maxwell Grant. Private road beyond gates over low pass from Tercio to vast Vermejo Park Ranch headquarters, seventeen miles. Vermejo (Canadian River)–Purgatoire (Arkansas).

SHAEFERS PASS (8787) — Cimarron area, Maxwell Grant–Philmont Scout Camp, trail. North fork, Urraca Creek–Bear Creek.

STONEWALL PASS (7903) — Cimarron area, Maxwell Grant–Philmont Scout Camp. Trail runs over pass from Aguila Trail Camp to south fork, Urraca Creek.

TAOS GAP: Common name, Santa Fe Trail days, for Cimarron Creek canyon between Cimarron and Eagle Nest on pack mule route from Raton Pass to Taos by Palo Flechado Pass. U.S. Route 64 uses Taos Gap today.

TAOS PASS: See Palo Flechado Pass.

UNA DE GATO PASS: About the same as Emery Pass across Ratons. The phrase, referring to a shrub, means "cat claw" in Spanish.

U.S. HILL SUMMIT (8500) — Sangre de Cristos, State Route 3, all-weather, Mora–Taos, forty-seven miles. Rio Pueblo Rio Grande. Summit of this ancient route named by United States Army, 1847.

UTE PARK PASS (8400) — Cimarron area, Maxwell Grant–Philmont Scout Camp. Horseback trail crosses pass from Cimarroncita. Cimarron Creek drainage.

WEBSTER PASS (9489) — Cimarron area, Maxwell Grant–Philmont Scout Camp. Trail runs over pass from Rayado Creek to Bonito Creek below Lookout Peak. Kit Carson used to live in this region, 1840's.

Utah Passes

(Including Uinta and Wasatch Ranges)

ANDERSON PASS (12,800) — Near Kings Peak (13,498), highest point in Utah, Ashley National Forest. Uinta River–Henrys Fork, Green River drainages.

BALD MOUNTAIN PASS (11,000) — Kamas area, northeast, Uinta Range. From Kamas, State Route 150, highest auto road in Utah, zigzags past Mirror Lake, over pass and on north to Evanston, Wyoming. Provo River–Bear River drainages.

BEAVER SUMMIT: See Logan Canyon Summit.

C.O.C. PASS: Edward L. Berthoud's name in 1861 for Daniels (Strawberry) Pass, U.S. Route 40. The initials stood for Central Overland California Express, the big stage outfit which employed Berthoud.

DANIELS PASS: See Strawberry Pass.

DEAD HORSE PASS (ca. 11,500) — Hanna area (State Route 35), north. Crest crossing, Wasatch National Forest. Duchesne River–Black's Fork drainages, Green watershed.

DUCHESNE PASS: Captain Howard Stansbury's name for Strawberry Pass (1850).

EMIGRATION CANYON PASS (ca. 7200) — Salt Lake City area. From Henifer, State Route 65 crosses divide from Weber River and runs down Emigration Canyon to Salt Lake City. The Donner-Reed party was first to use this route, 1846. Thereafter, most of the early Mormon settlers used it, including Brigham Young, who first saw the Salt Lake Valley from the canyon mouth on July 24, 1847. Mormons call the crossing "the Pass."

GOLDEN PASS (ca. 6800) — Salt Lake City area. From Kimballs, U.S. Route 40 crosses Wasatch Range by this easy pass and descends rugged gorge of Parleys Canyon to Salt Lake City. Salt Lake–Colorado watersheds. Known today as Parleys Summit. The name is said to have derived partly from the fact that Parley P. Pratt, builder of the original road in the early 1850's, charged tolls so high that they were "golden." This has always been the main route through the Wasatch Range.

LOGAN CANYON SUMMIT (7900) — Logan area, Wasatch Range. From Garden City, Utah, U.S. Route 89 climbs above Bear Lake to summit, eleven and a half miles, and descends spectacular Logan Canyon by way of Beaver Creek and Logan River to Cache Valley. This favorite canyon route of Green River trappers in the 1820's was not popular as a road until late in the nineteenth century, according to Jack Goodman.

MOFFIT PASS (10,402) — Bald Mountain Pass area, north, Wasatch National Forest. Weber River (Salt Lake)–Bear River (Columbia) drainages.

OGDEN CANYON (*ca.* 7000) — Ogden area. From Ogden, State Route 39 goes through the Wasatch Range by this rugged Ogden River Canyon passage. It was used by the Stansbury expedition in 1849.

PARLEYS SUMMIT: See Golden Pass.

PASS, THE: See Emigration Canyon Pass.

PROVO CANYON (*ca.* 6500) — Provo area. From Provo, U.S. Route 189 ascends Provo River Canyon and Upper Provo Canyon and on to Weber River and U.S. 30. In 1850, Captain Howard Stansbury spoke highly of this route through the Wasatch. He called it Timpanagos Canyon.

RED KNOB PASS (*ca.* 11,600) — Hanna area, northeast, Wasatch National Forest, Uinta Range. This crest pass links Lake Fork Creek (Duchesne) and East Fork of Black's Fork, Green River watershed.

SOLDIER SUMMIT (7440) — Helper area, Wasatch Range. From Helper, where booster engines push Denver and Rio Grande Western trains over the divide, U.S. Route 50 runs up Price River Canyon to summit and down Soldier Creek and Spanish Fork Canyon to Utah Lake and Provo. Father Escalante's party descended Spanish Fork Canyon in 1776, but reached it from near Strawberry Pass and Diamond Creek instead of by Soldier Summit. Colorado–Salt Lake watersheds.

SQUAW PASS (*ca.* 11,500) — Hanna area, northeast, Wasatch National Forest, Uinta Range. Pass links Oweep Creek–Lake Fork Creek–Duchesne drainage and that of Black's Fork of Green River.

STRAWBERRY PASS (7994) — Fruitland–Heber area, Wasatch Range. From Fruitland, U.S. Route 40 ascends Strawberry River to pass and descends Daniels Canyon to Heber and Golden Pass road to Salt Lake City. Colorado–Salt Lake watersheds. Has been called Daniels Pass, Duchesne Pass, C.O.C. Pass.

TIMPANAGOS CANYON: Today's Provo Canyon.

UINTA SUMMIT (8400) — Vernal area, north, Ashley National Forest. From Vernal, fascinating road State Route 44, runs north over crest of Uinta Range to Red Canyon overlook of Green River and on down through Sheep Creek Canyon to Manila, Utah, and Green River, Wyoming. Excellent alternate route forks right north of crest to Dutch John and Flaming Gorge Dam.

WASATCH DIVIDE (6816) — Wasatch Range. U.S. Route 30 and the Union Pacific Railroad cross this sage divide between Bear and Weber rivers on way west to Ogden and Salt Lake City. The Harlan–Young party of California-bound emigrants and the Donner–Reed party used this old Indian trail through Echo Canyon in 1846. The advance group of Mormon pioneers went over the divide and through Echo Canyon in July, 1847. Weber (Salt Lake)–Columbia River watersheds.

WASATCH PASS (*ca.* 7980) — Crossing through the Wasatch Range used by the Gunnison expedition of 1853. It was called Salina Pass in 1881 when the Rio Grande Western Railroad planned a line across Castle Valley to Green River. The pass is practically the same as the Summit on State Route 10 between Salina and Fremont Junction.

Wyoming Passes

(Including Big Horns)

ANGEL PASS (11,500), CD — Pinedale–Fremont Lake area, Wind River Range. High climber's trail crosses pass one mile east of Bald Mountain Basin, perhaps seven miles south of Fremont Peak (13,730). Bull Lake Creek (Wind River)–Green River drainages. (Data from *Guide to the Wyoming Mountains*, by Orrin H. and Lorraine Bonney).

ANTELOPE PASS (*ca.* 8050) — Near source of Dale Creek in Sherman Hill area. Dale Creek (Cache la Poudre)–Willow Creek (Laramie River) drainages, South Platte–North Platte watersheds.

ARTHUR PASS: See Sheridan Pass.

BACKPACKERS PASS (12,900), CD — Green River Pass area, northeast, Wind River Range. In wildest climber's trail country of Dinwoody–Helen Glacier region around Gannett Peak (13,785). New Fork River (Green)–Dinwoody Creek (Wind) drainages. (From the Bonney *Guide to the Wyoming Mountains*.)

BAD PASS: Old name for Powder River Pass, Pryor's Gap (Mont.).

BALDY PASS (9829) — Big Horn Range. From near Burgess Junction, U.S. Route 14 out of Sheridan, State Route 14 diverges right, runs along Big Horn Crest for four miles to Baldy Pass (a divide really) and descends many hairpins past fascinating Indian Medicine Wheel detour to reach Kane, forty-nine miles. The Medicine Wheel is reached by three-mile scary shelf-road. Just east of pass, Hunt Mountain Road goes off south deep into wilderness. The Baldy Pass route is a beautiful drive.

BATTLE LAKE PASS (9916), CD — Encampment area, west, Sierra Madre Range. From Encampment, this charming, woodsy road runs over pass in summer to Slater, forty-seven miles. Encampment Creek (North Platte)–Battle Creek (Little Snake) drainages. Missouri–Colorado watersheds. Battle Creek was so named because Henry Fraeb was killed along it in 1841 during a scrap between trappers and Indians.

BEAR CREEK PASS (11,202) — Dubois area, north, Absaroka Range. From East Fork, Wind River–Bear Creek road at Waynes Hole, trail runs to top of pass, fifteen rugged miles, and descends north side five miles to Kirwin and the Wood River road to Meeteetse. Bear Creek (Wind River)–Wood River (Greybull) drainages, Bighorn–Yellowstone watershed. Pass is mile or so west of East Fork Pass.

BEAR CUB PASS (9200), CD — Absaroka Range. From U.S. Route 26–287 near top of Togwotee Pass, east side, road and then trail leads through Diamond G Ranch, past Brooks Lake, to top of pass, nine miles. Trail descent down Buffalo Fork of Snake River to highway again, twenty miles. Brooks Lake Creek (Wind River)–Buffalo Fork (Snake River) drainages, Missouri–Columbia watersheds. Superb uplands with good fishing lakes.

BEARTOOTH PASS (10,940) — Beartooth Plateau, Absaroka Mountains (running north into Montana). From Cooke City near northeast entrance of Yellowstone Park, splendid U.S. Route 212 runs east over Cooke Pass and then over the spectacular Beartooth Pass — along plateau traverse — swinging down north in steep switchbacks to end at Red Lodge, Montana, sixty-four miles. This road, build in 1932–1936, is the highest highway in the Rockies outside of Colorado. It follows the old "Sheridan Trail" laid out in September, 1882, when General Philip H. Sheridan and a force of 129 officers, soldiers, civilians and Indians crossed the pass with only one casualty — a mule which toppled from a cliff into the top of a tree.

BIGHORN PASS (9110) — Yellowstone National Park. From highway eight miles south of Mammoth Hot Springs, horse trail runs west of Panther Creek, over pass to headwater lakes of Gallatin River and down to West Gallatin road, twenty miles. Gardiner River (Yellowstone)–Gallatin drainages, Missouri watershed.

BIG SANDY PASS: See Jackass Pass.

BIRDSEYE PASS (6993) — Owl Creek Range. From U.S. Route 20 near Boysen Reservoir, back road runs north over pass and down north side to Buffalo Creek road, twenty miles, and then Thermopolis. Wind River drainage. This road was the main route from Casper to Thermopolis until the road was built through Wind River Canyon in 1924, Wyoming's first major highway project.

BLACKROCK PASS: A section of Togwotee Pass twelve miles down west side from top.

BLAUROCK PASS (ca. 12,500), CD — Green River Pass area, northeast, Wind River Range. In wild climber's trail country of Dinwoody–Helen Glacier region around Gannett Peak. It is reached from the east side by trail southwest from Burris and U.S. Route 287. New Fork River (Green River)–Dinwoody Creek (Wind River) drainages, Colorado–Missouri watersheds. Named for Carl Blaurock of the Colorado Mountain Club.

BONNEVILLE PASS (9922) — Dubois area, Absaroka Range. From end of DuNoir Creek road northwest of Dubois, trail runs up west fork and southeast over pass to Brooks Lake, thirteen miles. Pass is about a mile from CD and near Bear Cub Pass. Wind River drainage. Named for Captain Benjamin L. E. Bonneville, who explored in this region during 1832–1833.

BONNEY PASS (ca. 12,700), CD — Green River Pass area, east. Expert climber's trail crosses this pass in Titcomb Lake–Fremont Peak–Mount Helen–Gannett Peak area. Green River (Colorado)–Wind River (Missouri) watersheds. Also called Dinwoody Pass, for nearby Dinwoody Peak (ca. 13,400), which is a different summit from lower Dinwoody Peak fifteen miles northeast. Named for Orrin H. Bonney of the American Alpine Club, who used it in 1936.

BOOTJACK GAP (9180) — Cooke City area, south, Absaroka Range. From Crandall Ranger Station on Cooke City–Cody road, trail runs up Crandall Creek and Papoose Creek to pass, descending west side along Miller Creek and Lamar River to the Yellowstone. Clarks Fork–Yellowstone drainages. (Bonney) Also called Papoose Pass.

BRIDGER PASS (7523), CD — Rawlins area, about twenty air miles south and slightly west of town near extreme north end of Sierra Madre Range. This unmarked pass, though famed in history, is hard to find without a compass in the car, and hard to recognize at the top because the grade is slight. The best approach is to leave U.S. Route 30 from the west edge of Rawlins southwesterly on the Sulphur Springs road. After twenty-six miles, near the old Sulphur Springs stage stop, take a southeast (left) fork for four miles up Muddy Creek and backtrack north six miles more to the top of the pass. From thence the old Overland Trail descends northeast along Emigrant Creek for fifteen miles to its junction with Pine Grove Creek, Little Sage Creek (almost) and the paved road to Rawlins. Green River–North Platte watersheds. The pass was named for Jim Bridger, who knew it well when he guided Captain Stansbury's party over it on September 20, 1850. In 1862, when the Oregon Trail was closed by Indians guarding South Pass, the Overland Trail over Bridger Pass took its place. It was astonishingly direct, with almost continuous water all the way west from the North Platte crossing to Fort Bridger. The Bryan's Pass on Lieutenant G. T. Warren's map of 1857 is a variant of Bridger Pass.

BRYAN'S PASS (ca. 7600), CD — Named for Lieutenant Francis T. Bryan, who took a troop of men and thirty-three wagons from Fort Riley, Kansas, over this pass August 14-16, 1856, having missed Bridger Pass by a mile or less. It appears that Bryan crossed at the head of Pine Grove Creek instead of Emigrant Creek. Bryan's geologist on the trip was the St. Louisan, Henry Engelmann, for whom the beautiful spruce of the Rockies high country was named.

CACHE LA POUDRE PASS (ca. 8000) — Just south of Tie Siding on Laramie–Fort Collins road, U.S. Route 287. Willow Creek (Laramie River)–Dale Creek (Cache la Poudre) drainages. Pass runs into Colorado to Virginia Dale, once an important stage stop on the Overland Trail from Denver to Salt Lake City via Bridger Pass (1862-1868).

CANOE LAKE PASS (ca. 9200) — Cooke City area, south, Absaroka Range. From Cody–Cooke City road, trail runs west up Crandall Creek and Timber Creek to pass and down Miller Creek in Yellowstone Park to Lamar River and Tower Falls. This was once a branch of the Bannock Indian trail. (Bonney) Crandall Creek (Clarks Fork)–Miller Creek (Yellowstone) drainages.

CEDAR CREEK PASS (ca. 8200) — Saratoga area, Medicine Bow Range. From Cedar Creek road end, trail crosses pass on northeast side of Pennock Mountain to North Rankin Creek and Pass Creek road. North Platte watershed.

CEDAR GAP (6566) — Big Horn Mountains (south). Gap is on back road from Badwater south to Arminto. Badwater-Alkali creeks drainage, north side. Jim Bridger led the Raynolds party through it to the Badwater in May, 1860.

CHEESE PASS (ca. 10,000) — Wyoming Range, in high country east of Smoot and the cheese factories of Star Valley. Pass is just north of Mount Thompson and Thompson Pass on old Big Piney–Smoot road. Middle fork, South Piney Creek (Green River)–Greys River (Snake) drainages, Colorado–Columbia watersheds.

CHEYENNE PASS (8591) — Laramie area, east. From Chcyenne,

pleasant Happy Jack road runs up Lodgepole Creek drainage to pass and Happy Jack winter sports area, where it meets U.S. Route 30 near the top of Telephone Canyon. Lodgepole Creek (South Platte)–Laramie River (North Platte) drainages. Pass is marked on Lieutenant G. T. Warren's 1857 map. This ancient traverse was used on September 27, 1850, by the Captain Stansbury party, and in the summer of 1856 by Lieutenant F. T. Bryan's group. Also called Pole Creek Pass, Tie City Pass. Wagons were going over it by 1860.

"CHEYENNE PASS": Name of area between Crow Creek and Chugwater Creek at east foot of Laramie Hills used by Cheyenne tribe in annual migrations.

CHRISTINA PASS (10,760) — South Pass area, north, Wind River Range. From Christina Lake Road (off Louis Lake road south from Lander), trail crosses pass and descends west to Sweetwater Guard Station. Superb lake country. Sweetwater–Popo Agie (Wind River) drainages, Missouri watershed.

CLIFF CREEK PASS (9000) — Jackson area, south, Wyoming Mountains. From U.S. Route 187 near Bondurant, trail goes south up Cliff Creek to top of pass, fourteen miles. Little Grey's River trails on other side. Hoback–Snake River drainage. Cliff Creek is just east of Pickle Pass.

COMMISSARY RIDGE (9255) — Wyoming Mountains. From near La Barge (U.S. Route 189), charming back road crosses ridge after long haul up La Barge Creek to Smiths Fork of Bear River, and then over Salt River Range to Smoot and Star Valley. Ridge is drained by branches of Green River, Bear River and Greys River. Colorado–Columbia watersheds.

CONANT PASS (*ca.* 9000) — From north end of Jackson Lake, trail runs up Berry Creek west and over low Teton Range crest to Conant Basin and 4WD road descending Conant Creek drainage into Idaho (Ashton). Snake River watershed.

CONY PASS (10,400) — Wind River Range, east side. From Ferguson Gulch road end southwest of Lander (or from Mormon Basin road end), Farlow Pack Trail runs to Cony and Cyclone passes. Popo Agie (Wind River) drainage.

COTTONWOOD PASS (6727) — Lysite Mountains, Big Horn Range, south. From Lost Cabin north of U.S. Route 20 and Lysite, back road runs sixteen miles north to pass and on north down No Wood Creek fifty-three miles to Tensleep. Cottonwood Creek (Wind River)–No Wood Creek (Big Horn) drainages, Missouri watershed. Wilson Price Hunt passed this way westbound in September, 1811.

COUGAR PASS (11,300) — Dubois area, northwest, Absaroka Mountains. From Wiggins Fork road end north of Dubois, trail goes on up Wiggins Fork, Frontier Creek and Cougar Creek to rimrock pass, twenty-two miles. Wind River–South Fork, Shoshone River drainages, Missouri watershed. According to Robert Tripp of Dubois, the trail going up is so steep that the "horse is on his tail more than on his legs." The Bonneys report that the pass was discovered by Ned Frost, 1902–1903.

COW CREEK PASS: See Greybull Pass.

CRAIG PASS (8260), CD — Yellowstone National Park. The CD has strange ways. The Old Faithful and West Thumb road crosses from the Western Slope to the Eastern Slope while running *west*. And, on top of the pass itself, Isa Lake flows both toward the Pacific via Snake River, and to the Gulf of Mexico via Yellowstone River. See Norris Pass also for more shenanigans.

CRANDALL PASS (9920) — Cooke City area, south, Absaroka Range. From Cooke City–Cody road at Crandall Ranger Station, a trail runs up north fork, Crandall Creek, over pass to Cache Creek in Yellowstone Park. Crandall Creek (Clarks Fork)–Cache Creek (Yellowstone) drainages. Jack Crandall, a prospector, was killed by Indians on Crandall Creek, July 1, 1870. (Bonney) Chief Joseph's people could have used this pass or Bootjack Gap (Papoose Pass) during their flight in August, 1877.

CROOK'S GAP (ca. 7500) — Green Mountains–Three Forks area. From U.S. Route 287 at Lamont just south of Whiskey Gap and Muddy Gap, back road goes west and north through oil country and over gap to rejoin U.S. 287 on way to Lander. Crooks Creek (Sweetwater) drainage. Named for the United States cavalry leader, General George Crook. The gap used to be on a shortcut road to Green River which veered left from Oregon Trail ten miles west of Devil's Gate. Though more level than the Oregon Trail, it involved an eighty mile stretch without water. F. V. Hayden called it Elkorn Gap.

CUBE ROCK PASS (ca. 10,700) — Near Green River Pass, Wind River Range. From Upper Green River, rugged trail crosses pass to Peak Lake southwest of Gannett Peak, Green River drainage.

CYCLONE PASS (10,400) — Wind River Range, east side. From Ferguson Gulch road end southwest of Lander, or from Mormon Basin road end, Farlow Pack Trail runs to Cony and Cyclone passes. Popo Agie (Wind) drainage.

DEAD INDIAN PASS (8048) — Absaroka Range. Pass is near top of Dead Indian Hill on Cody–Cooke City road thirty miles northwest of Cody. Paint Creek–Dead Indian Creek (Clarks Fork) drainage of the Yellowstone. John Colter reached this pass in 1807–1808.

DEER CREEK PASS (10,500) — Cody area, southwest, Absaroka Range. From Valley, forty-two miles southwest of Cody on South Fork, Shoshone River road, heavily used trail crosses pass to Thorofare hunting country, eleven miles, and on to Thorofare Creek and Bridger Lake, twenty-nine miles more, at southeast corner of Yellowstone Park. (Bonney) Shoshone–Yellowstone drainages.

DEVILS GAP (ca. 7200) — Three Crossings area, Sweetwater River. Gap links Cottonwood–Beaver Creek–Popo Agie and Sweetwater–North Platte drainage. Missouri watershed.

DINWOODY PASS: See Bonney Pass.

"DODGE'S PASS": See Separation.

DULL KNIFE PASS (ca. 8300) — Kaycee (U.S. Route 87) area. Pass is reached from Mayoworth, which is twelve miles northwest of Kaycee up the North Fork of Powder River. From Mayoworth, back road running southwest six miles near the Condit Ranch, arrives at pass in beautiful "Red Wall" country of Johnson County. The famous site of General Ranald Mackenzie's fight with Dull Knife's village of runaways from the reservation, November 25, 1876, is reached by driving west from Kaycee to Barnum, seventeen miles, and then north seven miles among incredible ledges of bright red sandstone and over a little divide to Red Fork of the

Powder and the road end at the Graves Ranch. There is a marker at the battle site which is about three miles southwest of Dull Knife Pass. Some of Dull Knife's people escaped from Mackenzie first through Fraker and then Dull Knife passes.

DUNRAVEN PASS (8859) — Yellowstone Park. Pass, named for the Earl of Dunraven who visited Yellowstone in 1874, is on the Canyon Village–Tower Falls highway. In January, 1887, the pioneer Yellowstone photographer, Frank Jay Haynes, and his party nearly perished on Dunraven Pass during a blizzard.

DUTCH OVEN PASS (10,400) — Shell-Granite Pass (U.S. Route 14) area, Big Horn Range. From Shell Creek picnic ground, Shell Creek trail goes to Shell Lakes and over pass to Medicine Lodge Lakes. Bighorn drainage.

EAGLE PASS (ca. 10,200) — Cody area, Absaroka Range. Trail from North Fork, Shoshone River, out of Cody runs up Eagle Creek and over pass to Mountain Creek and Yellowstone River. Bighorn–Yellowstone drainage.

EAST FORK PASS (11,200) — Dubois area, north, Absaroka Range. From end of East Fork of Wind River road, trail climbs ten miles to pass and descends north side five miles more to Kirwin and then Meeteetse. Wind River–Wood River (Greybull) drainages, Missouri watershed. Pass is near Bear Creek Pass in area of Wiggins Peak (12,160).

EAST INDIAN PASS (ca. 11,500) — Green River Pass area east. This remote climber's pass, about three miles northeast of Fremont Peak, connects north fork of Bull Lake Creek and Dry Creek of Wind River drainages. (Bonney) It is usually reached from east side of Range, Burris (U.S. Route 26–287), via the Dry Creek trail.

EDELMAN PASS (ca. 10,400) — Shell-Granite Pass (U.S. Route 14) area, Big Horn Range. From Shell Lakes, trail crosses pass to Edelman Creek and Big Goose Creek road to Sheridan. Tongue River–Bighorn watersheds.

ELKHORN GAP: Hayden's name for Crook Gap.

ELK PASS (ca. 10,600) — Cloud Peak Wilderness area southwest of Dome Lake, Big Horn Range. Dim trail crosses pass from West Goose Creek to Shell Creek drainage. (Bonney)

EMIGRANT GAP (5600) — Near Rattlesnake Range. Poison Spider Road runs through gap nine miles due west of Casper. North Platte drainage. The Oregon Trail left the North Platte to go through gap and on to Willow Springs, Independence Rock and the Sweetwater. See Red Buttes Pass also.

EVANS PASS: See Sherman Hill Summit.

EXIT PASS (ca. 11,000) — Cloud Peak Wilderness Area, Big Horn Range. Climbers' route from Kearney Lake and Creek goes over pass to Lake Elsie and Cliff Lake Camp Ground. Piney Creek (Powder River)– North Paint Rock Creek (Bighorn River) drainages.

FALLS RIVER PASS (ca. 7500) — Jackson Lake area, north end Teton Range. In 1872, Hayden's men planned railroad from Corinne, Utah, over this pass to enter Yellowstone Park in Beula Lakes area.

FAWN PASS (9100) — Yellowstone Park. From Mammoth Hot Springs, horse trail runs west up Fawn Creek over pass and down to Gallatin River road, twenty miles. Farn Creek–Gardiner River and Gallatin River drainages.

FLORENCE PASS (11,000) — Cloud Peak Wilderness Area, Big Horn Range. Trail crosses pass at Florence Lake on three-mile run from Medicine Park to Fortress Lakes. Tensleep Creek (Bighorn River)–North Clear Creek (Powder River) drainages.

FOX CREEK PASS (10,315) — Teton Range. From Victor, Idaho, long hiking trail runs up Fox Creek to Pass Lake, over crest, and northerly on east side to Fox Creek Pass under Mount Meek (10,677), and westerly again to Driggs, Idaho, by way of Devil's Stairs and south fork of Teton Creek. Teton River (Snake) drainage. This pass is one of very few in Teton Range.

FOXPARK DIVIDE (9142) — Medicine Bow Range. State Route 230 crosses pass from Woods Landing out of Laramie to Mountain Home on way to North Park and Walden in Colorado, fourteen miles. Laramie–North Platte drainages. Coalmont branch of U. P. Railroad has followed this route.

FRAKER PASS (8300) — Kaycee area, northwest, Big Horn Range. From Kaycee, road runs seventeen miles west to Barnum and seven miles north over little divide to Graves Ranch on Red Fork, Powder River, and site of Dull Knife Battle of November 25, 1876. Fraker Pass is just over ridge northeast from this point. It was named for the pioneer rancher, Harmon Fraker, a former Wisconsin lumberjack who came to Red Fork in 1877, just in time to salvage and repair for his own use guns dropped during Dull Knife Battle. See also Dull Knife Pass which, like Fraker Pass, was on the old Sioux trail from Powder River to the Sweetwater country.

FREMONT'S PASS: See South Pass.

GENEVA PASS (10,600) — Cloud Peak Wilderness Area, Big Horn Range. Trail from Lake Geneva and east fork, Big Goose Creek, crosses pass to Cliff Lake Camp Ground and North Paint Rock Creek. Tongue River–Bighorn River watersheds.

GLACIER PASS (ca. 12,900), CD — Green River Pass area, east, Wind River Range. Very high climber's pass south of Gannett Peak linking Dinwoody Glacier (east) and Mammoth Glacier (west). (Bonney)

GRANITE PASS (8950) — Big Horn Range. From Greybull and Shell, U.S. Route 14 winds spectacularly out of Big Horn Valley up Shell Canyon in hairpin turns (recalling Swiss Alps highways) to Ranchester and Sheridan. One of Wyoming's most exciting roads.

GREEN RIVER PASS (10,370) — Pinedale area, north, Wind River Range, west side. From Pinedale, road north through Cora reaches Green River Lakes road end from whence trail runs fifteen miles south, having reversed direction, to pass and Summit Lake. Route is important part of Highline trail running south through Bridger Wilderness Area just below crest of Wind River Range all the way to Christina Pass. Green River Pass is three miles or so west of CD.

GREYBULL PASS (ca. 12,200) — Dubois area, north, Absaroka Range. From Horse Creek Basin road end, Wiggins Fork–Greybull trail, extremely rugged, climbs to high pass and falls down Cow Creek and Greybull River to Pitchfork and Meeteetse, sixty-five miles. Wind River–Greybull River drainages. Missouri watershed.

HAILEY PASS (11,165), CD — Fort Washakie area, southwest, Wind River Range. From end of Moccasin Lake road out of Fort Washakie, horse trail runs to top of pass and on to trail network and Marms Lake on west side. South fork, Little River–New Fork River (Green) drainages, Missouri-Colorado watersheds. Named for Sheepman and State Senator Ora Hailey.

HAY PASS (*ca.* 11,160), CD — Pinedale area, northeast, Wind River Range. Pass is in Mt. Victor area just west of Milk Lakes and east of Timico Lake. Bull Lake Creek (Wind River)–Falls Creek (Green River) drainages, Missouri-Colorado watersheds. Named for John Hay, Rock Springs banker. (Bonney)

HORSE CREEK PASS (*ca.* 11,200) — Dubois area, north, Absaroka Range. From Horse Creek road end, trail runs up Horse Creek to top of pass below Ragged Top Mountain (11,848) in Pierpont Pass section so beloved by rock hounds. Horse Creek (Wind River)–South Fork, Shoshone River drainages. Missouri watershed. (Robert Tripp)

HUNT'S PASS: See Teton Pass.

ILLINOIS PASS (*ca.* 11,750), CD — Pinedale area, east, Wind River Range. Climber's pass in Washakie Pass–Marms Lake sector. (Bonney)

INDIAN PASS (12,130), CD — Pinedale–Green River Pass area, Wind River Range. Climber's pass between Jackson Peak and Knife Point Mountain just south of Fremont Peak. Indians may have used this high traverse, though horses cannot get over it. North fork, Bull Lake Creek (Wind River)–Fremont Lake (Green River) drainage. Missouri–Colorado watersheds.

ISHAWOOA PASS (9870) — Cody area, southwest, Absaroka Range. From South Fork, Shoshone River, trail branches west up Ishawooa Creek to pass and down Pass Creek on Yellowstone Park side to Thorofare Creek and Yellowstone River. In 1873, Captain W. A. Jones gave pass its Indian name meaning "a finger-shaped column" — referring to such a rock column which he observed three miles up Ishawooa Creek from the South Fork, Shoshone River. Missouri watershed.

JACKASS PASS (*ca.* 10,800), CD — Fort Washakie area, southwest, Wind River Range. From Moccasin Lake road end out of Fort Washakie, trail runs up North Popo Agie River to Lonesome Lake and south over pass to Big Sandy Lake trails. Missouri–Colorado watershed. This old Indian crossing has been called Big Sandy Pass. According to Orrin H. Bonney, name derives from claim of early packers that only a jackass could be driven through it.

JONES PASS (9450) — Yellowstone Park just north of Sylvan Pass and U.S. Route 14. From North Fork, Shoshone River, trail leads up Jones Creek to pass and down Bear Creek to East Entrance road and Yellowstone Lake. Missouri drainage. Named for Captain W. A. Jones, who led army party into park in 1873 through or near this gate.

LINCOLN PASS: See Sheridan Pass, Union Pass.

LIZARD HEAD PASS (11,750) — Fort Washakie area, southwest, Wind River Range, east side. From Lizard Head Meadows near source of North Fork, Popo Agie, climber's trail runs north over pass circling Cathedral Peak and on to Valentine Lake and Creek and South Fork of Little Wind River.

LOST SOLDIER GAP (*ca.* 7000) — Rawlins area, north, Green Mountains. Gap is very near Bairol (U.S. Route 287), and near source of Lost Soldier Creek, which vanishes by evaporation at Lost Soldier Lake. Robert Stuart's Astorians went through gap eastbound on October 26, 1812.

MCDOUGAL GAP (8500) — Pinedale area, northwest, Wyoming Range. From Cottonwood Guard Station, back road leads to gap and trail beyond down Sheep Creek drainage to Greys River road, 15 miles. North Cottonwood Creek (Green River)–Greys River (Snake) watersheds. May have been named for Duncan McDougall, of Astor's Pacific Fur Company and the North West Company later.

MCDOUGAL'S PASS (9236) — Star Valley area, east, Salt River Range. From Turnerville–U.S. Route 89, trail runs east up Willow Creek to pass and down Dead Horse Creek to Greys River. Salt River–Greys River drainages, Snake watershed. Probably named for Duncan McDougall (see above).

MERVIT PASS (*ca.* 8105) — Thermopolis area, southwest, Owl Creek Range. Owl Creek road west of Thermopolis crosses pass south by hairpins to Wind River and U.S. Route 26 at Pilot Butte Oil Field. Owl Creek–Holland Creek drainages, Wind River–Missouri watershed. One of the few road passes over Owl Creek Range. Others are Sheep Creek and Mexican.

MEXICAN PASS (6253) — Owl Creek Range. From Thermopolis, back road winds through powdery Red Canyon area and over pass to gumbo and salt sage flats and sandstone ridges sixty miles and more to Kinnear and U.S. Route 26–287 on Wind River. Wind River–Missouri watershed. This was the main route bypassing Wind River Canyon from the Dubois area of Wind River to Thermopolis in early days. Casper travelers crossed Birdseye Pass to Thermopolis.

MORTON PASS: See Sybille Pass.

MOSQUITO PASS (*ca.* 9000) — Jackson area, southwest, Snake River Range. Pass is at head of Mosquito Creek up which back road runs about seven miles from below Wilson. The pass can be reached also from top of Teton Pass (State Route 22), where sign points south to it, seven miles along crest. Snake River watershed.

MUDDY GAP (6350) — Rawlins area, north, between Green and Ferris Mountains. Gap is at junction of U.S. Route 287 from Rawlins and State Route 220, on way to Lander. Muddy Creek drains north into the Sweetwater (North Platte). Waters to the south just evaporate into Great Basin, as they do around Salt Lake, Utah. Gap is five miles northwest of Whiskey Gap. It was discovered October 26, 1812, by Robert Stuart's eastbound Astorians. Muddy Gap and Whiskey Gap were on routes to Oregon Trail from south.

MUDDY PASS: See Munkres Pass.

MUD PASS (9487) — Jackson area, southwest. Snake River Range. From top of Teton Pass, long trail runs south along crest to Mosquito Pass, seven miles, and seven miles more to Mud Pass, joining on the way the crest sheep driveway which continues to Indian Creek Pass, and from thence to Little Dog Creek road and U.S. Route 26, eighteen miles south of Jackson. Snake watershed.

MUNKRES PASS (*ca.* 9500) — Tensleep area, east, Big Horn Range.

U.S. Route 16 crosses this pass about four miles east of Powder River Pass and two miles north of Hesse Mountain (10,460). North fork, Crazy Woman Creek–North Fork, Powder River drainages, Missouri watershed. Also called Muddy Pass, for Muddy Creek, a branch of north fork, Crazy Woman Creek.

NEW YORK PASS (11,450), CD — Lander area, west, Wind River Range. From Lander, trail ascends North Fork, Popo Agie River, to Lizard Head Meadows and Lonesome Lake, where climber's route scales pass to Shadow Lake below Dimpingora Peak (12,378). Popo Agie (Wind River)–East Fork River (Green) drainages, Missouri–Colorado watersheds. New York alpinists named this new traverse in 1955. (Bonney)

NH TRAIL PASS (ca. 8000) — Back country Red Wall crossing, Big Horn Range (south). From Barnum west of Kaycee (U.S. Route 87), confusing ranch road on old Indian route, pushes farther west up Beaver Creek, more or less over low Big Horn crest, and down Canyon Creek to Bigtrails community and No Wood Creek, thirty miles. Powder River–Bighorn drainages, Missouri watershed. Dull Knife Pass and battle site are north of Barnum. Some students believe that Wilson Price Hunt's Astorians came this way westbound in September, 1811, rather than over Powder River Pass to the north.

NORRIS PASS (ca. 8200), CD — Yellowstone Park. From Craig Pass, where the Old Faithful road crosses to the Eastern Slope of the CD by running *west*, a trail runs over Norris Pass to the Western Slope by running *east*. Everything is peculiar in Yellowstone. Firehole River (Madison)–Lewis River (Snake) drainages, Missouri–Columbia watersheds.

NORTH INDIAN CREEK PASS (9191) — Jackson area, southwest, Snake River Range. From U.S. Route 26–89 south of Jackson, trail runs up South Fall Creek over pass and down North Indian Creek to the beautiful Palisades Reservoir in Idaho. Snake River watershed. Pass is on sheep driveway from U.S. Route 26 up Little Dog Creek along crest to Mud Pass and northwest into Teton Basin, Idaho.

OBERG PASS (8206) — Saratoga area northeast, Medicine Bow Range. Rough road from Pass Creek goes up Oberg Creek over pass to Pass Creek again, just north of Pennock Mountain (9965). North Platte drainage.

PAPOOSE PASS: See Bootjack Gap.

PARADISE PASS (10,970) — Fort Washakie area, Wind River Range, east side. From St. Lawrence Ranger Station road end (west of Fort Washakie, trail runs up St. Lawrence Creek and over pass on Windy Ridge just south of Tybo Peak to Paradise Basin and Paradise Creek. Sage Creek–Paradise Creek–Bull Lake Creek drainages, Wind River watershed.

PHILLIPS PASS (ca. 9200) — Jackson area, northwest, Teton Range. Trail crosses the minor pass up Fish Creek and Phillips Canyon to Moose Creek and Teton River. Phillips is immediately north of Teton Pass.

PHOTO PASS (ca. 11,237), CD — Fort Washakie area, west, Wind River Range. From St. Lawrence Ranger Station road end west of Fort Washakie, climber's trail runs to Raft Lake and Movo Lake, up North Fork of Little Wind River to Wykee Lake, and over pass and CD to Middle Fork Lake (Boulder Creek). Wind River–Green River drainages, Missouri–Colorado watersheds. Photo Pass was named in 1950 by members of the Colorado Mountain Club. (Bonney) It can be reached also from west side, Boulder town on U.S. Route 187.

PICKLE PASS (9400) — Wyoming Mountains near Bondurant. From U.S. Route 187 in Hoback Canyon, trail runs south up Willow Creek to pass, fifteen miles. Little Greys River trails on other side. Snake watershed.

PIERPONT PASS (10,300) — Dubois area, north, Absaroka Range. From Wiggins Fork road end, trail goes over Cougar Pass and then Pierpont Pass to South Fork, Shoshone River. Wind River–Shoshone River drainages, Missouri watershed. Pierpont is popular rock hound pasture.

POLE CREEK PASS: See Cheyenne Pass.

POWDER RIVER PASS (9666) — Big Horn Range. From Buffalo, U.S. Route 16, a fine highway, winds west, south and west again with great leisure through the Big Horn forests and grassy spaces to top of pass, forty miles, north of which rise the gray rubble crests of the range's highest peak, Cloud (13,165) and others. The road becomes melodramatic as it descends the Swiss-like hairpins of Tensleep Creek to Tensleep town, thirty miles, and enters the fantastic, tortured, blistered, tawny-cream-red humpy landscape which extends most of twenty-eight miles to Worland and Bighorn River. Pass is on Crazy Woman–Muddy Creek (Powder River) and Tensleep–No Wood creeks (Bighorn) drainages. The scenery is most unlike the usual in the Rockies. The trappers called this one Bad Pass, because of the badlands on west side.

RAMPART PASS (ca. 11,300) — Cody area, west, Absaroka Range. From Elk Fork Camp Ground west of Cody, horse trail runs up Elk Fork Creek and over high, rugged pass at Overlook Mountain and down Open and Thorofare creeks to Bridger Lake and Yellowstone River, sixty miles. Bighorn–Yellowstone drainages. Missouri watershed. Orrin H. Bonney, the Wyoming expert, calls this trail one of the finest in Absarokas, but requiring expert horsemanship. The pass is knife-edged rimrock.

RATTLESNAKE PASS (7518) — Saratoga area, northeast, Medicine Bow Range, Elk Mountain. From State Route 130 at point twelve miles south of U.S. Route 30, gravel road parallels Overland Trail of 1860's east up Pass Creek and Rattlesnake Creek over pass to site of Fort Halleck. Laramie–North Platte drainages. U.S. 30 may be relocated through Rattlesnake Pass. Frémont crossed it August 3, 1843. Lieutenant Francis T. Bryan got wagons through August 9–11, 1856.

RED BUTTES PASS (5578) — Oregon Trail landmark on present State Route 220, twelve miles southwest of Casper, where North Platte cuts through low red and white sandstone formations. Emigrants on the trail passed north of these Buttes through Emigrant Gap to Willow Springs and Independence Rock on the Sweetwater. Red Buttes marked the end of the good grass country of eastern Wyoming and the start of the South Pass arid region. Some miles west of Red Buttes was the Devil's Back Bone, said to be the worst hill on the Oregon Trail short of Snake River.

RED PASS (8800) — Jackson area, southwest, Snake River Range. From Snake River (U.S. Route 89), trail runs seven miles to top of pass, and down Dog Creek on other side to Snake again.

REPUBLIC PASS (ca. 10,000) — Absaroka Range. From Lamar River in Yellowstone Park, east side, trail runs up Cache Creek, over pass and down Republic Creek to Montana border and Clarks Fork. Missouri watershed. Trail passes near the spectacular Absaroka summits, Pilot Peak (11,708) and Index Peak (11,740).

RIM, THE (7921) — Gros Ventre Range. From Pinedale, U.S. Route

187 runs over divide from Green to Hoback River on its way to Jackson and Grand Teton National Park. Green (Colorado)–Snake (Columbia) drainages.

SALT RIVER PASS (7616) — Gannett Hills area. From Smoot, U.S. Route 89 leaves Star Valley south up Salt River, over easy pass and through Thomas Fork Canyon to Geneva, seventeen miles, on way to Montpelier, Idaho, and Bear Lake. Snake (Columbia)–Bear River (Salt Lake) watersheds.

SCENIC PASS (11,797) — Dubois area, south, Wind River Range, east side. From near Burris on U.S. Route 26–287, rough road runs southwest between between Little Dry and Dry Creek, becoming 4WD track near entrance to Shoshone National Forest. Horse trail continues up to Scenic Pass between Dry Creek and Dinwoody Creek. Breathtaking view up Dinwoody Creek of Gannett Peak (13,785), highest in Rockies north of Colorado. Wind River drainage.

SEPARATION (7107), CD — Union Pacific name for divide west of Rawlins crossed by railroad from Wyoming's Great Basin to Green River drainage. The spot is at Creston, Wyoming. Also called "Dodge's Pass," after General Grenville M. Dodge, the U. P.'s great chief engineer.

SHANNON PASS (ca. 11,100) — Green River Pass area, Wind River Range, west side. This climber's pass, noted by Bonney, is on trail just west of Stroud Peak (12,222). Green River drainage. It was named for Ranger Harmon Shannon, who created many Upper Green River trails.

SHEEP CREEK PASS (8400) — Thermopolis area, southwest, Owl Creek Range. From Thermopolis, road ascends Owl Creek and Red Creek and over pass to West Sheep Creek and Sheep Creek, winding up eventually at Pilot Butte Oil Field area and U.S. Route 26 short of Dubois. A nearby second Sheep Creek Pass ascends by north fork of Mud Creek instead of by Red Creek. These passes over Owl Creek Range are between Mervit (west) and Mexican passes.

SHEEP PASS (ca. 10,000) — Smoot area, east, Salt River Range. Pass on north side of Mount Wagner links Spring Creek (Greys River) and Wagner Creek–Cottonwood Creek–Salt River drainages. Today's Sheep Trail from Star Valley over pass may have been used by Robert Stuart's eastbound Astorians on September 16, 1812.

SHERIDAN PASS (9100), CD — Dubois area, west, Wind River Range, north end. From U.S. Route 287, trail runs up Sheridan Creek to pass and down Squaw Creek and north fork of Fish Creek to Gros Ventre River in Jackson Hole. Wind River–Snake River watersheds. The pass, nine and one fourth miles southeast of Togwotee Pass, is reached also from Du Noir lumber camp on Union Pass road. It is distinguished particularly because it was crossed by President Chester A. Arthur during his trip to Yellowstone Park in August, 1883. The Arthur party was conducted by Lieutenant General Philip H. Sheridan, and it included Secretary of War Robert T. Lincoln, son of Abraham Lincoln, and Governor John Schuyler Crosby of Montana. The group reached Green River, Wyoming, from Omaha on the Union Pacific and rode to Fort Washakie in a Concord coach. Near South Pass, some cowboys pretended to hold up the President — the same routine practiced at dude ranches today. The group shifted to horseback at Fort Washakie and moved up Wind River with a cavalry escort of seventy-five soldiers. Couriers galloped up every twenty miles with reports from Washington which had been telegraphed to Green River. The Indian guide was Captain Jones's man of 1873, Togwotee, but he did not lead the way over Togwotee Pass this time. Instead, he used what we call Sheridan Pass. The President paid little attention to the magnificent views of the Tetons, but was utterly absorbed by the trout fishing. While encamped on the Gros Ventre River side of the pass, he offered twenty-five dollars to the soldier catching the largest trout. The winning fish was only eight inches long but heavy as lead. In fact, as Arthur learned later, the soldier had stuffed it with lead bullets to give the poor little thing a chance. Legend has it that this Presidential crossing was celebrated with a champagne dinner party, the champagne and ice having been brought to the wilderness by a pack train of mules. After the President's visit, the pass was named Robert Lincoln Pass by General Sheridan, but he couldn't make it stick and his own name has been used ever since. Occasionally it is called Arthur Pass.

SHERMAN HILL SUMMIT (8235) — Laramie Mountains. From Cheyenne, present U.S. Route 30–Interstate 80 crosses crest a mile northwest of Sherman Hill Summit to descend Telephone Canyon to Laramie. The Happy Jack road through Cheyenne Pass falls into Telephone Canyon too. Sherman Hill Summit, the highest point on the U. P. before the line was rerouted a mile south at 8061 feet, is marked by the ugly Ames Monument to the Ames brothers, Boston backers of the U. P. The Summit used to be a very busy place, with the station, five-stall roundhouse, turntable, two section houses, tool house, twenty-five log homes, a store, two hotels, two saloons, a car repair shop and 5307 feet of siding track. Only the lonely monument and bits of grade remain. The highway crest (8835) contains a twelve-foot bronze head of Abraham Lincoln atop a thirty-foot granite base, created by the sculptor Robert I. Russin, of the University of Wyoming faculty. It was contributed by Dr. Charles W. Jeffrey of Rawlins to mark the highest point on what used to be known as Lincoln Highway, and it was unveiled in October, 1959. Sherman Hill Summit has been called Evans Pass after James A. Evans, a Union Pacific engineer.

SHOSHONE PASS (9730) — Dubois area, north, Absaroka Range. A major and ancient Indian trail runs up Du Noir Creek from U.S. Route 26–287 and then up its east fork to pass. Descent is down South Fork, Shoshone River, to Stinking Water Mines and the Cody road. Wind River–Bighorn drainage, Missouri watershed. Captain William A. Jones called it Stinking Water Pass in his report of 1873.

SIOUX PASS (9760) — South Pass area, north, south end of Wind River Range. From Christina Lake road (off Louis Lake road to Lander, trail climbs one mile to pass and down other side, five miles, to East Sweetwater road end. Sweetwater–Wind River drainages, Missouri watershed. State Route 28 is about ten miles east of this Wind River Sioux Pass.

SIOUX PASS (ca. 5400) — Near Lysite Mountains, adjoining southern Big Horns. Pass is on old Indian trail, now a road, from Lysite north over Cottonwood Pass to No Wood, thirty-two miles, which carries on to Tensleep and the Powder River Pass highway. Badwater–Cottonwood creeks (Bighorn River) drainages. The Hunt Astorians seemed to have crossed Sioux Pass in 1811.

SNOWSHOE PASS (ca. 9600) — Yellowstone National Park, west

side. Snowshoe Pass connects Fawn Pass with Fan Creek drainage a few miles northwest of Fawn Pass.

SNOWY RANGE PASS (10,800) — Medicine Bow Range and Forest near Medicine Bow Peak (12,005). From Laramie a beautiful highway (State Route 130) runs west through Centennial and by easy grades to Lake Marie and over picturesque pass to Saratoga, eighty miles. North Platte–Laramie drainages. Second highest road pass in Wyoming. Beartooth is first (10,940).

SOUTHERN PASS: Usually refers to South Pass.

SOUTH PASS (7550), CD — Twelve miles south of south end, Wind River Range. It is at the northwest edge of a vast desert known as Wyoming Basin, extending northwest 150 miles from Bridger Pass and the Sierra Madre Range to Wind River Range. This basin is a complete break in the Rockies chain. The Oregon Trail crossed South Pass near State Route 28 (Lander to Farson, sixty-five miles). The trail ran up Sweetwater River until the river veered north to its Wind River source. Then the trail went over South Pass and down to Pacific Springs, four miles, and on down Pacific Creek and Sandy Creek to Green River. Sweetwater (North Platte)–Pacific Creek (Green River) drainages, Missouri–Colorado watersheds. The low flat divide is easily crossed anywhere in this rolling area but the narrow treeless South Pass part drew all the traffic because it alone has almost continuous running water. Two brides, Narcissa Whitman and Eliza Spalding, were the first white women to cross the CD — South Pass in 1836.

STINKING WATER PASS: See Shoshone Pass.

STONE PILLAR PASS (ca. 12,200) — Green River Pass area, Wind River Range, west side. Pass is climber's couloir from east inlet of Stonehammer Lake north-northeast to glacier area under west side of Gannett Peak. Green River drainage.

SUMMIT: See Sherman Hill Summit.

SWEETWATER GAP (10,327) — South Pass area, north. From Louis Lake road out of Lander, trail runs up Middle Popo Agie River to gap and continues south to Sweetwater Guard Station, twenty-nine miles. Sweetwater–Wind River drainages, Missouri watershed. Gap is ultimate source of historic Sweetwater. Since CD is only two miles west of it, the gap is almost a triple divide — Green River (Gulf of Mexico), Sweetwater to North Platte, and Popo Agie to Yellowstone and the Missouri.

SYBILLE PASS (ca. 7301) — Laramie area, north, Laramie Range. From near Bosler at U.S. Route 30–287, road rises to pass through pastures and pine-tipped ledges and descends Sybille Creek through Cooney Hills to Wheatland and U.S. 87, sixty-five miles. Laramie drainage. Also called Morton Pass. Named for John Sybille, a French trader who worked among the Sioux out of Fort Laramie.

SYLVAN PASS (8559) — Cody area, west, Absaroka Range. From Cody, U.S. Route 14–20, revolutionized in 1961 by a $3,000,000 tunnel bypassing the notorious Dam Hill to the top of Buffalo Bill Dam, runs fifty-three miles up Shoshone Canyon and the North Fork, Shoshone River, to Yellowstone Park's east entrance and Sylvan Pass. The west-side descent to Yellowstone Lake past Sylvan Lake is along Cub Creek drainage. This low road pass is still one of the highest in the park.

TELEPHONE PASS (8025): Near Pickle Pass in Bridger National Forest.

TELEPHONE CANYON SUMMIT: See Sherman Hill Summit.

TETON PASS (8429) — Jackson area, west, Teton–Snake River ranges. From Jackson, State Route 22 wriggles quite steeply by many switchbacks over pass to Victor, Idaho, twenty-five miles, and on to the lush Pierre's Hole country around Driggs which is called Teton Basin today. Until recent years, this ancient traverse was avoided by conservative motorists because of its excessive grade. Teton: French for "breast."

TEXAS PASS (*ca.* 11,400), CD — Wind River Range, Mount Washakie area, in Lonesome Lake climber's sector east of New York Pass. From Shadow Lake, Billys Lake and Barren Lake, the route scales a ridge to Little Skunk Lake and Lonesome Lake. Orrin H. Bonney, of Houston, Texas, named this gap when he climbed over it in 1940.

THOMPSON PASS (*ca.* 9500) — Pinedale area, west, Wyoming Range. From Big Piney, entrancing back road runs up South Piney Creek twenty-nine miles to pass, Commissary Ridge, and then continues westerly over Wagner Pass of Salt River Range and on to Smoot (U.S. Route 89) in Star Valley. Thompson's Pass was on Frederick W. Lander's Fort Kearny, South Pass and Honey Lake (California) Wagon Road, built in 1858–1860 — the so-called Lander Cut-off as an improvement to the Oregon Trail. South Piney Creek–La Barge Creek–Greys River triple drainages. Colorado–Snake watersheds. Named by Lander for Jacob Thompson, Secretary of the Interior under Buchanan.

TIE CITY PASS: See Cheyenne Pass.

TOGWOTEE PASS (9658), CD — Dubois area, northwest, separating Wind River Range (south) from Absarokas. From Dubois, splendid scenic highway, U.S. Route 26–287, runs to extreme Wind River source, over this forested traverse and down (watch for moose!) Blackrock Creek to Snake River and Jackson Lake in full overwhelming view of the Teton Range. An old route between Wind River Valley and Jackson Hole. Missouri–Columbia watershed. Named in 1873 by Captain William A. Jones for his Snake Indian guide, though it had been known from at least 1811. The word is pronounced "Towgut-er," accent on first syllable. Spelled variously To-Gwo-Tee, Togwoda, Togwater; the word means Shoshoni "goes from this place" or "shoots with a spear." Also called Wind River Pass. Army built first wagon road over in 1898 (they called it a "model" road even though the wagons had to be let down west side by windlass). First auto road about 1922.

TRAIL CREEK PASS (*ca.* 8300) — Absaroka Range. From Dick Turpin Meadow on west side of Togwotee Pass highway, fine trout-moose trail runs far up North Buffalo Fork and over pass to Trail Creek, Pacific Creek and Two Ocean Pass. Snake drainage, Columbia watershed.

TWILIGHT PASS (*ca.* 11,600) — Dubois area, north, Absaroka Range. Robert Tripp reports on this pass at head of Twilight Creek off Horse Creek, crossing Absaroka crest just east of Ragged Top Mountain (11,848). Pass is two miles south of where Shoshone trail crosses Cougar Pass on way to Pierpont Pass and South Fork, Shoshone River. Wind River–Shoshone River drainages, Missouri watershed.

TWO OCEAN PASS (8200), CD — Togwotee Pass area, north, Absaroka Range. Horseback trails run northwest over this unusual pass from Jackson Lake, Snake River and Pacific Creek to imperceptible top at Two Ocean Creek, and north down Atlantic Creek and Yellowstone River into Yellowstone Park. Yellowstone–Snake River drainages. Jim Bridger claimed discovery of this pass as of 1832, though John Colter may have crossed it in 1807–1808.

UNION PASS (9210), CD — Dubois area, southwest. From U.S. Route 26–287 at point nine miles northwest of Dubois, Union Pass road takes off left to southwest up Warm Springs Creek branches and reaches top of pass beyond Du Noir lumber camp in about twelve miles, with the pretty Lake of the Woods just imperceptibly over pass. Road is rough and steep in spots but standard cars usually make it. 4WD descent only on west side to Green River road (twelve miles) which winds up at Kendall, Cora and Pinedale in forty-four more miles. This descent from top includes first six miles on Gros Ventre (Snake) drainage — Fish Creek — ending at a 9253-foot divide between this Fish Creek source and Wagon Creek (Green River) source. From Union Pass, a scenic cowboy 4WD road runs northwest along CD for miles to Fish Lake and more Fish Creek past Sheridan Pass Trail and returns to U.S. Route 26–287 down Warm Springs Creek. Hunt's Astorians crossed this old Union Pass Indian route westbound on September 16, 1811. Captain William F. Raynolds named it in 1860. Also called Lincoln Pass.

VISTA PASS (*ca.* 10,000) — Green River Pass and Vista Lake area, Wind River Range, west side.

WAGNER PASS (9026) — Smoot area, east, Salt River Range. From near top of Salt River Pass out of Star Valley, delightful back road runs easterly over Salt River Range by Wagner Pass on way to Commissary Ridge, Thompson Pass (Wyoming Range) and South Piney Creek route to Big Piney — the old Lander Cut-off (See Thompson Pass). Wagner Pass was named by Lander for his chief engineer, William H. Wagner. The area is replete with picnic parks, trout streams and groves of trees.

WASHAKIE PASS (11,610), CD — Fort Washakie area, southwest, Wyoming Range. From end of Moccasin Lake road out of Fort Washakie, horse trail runs to top of pass and on to trail network on west side. South Fork, Little Wind River–East Fork River (Green) drainages. Hayden's men noted this old Indian trail in 1870's.

WHISKEY GAP (6380) — Rawlins area, north, Ferris Mountains, reached by back road three miles east of U.S. Route 287 from starting point two miles south of Muddy Gap. Whiskey Gap was on popular wagon road from Rawlins country to Mormon Trail below Three Crossings and Split Rock. Sweetwater (North Platte)–Great Basin drainages. Name derived from tee-totaling army officer dumping barrel of whiskey into spring near gap giving it a bourbon flavor and causing soldiers to line up for a drink of "water."

WHITE PASS (8000) — Dubois area, north, Absaroka Range. Pass is south of Ramshorn Peak and four miles north of U.S. Route 26–287.

WIND RIVER PASS: See Togwotee Pass.

WINDY GAP (11,640) — Hay Pass area, Wind River Range, east side. Climber's pass on Paradise Basin–Steamboat Lake–Hatchet Lake trail. Bull Lake Creek (Wind River) drainage.

INDEX

For a full list of passes, see the ROSTER OF PASSES, pages
373-456. The Roster is not included in this index.
Numbers in italic below refer to numbered illustrations, not pages.

Blaeberry River (of the Columbia), 65
Blanca Peak (14,317), 22-23, 109, 148
Blue Mesa Summit, Colo., 111; Mears road over, 259
Blue River (of the Colorado), 136
Boat Encampment, B.C., 91
Bonners Ferry, Idaho, 72
Bonneville, Captain Louis Eulalie de Bonneville, exploration, 128-130; what peak did he climb?, 333
Boreas (Breckenridge) Pass, Colo., 53; skiing miners over, 175; wagon road, 182; rails over, 276, 324; *18*
Boulder Pass, Colo., *see* Rollins Pass
Boundaries: U.S.-Can., 64, 142; 49th parallel "fatal error," 163-164; Louisiana Purchase, 48, 93, 324
Bow Pass, Can., crossed by Hector, 168; Banff-Jasper highway over, 318
Bow River (of the South Saskatchewan), 163
Bozeman, Mont., 41, 213; rails arrive, 287
Bozeman, John M., leads train to Virginia City, creates Bozeman Trail, 204-206; death, 342
Bozeman Pass, Mont., William Clark over, 42, 66; Colter over, 68; Henry over, 70; emigrants over, 205; rail tunnel, 287, 313; superhighway, 321
Breckenridge Pass, *see* Boreas Pass
Bridger, James, 113; visits Great Salt Lake, 117-118; discovers Two Ocean Pass, maybe, 121; guides Stansbury, 143; guides Berthoud, 184-188; guides Raynolds, 198-200; guides train to Virginia City, 204-205
Bridger Pass, Mont., 42; Bridger over, 205; 213, 341
Bridger Pass, Wyo., Ashley over, 119; Fremont over, 134; Stansbury over, 145; stage line over, 187; *7*
Bross, Mount (14,169), 137
Brown, Mount (9156), demoted, 123, 300
Brown's Canyon (of the Arkansas), 53
Brown's Hole (Park), 120, 121, 134
Buckhorn Pass, Colo., 310
Buena Vista, Colo., 246, 270
Buffalo, Wyo., 114
Buffalo Pass, Colo., Steamboat Springs area, 136; road over, 333
Buffalo Peaks (13,541), 53, 242
Bull Pen, *see* North Park
Burgess Pass, Can., 305
Butte, Mont., 35, 92; first rails, 282-284; booms, 288; origins, 342
Byers, Editor William Newton, attacks Baker's Park, 179-180; promotes Berthoud and road west, 184; blasts Bannack, 191; buys Hot Sulphur Springs, 230-231

CACHE VALLEY, Utah, 117
Cache La Poudre River (of the South Platte), 71, 118; source, 248
Cadotte, Pierre, 155, 336
Cadotte Pass, Mont., 35, 42; crossed by Stevens, named, 155; dogsleds over, 159-160, 284
Calgary, Alberta, Can., 64
Calico Pass, Colo., 250, 391

Cameahwait, Chief, Sacajawea's brother, 37
Cameron Pass, Colo., named for, road over, 248; cars over, 314
Camp Augur, Lander, Wyo., 225
Camp Hale, Pando, Colo., 248, 414
Canadian River (of the Arkansas), 7, 9-10, 14, 48, 126
Canon City, Colo., 51, 55-56
Cantonment Jordan, Mont., 197
Cantonment Loring, Idaho, 158
Cantonment Stevens, Mont., 156
Cariboo, B.C., gold rush, 206-209
Carnero Pass (Gunnison's, Fremont's), 150, 334
Carson, Christopher, 97, 131, 133
Cartier, Jacques, 25
Casper, Wyo., 313
Cass, Martin, 82, 330
Castle Rock, Colo., 133
Cataract Pass, Can., 302
Cebolla Pass, Colo., 258
Cecere, Gaetano, 291
Central City, Colo., 233, 237
Central Overland California and Pikes Peak Express Company ("C.O.C."), 184-188
Central Overland Route (Fort Kearny, Neb.-Honey Lake, Calif.), 193-195
Cerro Summit, Colo., 111; Gunnison over, 150; Mears road over, 259; cars over, 315
Chalk Creek Pass, Colo., 249
Chama River (of the Rio Grande), 8, 15, 16
Charbonneau, Baptiste (Little Pomp), 32, 37, 38, 66
Charbonneau, Toussaint, with Lewis and Clark, 32, 41
Charles III, King of Spain, 14-15; loses interest in Rockies, dies, 23-24
Cheadle, Dr. W. B. C., over Yellowhead, 342
Cherokee Trail, forerunner of Overland Trail, 185
Cherry Creek (of the South Platte), 133, 230
Cheyenne Pass, Wyo., crossed by Stansbury, 146; rails over area, 262-264
Chicago Creek (of Clear Creek-South Platte), 172
Chief Joseph Pass, Mont., brand-new, 325
Chivington, Major John M., hero of La Glorieta battle, 188-191
Cibola, Seven Cities of, 4-6
Cimarron, N.M., 96, 127
Cimarron Creek (of the Canadian), 18, 96
Cimarron Cut-Off, 98-99, 127
Cimarron River (of the Arkansas), 10-11, 98
Cinnamon Pass, Colo., crossed by Baker, 178-179; by Hayden men, 221-222; road over, 258-259; modern 4WD road, 339
Civil War in the Rockies, 177; effect of, 183-184; La Glorieta Pass battle, 188-191
Clark, Captain William, 30-31; over Lemhi, 37; side trip homeward over Gibbons, Bull Creek, Bozeman, 41-42
Clark Fork (of the Columbia), 34; named, described by Lewis and Clark, 72
Clarks Fork (of the Yellowstone), 66, 67
Clearwater River (of the Blackfoot), 160
Cloud Peak (13,165), highest in Big Horns, 78, 115
Clyman, Jim, 115, 116, 119

Gregory Gulch (of North Clear Creek), 171
Greybull River (of the Bighorn), 66
Greys River (of the Snake), 70, 86
Gros Ventre River (of the Snake), 129, 199
Grover, Lieutenant Cuvier, 159-160
Guanella, Thomas, 233-234
Guanella Pass, Colo., 172, 235; modern road over, 347
Gunnison, Colo., 111, 251, 273
Gunnison, Captain John W., shoots horse, 145; expedition, 146-150; death, 151
Gunnison River (of the Colorado), Gunnison visits, 150; passes of, 219

HABEL, JEAN, explores Yoho Valley, 305
Hagerman, James J., 276-279
Hagerman (Frying Pan) Pass, Colo., 247; rail tunnel, 277-278
Ham, Zacharias, 110
Ham's Fork (of the Green), 119
Handcart Pass, see Webster Pass
Hard Pan Triangle Auto Route, 314
Hardscrabble Pass, Colo., 52
Hart Highway, Can., 29, 44
Harvard, Mount (14,420), second highest in Rockies, 21, 53; naming of, 390
Hawse, Jasper, 207, 327
Hayden, Dr. Ferdinand Vandeveer, early career, 211; surveys, 212-225; his *Atlas of Colorado*, 244
Hayden Pass, Colo., 54, 218
Hayden Survey, 211-225; Colo. mapping, 214; quality of men, methods, 216; altitudes versus modern altitudes, 345; *13*
Hector, Dr. James, explorations, 164-169
Helena, Mont. (Last Chance Gulch), 35, 155; birth of, named, 201-202; rails arrive, 287
Hell Gate (of Clark Fork) near Missoula, 42, 92; origin of name, 155, 201; grabbed by Northern Pacific, 285
Henry, Major Andrew, joins Lisa expedition, crosses Raynolds (Targhee?) Pass, 69-70, 74, 112; up Yellowstone for Ashley, 114; other passes noted, 328
Henrys Fork (of the Green), 120
Henrys Fork (of the Snake), 69, 70
Henrys Lake, Idaho, 69, 70, 200, 212-213
High Rockies Passes (trail or 4WD):
　Canada, see Wolverine (9500), President (9469), Cline (9370)
　Colorado, see Electric (13,200), Elkhead (13,200), Mosquito (13,188), Argentine (13,132), Imogene (13,114), New York (13,100), Grizzly (13,093)
　Montana, see Sundance (11,040), Expedition (10,000), Deadman (9800)
　New Mexico, see Costilla (10,100)
　Utah, see Anderson (12,800)
　Wyoming, see Backpackers (12,900), Glacier (12,900), Bonney (12,700), Blaurock (12,500), Stone Pillar (12,200), Greybull (12,200), Indian (12,130)
High Rockies Road Passes (standard cars):
　Canada, see Highwood (8000), Bow (6878), Sunwapta (6675)
　Colorado, see Cumberland (12,200), Cottonwood (12,126), Independence (12,-095), Loveland (11,992)

Montana, see Cooke (8066)
New Mexico, see Red River (9852)
Utah, see Bald Mountain (11,000)
Wyoming, see Beartooth (10,940), Snowy Range (10,800)
High Rockies Roads over passes, steepness compared, 349
Hill, James Jerome, 288-292
Hoback, John, 70, 77, 79-82, 84
Hoback River (of the Snake), 70
Holladay, Ben, Mont. stage line, 204
Homans, Sheppard, 147
Homestake Pass, Mont., 354
Hooker, Mount (10,782), demoted, 123, 300
Hoosier Pass, Colo., 53, 63; Frémont over, 137; named, 176; wagons over, 182; *10, 16*
Horse Lake Pass, N.M., described, 16-18; De Anza's attitude, 23; on Mont. trade route, 37, 62; crossed by Ewing Young, 106-107
Horse Prairie Creek (of the Red Rock-Beaverhead), 36, 41
Horseshoe Pass, Colo., 242
Hot Sulphur Springs, Colo., 183, 230-231
Howse, Joseph, 73, 327
Howse Pass, Can., crossed by Thompson, 64-65; closed by Blackfeet, 72-74, 93; crossed by Hector, 169; *9*
Hudson's Bay Fur Company, 25-26, 68, 72, 73; merges with North West, 92
Huerfano River (of the Arkansas), 8, 12, 50
Hughes, Bela M., blocked at Berthoud, 231
Hunchback Pass, Colo., 179; crossed by Hayden men, 224, 260; *15*
Hunt, Wilson Price, leads Astorians, 76-83; modern version of his route, 330-331
Hunters' Pass, see Independence Pass

IDAHO SPRINGS, Colo., 175, 230
Illecillewaet Glacier, 299-300
Immell, Michael, 112
Independence Pass, Colo., 54, 219, 252; road over, 254-258; cars over, 314
Indian Creek Pass, Colo., 96, 148
Indian Pass, Wyo., 132-133
Indians, Apache (Jicarilla), 5, 7-8, 11-121; reservation, 17; Arapaho, 84, 136; Arikara, 114; Bannock, 69; Blackfoot, trouble with Lewis, 43-44, 65-66, 68; chastise Colter party, 69; blacklist trappers, 74, 153; Cheyenne, 196; close Bozeman Trail, 206; Comanche, 9, 11, 13, 15; subdued by De Anza, 18-22, 95, 96, 97; Crow (Absaroka), 63, 65, 66, 68, 77; tail Stuart group, 85, 114; Flathead, guide Lewis and Clark, 39-41, 65; Marias Pass battle, 72-74; Kootenai, 72; Mandan, 30, 114; Navajo, 18; Nez Perce, 196; Chief Joseph flight, 343-344; Pend d'Oreille (Kalispel), 72-73; Salish, 73; Sioux, 144, 196; close Bozeman Trail, 205-206; Snake (Shoshoni), 32; help Lewis and Clark, 37-38, 67, 196; guide Astorians, 80; Stoney, 166, 168, 303; Ute, with Escalante, 15-16, 18; with De Anza, 19; Muaches, 95-96; habitat, 103-104; Colo. real estate, 214-215; wealth, 345
Ingersoll, Ernest, 274
Irving, Washington, 128-130

Pikes Peak Ocean-to-Ocean Highway, 313
Pine River Pass, Can., 29, 292
Pinedale, Wyo., 67, 70, 87, 132
Pinkham Pass, Colo., 270
Pinto Pass, Can., naming of, 302
Pipestone Pass, Can., crossed by Hector, 168, 307
Pipestone Pass, Mont., 35, 285, 313
Pitamakan Pass, Mont., Tinkham over, 162
Pitcock Hot Springs, Idaho, 86
Plummer, Henry, 203
Pocatello, Idaho, 85
Pocket Creek (of East Fork River-Green), 87
Pomeroy Pass, Colo., 250
Pompey, *see* Charbonneau, Baptiste
Poncha Pass, Colo., De Anza over, 20, 23-24, 53, 54, 62, 108, 122; Gunnison over, 149, 177; Mears road, 251; Tenderfoot Trail, 315
Popo Agie River (of the Wind-Bighorn), 67, 80, 116; how to pronounce, 328
Potts, Daniel T., 114
Powder River Pass, Wyo., crossed by Astorians, 78-79; Potts party over, 114; Black and Yellow Auto Trail, 320; 6
President Pass, Can., Whymper over, 306
Price, W. W., drives car over Tennessee, 310
Priest Pass, Mont., 35, 313
Princeton, Mount (14,197), 53; named, 390
Promontory Divide, Colo., crossed by Pike, 57
Provo Canyon, Utah, 118, 264
Provost, Etienne, 109, 118, 120
Pryor, Nathaniel, 128, 327-328
Pryor's Gap, Mont., 66, 67
Pueblo, Colo., 50, 71, 101, 133
Purcell, James, 97, 326
Purgatoire River (of the Arkansas), 7, 10; area described, 11-12, 50, 126; source, 148
Purity Pass, Can., 300

QUIVERA, Kingdom of, 6-7, 12

RABBIT EARS PASS, Colo., oddity of, 38, 89, 121, 136, 217; Victory Highway over, 314
Railroad over Rockies, altitude records, all lines, 353-354; *Burlington Railroad,* 79; *Canadian National Railways,* 75, 354; over Yellowhead, formation of, 385-386; *Canadian Pacific,* 168, 288; building over Kicking Horse, Rogers, 292-297; over Crowsnest, 296, 376; Kicking Horse spiral tunnels, 378; Rogers Pass tunnel, etc., 382; *Chicago, Milwaukee and St. Paul,* 158, 293; Pipestone Pass tunnel, reason for electrification, 354, 431; tunnel at St. Paul Pass, 434; *Colorado Central and Pacific Railroad,* 239, 266, 269, 275; *Colorado Midland Railroad* over Ute, Trout Creek, Hagerman passes, 277-278; tunnels, etc. 352; *Denver and Rio Grande (Western) Railroad,* 17, 55; at Crested Butte, 255; over La Veta, 267-268; *24;* to Leadville, 271; over Fremont, Tennessee, Marshall and Cumbres passes, 273; reaches Aspen, 278; La Veta Pass route changed, 351; over Soldier Summit, Utah, 440; *Denver, George-*

town and Utah Railway, paper road to all over, 267; *Denver, Northwestern and Pacific* (Moffat Line), over Rollins (Corona) Pass, 280; history, 353, 410; *Denver Pacific Railroad,* 264; *Denver, South Park and Pacific Railroad,* 242; built by John Evans to Morrison, 267; John Evans continued toward St. Elmo, sold out, 270-271; James A. Evans pushes through Alpine Tunnel to Gunnison, 271-272; James A. Evans builds over Boreas and Fremont passes to Leadville for Sidney Dillon and the U. P., 276; *25;* later tribulations, 352; *Gilmore and Pittsburgh Railroad,* Bannock Pass history, 420; *Great Northern Railway,* 34, 43; building over Marias, etc., 285-292; *27; Kansas Pacific Railroad,* 264, 286; *Laramie, North Park and Western (U. P.),* 408; *Montana Central,* reaches Butte, 288; *Northern Pacific Railroad,* 158; building over Bozeman, Mullan, Lookout passes, 284-287; reaches Butte over Homestake, 354; tunnels, 421 (Bozeman), 430 (Mullan); *Rio Grande Southern Railroad,* over Lizard Head Pass, 279-280; *Santa Fe Railroad,* over La Glorieta, 6; Raton, 10, 141; Raton Pass seizure, 269; buys Colorado Midland, 278; Raton Pass tunnel data, more history, 351; *Silverton Railroad,* built by Mears, 279-280; *Uintah Railroad,* Baxter Pass history, 387-388; *Union Pacific Railroad,* 86, 92, 144, 146, 206, 218; over Sherman Hill Summit of Cheyenne Pass area, etc., 262-264; threats to take over northern Colorado via Pinkham Pass and Muddy Pass to Middle Park, 269-270, 281; Pinkham Pass line, 408; *Utah and Northern Railroad,* over Monida, Deer Lodge passes to Butte, etc., 282-284, 354
Raton Pass, Colo.-N.M., 6, 8-9; described, 10-11; crossed by Valverde, Villasur, Mallets, 13-14, 18, 22, 23, 50; crossed by McKnight, 70-71, 95-96; Becknell over, 97; first wagons, 128; described by Abert, 140-144; Army of the West over, 141; Denver army over, 189; seized by Santa Fe Railroad, 269; highway, 313; road, rail, 351; *2*
Rattlesnake Pass, Wyo., 119, 133-134, 145
Ravalli, Father Anthony, 157
Rawlins, Wyo., 85, 88, 218
Raynolds, Captain William F., 197-200
Raynolds Pass, Mont.-Idaho, crossed by Henry, 69, 122; crossed, described by Raynolds, 200, 203, 213; modern road, *14*
Red Desert, of Wyoming's Great Basin, 89
Red Mountain Pass, Colo.-San Juans, crossed by Hayden men, 222; Mears "Rainbow Route" over, 259; *23;* Mears rails over, 279; Million Dollar Highway, 314
Red River Pass, N.M., Stonewall area, 11
Red River Pass, N.M., Taos area, 11, 242
Red River (of the Mississippi), Pike misses it, 53-55; misses again, 59; Long misses it, 126
Red Rock Pass, Mont.-Idaho, 36, 38, 213, 283
Rendezvous trapper sites, 332
Reznor, Jacob, 70, 77, 79-82, 84
Rhoda, Franklin, 220-225
Rim, The, Wyo., 70, 81, 86, 320